THE AUDITORY CORTEX

A SYNTHESIS OF
HUMAN AND ANIMAL RESEARCH

THE AUDITORY CORTEX

A SYNTHESIS OF HUMAN AND ANIMAL RESEARCH

Edited by

Reinhard König
Peter Heil
Eike Budinger
Henning Scheich

Leibniz Institute for Neurobiology
Center for Learning and Memory Research
Magdeburg, Germany

2005

LAWRENCE ERLBAUM ASSOCIATES, PUBLISHERS
Mahwah, New Jersey   London

MW

Camera ready copy for this book was provided by the editors.

Lawrence Erlbaum Associates, Inc., Publishers
10 Industrial Avenue
Mahwah, New Jersey 07430
www.erlbaum.com

Cover design by Kathryn Houghtaling Lacey

Library of Congress Cataloging-in-Publication Data

The auditory cortex : a synthesis of human and animal research / [edited by] Reinhard König … [et al.].
     p. cm.
Includes bibliographical references and index.
ISBN 0-8058-4938-6 (cloth : alk. paper)
1. Auditory cortex. I. König, Reinhard, 1960– [DNLM: 1. Auditory Cortex. 2. Auditory Perception. 3. Psysiology, Comparative. WL 307 A912 2005]
QP383.15.A93   2005
612.8'255—dc22   2004061937
                                                CIP

Books published by Lawrence Erlbaum Associates are printed on acid-free paper, and their bindings are chosen for strength and durability.

Printed in the United States of America
10 9 8 7 6 5 4 3 2 1

5/8/06

CONTENTS

PART II
CODING OF SOUNDS

PART III
PLASTICITY, LEARNING, AND COGNITION

PREFACE

Sometime in 2002, Henning Scheich expressed his feeling that it was about time to bring together scientists who work on the auditory cortex of humans with those who work on that part of the brain in animals. A meeting would enable these scientists to learn and benefit from each other's knowledge and experience by exchanging their concepts, approaches, and in-between-the-lines thoughts. As a matter of fact, the idea of an encounter of experts from the two areas fell on fertile grounds – evidently, a meeting of that kind was urgently needed. The "human fraction", using sophisticated, mainly non-invasive techniques such as functional magnetic resonance imaging, magneto- and electroencephalography to study its subject, often seemed rather unaware, or at least not well informed, of the progress that the "animal fraction" had made, and vice versa. In any event, we asked a bunch of representative outside experts what they thought about such a get-together, and much to our surprise all thought it was a very good idea (a rare event in a scientist's life).

So, we started organizing and – thanks to the more than 200 participants from all over the world, our numerous sponsors, and our hosts at the Herrenkrug Park Hotel, the organizing team, and many other people – enjoyed an exciting and successful meeting, termed the "International Conference on Auditory Cortex – Towards a Synthesis of Human and Animal Research", in Magdeburg from September 13-17, 2003. You may get an idea by studying the Proceedings of the conference, edited by Eike Budinger and Birgit Gaschler-Markefski and published by the Shaker-Verlag.

The meeting tried to cover three themes: i) Auditory cortical fields and their functions, ii) coding of sounds, and iii) plasticity, learning, and cognition. No doubt, the presentations were excellent and, thus, an appropriate publication seemed in order. Here it is. The book is organized around the same three schemes as the conference. Some readers may disagree with where we have placed individual chapters, but this reflects the fact that the themes are really closely tied together. Those readers who also attended the conference may note that the chapters in this book go beyond or may even differ significantly from the content of the presentations during the conference. But all chapters succeed in achieving the desired synthesis even better than did the talks. This is so also because most authors have incorporated ideas, questions, and critique brought up during the conference (although one invited speaker "complained" that the atmosphere during the conference was so nice that he felt reluctant to make any critical comments about the science presented).

We are most grateful to our authors for their contributions and their patience with us, to our numerous reviewers, who shall remain anonymous although they did excellent jobs and helped to improve each and every chapter, and to Emily Wilkinson, Bonita D'Amil, and Art Lizza at Lawrence Erlbaum Associates without whom this book would not have become a reality.

Dear Reader, enjoy!

Reinhard König, Peter Heil, Eike Budinger, Henning Scheich

LIST OF AUTHORS

Hermann Ackermann
Department of Neurology
Eberhard-Karls University Tübingen
Hoppe-Seyler-Strasse 3
72076 Tübingen
Germany
hermann.ackermann@uni-tuebingen.de

Michela Adriani
Division de Neuropsychologie
CHUV
1011 Lausanne
Switzerland
Michela.Adriani @chuv.hospvd.ch

Ehud Ahissar
Department of Neurobiology
The Weizmann Institute
Rehovot 76100
Israel
Ehud.Ahissar@weizmann.ac.il

Merav Ahissar
Department of Psychology &
    Interdisciplinary Center for
    Neural Computation
Hebrew University
Jerusalem 91905
Israel
msmerava@pluto.mscc.huji.ac.il

Pascal Belin
Département de Psychologie
Université de Montréal
CP 6128 succ Centre-Ville
Montréal (Québec), H3C 3J7
Canada
pascal.belin@umontreal.ca

André Brechmann
Special Laboratory Non-Invasive Brain
    Imaging
Leibniz Institute for Neurobiology
Brenneckestraße 6
39118 Magdeburg
Germany
andre.brechmann@ifn-magdeburg.de

Michael Brosch
Department Auditory Learning and
    Speech
Leibniz Institute for Neurobiology
Brenneckestraße 6
39118 Magdeburg
Germany
michael.brosch@ifn-magdeburg.de

Mel Brown
Department of Psychology
School of Psychology, Psychiatry, and
    Psychological Medicine
Faculty of Medicine, Nursing, and
    Health Sciences
Monash University
Vic 3800
Australia
mel.brown@med.monash.edu.au

John F. Brugge
Waisman Center
1500 Highland Avenue
University of Wisconsin

Madison, WI 53705
USA
brugge@waisman.wisc.edu

Eike Budinger
Leibniz Institute for Neurobiology
Department Auditory Learning and
    Speech
Brenneckestraße 6
39118 Magdeburg
Germany
Eike.Budinger@ifn-magdeburg.de

Stephanie Clarke
Division de Neuropsychologie
CHUV
1011 Lausanne
Switzerland
Stephanie.Clarke@chuv.hospvd.ch

Jean-Marc Edeline
NAMC UMR 8620, Bât 446
Université Paris Sud
91405 Orsay cedex
France
Jean-Marc.Edeline@ibaic.u-psud.fr

Jos J. Eggermont
Departments of Physiology &
    Biophysics and Psychology
Neuroscience Research Group
University of Calgary
3330, Hospital Drive N.W.
Calgary (Alberta), T2N 4N1
Canada
eggermon@ucalgary.ca

Mounya Elhilali
Centre for Auditory and Acoustic
    Research
Institute for Systems Research
Electrical and Computer Engineering
University of Maryland
College Park, MD 20742
USA
mounya@isr.umd.edu

Steven J. Eliades
Department of Biomedical Engineering
Johns Hopkins University
720 Rutland Ave., Ross 424
Baltimore, MD 21205
USA

seliades@jhu.edu

Dina Farkas
Department of Neurobiology
The Alexander Silberman Institute of
    Life Science
Edmund Safra Campus, Givat Ram
91904 Jerusalem
Israel
farkad@md.huji.ac.il

Walter J. Freeman
MCB LSA IMLSAP 142 Life Science
Addition, #3200
University of California at Berkeley
Berkeley, CA 94720-3200
USA
wfreeman@socrates.berkeley.edu

Jonathan Fritz
Centre for Auditory and Acoustic
    Research
Institute for Systems Research
Electrical and Computer Engineering
University of Maryland
College Park, MD 20742
USA
ripple@isr.umd.edu

Shigeto Furukawa
Human and Information Science
    Laboratory
NTT Communication Science
    Laboratories
3-1 Morinosato Wakamiya, Ataugi,
Kanagawa, 243-0198
Japan
shig@avg.brl.ntt.co.jp

P. Charles Garell
Department of Neurosurgery
University of Wisconsin
Madison, WI 53711
USA
garell@neurosurg.wisc.edu

Troy A. Hackett
Bill Wilkerson Center
Department of Psychology
Vanderbilt University
111 21st Avenue South
Nashville, TN 37240
USA

troy.a.hackett@vanderbilt.edu

Deborah A. Hall
Medical Research Council
Institute of Hearing Research
University Park
Nottingham NG7 2RD
UK
D.Hall@ihr.mrc.ac.uk

Henry E. Heffner
Department of Psychology
University of Toledo
2801 West Bancroft
Toledo, OH 43606
USA
hheffne@pop3.utoledo.edu

Peter Heil
Department Auditory Learning and
   Speech
Leibniz Institute for Neurobiology
Brenneckestraße 6
39118 Magdeburg
Germany
peter.heil@ifn-magdeburg.de

Ingo Hertrich
Department of General Neurology
Hertie-Institute for Clinical Brain
   Research
Eberhard-Karls University Tübingen
Hoppe Seyler-Strasse 3
D-72076 Tübingen
Germany
ingo.hertrich@uni-tuebingen.de

Andreas Hess
Institute for Pharmacology and
   Toxicology
Fahrstrasse 17
91054 Erlangen
Germany
andreas.hess@pharmakologie.uni-
   erlangen.de

Junsei Horikawa
Toyohashi University of Technology
1-1 Hibarigaoka, Tempaku
Toyohashi, 441-8580
Japan
horikawa@tutkie.tut.ac.jp

Yutaka Hosokawa
Tokyo Medical and Dental University
2-3-10 Kanda-surugadai, Chiyoda-ku
Tokyo 101-0062
Japan
hosokawa.nphy@mri.tmd.ac.jp

Matthew A. Howard III
Department of Neurosurgery
University of Iowa
Iowa City, IA 52242
USA
matthew-howard@uiowa.edu

Kazuo Imaizumi
Coleman Memorial Laboratory
WM.Keck Center for Integrative
   Neuroscience
Department of Otolaryngology
University of California at San
   Francisco
513 Parnassus Ave., Box 0732
San Francisco, CA 94143-0732
USA
kazuo@phy.ucsf.edu

Dexter R. F. Irvine
Department of Psychology
School of Psychology, Psychiatry, and
   Psychological Medicine
Faculty of Medicine, Nursing and
   Health Sciences
Monash University
Vic 3800
Australia
dexter.irvine@med.monash.edu.au

Jon H. Kaas
Department of Psychology
Vanderbilt University
111 21st Ave South
Nashville (Tennessee), 37203
USA
jon.h.kaas@vanderbilt.edu

Hiroto Kawasaki
Department of Neurosurgery
University of Iowa
Iowa City, IA 52242
USA
hiroto-kawasaki@uiowa.edu

Reinhard König
Special Laboratory Non-Invasive Brain
    Imaging
Leibniz Institute for Neurobiology
Brenneckestraße 6
39118 Magdeburg
Germany
rkoenig@ifn-magdeburg.de

Nina Kraus
Auditory Neuroscience Laboratory
Northwestern University
2240 Campus Drive
Evanston, IL 60208
USA
nkraus@northwestern.edu

Liora Las
Department of Neurobiology
The Alexander Silberman Institute of
    Life Science
Edmund Safra Campus, Givat Ram
91904 Jerusalem
Israel
lioraa@md.huji.ac.il

Charles C. Lee
Division of Neurobiology
Department of Molecular and Cell
    Biology
University of California at Berkeley
Life Science Addition
Berkeley, CA 94720-3200
USA
chazwell@uclink4.berkeley.edu

Qingyu Li
Department of Neurosurgery
University of Iowa
Iowa City, IA 52242
USA
qingyu-li@uiowa.edu

Jennifer F. Linden
Coleman Memorial Laboratory
WM.Keck Center for Integrative
    Neuroscience
Department of Otolaryngology
University of California at San
    Francisco
513 Parnassus Ave., Box 0732
San Francisco, CA 94143-0732

USA
linden@phy.ucsf.edu

Werner Lutzenberger
MEG Center
Eberhard-Karls University Tübingen
Otfried-Müller-Strasse 47
72076 Tübingen
Germany
werner.lutzenberger@uni-tuebingen.de

Russell Martin
Aeronautical and Maritime Research
    Laboratory
Defence Science and Technology
    Organisation
P.O. Box 4331
Melbourne, Vic. 3001
Australia
russell.martin@dsto.defence.gov.au

Klaus Mathiak
MEG Center
Eberhard-Karls University Tübingen
Otfried-Müller-Straße 47
72076 Tübingen
Germany
klaus.mathiak@uni-tuebingen.de

Brian J. Mickey
Kresge Hearing Research Institute
University of Michigan
1301 E. Ann St.
Ann Arbor, MI 48109-0506
USA
bmickey@umich.edu

John C. Middlebrooks
Kresge Hearing Research Institute
University of Michigan
1301 E. Ann St.
Ann Arbor, MI 48109-0506
USA
jmidd@umich.edu

Janine Möbes
Department of Neurology
Medizinische Hochschule Hannover
Carl-Neuberg. Str. 1
30623 Hannover
Germany
moebes.janine@mh-hannover.de

Patricia Morosan
Institute for Medicine
Research Center Jülich
52425 Jülich
Germany
p.morosan@fz-juelich.de

Thomas F. Münte
Department of Neuropsychology
Otto-von-Guericke University
P.O. Box 4120
39016 Magdeburg
Germany
thomas.muente@nat.uni-magdeburg.de

Wido Nager
Department of Neurology
Medizinische Hochschule Hannover
Carl-Neuberg. Str. 1
30623 Hannover
Germany
nager.wido@mh-hannover.de

Israel Nelken
Department of Neurobiology
The Alexander Silberman Institute of
  Life Science
Edmund Safra Campus, Givat Ram
91904 Jerusalem
Israel
Israel@md.huji.ac.il

Heinrich Neubauer
Department Auditory Learning and
  Speech
Leibniz Institute for Neurobiology
Brenneckestraße 6
39118 Magdeburg
Germany
heinrich.neubauer@ifn-magdeburg.de

Trent Nicol
Auditory Neuroscience Laboratory
Northwestern University
2240 Campus Drive
Evanston, IL 60208
USA
tgn@northwestern.edu

Frank W. Ohl
Department Auditory Learning and
  Speech
Leibniz Institute for Neurobiology

Brenneckestraße 6
39118 Magdeburg
Germany
frank.ohl@ifn-magdeburg.de

Hiroyuki Oya
Department of Neurosurgery
University of Iowa
Iowa City, IA 52242
USA
hiroyuki-oya@uiowa.edu

Nicola Palomero-Gallagher
Institute for Medicine
Research Center Jülich
D-52425 Jülich
Germany
n.palomero-gallagher@fz-juelich.de

Valerie Park
Department of Psychology
School of Psychology, Psychiatry, and
  Psychological Medicine
Faculty of Medicine, Nursing and
  Health Sciences
Monash University
Vic 3800
Australia
vnpark@excite.com

Jörg Rademacher
CEA Service Hospitalier F. Joliot
4, place du Général Leclerc
91 401 Orsay
France
j.rademacher@fz-juelich.de

Richard A. Reale
Waisman Center
1500 Highland Avenue
University of Wisconsin
Madison, WI 53705
USA
reale@cortex.waisman.wisc.edu

Jascha Rüsseler
Department of Neuropsychology
Otto-von-Guericke University
P.O. Box 4120
39016 Magdeburg
Germany
jascha.ruesseler@nat.uni-
  magdeburg.de

Henning Scheich
Department Auditory Learning and
    Speech
Leibniz Institute for Neurobiology
Brenneckestraße 6
39118 Magdeburg
Germany
henning.scheich@ifn-magdeburg.de

Christoph E. Schreiner
Coleman Memorial Laboratory
WM.Keck Center for Integrative
    Neuroscience
Department of Otolaryngology
University of California at San
    Francisco
513 Parnassus Ave., Box 0732
San Francisco, CA 94143-0732
USA
chris@phy.ucsf.edu

Holger Schulze
Department Auditory Learning and
    Speech
Leibniz Institute for Neurobiology
Brenneckestraße 6
39118 Magdeburg
Germany
holger.schulze@ifn-magdeburg.de

Shihab Shamma
Institute for Systems Research
Neural Systems Laboratory
University of Maryland
College Park, MD 20742
USA
sas@Glue.umd.edu

G. Christopher Stecker
Kresge Hearing Research Institute
University of Michigan
1301 E. Ann St.
Ann Arbor, MI 48109-0506
USA
cstecker@umich.edu

Shunji Sugimoto
Department Auditory Learning and
    Speech
Leibniz Institute for Neurobiology
Brenneckestraße 6
39118 Magdeburg

Germany
shunji.sugimoto@ifn-magdeburg.de

Ikuo Taniguchi
Tokyo Medical and Dental University
2-3-10 Kanda-surugadai, Chiyoda-ku
Tokyo 101-0062
Japan
riji-kenkyu.adm@cmn.tmd.ac.jp

Eric Tardif
Institut de Physiologie
Université de Lausanne
Rue du Bugnon 7
1005 Lausanne
Switzerland
Eric.Tardif@iphysiol.unil.ch

Nachum Ulanovsky
Department of Neurobiology
The Alexander Silberman Institute of
    Life Science
Edmund Safra Campus, Givat Ram
91904 Jerusalem
Israel
nachumu@md.huji.ac.il

Alessandro E. P. Villa
University Joseph Fourier
Faculty of Medicine
Laboratory of Neurobiophysics
38043 Grenoble
France
avilla@neuroheuristic.org

Igor Volkov
Department of Neurosurgery
University of Iowa
Iowa City, IA 52242
USA
igor-volkov@uiowa.edu

Xiaoqin Wang
Department of Biomedical Engineering
Johns Hopkins University
720 Rutland Ave, Ross 424
Baltimore, MD 21205
USA
xwang@bme.jhu.edu

Brad Wible
Auditory Neuroscience Laboratory
Northwestern University

2299 North Campus Drive
Evanston, IL 60208
USA
b-wible1@northwestern.edu

Jeffery A. Winer
Division of Neurobiology
Department of Molecular and Cell
    Biology
University of California at Berkeley
Life Science Addition
Berkeley, CA 94720-3200
USA
jawiner@socrates.berkeley.edu

Robert J. Zatorre
Montreal Neurological Institute
Department of Neuropsychology
3801 rue University Montreal
Montreal (Québec), H3A 2B4
Canada
Robert.Zatorre@staff.mcgill.ca

Karl Zilles
Institute for Medicine
Research Center Jülich
52425 Jülich
Germany
k.zilles@fz-juelich.de

PART I

AUDITORY CORTICAL FIELDS AND THEIR FUNCTIONS

1. INTRODUCTION:
AUDITORY CORTICAL FIELDS AND THEIR FUNCTIONS

Eike Budinger

The auditory cortex represents the centralmost largely unimodal processing stage of auditory information along the auditory pathway. It seems to be essential, for example, for discrimination and localization of sounds, recognition of species-specific vocalization, embedding of acoustical cues into the behavioral context, and auditory learning and memory. The auditory cortex is not a homogenous region; like all other sensory cortices it consists of multiple areas or fields. Each field is commonly defined by a unique combination of anatomical and physiological features and a field border by a rather abrupt change of at least one of these features.

From an anatomist's point of view an auditory field is designated by its specific pattern of the cyto-, fiber-, and chemoarchitecture and by its thalamocortical, corticocortical, and corticofugal connections. For example, in all species investigated so far, a central auditory field, usually termed the primary field AI, can be distinguished from other fields by its koniocortical architecture and dense network of myelinated fibers, by the highest expression and activity of certain proteins (like calcium-binding and neurofilament proteins, cytochrome oxidase), and by its strong connections with the principle nucleus of the medial geniculate body of the auditory thalamus. At the borders of AI with the adjoining fields, some of these anatomical characteristics change markedly, for example the koniocortical lamination pattern and/or the pattern of connections with the auditory thalamus. However, the differentiation of those fields, which surround AI, is still difficult and often depends on the observer's subjective view and on the thoroughness of the methods used.

From a physiologist's point of view auditory cortical fields can sometimes be distinguished based upon single receptive field properties of their neurons, for example, the characteristic (or best) frequency, spectral bandwidth, latency to the first spike, spatial response characteristics (e.g., binaural interactions, direction sensitivity), amplitude modulation properties, and frequency modulation rates. Up to now there seems to be only one of these properties, *viz.* the characteristic frequency (CF), which can relatively reliably help to identify at least some auditory fields, since the CF often forms orderly, that is, topographic, maps or gradients across the cortical surface. The orientation of these so-called tonotopic maps or gradients is usually typical for a field within a species, but can be different for homologue fields of different species. During electrophysiological recordings, the tonotopic map of AI is most prominent, corroborated by the sharply tuned, frequently phasic, and short-latency responses of the AI neurons. The tonotopic gradient of this map is commonly reversed at the borders of AI with the surrounding fields, but often the neurons of these fields do not always represent the full audible frequency-range of the animal, that is, the tonotopic map is not "complete". Moreover, neurons of these fields usually exhibit a much more complex firing pattern than those of AI in terms of, for example, more tonic, more variable, and longer lasting responses. Thus again, the physiological differentiation between the fields surrounding AI is difficult. In addition, the constitution of the experimental animal (e.g., anesthesia, motivation, deprivation, learning tasks, etc.) can substantially influence the receptive field properties of neurons and thus hamper the delineation of all field borders.

In consequence, aside from the description of AI and its directly neighboring fields, the exact number and location of all other auditory fields is still controversial for nearly every mammalian species investigated so far. Detailed studies are available of the auditory cortex of some carnivores (cat, ferret, dog), several bat species (mustache, big brown, horseshoe bat), rodents (gerbil, mouse, guinea pig), and non-human primates (macaque, owl monkey), but for most other taxa, and even for several common laboratory animals like rabbit and rat, our knowledge is much more limited.

In humans, the functional organization of the auditory cortex remains even more obscure. This is largely due to the limited applicability of most invasive experimental techniques. Our recent knowledge is mainly based on *post mortem* anatomy, studies of patients with cerebral lesions, and on anatomical and functional non-invasive brain imaging methods, like functional magnetic resonance imaging (fMRI), positron emission tomography (PET), electroencephalography (EEG), and magnetoencephalography (MEG). Hence, we are still not able to exactly match the anatomical parcellation of the human auditory cortex with the loci of functional activation, furthermore, even the exact borders and the tonotopic organization of the human AI have not been shown convincingly, yet. Additional problems for precisely localizing auditory fields in the human cortex are the high interindividual variability and the pronounced interhemispheric asymmetry of even gross morphological features of the supratemporal plane. Nevertheless, as it is the case with animals, only the coincidence of distinct microstructural *and* physiological changes can define borders between auditory fields. Thus, for example, the variable outlines of Heschl's gyrus or of the *planum temporale* cannot mark the location of a field, because they do not coincide with changes of, for example, the cellular or fibritic lamination pattern, nor does a single focus of activation above some arbitrary threshold, for example, in an fMRI experiment, define an auditory field.

More recently scientists try to link the search for characteristic anatomical and physiological features of the auditory fields with the search for their putative specific functions. The functions of a field, that is, actually measured as the activity of their neurons with respect to a given acoustic situation, can be described either by the analysis of the incoming stimulus ("bottom-up" approach) or by the task which has to be solved by the animal ("top-down" approach). Thus, neurons of a given field can respond to the same acoustic stimulus with different activation pattern, which makes it difficult to identify the putative functions of auditory fields, if such functions exist at all. However, in analogy to the visual system, where attributes like luminance, color, motion, orientation, depth, and form of visual objects are processed to a certain degree by separate visual fields before they are conveyed into a single visual percept, acoustic features like intensity, pitch and timbre, sound transients and periodicities, sound source motion and location have been suggested to be some of the key qualities required for the recognition and processing of auditory objects and scenes. Nonetheless, up to now these attributes seem not to be separately processed by individual fields and thus seem not to be sufficient to unequivocally characterize an auditory field. In addition, it is not clear yet, in which way the cortical processing of these features really differs from that in some of the lower levels of the auditory pathway.

Another key question is to what extent the auditory cortices of different species differ or whether their organization follows mainly the same principles. In the latter case it should be possible to develop a common concept and a common nomenclature of auditory cortex and its fields. Recent attempts to generalize the results of auditory research of the last decades suggest several, but mutually not exclusive, concepts of the functional organization of the auditory cortex:

Auditory cortical information processing is most likely organized in a serial (hierarchical) fashion, originating from primary-like core fields of auditory cortex and extending via fields of the so-called surrounding belt and parabelt to target areas of the multimodal association cortex, like the prefrontal cortex. Concurrently, there seem to be several parallel (functional) processing streams, originating from and involving different fields at each cortical level. It is disputed, whether two of these functional streams can account for a bipartite information processing based on rather abstract aspects of sound, *viz.* what is heard (object identification) and where it comes from (object localization). Another concept proposes a dichotomy of information processing based on rather physical characteristics of sound, with a left-hemisphere specialization for rapid temporal processing and a right-hemisphere specialization for fine spectral processing. It is unclear, how the cortical neurons extract from a complex acoustic signal the respective information about an auditory object's or subject's identity and location, nor how they differentiate between speech and music, but neurons of some fields seem to be more tuned to one or the other aspect.

The ten chapters of this book section reflect the variety of experimental approaches in investigating auditory cortical areas and their possible functions in different species. The chapters combine and discuss results from anatomical work on human (Morosan et al., Hall, Clarke et al.), monkey (Kaas & Hackett), and cat (Imaizumi et al.), electrophysiological investigations on human (Brugge et al.), monkey (Brosch & Scheich), cat, and mouse (Imaizumi et al.), lesion studies on human (Clarke et al.) and monkey (Heffner), and findings from non-invasive functional imaging studies on human (Hall, Clarke et al., Belin & Zatorre, Ackermann et al.). Main topics of the following chapters are the identification and the anatomical, physiological, and functional characterization of auditory cortical fields; the representation of spectral and temporal properties of simple and complex sounds within these fields; the possible functions of the auditory cortex and its fields in the detection, identification, discrimination, and localization of sound; the non-acoustical influences on auditory cortical fields; their putative positions in serial and parallel processing streams of auditory information; and the (often lateralized) voice and speech processing in the brain. All chapters present superb overviews about the functional organization of the auditory cortex and provide a broad basis for the following book sections on coding of sound as well as on learning, cognition, and plastic processes within auditory cortical fields.

2. SUBDIVISIONS AND CONNECTIONS OF THE AUDITORY CORTEX IN PRIMATES: A WORKING MODEL

Jon H. Kaas, Troy A. Hackett

INTRODUCTION

Our goal in this chapter is to provide a model of the auditory system, especially at the cortical level, that is mainly based on experimental observations on monkeys but largely applies to humans. Such models or theories of subcortical and cortical processing networks have been elaborated repeatedly for the visual system (e.g., Felleman & Van Essen, 1991), and, to a lesser extent, the somatosensory system (e.g., Kaas, 2004). These models include proposed subdivisions (areas and nuclei) of systems and their interconnections. We prefer to refer to such depictions of systems as models or theories rather than descriptions because of uncertainties about interpretations of results, and the limitations of many results. In the outline of the primate visual system of Felleman and Van Essen (1991), for example, the authors indicated the locations of 32 visual areas on a surface of the flattened cortex of a macaque monkey brain, and diagramed the cortical connections of all 32 visual areas. This effort necessarily involved interpretations of the results of many studies where uncertainties exist over the locations of injection sites for revealing connections, the locations of transported label indicating projecting neurons or axon terminations, and the architectonic and physiological evidence for the areas. In recognition of these uncertainties, the authors assigned confidence levels to proposed areas from 1 to 3, with only five areas getting the rating of 1 for being well defined. However, there are even uncertainties about two of these five areas. Of these five, three (V1, V2, and MT) are widely accepted as valid visual areas, but the other two (dorsal V3 and VP) are not (see Kaas & Lyon, 2001). Instead, V3d and VP might be parts of the same visual area.

Given such uncertainties, which apply even more to the understudied auditory cortex, it seems more advisable to refer to such depictions of the obviously complicated processing networks as theories or models, rather than to infer that they are fully accurate descriptions of real systems. By stressing the tentative nature of such proposals, critical examinations, revisions, additions, and the recognition of species and taxa differences are invited. For instance, the basic auditory system of primates must have been modified with the evolution of humans to accommodate speech and other higher cognitive functions. The tendency to view the models of the visual system and the somatosensory system as descriptions rather than models has had the unfortunate impact of discouraging rather that encouraging further research on the organization of these systems.

Given, the probable differences in systems across primate taxa, the limitations of the supportive data, and the potential for misleading conclusions, what is the value of such models? To the extent that proposals are specific about the locations of areas and nuclei, their connections and other anatomical features, and their physiological characteristics, they became challengeable, and components can be shown to be wrong and changed. Thus, it becomes possible for the models to evolve and become increasingly accurate descriptions of sensory systems. In addition, at all stages of development, models have the potential to usefully guide research, including research related to further development of the model. For example, when visual area MT was first identified and became one of the three well defined areas of the model of visual cortex, MT became popular for further investigation in physiological experiments. The recently proposed auditory area, CM, is starting to emerge as such an area of increased study (e.g., Foxe et al, 2002; Fu et al., 2003; Rauschecker et al., 1997; Schroeder et al., 2001) for a similar reason.

THE BASIC FEATURES OF THE MODEL

A version of a model of the auditory system of simian primates is shown in Figure 2.1. The proposal includes basic subdivisions of the subcortical auditory system that appear to exist in most mammals. As homologous subdivisions of the cochlear nuclear complex, superior olivary complex, and inferior colliculus of the midbrain have been identified in both primate and non-primate species, the common assumption is that these structures are similar in connections and functions across mammalian taxa. Yet, we should be cautious in this assumption, as there have been few studies of the connections and physiology of subcortical auditory nuclei in primates, and the methods of early studies on connections limit the certainties of conclusions. Nevertheless, we have been able to establish many of the illustrated connections of the auditory midbrain in ongoing studies of the connections of the inferior colliculus of monkeys

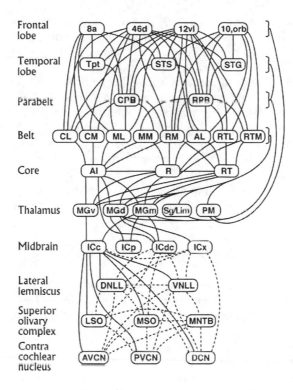

Fig. 2.1. Some of the proposed subcortical and cortical subdivisions and connections of the auditory system of primates. Connections based on studies in primates are in solid lines, while dashed lines indicate connections surmised from studies in non-primates. Abbreviations follow from bottom to top in the diagram. The cochlear nuclear complex has anteroventral (AVCN), posteroventral (PVCN), and dorsal (DCN) cochlear nuclei. The superior olivary complex has the lateral superior olive (LSO), the medial superior olive (MSO), and the medial nucleus of the trapezoid body (MNTB). The lateral lemniscus includes dorsal (DNLL) and ventral (VNLL) nuclei. The inferior colliculus includes a central nucleus (ICc), a pericentral nucleus (ICp), dorsal cortex (ICdc), and an external nucleus (ICX). The thalamus includes ventral (MGv), dorsal (MGd) and medial or magnocellular (MGm) nuclei of the medial geniculate complex, as well as the suprageniculate (Sg) and limitans (Lim) nuclei, and the medial pulvinar (PM). At the level of the cortex, the auditory core includes the primary area (A1), the rostral area (R) and the rostrotemporal area (RT). Belt areas named by position are caudolateral (CL), caudomedial (CM), middle lateral (ML) middle medial (MM), rostromedial (RM), anterolateral (AL), rostrotemporal medial (RTL) and rostrotemporal medial (RTM). The parabelt has caudal (CPB) and rostral (RPB) divisions. The temporal lobe has temporoparietal (Tpt), superior temporal sulcus (STS) and superior temporal gyrus (STG) regions. Frontal lobe regions are numbered after the tradition of Brodmann (see Preuss and Goldman-Rakic, 1991) and include periarcuate cortex in the region of the frontal eye field (8a), working memory cortex of the dorsal bank of the principal sulcus (46d), ventrolateral prefrontal cortex (12vl), the frontal pole (10) and orbitofrontal cortex (orb). Modified from Kaas and Hackett, 2000.

Blumell et al., 2002; Neagu et al., 1998). In regard to the auditory thalamus, the ventral or principle division of the medial geniculate complex, MGv, as well as the dorsal (MGd) and medial or magnocellular (MGm) divisions are widely recognized in both primate and non-primate taxa (e.g., Jones, 1985). The somewhat vaguely defined suprageniculate nucleus (Sg) and limitans nucleus (Lim), with auditory and other functions, are identified as homologous across taxa with less certainty. The brainstem inputs to divisions of the medial geniculate complex seem similar in primates and non-primates, but the cortical connections of these divisions differ as the number and types of cortical auditory areas differ. Less is known about the connections of Sg and Lim. Finally, the medial division of the pulvinar complex in primates (PM) is implicated by connections with auditory cortex in the processing of auditory information, but PM has no established homologue in non-primate mammals.

THE CORE OF PRIMARY-LIKE AUDITORY CORTEX

All mammals have one or more cortical areas that represent the first stage of cortical processing. (see Luethke et al., 1988, for review). This area or one of these areas is termed primary auditory cortex, A1, but often other areas with very similar features exist and are given other names. The features that distinguish A1 and other primary-like areas include histological, characteristics such as a layer 4 that is densely packed with small cells, dense myelination, and abundant cytochrome oxidase. The most dense thalamic inputs are from MGv. Neurons in the core respond well to tones and have best characteristic frequencies. Neurons with differing best frequencies are distributed in a spatial pattern that forms a tonotopic array or arrays of isofrequency bands. We propose that most or all primates, including humans, have three such areas, termed A1, R (for rostral), and RT (for rostrotemporal). Together, these three areas constitute the core of auditory processing at the cortical level. As the three areas have similar thalamic inputs from MGv, they are activated in parallel (see below). However, each core area distributes somewhat differently to adjoining cortical areas, implying an early separation of MGv information into processing streams of differing functional roles.

The auditory core in the brain of a macaque monkey is located on the lower bank of the lateral fissure (Fig. 2.2). The three areas are arranged in a caudorostral (or dorsoventral) sequence along the plane of the fissure with A1 most caudal, R just rostral to A1, and RT rostral to R. Because each area is somewhat longer than wide, and the three areas are strung together, the total length is about 6–7 times the width. The position of the core varies slightly across primate species, so that in primates with a shallow lateral fissure, such as marmoset monkeys (e.g., Aitkin et al., 1988; Luethke et al., 1989) and prosimian galagos (Brugge, 1982), the core extends onto the surface of the temporal lobe. In humans, with a deep lateral fissure that contains additional fissures, the core occupies much of Heschl's gyrus, where the core is

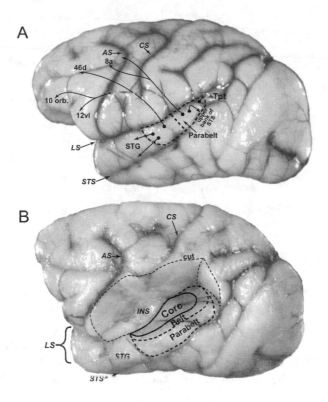

Fig. 2.2. A lateral view of the brain of a macaque monkeys before (A) and after (B) some of the parietal and frontal cortex has been removed to expose auditory cortex in the lower bank of the lateral sulcus. Auditory and auditory related areas include the core, belt, parabelt, Tpt, STG, and STS regions of the temporal lobe; and 8a, 46d, 12vl, 10 and orbitofrontal regions of the frontal lobe. See Figure 2.1 for abbreviations. Modified from Hackett et al., 1999.

rotated in a manner that would place A1 deepest in the lateral fissure (Hackett et al., 2001).

The reasons for dividing the core into three areas stem from the early microelectrode studies of Merzenich and Brugge (1973), Imig et al (1977), and Morel and Kaas (1992). In macaque monkeys, Merzenich and Brugge (1973) defined two similar tonotopically organized fields with primary-like features, A1 and RL (for rostrolateral). Imig et al. (1977) subsequently identified these two fields in owl monkeys, but renamed RL the rostral area, R, the term we have retained in our model. Morel and Kaas (1992) later added the rostrotemporal area, RT, at the rostral border of R. Because studies of the core region tended to concentrate on A1, we know most about A1, less about R, and very little about RT. Yet, there is evidence from studies on both New World monkeys (Imig et al., 1977; Morel & Kaas, 1992) and Old World macaque

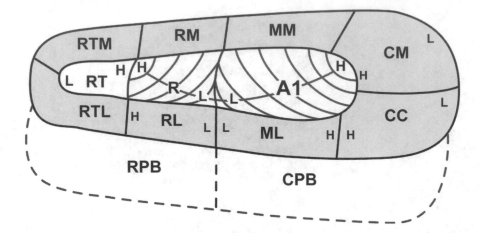

Fig. 2.3. The relative locations of core, belt and parabelt areas, with tonotopic patterns in core and some of the belt areas. Isofrequency contours from high (H) to low (L) are indicated for A1 and R, and the general best frequency progressions are indicated in other areas. See Figure 2.1 for abbreviations.

monkeys (Kosaki et al., 1997; Merzenich & Brugge, 1973; Morel et al., 1993) that A1 and R approximate mirror-image representations of each other's tonotopic organization. Tonotopic order proceeds from representing high best frequencies to low best frequencies in a caudorostral direction in A1, reversing to a low to high sequence in R (Fig. 2.3).

However, the isofrequency bands are tilted so that portions of A1 and R, deeper in the lateral sulcus, consistently represent higher tones for the same rorstrocaudal level (see also Aitkin et al., 1986; Cheung et al., 2001). This tilt can be especially pronounced in New World monkeys RT appears to form a reversal of the tonotopic organization of R, but there is only limited data (Morel & Kaas, 1992).

In humans, there is evidence from neuromagnetic MEG studies (e.g., Lütkenhöner & Steinsträter, 1998; Pantev et al., 1995), recordings with implanted electrodes (e.g., Howard et al., 1996), and functional imaging (fMRI) studies (e.g., Talavage et al., 2000) for tonotopic organization in the core region from high to low in a mediolateral sequence, (see Formisano et al., 2003 for further review), which likely reflects A1 (because of the rotation of the core). As the noninvasive imaging techniques in humans are of low resolution, other patterns have not been obvious, but there have been suggestions of other tonotopic areas (e.g., Lütkenhöner et al., 2001; Talavage et al., 2000). However, a recent fMRI study at seven Tesla provided clear evidence of two tonotopic maps sharing a low-frequency border that were judged to be homologous with A1 and R of monkeys (Formisano et al., 2003). Further evidence for the existence of three core areas in humans and apes (where there is no data on tonotopy) is limited to architectonic descriptions of a core that is elongated in each of these primates as in monkeys, providing room for three similar representations. In monkeys, chimpanzees and humans, the core is readily identified by its distinctive architectonic characteristics (see Hackett et al., 2001; Hackett, 2002; Rivier & Clarke, 1997; Wallace et al., 2002).

In monkeys, both early and more recent studies provide evidence for MGv projections to A1 and R, with most of the evidence involving A1 (Burton & Jones, 1976; Hashikawa et al, 1995; Luethke et al., 1989; Mesulam & Pandya, 1973; Morel & Kaas, 1992; Morel et al., 1993). RT also receives input from MGv, but the evidence is limited to data from owl monkeys (Morel & Kaas, 1992). Thus, the evidence for thalamic connections and tonotopic organization in RT is weaker than it is for A1 and R, and the evidence for RT as a core area is weaker. In addition, the architectonic features that distinguish the core are less pronounced in RT, although all three areas are distinctly different from the cortex of the surrounding belt (Hackett et al., 1999). However, an additional argument for including RT in the core is that all three proposed areas of the core project only sparsely, if at all, to the large region of the temporal lobe we define as the parabelt, while belt areas surrounding the core project densely to the parabelt (Hackett et al., 1998a). As neurons in R were not deactivated by a lesion of A1 (Rauschecker et al., 1997), R and A1 appear to be independently activated by parallel projections from MGv. It seems likely that RT is also independently activated, but physiological evidence is lacking.

THE SECOND LEVEL OF CORTICAL PROCESSING: AREAS OF THE AUDITORY BELT

As a second stage of auditory processing in cortex, our model includes a narrow belt of eight areas surrounding the core (Fig. 2.3). The concept of auditory core of primary cortex surrounded by a non-primary belt is an idea derived from early architectonic studies of auditory cortex (Galaburda & Pandya, 1983; Pandya & Sanides, 1973). These investigators described an elongated primary area of auditory koniocortex, KA, as a "core" bordered medially by a "root" area and laterally by a "belt" area, in congruence with a broader theoretical interpretation of cortical architecture. The KA core appears by position to include both A1 and R of the present proposal, but not RT, while the root area overlaps the present medial belt areas and the belt area overlaps the present lateral belt areas. As in the present model, Galaburda and Pandya (1983) proposed from their study of connections that the core is connected with the root (medial belt) and the belt (lateral belt). The present 2–3 mm wide belt in macaque monkeys is narrower than the previously proposed root-belt, has dense interconnections with the core, and only sparse inputs form MGv with most of the thalamic inputs from MGd and MGm. However, the belt is not architectonically uniform. Patterns of tonotopic organizations, connections with core areas and other fields, and architectonic differences have all been used to divide the belt into the 8 areas described below.

Area CM

Merzenich and Brugge (1973) first defined CM as caudomedial field roughly in the position of CM of the present proposal. While neurons in CM did not respond well to tones, Merzenich and Brugge (1973) were able to determine best frequencies of neurons at enough sites to suggest that CM represents tones in a reversal of the pattern in A1. Neurons have high to low best frequencies as they distribute in a rostrocaudal progression away from the CM border. More recently, Rauschecker et al., (1995; 1997) and Kosaki et al., (1997) provided further evidence for a weak tonotopic gradient in CM. CM is also distinguished from A1 by other neuron response characteristics. The latencies of response to tones is longer for neurons in CM than A1, and the neurons in CM have much broader frequency tuning (Recanzone et al., 2000a).

CM also differs from A1 in that many CM neurons respond to somatosensory stimulation of the head and neck (Fu et al., 2003; Schroeder et al., 2001). A homolog of CM has been proposed for humans after fMRI results showed auditory and somatosensory overlap in a region of cortex next to the auditory core (Foxe et al., 2002). In comparison to other belt areas, CM more closely resembles the core in being more densely stained for myelin (Hackett et al., 1998a; Morel & Kaas, 1992; Morel et al., 1993) and parvalbumin (Hackett et al., 1998a; Jones et al., 1995), but less densely than the core. However, CM is clearly excluded from the core as it receives few inputs form MGv while having dense inputs from MGd (Molinari et al., 1995; Rauschecker et al., 1995, 1997). CM receives dense inputs form A1 (Fitzpatrick & Imig, 1980; Jones et al., 1995; Morel et al., 1993), and lesions of A1 greatly depress the responsiveness of neurons in CM to auditory stimuli (Rauschecker et al., 1997). CM is densely connected with the caudal parabelt (Hackett et al., 1998a).

Area CL

The caudolateral area, CL, is one of three coarsely tonotopically organized areas distinguished by Rauschecker et al. (1995) in the lateral belt. Neurons in rostral CL, near the A1 border, responded better to higher frequency tones and band-passed noise burst centered at higher frequencies, while more caudal neurons in CL preferred lower frequencies. CL also expresses less parvalbumin than CM, but more than the adjoining belt area, ML (Hackett et al., 1998a). Connections of the CL region include A1, adjoining areas of the belt, and the caudal parabelt (Hackett et al., 1998a; Jones et al., 1995; Morel et al., 1993). As for other belt areas, thalamic inputs are from MGd and MGm, rather than from MGv (Molinari et al., 1995). The present CL includes the lateral part of CM of Merzenich and Brugge (1973) and the caudal area, C, of Morel and Kaas (1992) and Morel et al. (1993). As CL and CM have parallel tonotopic progressions, and histological and connectional differences are not marked, CL and CM could be considered to be parts of the same area. Neurons sensitive to the spatial locations of sound sources are more common in CL than in other divisions of the lateral belt (Tian et al., 2001), but they are also common in CM (Recanzone et al., 2000b).

Area ML

The portion of the belt just lateral to A1 contains a coarsely tonotopic representation from high to low tones in a caudorostral sequence in parallel with the representation in A1 (Kosaki et al., 1997; Merzenich & Brugge, 1973; Morel et al., 1993; Rauschecker et al., 1995). This portion of the belt was originally called the lateral field (L) by Merzenich and Brugge (1993), but was renamed the posterior lateral field (PL) to distinguish it from the anterior lateral area (AL) bordering the core area R (Fitzpatrick & Imig, 1980). More recently, Rauschecker et al. (1995) substituted the term ML when they distinguished the caudolateral field (CL) from the caudal or caudomedial fields of earlier reports. To avoid the problem of having both caudolateral and posterior lateral areas, we adopted the terms ML (middle lateral) and CL from Rauschecker et al. (1995).

Besides the electrophysiological evidence for a weak level of tonotopic organization, ML is distinguished by dense connections with A1, with sparse connections coming from R (Aitkin et al., 1988; Fitzpatrick & Imig, 1980; Luethke et al., 1989; Morel et al., 1993). These connections appear to be weakly topographical, with rostral A1 having more connections with rostral ML. In addition, ML is strongly interconnected with the caudal parabelt in a weak topographic pattern, with rostral ML more densely connected with rostral parabelt (Hackett et al., 1998a). ML also has connections with frontal cortex near or within the frontal eye field, and more rostrally in cortex of the principal sulcus (area 46d) involved in working memory (Morel & Kaas, 1992; Romanski et al., 1999a, 1999b). Thalamic connections have not been fully investigated, but limited results indicate that ML receives inputs from MGd, MGm, Sg-Lim, and the medial pulvinar, PM (Morel & Kaas, 1992). Neurons in ML and adjoining areas of the lateral belt respond better to band-pass noise bursts with defined center frequencies than tones, and better to monkey calls than energy-matched tones (Rauschecker et al., 1995). The responsiveness of ML neurons to more complex sounds is consistent with the anatomical evidence that the belt areas represent a second level of cortical processing.

Area MM

The middle medial field (MM) is one of the more tentative divisions of the auditory belt. Connection patterns and limited results from microelectrode recording provide some support for considering MM as a valid area, similar to ML in forming a crude parallel representation to that in A1 (Imig et al., 1977; Morel et al., 1993). In these experiments, MM was included as a wing of CM, which remains as an alternative interpretation of the organization of the belt. Merzenich and Brugge (1973) included MM in a field, "a" which adjoined both A1 and R (their RL) medially. They commented only that "a" was cytoarchitechronically distinct from A1, and that in the few recordings from "a," the best frequencies of neurons did not correspond to the progression in A1. Connections of MM are most dense with A1 (Fitzpatrick & Imig, 1980; Morel & Kaas, 1992; Morel et al., 1993). Other connections are with the lateral belt (CL and MM) and with the caudal parabelt (Hackett et al., 1998a; Morel et al., 1993). Injections of tracers in cortex near and rostral to the frontal eye field of the frontal lobe labeled neurons medial to A1 in cortex defined here as MM (Romanski et al., 1999a).

Area AL

The anterior lateral area AL is located in the portion of the auditory lateral belt that borders R. Merzenich and Brugge (1973) recorded from a few neurons in the region, and found the neurons difficult to excite but somewhat responsive to tones. They referred to the region as area "b." In owl monkeys, Imig et al. (1977) renamed the region the anterolateral field (AL), and found that neurons were broadly tuned to tone frequency in a tonotopic pattern that roughly paralleled that of adjoining R. Limited, but comparable results were obtained in macaques by Morel et al. (1993), and more extensively by Rauschecker et al. (1995); also see Kosaki et al. (1997). As for areas CL and MM, AL was described as coarsely tonotopic, with neurons being much more responsive to broadband noise and complex sounds than neurons in the core (Rauschecker et al., 1995). In addition, Tian et al. (2001) reported that neurons in AL were more responsive to the species-specific communication calls and less tuned to the locations of such calls than were neurons in CL. Thus, AL appears to be more involved in identifying rather than localizing sounds. AL connects more densely with R than with A1 (Fitzpatrick & Imig, 1980; Morel & Kaas, 1992). Cortical connections of AL are more dense with the adjoining rostral parabelt (RPB) than the caudal parabelt (CP) (Hackett et al., 1998a), while more distant connections are with orbital polysensory and prefrontal regions of the frontal lobe (Romanski et al., 1999a, 1999b). Thalamic connections include PM and Sg-Lim, (Morel & Kaas, 1992), as well as MGm and MGd (Molinari et al., 1995).

Area RM

Because of its medial location, the rostromedial area, RM, has not been well studied. RM is part of area "a" of Merzenich and Brugge (1973). The field was named RM by Imig et al. (1977), as they found neurons responsive to auditory stimuli in this region in owl monkeys, while being uncertain about distinguishing the region as a separate field. RM is strongly connected with R, and to a much lesser extent, with A1 and RT (Fitzpatrick & Imig, 1980; Jones et al., 1995; Morel & Kaas, 1992). In contrast to other areas of the belt, RM is strongly connected with both RPB and CPB of the parabelt (Hackett et al., 1998a). This suggests that the outputs of RM are more broadly distributed than those other belt fields, and contribute to both the dorsal and ventral streams of cortical processing that have been proposed as being more involved in processing "where" a sound is located (dorsal stream) or "what" the sound signifies (ventral stream, see Kaas & Hackett, 1999; Rauschecker & Tian, 2000). Injections of tracers into ML and AL demonstrate RM connections with those fields (Morel et al., 1993). The results of more recent studies involving injections placed directly in RM have not been fully published, but a preliminary analysis indicates that RM is broadly connected with other subdivisions of auditory cortex, including RT and R of the core, AL and ML of the belt, and RPB and CPB of the parabelt (de la Mothe et al., 2002).

Areas MRT and LRT

With the evidence that a third area, RT, is part of the auditory core, the lateral (rostrotemporal lateral, LRTL) and medial (medial rostrotemporal) bordering zones were assumed to be part of the auditory belt (Morel & Kaas, 1992). An injection in RT demonstrated connections with the RTM and RTL regions, and both fields have connections with RPB of the auditory parabelt (Hackett et al., 1998a). RTM also appears to be sparsely connected to part of the superior temporal gyrus just rostral to the parabelt (Hackett et al., 1998a).

THE PARABELT AS A THIRD LEVEL OF CORTICAL PROCESSING OF AUDITORY INFORMATION

The parabelt of auditory cortex is the region of temporal cortex just lateral (on a flattened view of cortex) or ventral to the lateral belt (Fig. 2.2). Injections in the belt areas label the parabelt (see above) and injections in the parabelt densely label the belt, but label few or no neurons in the core (Hackett et al., 1998a). Thus, auditory stimuli activate the parabelt cortex indirectly via the belt, and the parabelt can be considered a third level of cortical processing. The extent of the parabelt is known only approximately, as architectonic boundaries are not obvious, and the response properties of neurons in the region have not been systematically studied. Hackett et al (1998a) divided the parabelt into rostral and caudal regions or areas on the basis of differences in connections. The RPB has the densest connection with rostral belt areas, while the CPB connects more densely with the caudal belt. However, the connections patterns vary for different locations within each division of the parabelt, and a sharp, distinctive change in connection patterns was not apparent near the RPB and CPB border. Thus, the connection pattern may change gradually along the length of the parabelt in a manner that would be compatible with considering the area to be a single area, or the parabelt may have more than two divisions. Parts of the temporal lobe were considered outside the parabelt when injections failed to significantly label the belt.

Injections in the parabelt labeled a few neurons in MGd and MGm, but none in MGv (Hackett et al., 1998b). Most of the neurons labeled in the thalamus were in the Sg, Lim, and the PM. The parabelt likely depends on the belt areas for above threshold activation of neurons, but activation via MGd and MGm projections may be important sources of auditory information, and other thalamic inputs may be part of a cortico-thalamic-cortical relay (Sherman & Guillery, 2001).

The parabelt connects with adjacent regions of cortex in the superior temporal sulcus. Some of this cortex is considered polysensory (see Cusick, 1997 for review). RPB connects more with rostral portions of the superior temporal sulcus and gyrus, which both largely auditory and visual functions (Poremba et al., 2003). CPB has more connections with the caudal end of the superior temporal gyrus and sulcus, as well as the adjoining posterior parietal cortex; regions involved in somatosensory and visuomotor as well as auditory functions (Anderson et al., 1997). Yet, there is considerable overlap in the pattern of RPB and CPB connections with cortex of the superior temporal gyrus and sulcus.

The parabelt is also connected with several regions of the frontal lobe (Hackett et al., 1999; Romanski et al., 1999a, 1999b). The caudal parabelt connects with frontal cortex just rostral and possibly overlapping the frontal eye field (area 8a). These connections likely have a role in directing eye movements towards sounds of interest. Other connections of the caudal parabelt are with dorsolateral prefrontal cortex of the principal sulcus of macaque monkeys (area 46d). This cortex is involved in the short-term storage of information in working memory, especially in visuospatial working memory (Goldman-Rakic, 1996). Neurons that respond to auditory stimuli in dorsolateral prefrontal cortex are sensitive to the location of a sound source (Azuma & Suzuki, 1984; Suzuki, 1985), suggesting that this cortex is also involved in directing gaze and attention to sounds. The rostral parabelt is more connected with other parts of the frontal lobe, including a sector of ventrolateral prefrontal cortex where neurons responsive to auditory stimuli are bordered by neurons responsive to visual stimuli (Romanski & Goldman-Rakic, 2001). As species-specific vocalizations were highly effective in activating neurons, this region of cortex may be more involved in identifying sounds, rather than locating the sound source. Other connections of the rostral parabelt were with orbital frontal cortex, a multi-sensory region involved in assigning emotional value to stimuli (Zald & Kim, 2001). Early studies demonstrated that many neurons in orbital frontal cortex are activated by auditory stimuli (Benevento et al., 1977).

Is there a medial parabelt?

One question that the present model raises is whether there is a medial parabelt to match the lateral parabelt? First, all of the belt areas are densely connected with the lateral parabelt, and none of the injections that have been placed in the more accessible lateral belt areas have labeled regions of cortex that "medially" adjoin the medial auditory belt. As the belt areas all connect with the lateral parabelt, a comparable medial parabelt would also be expected to have belt connections. More importantly, much of the cortex adjoining the medial auditory belt in the depths of the lateral sulcus, including cortex of insular and upper bank of the sulcus, has somatosensory functions (Kaas, 1990). Areas in the lateral sulcus that systematically represent cutaneous receptors of the body include area S2, the parietal ventral area, PV, and the ventral somatosensory area, VS (see Qi et al, 2002). These areas appear to closely border the medial auditory belt. As they are at least predominately somatosensory in function, there is little or no space for a "medial" auditory parabelt that matches the lateral auditory parabelt. Nevertheless, some of these somatosensory areas appear to be involved in auditory functions. Area PV has a few connections with the medial auditory belt (Disbrow et al., 2003), and some neurons in VS respond to auditory stimuli (see Krubitzer et al., 1995; Qi et al., 2002). In addition, portions of somatosensory cortex of the lateral sulcus expressed increased metabolic activity in response to auditory stimuli (Poremba et al., 2003), identifying this cortex as having a role in the auditory-somatosensory interactions.

HIGHER LEVELS OF AUDITORY PROCESSING

Collectively, the regions of the temporal, parietal, and frontal lobes with direct connections with the auditory belt can be considered as representing a distributed and functionally diverse fourth level of cortical processing of auditory information. The connections of these areas in turn involve others (e.g., Tranel et al., 1988). The full extent of cortex that is involved in auditory processing in macaque monkeys was recently estimated by sectioning the corpus callosum to isolate the two hemispheres, and sectioning the afferents from the inferior colliculus to the thalamus to remove auditory inputs to one hemisphere (Poremba et al., 2003). As one hemisphere received auditory inputs and the other did not, the difference in the glucose utilization (2DG) patterns in the two hemispheres produced by a rich auditory environment revealed the probable extent of auditory and auditory-related cortex. This cortex included all of the cortex of the superior temporal gyrus and sulcus, inferior parietal cortex including the lateral bank of the intraparietal sulcus, much of the cortex of the lateral sulcus, large regions of prefrontal and orbital frontal cortex, portions of limbic cortex, and even the pole of the temporal lobe. Quite possibly, these extensive regions of cortex activated by auditory stimuli do not include all of the cortex that is influenced by auditory stimuli, as the monkeys were not required to process the auditory stimuli. Recently, the region of the auditory belt and perhaps the core has been described as having sparse projections to primary visual cortex (Falchier et al., 2002; Rockland & Ojima, 2003), suggesting that even more regions of cortex are influenced by auditory stimuli. Thus, the model in Figure 2.1 can be extended to include areas of the cortex that are beyond the fourth level of auditory processing.

THE INTERHEMISPHERIC CONNECTIONS OF AUDITORY CORTEX

Another shortcoming of the present model is that it doesn't include the connections between auditory areas of the two cerebral hemispheres. Although the callosal connections of core, belt, and parabelt auditory areas have been studied (e.g., Fitzpatrick & Imig, 1980; Hackett et al., 1999; Morel & Kaas, 1992; Morel et al., 1993), these connections were not included here in order to avoid an overly complicated diagram. In general, each auditory area is interconnected with its counterpart in the other hemisphere, as well as 1–3 areas at the same level, and 2–3 areas at the next higher and lower levels. Thus, callosal connections would add to the network properties of the model by including additional pathways of interaction. Each auditory area appears to be integrating inputs from several areas in the same and the opposite hemispheres, while receiving feedback from several areas of higher levels in both hemispheres.

SUMMARY AND CONCLUSIONS

1. We have presented a model of the auditory systems in primates that reflects the complexity of the system at subcortical and early cortical levels, but is less specific about subdivisions and connections at higher levels. As the model is based on a number of experimental observations on the auditory systems of New and Old World monkeys, it is likely to closely reflect the organization of the auditory systems of these primates, especially subcortically, where there appears to be considerable consistency across mammalian species, and for the first 3–4 levels of cortical processing. Less is known about how the model applies to prosimian primates, where there are few experimental studies. The somatosensory and visual systems are less elaborated at the cortical levels in prosimian primates. Likewise, little is known about how the model applies to auditory cortex of apes and humans, although the core of both taxa may include three areas.
2. The components of the model can be tested, and the model can be modified and expanded as additional results are obtained. Hopefully, the validity of the model for designated subcortical nuclei and connections can be evaluated with relatively few experiments, as primates appear to resemble non-primates in subcortical organization. The evidence for A1 and R, and their connection patterns is good, but more experiments with multiple tracers in the same cases would be useful. The connections of some of the proposed belt areas have been described, but little is known about others, especially the medial belt areas. Two

divisions of the parabelt have been proposed, but additional evidence might subdivide the region further. We know little about how regions connected with the parabelt are subdivided into areas, and how these areas relate to other fields. Finally, the model needs to be expanded to consider the subcortical targets of areas of auditory and multisensory cortex, including interconnections with the pulvinar and other thalamic nuclei, the basal ganglia, the limbic system, and the inferior colliculus. We need to know more about how neurons in proposed subdivisions are similar and different in how they respond to auditory stimuli, and how inactivation of areas affect auditory behavior. The research that needs to be done is considerable, but a model of the auditory system can be a useful guide to this research; and research results can feedback to reform and elaborate the model.

REFERENCES

Aitkin, L.M., Kudo, M., & Irvine, D.R. (1988). Connections of the primary auditory cortex in the common marmoset (*Callithrix jacchus jacchus*). The Journal of Comparative Neurology, 269, 235–248.

Aitkin, L.M., Merzenich, M.M., Irvine, D.R., Clarey, J.C., & Nelson, J. E. (1986). Frequency representation in auditory cortex of the common marmoset (*Callithrix jacchus jacchus*). The Journal of Comparative Neurology, 252, 175–185.

Anderson, R.A., Synder, L.H., Bradley, D.C., & Xing, J. (1997). Multimodal representation of space in the posterior parietal cortex and its use in planning movements. Annual Review of Neuroscience, 20, 303–330.

Azuma, M., & Suzuki, H. (1984). Properties and distribution of auditory neurons in the dorsolateral prefrontal cortex of the alert monkey. Brain Research, 90, 57–73.

Benevento, L.A., Fallon, J.H., Davis, B.J., & Rezak, M. (1977). Auditory-visual interaction in single cells of the superior temporal sulcus and orbitofrontal cortex of the macaque monkey. Experimental Neurology, 57, 849–872.

Blumell, S., de la Mothe, L.A., Y. Kajikawa, Kaas, J.H., & Hackett, T.A. (2002). Architectonic subdivisions and subcortical connections of the primate inferior colliculus. Abstracts – Society for Neuroscience, 261.12.

Brugge, J.F. (1982). Auditory cortical areas in primates. In C.N. Woolsey (Ed.), Cortical Sensory Organization (pp. 59–70). Clifton, NJ: Humana Press.

Burton, H., & Jones, E.G. (1976). The posterior thalamic region and its cortical projection in New World and Old Word monkeys. The Journal of Comparative Neurology, 168, 249–302.

Cheung, S.W., Bedenbaugh, P.H., Nagarajan, S.S., & Schreiner, C.E. (2001). Functional organization of squirrel monkey primary auditory cortex: Responses to pure tones. Journal of Neurophysiology, 85, 1732–1749.

Cusick, C.G. (1997). The superior temporal polysensory region in monkeys. In K.S. Rockland, J.H. Kaas, & A. Peters (Eds.), Cerebral cortex: Extrastriate cortex in primates (pp. 435–463). New York: Plenum Press.

de la Mothe, L., Blumell, S., Kajikawa, Y., & Hackett, T.A. (2002). Cortical connections of medial belt cortex in marmoset monkeys. Abstracts – Society for Neuroscience, 261.6.

Disbrow, E., Litinas, E., Recanzone, G.H., Padberg, J., & Krubitzer, L. (2003). Cortical connections of the second somatosensory area and the parietal ventral area in macaque monkeys. The Journal of Comparative Neurology, 462, 382–399.

Falchier, A., Clavagnier, S., Barone, P., & Kennedy, H., (2002). Anatomical evidence of multimodal integration in primate striate cortex. Journal of Neuroscience, 22, 5749–5759.

Felleman, D.J., & Van Essen, D.C. (1991). Distributed hierarchical processing in the primate cerebral cortex. Cerebral Cortex, 1, 1–47.

Fitzpatrick, K.A., & T.J. Imig, (1980). Auditory cortico-cortical connections in the owl monkey. The Journal of Comparative Neurology, 177, 537–556.

Formisano, E., Kim, D.-S., DiSalle, F., van de Moortele, P.-S., Ugurbil, K., & Goebel, R. (2003). Mirror-symmetric tonotopic maps in human primary auditory cortex. Neuron, 40, 859–869.

Foxe, J.J., Wylie, G.R., Martinez, A., Schroeder, C.E., Javitt, D.C., Guilfoyle, D., Ritter, W., & Murray, M.M. (2002). Auditory-somatosensory multisensory processing in auditory association cortex: An fMRI study. Journal of Neurophysiology, 88, 540–543.

Fu, K.M., Johnston,T.A., Shah, A.S., Arnold, L., Smiley, J., Hackett, T.A, Garraghty, P.E., & Schroeder, C.E. (2003). Auditory cortical neurons respond to somatosensory stimulation. Journal of Neuroscience, 23, 7510–7515.

Galaburda, A.M., & Pandya, D.N. (1983). This intrinsic architectonic and connectional organization of the superior temporal region of the rhesus monkey. The Journal of Comparative Neurology, 221, 169–184

Goldman-Rakic, P.S. (1996). The prefrontal landscape: implications of functional architecture for understanding human mentation and the central executive. Philosophical Transactions of the Royal Society of London. Series B. Biological Sciences, 351, 1445–1453.

Hackett, T.A. (2002). The comparative anatomy of the primate auditory cortex. In A.A. Ghazanfar (Ed.), Primate Audition, Ethology and Neurobiology (pp. 199–219). Boca Raton: CRC Press.

Hackett, T.A., Preuss, T.M., & Kaas, J.H. (2001). Architectonic identification of the core region in auditory cortex of macaques, chimpanzees, and humans. The Journal of Comparative Neurology, 441, 197–222.

Hackett, T.A., Stepniewska, I., & Kaas, J.H. (1998a). Subdivisions of auditory cortex and ipsilateral cortical connections of the parabelt auditory cortex in macaque monkeys. The Journal of Comparative Neurology, 394, 475–495.

Hackett, T.A., Stepniewska, I., & Kaas, J.H. (1998b). Thalamocortical connections of parabelt auditory cortex in macaque monkeys. The Journal of Comparative Neurology, 400, 271–286.

Hackett, T.A., Stepniewska, I., & Kaas, J.H. (1999). Prefrontal connections of the auditory parabelt cortex in macaque monkeys. Brain Research, 817, 45–58.

Hashikawa, T., Molinari, M., Rausell, E., & Jones, E.G. (1995). Patchy and laminar terminations of medial geniculate axons in monkey auditory cortex. The Journal of Comparative Neurology, 362, 195–208.

Howard, M.A., Volkov, I.O., Abbas, P.J., Damasio, H., Ollendieck, M.C., & Granner M.A. (1996). A chronic microelectrode investigation of the tonotopic organization of human auditory cortex. Brain Research, 724, 260–264.

Imig, T.J., Ruggero, M.A., Kitzes, L.M., Javel, E., & Brugge, J.F. (1977). Organization of auditory cortex in the owl monkey (*Aotus trivirgatus*). The Journal of Comparative Neurology, 171, 111–128.

Jones, E.G. (1985). The thalamus. New York: Plenum Press.

Jones, E.G., Dell'Anna, M.E. Molinari, M., Rausell, E., & Hashikawa, T. (1995). Subdivisions of macaque monkey auditory cortex revealed by calcium-binding protein immunoreactivity. The Journal of Comparative Neurology, 362, 153–170.

Kaas, J.H. (2000). Somatosensory system. In G. Paxinos & J.K. Mai (Eds.), The Human Nervous System (pp. 1059–1092). New York: Elsevier.

Kaas, J.H., & Hackett, T.A. (1999). 'What' and 'where' processing in auditory cortex. Nature Neuroscience, 2, 1045–1047.

Kaas, J.H., & Hackett, T.A. (2000). Subdivisions of auditory cortex and processing streams in primates. Proceedings of the National Academy of Sciences USA, 97, 11793–11799.

Kaas, J.H., & Lyon, D.C. (2001). Visual cortex organization in primates: Theories of V3 and adjoining visual areas. Progress in Brain Research, 134, 285–295.

Kosaki, H., Haskikawa, T., He, J., & Jones, E.G. (1997). Tonotopic organization of auditory cortical fields delineated by parvalbumin immunoreactivity in macaque monkeys. The Journal of Comparative Neurology, 386, 304–316.

Krubitzer, L.A., Clarey, J., Tweedale, R., Elson, G., & Calford, M. (1995). A redefinition of somatosensory areas in the lateral sulcus of macaque monkeys. Journal of Neuroscience, 15, 3821–3839.

Luethke, L.E., Krubitzer, L.A., & Kaas, J.H. (1988). Cortical connections of electrophysiologically and architectonically defined subdivisions of auditory cortex in squirrels. The Journal of Comparative Neurology, 268, 181–203.

Luethke, L.E., Krubitzer, L.A., & Kaas, J.H. (1989). Connections of primary auditory cortex in the New World monkey, Saguinus. The Journal of Comparative Neurology, 285, 487–513.

Lütkenhöner, B., Lammertamann C., Ross, D., & Steinstäter, O. (2001). Tonotopic organization of the human auditory cortex revisited: High-precision neuromagnetic studies. In D.J. Breebaart, A.J.M. Houstma, A. Kohlrausch, V.F. Prijs, & R. Schoonhoven (Eds.), Proceedings of the 12th International Symposium on Hearing. Physiological and psychophysical bases of auditory function (pp 129–136). Maastricht: Shaker.

Lütkenhöner, B., & Steinstäter, O. (1998). High-precision neuromagnetic study of the functional organization of the human auditory cortex. Audiology & Neuro-otology, 3, 191–213.

Merzenich, M.M., & Brugge, J.F. (1973). Representation of the cochlear partition on the superior temporal plane of the macaque monkey. Brain Research, 50, 275–296.

Molinari, M., Dell'Anna, M.E, Rausell, E., Leggio, M.G., Hashikawa, T., & Jones. E.G. (1995). Auditory thalamocortical pathways defined in monkeys by calcium-binding protein immunoreactivity. The Journal of Comparative Neurology, 362, 171–194.

Mesulam, M.M., & Pandya, D.N. (1973). The projections of the medial geniculate complex within the sylvian fissure of the rhesus monkey. Brain Research, 60, 315–333.

Morel, A., Garraghty, P.E., & Kaas, J.H. (1993). Tonotopic organization, architectonic fields, and connections of auditory cortex in macaque monkeys. The Journal of Comparative Neurology, 335, 437–459.

Morel, A., & Kaas, J.H. (1992). Subdivisions and connections of auditory cortex in owl monkeys. The Journal of Comparative Neurology, 318, 27–63.

Neagu, T.A., Hackett, T.A., & Kaas, J.H. (1998). Architectonic subdivisions and commissural connections of the inferior colliculus in squirrel and macaque monkeys. Abstracts – Society for Neuroscience, 24, 1881.

Pandya, D.N., & Sanides, F. (1973). Architectonic parcellation of the temporal operculum in rhesus monkey and its projection pattern. Zeitschrift für Anatomie und Entwicklungsgeschichte, 139, 127–161.

Pantev, C., Bertrand, O., Eulitz, D., Verkindt, C., Hampson, S., Schuierer, G., & Elbert, T. (1995). Specific tonotopic organizations of different areas of the human auditory cortex revealed by simultaneous magnetic and electric recordings. Electroencephalography and Clinical Neurophysiology, 94, 26–40.

Poremba, A., Saunders, R.C., Crane, A.M., Cook, M., Sokoloff, L., & Mishkin. M. (2003). Functional mapping of the primate auditory system. Science, 299, 568–572.

Preuss, T.M., & Goldman-Rakic, P.S. (1991). Myelo- and cytoarchitecture of the granular frontal cortex and surrounding regions in the strepsirhine primate Galago and the anthropoid primate Macaca. The Journal of Comparative Neurology, 310, 429–474.

Qi, H.-X., Lyon, D.C., & Kaas, J.H. (2002). Cortical and thalamic connections of the parietal ventral somatosensory area in marmoset monkeys (Callithrix jacchus). The Journal of Comparative Neurology, 443, 168–182.

Rauschecker, J.P., & Tian, B. (2000). Mechanisms and streams for processing of "what" and 'where" in auditory cortex. Proceedings of the National Academy of Sciences USA, 97, 11800–11806.

Rauschecker, J.P., Tian, B., & Hauser, M. (1995). Processing of complex sounds in the macaque nonprimary auditory cortex. Science, 268, 111–114.

Rauschecker, J.P., Tian, B., Pons, T., & Mishkin, M. (1997). Serial and parallel processing in rhesus monkey auditory cortex. The Journal of Comparative Neurology, 382, 89–103.

Recanzone, G.H., Guard, D.C. & Phan, M.L. (2000a). Frequency and intensity response properties of single neurons in the auditory cortex of the behaving macaque monkey. Journal of Neurophysiology, 83, 2315–2331.

Recanzone, G.H., Guard, D.C., &. Phan, M.L. (2000b). Correlations between the activity of single auditory cortical neurons and sound-localization behavior in the macaque monkey. Journal of Neurophysiology, 83, 2723–2739.

Rivier, F., & Clarke, S. (1997). Cytochrome oxidase, acetylcholinesterase, and NADPHDiaphrose staining in human supratemporal and insular cortex: Evidence for multiple auditory areas. NeuroImage, 6, 288–304.

Rockland, K.S., & Ojima, J., (2003). Multisensory convergence in calcarine visual areas in macaque monkey. International Journal of Psychophysiology, 50, 19–26.

Romanski, L.M., Bates, J.F., & Goldman-Rakic, P.S. (1999a). Auditory belt and parabelt projections to the prefrontal cortex in the rhesus monkey. The Journal of Comparative Neurology, 403, 141–157.

Romanski, L.M., & Goldman-Rakic, P.S. (2001). An auditory domain in primate prefrontal cortex. Nature Neuroscience, 5, 15–16.

Romanski, L.M., Tian, B., Fritz, J., Mishkin, M., Goldman-Rakic, P., & Rauschecker, J.P. (1999b). Dual streams of auditory afferents target multiple domains in the primate prefrontal cortex. Nature Neuroscience, 2, 1131–1136.

Schroeder, C.E., Lendsley, R.W., Specht, C., Marcovici, A., Smiley, J.F., & Javitt, D.C. (2001). Somatosensory input to auditory association cortex in the macaque monkey. Journal of Neurophysiology, 85, 1322–1327.

Sherman, S.M., & Guillery, R.W. (2001). Exploring the thalamus. San Diego: Academic Press.

Suzuki, H. (1985). Distribution and organization of visual and auditory neurons in the monkey prefrontal cortex. Vision Research, 25, 465–469.

Talavage, T.M., Ledden, P.J., Benson, R.R., Rosen, B.R., & Melcher, J.R. (2000). Frequency-dependent responses exhibited by multiple regions in human auditory cortex. Hearing Research, 150, 224–244.

Tian, B., Reser, D., Durham, A., Kustove, A., & Rauschecker, J.P. (2001). Functional specialization in rhesus monkey auditory cortex. Science, 292, 290–293.

Tranel, D., Brady, D.R.. van Hoesen, G.W., &. Damasio. A.R. (1988). Parahippocampal projections to posterior auditory association cortex (area Tpt) in Old World Monkeys. Experimental Brain Research, 70, 406–416.

Wallace, M.N., Johnston, P.W., & Palmer, A.R. (2002). Histochemical identification of cortical areas in the auditory region of the human brain. Experimental Brain Research, 143, 499–508.

Zald, D.H., & Kim, S.W. (2001). The orbitofrontal cortex. In S.P. Salloway, P.F. Malloy & J.D. Duffy (Eds.), The frontal lobes and neuropsychiatric illness. Washington, DC: American Psychiatric Press.

3. ANATOMICAL ORGANIZATION OF THE HUMAN AUDITORY CORTEX: CYTOARCHITECTURE AND TRANSMITTER RECEPTORS

Patricia Morosan, Jörg Rademacher,
Nicola Palomero-Gallagher, Karl Zilles

THE HUMAN AUDITORY CORTEX IS NOT A SINGLE ARCHITECTONIC FIELD

It is generally accepted, that the human auditory cortex consists of various anatomically and functionally distinct areas located in the dorsal (anterior: planum polare Pp; central: Heschl's gyrus HG, posterior: planum temporale Pt) and lateral parts of the superior temporal gyrus (STG) as well as in the inferior parietal lobule (Belin & Zatorre, 2000; Griffiths & Warren, 2002; Morosan et al., 2001, Warren & Griffiths, 2003; Zatorre et al., 2002). Amongst these different auditory fields, the putative primary auditory cortex (PAC) is found on the transverse gyrus (Heschl's gyrus) of the STG (Clarke & Rivier, 1998; Hackett et al, 2001; Rademacher et al., 2001, 2002). However, there is no agreement on the number, extent and nomenclature of human auditory areas. Furthermore, the functions of the different anatomically defined putative auditory areas in the human cortex are not known in sufficient detail.

Brodmann (1909) described the heterogeneous microstructural organization of the STG in his pioneering cytoarchitectonic studies (Figs. 3.1A and 3.1B). He identified four areas, the Brodmann areas (BA) 22, 41, 42, and 52. Systematic attempts to correlate cytoarchitecture and auditory dysfunctions of the human cerebral cortex have been done by Kleist (1934), who compared the localization of cortical lesions and the resulting dysfunctions with Brodmann's map. Lesion studies in the human brain are difficult to interpret (e.g., lesions are mostly large, covering several areas, postlesional plasticity), and therefore, there was no way of studying the *normal* functions of BA 22, 41, 42, and 52 until the advent of non-invasive functional neuroimaging techniques. Presently, Brodmann's map is frequently used to designate the anatomical sites of human brain functions by using the version of his map in the atlas of Talairach and Tournoux (1988).

The advances in functional brain mapping have stimulated recent cytoarchitectonic and histochemical studies of the human auditory cortex (e.g., Clarke & Rivier, 1998; Hackett et al., 2001; Kaas & Hackett, 2000; Morosan et al., 2001; Rademacher et al., 1993, 2001; Rivier & Clarke, 1997). In particular, a new method for observer-independent identification and localization of borders of cortical areas has been developed (Amunts et al., 2002; Schleicher et al., 1999; Zilles et al., 2002b) and applied to the cytoarchitectonic parcellation of the human auditory cortex (Morosan et al., 2001). Recently, the visualization of various transmitter receptors has been used to identify the human PAC (Zilles et al., 2002a).

The number, position, and size of primary, or primary-like auditory areas is still a matter of debate (Brodmann, 1909; Galaburda & Sanides, 1980; Hackett et al., 2001; Morosan et al., 2001; von Economo & Horn, 1930; von Economo & Koskinas, 1925), since the techniques for functional-structural analysis of the cerebral cortex as used in animal research (e.g., tracing of long fiber tracts, electrophysiology and single cell labeling) cannot be applied to living human subjects. Furthermore, it is only recently that functional imaging data could be directly compared with cytoarchitectonic studies in the same spatial reference system (e.g., Mazziotta et al., 2001; Roland & Zilles, 1998; Zilles et al., 2002b). Thus, the present chapter will present

- recent concepts of the architectonic organization of the putative auditory cortex in the human brain based on observer-independent, quantitative cyto- and receptorarchitectonic mapping, and
- 3-D population maps of architectonically defined auditory areas in a stereotaxic reference system ("reference brain") which can be used for direct comparisons with functional imaging studies.

BRODMANN'S AREAS 22, 41, AND 42 REVISITED

According to Brodmann (1909), the STG contains four cytoarchitectonically distinct areas: 22, 41, 42, and 52 (Figs. 3.1A and 3.1B). BA 41 is located on HG, contains densely packed small granular neurons in layer IV invading layer III, and thus, represents the koniocortical region of HG. The koniocortical structure of BA 41 is an important argument for its classification as the putative primary auditory cortex, because the only other koniocortical areas in the human isocortex are the primary somatosensory (S1) and visual (V1) areas. A further argument is the finding, that HG is the cortical target of the auditory radiation originating in the medial geniculate body (Flechsig, 1908). The less granular

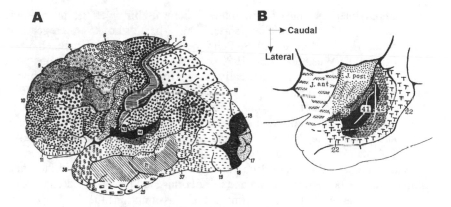

Fig. 3.1. Cytoarchitectonic map of the human auditory cortex (Brodmann, 1909). **A.** Lateral view. **B.** View of the supratemporal plane in the depth of the Sylvian fissure.

areas BA 42 and 22 as well as BA 52 may represent cytoarchitectonic correlates of further levels of auditory processing surrounding PAC (BA 41). The localization of unimodal secondary and tertiary auditory areas adjacent to the respective primary area would parallel similar spatial relations in the somatosensory and visual domains.

Although the parcellation of the human auditory cortex into the primary area BA 41, surrounded by unimodal secondary areas (BA 42, BA 52), and the higher order area BA 22 has been adopted in the atlas of Talairach and Tournoux (1988) and is widely used for the anatomical identification in functional imaging studies, Brodmann's identification of only a few auditory areas is difficult to reconcile with recent comparative studies in macaque monkeys showing many more areas, and with the enormous functional heterogeneity of the human auditory cortex as revealed by neuroimaging studies. Thus, a critical evaluation of Brodmann's parcellation (Brodmann, 1909) and similar cytoarchitectonic maps by others (Sarkisov et al., 1949; von Economo & Horn, 1930; von Economo & Koskinas, 1925) seems to be timely.

Some problems of Brodmann's and other's architectonic mapping are caused by methodical aspects, for example: (1) The restricted sensitivity for detecting microstructural borders in studies based on histological sections stained by a single technique (e.g., only Nissl-stain or myelin stain, no comparison with other techniques). (2) The parcellations are based on observer-dependent definitions of areal borders by simple visual inspection without quantification and rigorous testing of the significance of the findings, thereby introducing a major element of subjectivity into the definition of borders, as well as into the extent and shape of each cortical area. (3) The schematic presentation of the cortical surface and areal borders results in a lack of 3-D information, and in most cases, a nearly complete lack of the parcellation of the cortical surface hidden in the sulci. (4) The lack of analysis of the considerable intersubject variability of human brain morphology and particular borders of cortical areas.

A substantial interhemispheric and intersubject variability of the macro- and microanatomy of the auditory cortex has been, however, repeatedly demonstrated (Leonard et al., 1998; Penhune et al., 1996; Rademacher et al., 1993, 2001, 2002; Westbury et al., 1999). Until recently, further problems were caused by the lack of a sufficiently powerful technique for the spatial transformation ("warping") of microscopical data from histological sections into a common spatial reference system, which enables a direct comparison of the microstructural postmortem results with in vivo functional imaging data. The depiction of Brodmann's parcellation and numbering scheme in the stereotaxic atlas of Talairach and Tournoux (1988) is based on a projection of macroanatomical landmarks in Brodmann's *schematic* map and description onto landmarks of the postmortem brain and its sections, and not on cytoarchitectonic studies of those sections. Furthermore, the assumption that BA 41 is a cytoarchitectonically uniform region has not been confirmed in other studies, since subdivisions of the *koniocortex* into two (Galaburda & Sanides, 1980; Sarkisov et al., 1949; von Economo & Horn, 1930; von Economo & Koskinas, 1925), or three (Morosan et al., 2001) distinct cortical areas have been reported. It is also not entirely clear which of the reported subdivisions in one study (Brodmann, 1909; Clarke & Rivier, 1998; Galaburda & Sanides, 1980; Hackett et al., 2001; Hopf, 1954; Morosan et al., 2001; Rivier & Clarke, 1997; Sarkisov et al., 1949; von Economo & Horn, 1930; von Economo & Koskinas, 1925) is comparable to which subdivision in another study. Therefore, the approximate region of BA 41 has recently been remapped (Morosan et al., 2001) using a novel, quantitative and statistically testable cytoarchitectonic method for identification of areal borders (Amunts et al., 2002; Schleicher et al., 1999; Zilles et al., 2002b). In this study, koniocortical areas have been identified along the medio(posterior)-to-lateral(anterior) axis of HG, such as areas Te1.1, Te1.0 and Te1.2. More subdivisions of Te1 may be found if other staining methods are applied. Since cytoarchitectonic mapping was performed in a sample of ten brains (twenty hemispheres), interhemispheric and intersubject differences could be analyzed and the results were compared with the template anatomy of BA 41 as depicted in the Talairach and Tournoux (1988) atlas. Large differences between the BA 41 map of Talairach and Tournoux (1988) and the Te1 map of Morosan et al. (2001), particularly in the rostro-caudal direction, were found (Rademacher et al., 2001). The positions and borders of area Te1 of all ten examined brains were transformed by non-linear morphing procedures to the standard format of a widely used 3-D reference system represented by a MR-data set of a living brain. The resulting population map of Te1 quantitatively describes for the first time the existence of considerable intersubject and interhemispheric variability (Rademacher et al., 2001, 2002).

We think that area Te1 (Morosan et al., 2001; Rademacher et al., 2001) provides a more appropriate cytoarchitectonic depiction of PAC than the schematic concept of BA 41. The definition of further subdivisions of Te1 can serve as an anatomical reference in a systematic search for functionally defined auditory areas. The region of BA 42 (corresponding to Te2 in the present

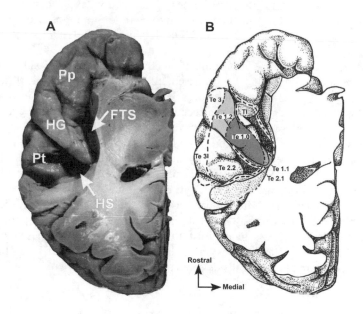

Fig. 3.2. Superior temporal plane after removal of the frontoparietal operculum in one individual brain (not included in the present study). **A.** Macroanatomical landmarks of the superior temporal plane. FTS = first transverse temporal sulcus; HS = Heschl's sulcus; HG = Heschl's gyrus; Pp = planum polare; Pt = planum temporale. **B.** Schematic drawing showing our cytoarchitectonic parcellation of the superior temporal cortex. Areas Te1.1, Te1.0, Te1.2, and Te1.3 are for their most part located on Heschl's gyrus. Te1.3 is located in the depth of Heschl's sulcus, but, in the selected view of the superior temporal plane, its topology is hidden from view by the crown of Heschl's gyrus. Areas Te2.1 and Te2.2 occupy the major part of the planum temporale, while area TI takes only a small stripe of the planum polare. Note that the borders between Te3 on the one hand and Te1.2, Te2.1, and Te2.2 on the other hand do not follow any macroanatomic landmark of the superior temporal plane.

chapter) and the posterior portion of Brodmann area 22 (corresponding to area TA$_1$ of von Economo & Koskinas (1925) or Te3 in this chapter) were also recently remapped using the quantitative cytoarchitectonic approach.

MACROANATOMICAL LANDMARKS AND THE AUDITORY CORTEX

The human auditory cortex has a complex and highly variable macroanatomic folding pattern (Fig. 3.2). After removal of the frontoparietal operculum, HG can be easily identified by its prominent size and shape (Steinmetz et al., 1989; von Economo & Koskinas, 1925). Its oblique course extends from the retroinsular region medially, to the bulge of STG laterally. An intermediate transverse sulcus occurs in some cases and subdivides – completely or incompletely – HG along its long axis into anterior and posterior portions termed "duplications" (Leonard et al., 1998; Penhune et al., 1996; Rademacher et al., 2002).

Posterior to HG there is a prominent sulcus, termed Heschl's sulcus (HS), and the planum temporale (Pt), a structure which may exhibit additional transverse gyri, unilaterally or bilaterally (Kulynych et al., 1994; Leonard et al., 1998; Musiek & Reeves, 1990). In a recent study, a single transverse gyrus was found in 70% of hemispheres, two transverse gyri in 24% of hemispheres, and three transverse gyri in the remaining 6% (Rademacher et al., 2001). Up to five transverse gyri have been described by others (Campaign & Minckler, 1976). Rostrally, the first temporal transverse sulcus separates HG from the planum polare, where no additional transverse gyri can be found. It is generally accepted that right-sided HG is shifted more rostrally than left-sided HG and that maximum side differences may result in more than 1 cm (Penhune et al., 1996; Rademacher et al., 2002). In contrast to earlier reports (e.g. Geschwind & Lewitsky, 1968), no "standard" asymmetric pattern with a larger Pt on the left side when compared to the right side seems to exist (Westbury et al., 1999).

QUANTITATIVE CYTOARCHITECTONIC MAPPING

Microscopical inspection

Area Te1 can be delimited from the adjacent less granular areas Te2 and Te3 on HG by the extremely high packing density of small round cell bodies ("granule cells") throughout the cortical layers II-IV, the lack of large or medium-sized pyramidal cells in the depth of the outer pyramidal layer (layer IIIc), a prominent inner granular layer (layer IV), and a characteristic paler-staining of the inner pyramidal layer (layer V).

The area located directly rostro-medially to Te1 has a large and cell sparse layer III, a strikingly narrower layer IV and thin but cell dense layers V and VI. It is termed *proisocortex* and it corresponds to area TI in the present chapter. Unlike area Te3, area Te2 has smaller pyramidal cells in layer IIIc, a more prominent inner granular layer, and a rather cell sparse layer V. The cytoarchitecture of the planum polare clearly contrasts that of HG and its posteriorly and laterally neighboring regions.

A sharp border separates Te3 from the neighboring area within the ventral lip of the superior temporal sulcus (area Te4). In contrast to Te3, Te4 is characterized by a rather cell dense layer II, a "cluster-like" arrangement of medium-sized IIIc pyramidal cells, a small layer IV, and rather cell dense layers V and VI.

In strictly orthogonal orientated histological sections, vertical, columnar arrangements of neurons can be observed in all three areas Te1, Te2, and Te3. Columns of neurons have already been described in auditory areas by von

Economo and Koskinas (1925). According to these authors, PAC shows short, "raindrop" like columns, while neuronal columns in non-primary areas TB and TA are larger, thus rather resembling "organ-pipes". By measuring the center-to-center distances between neighboring columns, Seldon (1985) reported that columnar width is similar in ipsilateral areas TC and TA, while in area TB spacing between columns is slightly decreased. Seldon (1985) also found significant side differences, with spacing being greater in the left hemisphere than in its right counterpart.

Observer-independent localization of areal borders

The exact positions of the borders of areas Te1, Te2 and Te3 were determined using an observer-independent quantitative method, which allows the statistical testing of the significance of changes in cytoarchitecture at interareal borders.

Ten brains from clinically and neuropathologically normal subjects ranging in age from 37 to 85 years (mean age = 65±17 years) were studied. In view of the extremes of ages analyzed, it should be mentioned, that the observer-independent method used by us for localization of areal borders is based on measurements of packing density of neurons, a cytoarchitectonic feature that, to our knowledge, does not change with age (Pakkenberg & Gundersen, 1997; Terry et al., 1987). Thus, putative variations in cell packing density may rather indicate architectonic variability than age-related changes in cytoarchitecture between subjects. Moreover, even decreases in the sizes of larger neurons, that in general can be expected in the human brain (Terry et al., 1987), have not been observed in the auditory cortex of the ten brains.

Figure 3.3 shows the cytoarchitecture of area Te3 in the youngest (37 years old) and oldest (85 years old) brain. Note that the sizes of IIIc pyramidal cells are similar across the two specimens. However, over the life span, the total amount of cortical neurons decreases at about 10% (Cragg, 1975; Pakkenberg & Gundersen, 1997), and we cannot exclude that, in our sample of ten postmortem brains, age had similar effects on neuronal number. But larger losses of neurons do not seem to occur in the superior temporal region, where, in normal subjects, no significant age-related differences in the number of neurons have been found (Gomez-Isla et al., 1997).

Independently of age, the cytoarchitecture of the brain may be affected by peri- and postmortal swelling of astrocytes. Since the ten postmortem brains were extensively dehydrated in a series of alcohol during histological processing, the swelling of cells is generally reduced to a similar level in the cell-body stained histological sections used for cytoarchitectonic analysis.

The observer-independent method for localization of areal borders was already published in detail (Schleicher et al., 1999), therefore, only a brief description of the principles will be given here. After digitization of cell-body stained histological whole brain sections with high resolution and quantification of cell body volume densities using the grey level index (GLI) procedure (Schleicher & Zilles, 1990), the laminar distribution pattern of the GLIs is

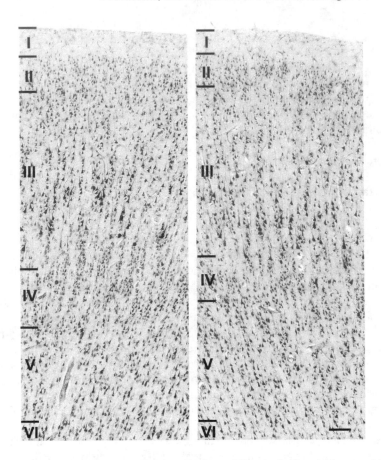

Fig. 3.3. Cytoarchitecture of area Te3 in a 37 years old brain (left) and 85 years old brain (right). Note that the sizes of the larger neurons in layer III do not significantly differ between the two brains, and the cytoarchitecture is nearly identical in both brains; scale bar = 0.1 mm.

continuously registered vertically to the cortical surface along traverses throughout the cortex. Each traverse represents an individual GLI profile (ordinate: cell body volume density (%); abscissa: cortical depth with entire cortical thickness normalized to 100%). Each profile is characterized by a set of ten features (represented together in a feature vector). To detect areal borders, the Mahalanobis distances D are calculated continuously using a sliding window procedure as a multivariate measure of the degree of dissimilarity between feature vectors of adjacent sets of profiles. Thus, the working hypothesis of this method is that feature vectors extracted from profiles located within a cortical area are more or less similar. Significant changes between the shapes of adjacent sets of profiles occur at the border between two cortical areas. The D values were then plotted in the sequence of the respective profiles (Mahalanobis distance function) along the cortical surface contour. A significant maximum of the Mahalanobis distance function may indicate a putative areal border. The following definitions and criteria must be fulfilled, before a significant maximum of the Mahalanobis distance can be accepted as a putative areal border: (i) discard maxima with $p > 0.05$ in the Hotelling's T^2 test (*statistical criterion*), (ii) accept only the absolutely highest maximum as a putative areal border, if two or more significant ($p < 0.05$) maxima are spatially separated by less than the actual size of one set of profiles (*resolution criterion*), (iii) consider only those maxima as areal borders, which were found at comparable positions across a series of at least three adjoining histological sections (*consistency criterion*).

Figure 3.4 shows an example of observer-independent localization of areal borders between Te2, Te3, and Te4. A digitized high-resolution image of a coronal brain section (Fig. 3.4A) was converted into the corresponding GLI image, where 113 individual profiles were equidistantly traced (Fig. 3.4B). Positions a and b in Figure 3.4B correspond to the position of significant maxima of the Mahalanobis distance function shown in Figure 3.4C. Index "a" corresponds to the border between Te2 and Te3, and index "b" corresponds to the border between Te3 and Te4. Figure 3.5 shows the results of the observer-independent localization of areal borders between TI, Te1, Te2, Te3, and Te4 in an additional brain. Here, "a," "e," and "f" correspond to interareal borders (TI/Te1, Te2/Te3, and Te3/multimodal area of the superior temporal sulcus, respectively). Note that the borders between Te2/Te3 and Te3/superior temporal sulcus closely correspond to the areal borders shown in Figure 3.4. Index "b" corresponds to the border between T1.1 and Te1.0, "c" corresponds to the areal border between Te1.0 and Te1.3/Te2.1, and "d" corresponds to the border between Te1.3/Te2.1 and Te2.2. The border between Te1.3 and Te2.1 was not found in the cytoarchitectonic studies at this level, but the receptor-architectonic studies (see below) suggest that an area Te1.3 may be interposed between Te1.0 and Te2.1 at more posterior levels. This demonstrates that receptor-architectonic studies may detect additional subdivisions not visible in cytoarchitectonic specimens.

Results from the observer-independent localization of areal borders confirm the parcellation of the auditory cortex into three major cytoarchitectonically distinct areas Te1, Te2, and Te3, but also introduce additional subdivisions of Te1 and Te2. The borders of Te1 show a considerable intersubject variability compared with the extent of HG (Rademacher et al., 2001). In contrast to the popular assumption, a spatial coincidence of the cytoarchitectonically defined borders of PAC with the borders of the medial two thirds of HG cannot be found in all cases. The border of Te1 is not correlated consistently with the macroanatomical geometry of landmarks such as HS, intermediate or first transverse temporal sulcus. Furthermore, the border between Te1 and Te2 cannot be related to the intermediate sulcus or to HS. Thus, the extent of HG does not provide a reliable macroanatomical landmark for the borders of PAC (Rademacher et al., 2001), and consequently variations in the shape of HG are

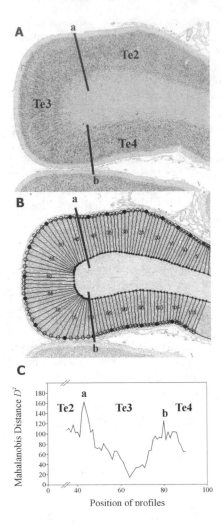

Fig. 3.4. Example of an observer-independent definition of cytoarchitectonic borders. **A.** Digitized histological and cell-body stained section comprising areas Te2, Te3, and Te4. **B.** GLI-image of A. A high GLI is represented by a dark pixel, a lower GLI is visualized by a lighter pixel. The GLI-distribution throughout the cortical depth was sampled by equidistant traverses (GLI profiles) from layer II to the grey/white matter boundary. The positions of the profiles were numbered from 1 to 113. **C.** The Mahalanobis distance D was plotted against the position of profiles (distance function). The significant maxima of the distance function at position "a" and "b" correspond to the borders between Te2/Te3 and Te3/Te4.

not correlated with parallel positional changes of the borders of PAC in a predictable way, although major or at least minor parts of the human auditory koniocortex are always found on HG.

Area Te2 occupies large portions of Pt, but the site of the upward deflection of the Sylvian fissure does not represent the posterior border of Te2. On both sides, the posterior border of Te2 is frequently located on Pt, but, occasionally, it can also encroach on the ascending part of the Sylvian fissure. Therefore, macroanatomical differences between the left and right Pt do not reflect an asymmetry of area Te2. A novel intraareal border has been identified by us within Te2 (Fig. 3.5), which subdivides this area into a more medially situated area Te2.1 and a more lateral area Te2.2. The latter area has a common border with area Te3, which is found on the free lateral surface of STG (Figs. 3.4 and 3.5). The subdivision of Te2 supports our introductory statement that, like in the primate brain, the human auditory region consists of many more cytoarchitectonic areas than shown in Brodmann's map. This finding supports recent comparative architectonic observations in macaques, chimpanzees and humans by Hackett et al. (2001). In the human, areas Te2.1 and Te2.2 probably represent counterparts of myeloarchitectonically identified areas ttr.2ai and ttr.2ae (Hopf, 1954), as well as of histochemically identified areas LP and LA (Rivier & Clarke, 1997; Wallace et al., 2002).

The border between area Te3 and Te4 is located on the ventral (Figs. 3.4 and 3.5) or ventrolateral surface of STG, but never encroaches on the middle temporal gyrus (MTG). This finding indicates that Te3 is not equivalent to BA 22, since the posterior part of BA 22 extends up to the lateral convexity of MTG. As far as one can infer from the schematic drawings of the superior temporal plane given by Rivier and Clarke (1997) and Wallace and co-workers

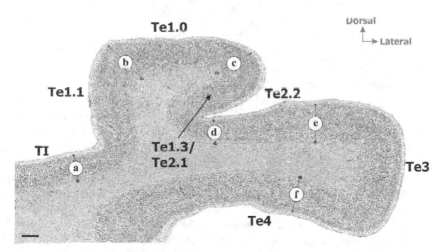

Fig. 3.5. GLI image of the superior temporal gyrus (STG) in the coronal plane. Labeled (a-f) profile positions indicate the observer-independent localization of areal borders between TI and Te1.1 ("a"), Te1.1 and Te1.0 ("b"), Te1.0 and Te1.3/Te2.1 ("c"), Te1.3/Te2.1 and Te2.2 ("d"), Te2.2 and Te3 ("e"), and Te3 and Te4 ("f"). Note that the cytoarchitectonically defined areal borders do not precisely match the macroanatomical landmarks of STG; scale bar = 1 mm.

(2002), Te3 extends both, more rostrally and more caudally than histochemically identified superior temporal area STA, probably including brain sectors that have yet not been mapped histochemically.

Subdivisions of the auditory koniocortex

Three areas, Te1.2, Te1.0, and Te1.1, have been identified along the medio-lateral axis of HG in Nissl-stained sections using the observer-independent cytoarchitectonic method. These areas share typical *koniocortical* features. Compared to the neighboring areas Te1.2 and Te1.1, the centrally located area Te1.0 is characterized by the highest packing density of small round cell bodies, the broadest layer IV and particularly small-sized IIIc pyramidal cells. In strictly orthogonal sections, the arrangement of neuronal perikarya in vertical cell columns is most clearly seen in area Te1.0 compared to Te1.1 or Te1.2. The medially located area Te1.1 is characterized by a less obvious layering and by the appearance of single, medium-sized pyramidal cells in layer IIIc. Lateral area Te1.2 shows a lower packing density of small granular cells than Te1.0 and Te1.1, and has a broader layer III with clusters of medium-sized IIIc pyramids. Layer IV is significantly wider in Te1.0 if compared to Te1.1 and Te1.2, which may indicate differences in densities of thalamo-cortical projections between the three auditory areas Te1.0, Te1.1, and Te1.2, since the primary target of the geniculo-cortical input is cortical layer IV.

Cytoarchitectonically, area Te1.2 probably corresponds to area TBC of von Economo and Horn (1930). The authors emphasize the cytoarchitectonic similarity of this area with both, area TC, which corresponds to area Te1.0, and area TB, which corresponds to area Te2. Area Te1.1 corresponds to medial area TD in the terminology of von Economo and Koskinas (1925).

More detailed subdivisions of the putative architectonic correlate of human PAC were reported in myeloarchitectonic observations (Beck, 1928; Hopf, 1954). Both authors identified a "subregio temporalis transversa profunda (ttr.1)" on HG, which shows a very high myelin density and was further subdivided into nine areas and subareas (Fig. 3.6). Subregion ttr.1 is probably the myeloarchitectonic correlate of our area Te1, and occupies most of HG.

More recently, the expression of acetylcholinesterase (AchE) has been studied in the human PAC (Clarke & Rivier, 1998; Hackett et al., 2001; Hutsler & Gazzaniga, 1996; Rivier & Clarke, 1997; Wallace et al., 2002). According to these observations PAC, as defined by intensive AchE-staining, corresponds to area TC of von Economo and Koskinas (1925) and to our area Te1.0 (Clarke & Rivier, 1998; Hackett et al., 2001; Wallace et al., 2002). It has been suggested that our medial area Te1.1 does not represent a part of the human auditory core region, but may correspond to the macaque caudomedial belt area CM (Hackett et al., 2001). Similarly, Te1.2 has been assigned to the histochemically identified anterolateral area (ALA), thus being interpreted as a part of the non-primary auditory cortex (Wallace et al., 2002). Since tracing studies of the geniculo-cortical system are not possible in the human brain, a definite decision about the

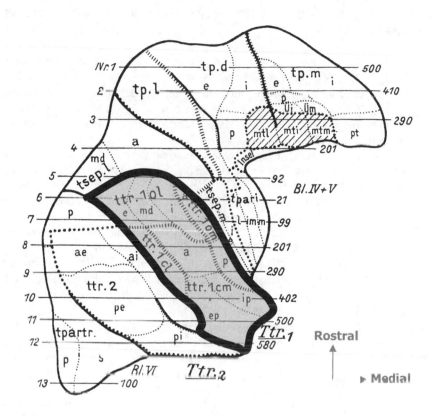

Fig. 3.6. Parcellation of the dorsal plane of superior temporal gyrus (STG) in a myeloarchitectonic study of Hopf (1954). More than 35 cortical areas and suburous were delineated in this part of the STG (modified after Hopf, 1954). The putative correlate of our area Te1 is indicated by the shaded grey area surrounded by a thick black line.

classification of the human areas Te1.2 and Te1.1 as core or belt areas is difficult.

Several components of auditory evoked potentials (MLAEPs, N30, P50, N60, and N75) have been differentiated along the medio-lateral axis of HG (Liegeois Chauvel et al., 1994). N30 is generated in the medial and P50 in the central part of HG. Both activations were interpreted as responses of the primary auditory cortex to tone burst. The generator sources of N60 and N75 are located in the lateral part of HG. Recent functional imaging studies of foreground-background decomposition of auditory perception cortex show two regional specific activations of HG, T1a and T1b (Scheich et al., 1998). These foci of activation are probably located in our areas Te1.1, Te1.0 (T1b), and Te1.2 (T1a).

REGIONAL AND LAMINAR DISTRIBUTION PATTERNS OF NEUROTRANS-MITTER RECEPTORS

The areal and laminar distribution of receptors of different transmitters (cholinergic nicotinic and muscarinic M2 receptors; serotoninergic 5-HT_2 receptors; glutamatergic AMPA and kainate receptors; adrenergic α_1 and α_2 receptors; GABAergic GABA_A receptors) were visualized in six human hemispheres by means of a previously described in vitro autoradiographic labeling procedure (Zilles et al., 2002a).

A major finding is, that our cytoarchitectonic parcellation of the human auditory cortex into areas Te1, Te2 and Te3 shows a perfect agreement with the regional distribution of the densities of the presently analyzed eight different transmitter receptors (Figs. 3.7 and 3.8). As all primary sensory cortices (Zilles et al., 2002a, 2002b), Te1 shows an exceptionally high density of muscarinic M2 receptors which is significantly higher than that measured in Te2 or Te3 (Fig. 3.7) of six hemispheres (Figs. 3.7B, C). Area Te4 shows a low mean (averaged over all cortical layers) density of M2 receptors. By contrast, medial area TI exhibits a rather high density of M2 receptors in the infragranular layers.

The 5-HT_2, α_2, and GABA_A receptors reach higher supragranular than infragranular densities, and are present in higher densities in Te1 than in Te2 or Te3 (Fig. 3.8). Compared to areas Te2 and Te3, Te1 shows higher mean concentrations of nicotinic receptor densities (Fig. 3.8). AMPA, kainate and α_1 receptors, however, show lowest densities in Te1. AMPA receptor densities are highest in layers I-III, and decrease towards deeper layers, reaching lowest values in layer VI. Kainate receptors show highest concentrations in layers V-VI, and slightly higher values in layers I-II than in the adjacent layers III and IV. The α_1 receptors have a clear bilaminar distribution pattern, with higher densities in layers I-III and V-VI than in layer IV. The mean density of α_1 receptors is lowest in area Te1.0.

The cytoarchitectonic subdivision of the koniocortex Te1 into areas Te1.0, Te1.1 and Te1.2 is also reflected by changes in receptor densities. Additionally, a further subdivision of Te1, area Te1.3, was found in the receptor architectonically studies laterally of Te1.0 and posteriorly to Te1.2. Te1.0 shows highest nicotinic, M2, 5-HT_2, α_2 and GABA_A but lowest kainate receptor densities averaged over all cortical layers. A careful inspection of the autoradiograph showing the nicotinic receptor distribution reveals that, like in area Te1.0, a sharp line of higher receptor density can also be seen at precisely the location Te1.1. Compared to Te1.3, Te1.1 shows higher densities of the M2 receptors (Fig. 3.7). AMPA receptors are most densely expressed in Te1.1. The laminar distribution pattern of the AMPA receptor in Te1.0 shares features with the laminar patterns both in area Te1.3 (low densities in the infragranular layers) and Te1.1 (high densities in the supragranular layers).

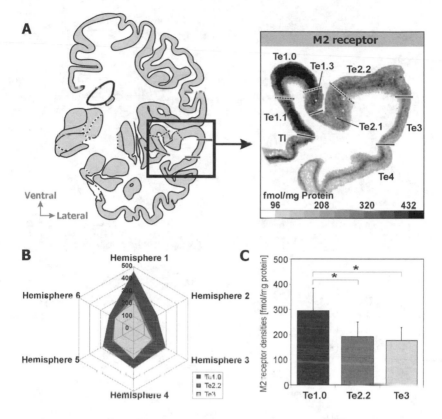

Fig. 3.7. A. Distribution of the muscarinic M2 receptors in a coronal section through the superior temporal gyrus. The lines indicate areal borders. **B.** Polar plot showing the mean density (averaged over all cortical layers) of M2 receptors in six individual human hemispheres. **C.** Mean M2 receptor densities were significantly higher in Te1.0 than in Te2.2 and Te3.

INTERSUBJECT VARIABILITY OF HUMAN PRIMARY AUDITORY CORTEX

The intersubject variability of human PAC has been studied by von Economo and Horn (1930), but it was only much later that systematic observations on topographic variability were reported. Galaburda and Sanides (1980) found large interindividual differences in the size of primary and non-primary auditory areas, and, in the early 1990s, intersubject differences in position and extent of PAC were described by Rademacher et al. (1993). Recently, the intersubject variability of area Te1 was studied in a sample of 27 brains (Rademacher et al., 2001). As expected from earlier studies, the volume of PAC varied to a high degree between the individual brains. The volume of Te1 reached 1683±538

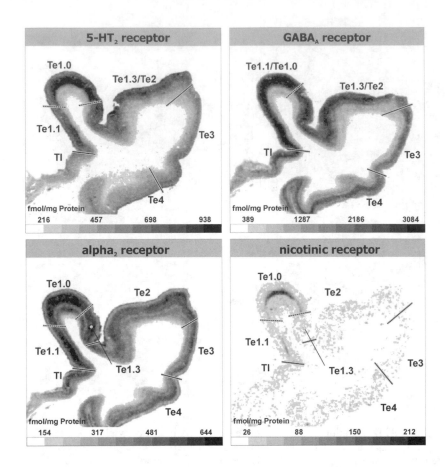

Fig. 3.8. Distribution of the serotoninergic $5HT_2$, the GABAergic $GABA_A$, the adrenergic α_2 and the cholinergic nicotinic receptors in coronal sections through the superior temporal gyrus. The lines indicate areal borders.

mm^3 in the left and 1581 ± 564 mm^3 in the right hemisphere, but no significant interhemispheric differences were found.

Since the borders of Te1 cannot be determined reliably in MR images of living brains using macroanatomical landmarks (see part III above), postmortem studies on intersubject variability in position, extent and shape of Te1 can provide useful information.

The average location of area Te1, for example, differs largely from the average location of HG (Rademacher et al., 2001). Maximal differences were found at the lateral border. The lateral border of Te1 is located more medially by ~10 mm on the left side and by ~6 mm on the right side than the lateral border of HG. Thus, the extent of the cytoarchitectonically defined area Te1 (koniocortex, putative PAC) is grossly overestimated by this macroanatomical landmark. Furthermore, the HG or BA 41 in a single hemisphere, such as in the Talairach atlas, cannot sufficiently represent the range of intersubject and interhemispheric variations in a population. Maximum differences between the extent of area Te1 in the right or left hemispheres and BA 41 as derived from the Talairach atlas were 16 mm in the sagittal plane, 18 mm in the coronal plane, and 14 mm in the axial plane. Topographical ambiguity on the order of centimeters is, however, relevant, because functional studies have indicated that specific auditory functions may be located only a few millimeters apart. For example, the auditory peak N1m arises from a cortical generator located about 5 mm posterior to the middle-latency peak of Pam (Pantev et al., 1995).

In view of the huge intersubject topographical variability of cortical areas, maps of the human cortex should not display borders of cortical areas without giving at least an impression of the intersubject variability. Thus, schematic maps and macroanatomical landmarks can be heavily misleading when they are used for the anatomical localization of functional foci. Therefore, probability (or population) maps of cortical areas seem to be the only way to bring architectonic findings on intersubject variability into a spatial reference system, which can be used for the interpretation of functional imaging data (Amunts et al., 1999, 2000; Geyer et al., 1999, 2000; Mazziotta et al., 2001; Roland & Zilles, 1994, 1996; Zilles et al., 1995).

POPULATION MAPS: IMPLICATIONS FOR FUNCTIONAL NEURO-IMAGING

The cell body-stained serial sections of each individual brain were digitized and used for 3-D reconstructions ("histological volume"). The histological volume was then warped to the 3-D reconstruction from MR images of the same brain ("MR volume"), which had been obtained prior to histological procedure in order to compensate for inevitable distortions caused by the histological technique. This warping step (i.e., histological to MR volume) used both linear and nonlinear transformations, and provides a correction of the histological distortions.

Following the observer-independent definition of cytoarchitectonic borders of auditory cortical areas, the areas were interactively traced onto the respective sections of the histological volume. As a result, volume data sets of ten brains including cytoarchitectonically defined areas were created, which demonstrate the considerable interindividual topographical variability of cortical areas.

Finally, the histological volumes with the labeled cortical areas were warped using a nonlinear, elastic transformation procedure to a common spatial reference system, which can be the MR volume of a "mean" brain or a single in vivo MR-imaged individual brain (Roland & Zilles, 1994, 1996, 1998). We prefer a single individual brain as "standard reference brain," since its 3-D reconstruction clearly shows a gyral and sulcal pattern, which is not visible on the smooth surface of a "mean" brain but useful for the comparative identification of macroanatomical landmarks. This complex procedure allows to compensate for the macroanatomical intersubject variability of the brains, and to achieve a maximal anatomical overlap between the different *post mortem* brains and between them and the reference brain (Schormann & Zilles, 1997, 1998). All ten individual maps of cortical areas were superimposed during this warping procedure in the standard reference brain. As a result, population (or probability) maps were obtained, which quantify and display the intersubject variability in the extent, shape and topography of cortical areas (Amunts & Zilles, 2001). Each voxel in the standard reference brain shows by color- or greyvalue coding (Figs. 3.9 and 3.10), whether the same cortical area in one brain (10% population map) or more brains (up to ten brains, 100% population map) occurs in these voxels.

Figure 3.9 shows population maps of Te1, Te2 and Te3 in MR images of a reference brain. The coronal and axial planes are depicted to demonstrate the principle and utility of multiple views in the 3D reference system. Figure 3.10 is an example of a probability atlas of Te1 shown in the axial plane, which shows most clearly that Te1 in the right hemisphere is shifted rostrally when compared to its homologue area in the left hemisphere. Such left-right differences in location of Te1 imply that there is considerable interhemispheric difference in the spatial position of cortical neurons corresponding to the same level of auditory processing. This is important for the anatomical interpretation of functional imaging data. For example, an interhemispheric shift in the center of functional activation does not necessarily mean that different auditory areas are activated, and vice versa, symmetrical activations in both hemispheres may be

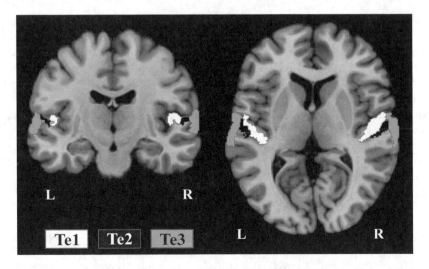

Fig. 3.9. Population maps of Te1, Te2 and Te3 in the spatial format of the reference brain (coronal (left) and axial (right) planes). White = area Te1 (voxels with overlap of at least 5 out of 10 brains); black = area Te2 (overlap of at least 3 out of 4 brains); gray = area Te3 (overlap of at least 5 out of 10 brains).

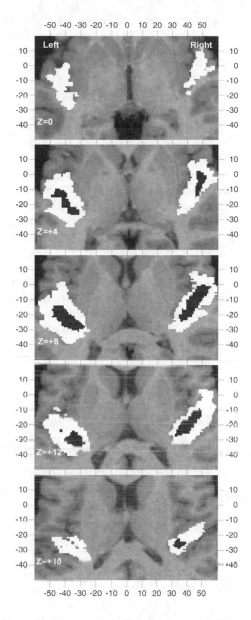

Fig. 3.10. Probability atlas of area Te1. Population maps of Te1 in five axial slices overlaid on a grid in stereotaxic space (z separation = 4 mm); x coordinates labeled horizontally, y coordinates labeled vertically. The left hemisphere is shown on the left side. White = maximal extent of Te1 (overlap of one out of ten brains in stereotaxic space); black = 50 % map of Te1 (overlap of at least 5 out of 10 brains).

located in different architectonic areas. In Figure 3.10, the population maps of Te1 in 5 horizontal sections are shown in the common spatial reference system at 4 mm intervals. These maps can be used to localize area Te1 for a given range of probability.

CONCLUSION

The quantitative cytoarchitectonic analysis of the human temporal cortex enables the identification of multiple, putative auditory areas on HG and STG. This parcellation is fully supported by specific regional and laminar distribution patterns of various neurotransmitter receptors in the various areas. Since the receptors play a major role in brain function, the combination of cytoarchitectonic and neurochemical mapping techniques provides new insights into the organization of the auditory cortex. The putative primary auditory cortex (Te1) can be characterized by a set of criteria, (i) cytoarchitectonically by its koniocortical structure, (ii) myeloarchitectonically by a very high packing density of myelinated fibers, and (iii) receptorarchitectonically by a particularly high expression of muscarinic M2 receptors. This combination of criteria is found – in addition to its occurrence in Te1 – only in the primary visual (V1) and somatosensory (S1) areas of the primate isocortex. Architectonic, i.e. microscopical, identifications of putative auditory areas are mandatory for the anatomical localization of auditory functions, since no sufficiently precise and consistent correlations can be found between the architectonically verified borders of auditory areas and macroanatomical landmarks. Furthermore, results from architectonic mapping in a larger sample of postmortem brains demonstrate a considerable interhemispheric and intersubject variability of these borders. Thus, only population maps of cortical areas reflect this topographical variability and provide a reliable tool for identifying the anatomical location of auditory functions in functional imaging techniques.

ACKNOWLEDGMENTS

This Human Brain Project/Neuroinformatics research is funded by the National Institute of Biomedical Imaging and Bioengineering, the National Institute of Neurological Disorders and Stroke, and the National Institute of Mental Health. Additional funding of the receptor studies by VW-Stiftung and DFG (Klinische Forschergruppe).

REFERENCES

Amunts, K., Malikovic, A., Mohlberg, H., Schormann, T., & Zilles, K. (2000). Brodmann's areas 17 and 18 brought into stereotaxic space – where and how variable? NeuroImage, 11, 66–84.

Amunts, K., Schleicher, A., Bürgel, U., Mohlberg, H., Uylings, H.B.M., & Zilles, K. (1999). Broca's region revisited: Cytoarchitecture and intersubject variability. The Journal of Comparative Neurology, 412, 319–341.

Amunts, K., Schleicher, A., & Zilles, K. (2002). Architectonic mapping of the human cerebral cortex. In A. Schüz & R. Miller (Eds.), Cortical Areas: Unity and Diversity (pp. 29–52). London, New York: Taylor & Francis.

Amunts, K., & Zilles, K. (2001). Advances in cytoarchitectonic mapping of the human cerebral cortex. In T. Naidich, T. Yousry, & V. Mathews (Eds.), Neuroimaging Clinics of North America, Vol.11 (pp.151–169). Philadelphia: W.B. Saunders Company.

Beck, E. (1928). Die myeloarchitektonische Felderung des in der Sylvischen Furche gelegenen Teiles des menschlichen Schläfenlappens. Journal für Psychologie und Neurologie, 36, 1–21.

Belin, P., & Zatorre, R.J. (2000). «What», «where» and «how» in auditory cortex. Nature Neuroscience, 3, 965–966.

Brodmann, K. (1909). Vergleichende Lokalisationslehre der Grosshirnrinde in ihren Prinzipien dargestellt auf Grund des Zellenbaues. Leipzig: Barth.

Campain, R., & Minckler, J. (1976). A note on the gross configurations of the human auditory cortex. Brain and Language, 3, 318–323.

Clarke, S., & Rivier, F. (1998). Compartments within human primary auditory cortex: Evidence from cytochrome oxidase and acetylcholinesterase staining. European Journal of Neuroscience, 10, 741–745.

Cragg, B.G. (1975). The density of synapses and neurons in normal, mentally defective ageing human brains. Brain, 98, 81–90.

Flechsig, P. (1908). Bemerkungen über die Hörsphäre des menschlichen Gehirns. Neurologisches Zentralblatt, 27, 2–7.

Galaburda, A., & Sanides, F. (1980). Cytoarchitectonic organization of the human auditory cortex. The Journal of Comparative Neurology, 190, 597–610.

Geyer, S., Schleicher, A., & Zilles, K. (1999). Areas 3a, 3b, and 1 of human primary somatosensory cortex: 1. Microstructural organization and interindividual variability. NeuroImage, 10, 63–83.

Geyer, S., Schormann, T., Mohlberg, H., & Zilles, K. (2000). Areas 3a, 3b, and 1 of human primary somatosensory cortex. 2. Spatial normalization to standard anatomical space. NeuroImage, 11, 684–696.

Geschwind, N., & Levitsky, W. (1968). Human brain: left-right asymmetries in temporal speech region. Science, 161, 186–187.

Gomez-Isla, T., Hollister, R., West, H., Mui, S., Growdon, J.H., Petersen, R.C., Parisi, J.E., & Hyman, B.T. (1997). Neuronal loss correlates with but exceeds neurofibrillary tangles in Alzheimer's disease. Annals of Neurology, 41, 17–24.

Griffiths, T.D., & Warren, J.D. (2002). The planum temporale as a computational hub. Trends in Neuroscience, 25, 348–353.

Hackett, T.A., Preuss, T.M., & Kaas, J.H. (2001). Architectonic identification of the core region in auditory cortex of macaques, chimpazees, and humans. The Journal of Comparative Neurology, 441, 197–222.

Hopf, A. (1954). Die Myeloarchitektonik des Isokortex temporalis beim Menschen. Journal für Hirnforschung, 1, 208–279.

Hutsler, J.J., & Gazzaniga, M.S. (1996). Acetylcholinesterase staining in human auditory and language cortices: Regional variation of structural features. Cerebral Cortex, 6, 260–270.

Kaas, J.H., & Hackett, T.A. (2000). Subdivisions of auditory cortex and processing streams in primates. Proceedings of the National Academy of Sciences USA, 97, 11793–11799.

Kleist, K. (1934). Gehirnpathologie. Barth: Leipzig.

Kulynych, J.J., Vladar, K., Jones, D.W., & Weinberger, D.R. (1994). Gender differences in the normal lateralization of the supratemporal cortex: MRI surface-rendering morphometry of Heschl's gyrus and the planum temporale. Cerebral Cortex, 4, 107–118.

Leonard, C.M., Puranik, C., Kuldau, J.M., & Lombardino, L.J. (1998). Normal variation in the frequency and location of human auditory cortex landmarks. Heschl's gyrus: where is it? Cerebral Cortex, 8, 397–406.

Liegeois-Chauvel, C., Musolino, A., Badier, J.M., Marquis, P., & Chauvel, P. (1994). Evoked potentials recorded from the auditory cortex in man: Evaluation and topography of the middle latency components. Electroencephalography and Clinical Neurophysiology, 92, 204–214.

Mazziotta, J., Toga, A., Evans, A., Fox, P., Lancaster, J., Zilles, K., Woods, R., Paus, T., Simpson, G., Pike, B., Holmes, C., Collins, L., Thompson, P., MacDonald, D., Iacobini, M., Schormann, T., Amunts, K., Palomero-Gallagher, N., Geyer, S., Parsons, L., Narr, K., Kabani, N., Le Goualher, G., Boomsma, D., Cannon, T., Kawashima, R., & Mazoyer, B. (2001). A probabilistic atlas and reference system for the human brain: International Consortium for Brain Mapping (ICBM). Philosophical Transactions of the Royal Society of London. Series B. Biological Sciences, 356, 1293–1322.

Morosan, P., Rademacher, J., Schleicher, A., Amunts, K., Schormann, T., & Zilles, K. (2001). Human primary auditory cortex: Cytoarchitectonic subdivisions and mapping into a spatial reference system. NeuroImage, 13, 684–701.

Musiek, F.E., & Reeves, A.G. (1990). Asymmetries of the auditory areas of the cerebrum. Journal of the American Academy of Audiology, 1, 240–245.

Pakkenberg, B., & Gundersen, H.J. (1997). Neocortical neuron number in humans: effect of sex and age. The Journal of Comparative Neurology, 384, 312–320.

Pantev, C., Bertrand, O., Eulitz, C., Verkindt, C., Hampson, S., Schuierer, G., & Elbert, T. (1995). Specific tonotopic organizations of different areas of the human auditory cortex revealed by simultaneous magnetic and electric recordings. Electroencephalography and Clinical Neurophysiology, 94, 26–40.

Penhune, V.B., Zatorre, R.J., MacDonald, J.D., & Evans, A.C. (1996). Interhemispheric anatomical differences in human primary auditory cortex: probabilistic mapping and volume measurement from magnetic resonance scans. Cerebral Cortex, 6, 661–672.

Rademacher, J., Bürgel, U., & Zilles, K. (2002). Stereotaxic localization, intersubject variability, and interhemispheric differences of the human auditory thalamocortical system. NeuroImage, 17, 142–160.

Rademacher, J., Caviness, V.S., Steinmetz, H., & Galaburda, A.M. (1993). Topographical variation of the human primary cortices: Implications for neuroimaging, brain mapping, and neurobiology. Cerebral Cortex, 3, 313–329.

Rademacher, J., Morosan, P., Schormann, T., Schleicher, A., Werner, C., Freund, H.J., & Zilles, K. (2001). Probabilistic mapping and volume measurement of human primary auditory cortex. NeuroImage, 13, 669–683.

Rivier, F., & Clarke, S. (1997). Cytochrome oxidase, acetylcholinesterase, and NADPH-diaphorase staining in human supratemporal and insular cortex: Evidence for multiple auditory areas. NeuroImage, 6, 288–304.

Roland, P.E., & Zilles, K. (1994). Brain atlases – a new research tool. Trends in Neuroscience, 17, 458–467.

Roland, P. E., & Zilles, K. (1996). The developing European computerized human brain database for all imaging modalities. NeuroImage, 4, 39–47.

Roland, P. E., & Zilles, K. (1998). Structural divisions and functional fields in the human cerebral cortex. Brain Research. Brain Research Reviews, 26, 87–105.

Sarkisov, S.A., Filimonoff, I.N., & Preobrashenskaya, N.S. (1949). Cytoarchitecture of the Human Cortex Cerebri (Russ.). Medgiz: Moscow.

Scheich, H., Baumgart, F., Gaschler-Markefski, B., Tegeler, C., Tempelmann, C., Heinze, H.J., Schindler, F., & Stiller, D. (1998). Functional magnetic resonance imaging of a human auditory cortex area involved in foreground-background decomposition. European Journal of Neuroscience, 10, 803–809.

Schleicher, A., Amunts, K., Geyer, S., Morosan, P., & Zilles, K. (1999). Observer-independent method for microstructural parcellation of cerebral cortex: A quantitative approach to cytoarchitectonics. Neuroimage, 9, 165–177.

Schleicher, A., & Zilles, K. (1990). A quantitative approach to cytoarchitectonics: Analysis of structural inhomogeneities in nervous tissue using an image analyser. Journal of Microscopy, 157, 367–381.

Schormann, T., & Zilles, K. (1997). Limitations of the principle axes theory. IEEE Transactions on Medical Imaging, 16, 942–947.

Schormann, T., & Zilles, K. (1998). Three-dimensional linear and nonlinear transformations: An integration of light microscopical and MRI data. Human Brain Mapping, 6, 339–347.

Seldon, H.L. (1985). The anatomy of speech perception. In A. Peters & E.G. Jones (Eds.), Cerebral cortex: Vol. 5. Association and auditory cortices (pp. 273–327). London: Plenum Press.

Steinmetz, H., Rademacher, J., Huang, Y., Hefter, H., Zilles, K., Thron, A., & Freund, H.-J. (1989). Cerebral asymmetry: MR planimetry of the human planum temporale. Journal of Computer Assisted Tomography, 13, 996–1005.

Talairach, J., & Tournoux, P. (1988). Coplanar Stereotaxic Atlas of the Human Brain. Stuttgart: Thieme.

Terry, R.D., DeTeresa, R., & Hansen L.A. (1987). Neocortical cell counts in normal human adult aging. Annals of Neurology, 21, 530–539.

von Economo, C., & Horn, L. (1930). Über Windungsrelief, Masse und Rindenarchitektonik der Supratemporalfläche, ihre individuellen und ihre Seitenunterschiede. Z. Neurol. Psychiat., 130, 678–757.

von Economo, C., & Koskinas, G.N. (1925). Die Cytoarchitektonik der Hirnrinde des erwachsenen Menschen. Berlin: Springer Verlag.

Wallace, M.N., Johnston, P.W., & Palmer, A.R. (2002). Histochemical identification of cortical areas in the auditory region of the human brain. Experimental Brain Research, 143, 499–508.

Warren, J.D., & Griffiths, T.D. (2003). Distinct mechanisms for processing spatial sequences and pitch sequences in the human auditory brain. Journal of Neuroscience, 23, 5799–5804.

Westbury, C.F., Zatorre, R.J., & Evans, A.C. (1999). Quantifying variability in the planum temporale: A probability map. Cerebral Cortex, 9, 392–405.

Zatorre, R.J., Bouffard, M., Ahad, P., & Belin, P. (2002). Where is "where" in the human auditory cortex? Nature Neuroscience, 5, 905–909.

Zilles, K., Schlaug, G., Matelli, M., Luppino, G., Schleicher, A., Qü, M., Dabringhaus, A., Seitz, R., & Roland, P.E. (1995). Mapping of human and macaque sensorimotor areas by integrating architectonic, transmitter receptor, MRI and PET data. Journal of Anatomy, 187, 515–537.

Zilles, K., Palomero-Gallagher, N., Grefkes, C., Scheperjans, F., Boy, C., Amunts, K., & Schleicher, A. (2002a). Architectonics of the human cerebral cortex and transmitter receptor fingerprints: Reconciling functional neuroanatomy and neurochemistry. European Neuropsychopharmacology, 12, 587–599.

Zilles, K., Schleicher, A., Palomero-Gallagher, N., & Amunts, K. (2002b). Quantitative analysis of cyto- and receptorarchitecture of the human brain. In A.W. Toga, & J.C. Mazziotta (Eds.), Brain Mapping: The Methods, 2nd edition (pp. 573–602). Academic Press.

4. SENSITIVITY TO SPECTRAL AND TEMPORAL PROPERTIES OF SOUND IN HUMAN NON-PRIMARY AUDITORY CORTEX

Deborah A. Hall

INTRODUCTION

Relative to a silent baseline, sound-evoked activation engages much of the auditory cortex irrespective of the acoustic properties of the signal. However, particular response preferences can be localized within discrete subregions by contrasting sound conditions that possess different values of the acoustical property of interest. Using these simple subtraction and linear regression approaches, numerous functional magnetic resonance (fMRI) studies have measured the relative distribution across the human auditory cortex of sensitivities to a range of fundamental sound properties including frequency, bandwidth, sound level, temporal structure, spatial location, and auditory motion (see Hall et al., 2003, for a general review). In perhaps every case except that of sound intensity encoding (Hart et al., 2002, 2003a), these features evoke differential activation that clearly extends across the non-primary, as well as the primary, auditory cortex. Spectral and temporal sound features convey information about the identity and source of that sound. Although many computational transformations have been completed before the acoustic signal reaches the auditory cortex, the cortex significantly contributes to auditory analysis. The neural computations performed by non-primary auditory cortex are uncertain but they may involve stages in identifying auditory objects, including the integration of spectral and temporal sound features (Zatorre et al., 2002) and the matching of these components with learned spectro-temporal representations (Griffiths & Warren, 2002).

From both ecological and clinical viewpoints, neuroimaging is an important tool for understanding the cortical mechanisms involved in processing speech, music and environmental sounds that have complex spectro-temporal patterns. However, basic underlying operations can be usefully explored by using synthesized signals that have a highly-constrained spectro-temporal pattern. Here, I shall review the literature on two specific sound properties (frequency spectrum and temporal structure) that can be precisely manipulated in the laboratory. These acoustic manipulations generate distinctive response patterns across the non-primary subregions, revealing a sensitivity to certain spectral and temporal features (and combinations of those features) that underlies complex sound processing.

In humans, as in non-human primates, our understanding of the architectonic structure and functional specialization of the non-primary auditory cortex is much more limited than that of the primary auditory cortex (Hackett, 2003). Auditory fMRI is a highly-informative methodology and has a rapidly-growing literature which has already made a significant contribution to this debate. However, specifying the precise location of the fMRI signal is more difficult than is commonly assumed. Although the spatial resolution of the raw image data is generally about 3 mm^3, the effective functional resolution is much coarser after the data have been spatially transformed into standard coordinate space, smoothed and averaged across subjects. Additionally, important insights may also be obscured by the highly disparate approaches to interpreting and reporting the distribution of functional activation (Brett et al., 2002). In the case of auditory brain function, the different nomenclature and methods for interpretation make the task of across-study comparisons particularly difficult. The present chapter therefore aims to consolidate this literature by using a consistent vocabulary and by discussing the localization of functional activations with respect to all three commonly-used schemes of interpretation: morphological, architectonic, and neurophysiological.

MORPHOLOGICAL SCHEMES FOR INTERPRETING THE DISTRIBUTION OF FUNCTIONAL RESPONSES IN HUMAN AUDITORY CORTEX

The auditory cortex lies on the upper surface of the superior temporal gyrus (STG). Figure 4.1 illustrates the highly undulating shape of the supra-temporal plane which hinders a clear view of the spatial layout of the auditory fields unless the image is transformed into a flattened cortical space. The cortical folding forms distinctive gyri and sulci that are generally present in all individuals. The absolute locations of these features can be somewhat variable and so a pragmatic data-driven scheme for interpreting functional activation acquired by fMRI describes the location of responses with respect to the key reliable morphological landmarks which are shown in Figure 4.2A. Heschl's gyrus (HG) is the name given to the transverse gyrus on the supra-temporal

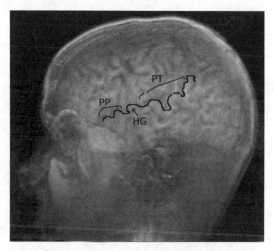

Fig. 4.1. Sagittal view of an individual's left hemisphere showing the rendered cortical surface taken from a structural MR scan. The thick black line follows the surface of the supra-temporal plane and illustrates the highly convoluted shape of the superior temporal gyrus. The location of key features are denoted: HG – Heschl's gyrus; PP – planum polare; PT– planum temporale.

plane. HG is identifiable by its prominent size and characteristic shape, having an oblique axis in the antero-lateral to postero-medial orientation.

The anterior border of HG is marked by the first transverse temporal sulcus (HA) and its posterior border is marked by Heschl's sulcus (H1S). Between individuals there may be one, two or even three transverse gyri, and the number can differ across the left and right hemispheres. When multiple transverse gyri are present, HG is the anterior-most one (Penhune et al., 1996). Behind H1S lies the planum temporale (PT) whose posterior border occurs at the end of the Sylvian fissure marked by the ascending and descending rami (Westbury et al., 1999). In front of HA lies the planum polare which extends forward across the temporal plane and has the insula cortex at its medial border. Although relating the distribution of functional activation to these morphological landmarks is limited in its gross description (Hart et al., 2002, 2003a), it does avoid the more speculative associations with other architectonic and functional schemes which cannot be validated for individual human listeners.

ARCHITECTONIC SCHEMES FOR INTERPRETING THE DISTRIBUTION OF FUNCTIONAL RESPONSES IN HUMAN AUDITORY CORTEX

Studies of human cortical architecture suggest that the auditory cortex consists of a primary field surrounded by non-primary fields (Morosan et al., 2004). The primary field overlaps considerably with the location of Heschl's gyrus

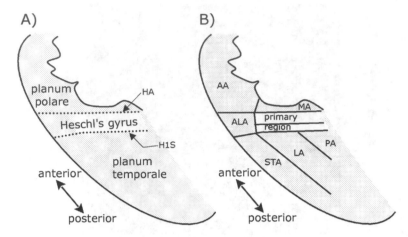

Fig. 4.2. Schematic outline of the flattened upper surface of the left superior temporal gyrus illustrating the regional subdivisions of the human auditory cortex. Non-primary auditory regions are shown by the dotted shading. **A)** Key sulcal landmarks identify the three principal morphologically-defined regions of the auditory cortex. **B)** One example of architectonic parcellation based on the distribution and density of neural cells identified by histochemical methods (after Rivier & Clarke, 1997; Wallace et al., 2002). In non-primary regions, the borders of these subdivisions are poorly defined by sulcal landmarks. Abbreviations are as follows: HA: first transverse temporal sulcus; H1S: Heschl's sulcus; AA: anterior area; ALA: antero-lateral area; LA: lateral area; MA: medial area; PA: posterior area; STA: supra-temporal area.

located on the upper plane of the STG. The non-primary fields encircle the primary field and extend across the STG. Undoubtedly, the non-primary fields are many in number, but at present there is no consensus upon precisely how many, the location of their borders, and the nomenclature used to describe them. To localize human brain activation as revealed by fMRI and other techniques, neuroimagers have turned to the anatomical literature that has identified auditory fields on the basis of their laminar characteristics. However, neuroimagers have interpreted their data according to a range of different anatomical parcellation schemes (including Brodmann, 1909; Galaburda & Sanides, 1980; Morosan et al., 2000; Rivier & Clarke, 1997) as well as defining novel variants (Scheich et al., 1998). This diversity makes it difficult to draw comparisons across neuroimaging studies. However, data from two separate labs have recently converged upon a common parcellation scheme of up to five or six putative non-primary auditory fields arranged immediately surrounding HG (Rivier & Clarke, 1997; Wallace et al., 2002). Not only do the borders broadly concur, but also the same nomenclature has been adopted. These fields are illustrated schematically in Figure 4.2B. HG contains both the primary field(s) and a non-primary field that is on the antero-lateral extent of HG and has been termed ALA (Wallace et al., 2002). At least two non-primary fields, AA and

MA, lie on the planum polare, while at least three non-primary fields, LA, PA, and STA, are located on PT. Such progress marks a small, but nonetheless, significant step towards promoting a shared concept of auditory cortex parcellation. Further progress in mapping the architecture of the human auditory cortex is likely to be achieved with the combined use of markers for histochemical, metabolic, and myelination distributions, so that these fields can be confirmed and new fields either added or subdivisions within them proposed. The challenge remains to develop a reliable method for applying this post-mortem information to in vivo brains where only morphological landmarks are visible. Given the intersubject variability between the cytoarchitectonic boundaries of the primary field and the sulci bordering HG (Morosan et al., 2001; Rademacher et al., 2001) it is likely that similar (or even greater) degrees of variability exist for non-primary subdivisions. Therefore, associations between functional and architectonic organization in human non-primary auditory regions are at best tentative. Although current anatomical knowledge is insufficient to drive the mapping of the functional organization, an initial step to link human functional architecture with its anatomy has been achieved by interpreting the location of functional activation with respect to the centre of mass of these anatomical non-primary fields (e.g., Hall et al., 2002; Schönwiesner et al., 2002; Talavage et al., 2000). Throughout the chapter, I will refer to the architectonic parcellation scheme illustrated in Figure 4.2B, reinterpreting the original anatomical localization of those fMRI studies that have used alternative schemes.

NEUROPHYSIOLOGICAL SCHEMES FOR INTERPRETING THE DISTRIBUTION OF FUNCTIONAL RESPONSES IN HUMAN AUDITORY CORTEX

Some researchers have turned to the literature on non-human primate electrophysiology to guide interpretations of the functional organization of the human auditory cortex. For example, neurons in the lateral non-primary auditory field of the macaque are better tuned to band-passed noise bursts than they are to pure tones at the same centre frequency (Rauschecker et al., 1995), presumably because they integrate over a broader range of the tonotopic gradient. Likewise in humans, band-passed noise bursts generate more widespread activation than do pure tones across the non-primary auditory cortex (Wessinger et al., 2001). More controversial is the proposal that the posterior portion of the non-primary auditory field of the macaque, which appears to be specialized for analyzing sound movement in space (Rauschecker, 1998; Rauschecker & Tian, 2000; Recanzone, 2000a), has a human analogue in part of the PT (e.g., Hart et al., 2004; Pavani et al., 2002; Warren et al., 2002; Zatorre et al., 2002). Whilst both intuitively appealing and potentially highly informative (see Semple & Scott, 2003), this across-species comparative approach warrants a number of theoretical and empirical caveats.

For a number of important reasons (non-human primate) neurophysiologists and (human) neuroimagers lack a common empirical basis for comparing the functional distribution of responses across the entire auditory cortex between the respective disciplines. Briefly stated, one drawback is that there is no validation for direct structural and functional homologies across species. For example, there is no simple one-to-one mapping between humans and macaque structural subdivisions, particularly in the non-primary auditory regions where the expansion of the posterior STG in humans may represent the addition of areas not presently accounted for in the macaque (Hackett, 2003). Second, there is a difference in the spatial coverage across the auditory cortex in terms of the measurement recordings obtained by the specialized data acquisition techniques in human and non-human species. Differences occur at many levels: single neurons, neuronal populations, laminar depth and cortical fields. Characterization of electrophysiological response properties is largely derived from recordings in the middle layers of the cortical sheet (layers III-V) where responses in anesthetized animals are most robust. This limitation can obscure the diversity of mechanisms that are known to exist at different depths through the cortical layers and gives more weight to properties expressed in the thalamo-cortical input than intrinsic cortical processing (see Semple & Scott, 2003). In contrast, the fMRI signal integrates the level of metabolic activity across a very large neuronal population within the cortical sheet because it has the neurovasculature as its source. Third, electrophysiology and fMRI are not equally sensitive to the two neural coding mechanisms of rate and time. fMRI activation reflects a complex interplay between oxygen consumption, blood oxygenation level and blood flow that is a consequence of the overall amount of neural metabolic activity in that brain region caused by synaptic and discharge activity (Bandettini et al., 1992; Kwong et al., 1992; Ogawa et al., 1992). The haemodynamic changes are sufficiently co-localized to the site of neural activity for fMRI to provide a good marker for functional localization, although the signal-to-noise ratio is probably not as good for fMRI as it is for multiunit recording (Logothetis et al., 2001). The precise relationship between the fMRI signal and neural activity is not yet fully understood. However, technical advances now enable simultaneous measurements of the two and so the ultimate goal is to define a predictive relationship between the fMRI signal and neural spiking activity, since this achievement would enable us to link the large body of non-human electrophysiological data to that of human fMRI data. The first study to make measurement comparisons was published in 2001 (Logothetis et al., 2001). Logothetis observed that while multiunit activity was transient, fMRI activity was sustained and so concluded that there was no simple quantitative relationship between the two. Contemporary theories favor a relatively direct correlation between the fMRI signal and inhibitory and excitatory synaptic activity in the neuronal population, with a secondary and potentially more variable correlation with neural spiking activity (Arthurs & Boniface, 2002). Under certain circumstances, the fMRI signal is directly proportional to the ensemble spiking frequency of neurons in cortical layer IV (Smith et al., 2002).

This new result associates the average neuronal population activity to the energy consumption required for neurotransmitter glutamate release (with this metabolic demand driving the fMRI response). Hence, rate coding is likely to be closely coupled to the location and magnitude of fMRI activity. Electrophysiological recording provides information not only about the rate, but also the timing of neural processing. Neurons explicitly encode the temporal features of a sound by their synchronization of neuronal firing, either to the phase of a pure tone or to the temporal envelope of the sound (e.g., Langner, 1992; Steinschneider et al., 1998). FMRI is insensitive to synchrony coding, but conveys gross information in the temporal dimension about the sustained or transient nature of the time-envelope of population neural activity (Harms & Melcher, 2002). In the context of temporal encoding discussed in this chapter, fMRI represents a model of temporal structure where the temporal regularity of the firing patterns is converted to a more sustained population rate code.

SENSITIVITY TO THE FREQUENCY SPECTRUM

Frequency is an obvious organizing feature of the auditory system and, in many animal species receptive field properties reveal an orderly progression across the surface of the auditory cortex. Tonotopic organization is defined by the arrangement of neurons tuned to the same frequency in iso-frequency bands that run parallel to the cortical surface, with a systematic change in frequency tuning orthogonal to those iso-frequency bands. Figure 4.3A illustrates the orientation of frequency bands that have been mapped in the primary fields and some of the non-primary auditory fields in the macaque monkey (see review by Kaas & Hackett, 1998). In macaque, non-primary subdivisions are less precisely tonotopically arranged than primary subdivisions and are generally more responsive to complex stimuli than to tones (Kaas et al., 1999, Merzenich & Brugge, 1973; Morel et al., 1993). Likewise in humans, sinusoidal tones typically evoke weak activity in non-primary auditory cortex. Single-frequency tones have been used widely to probe tonotopicity in the primary auditory cortex (Bilecen et al., 1998; Di Salle et al., 2001; Engelien et al., 2002; Formisano et al., 2003; Le et al., 2001). However, even within primary auditory fields, sinusoids may not be optimal for tonotopic mapping because their associated activation is not highly sustained (Hart et al., 2003) For example, a within-subject comparison between the responses to a 4-kHz tone and a bandpassed frequency-modulated signal with the same centre frequency showed that the pure tone elicited statistically weaker activity in the high-frequency part of Heschl's gyrus than did the modulated signal (Schönwiesner et al., 2003). If an acoustic signal generates weak or unreliable activation across listeners, then it will be more difficult to detect subtle activation differences driven by an experimental manipulation of that signal. The typical approach to determine the location and orientation of the tonotopic axis has been to reduce the analysis to that of shifts in the spatial location of the single maximum focus of activation as

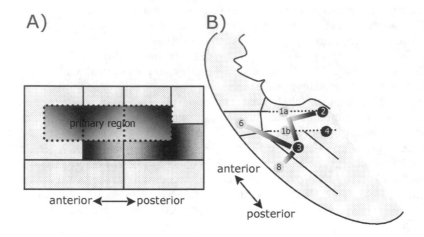

Fig. 4.3. Schematic outlines showing the representation of frequency-dependent responses across different subdivisions of the auditory cortex in macaques (A) and humans (B). The two drawings are angled differently, but in such a way that the primary regions share the same orientation. In the macaque, the primary region occurs along the superior temporal gyrus whereas in humans, its angle is more oblique. High-frequency selectivity is in dark grey and low-frequency selectivity is in light grey, with the orientation of the grey-scale shading denoting the axis of the tonotopic gradient. The non-primary auditory fields are indicated by the superimposed dots, with the borders between fields in solid lines. Dotted lines indicate the borders of the primary auditory fields. A) The box diagram summarizes the tonotopic organization of those primate auditory fields that have been mapped using neurophysiological recording and reviewed by Kaas & Hackett (1998). Tonotopy has not yet been established in many of the non-primary belt and parabelt subdivisions and these are shown in white. B) In humans, multiple frequency-dependent foci have been reliably identified across three fMRI studies and these are projected onto the same schematic outline as in Figure 4.1B. Numbered foci are described in more detail in the text. Those putative tonotopic gradients proposed by Talavage et al. (2004) are denoted by the grey-scale shading.

a function of stimulus frequency (Le et al., 2001; Wessinger et al., 1997) or of one centre of mass (Engelien et al., 2002) or to the visual inspection of a shift in the general response pattern (Bilecen et al., 1998). Reducing the frequency-dependent response to a single value is unlikely to be representative if multiple tonotopic fields are present.

Three fMRI studies are worthy of note (Schönwiesner et al., 2002; Talavage et al., 2000, 2004). These have sought evidence for multiple frequency-dependent sites of activation in both primary and non-primary human auditory regions using band-passed signals with dynamically-changing spectral features. Additionally, data have been represented by multiple frequency-dependent peaks of maximal activation, rather than being reduced to single low- and high-frequency foci. In those studies where signals with a discrete frequency were presented, frequency-dependent responses could be determined by contrasting low- and high-frequency conditions. In an alternative approach, a slowly presented frequency sweep evoked a traveling wave of neuronal activity across the tonotopic cortical surface so that frequency sensitivity smoothly covaried with response latency (Talavage et al., 2004). Generally, the locations of the frequency-dependent responses are in close agreement across studies and these are illustrated in Figure 4.3B. The sound-evoked activation mainly coincided with the anterior (foci 1a and 2) and posterior (foci 1b and 4) borders of HG and confirms a separation across the medial portion of HG with more vigorous responses to high frequencies medially and to low frequencies laterally. Beyond HG, three frequency-dependent activation foci were observed in all three studies: 1) focus 3, a high-frequency site half way along the length of HG, but lying posterior to it within the morphological boundary of PT. Anatomically, focus 3 may coincide with LA, 2) focus 6, a low frequency site at the antero-lateral extreme of HG that may lie in ALA and 3) focus 8, a low-frequency site also within the PT but lying further posterior and lateral to focus 3. The anatomical location of focus 8 is unclear, but it may reside in either LA or STA. Two other foci (5 and 7) have been reported by Talavage et al. (2000; 2004), but there is much greater intersubject variability in the frequency-dependent activity at these sites. Hence, I shall not discuss them further.

A consensus has yet to emerge about the functional significance of these frequency-dependent foci since the views of the authors are opposed. Talavage suggests that these foci represent the endpoints of multiple tonotopic gradients, whereas Schönwiesner proposes that they correspond to different auditory fields that are engaged in processing acoustic features associated with different frequency bands. Defining gradients between numerous frequency-dependent foci has been highly problematic, especially when the locations of only two points along each putative gradient are known. Recent high-field fMRI measurements of activation evoked by six tone frequencies support the presence of two mirror-symmetric gradients across HG with a common low frequency border (Formisano et al., 2003). This organization is consistent with electrophysiological data from the macaque (see Fig. 4.3A). It is unclear how the locations of the frequency-dependent foci reported by Talavage and Schönwiesner can be reconciled with Formisano's description of the functional anatomy. However Talavage et al. (2004) have speculated that the putative gradients first linking focus 2 (high frequency) to focus 1 (low frequency) and second linking focus 1 to focus 3 (high frequency) could represent the same mirror-reversed tonotopy.

The most reliable frequency-dependent responses (foci 1a, 1b, 2, and 4) involve portions of HG, which is traditionally considered to represent the primary auditory region. The multiple foci at the borders of HG may indicate that the anterior (HA) and posterior (H1S) borders of HG represent two distinct functional subdivisions. One suggestion is that the anterior stripe corresponds to the primary auditory field and the posterior stripe perhaps corresponds to a non-primary auditory field. First, Di Salle et al. (2001) observed an anterior/posterior difference in the response time course when the acoustical stimulus was presented against scanner noise, suggesting that the activation along the posterior border had reached saturation, but that activation along the anterior border had not. The second line of evidence is that the low-frequency foci (1a and 1b) are differently responsive to high frequencies, with focus 1a being completely unresponsive to high frequencies, but focus 1b being weakly responsive (Schönwiesner et al., 2002). In addition, recent architectonic evidence points to an anatomical border across HG that is consistent with these functional distinctions. This border occurs in the base and walls of H1S (Wallace et al., 2001), thus forming a strong anatomical candidate for the location of the functional activation along the posterior border of HG. However, the pattern of histochemical staining suggests that the anterior and posterior borders of HG form two primary auditory fields. Recent fMRI data that do not fit neatly with these observations is the absence of a frequency gradient linking the low and high frequency foci along H1S (1b and 4) (Talavage et al., 2004). Instead, foci 1 and 3 appear to be linked by a frequency gradient that cuts across this region, and may include LA which is a posterior non-primary auditory field. Thus, although there is no doubt that differential sensitivities to low- and high-frequency sounds exist, fMRI evidence for the presence of frequency gradients within different subdivisions of the auditory cortex is not yet compelling, nor does the pattern of frequency-dependent activation provide a clear marker for segregating the primary and non-primary auditory fields.

A number of methodological challenges arise in the use of fMRI to map frequency gradients across the auditory cortical surface. For example, frequency gradients may be more clearly revealed if studies probe the full frequency range of human hearing, particularly for non-primary auditory cortex where the subdivisions are likely to be less precisely tonotopically arranged. The audible range for human listeners extends from 60 Hz to up to 20 kHz, yet the widest range used for fMRI frequency mapping has been from 125 Hz to 8 kHz (Schönwiesner et al., 2002; Talavage et al., 2000, 2004), a noticeably truncated portion at the lower end of the continuum.

An issue that has received the most attention is the effect of the intense level of the background scanner noise which either masks or interacts with the pattern of stimulus-induced auditory activation (Bandettini et al., 1998). Solutions generally involve interposing long interscan intervals (up to 20 s) during which the stimulus is presented. A number of variants of this technique have been implemented for frequency-dependent mapping (Bilecen et al., 1998; Di Salle et al., 2001; Engelien et al., 2002; Formisano et al., 2003; Le et al., 2001).

Alternatively, the intensity of the scanner noise can be reduced by modifying the pulse sequence, for instance by slowing the onset and offset ramp times for the currents applied to the gradient coils (Hennel et al., 1990; de Zwart et al., 2002). When these techniques have not been applied to reduce the background noise, a common justification is that the peak frequencies of energy of the scanner noise do not overlap with those of the test frequencies and hence do not interact with the activation pattern (Schönwiesner et al., 2002; Wessinger et al., 1997). This is not true at the background levels typically occurring in fMRI

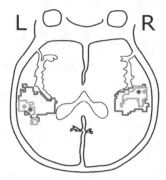

Fig. 4.4. Outline of the upper surface of the superior temporal gyrus showing the extent of activation by a 4.75 kHz sinusoidal tone presented at 42 dB SPL (light grey) and the same tone presented at 90 dB SPL (dark grey). Activation is computed relative to a silent baseline, P < 0.001. Dots indicate the location of the peak of activation located in lateral PT on the left and near H1S, the posterior border of lateral HG, on the right (42 dB, −58 −32 14 mm and 60 −18 8 mm; 90 dB, −52 −36 14 mm and 54 −18 12 mm in standard MNI brain space). In both hemispheres, the absolute location shifted by 7 mm as a function of sound level, principally in the medio-lateral dimension. Data are taken from Hart et al. (2003a).

(such as 87−96 dB SPL with ear protection, Foster et al., 2000). Although the peak energy of scanner noise and of the stimulus may be separated across the spectrum, the vibration pattern along the basilar membrane and the subsequent neural activation pattern will be much less so because of the spread of excitation by signals with a high sound energy.

The level of stimulus presentation has been a much less debated issue, but of equal importance. To be audible above the intense background noise, acoustic signals are presented at a level that exceeds their threshold in quiet by many 10s of decibels. Epidemiological data reveal that around 92% of the UK population in their 5th decade has an average hearing threshold better than 25 dB HL, measured at 0.5, 1, 2, and 4 kHz in the better ear (Davis, 1995). For the younger adults who are typical volunteers for fMRI studies, the prevalence of good hearing would be even greater. Despite this fact, in the fMRI studies of tonotopy reported above, sounds were generally presented at 70−80 dB SPL even during silent scanning protocols (Di Salle et al., 2001; Engelien et al., 2002; Formisano et al., 2003; Le et al., 2001), and in one case were presented at 100 dB SPL (Bilecen et al., 1998). The frequency specificity of neuronal responses is critically determined by sound level. Electrophysiological studies show that at levels close to threshold, the tuning curve is at its most narrow. However, as sound level increases the tuning curve broadens, so that neurons with adjacent best frequencies are also excited. Hence, the proportion of cortical neurons activated by a single-frequency tone increases with the sound level of that tone (Phillips et al., 1994). While the sensitivity of the auditory cortex undoubtedly differs between an anesthetized preparation and an awake human listener, our human fMRI data reveals a similar pattern of broadening activation as a function of level for 0.30 and 4.75 kHz tones (Hart et al., 2002, 2003a). A subset of these data is presented in Figure 4.4. Smearing across iso-frequency contours of frequency sensitivity could limit the resolution of frequency mapping for sounds at high presentation levels, although this may not be detectable given that fMRI integrates activity over large neuronal populations anyway. The degree of smearing may differ across frequencies because the shape of the growth in sound-level dependent activation differs for low and high frequencies, being greatest at 60–84 dB SPL (Hart et al., 2003a; Phillips et al., 1994). The fMRI data also reveal that the absolute locations of the peaks of activation are somewhat level sensitive, but not in any systematic manner.

RESPONSES TO THE SLOW-RATE TEMPORAL STRUCTURE IN SOUND

Many behaviorally-relevant sounds from the environment have a complex spectral composition that varies over time. Slow-rate modulations are important for speech and melody perception. For example, speech intelligibility is most profoundly impaired when temporal modulations below 16 Hz are removed (Drullman et al., 1994). Temporal fluctuations in the amplitude envelope of speech convey segmental cues to manner of articulation, voicing, vowel identity and prosody (Rosen, 1992). Imaging studies use well-controlled stimuli, such as tones or noise, in which the temporal characteristics are determined either by a sinusoid or a square-wave modulating waveform. Presentation of these signals has revealed that sites across the auditory cortex respond significantly to a wide range of modulation rates, but that the magnitude and response shape of such activation is rate dependent. The auditory cortex responds maximally to slow-rate modulations in the range 2–10 Hz and, as Figure 4.5A illustrates, this response is sustained across the duration of the stimulus (Giraud et al., 2000; Harms & Melcher, 2002; Tanaka et al., 2000). As the rate rises to 35 Hz, the response becomes more phasic with sharp peaks at the stimulus onset and offset. Differences in the response between human primary cortex on HG and non-primary regions on the STG are not clear, although the data suggest that, for slow rates of modulation, non-primary regions respond more strongly than does HG (Giraud et al., 2000) and that non-primary regions respond in a more strongly phasic manner than in HG (Seifritz et al., 2002).

In the primary and non-primary auditory cortices of non-human primates, temporal modulation in amplitude or frequency is essential to drive many neurons that are unresponsive or weakly responsive to steady-state sinusoids. Responses in primary auditory cortex of awake primates have been measured in detail (see review by Wang et al., 2003), but non-primary auditory fields have not yet been studied. A common observation in the primary region is that the discharge pattern varies as a function of modulation rate (Fig. 4.5B). Slow-rate modulations, up to about 30 Hz generate significant synchronized discharges so

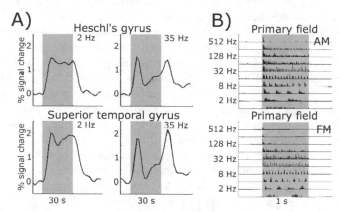

Fig. 4.5. Examples of auditory cortical responses to modulated signals measured **A)** in humans using fMRI (Harms & Melcher, 2002), and **B)** in primates using electrode recordings (Liang et al., 2002). Stimulus duration is shown by the grey shaded bar. For human listeners, the stimulus was a train of noise bursts presented at different rates. For primates, the stimulus was a tone at the unit's best frequency, modulated in amplitude and frequency by a sinusoid at different rates.

that the temporal pattern is explicitly encoded by the temporal discharge of the cortical neurons. Additionally, temporal modulations in the range of 16–32 Hz generate the maximal discharge rate in the primary auditory cortex. Higher temporal modulation frequencies are encoded by the average sustained discharge rate of the neuronal population, but as the modulation rate increases to 200 Hz and above, onset discharges become more prevalent. One interpretation of the phasic response in the human fMRI data at modulation rates > 35 Hz is that it reflects population coding of stimulus transients. Indeed, onset and offset responses have been recorded in cortical neurons of awake behaving primates in both primary and non-primary fields (Pfingst & O'Connor, 1981; Recanzone, 2000b; Wang et al., 2003). However, the precise correspondence is unclear since electrophysiological recordings are for stimuli whose duration does not exceed 500 ms, whereas fMRI measures are for stimuli which last several tens of seconds.

Here at the MRC Institute of Hearing Research, we have investigated which region of the auditory cortex is most sensitive to signals modulated in frequency and amplitude at a rate of 5 Hz (Hall et al., 2002; Hart et al., 2003b). Signals modulated in frequency (FM) differ from those modulated in amplitude (AM) in their spectral content, but they share the same modulation waveform. Relative to their unmodulated counterparts, 5-Hz frequency modulation generates greater activation in HG and in a region immediately posterior to it on PT, extending to the lateral convexity of the STG. Multiple peaks of activation have been identified within this non-primary auditory activation and strong candidates for their location are fields LA, STA, and possibly ALA. The greatest peak of activity (−64 −14 2 mm in standard MNI brain space, Hall et al., 2002) occurred closest to the low-frequency-dependent focus 6 which is compatible with the 300-Hz fundamental frequency of the carrier presented in our experiments. However, the peak of activation occurred somewhat closer to H1S than focus 6 itself. Data presented in Figure 4.6 reveal that the pattern of 5-Hz modulation sensitivity is co-localized for tones modulated in either frequency or amplitude (Hart et al., 2003b). One interpretation is that there is a common mechanism for the neuronal population coding of AM and FM. Recent electrophysiological evidence supports this view (see review by Wang et al., 2003). In the primary auditory cortex of awake primates, both individual and populations of neurons are selective to particular modulation frequencies, assessed by their mean firing rate and synchrony. Moreover, the best modulation frequency measured by the discharge rate is equivalent for both AM and FM sinusoidal modulations, irrespective of the type of carrier signal. Because amplitude and frequency modulations are produced along different stimulus dimensions, the equivalence between best modulation frequencies in various stimulus conditions suggests an inherent temporal selectivity in cortical neurons that is applicable to a wide range of slow-rate time-varying signals. The results from the fMRI studies in humans converge on the importance of non-primary auditory cortex, including the lateral portion of HG (field ALA), but particularly subdivisions of PT (fields LA and STA), in the analysis of these slow-rate temporal patterns in sound.

RESPONSES TO THE FAST-RATE TEMPORAL STRUCTURE IN SOUND

Temporal regularity, interaural timing differences (ITD) and interaural correlation (IAC) are examples of acoustic information conveyed by the fine temporal structure in sound. By fine timing information, I refer to that which is on a scale of 100s of microseconds or milliseconds. As discussed in the previous section, the accuracy of synchrony neural coding for conveying periodicity and fine temporal structure (> 50 Hz) is limited in the auditory cortex and so temporal microstructure must be converted into a different code. Computational models for the representation of temporal patterns in the auditory system use temporal correlation to encode the temporal patterns in the auditory signal, either of a signal with itself (to give the autocorrelation function) or of the different signals at the two ears (to give the cross-correlation function). One form of auditory autocorrelation correlates the auditory nerve activity within each frequency channel with a delayed version of itself (Meddis & Hewitt, 1991). A pitch can be generated from a noise if that noise is delayed and added to itself repeatedly. The resulting stimulus is perceived as a tone that has a pitch corresponding to the reciprocal of the delay, plus a background noise. The internal temporal regularity of this regular-interval noise is apparent in the autocorrelogram as a peak in the integration interval corresponding to the delay that is consistent across frequency channels. These peaks across frequency are illustrated in Figure 4.7A and can be contrasted with a random noise that has no

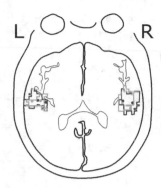

Fig. 4.6. Outline of the upper surface of the superior temporal gyrus showing the extent of the effect of amplitude (dark grey) and frequency (light grey) modulation. Activation is determined relative to the unmodulated carrier, p < 0.001. Dots indicate peaks of activation located close to H1S, the posterior border of HG, and within PT. Co-ordinates in standard MNI brain space for AM are −51 −18 3 mm, −42 −21 6 mm, 48 −18 6 mm and 60 −21 9 mm and for FM are −48 −18 3 mm, −57 −18 9 mm, 48 −21 6 mm and 60 −30 3 mm. Data are taken from Hart et al. (2003b).

temporal regularity shown in Figure 4.7B. With more repeats of the delay-and-add process, the peaks in the autocorrelogram become more pronounced and the strength of the pitch percept increases. The neural basis of temporal regularity has been explored by comparing noise stimuli that have temporal regularity to a control noise that does not (Griffiths et al., 1998, 2001; Patterson et al., 2002). Noises were highpass filtered at either 0.5 or 1 kHz to remove any low-frequency spectral peaks in the auditory nerve activity, thus ensuring that pitch information could only be extracted from the temporal pattern. The cochlear nucleus, inferior colliculus, medial geniculate body, and auditory cortex all responded more strongly to the regular-interval noise than to the control noise (Griffiths et al., 2001). To address where in the auditory cortex sensitivity to the temporal representation of pitch occurs, a recent fMRI study localized the differential activation for all the individual listeners as well as for the group-averaged data (Patterson et al., 2002). The most prominent activation by the fixed-pitch regular-interval noise relative to the control noise occurred bilaterally in lateral HG (average location: −55 −13 2 mm and 57 −9 −2 mm in standard MNI brain space). This activation centre was antero-lateral to that region of HG that is traditionally associated with the primary auditory field. The authors refer to the architectonic studies of the macaque (Kaas & Hackett, 2000), suggesting that the activation site may be located in the human homologue of either the rostral or rostro-temporal subdivision of the primate primary region. The architectonic features of the rostro-temporal subdivision make it the least certain member of the primary region. Turning to the architectonic scheme adopted for the purposes of this chapter, a strong candidate for the activation site might be field ALA, again a non-primary auditory field.

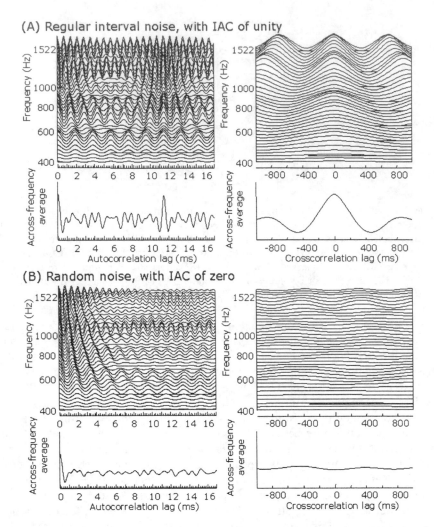

Fig. 4.7. Time-interval representations of the autocorrelation and cross-correlation for
(A) a regular interval noise that has 16 delay-and-add iterations and is perfectly
correlated across the two ears (IAC = 1), and **(B)** a random noise that is uncorrelated
across the two ears (IAC = 0). Correlograms illustrate the correlation within individual
frequency channels, plus the frequency-averaged correlation. The frequency-averaged
correlogram in (A) clearly shows a peak at 11 ms, corresponding to a pitch of 90 Hz.

The authors speculate that the role of this site in lateral HG is in calculating
the specific value of the pitch from the peak in the frequency-averaged
autocorrelogram (see also Griffiths, 2005). In contrast, the preserved synchrony
coding in the brainstem and thalamus mean that these lower auditory sites more

likely play a crucial role in extracting the time-interval information from the neural firing pattern.

Increasing the degree of temporal regularity in the noise increases the salience of the pitch. The autocorrelation model represents pitch salience by the height of the peak in the frequency-averaged autocorrelogram and hence this model would predict an increase in activation as a function of pitch strength in those sites sensitive to temporal regularity. A linear increase in activity as a function of the degree of temporal regularity was observed in the cochlear nucleus, inferior colliculus and the auditory cortex, bilaterally (Griffiths et al., 1998, 2001). The relationship between activation and the number of delay-and-add iterations in the noise is illustrated in Figure 4.8A, with the location of the most significant voxels marked in Figure 4.8B by the black stars. Although the authors describe the cortical effect as being primary, the group-averaged peak coordinates (−71 −16 −3 mm and 59 −2 −5 mm in standard MNI brain space) appear in a location close to the lateral portion of the auditory cortex, suggesting that activation could again be in the non-primary auditory field ALA. Hence, it remains possible that lateral HG plays a role in determining the salience, as well as the specific value, of a pitch. One conclusion therefore is that the non-primary field in lateral HG is the neural correlate of a pitch center. As it is described in this series of studies, pitch is extracted from the timing information in the auditory signal and does not arise from a detection of the harmonically-related spectral peaks. Further research will be needed to determine whether indeed the same area in lateral HG represents both temporal and spectral pitch values

While the temporal regularity in a regular-interval noise is determined by the monaural input from each ear, the temporal patterning of ITD information is extracted from a binaural comparison of the input from the two ears. ITDs are the main binaural cues used for localizing low-frequency sounds in the horizontal plane. For signals that differ in their time of arrival at the two ears, the neural input to the medial division of the superior olivary complex is the primary site of binaural convergence. The underlying neural mechanism is understood to rely on a coincidence of excitatory inputs from the two ears that are phase-locked to either the stimulus frequency or the stimulus envelope. Thus, a network of coincidence detectors converts ITDs into a profile of neural activity across a spatial array of neurons (Colburn et al., 1990; Jeffress, 1948).

Computationally speaking, coincidence detection is equivalent to a cross-correlation of the inputs from the two ears. Figure 4.7 presents examples of noise signals, one (Fig. 4.7A) that is perfectly correlated and one (Fig. 4.7B) that is uncorrelated across the two ears. Cross-correlation is a widely accepted model for the encoding of ITDs (Stern & Trahiotis, 1995; Yin et al., 1987). The IAC of a sound is one measure of the similarity between the signals at the left and right ears since it measures the randomness of the ITDs across all the frequency components of the sound. As IAC is reduced, both the ITD at the two ears and its representation in the crosscorrelogram become diffuse. Manipulating the IAC of a sound has salient perceptual consequences. When

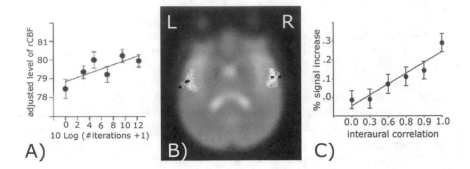

Fig. 4.8. Auditory cortical activation by the fine-temporal structure in sound. **A)** Linear relationship between activity and the temporal regularity of a regular-interval noise, as determined by the number of add-and-delay iterations. The graph plotted is for the activated region in the left hemisphere, $p < 0.05$ corrected (Griffiths et al., 1998). The black stars overlaid onto the supra-temporal plane in both hemispheres, shown in **B)**, represent the location of the peaks of the linear response to pitch salience. Co-ordinates have been converted into the same 3-D space as the underlying brain image. The white region in lateral HG is the probabilistic map of Te1.2 (Morosan et al., 2000), which is likely to be equivalent to the non-primary auditory field ALA. The black pixelated foci denote those voxels that are sensitive to IAC. **C)** Linear relationship between activity and IAC averaged across the two hemispheres (Budd et al., 2003).

presented over headphones a sound that has an IAC of unity appears to be a single intracranial event arising in the middle of the head, while a sound that has an IAC of zero is perceived as two separate events at each ear or as a single broad event occurring across the head (Blauert & Lindeman, 1986). Sensitivity to IAC has primarily been examined in the auditory brainstem (Brugge et al., 1969; Yin & Chan, 1990). However, recent fMRI evidence has revealed the organization of IAC sensitivity within the auditory cortex. A distinct bilateral sub-region in the lateral extent of Heschl's gyrus shows a positive linear relationship between activation and level of IAC (Budd et al., 2003). The data illustrating this relationship are shown in Figure 4.8C. The authors refer to the architectonic parcellation scheme of human HG given by Morosan et al. (2000) which defines the location of this activation site as Te1.2: the lateral third of the primary auditory cortex (see Fig. 4.8B). Although Morosan et al. (2000) represent Te1.2 as a primary subdivision, its architectonic features appear to be transitional between primary and non-primary zones. Indeed on the basis of a similar pattern of histological staining, Wallace et al. (2002) propose that Te1.2 probably corresponds to field ALA. The low-frequency specificity of field ALA (Schönwiesner et al., 2002; Talavage et al., 2000, 2004) is furthermore consistent with its role in computing IAC, since electrophysiological and psychophysical evidence indicates that sensitivity to ITD and IAC is largely confined to low-frequency stimulation (Yin et al., 1987).

Figure 4.8 shows that the lateral HG region shown to be linearly sensitive to binaural temporal regularity (Budd et al., 2003) is close to the region also shown to be linearly sensitive to monaural temporal regularity in the study of Griffiths et al. (1998). Group-averaged coordinates in stereotaxic space are difficult to compare across studies because they are affected by intersubject variability in brain anatomy, differences in the contrast of the images used for transformation into the standard space, as well as general statistical error. Despite these problems, the proximity of the two activation sites is provocative. If these two activation sites are indeed co-localized, then a common functional role is likely. Just as the salience of IAC is conveyed by the relationship between the cross-correlation pattern in many frequency channels, so the salience of the pitch in a regular-interval noise is greatest when the period of the temporal patterning is consistent across frequency channels. Therefore, an alternative interpretation for the role of the non-primary auditory region in lateral HG could be in the across-frequency integration of evidence of fast-rate temporal patterns in sound, rather than in detecting pitch. Given that the coherence of the temporal information across frequency channels and pitch strength co-vary, it is not clear from the current evidence which stimulus dimension is critical for cortical activity.

REPRESENTATION OF THE PERCEPTUAL ATTRIBUTES OF SOUND

There is a general agreement that the ascending auditory system comprises multiple stages of neural processing where the features of the sound that are encoded become an increasingly abstract representation of the sound stimulus. One clear example presented here is the case of slow-rate temporal structure in sound. In the auditory periphery, auditory nerve fibers faithfully represent fine details of sound up to approximately 4 kHz in their temporal discharge patterns. The temporal limit of stimulus-synchronized responses gradually degrades as the information is transmitted via the cochlear nucleus, inferior colliculus and medial geniculate body due to biophysical properties of neurons and temporal integration of converging neural inputs, such that synchronized responses in the auditory cortex markedly drop off beyond approximately 200 Hz and hence fast rates are coded by a different mechanism. FMRI measurements of the shape of the response reveal a similar shift in coding mechanism through the ascending auditory system (Harms & Melcher, 2002). The inferior colliculus shows a sustained time course irrespective of the rate, whereas auditory cortex has a time course that is highly rate dependent, with the medial geniculate body showing a response that is intermediate between the two.

Moreover, evidence from the fMRI studies indicates that cortical encoding is more closely associated with the overall perceptual attributes of the sound than its component acoustical features. For noise bursts at repetition rates between 2 and 35 Hz, this pattern is revealed by the change in the response shape. Specifically, the shift in the response from sustained to biphasic with increasing rate seems to correspond to a shift in perception from stimulus events that can be resolved individually to events that fuse to form a type of continuous percept. For the fused percept, the start and end of the train become the most salient perceptual changes and these are delineated by peaks in the activation. Interestingly, these high-rate stimuli appear to generate more highly phasic responses within the non-primary region of the STG that is lateral to HG, than within HG itself, suggesting an increasingly prominent coding of the sound borders in higher auditory centers (Harms & Melcher, 2003). The cortical representation of finer temporal structure is also driven by the perceptual attributes of the sound, both for temporal pitch and IAC as discussed in this chapter. With respect to pitch, non-primary auditory activation is not only strongly determined by the presence of a temporal pitch, but also by its salience (Griffiths et al., 1998). Non-primary auditory cortex is also strongly responsive to IAC level (Budd et al., 2003). Moreover, the moderate departure from a linear response to IAC level follows a positive accelerating function. Larger response increases occur between levels of IAC near unity than between levels near zero. This response pattern is qualitatively compatible with previous measures of psychophysical sensitivity to IAC. Human listeners are more sensitive to differences in IAC close to unity than zero (e.g., Pollack & Trittipoe, 1959). The neural representation of temporal pitch and IAC appears to evolve as one ascends the auditory pathway. In the brainstem, although both cochlear nucleus and inferior colliculus were sensitive to the changes in temporal regularity that generated a pitch percept, the preference in the inferior colliculus was the greater (Griffiths et al., 2001). The inferior colliculus and medial geniculate body were not found to be sensitive to IAC level (Budd et al., 2003). Thus, the evidence supports the notion of an increasing responsiveness to percept attributes of sound throughout the ascending auditory system, culminating in the non-primary auditory cortex.

Organisms have to effectively operate within complex auditory environments, containing simultaneous auditory objects located at dynamically-varying points in space. One of the primary challenges for the auditory brain is to analyze this auditory scene so that the organism can interact with its environment in a goal-directed manner. The spectral and temporal properties of sound convey all the information required to determine the identity and source of a sound. Computational stages in this sensory process involve feature analysis of the incoming acoustic signals, segregation of the spectro-temporal pattern into separate auditory objects, recoding of this information as invariant auditory objects and matching of these representations with previously stored knowledge. Encoding the perceptual properties of a sound is integral to determining it as an auditory object and the non-primary auditory cortex probably plays a key role in this process. The non-primary auditory cortex has widespread cortical projections to frontal and parietal brain regions (Romanski et al., 1999) and so it is ideally suited to access distinct higher-level cortical mechanisms for sound object identification and localization.

CONCLUSION

FMRI has made a valuable contribution to characterizing functional subdivisions of the non-primary auditory cortex across lateral HG and PT in terms of their responsiveness to spectral and temporal properties of sound stimuli. There is a widespread distribution of multiple discrete subregions that are sensitive to high- or low-frequency sounds. While this pattern broadly concurs with the multiple tonotopic fields measured in primate electrophysiology, on the basis of current fMRI data, we are not yet able to make a claim for separate functional fields because we need to gather more evidence on the orientation of the frequency gradients and the location of the borders between them. In this respect, non-invasive mapping of the human auditory cortex using fMRI still holds challenges that were solved some time ago for the visual cortex (e.g., Sereno et al., 1995). The non-primary subregions that are sensitive to temporal structure in sound are quite narrowly distributed across the auditory cortex. Sensitivity to the temporal envelope of sound activates lateral HG and postero-lateral parts of PT, whereas sensitivity to the fine temporal structure that defines temporal pitch and IAC is largely confined to the lateral portion of HG which overlaps with low-frequency dependent areas. Whether or not it is right to propose that these activated regions reflect functionally-separate subdivisions of the non-primary auditory cortex remains speculation at this stage. The field would gain much added value in the use of complementary techniques such as multi-unit recording in primates, where the mapping of responses in the non-primary lateral belt and parabelt regions has been much under-researched. Our understanding of the architectonic structure and functional specialization of the non-primary auditory cortex is much more limited than that of the primary auditory cortex. This holds true for both human and non-human primates, making across-species comparisons of non-primary auditory cortical structure and function rather speculative. Given these large gaps in our current understanding of the organization of the mammalian non-primary auditory cortex, it is in this area of research where the greatest challenges arise, but also where the opportunities for progress are greatest.

REFERENCES

Arthurs, O.J., & Boniface, S. (2002). How well do we understand the neural origins of the fMRI BOLD signal? Trends in Neurosciences, 25, 27–31.

Bandettini, P.A., Jesmanowicz, A., Van Kylen, J., Birn, R.M., & Hyde, J.S., (1998). Functional MRI of brain activation induced by scanner acoustic noise. Magnetic Resonance in Medicine, 39, 410–416.

Bandettini, P.A., Wong E.C., Hinks, R.S., Tikofsky, R.S., & Hyde, J.S. (1992). Time course EPI of human brain function during task activation. Magnetic Resonance in Medicine, 25, 390–397.

Bilecen, D., Scheffler, K., Schmid, N., Tschopp, K., & Seelig, J. (1998). Tonotopic organization of the human auditory cortex as detected by BOLD-fMRI. Hearing Research, 126, 19–27.

Blauert, J., & Lindeman, W. (1986). Spatial mapping of intracranial auditroy events for various degrees of interaural coherence. Journal of the Acoustical Society of America, 79, 806–813.

Brett, M., Johnsrude, I.S., & Owen A.M. (2002). The problem of functional localization in the human brain. Nature Reviews Neuroscience, 3, 243–249.

Brodmann, K. (1909). Vergleichende Lokalisationslehre der Grosshirnrinde in ihren Prinzipien dargestellt auf Grund des Zellaufbaus. Leipzig: Barth.

Brugge, J.F., Dubrovsky, N.A., Aitkin, L.M., & Anderson, D.J. (1969). Sensitivity of single neurons in auditory cortex of cat to binaural tonal stimulation: Effects of varying interaural time and intensity. Journal of Neurophysiology, 32, 1005–1024.

Budd, T.W., Hall, D.A., Gonçalves, M.S., Akeroyd, M.A. Foster, J.R., Palmer, A.R., Head, K., & Summerfield, A.Q. (2003). Binaural specialisation in human auditory cortex: An fMRI investigation of interaural correlation sensitivity. NeuroImage, 20, 1783–1794.

Colburn, H.S., Han, Y.A., & Culotta, C.P. (1990). Coincidence model of MSO responses. Hearing Research, 49, 335–346.

Davis, A. (1995). Hearing in adults: The prevalence and distribution of hearing impairment and reported hearing disability in the MRC Institute of Hearing Research's National Study of Hearing. London: Whurr Publishers Ltd.

Di Salle, F., Formisano, E., Seifritz, E., Linden, D.E.J., Scheffler, K., Saulino, C., Tedeschi, G., Zanella, F.E., Pepino, A., Goebel, R., & Marciano, E. (2001). Functional fields in human auditory cortex revealed by time-resolved fMRI without interference of EPI noise. NeuroImage, 13, 328–338.

Drullman, R., Festen, J.M., & Plomp, R. (1994). Effect of temporal envelope smearing on speech reception. Journal of the Acoustical Society of America, 95, 1053–1064.

Engelien, A., Yang, Y., Engelien, W., Zonana, J., Stern., E., & Silbersweig, D.A. (2002). Physiological mapping of human auditory cortices with a silent event-related fMRI technique. NeuroImage, 16, 944–953.

Formisano, E., Kim, D-S., Di Salle, F., van de Moortele, P-F., Urgibil, K., & Goebel, R. (2003). Mirror-symmetric tonotopic maps in human primary auditory cortex. Neuron, 40, 859–869.

Galaburda, A., & Sanides, F. (1980). Cytoarchitectonic organization of the human auditory cortex. The Journal of Comparative Neurology, 190, 597–610.

Giraud, A.L., Lorenzi, C., Asburner, J., Wable, J., Johnsrude, I., Frackowiak, R., & Kleinschmidt, A. (2000). Representation of the temporal envelope of sounds in the human brain. Journal of Neurophysiology, 84, 1588–1598.

Griffiths, T.D., Functional imaging of pitch processing. (2005). In C.J. Plack, A.J. Oxenham, R.R. Fay, & A.N. Popper (Eds.), Pitch: Neural processing and perception. New York: Springer.

Griffiths, T.D., Buchel, C., Frackowiak, R.S., & Patterson R.D. (1998). Analysis of temporal structure in sound by the human brain. Nature Neuroscience, 1, 422–427.

Griffiths, T.D., Uppenkamp, S., Johnsrude, I.S., Josephs, O., & Patterson, R.D. (2001). Encoding of the temporal regularity of sound in the human brainstem. Nature Neuroscience 4, 633–637.

Griffiths, T.D., & Warren, J.D. (2002). The planum temporale as a computational hub. Trends in Neurosciences, 25, 348–353.

Hackett, T.A. (2003). The comparative anatomy of the primate auditory cortex. In A.A. Ghazanfar (Ed.), Primate audition: Ethology and neurobiology (pp. 199–219). Boca Raton, FL: CRC Press LLC.

Hall, D.A., Hart, H.C., & Johnsrude, I.S. (2003). Relationships between human auditory cortical structure and function. Audiology and Neuro-Otology, 8, 1–18.

Hall, D.A., Johnsrude, I.S., Haggard, M.P., Palmer, A.R., Akeroyd, M.A., & Summerfield, A.Q. (2002). Spectral and temporal processing in human auditory cortex. Cerebral Cortex, 12, 140 149.

Harms, M.P., & Melcher, J.R. (2002) Sound repetition rate in the human auditory pathway: Representations in the waveshape and amplitude of fMRI activation. Journal of Neurophysiology, 88, 1433–1450.

Harms, M.P., & Melcher, J.R. (2003). Detection and quantification of a wide range of fMRI temporal responses using a physiologically-motivated basis set. Human Brain Mapping, 20, 168–183.

Hart, H.C., Hall, D.A., & Palmer, A.R. (2003a). The sound-level dependent growth of auditory cortical activation, as measured using fMRI, is different for low- and high-frequency tones. Hearing Research, 179, 104–112.

Hart, H.C., Palmer, A.R., & Hall, D.A. (2002). Heschl's gyrus is more sensitive to tone level than non-primary auditory cortex. Hearing Research, 171, 177–190.

Hart, H.C., Palmer, A.R., & Hall, D.A. (2003b). Regions outside primary auditory cortex in humans are more activated by modulated than by unmodulated stimuli. Cerebral Cortex, 13, 773–781.

Hart, H.C., Palmer, A.R., & Hall, D.A. (2004). Different areas of human non-primary auditory cortex are activated by sounds with spatial and nonspatial properties. Human Brain Mapping, 21, 178–190.

Hennel, F., Girard, F., & Loenneker, T. (1999). "Silent" MRI with soft gradient pulses. Magnetic Resonance in Medicine, 42, 6–10

Jeffress, L.A. (1948). A place theory of sound localization. Journal of Comparative Physiology and Psychology, 61, 468–486.

Kaas, J.H., & Hackett, T.A. (1998). Subdivisions of auditory cortex and levels of processing in primates. Audiology and Neuro-Otology, 3, 73–85.

Kaas, J.H., & Hackett, T.A. (2000). Subdivisions of auditory cortex and processing streams in primates. Proceedings of the National Academy of Sciences USA, 97, 11793–11799.

Kaas, J.H., Hackett, T.A., & Tramo, M.J. (1999). Auditory processing in primate cerebral cortex. Current Opinion in Neurobiology, 9, 164–170.

Kwong, K.K., Belliveau, J.W., Chesler, D.A., Goldberg, I.E., Weisskoff, R.M., Poncelet, B.P., Kennedy, D.N., Hoppel, B.E., Cohen, M.S., Turner, R., Cheng, H.M., Brady, T.J., & Rosen, B.R. (1992). Dynamic magnetic resonance imaging of human brain activity during primary sensory stimulation. Proceedings of the National Academy of Sciences USA, 89, 5675–5679.

Langner, G. (1992). Periodicity coding in the auditory system. Hearing Research, 60, 115–142.

Le, T.H., Patel, S., & Roberts, T.P.L. (2001). Functional MRI of human auditory cortex using block and event-related designs. Magnetic Resonance in Medicine, 45, 254–260.

Liang, L., Lu, T., & Wang, X. (2002). Neural representations of sinusoidal amplitude and frequency modulations in the primary auditory cortex of awake primates. Journal of Neurophysiology, 87, 2237–2261.

Logothetis, N.K., Pauls, J., Augath, M., Trinath, T., & Oeltermann, A. (2001). Neurophysiological investigation of the basis of the fMRI signal. Nature, 412, 150–157.

Meddis, R., & Hewitt, M.J. (1991). Virtual pitch and phase sensitivity of a computer-model of the auditory periphery 1. Pitch identification. Journal of the Acoustical Society of America, 89, 2866–2882.

Merzenich, M.M., & Brugge, J.F. (1973). Representation of the cochlear partition on the superior temporal plane of the macaque monkey. Brain Research, 50, 275–296.

Morel, A., Garraghty, P.E., & Kaas, J.H. (1993). Tonotopic organisation, architectonic fields, and connections of auditory cortex in macaque monkeys. The Journal of Comparative Neurology, 335, 437–459.

Morosan, P., Rademacher, J., Palomero-Gallagher N., & Zilles, K. (2004). Anatomical organization of the human auditory cortex: Cytoarchitecture and transmitter receptors. In R. König, P. Heil, E. Budinger, & H. Scheich (Eds.), The Auditory Cortex – A Synthesis of Human and Animal Research. Hillsdale, NJ: Lawrence Erlbaum Associates.

Morosan, P., Rademacher, J., Schleicher, A., Amunts, K., Schormann, T., & Zilles, K. (2001). Human primary auditory cortex: Cytoarchitectonic subdivisions and mapping into a spatial reference system. NeuroImage, 13, 684–701.

Ogawa, S., Tank, D.W., Menon, R., Ellerman, J.M., Kim, S.-G., Merkle, H., & Urgurbil, K. (1992). Intrinsic signal changes accompanying sensory stimulation: Functional brain mapping with magnetic resonance imaging. Proceedings of the National Academy of Sciences USA, 89, 5951–5955.

Patterson, R.D., Uppenkamp, S., Johnsrude, I.S., & Griffiths, T.D. (2002). The processing of temporal pitch and melody information in auditory cortex. Neuron, 36, 767–776.

Pavani, F., Macaluso, E., Warren, J.D., Driver, J., & Griffiths, T.D. (2002). A common cortical substrate activated by horizontal and vertical sound movement in the human brain. Current Biology, 12, 1584–1590.

Penhune, V.B., Zatorre, R.J., Macdonald, J.D., & Evans, A.C. (1996). Interhemispheric anatomical differences in human primary auditory cortex: Probabilistic mapping and volume measurement from magnetic resonance scans. Cerebral Cortex, 6, 661–672.

Pfingst, B.E., & O'Connor, T.A. (1981). Characteristics of neurons in auditory cortex of monkeys performing a simple auditory task. Journal of Neurophysiology, 45, 16–34.

Phillips, D.P., Semple, M.N., Calford, M.B., & Kitzes, L.M. (1994). Level-dependent representation of stimulus frequency in cat primary auditory cortex. Experimental Brain Research, 102, 210–226.

Pollack, I., & Trittipoe, W. J. (1959). Binaural listening and interaural noise correlation. The Journal of the Acoustical Society of America, 31, 1250–1252.

Rademacher, J., Morosan, P., Schormann, T., Schleicher, A., Werner, C., Freund, H.-J., & Zilles K. (2001). Probabilistic mapping and volume measurement of human primary auditory cortex. NeuroImage, 13, 669–683.

Rauschecker, J.P. (1998). Cortical processing of complex sounds. Current Opinion in Neurobiology, 8, 516–521.

Rauschecker, J.P., & Tian, B. (2000). Mechanisms and streams for processing "what" and "where" in auditory cortex. Proceedings of the National Academy of Sciences USA, 97, 11800–11806.

Rauschecker, J.P., Tian, B., & Hauser, M. (1995). Processing of complex sounds in the macaque non-primary auditory cortex. Science, 268, 111–114.

Recanzone, G.H. (2000a). Spatial processing in the auditory cortex of the macaque monkey. Proceedings of the National Academy of Sciences USA, 97, 11829–11835.

Recanzone, G.H. (2000b). Response profiles of auditory cortical neurons to tones and noise in behaving macaque monkeys. Hearing Research, 150, 104–118.

Rivier, F., & Clarke, S. (1997). Cytochrome oxidase, acetylcholinesterase, and NADPH-diaphorase staining in human supra-temporal and insular cortex: Evidence for multiple auditory areas. NeuroImage, 6, 288–304.

Romanski, L.M., Tian, B., Fritz, J., Mishkin, M., Goldman-Rakic, P., & Rauschecker, J. (1999). Dual streams of auditory afferents target multiple domains in the primate prefrontal cortex. Nature Neuroscience, 2, 1131–1136.

Rosen, S. (1992). Temporal information in speech: Acoustic, auditory and linguistic aspects. Philosophical Transactions of the Royal Society of London, Series B. 336, 367–373.

Scheich, H., Baumgart, F., Gaschler-Markefski, B., Tegeler, C., Tempelmann, C., Heinze, H.J., Schindler, F., & Stiller, D. (1998). Functional magnetic resonance imaging of a human auditory cortex area involved in foreground-background decomposition. European Journal of Neuroscience, 10, 803–809.

Schönwiesner, M., von Cramon, Y.D., & Rübsamen, R. (2002). Is it tonotopy after all? NeuroImage, 17, 1144–1161.

Seifritz, E., Esposito, F., Hennel, F., Mustovic, H., Neuhoff, J.G., Bilecen, D., Tedeschi, G., Scheffler, K., & Di Salle, F. (2002). Spatiotemporal pattern of neural processing in the human auditory cortex. Science, 297, 1706–1708.

Semple, M.N., & Scott, B.H. (2003). Cortical mechanisms in hearing. Current Opinion in Neurobiology, 13, 167–173.

Sereno, M.I., Dale, A.M., Reppas, J.B., Kwong, K.K., Belliveau, J.W., Brady, T.J., Rosen, B.R., & Tootell. R.B.H. (1995). Borders of multiple visual areas in humans revealed by functional magnetic-resonance-imaging. Science, 268, 889–893.

Smith, A.J., Blumfeld, H., Behar, K.L., Rothman, D.L., Shulman, R.G., & Hyder, F. (2002). Cerebral energetics and spiking frequency: The neurophysiological basis of fMRI. Proceedings of the National Academy of Sciences USA, 99, 10765–10770.

Steinschneider, M., Reser, D.H., Fishman, Y.I., Schroeder, C.E., & Arezzo, J.C. (1998). Click train encoding in primary auditory cortex of the awake monkey: Evidence for two mechanisms subserving pitch perception. Journal of the Acoustical Society of America, 104, 2935–2955.

Stern, R.M., & Trahiotis, C. (1995). Models of Binaural Interaction. In B.C.J. Moore (Ed.), Hearing (pp. 347–386). London: Academic Press Limited.

Talavage, T.M., Ledden, P.J., Benson, R.R., Rosen, B.R., & Melcher, J.R. (2000). Frequency-dependent responses exhibited by multiple regions in human auditory cortex. Hearing Research, 150, 225–244.

Talavage, T.M., Sereno, M.I., Melcher, J.R., Ledden, P.J., Rosen, B.P., & Dale, A.M. (2004). Tonotopic organization in human auditory cortex revealed by progressions of frequency sensitivity. Journal of Neurophysiology, 91, 1282–1296.

Tanaka, H., Fujita, N., Watanabe, Y., Hirabuki, N., Takanashi, M., Oshiro, T., & Nakamura, H. (2000). Effects of stimulus rate on the auditory cortex using fMRI with 'sparse' temporal sampling. Neuroreport, 11, 2045–2049.

Wallace, M.N., Johnston, P.W., & Palmer, A.R. (2002). Histochemical identification of cortical areas in the auditory region of the human brain. Experimental Brain Research, 143, 499–508.

Wang X., Lu, T., & Liang, L. (2003). Cortical processing of temporal modulations. Speech Communication, 41, 107–121.

Warren, J.D., Zielinski, B.A., Green, G.G.R., Rauschecker, J.P., & Griffiths, T.D. (2002). Perception of sound-source motion by the human brain. Neuron, 34, 139–148.

Wessinger, C.M., van Meter, J., Tian, B., van Lare, J., Pekar, J., & Rauschecker, J.P. (2001). Hierarchical organization of the human auditory cortex revealed by functional magnetic resonance imaging. Journal of Cognitive Neuroscience, 13, 1–7.

Westbury, C.F., Zatorre, R.J., & Evans, A.C. (1999). Quantifying variability in the planum temporale: A probability map. Cerebral Cortex, 9, 392–405.

Yin, T.C.T., & Chan, J.C.K. (1990). Interaural time sensitivity in medial superior olive of cat. Journal of Neurophysiology, 64, 465–488.

Yin, T.C.T., Chan, J.C.K., & Carney, L.H. (1987). Effects of interaural time delays of noise stimuli on low-frequency cells in the cats inferior colliculus 3. Evidence for cross-correlation. Journal of Neurophysiology, 58, 562–583.

Zatorre, R.J., Bouffard, M., Ahad, P., & Belin, P. (2002). Where is 'where' in the human auditory cortex? Nature Neuroscience, 5, 905–909.

de Zwart, J.A., van Gelderen, P., Kellman, P., & Duyn, J.H. (2002). Reduction of gradient acoustic noise in MRI using SENSE-EPI. NeuroImage, 16, 1151–1155.

5. "What" and "Where" in Human Audition: Evidence from Anatomical, Activation, and Lesion Studies

Stephanie Clarke, Michela Adriani, Eric Tardif

A sound that we hear in a natural setting allows us to identify the sound source and simultaneously to localize it in space. Converging evidence from non-human and human studies suggests that these two aspects are processed in at least partially independent cortical networks. This chapter will review the major studies that have led to this conception, starting with a brief review of anatomical and electrophysiological studies in non-human primates, and concentrating then on anatomical, activation and lesion studies in humans.

PARALLEL AND HIERARCHICAL ORGANISATION OF AUDITORY AREAS: EVIDENCE DERIVED FROM STUDIES IN NON-HUMAN PRIMATES

For over 2 decades the concept of parallel and hierarchical processing of sensory information has been well established in visual modality but it is relatively recent for the auditory system. The basic concept underlying parallel processing is that two or more attributes of a stimulus (e.g., color, movement, form, depth in vision) are processed by segregated neural pathways. On the other hand, the concept of hierarchical organization of sensory systems refers to a series of interconnected brain structures processing simple-to-complex aspects of stimuli. Low-order structures (e.g., subcortical sensory relays and primary sensory areas) deal with basic processing of information while high-order cortical areas are involved in the analysis of more complex features of stimuli.

In audition, two major attributes of a stimulus are of particular interest, namely its identification («what») and its location in space («where»). Anatomical and electrophysiological studies in non-human primates suggest that segregated pathways within the auditory system may process these two aspects of auditory information.

Parallel thalamo-cortical pathways defined by calcium-binding proteins immunoreactivity

The auditory cortex of non-human primates is divided in three cortical regions named core (containing AI and the rostral area R), belt (containing caudolateral, CL; caudomedial, CM; middle lateral, ML; rostromedial, RM; anterolateral, AL; lateral rostrotemporal, RTL; and medial rostrotemporal, RTM areas), and parabelt (containing caudal, CPB and rostral, RPB areas) that can be identified by cytoarchitectonic features, electrophysiological mapping, and the distribution of chemical markers such as cytochrome oxidase (CO), acethylcholinesterase (AchE) and calcium-binding proteins (CaBPs; Jones et al., 1995; Jones, 2003; Kaas & Hackett, 2000; Rauschecker & Tian, 2000). Auditory thalamic nuclei and some auditory cortical areas can be distinguished on the basis of immuno-reactivity to the CaBPs parvalbumin (PV) and calbindin (CB; Jones & Hendry, 1989; Jones et al., 1995; Molinari et al., 1995). Combined immunohisto-chemical and tracing studies revealed that PV-positive neurons in the medial geniculate body send dense cortical projections to layer IV of AI, and CB-positive cells to layer I (Hashikawa et al., 1991; Molinari et al., 1995). Moreover, tracing studies have shown that cortical areas of the core (areas AI and R) receive thalamic input from several nuclei of the medial geniculate body while area CM of the belt receives sparse thalamic projections (Rauschecker et al., 1997). It was subsequently shown that the anterior and posterior parts of the belt project to different targets in the prefrontal cortex (Romanski et al., 1999). These anatomical studies suggest that parallel thalamo-cortical as well as cortico-cortical pathways exist in the auditory system of non-human primates. These segregated pathways may underlie the "what" and "where" processing of sound.

Electrophysiological evidence for parallel and hierarchical organization of cortical auditory areas

In non-human primates, AI was shown to be tonotopically organized and its neurons to have narrow frequency tuning (Merzenich & Brugge, 1973; Morel et al., 1993). Neurons in the non-primary auditory areas appear to be less narrowly tuned; in area CM, they were shown to respond to a much broader range of frequencies than neurons in AI (Recanzone, 2000), a response which is abolished or greatly altered after a complete lesion of area AI (Rauschecker et al., 1997). While neurons respond strongly to pure tones in AI, they were reported to be selective for more complex stimuli in the superior temporal gyrus

(Rauschecker et al., 1995). These observations support a hierarchical organisation of core and belt areas.

Tian et al. (2001) have shown different specializations between lateral belt areas: AL for monkey calls (but not for position in space), and CL for positions (but not monkey calls). These findings strongly suggest the existence of parallel processing streams involved, respectively, in sound recognition (the "what" stream) and localization (the "where" stream; Rauschecker & Tian, 2000).

ARCHITECTURE OF THE HUMAN SUPRATEMPORAL PLANE – EVIDENCE FOR MULTIPLE AUDITORY AREAS WITH HIERARCHICAL ORGANIZATION

The human auditory cortex is classically subdivided into several architectonically defined areas. The number of these areas as well as their extent and exact position vary among authors (for detailed description, see Morosan et al., 2004). Using cytoarchitectonic criteria, Brodmann (1909) distinguished three areas, called 41, 42, and 22, and von Economo and Koskinas (1925) four, TC, TD, TB, and TA. More recent investigations, based on the visualization of enzymatic activity or specific epitopes suggest a more complex organization that is compatible with parallel and hierarchical processing.

The visualization of CO, AChE and NADPH-diaphorase activity in the supratemporal plane, the posterior part of the superior temporal gyrus, and the insula of normal human brains yielded specific patterns that are compatible with the presence of several distinct areas (Rivier & Clarke, 1997; Fig. 5.1A). Five putative areas had a high level of CO, namely the primary auditory area (AI, corresponding to area TC of von Economo and Koskinas), an area on the planum polare (called anterior auditory area = AA, located within area TC/TG), an area posterior to Heschl's gyrus (called posterior auditory area = PA, located within area TA), an area on the posterior convexity of the superior temporal gyrus (called superior temporal auditory area = STA, located within area TA), and an area on the postero-superior insula (called posterior insular auditory area = PIA, located in area IB). Two more areas were more lightly stained, namely an area between AI and STA (called lateral auditory area = LA, located within area TB); and an area on anterior insula (called anterior insular auditory area = AIA, located within area IA). A subsequent study using Nissl, myelin, AChE, CO, NADPH-diaphorase, and PV staining confirmed the characteristics of the above described areas and identified two additional areas called by the authors anterolateral auditory area (= ALA, located on the lateral part of Heschl's gyrus next to AI) and lateral auditory area (= LP, located next to AI in the base and walls of Heschl's sulcus, Wallace et al., 2002).

The laminar distribution of CO activity varied in different areas. The highest activity was in layer IV in the primary auditory area, while layer III was more active in the surrounding areas LA, PA, AA, and MA and even more so in area STA (Rivier & Clarke, 1997). The difference in laminar distribution of metabolic activity is likely to reflect different input-output relationships and hence different hierarchical levels within auditory cortical processing, with AI as the level of entry, surrounded by at least four areas of an intermediate hierarchical level. Currently only one higher level area has been identified, namely area STA. It is striking that, at an intermediate level, four areas are present, suggesting strongly the existence of parallel pathways.

Hierarchical processing is also suggested by differences in AchE activity. AchE-positive fibers predominated in the primary auditory area and pyramidal neurons in area STA; a mixture of fiber and neuronal staining was found in areas LA, MA, PA, and AA (Rivier & Clarke, 1997; Wallace et al., 2002). Mesulam and Geula (1994) found that in AchE-stained material, the primary sensory cortices, including AI, had a moderate density of axons and a low density of pyramidal neurons. The "upstream" auditory association cortex (defined as unimodal association cortex receiving direct input from the primary sensory cortex) contained slightly less axons and more pyramidal neurons than AI. Hustler and Gazzaniga (1996) analyzed AchE staining in human auditory and language cortices. They found that AI contained a dense mesh of fibers, but almost no neurons, whereas adjacent cortical regions contained less axons and more neurons. Posterior auditory regions contained a relatively high density of pyramidal neurons and axons.

Further evidence for parallel and hierarchical organization of human auditory areas comes from investigations of calcium binding protein immuno-reactivity patterns (Chiry et al., 2003). In AI, PV labeling was dark in layer IV and CB in layers I-III and V, while calretinin (CR) labeling was relatively light. These complementary patterns of CaBPs labeling in the neuropil are likely to reflect parallel thalamic input originating from PV-positive and CB-positive neurons that terminate in separated cortical layers, as shown by combined tracing and immunohistochemical studies in non-human primates (Hashikawa et al., 1991; Molinari et al., 1995). In non-primary auditory areas, the intensity of labeling tended to become progressively lighter while moving away from AI, with qualitative differences among cytoarchitectonically defined areas. This probably reflects a progressive diminution of thalamic afferents in high-order areas, suggesting a hierarchical organization of auditory areas in man. By analogy with non-human primates, these results suggest differences in intrinsic organization among auditory areas that are compatible with parallel and hierarchical processing of auditory information.

The complementary patterns of CaBPs observed in the auditory cortex raise the question about a possible similar organization of subcortical auditory structures. This is the case in the (human) inferior colliculus, where the CaBPs PV, CB and CR revealed distinct compartments, notably the central nucleus and the surrounding dorsal cortex being positive to PV or CB+CR, respectively (Tardif et al., 2003).

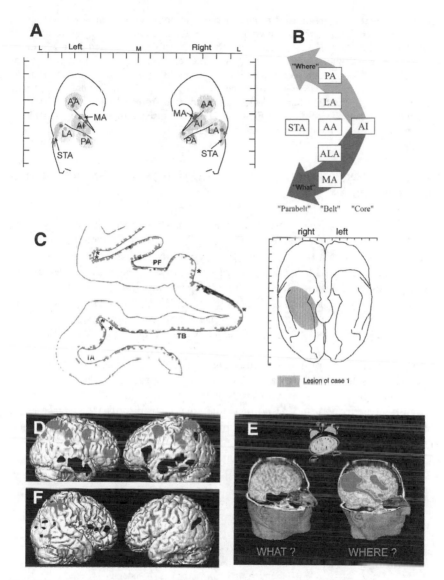

Fig. 5.1. A. Human auditory areas on supratemporal plane as revealed by cytochrome oxidase activity patterns (adapted from Rivier & Clarke, 1997). Dots indicate the Talairach coordinates of centers of auditory areas as determined on two brains. B. Parallel and hierarchical organization of human auditory areas as suggested by architectonic (Chiry et al., 2003; Rivier & Clarke, 1997) and fMRI studies (Clarke et al., 2004). C. Density of heterotopic interhemispheric afferents in human areas TA, TB, and PF, as traced by the Nauta method in a case of right hemispheric inferior temporal lesion (shown in right panel; adapted from Di Virgilio & Clarke, 1997); grey = low to medium density, black = high density of afferents. Asterisks mark the limits between

cytoarchitectonic areas (regions of progressive transition between areas are indicated by two asterisks. **D**. Cortical regions involved selectively in sound recognition (black) and sound localization (grey); mean value from 18 normal subjects (adapted from Maeder et al., 2001). **E**. Hemispheric lesions associated with a selective deficit in sound recognition (in black, on left) or sound localization (in grey, on right; adapted from Clarke et al., 2002). **F**. Disturbed processing within the auditory "what" and "where" processing streams in a case of a right hemispheric lesion (adapted from Adriani et al., 2003); the same paradigm has been used as in Figure 5.1D. Note absence of selective "What" and "Where" processing streams in the intact left hemisphere.

FUNCTIONAL SPECIALIZATION OF ANATOMICALLY DEFINED HUMAN AUDITORY AREAS

Several activation studies described their results in terms of auditory areas identified by Rivier and Clarke (1997) and allow thus to understand better the functional specialization of the non-primary auditory areas in man (Tab. 5.1). Areas LA, STA, MA, ALA, and PA have been shown to be activated selectively by frequency modulation (Hall et al., 2002; Schönwiesner et al., 2002) or have frequency-dependent responses (Talavage et al., 2000, 2004), suggesting some degree of tonotopic organization. Within AI two tonotopic maps have been described (Formisano et al., 2003; Talavage et al., 2004), suggesting functional subdivisions.

As in non-human primates distinct parts of the non-primary auditory cortex appear to be selective to spatial or non-spatial properties of sound (Hart et al., 2004), and specific non-primary areas were shown to be selective for sound recognition (areas MA and ALA) or sound localization (area PA; Clarke et al., 2004). Furthermore, areas STA, LA, and PA showed greater responses under verbal dichotic than diotic condition, which was interpreted by the authors as reflecting the increased attentional load; the activation under this condition was greater in STA than in LA and PA (Hashimoto et al., 2000).

Table 5.1. Functional specialization of anatomically defined auditory areas, as described in activation studies.

Reference	Area(s)	Selectively activated by
Hashimoto et al., 2000	STA, PA, LA (STA more than PA and LA)	Dichotic presentation of speech
Talavage et al., 2000	MA, LA, STA, PA	Frequency dependent responses
Hall et al., 2002	LA, STA	Frequency modulation
Schönwiesner et al., 2002	LA, PA, STA	Frequency modulation
Talavage et al., 2004	MA ,LA, AA, ALA	Frequency progression
Clarke et al., 2004	MA, ALA	Sound recognition
Clarke et al., 2004	PA	Sound localization

Although not linked to specific auditory areas, some activation studies also suggest a hierarchical organization within and beyond the human supratemporal plane. The presentation of an iterated noise activating all frequency regions but producing strong pitch perception was shown to produce activation in non-primary auditory areas, suggesting a hierarchical organization of time analysis in the auditory cortex (Griffiths et al., 1998) The concept of parallel and hierarchical processing of sounds was also proposed for speech perception and to involve not only auditory areas of the supratemporal plane but also frontal, parietal, and other temporal areas (Scott & Johnsrude, 2003).

INTRAAREAL COMPARTMENTS IN THE HUMAN PRIMARY AUDITORY CORTEX

The human primary auditory area contains distinct intraareal compartments, as revealed by CO and AChE activity patterns (Clarke & Rivier, 1998). A 2.0 to 2.5 mm wide antero-posterior band that has a high level of CO and AChE activity is present at mid-AI. It corresponds to the highly granular part of AI. A different set of compartments can be observed in tangential, CO stained sections through layers III and IV, namely ca. 500 μm thick alternating dark and light CO stripes. They are perpendicular to the dark band. Comparison with tonotopic maps of human AI obtained by activation studies (Pantev et al., 1995; Romani et al., 1982; Tiitinen et al., 1993; Verkindt et al., 1995) suggests that the CO and AChE dark band is most likely parallel to iso-frequency lines and may correspond to the representation of frequencies critical for speech comprehension. The narrow stripes may be related to particular binaural or ampliotopic domains, whose presence is suggested by evidence from electrophysiological recordings in cat AI (Imig & Adrian, 1977; Middlebrooks et al., 1980) and from magnetoencephalographic studies in man (Tiitinen et al., 1993). The significance of intraareal CO patterns in human AI is not known but it suggests the existence of parallel auditory pathways. Combined electrophysiological and tracing studies in monkeys have shown that the pattern of dark CO blobs in visual area V1 are indeed indicative of segregated parallel pathways (Livingstone & Hubel, 1983; 1988) and a similar organization has been shown in human V1 (Clarke, 1994; Horton & Hedley-Whyte, 1984).

DIFFERENT INTRINSIC CONNECTIVITY IN THE PRIMARY AND HIGHER LEVEL HUMAN AUDITORY AREAS

The human auditory areas on the supratemporal plane have different patterns of intrinsic connections (Tardif & Clarke, 2001). Most of these connections originate from layer II-III pyramids and only a few from non-pyramidal neurons. Very short intrinsic connections run in all cortical layers, while longer connections tend to avoid layer IV. The tangential spread of intrinsic connections differs among auditory areas (Fig. 5.2). In the primary auditory area intrinsic connections are short. In areas located on the plana polare and temporale they spread further out. Anisotropic connectivity was observed in these two regions. Differences in intrinsic connectivity are likely to reflect different types of cortical integration. In the primary auditory area, intrinsic connections involve mainly nearby units or modules, probably with similar coding properties, whereas in surrounding areas, connections spread over more distant units and may play an important role in the integration of different auditory features.

CONNECTIVITY OF HUMAN AUDITORY AND SPEECH AREAS

Interareal connections have been demonstrated with electrical stimulation and recording paradigm and suggest serial processing stream from AI to the posterior part of the superior temporal gyrus (probably area STA) in man (Brugge et al., 2003). Although the segregation into "what" and "where" streams is an important feature of human auditory areas, some other features of cortical organization have been demonstrated in high-order areas, particularly those related to language processing.

Asymmetry of intrinsic connections

Left-right asymmetries were demonstrated for intrinsic connectivity of higher order auditory areas and of areas which are involved on the left side in speech processing (Hutsler & Galuske, 2003). In particular, intrinsic connections of the posterior part of Brodmann's area 22, corresponding in the left hemisphere to part of Wernicke's areas have been shown to have a patchy pattern, which has a larger spacing in the left than in the right hemisphere (Galuske et al., 2000).

Widely heterotopic interhemispheric afferents to higher order auditory areas

Very little is known about the long cortico-cortical connections (both intra- and interhemispheric) of the human auditory and associated cortex. They are believed to obey similar organizational principles as in non-human primates. Although this may be the case for a large number of connections, very unexpected connections have been found in man. Using the Nauta method for anterogradely degenerating axons, we have described monosynaptic inter-hemispheric input from the right inferior temporal cortex to Broca's and Wernicke's areas, including auditory areas on the left planum temporale (Di Virgilio & Clarke, 1997; Fig. 5.1C). This study revealed three organizational principles of the auditory association cortex and of the speech areas. First, the presence of direct connections from the right inferior temporal cortex to higher order auditory areas on the left planum temporale and the speech areas indicates

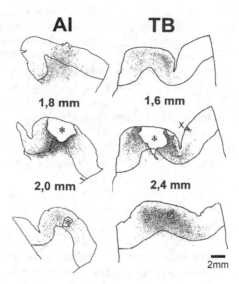

Fig. 5.2. Intrinsic connections of the human primary (AI) and higher order (TB) auditory association areas. White areas with asterisks indicate DiI injections, black lines represent individual axon segments. Distance between charted sections are indicated in mm. Note the relatively short cortical projections in AI and the longer, often asymmetrical projections in TB. Medial sections are on top, lateral ones are at the bottom of the column. On individual sections, posterior is to the right and dorsal is up. Adapted from Tardif and Clarke (2001).

that human interhemispheric connections can be widely heterotopic. Second, the fact that connections from the inferior temporal cortex terminate in auditory areas as well as Wernicke's and Broca's areas speaks in favor of parallel pathways in visuo-verbal processing. And third, the patchy distribution of visual interhemispheric afferents, which was observed in auditory and Wernicke's area hints at a possible functional compartmentalization within this region.

The heterotopic interhemispheric afferents to auditory association and speech areas are part of a more widely spread system of parallel interhemispheric pathways, involving telencephalic (Clarke & Miklossy, 1990; Di Virgilio et al., 1999) and subcortical connections (Tardif & Clarke, 2002).

PARALLEL PROCESSING STREAMS FOR SOUND RECOGNITION AND SOUND LOCALIZATION: EVIDENCE FROM PSYCHOPHYSICAL AND ACTIVATION STUDIES IN NORMAL SUBJECTS

Distinct neural populations are likely to be involved in the processing of auditory recognition and auditory spatial information. This is implied by the observation of specific interference in a short-term memory task for sound content and sound localization (Anourova et al., 1999; Clarke et al., 1998).

Anatomical evidence for distinct processing streams involved in sound recognition and sound localization was presented in two fMRI studies (Alain et al., 2001; Maeder et al., 2001). In one study (Maeder et al., 2001), three conditions were used: 1) a sound localization task, 2) a sound identification task, and 3) rest. Tasks of sound recognition and localization activated, as compared to rest, inferior colliculus, medial geniculate body, Heschl gyrus, and parts of the temporal, parietal, and frontal convexity bilaterally. The activation pattern on the fronto-temporo-parietal convexity differed in the two conditions (Fig. 5.1D). Middle temporal gyrus and precuneus bilaterally and the posterior part of left inferior frontal gyrus were more activated by recognition than by localization. The lower part of inferior parietal lobule and posterior parts of middle and inferior frontal gyri were more activated, bilaterally, by localization than by recognition. Parts of this network were also activated in a passive listening paradigm, a focus on the superior temporal gyrus by semantic stimuli and another focus, on the inferior parietal lobule, by stimuli carrying spatial information. Thus, anatomically distinct networks are involved in sound recognition and sound localization.

A second study used a different paradigm, namely pitch or location comparisons (Alain et al., 2001). It demonstrated a partial dichotomy of the two processing pathways; location comparison activated selectively parietal regions, while activation associated with pitch comparison remained limited to the supratemporal plane and parts of the superior temporal gyrus.

The involvement of distinct cortical networks in spatial and non-spatial auditory processing is further supported by electrophysiological studies (Alain et al., 2001; Anourova et al., 2001). While the existence of a ventral pathway dedicated to sound recognition – the "what" pathway – is generally accepted, the specialization of the dorsal one remains more controversial, and it has been proposed that the dorsal pathway plays a role in the analysis of spectral motion rather than sound localization (Belin & Zatorre, 2000). Although the precise organization of the dorsal – the "where" pathway – is not fully understood, there is growing evidence of its involvement in auditory spatial aspects (Bushara et al., 1999; Griffiths et al., 1996, 2000; Warren et al., 2002; Weeks et al., 1999; Zatorre et al., 2002). Functional subsystems may, however, exist within the dorsal pathway. An auditory evoked potential study demonstrated that distinct neural populations are involved in sound localization and in sound motion perception (Ducommun et al., 2002).

EFFECTS OF FOCAL HEMISPHERIC LESIONS

Further evidence for separate neural networks for sound recognition and sound localization comes from patient studies. Sound recognition and sound localization can be disrupted independently as shown in a study of 15 patients with focal right-hemispheric lesions (Clarke et al., 2002; Thiran & Clarke, 2003). In this series, four patients were normal in sound recognition but severely impaired in sound localization, whereas 3 other patients had difficulties in recognizing sounds but localized them well. In patients with selective sound localization deficit, the lesions involved the inferior parietal and frontal cortices, and the superior temporal gyrus, i.e., parts of the auditory "where" processing stream, while in patients with selective sound recognition deficit, the lesions involved the temporal pole and anterior part of the fusiform, inferior and middle temporal gyri, i.e., parts of the auditory "what" processing stream (Fig. 5.1E). These observations confirm and expand previous case reports of two patients with right-hemispheric lesions associated with selective deficit in sound recognition (Fujii et al., 1990; Spreen et al., 1965) and of one patient with selective deficit in sound localization (Griffiths et al., 1996, 1997).

Left unilateral hemispheric lesions can yield similar dissociation between deficits in sound recognition and sound localization with very similar anatomoclinical correlations. Two cases have been reported with selective deficits in sound recognition and one case with a selective deficit in sound localization (Clarke et al., 2000). Two cases of selective deficits in sound recognition have been described following bilateral temporal lesions (Jerger et al., 1972; Rosati et al., 1982). The double dissociation of deficits in sound localization or sound recognition and the specific anatomoclinical correlations support further the hypothesis of separate cortical processing pathways for auditory recognition and localization.

Patient studies suggest further a possible dichotomy between sound recognition and sound localization in the attentional domain (Clarke & Bellmann-Thiran, in press). Two behaviorally and anatomically distinct types of auditory neglect have been described following right-hemispheric lesions, one corresponding to deficits in allocation of auditory spatial attention following lesions centered on basal ganglia and the other to distortions of auditory spatial representation following fronto-temporo-parietal lesions (Bellmann et al., 2001).

THE AUDITORY "WHAT" AND "WHERE" PROCESSING STREAMS LOSE THEIR SPECIFICITY IN THE ACUTE STAGE AFTER A LESION

The organization of the auditory "what" and "where" processing streams is not fully understood. They can be thought of as regions specialized in a particular processing or as parts of a larger network in which specific processing is not entirely independent from the other parts. We have addressed these two hypotheses by investigating the acute effects of small focal lesions to the auditory "what" and "where" processing streams (Adriani et al., 2003b). Thirty patients with a first unilateral hemispheric lesion, 15 with right-hemispheric damage and 15 with left-hemispheric damage, were evaluated for their capacity to recognize environmental sounds, to localize sounds in space and to perceive sound motion. Selective deficits in one of the functions or combined deficits in two or the three functions were observed in cases with right- or left-hemispheric lesions.

Deficient performance in sound recognition, sound localization and/or sound motion perception was always associated with a lesion that involved the shared auditory structures and the specialized "what" and/or "where" networks, while normal performance was associated with lesions within or outside these territories. Thus, damage to regions known to be involved in auditory processing in normal subjects is necessary, but not sufficient for a deficit to occur.

In the acute stage, lesions of a specialized network were not always associated with the corresponding deficit. Conversely, specific deficits tended not to be associated predominantly with lesions of the corresponding network, e.g. selective deficits in auditory spatial tasks were observed in patients whose lesions involved the shared auditory structures and the specialized "what" network but not the specialized "where" network. This observation supports the hypothesis that the auditory "what" and "where" processing streams function as parts of a larger auditory network, in which an acute lesion of one network disturbs the processing in the other.

BILATERAL AUDITORY "WHAT" AND "WHERE" PROCESSING STREAMS – WHY DO UNILATERAL LESIONS CAUSE DEFICITS?

Activation studies in normal subjects demonstrated the presence of auditory "what" and "where" processing streams in either hemisphere and yet sound recognition and/or localization may be disrupted by purely unilateral damage. This suggests that processing within one hemisphere may not be sufficient or may be disturbed by the contralateral lesion. To address this issue we have investigated sound recognition and sound localization psychophysically and with fMRI in seven patients with unilateral right hemispheric lesions (Adriani et al., 2003a). Two patients had a combined deficit in sound recognition and sound localization, two a selective deficit in sound localization, one a selective deficit in sound recognition and two had normal performance in both. In comparison to normal subjects the sound recognition and the sound localization tasks activated less the intact, left hemisphere, both in patients with normal and deficient performance. Specialized networks for sound recognition and sound localization in the left hemisphere were activated very similarly to normal subjects in patients with normal performance, but failed to be so in patients with deficient performance (Fig. 5.1F).

Thus, unilateral lesions disturb the processing in the contralateral, intact hemisphere including, in some cases, the breakdown of parallel processing in the auditory "what" and "where" streams. This breakdown is then associated with deficient performance in sound recognition and/or sound localization.

SUMMARY

Evidence from anatomical, activation and lesion studies suggest that sound recognition and sound localization are processed into two networks, the "what" and the "where" streams. Although these networks process the two types of information in parallel and to some extent independently, interactions between them occur, such as revealed by early and/or contralateral effects of lesions.

ABBREVIATIONS

AI   Primary auditory area
AchE   Acethylcholinesterase
AL   Anterolateral area (monkey)
CaBPs   Aalcium-binding proteins
CB   Calbindin
CL   Caudolateral area (monkey)
CM   Caudomedial area (monkey)
CO   Cytochrome oxidase
CPB   Caudal parabelt (monkey)
CR   Calretinin
IID   Interaural intensity difference
ITD   Interaural time difference
ML   Mediolateral area (ML)
PV   Parvalbumin
R   Rostral area (monkey)
RM   Rostromedial area (monkey)
RPB   Rostral parabelt (monkey)
RTL   Lateral rostrotemporal area (monkey)
RTM   Medial rostrotemporal area (monkey)

Auditory areas as described by Rivier and Clarke, 1997:
AA   Anterior auditory area
AIA   Anterior insular auditory area
LA   Lateral auditory area
MA   Medial auditory area
PA   Posterior auditory area
PIA   Posterior insular auditory area
STA   Superior temporal auditory area

REFERENCES

Adriani, M., Bellmann, A., Meuli, R., Fornari, E., Frischknecht, R., Bindschaedler, C., Rivier, F., Thiran, J.-Ph., Maeder, P., & Clarke, S. (2003a). Unilateral hemispheric lesions disrupt parallel processing within the contralateral intact hemisphere: An auditory fMRI study. NeuroImage, 20, Suppl. 1, S66–74.

Adriani, M., Maeder, P., Meuli, R., Bellmann Thiran, A., Frischknecht, R., Villemure, J. G., Mayer, J., Annoni, J.M., Bogousslavsky, J., Fornari, E., Thiran, J.-Ph., & Clarke, S. (2003b). Sound recognition and localization in man: Specialized cortical networks and acute effects of circumscribed lesions. Experimental Brain Research, 153, 591–604.

Alain, C., Arnott, S.R., Hevenor, S., Graham, S., & Grady C.L. (2001). "What" and "Where" in the human auditory system. Proceedings of the National Academy of Sciences USA, 98, 12301–12306.

Anourova, I., Nikouline, V.V., Ilmoniemi, R.J., Hotta, J., Aronen, H.J., & Carlson, S. (2001). Evidence for dissociation of spatial and nonspatial auditory information processing. NeuroImage, 14, 1268–1277.

Anourova, I., Rämä, P., Alho, K., Koivusalo, S., Kalmari, J., & Carlson, S. (1999). Selective interference reveals dissociation between auditory memory for location and pitch. Neuroreport, 10, 3543–3547.

Belin, P., & Zatorre, R.J. (2000). 'What', 'where' and 'how' in auditory cortex. Nature Neuroscience, 3, 965–966.

Bellmann, A., Meuli, R., & Clarke, S. (2001). Two types of auditory neglect. Brain, 124, 676–687.

Brodmann, K. (1909). Vergleichende Localisationslehre der Grosshirnrinde in ihren Prinzipien dargestellt auf Grund des Zellenbaues. Leipzig: Johann Ambrosius Barth.

Brugge, J.F., Volkov, I.O., Garell, P.C., Reale, R.A., & Howard, M.A., 3rd. (2003). Functional connections between auditory cortex on Heschl's gyrus and on the lateral superior temporal gyrus in humans. Journal of Neurophysiology, 90, 3750–3763.

Bushara, K.O., Weeks, R.A., Ishii, K., Catalan, M.J., Tian, B., Rauschecker, J.P., & Hallett, M. (1999). Modality-specific frontal and parietal areas for auditory and visual spatial localization in humans. Nature Neuroscience, 2, 759–766.

Chiry, O., Tardif, E., Magistretti, P.J., & Clarke, S. (2003). Patterns of calcium-binding proteins support parallel and hierarchical organization of human auditory areas. European Journal of Neuroscience, 17, 397–410.

Clarke, S. (1994). Modular organization of human extrastriate visual cortex: Evidence from cytochrome oxidase pattern in normal and macular degeneration cases. European Journal of Neuroscience, 6, 725–736.

Clarke, S., Adriani, M., & Bellmann, A. (1998). Distinct short-term memory systems for sound content and sound localization. Neuroreport, 9, 3433–3437.

Clarke, S., Bellmann, A., Meuli, R.A., Assal, G., & Steck, A.J. (2000). Auditory agnosia and auditory spatial deficits following left hemispheric lesions: Evidence for distinct processing pathways. Neuropsychologia, 38, 797–807.

Clarke, S., & Bellmann-Thiran, A. (2004). Auditory neglect: What and where in auditory space. Cortex (in press).

Clarke, S., Bellmann-Thiran, A., Maeder, P., Adriani, M., Vernet, O., Regli, L., Cuisenaire, O., & Thiran, J.-P. (2002). What and Where in human audition: Selective deficits following focal hemispheric lesions. Experimental Brain Research, 147, 8–15.

Clarke, S., & Miklossy, J. (1990). Occipital cortex in man: organization of callosal connections, related myelo- and cytoarchitecture, and putative boundaries of functional visual areas. The Journal of Comparative Neurology, 298, 188–214.

Clarke, S., & Rivier, F. (1998). Compartments within human primary auditory cortex: evidence from cytochrome oxidase and acetylcholinesterase staining. European Journal of Neuroscience, 10, 741–745.

Clarke, S., Viceic, D., Maeder, P.P., Meuli, R.A., Adriani, M., Fornari, E., & Thiran, J.-P. (2004). What and where specialization within non-primary auditory areas: An fMRI study. Forum of European Neuroscience Abstracts.

Di Virgilio, G., & Clarke, S. (1997). Direct interhemispheric visual input to human speech areas. Human Brain Mapping, 5, 347–354.

Di Virgilio, G., Clarke, S., Pizzolato, G., & Schaffner, T. (1999). Cortical regions contributing to the anterior commissure in man. Experimental Brain Research, 124, 1–7.

Ducommun, C.Y., Murray, M.M., Thut, G., Bellmann, A., Viaud-Delmon, I., Clarke, S., & Michel, C.M. (2002). Segregated processing of auditory motion and auditory location: An ERP mapping study. NeuroImage, 16, 76–88.

Formisano, E., Kim, D.S., Di Salle, F., van de Moortele, P.F., Ugurbil, K., & Goebel, R. (2003). Mirror-symmetric tonotopic maps in human primary auditory cortex. Neuron, 40, 859–869.

Fujii, T., Fukatsu, R., Watabe, S., Ohnuma, A., Teramura, K., Saso, S., & Kogure, K. (1990). Auditory sound agnosia without aphasia following a right temporal lobe lesion. Cortex, 26, 263–268.

Galuske, R.A., Schlote, W., Bratzke, H., & Singer, W. (2000). Interhemispheric asymmetries of the modular structure in human temporal cortex. Science, 289, 1946–1949.

Griffiths, T.D., Buchel, C., Frackowiak, R.S., & Patterson, R.D. (1998). Analysis of temporal structure in sound by the human brain. Nature Neuroscience, 1, 422–427.

Griffiths, T.D., Green, G.G.R., Rees, A., & Rees, G. (2000). Human brain areas involved in the analysis of auditory movement. Human Brain Mapping, 9, 72–80.

Griffiths, T.D., Rees, A., Witton, C., Cross, P.M., Shakir, R.A., & Green, G.G.R. (1997). Spatial and temporal auditory processing deficits following right hemisphere infarction: A psychophysical study. Brain, 120, 785–794.

Griffiths, T.D., Rees, A., Witton, C., Shakir, R.A., Henning, G.B., & Green, G.G.R. (1996). Evidence for a sound movement area in the human cerebral cortex. Nature, 383, 425–427.

Hall, D.A, Johnsrude, I.S., Haggard, M.P., Palmer, A.R., Akeroyd, M.A., & Summerfield, A.Q. (2002). Spectral and temporal processing in human auditory cortex. Cerebral Cortex, 12, 140–149.

Hart, H.C., Palmer, A.R., & Hall, D.A. (2004). Different areas of human non-primary auditory cortex are activated by sounds with spatial and nonspatial properties. Human Brain Mapping, 21, 178–190.

Hashimoto, R., Homae, F., Nakajima, K., Miyashita, Y., & Sakai, K.I. (2000). Functional differentiation in the human auditory and language areas revealed by a dichotic listening task. NeuroImage, 12, 147–158.

Hashikawa, T., Rausell, E., Molinari, M., & Jones, E.G. (1991). Parvalbumin and calbindin-containing neurons in the monkey medial geniculate complex: Differential distribution and cortical layer-specific projections. Brain Research, 544, 335–341.

Horton, J.C., & Hedley-Whyte, E.T. (1984) Mapping of cytochrome oxidase patches and ocular dominance columns in human visual cortex. Philosophical Transactions of the Royal Society of London. Series B. Biological Science, 304, 255–272.

Hutsler, J.J., & Galuske, R.A.W. (2003). Hemispheric asymmetries in cerebral cortical networks. Trends in Neuroscience, 26, 429–435.

Hutsler, J.J., & Gazzaniga, M.S. (1996). Acetylcholinesterase staining in human auditory and language cortices: Regional variation of structural features. Cerebral Cortex, 6, 260–270.

Imig, T.J., & Adrian, H.O. (1977). Binaural columns in the primary field (A1) of cat auditory cortex. Brain Research, 138, 241–257.

Jerger, J., Loverling, L., & Wertz, M. (1972). Auditory disorder following bilateral temporal lobe insult: Report of a case. The Journal of Speech and Hearing Disorders, 37, 523–535.

Jones, E.G. (2003). Chemically defined parallel pathways in the monkey auditory system. Annals of the New York Academy of Sciences, 999, 218–33.

Jones, E.G., Dell'Anna, M.E., Molinari, M., Rausell, E., & Hashikawa T. (1995). Subdivisions of macaque monkey auditory cortex revealed by calcium-binding protein immunoreactivity. The Journal of Comparative Neurology, 362, 153–170.

Jones, E.G., & Hendry, S.H. (1989). Differential calcium binding protein immuno-reactivity distinguishes classes of relay neurons in monkey thalamic nuclei. European Journal of Neuroscience, 1, 222–246.

Kaas, J.H. & Hackett, T.A. (2000). Subdivisions of auditory cortex and processing streams in primates. Proceedings of the National Academy of Sciences USA, 97, 11793–11799.

Livingstone, M.S., & Hubel, D.H. (1983). Specificity of cortico-cortical connections in monkey visual system. Nature, 304, 531–534.

Livingstone, M.S., & Hubel, D.H. (1988). Segregation of form, color, movement, and depth: anatomy, physiology, and perception. Science, 240, 740–749.

Maeder, P., Meuli, R., Adriani, M., Bellmann, A., Fornari, E., Thiran, J.-Ph., Pittet, A., & Clarke, S. (2001). Distinct pathways involved in sound recognition and localization: A human fMRI study. NeuroImage, 14, 802–816.

Merzenich, M.M., & Brugge, J.F. (1973). Representation of the cochlear partition of the superior temporal plane of the macaque monkey. Brain Research, 50, 275–296.

Mesulam, M.M., & Geula, C. (1994). Chemoarchitectonics of axonal and perikaryal acetylcholinesterase along information processing systems of the human cerebral cortex. Brain Research Bulletin, 33, 137–153.

Middlebrooks, J.C., Dykes, R.W., & Merzenich M.M. (1980). Binaural response-specific bands in primary auditory cortex (AI) of the cat: Topographical organization orthogonal to isofrequency contours. Brain Research, 181, 31–48.

Molinari, M., Dell'Anna, M.E., Rausell, E., Leggio, M.G., Hashikawa, T., & Jones, E.G. (1995). Auditory thalamocortical pathways defined in monkeys by calcium-binding protein immunoreactivity. The Journal of Comparative Neurology, 13, 171–194.

Morel, A., Garraghty, P.E., & Kaas, J.H. (1993). Tonotopic organization, architectonic fields, and connections of auditory cortex in macaque monkeys. The Journal of Comparative Neurology, 335, 437–459.

Morosan, P., Rademacher, J., Palomero-Gallagher, N., & Zilles, K. (2004). Anatomical organization of the human auditory cortex: Cytoarchitecture and transmitter receptors. In R. König, P. Heil, E. Budinger, & H. Scheich (Eds.), The Auditory Cortex – A Synthesis of Human and Animal Research. Hillsdale, NJ: Lawrence Erlbaum Associates.

Pantev, C., Bertrand, O., Eulitz, C., Verkindt, C., Hampson, S., Schuierer, G., & Elbert, T. (1995). Specific tonotopic organizations of different areas of the human auditory cortex revealed by simultaneous magnetic and electric recordings. Electroence-phalography and Clinical Neurophysiology, 94, 26–40.

Rauschecker, J.P., & Tian, B. (2000). Mechanisms and streams for processing of "what" and "where" in auditory cortex. Proceedings of the National Academy of Sciences USA, 97, 11800–11806.

Rauschecker, J.P., Tian, B., & Hauser, M. (1995). Processing of complex sounds in the macaque non-primary auditory cortex. Science, 268, 111–114.

Rauschecker, J.P., Tian, B., Pons, T., & Mishkin M. (1997). Serial and parallel processing in rhesus monkey auditory cortex. The Journal of Comparative Neurology, 382, 89–103.

Recanzone, G.H. (2000). Spatial processing in the auditory cortex of the macaque monkey. Proceedings of the National Academy of Sciences USA, 97, 11829–11835.

Rivier, F., & Clarke, S. (1997). Cytochrome oxidase, acetylcholinesterase and NADPH-diaphorase staining in human supratemporal and insular cortex: Evidence for multiple auditory areas. NeuroImage, 6, 288–304.

Romani, G.L., Williamson, S.J., & Kaufman, L. (1982). Tonotopic organization of the human auditory cortex. Science, 216, 1339–1340.

Romanski, L.M., Tian, B., Fritz, J., Mishkin, M., Goldman-Rakic, P.S., & Rauschecker, J.P. (1999). Dual streams of auditory afferents target multiple domains in the primate prefrontal cortex. Nature Neuroscience, 2, 1131–1136.

Rosati, G., De Bastiani, P., Paolino, E., Prosser, S., Arslan, E., & Artioli, M. (1982). Clinical and audiological findings in a case of auditory agnosia. Journal of Neurology, 227, 21–27.

Schönwiesner, M., von Cramon, D.Y., & Rübsamen, R. (2002). Is it tonotopy after all? NeuroImage, 17, 1144–1161.

Scott, S.K. & Johnsrude, I.S. (2003). The neuroanatomical and functional organization of speech perception. Trends in Neuroscience, 26, 100–107.

Spreen, O., Benton, A.L., & Fincham, R.W. (1965). Auditory agnosia without aphasia. Archives of Neurology, 13, 84–92.

Talavage, T.M., Ledden, P.J., Benson, R.R., Rosen, B.R., & Melcher, J.R. (2000). Frequency-dependent responses exhibited by multiple regions in human auditory cortex. Hearing Research, 150, 225–244.

Talavage, T.M., Sereno, M.I., Melcher, J.R., Ledden, P.J., Rosen, B.R., & Dale, A.M. (2004). Tonotopic organization in human auditory cortex revealed by progressions of frequency sensitivity. Journal of Neurophysiology, 91, 1282–1296.

Tardif, E., Chiry, O., Probst, A., Magistretti, P.J., & Clarke, S. (2003). Patterns of calcium-binding proteins in human inferior colliculus. Identification of subdivisions and evidence for putative parallel systems. Neuroscience, 116, 1111–1121.

Tardif, E., & Clarke, S. (2001). Intrinsic connectivity of human auditory areas: A tracing study with DiI. European Journal of Neuroscience, 13, 1045–1050.

Tardif, E., & Clarke, S. (2002). Commissural connections of human superior colliculus. Neuroscience, 111, 363–372.

Thiran, A.B., & Clarke, S. (2003). Preserved use of spatial cues for sound segretation in a case of spatial deafness. Neuropsychologia, 41, 1254–1261.

Tian, B., Reser, D., Durham, A., Kustov, A. & Rauschecker, J.P. (2001). Functional specialization in rhesus monkey auditory cortex. Science, 292, 290–293.

Tiitinen, H., Alho, K., Huotilainen, M., Ilmoniemi, R.J., Simola, J., & Näätänen, R. (1993). Tonotopic auditory cortex and the magnetoencephalographic (MEG) equivalent of the mismatch negativity. Psychophysiology, 30, 537–540.

Verkindt, C., Bertrand, O., Perrin, F., Echallier, J.F., & Pernier, J. (1995). Tonotopic organization of the human auditory cortex: N100 topography and multiple dipole model analysis. Electroencephalography and Clinical Neurophysiology, 96, 143–156.

von Economo, C., & Koskinas G.N. (1925). Die Zytoarchitectonik der Hirnrinde des erwachsenen Menschen. Berlin: Julius Springer.

Wallace, M.N., Johnston, P.W., & Palmer, A.R. (2002). Histochemical identification of cortical areas in the auditory region of the human brain. Experimental Brain Research, 143, 499–508.

Warren, J.D., Zielinski, B.A., Green, G.G.R., Rauschecker, J.P., & Griffiths, T.D. (2002). Perception of sound-source motion by the human brain. Neuron, 34, 139–148.

Weeks, R.A., Aziz-Sultan, A., Bushara, K.O., Tian, B., Wessinger, C.M., Dang, N., Rauschecker, J.P., & Hallett, M. (1999). A PET study of human auditory spatial processing. Neuroscience Letters, 262, 155–158.

Zatorre, R. J., Bouffard, M., Ahad, P., & Belin, P. (2002). Where is 'where' in the human auditory cortex? Nature Neuroscience 5, 905–909.

6. THE ANTERIOR FIELD OF AUDITORY CORTEX: NEUROPHYSIOLOGICAL AND NEUROANATOMICAL ORGANIZATION

Kazuo Imaizumi, Charles C. Lee, Jennifer F. Linden, Jeffery A. Winer, Christoph E. Schreiner

INTRODUCTION

Auditory cortex in mammals, including humans, consists of multiple fields. Discerning differences in response properties, functional organization, and neural connectivity among these fields is key to understanding global organization and, ultimately, the functional roles in concurrent processing of auditory information. In the cat, the primary auditory cortex (AI) and the anterior auditory field (AAF) represent the earliest stages of cortical information processing. Both AI and AAF are tonotopically organized, and contain neurons that respond strongly, with short latencies, to pure tone stimuli (Knight, 1977; Merzenich et al., 1974; Phillips & Irvine, 1982). Analysis of anatomical connectivity among cortical layers indicates that AI and AAF are situated at a hierarchically similar level (Rouiller et al., 1991). Thus, comparing AI and AAF provides a unique opportunity to study how topographic projections create global and local maps in hierarchically equivalent cortical fields, and to evaluate response properties and functional organization in concurrent cortical processing streams.

While receptive field properties and their functional organization in cat AI have been extensively studied (Imig & Adrián, 1977; Merzenich et al., 1974; Nelken, 2002; Read et al., 2002; Schreiner & Mendelson, 1990; Sutter et al., 1999), knowledge about AAF response properties is more limited (Eggermont, 1998, 1999; Knight, 1977; Phillips & Irvine, 1982; Schreiner & Urbas, 1986). In particular, functional organization beyond tonotopy is essentially unknown for

AAF in cat and other mammals. In this chapter, we review our recent findings about AAF spatial organization, functional properties, and neuroanatomical connectivity (Imaizumi et al., 2004; Lee et al., 2004). In addition, we compare some basic response parameter distributions for AI and AAF in two different mammals (Imaizumi et al., 2004; Linden et al., 2003): the cat, which has long been the species of choice for most auditory cortex research; and the mouse, a model system for studies of the genetics of hearing. This cross-species comparison reveals possible common themes for early auditory cortical processing in mammals, and also possible species-specific differences in AI and AAF physiology.

CHARACTERISTIC FREQUENCY REPRESENTATION IN AI AND AAF

AI and AAF in the cat are flanked by three sulci, the suprasylvian sulcus (sss), the posterior ectosylvian sulcus (pes), and the anterior ectosylvian sulcus (aes) (Fig. 6.1). In cat and some other mammals, AI and AAF are equally exposed on the gyral surface, and, thus, their study minimizes potential experimental biases of differential responses among cortical layers. Extracellular recordings (both single- and multi-units) were obtained from the main thalamo-cortical recipient layers, IIIb and IV (Huang & Winer, 2000), for large areas of AI and AAF (Imaizumi et al., 2004). Spatial reconstruction of the response distributions was created by Voronoi-Dirichlet tessellation (Fig. 6.1). Each polygon represents a recording position, and polygon borders were determined from the midpoints of a straight line between adjacent recording positions (Kilgard & Merzenich, 1998). At each recording point, receptive field parameters (RFPs) were extrapolated from frequency response areas obtained by presenting 675 pseudorandomized tone bursts at different frequencies (3–5 octaves) and sound levels (70 dB range). Characteristic frequency (CF), threshold, quality factors (Q_{10} and Q_{40}: CF divided by bandwidth at 10 or 40 dB SPL above threshold), and minimum first-spike latency (hereafter, latency) were determined. The use of tonal receptive fields provides direct comparisons of neural functions within and across species for these early cortical areas.

AI and AAF have clear tonotopic gradients in opposite directions, with a steeper CF gradient in AAF; the two fields share a border (dashed line) at high CFs (Fig. 6.1; Imaizumi et al., 2004). Previous physiological studies have shown considerable overlap of frequency representations in AI and AAF (Knight, 1977; Merzenich et al., 1974; Phillips & Irvine, 1982). However, the CF gradient in AAF is less uniform than in AI, with under-representation of some CFs (Imaizumi et al., 2004). For example, the case illustrated in Figure 6.1 shows that the representation of 10–15 kHz is nearly absent in AAF while the same CF range is robustly represented in AI. To quantify this phenomenon, each polygon area in tessellation maps was computed and compared in a sliding window of 1/3-CF octave steps (Imaizumi et al., 2004). Dense mapping of the AAF cortical surface region in five hemispheres revealed a consistent under-

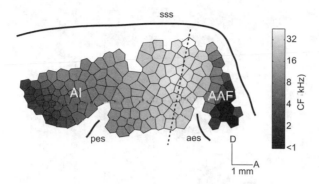

Fig. 6.1. Location of AI and AAF relative to the suprasylvian sulcus. The reversal of characteristic frequencies (CFs) at the AI and AAF border is illustrated by a dashed line. CF gradient was smoothed by a second order, weighted least-squares linear regression model, and coded in gray scale. *sss*: suprasylvian sulcus, *pes*: posterior ectosylvian sulcus, *aes*: anterior ectosylvian sulcus, *D*: dorsal, *A*: anterior. Modified from Imaizumi et al. (2004).

representation of the mid-frequency range in all cases, most often for CF ranges 1–5 kHz and ~11 kHz (Imaizumi et al., 2004). No such under-representation of mid-frequency was observed in AI. An over-representation of 20–30 kHz was also found in AAF (Knight, 1977). These observations indicate that the arrangement of frequency representation is specific in AI and AAF.

MODULAR ORGANIZATION OF AAF

To pinpoint the functional differences between AI and AAF, it is necessary to understand the distribution of RFPs as a function of CF across the fields. The most sensitive CF ranges for AI and AAF are at mid-frequencies, 5–20 kHz and 10–20 kHz, respectively (Imaizumi et al., 2004, Imaizumi & Schreiner, 2004). Thresholds are higher toward lower and higher CFs. Spectral bandwidth, expressed as Q_{10} or Q_{40}, increases with increasing CFs in both fields. Response latency is clearly related to CF in AI (shorter latencies with increasing CFs) but less so in AAF. Overall, several RFPs are CF-dependent, although the trends are not necessarily the same for both fields.

In cat AI, spatial clusters of neurons with similar RFPs such as binaurality, intensity sensitivity, and spectral bandwidth (e.g., Q_{40}) exist along iso-frequency contours (Middlebrooks et al., 1980; Phillips et al., 1994; Read et al., 2001; Schreiner & Mendelson, 1990; Schreiner et al., 2000). To assess whether similar spatial clustering exists in AAF, co-variations of RFPs with CF need to be eliminated by removal of trends evident in non-parametric, local regression fits. Spatial analysis of RFP residuals (differences between the model and observed values) revealed that a modular organization of RFPs also exists in AAF. Figure

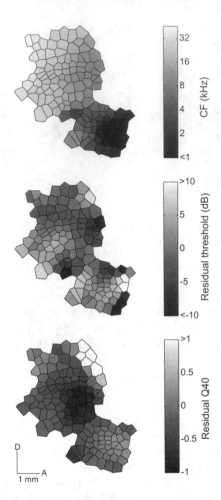

Fig. 6.2. Tessellation maps for CF and residual receptive field parameters (threshold and Q_{40}) in AAF. Tessellation maps were smoothed. See Figure 6.1 legend for further explanation. Modified from Imaizumi et al. (2004).

6.2 illustrates a tonotopic map (CF) and residual maps for threshold and Q_{40} in cat AAF. In the residual scale, zero corresponds to the mean residual value for each RFP. Along iso-frequency contours, clusters with similar residual values are evident, in particular for threshold. For Q_{40} residuals, a large low-value cluster (broadly tuned neurons) and a small high-value cluster (sharply tuned neurons) are located in the central and dorsal areas, respectively. Residuals for other parameters (Q_{10} and latency) are also distributed non-homogeneously in local clusters (Imaizumi et al., 2004). Thus, a parameter-specific modular organization occurs in AAF. However, this modular organization appears to be less robust than in AI, where a large module of high Q_{40} values (sharply tuned

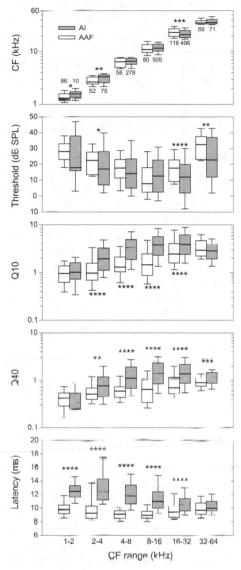

Fig. 6.3. A comparison of receptive field parameters between AAF and AI in cat auditory cortex. Samples were pooled from seven and 16 hemispheres, respectively, for AAF and AI. An entire group was divided into six groups in octave CF bins from 1 to 64 kHz. Box plots illustrate medians (horizontal lines), quartiles (box heights), and 10th and 90th percentiles (whiskers). A Mann-Whitney U test was performed: *: $p < 0.05$, **: $p < 0.01$, ***: $p < 0.001$, ****: $p < 0.0001$. Numbers (top panel) indicate sample size for each group. Modified from Imaizumi et al. (2004).

neurons) consistently dominates the center of isofrequency contours (at least for CF > 5 kHz), and is flanked by low Q_{40} values (broadly tuned neurons) in the dorsal and ventral areas (Imaizumi & Schreiner, 2004). The less robust modular organization in AAF may be related to its smaller size relative to AI, the fact that only the exposed cortex was mapped, and/or a different constellation of anatomical connections with thalamus or other cortical fields (see below).

RECEPTIVE FIELD PARAMETERS IN CAT AND MOUSE AI AND AAF

AI and AAF are the primary tonotopic fields involved in early cortical processing. Thus far, the evidence presented in this chapter has shown that cat AAF differs from AI in details of CF representation and, potentially, in the extent and spatial consistency of its modular organization. How are these differences related to RFPs in these two fields, and are analogous differences evident in other species? Previous studies in the cat (Eggermont, 1998; Phillips & Irvine, 1981, 1982) did not find prominent global differences in the RFP distributions of the two fields. The CF-dependence of RFPs in AI and AAF requires limiting comparisons to narrow CF ranges. Pooling AAF and AI recordings from current and previous studies in cat (seven AAF and 16 AI hemispheres) (Imaizumi et al., 2004; Imaizumi & Schreiner, 2004; Lee et al., 2004; Read et al., 2001; Schreiner & Raggio, 1996) and, similarly, for AAF and AI in mice (12 hemispheres) (Linden et al., 2003) allows a quantitative evaluation of RFP differences in these species. Each RFP between AAF ($n = 461$) and AI ($n = 1.435$) units in cats was compared by Mann-Whitney U test in octave CF bins from 1 to 64 kHz (Fig. 6.3). Box plots in Figure 6.3 compare RFP values for both fields in octave bins. Clear differences between the two fields were found in spectral bandwidth (Q_{10} and Q_{40} values) and latency (Imaizumi et al., 2004). AAF neurons were more broadly tuned to frequency than AI neurons in most CF bins except for low (1–2 kHz) and high CFs (32–64 kHz for Q_{10}). In the mid-CF range, large modules with sharply tuned neuron clusters are found in AI (Imaizumi & Schreiner, 2004; Read et al., 2001; Schreiner & Mendelson, 1990), which may account for the significant difference in spectral bandwidth between AAF and AI. AAF neurons also had shorter latencies than AI neurons in all CF bins except for the highest frequencies (32–64 kHz). Threshold differences were also noticed, with slightly higher thresholds for AAF neurons between 2–4 kHz and 16–64 kHz. The differences may be a consequence of differences in the CF distribution in these frequency bins.

RFPs in AI and AAF have also been compared in mice (Linden et al., 2003). Frequency response areas were mapped using tone bursts, and spectro-temporal receptive fields were estimated from neural responses to dynamic random chord stimuli. AI neurons had longer receptive field durations than AAF neurons, suggesting a longer integration time window for AI neurons (Linden et al., 2003). As in the cat, mouse AAF neurons had shorter latencies (Fig. 6.4).

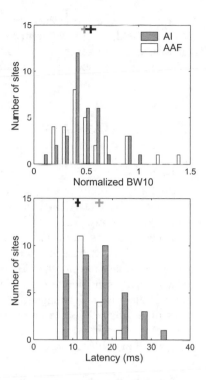

Fig. 6.4. A comparison of receptive field parameters between AAF and AI in mouse auditory cortex (12 hemispheres). Normalized bandwidth 10 (BW10) was defined as bandwidth at 10 dB above threshold divided by CF (inverse of Q_{10}): the higher the value, the more broadly the neurons are tuned. Kolmogorov-Smirnov test was performed for statistical significance. There was significant difference for latency ($p < 0.0001$) but not for normalized *BW10*. Modified from Linden et al. (2003).

Spectral bandwidths at 10 dB above threshold divided by CF (i.e., inverse of Q_{10}) were similar between AI and AAF (Fig. 6.4). However, bandwidths estimated from responses to dynamic random chord stimuli were broader for AI (Linden et al., 2003).

The observations that latencies are shorter in AAF than AI both in cat and mouse as well as ferret and rat (Kowalski et al., 1995; Rutkowski et al., 2003) suggest a functional contrast between the two fields that may extend to other mammals (see an exception in Harel et al., 2000). By contrast, analyses of tuning sharpness did not reveal a similar pattern of results in the two species. This may be related to species-specific differences in internal features of auditory cortical organization, such as GABAergic organization (Prieto et al., 1994) and horizontal connectional patterns (Lee et al., 2004; Read et al., 2001). Alternatively, the differences in sharpness of tuning between AI and AAF neurons observed in cat may depend on the presence of highly developed bandwidth modules, which may not exist in mice. In summary, latency differences between AI and AAF are observed across different species, suggesting that the two auditory fields may have contrasting roles in temporal processing of auditory information; however, bandwidth analyses seem to indicate that the roles of AI and AAF in spectral processing could be species-specific.

ANATOMICAL CONNECTIONS OF AI AND AAF

The possibility of concurrent projection streams for AI and AAF has a long history (Andersen et al., 1980; Morel & Imig, 1987; Tian & Rauschecker, 1994). To evaluate this possibility experimentally, it is most appropriate to compare the neural connections in AI and AAF neurons that share a similar physiological property. Moreover, because RFPs of cortical neurons may be influenced by the combined neural inputs from thalamic, cortico-cortical, and commissural sources, it is logical to use retrograde anatomical tracers to find the origins of cortical input. With this goal in mind, the CF gradients in cat AI and AAF were identified, and two equally sensitive retrograde tracers, cholera toxin β subunit and cholera toxin β subunit-gold conjugate, were injected into the same iso-frequency contours of AI and AAF (Lee et al., 2004). To compensate for different magnification factor between AI and AAF (Knight, 1977), two to three tracer deposits were made in AI and only one deposit in AAF. This approach also reduced potential differences in connectivity due to module-specific properties such as sharp or broad tuning areas. Cytoarchitechtonic borders among different cortical fields were identified with the Nissl stain and the SMI-32 antibody that recognizes neurofilaments of apical dendrites in pyramidal neurons (Lee et al., 2004).

Retrogradely labeled cell bodies were identified in the medial geniculate body (MGB) and all auditory and auditory-associated cortical fields. The most striking result was that < 2% of the neurons were double-labeled in the MGB and all auditory and auditory-associated cortical fields (Lee et al., 2004). That is, almost all thalamic and cortical neurons project independently to AI and AAF; this suggests that thalamic and cortical neurons representing the same frequency are members of concurrent projection systems. Sixty percent of cortical projections to the injection sites originated intrinsically in both fields, but spanned a broader frequency range in AAF (Lee et al., 2004). Intrinsic connections within AI are related to long horizontal connections between bandwidth-modules (Read et al., 2001).

Thalamo-cortical projections provide excitatory inputs to AI and AAF. AI receives ~80% of its thalamic input from the tonotopically organized ventral division of the MGB (Fig. 6.5). By contrast, AAF receives almost equal projections (~75%) from the tonotopically organized ventral and the rostral pole divisions (also termed the lateral part of the posterior group; Imig & Morel, 1985a) and ~25% from the non-tonotopically organized dorsal and medial divisions of the MGB (Lee et al., 2004). Differences in modular organization

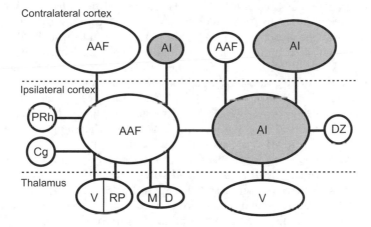

Fig. 6.5. Anatomical connections from the thalamus and ipsilateral and contralateral cortices to AAF and AI. The area of each contour is proportional to the relative strength of the projections from each thalamic or cortical source. Dashed lines divide projection sources. For cortico-cortical connections, only the projections that differed for the two fields are illustrated. *PRh*: perirhinal cortex, *Cg*: cingulate cortex, *DZ*: dorsal zone, *V*: auditory thalamic ventral division, *RP*: thalamic rostral pole, *M*: thalamic medial division, *D*: thalamic dorsal division. Modified from Lee et al. (2004).

and RFPs between AI and AAF may be directly related to differences in thalamo-cortical projections to AI and AAF. The organization of binaural response properties in the MGB appears to contribute directly to the modular organization of AI (Middlebrooks & Zook, 1983; Velenovsky et al., 2003). Although the intrinsic organization of RFPs in the MGB is not fully understood, the robust modular organization of AI may be related to the intrinsic organization of the ventral division of the MGB. By contrast, the less robust modular organization of AAF may be related to convergent projections from four different divisions of the MGB. Some RFPs of AAF, such as shorter latency and wider spectral bandwidth, are well-matched to the neural properties of these tonotopic and non-tonotopic divisions of the MGB (Calford & Aitkin, 1983; Imig & Morel, 1985a, 1985b; Rodrigues-Dagaeff et al., 1989). Neurons in the ventral and the rostral pole divisions of the MGB have relatively short latency, and neurons in the dorsal and medial divisions of the MGB are broadly tuned. Moreover, the rostral pole of the MGB contains a sparse CF representation in the mid-frequency range and an over-representation in the high frequency range (Imig & Morel, 1985a), which corresponds to the observed under- and over-represented CF ranges of AAF. Therefore, RFPs and the modular organization in AI are strongly influenced by the projection from the ventral division of the MGB, while those in AAF may be created by convergent projections from several divisions of the MGB.

Beside these thalamic projections, AI and AAF receive projections from virtually all tonotopic and non-tonotopic auditory fields and from many non-auditory cortical fields (Lee et al., 2004). Three cortical fields had significantly larger projections either to AI or AAF (Fig. 6.5). AI receives greater feedback projections from the dorsal zone (DZ) that is located dorsal to AI (Middlebrooks & Zook, 1983). DZ neurons often have multi-peaked frequency tuning curves (He & Hashikawa, 1998; Sutter & Schreiner, 1991), can be tuned to particular stimulus durations (He et al., 1997), and may have an auditory spatial modular map (Stecker & Middlebrooks, 2003). AAF receives greater feedback projections from the perirhinal (PRh) and cingulate (Cg) cortices (Fig. 6.5), which may be involved in cognitive functions such as learning and memory (Lindquist et al., 2004) and auditory attention (Benedict et al., 2002), respectively. Although the functional roles of the feedback projections from DZ to AI or from PRh and Cg to AAF are not known, these differences in extrinsic cortico-cortical connectivity set these fields apart (Lee et al., 2004).

AI and AAF receive commissural projections largely from the same fields (Fig. 6.5). However, the relative contributions of feedforward and feedback projections might differ between AI and AAF. In AI, feedforward projections through layers III (~70%) surpass feedback projections through layers VI (~30%). By contrast, AAF had equal proportions of feedforward and feedback projections (~50%/50%) (Lee et al., 2004). The functional role for commissural connections may be hemispheric lateralization of sound processing, at least, in the monkey (Poremba et al., 2004). Another possibility is in clustering of binaural response properties (Imig & Brugge, 1978; Liu & Suga, 1997).

DISCUSSION

Despite the hierarchical equivalency of the two fields, physiological and anatomical evidence suggests that AAF differs from AI in several properties, including frequency representation, modular functional organization, RFP distributions, and anatomical connectivity. In the cat auditory system, tonotopic pathways to AI and AAF are largely independent, concurrent streams, and already separated at subcortical levels. Presumably, other concurrent streams exist (e.g., for spectral bandwidth or latency) within each field that may subserve different neural functions.

In macaque auditory cortex, two task-specific parallel pathways have been proposed: one for sound identification and another for sound location processing (Rauschecker & Tian, 2000; Romanski et al., 1999; Tian et al., 2001). These pathways have been associated with the caudolateral and the anterior lateral cortical areas, respectively, and project with little overlap to largely segregated areas of the prefrontal cortex (Romanski et al., 1999). A similar segregation may exist in cat auditory cortex. In behavioral experiments, bilateral deactivation of AAF with cryoloops disrupted performance in a temporal pattern discrimination task, but did not affect performance in a sound localization task (Lomber & Malhotra, 2003). Bilateral deactivation of AI disrupted performance both in sound localization and temporal pattern discrimination tasks (Barnes & Lomber,

2003; Malhotra et al., 2004), which suggests that AI is less specialized. By contrast, cooling of the posterior auditory field disrupted performance in a sound localization task but not in a temporal pattern discrimination task (Lomber & Malhotra, 2003). The shorter latencies, shorter receptive field durations (shorter integration time window), and higher repetition following rates observed in cat and mouse AAF (Imaizumi et al., 2003, 2004; Linden et al., 2003; Schreiner & Urbas, 1988) supports the idea that this field may be involved in the processing of temporal structure necessary, for example, in the analysis of vocalizations. The functional differences between AI and the anterior and posterior cortical areas may reflect similar task-related parallel pathways as proposed for the monkey auditory system.

The present results have significance for several issues relating to auditory cortex organization. Thus, while both AI and AAF represent the cochlear sensory epithelium, these maps are not mirror images (Winer, 1992) nor are they equivalent physiologically (Imaizumi et al., 2004). This leads to the question of why there are multiple, non-equivalent basilar membrane maps in auditory cortex. One answer is that AI and AAF are involved in different facets of processing. AI, with its complete and near-linear representation of CF, might then be proposed to have a role analogous to the primary visual cortex (area 17), where the retinotopic map in the cat is complete (Tusa et al., 1978) and proportionately far larger than that of the more than ten other cortical areas recognized as visual (Tusa et al., 1981). Since the AAF map is more complete at the lowest and highest CFs, we propose two possible, more specialized roles for AAF. The first is for temporal coding of cat (or kitten) vocalizations (Brown et al., 1978) based on the robust latency modular organization in the low frequency area (Imaizumi et al., 2004). In contrast, the high-frequency AAF representation might be specialized for processing rodent startle (Kaltwasser, 1991) or isolation (Insel et al., 1989) calls, both of which involve such frequency ranges (Sewell, 1970).

The comparatively low incidence of branched thalamo-cortical, cortico-cortical and commissural connections to AI and AAF suggests that their operations are performed largely in parallel. This differs from the prevailing model of thalamo-cortical visual system organization, where, for example, the bifurcating axons of Y-cells project both to areas 17 and 18 (Humphrey et al., 1985), and it is consistent with different forms of global organization in the auditory and visual forebrain (Linden & Schreiner, 2003). Thus, each lateral geniculate layer represents one eye exclusively (Sur & Sherman, 1982), while the ventral division of the MGB has a complex, interleaved representation of both ears (Middlebrooks & Zook, 1983). The laminar specificity of auditory thalamo-cortical input to AI and AAF (Huang & Winer, 2000) and the rarity of branched axons (Lee et al., 2004) support the notion that they are parallel in a different way than areas 17 and 18, which share extensive and highly branched cortico-cortical projections (Bullier et al., 1984). Insofar as this model of AI and AAF is valid, it could shed light on possible operations of the three other tonotopic regions (the posterior, the ventroposterior, and the ventral auditory fields) in cat auditory cortex. Each field appears to have an incomplete representation of the basilar membrane (Imig et al., 1982). Given the breadth of cortico-cortical connectivity, removal of one primary field may have little effect on the operations of another (Kitzes & Hollrigel, 1996). Because of the apparent rarity of fields with a complete map of the basilar membrane, frequency-specific lesions to such a field would have the most deleterious effect on sound localization (Jenkins & Merzenich, 1984). Finally, lesions to non-tonotopic fields would affect preferentially aspects of auditory performance (e.g., temporal pattern discrimination) other than frequency analysis or sound localization (Colavita et al., 1974). While it is beyond the immediate scope of these comments to suggest that such principles extend universally to neocortical sensory processing, it may not be coincidental that many of these observations apply to the visual and somatic sensory systems (Dykes, 1983; Dykes & Lamour, 1988), suggesting even more global implications.

ACKNOWLEDGMENTS

This work was supported by National Institutes of Health grants R01 DC2260-09 and PO1 NS34835 (C.E.S.) and R01 DC2319-25 (J.A.W.). We thank Andrew Tan, Poppy Crum, and Dr. Bénédicte Philibert for assistance in the physiological recordings and David Larue and Tania Bettis for histological expertise.

REFERENCES

Andersen, R.A., Knight, P.L., & Merzenich, M.M. (1980). The thalamocortical and corticothalamic connections of AI, AII, and the anterior auditory field (AAF) in the cat: Evidence for two largely segregated systems of connections. Journal of Comparative Neurology, 194, 663–701.

Barnes, W.H., & Lomber, S.G. (2003). Cerebral areas mediating pattern discrimination in auditory cortex of the behaving cat. Abstracts - Society for Neuroscience, 182.13.

Benedict, R.H., Shucard, D.W., Santa Maria, M.P., Shucard, J.L., Abara, J.P., Coad, M. L., Wack, D., Sawusch, J., & Lockwood, A. (2002). Covert auditory attention generates activation in the rostral/dorsal anterior cingulate cortex. Journal of Cognitive Neuroscience, 14, 637–645.

Brown, K.A., Buchwald, J.S., Johnson, J.R., & Mikolich, D.J. (1978). Vocalization in the cat and kitten. Developmental Psychobiology, 11, 559–570.

Bullier, J., Kennedy, H., & Salinger, W. (1984). Bifurcation of subcortical afferents to visual areas 17, 18, and 19 in the cat cortex. Journal of Comparative Neurology, 228, 309–328.

Calford, M.B., & Aitkin, L.M. (1983). Ascending projections to the medial geniculate body of the cat: Evidence for multiple, parallel auditory pathways through thalamus. Journal of Neuroscience, 3, 2365–2380.

Colavita, F.B., Szeligo, F.V., & Zimmer, S.D. (1974). Temporal pattern discrimination in cats with insular-temporal lesions. Brain Research, 79, 153–156.

Dykes, R.W. (1983). Parallel processing of somatosensory information: A theory. Brain Research, 286, 47–115.

Dykes, R., & Lamour, Y. (1988). Neurons without demonstrable receptive fields outnumber neurons having receptive fields in samples from the somatosensory cortex of anesthetized or paralyzed cats and rats. Brain Research, 440, 133–143.

Eggermont, J.J. (1998). Representation of spectral and temporal sound features in three cortical fields of the cat. Similarities outweigh differences. Journal of Neurophysiology, 80, 2743–2764.

Eggermont, J.J. (1999). The magnitude and phase of temporal modulation transfer functions in cat auditory cortex. Journal of Neuroscience, 19, 2780–2788.

Harel, N., Mori, N., Sawada, S., Mount, R.J., & Harrison, R.V. (2000). Three distinct auditory areas of cortex (AI, AII, and AAF) defined by optical imaging of intrinsic signals. NeuroImage, 11, 302–312.

He, J., & Hashikawa, T. (1998). Connections of the dorsal zone of the cat auditory cortex. Journal of Comparative Neurology, 400, 334–348.

He, J., Hashikawa, T., Ojima, H., & Kinouchi, Y. (1997). Temporal integration and duration tuning in the dorsal zone of cat auditory cortex. Journal of Neuroscience, 17, 2615–2625.

Huang, C.L., & Winer, J.A. (2000). Auditory thalamocortical projections in the cat: Laminar and areal patterns of input. Journal of Comparative Neurology, 427, 302–331.

Humphrey, A.L., Sur, M., Uhlrich, D.J., & Sherman, S.M. (1985). Termination patterns of individual X- and Y-cell axons in the visual cortex of the cat: Projections to area 18, to the 17/18 border region, and to both areas 17 and 18. Journal of Comparative Neurology, 233, 190–212.

Imaizumi, K., Priebe, N. J., Cheung, S.W., & Schreiner, C.E. (2003). Spatial distribution of temporal information in cat anterior auditory field. In E. Budinger & B. Gaschler-Markefski (Eds.), Proceedings of the international conference on auditory cortex: Towards a synthesis of human and animal research (p. 27). Aachen: Shaker.

Imaizumi, K, Priebe, N.J., Crum, P.A.C., Bedenbaugh, P.H., Cheung, S.W., & Schreiner, C.F. (2004). Modular functional organization in cat anterior auditory field. Journal of Neurophysiology, 92, 444–457.

Imaizumi, K., & Schreiner, C.F. (2004). Non-homogeneous modular organization of cat primary auditory cortex. In P. Santi (Ed.), Abstracts of the 27th Annual Mid-Winter Research Meeting of the Association of Research in Otolaryngology (p. 193).

Imig, T.J., & Adrián, H.O. (1977). Binaural columns in the primary field (AI) of cat auditory cortex. Brain Research, 138, 241–257.

Imig, T.J., & Brugge, J.F. (1978). Sources and terminations of callosal axons related to binaural and frequency maps in primary auditory cortex of the cat. Journal of Comparative Neurology, 182, 637–660.

Imig, T.J., & Morel, A. (1985a). Tonotopic organization in lateral part of posterior group of thalamic nuclei in the cat. Journal of Neurophysiology, 53, 836–851.

Imig, T.J., & Morel, A. (1985b). Tonotopic organization in ventral nucleus of medial geniculate body in the cat. Journal of Neurophysiology, 53, 309–340.

Imig, T.J., Reale, R.A., & Brugge, J.F. (1982). The auditory cortex. Patterns of cortico-cortical projections related to physiological maps in the cat. In C. N. Woolsey (Ed.), Cortical sensory organization, Volume 3, Multiple auditory areas (pp. 1–41). Clifton, NJ: Humana Press.

Insel, T.R., Gelhard, R.E., & Miller, L.P. (1989). Rat pup isolation distress and the brain benzodiazepine receptor. Developmental Psychobiology, 22, 509–525.

Jenkins, W.M., & Merzenich, M.M. (1984). Role of cat primary auditory cortex for sound-localization behavior. Journal of Neurophysiology, 52, 819–847.

Kaltwasser, M.T. (1991). Acoustic startle induced ultrasonic vocalization in the rat: A novel animal model of anxiety? Behavioral Brain Research, 43, 133–137.

Kilgard, M.P., & Merzenich, M.M. (1998). Cortical map reorganization enabled by nucleus basalis activity. Science, 279, 1714–1718.

Kitzes, L.M., & Hollrigel, G.S. (1996). Response properties of units in the posterior auditory field deprived of input from the ipsilateral primary auditory cortex. Hearing Research, 100, 120–130.

Knight, P.L. (1977). Representation of the cochlea within the anterior auditory field (AAF) of the cat. Brain Research, 130, 447–467.

Kowalski, N., Versnel, H., & Shamma, S.A. (1995). Comparison of responses in the anterior and primary auditory fields of the ferret cortex. Journal of Neurophysiology, 73, 1513–1523.

Lee, C.C., Imaizumi, K., Schreiner, C.E., & Winer, J.A. (2004). Concurrent tonotopic processing streams in auditory cortex. Cerebral Cortex, 14, 441–451.

Linden, J.F., Liu, R.C., Sahani, M., Schreiner, C.E., & Merzenich, M. M. (2003). Spectrotemporal structure of receptive fields in areas AI and AAF of mouse auditory cortex. Journal of Neurophysiology, 90, 2660–2675.

Linden, J.F., & Schreiner, C.E. (2003). Columnar transformations in auditory cortex? A comparison to visual and somatosensory cortices. Cerebral Cortex, 13, 83–89.

Lindquist, D.H., Jarrard, L.E., & Brown, T.H. (2004). Perirhinal cortex supports delay fear conditioning to rat ultrasonic social signals. Journal of Neuroscience, 24, 3610–3617.

Liu, W., & Suga, N. (1997). Binaural and commissural organization of the primary auditory cortex of the mustached bat. Journal of Comparative Physiology [A] 181, 599–605.

Lomber, S., & Malhotra, S. (2003). Double dissociation of "what" and "where" processing in auditory cortex. In E. Budinger, & B. Gaschler-Markefski (Eds.), Proceedings of the international conference on auditory cortex: Towards a synthesis of human and animal research (p. 33). Aachen: Shaker.

Malhotra, S., Hall, A.J., & Lomber, S.G. (2004). Cortical control of sound localization in the cat: Unilateral cooling deactivation of 19 cerebral areas. Journal of Neurophysiology, 92, 1625–1643.

Merzenich, M.M., Knight, P.L., & Roth, G.L. (1974). Representation of cochlea within primary auditory cortex in the cat. Journal of Neurophysiology, 38, 231–249.

Middlebrooks, J.C., Dykes, R.W., & Merzenich, M.M. (1980). Binaural response-specific bands in primary auditory cortex (AI) of the cat: Topographical organization orthogonal to isofrequency contours. Brain Research, 181, 31–48.

Middlebrooks, J.C., & Zook, J.M. (1983). Intrinsic organization of the cat's medial geniculate body identified by projections to binaural response-specific bands in the primary auditory cortex. Journal of Neuroscience, 3, 203–224.

Morel, A., & Imig, T.J. (1987). Thalamic projections to fields A, AI, P, and VP in the cat auditory cortex. Journal of Comparative Neurology, 265, 119–144.

Nelken, I. (2002). Feature detection by the auditory cortex. In D. Oertel, R. R. Fay, & A. N. Popper (Eds.), Springer handbook of auditory research. Volume 15, Integrative functions in the mammalian auditory pathway (pp. 358–416). New York: Springer-Verlag.

Phillips, D.P., & Irvine, D.R.F. (1981). Responses of single neurons in physiologically defined primary auditory cortex (AI) of the cat: Frequency tuning and response intensity. Journal of Neurophysiology, 45, 48–58.

Phillips, D.P., & Irvine, D.R.F. (1982). Properties of single neurons in the anterior auditory field (AAF) of cat cerebral cortex. Brain Research, 248, 237–244.

Phillips, D.P., Semple, M.N., Calford, M.B., & Kitzes, L.M. (1994). Level-dependent representation of stimulus frequency in cat primary auditory cortex. Experimental Brain Research, 102, 210–226.

Poremba, A., Malloy, M., Saunders, R.C., Carson, R.E., Herscovitch, P., & Mishkin, M. (2004). Species-specific calls evoke asymmetric activity in the monkey's temporal poles. Nature, 427, 448–451.

Prieto, J.J., Peterson, B.A., & Winer, J.A. (1994). Morphology and spatial distribution of GABAergic neurons in cat primary auditory cortex (AI). Journal of Comparative Neurology, 344, 349–382.

Rauschecker, J.P., & Tian, B. (2000). Mechanisms and streams for processing of "what" and "where" in auditory cortex. Proceedings of the National Academy of Sciences USA, 97, 11800–11806.

Read, H.L., Winer, J.A., & Schreiner, C.E. (2001). Modular organization of intrinsic connections associated with spectral tuning in cat auditory cortex. Proceedings of the National Academy of Sciences USA, 98, 8042–8047.

Read, H.L., Winer, J.A., & Schreiner, C.E. (2002). Functional architecture of auditory cortex. Current Opinion in Neurobiology, 12, 433–440.

Rodrigues-Dagaeff, C., Simm, G., De Ribaupierre, Y., Villa, A., De Ribaupierre, F., & Rouiller, E.M. (1989). Functional organization of the ventral division of the medial geniculate body of the cat: Evidence for a rostro-caudal gradient of response properties and cortical projections. Hearing Research, 39, 103–125.

Romanski, L.M., Tian, B., Fritz, J., Mishkin, M., Goldman-Rakic, P.S., & Rauschecker, J.P. (1999). Dual streams of auditory afferents target multiple domains in the primate prefrontal cortex. Nature Neuroscience, 2, 1131–1136.

Rouiller, E.M., Simm, G.M., Villa, A.E.P., De Ribaupierre, Y., & De Ribaupierre, F. (1991). Auditory corticocortical interconnections in the cat: Evidence for parallel and hierarchical arrangement of the auditory cortical areas. Experimental Brain Research, 86, 483–505.

Rutkowski, R.G., Miasnikov, A.A., & Weinberger, N.M. (2003). Characterisation of multiple physiological fields within the anatomical core of rat auditory cortex. Hearing Research, 181, 116–130.

Schreiner, C.E., & Mendelson, J.R. (1990). Functional topography of cat primary auditory cortex: Distribution of integrated excitation. Journal of Neurophysiology, 64, 1442–1459.

Schreiner, C.E., & Raggio, M.W. (1996). Neuronal responses in cat primary auditory cortex to electrical cochlear stimulation. II. Repetition rate coding. Journal of Neurophysiology, 75, 1283–1300.

Schreiner, C. E., Read, H. L., & Sutter, M. L. (2000). Modular organization of frequency integration in primary auditory cortex. Annual Review of Neuroscience, 23, 501–529.

Schreiner, C.E., & Urbas, J.V. (1986). Representation of amplitude modulation in the auditory cortex of the cat. I. The anterior auditory field (AAF). Hearing Research, 21, 227–241.

Schreiner, C.E., & Urbas, J.V. (1988). Representation of amplitude modulation in the auditory cortex of the cat. II. Comparison between cortical fields. Hearing Research, 32, 49–64.

Sewell, G.D. (1970). Ultrasonic signals from rodents. Ultrasonics, 8, 26–30.

Stecker, G.C., & Middlebrooks, J.C. (2003). Distributed coding of sound locations in the auditory cortex. Biological Cybernetics, 89, 341–349.

Sur, M., & Sherman, S.M. (1982). Retinogeniculate terminations in cats: Morphological differences between X and Y cell axons. Science, 218, 389–391.

Sutter, M.L., & Schreiner, C.E. (1991). Physiology and topography of neurons with multipeaked tuning curves in cat primary auditory cortex. Journal of Neurophysiology, 65, 1207–1226.

Sutter, M.L., Schreiner, C.E., McLean, M., O'Connor, K.N., & Loftus, W.C. (1999). Organization of inhibitory frequency receptive fields in cat primary auditory cortex. Journal of Neurophysiology, 82, 2358–2371.

Tian, B., & Rauschecker, J.P. (1994). Processing of frequency-modulated sounds in the cat's anterior auditory field. Journal of Neurophysiology, 71, 1959–1975.

Tian, B., Reser, D., Durham, A., Kustov, A., & Rauschecker, J.P. (2001). Functional specialization in rhesus monkey auditory cortex. Science, 292, 290–293.

Tusa, R.J., Palmer, L.A., & Rosenquist, A.C. (1978). The retinotopic organization of area 17 (striate cortex) in the cat. Journal of Comparative Neurology, 177, 213–235.

Tusa, R.J., Palmer, L.A., & Rosenquist, A.C. (1981). Multiple cortical visual areas: Visual field topography in the cat. In C.N. Woolsey (Ed.), Cortical sensory organization, Volume 2, multiple visual areas (pp. 1–31). Clifton, NJ: Humana Press.

Velenovsky, D.S., Cetas, J.S., Price, R.O., Sinex, D.G., & McMullen, N.T. (2003). Functional subregions in primary auditory cortex defined by thalamocortical terminal arbors: An electrophysiological and anterograde labeling study. Journal of Neuroscience, 23, 308–316.

Winer, J.A. (1992). The functional architecture of the medial geniculate body and the primary auditory cortex. In D.B. Webster, A.N. Popper, & R.R. Fay (Eds.), Springer handbook of auditory research. Volume 1. The mammalian auditory pathways: Neuroanatomy (pp. 222–409). New York: Springer-Verlag.

7. THE NEUROBEHAVIORAL STUDY OF AUDITORY CORTEX

Henry E. Heffner

INTRODUCTION

The use of ablation-behavior experimentation to study auditory cortex began during the second half of the 19th century when it was discovered that sensory and motor functions could be localized to different parts of neocortex. Since that time, our views on the role of auditory cortex have gradually evolved as the results of new studies have added to, or revised, previous findings. Sometimes new findings have met with general acceptance; at other times, they have been accompanied by controversy, and the view that prevailed at the time has not always been the correct one. The purpose of this chapter is not only to present our views of the function of auditory cortex, but to describe how we arrived at them.

HISTORY

19th Century

During the first half of the 19th century, it was generally believed that the cerebral hemispheres were the seat of consciousness, although, contrary to the claims of the phrenologists, the various functions were not localized to specific areas (e.g., James, 1890). This view was based primarily on the ablation studies of Pierre Flourens, who claimed that the cerebral lobes were "... the seat of sensations, perception and volition", and that the degree to which these functions were affected depended on the size of the lesion, with total removal of the lobes resulting in a total deficit (Flourens, 1824). However, Flourens' work was conducted primarily on birds and the cerebral lobes of birds are not homologous to the neocortex of mammals. Thus, Flourens' generalization of his results from birds to mammals is an early example of the pitfalls encountered in generalizing results obtained on one species to others.

The strong anti-localization views held by early researchers was a reaction to the localizationist claims of the phrenologists. Indeed, phrenology played such a prominent role in the early study of cerebral cortex that well into the 20th century, Charles Sherrington was still giving a relatively detailed discussion of the theories of Franz Gall (Sherrington, 1926). As a result, 19th century researchers were cautious about making claims regarding the localization of function in the cortex. The first serious inkling that functions were localized in the cortex came from the work of Paul Broca, who described a patient with a frontal lobe lesion that all but abolished the ability to speak – interestingly, Broca noted in his paper that his placement of the "seat of the faculty of language" differed from that of the phrenologists, which he likely did as a way of distancing himself from them (Broca, 1861). However, it was the publication by Fritsch and Hitzig (1870) of their results of electrically stimulating cortex in the dog that finally convinced researchers that different functions could be localized in the cortex. (It may be noted that Fritsch and Hitzig were not the first to electrically stimulate cortex, and much of their paper is devoted to attempting to explain the negative results of others, as well as the ablation results of Flourens.)

Following on the work of Fritsch and Hitzig, a number of researchers began to search for the various functional areas they expected to find in the cortex, including an auditory area. One of the leading localizationists in this search was a British physician, David Ferrier, who conducted a series of experiments to find auditory cortex in monkeys (for references, see Heffner, 1987; James, 1890). The standard procedure at that time was to initially identify a functional area by electrical stimulation. Once an area had been delineated, it was then removed surgically to see if that particular function was abolished. Thus, Ferrier began by electrically stimulating cortex and looking for an auditory startle response, which he found when he stimulated the posterior two thirds of the superior temporal gyrus (Fig. 7.1; Ferrier, 1875). The next step was to surgically remove that area and, based on Flourens' view that the cerebral lobes were the seat of consciousness, it was expected that such lesions would completely abolish hearing (e.g., James, 1890). Ferrier found that bilateral ablations that included the superior temporal gyrus did indeed render monkeys unresponsive to sound. In addition, unilateral lesions resulted in a lack of response to sounds presented to the ear contralateral to the lesion, a phenomenon Ferrier demonstrated by plugging the ipsilateral ear.

Although Ferrier's findings met with initial acceptance, this soon changed. One source of doubt was the finding by Luciani that temporal lobe lesions did not produce permanent absolute deafness in dogs – Ferrier's response to this was that there were species differences and dogs would not show the same

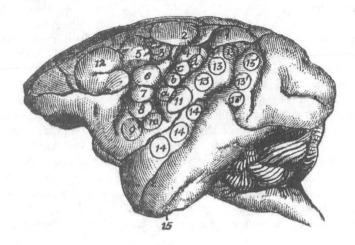

Fig. 7.1. Auditory cortex in the macaque brain (14) as defined by David Ferrier (1875).

degree of impairment as monkeys and humans (see Heffner, 1987). However, a more serious problem was the failure of Edward Schäfer and his colleagues in 1889 to replicate Ferrier's results in monkeys. Although Schäfer's initial results appeared to support Ferrier's, a later series of cases failed to show deafness following bilateral lesions of the superior temporal gyrus. Ferrier's response was that Schäfer's lesions were incomplete, though he eventually was willing to concede that cortical lesions might not cause total deafness. However, in the opinion of William James, it was Schäfer's failure to find total deafness in monkeys that was the more important of the two results, by which James implied that auditory cortex was probably not located in the superior temporal gyrus of monkeys. [In contrast, James felt that the work on sensory aphasia definitely indicated that auditory cortex in man was located in the temporal lobe, particularly the posterior two thirds of the superior temporal gyrus, which he labeled as "Wernicke's Area" (James, 1890, p. 39, Fig. 11).]

The reason for William James favoring Schäfer's negative results lay in the view that "... the *loss* of [a] function does not necessarily show that it *is* dependent on the part cut out; but its *preservation* does show that it is *not* dependent: and this is true though the loss should be observed ninety-nine times and the preservation only once in a hundred similar excisions." (James, 1890; p. 43; emphasis in the original). Indeed, this rule still applies today, assuming, of course, that the difference in results is not due to differences in the lesions. Thus, a hundred years elapsed before it was discovered that Ferrier was correct: ablation of auditory cortex in primates *does* result in a hearing loss, the failure of Schäfer to find such a deficit was probably because his lesions were incomplete, and not all species show a cortical hearing loss (H.E. Heffner & R.S. Heffner, 1990a).

Middle 20th Century

It has been noted that the modern era of auditory neurobehavioral studies dates
to the late 1940s, when Dewey Neff and others returned from the armed forces
to set up experimental laboratories (Masterton, 1997). Together with their
students, they began to use the ablation-behavior method to study the auditory
system. A major advance in their work was that, where previous studies had
looked at an animal's *un*conditioned response to sound, animals were now
trained to detect and discriminate sounds using conditioning procedures. Thus,
after pre-training and testing of auditory discriminations, using carefully
controlled auditory stimuli, circumscribed lesions were made and postoperative
testing of the same discriminations was conducted. Another advance was the
careful histological verification of the lesions along with a description of the
resulting thalamic retrograde degeneration added by Irving Diamond, a
substantial improvement over the gross verification of lesions conducted during
the 19th century.

   Frequency discrimination. The 1940s witnessed advances in the
electrophysiological study of the brain and it was soon discovered that auditory
cortex could be divided into different areas, many of which were tonotopically
organized (for a well-known summary, see Woolsey, 1960). To many
researchers, the tonotopic arrangement suggested that auditory cortex was
necessary for the discrimination of frequency and ablation studies were soon
performed to test that hypothesis (e.g., Butler & Neff, 1950; Evarts, 1952).
Although most studies found that cortical lesions did not abolish frequency
discrimination, Meyer and Woolsey (1952) reported that cats with large auditory
cortex lesions were no longer able to discriminate frequency. This finding
resulted in some controversy and the search for an explanation of the
discrepancy focused on differences in the behavioral and stimulus presentation
procedures (Neff et al., 1975).
   That procedural differences accounted for the different results was suggested
by R.F. Thompson in Woolsey's laboratory (Thompson, 1960). The main
difference between the two procedures was that Neff's group required animals
to respond to a change in the frequency of an ongoing train of tone pulses;
Meyer and Woolsey, on the other hand, required animals to discriminate a train
of tone pulses in which the last pulse differed in frequency from the preceding
pulses from another train in which all the tone pulses were the same frequency.
Thompson found that although operated animals could detect a change in
frequency when tested with Neff's procedure, they failed to respond
differentially to the two tone trains in Meyer and Woolsey's procedure. Because
the animals responded equally to both pulse trains (i.e., their false positive rate
increased), he concluded that removal of auditory cortex interfered with their
ability to inhibit a response to the non-target or neutral stimulus.
   Neff and his colleagues, however, had a different interpretation (e.g., Neff et
al., 1975). They focused on whether the sounds to be discriminated were

presented against a background of silence (Meyer and Woolsey's task) or whether there was an on-going signal with the animal simply required to detect a change in the signal (Neff's task). Specifically, they proposed that neural habituation takes place when a neutral stimulus is presented for some time and that changing to a new frequency then elicits a larger neural response to which an animal with an auditory cortex lesion is able to respond (Neff, 1960; Neff et al., 1975). This formulation, which came to be known as the "Neff Neural Model," was more a description of what the auditory system did in the absence of auditory cortex, than a theory of what auditory cortex did.

Our current views differ from both previous ones. With the development of advanced behavioral techniques, we now know that although cortical lesions result in increased frequency discrimination thresholds, they do not abolish the ability of an animal to respond to tone trains that differ in frequency (Harrington et al., 2001). The fact that both Meyer and Woolsey (1952) and Thompson (1960) were unable to get their animals to perform was because a Go/NoGo procedure gives little control over an animal's false positive rate with the result that an animal may adopt the strategy of responding to both the target signal and the neutral signal when a task becomes difficult (H.E. Heffner & R.S. Heffner, 1995). Thus, auditory cortex lesions do not abolish simple frequency discrimination regardless of whether the animals are trained to detect a change in frequency or to discriminate between two different frequencies (Cranford, 1979).

Tone patterns. A second line of inquiry concerned the role of auditory cortex in discriminating tone patterns, an investigation that was prompted by the discovery that visual cortex played a role in the discrimination of visual patterns (Neff, et al., 1975). For example, cats were tested before and after auditory cortex ablation for their ability to discriminate a "low-high-low" set of tones from a "high-low-high" set (where low might be 800 Hz and high 1000 Hz). A number of studies were conducted using a variety of tone patterns, each with a well-defined rationale (for a review, see Elliott & Trahiotis, 1972). However, this line of research did not yield any new insights into the function of auditory cortex. Part of the problem was that normal animals sometimes had difficulty discriminating the tone patterns, making the inability of an animal to discriminate them after cortical ablation difficult to interpret; that is, did the cortical ablation abolish the ability to discriminate a particular pattern or did the general effects of the lesion just make the task a little more difficult. Thus, although one can make a compelling rationale that analogous anatomical structures, such as auditory and visual cortex, might have analogous functions, this line of reasoning did not meet with success in this case.

Sound localization. One line of research that did lead to an important finding was the study of the role of auditory cortex in sound localization. Specifically, Neff and his colleagues demonstrated that cats with bilateral auditory cortex lesions were unable to walk to the source of a brief sound, that is, one too brief to be scanned or tracked (Neff et al., 1956). They considered this to be a perceptual deficit, i.e., a loss of auditory space, as opposed to a sensory deficit, such as an increase in sound localization thresholds, an interpretation that has been borne out by subsequent research.

In a later study, Masterton and Diamond (1964) investigated the effect of bilateral auditory cortex lesions in cats on the discrimination of binaural clicks. Although their results are sometimes *mis*interpreted as indicating that the lesions abolished an animal's ability to discriminate binaural clicks, what they showed is that, unlike normal animals, the operated animals did not generalize from a single click to the left or right ear to binaural clicks in which the left or right ear received the leading sound. In other words the animals had a perceptual deficit in which they no longer equated binaural clicks (which differed in their time of arrival at the two ears) with single clicks. The perceptual nature of the cortical sound-localization deficit has also been supported by additional studies that have demonstrated that although carnivores and primates with bilateral cortical lesions retain some ability to discriminate left sounds from right sounds, they no longer associate the sounds with locations in space (Heffner, 1978; H.E. Heffner & R.S. Heffner, 1990b).

Latter Part of the 20th Century

Beginning in the mid 1960s, R.B. Masterton made several methodological and theoretical contributions to the study of auditory cortex. One was to improve on the regimen of behavioral methods used to assess the effects of lesions. Although postoperative testing would begin with a repetition of the preoperative tests, it now included further intensive and extensive testing to circumscribe any deficit that might be present, or to illustrate the absence of ancillary deficits over a wide variety of discriminations (Masterton, 1997).

Testing methods. Detailed testing of animals with cortical lesions was facilitated by the use of advanced testing procedures. The method of "conditioned suppression" was borrowed from the behavioral psychologists (Estes & Skinner, 1941), by way of James C. Smith of Florida State University, and adapted for auditory testing (H.E. Heffner & R.S. Heffner, 1995). This method simply requires an animal to drink from a water spout and break contact with the spout whenever it hears a particular sound (or a different sound). Not only does it fix an animal's head within the sound field, but it requires little cognitive ability on the part of the animal, making it well-suited for testing brain-damaged and other difficult-to-test animals.

Another important factor was the automation of testing procedures, which both removed the experimenter from direct contact with the animal, a potential distraction to the animal, and dramatically increased the number of trials that could be obtained. For example, the original sound-localization procedure used by Neff involved placing an animal in a start box, presenting a sound from behind the correct goal box, releasing the animal, and then physically returning the animal to the start box after it had made its response (Neff et al., 1975). Automating this procedure by having the animal begin a trial by placing its mouth on a "start" water spout and then contacting a "goal" spout to indicate its response not only fixed the animal's head in the sound field at the beginning of each trial, but increased the number of trials that could be obtained in a session from 20 to over 200 (Thompson et al., 1974).

The delineation of a deficit involves multiple and detailed tests. Although postoperative testing always begins with a repetition of the preoperative test, it is necessary to include additional tests to determine the nature of a deficit or to rule out the possibility that an animal is using alternative strategies to solve a task. In addition, ablation/behavior studies typically include control tests to demonstrate that an observed deficit is not due to any attention, motivation, cognitive, or motor disorder. Thus, for example, such control tests have established that the cortical deficits observed using the conditioned suppression procedure are not the result of any reduction in fear conditioning (H.E. Heffner & R.S. Heffner, 2003). [On the other hand, the possibility that the reduced fear response observed following lesions of the amygdala (and other sites) may be due to a hearing loss has never been ruled out. Not only does the possibility exist that such lesions themselves may cause a hearing loss, but the lesions are made stereotaxically and the earbars used to position an animal's head in a stereotaxic device are known to rupture the eardrums.]

Evolutionary approach. Influenced by Irving Diamond at Duke University, Masterton brought an evolutionary approach to the study of auditory cortex. Arguing that the functions of auditory cortex might differ between animals at different levels of a phyletic scale, he proposed to determine the evolution of auditory cortex in man's lineage. This would be done by determining the effects of cortical ablation in animals selected for their neurological similarity to various ancestors of man. The animals he chose were the Virginia opossum (marsupial), the hedgehog (insectivore), the Malaysian tree shrew (believed at the time to be a primitive primate), the bushbaby (a prosimian), and macaques (monkey) (see Fig. 1 of Masterton et al., 1969).

An unstated assumption underlying this approach was that if auditory cortex was not necessary for a basic sensory function in animals lower on the phylogenetic scale, then it would not be necessary for animals that were higher on the scale. This assumption, however, resulted in an error. Because auditory cortex lesions have little or no effect on absolute thresholds in such animals as opossums, rats, and cats, it was firmly believed that the cortex played no role in the detection of sound in any species (e.g., Neff et al., 1975). As a result, reports of "cortical deafness" in humans following bilateral stokes were brushed off as the result of damage to non-auditory areas of cortex, that is, cognitive deficits. This changed when it was discovered that bilateral auditory cortex ablation resulted in a hearing loss that could not be ignored (H.E. Heffner & R.S. Heffner, 1986a). Thus, auditory cortex in primates has extended its influence to include so basic a function as the detection of sound, which, because one sees substantial recovery of hearing over time, is probably due to the sudden removal of descending cortical input to lower auditory centers.

Sounds vs. sound sources. The observation that in cats, at least, auditory cortex ablation seems to have little effect on the sensory aspects of hearing (e.g., sound detection, frequency and intensity discrimination), while it has a profound effect on the ability of an animal to locate the source of a sound, led to a distinction between the discrimination of sounds and the discrimination of sound sources (Masterton, 1992, 1993, 1997; Masterton & Diamond, 1973). A broader way of expressing this distinction is "sensation vs. perception" with auditory cortex having a perceptual role. One opportunity to test this hypothesis arose when Bill Stebbins' group at the University of Michigan demonstrated a right-ear advantage in Japanese macaques for the discrimination of two forms of their coo calls (e.g., Peterson et al., 1978). Drawing an analogy between monkey vocalizations and human speech, their finding suggested that the left cortical hemisphere of these monkeys was responsible for the perception of vocal communications.

The demonstration that bilateral ablation of auditory cortex in Japanese macaques permanently abolished their ability to discriminate the coo calls, with left (but not right) unilateral lesions resulting in a small, transient deficit demonstrated that, indeed, cortex was involved in this ability (H.E. Heffner & R.S. Heffner, 1986b). At this point, however, the deficit could be explained as either a perceptual or a sensory deficit. It would be a perceptual deficit if the animals were unable to discriminate the biological meaning of the coos. However, because the two classes of coos are physically different, one rising, the other falling in frequency, there was always the possibility that the deficit was sensory in that the animals were unable to physically distinguish between the two types of coos. We now know that this deficit is sensory in nature, that bilateral auditory cortex ablation renders macaques being unable to determine if a sound is changing in frequency (Harrington et al., 2001). Thus, although we are reluctant to abandon the idea that auditory cortex is responsible for the perception of sound, this particular result is a sensory deficit.

EFFECTS OF AUDITORY CORTEX ABLATION

The following is a brief summary of the main effects of auditory cortex lesions on hearing. The citations are not exhaustive and additional studies can be found by consulting those referenced here. A comprehensive review of the pre-1975 studies can be found in the chapter by Neff et al. (1975).

Absolute sensitivity

In macaque monkeys, unilateral ablation of auditory cortex (the posterior two thirds of the superior temporal gyrus; Fig. 7.2) results in a definite, and often

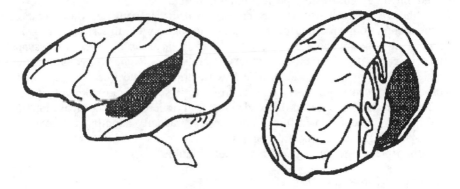

Fig. 7.2. Typical lesion of auditory cortex in the Japanese macaque (blackened area), encompassing the posterior two-thirds (or more) of the superior temporal gyrus.

severe, hearing loss in the ear contralateral to the lesion (H.E. Heffner & R.S. Heffner, 1989). The initial hearing loss is followed by rapid, but incomplete recovery during the first month after surgery. A small hearing loss can still be seen 4 months later, although it is necessary to compare pre- and post-operative thresholds to conclusively demonstrate that a hearing loss exists. A unilateral cortical hearing loss undoubtedly occurs in humans, however, the rapid recovery of sensitivity and the lack of premorbid audiograms for such patients has prevented it from being conclusively demonstrated.

The hearing loss that results in macaque following bilateral ablation of auditory cortex is much more severe than the combination of two unilateral hearing losses (H.E. Heffner & R.S. Heffner, 1986a, 1989, 1990a). Indeed, an animal may initially be totally unresponsive to sound, especially if auditory cortex in both hemispheres is ablated at the same time. The animals show substantial recovery during the first 1–2 months after surgery, at which time the hearing loss becomes moderate. Although little recovery is seen during the next year or so, recent work indicates that thresholds do continue to improve with additional recovery observed 3–5 years later (Harrington, 1999, 2002). Control tests have indicated that the threshold shift cannot easily be accounted for by non-sensory factors such as attention or vigilance (H.E. Heffner & R.S. Heffner, 1990a). Cortical hearing loss following bilateral auditory cortex damage is well established in humans (e.g., Jerger et al., 1969; for a review, see H.E. Heffner & R.S. Heffner, 1986a).

A significant cortical hearing loss has only been demonstrated in humans and macaques; no cortical hearing loss has been noted in opossums or rats and only small hearing losses have been noted in cats, dogs, and ferrets (R.S. Heffner & H.E. Heffner, 1984; H.E. Heffner & R.S. Heffner, 1986a; Kavanagh & Kelly, 1986; Ravizza & Masterton, 1972). So far, the survey of different species is too small to reach any conclusions as to which animals might show cortical deafness, although the undoubtedly simplistic hypothesis that it will be found only in gyrencephalic species comes to mind.

Although the recovery of hearing seen in primates could be due to other cortical areas compensating for the loss of auditory cortex, this seems unlikely to us. Not only are there relatively few cortical neurons outside of classical auditory cortex that respond to auditory stimuli (e.g., Romanski & Goldman-Rakic, 2002), but for them to assume new functions would likely disrupt their ability to perform their normal ones. Instead, it seems more likely that the cortical hearing loss is due to the sudden removal of descending cortical input to lower auditory centers with the lower centers gradually adapting to the loss. Thus, one might expect neural responses in the lower auditory centers to be initially depressed following auditory cortex ablation.

Intensity discrimination

Auditory cortex lesions do not abolish the ability of carnivores or primates to discriminate intensity (Neff et al., 1975). However, recent research suggests that there may be some effect of cortical lesions on intensity discrimination thresholds in primates, depending on the direction of the intensity change (Harrington, 2002). Specifically, bilateral ablation results in, at most, a slight rise in thresholds for detecting an *increase* in intensity, whereas thresholds for detecting a *decrease* in intensity are noticeably raised. Higher than normal thresholds for an intensity decrement can also be observed in unilateral cases for sounds presented to the ear opposite the lesion. The observation that auditory cortex lesions result in raised thresholds for detecting a decrease, but not an increase, in threshold brings to mind the Neff Neural model, which, as previously discussed, states that animals without auditory cortex can detect an increase in neural activity.

Frequency discrimination

Auditory cortex ablation results in increased frequency discrimination thresholds in some species. The work of Massopust and his colleagues demonstrated reliable increases in discrimination thresholds in monkeys following cortical lesions (e.g., Massopust et al., 1970), a result that has been supported by subsequent research (Harrington et al., 2001; H. Heffner & Masterton, 1978). Cats also appear to have increased thresholds following cortical lesions (Cranford, 1979). On the other hand, cortical ablation does not appear to have any effect on frequency discrimination in rats (Kelly, unpublished doctoral dissertation). It has been demonstrated that chemical inactivation of auditory cortex by the application of muscimol temporarily causes rats to fail to respond on a frequency discrimination task (Talwar et al., 2001); however, no control tests were conducted so it is not known if the results are due to an auditory, attentional, cognitive, or motor deficit (H.E. Heffner & R.S. Heffner, 2003).

In what may be a related phenomenon, Whitfield (1980) found that auditory cortex lesions abolished the ability of cats to perceive the pitch of complex tones, a pitch referred to as the "missing fundamental." However, of the 13 animals in the study, only 2 were able to learn the discrimination preoperatively. As a result, it is possible that the effect was due to the cortical lesions increasing the difficulty of an already difficult task. However, the question of whether auditory cortex is necessary for the perception of the missing fundamental is important and it would be worth replicating this study with advanced behavioral procedures.

Frequency change

In monkeys, auditory cortex ablation abolishes the ability to determine if a sound is changing in frequency. Specifically, the animals can no longer discriminate a steady tone from one that is rising or falling in frequency (Harrington, 2002; Harrington et al., 2001). Because the animals can still discriminate frequency, it is necessary to test them in a way that prevents them from solving the task on the basis of absolute frequency. This is done by requiring the animals to discriminate swept tones from steady tones with the frequency of the steady tone varied from trial to trial. In addition, the range of frequencies of the steady tones must span the frequency range of the swept tones. It should be noted that normal monkeys easily learn this discrimination when tested with the method of conditioned suppression; on the other hand, an attempt to test this discrimination using a Go/NoGo procedure failed because the procedure lacked sufficient control over the animals' false positive rates (May et al., 1988).

The inability to determine if a sound is changing in frequency is a profound deficit that would be expected to render an individual unable to make much sense of the auditory world. This deficit may also occur in cats as cortical lesions are known to impair the ability to discriminate a rising from a falling swept tone; that the discrimination was not abolished may be due to the fact that an animal tested on rising versus falling tones may resort to using absolute frequency as a cue by attending just to the beginning or ending portion of the signal (Kelly & Whitfield, 1971). Whether a deficit may be found in rodents is not known; a study of the effect of cortical lesions on the discrimination of frequency sweeps by gerbils presented only group data with relatively large variance so it is not known if the deficit occurred in all of the animals (Ohl et al., 1999).

Sound localization

Unilateral lesions of auditory cortex result in a complete inability to discriminate the locus of a sound in the hemifield opposite the lesions, an effect that has been demonstrated in both macaques and squirrel monkeys (Heffner, 1997; H.E. Heffner, & R.S. Heffner, 2003; Thompson & Cortez, 1983). Some residual ability to localize sound in the contralesional hemifield remains for sound sources within about 15E of midline. Bilateral ablation appears to be the sum of two unilateral lesions. Although an animal can distinguish left sounds from right sounds, it shows no awareness of the location of the sound source (H.E. Heffner & R.S. Heffner, 1990b).

Among the other species that have been tested, ferrets, cats, and dogs appear to have the same cortical sound localization deficit as monkeys (Heffner, 1978; H.E. Heffner & R.S. Heffner, 1990b; Kavanagh & Kelly, 1987; Neff et al., 1975). On the other hand, cortical lesions do not appear to affect the ability of laboratory rats or wild wood rats to localize sound. The studies of opossums, hedgehogs, and bushbabies with cortical lesions were not sufficiently detailed to determine whether the animals were localizing sound sources as opposed to just discriminating left and right sounds (H.E. Heffner & R.S. Heffner, 1990b).

Some effects of partial lesions of auditory cortex

In macaques, it has been suggested on the basis of electrophysiological evidence that the identification of complex sounds is processed in the rostral portion of auditory cortex and that the localization of sounds in space is processed in the caudal portion (e.g., Rauschecker & Tian, 2000). To test this hypothesis, three Japanese macaques with complete auditory cortex lesions in one hemisphere received lesions in the other hemisphere that were restricted either to the rostral, core, or caudal areas of auditory cortex (Harrington, 2002). The animals were then tested on both their ability to determine if a sound was changing in frequency and to localize sound in the left and right hemifields. It was found that lesions of either the rostral or core portions of auditory cortex result in an inability to determine if a sound is changing in frequency whereas a lesion of the caudal portion had no effect. On the other hand, the rostral lesion appeared to have no effect on sound localization in the contralesional hemifield whereas the other two lesions resulted in threshold shifts, with the caudal lesion resulting in the largest shift (unlike complete unilateral lesions, none of the restricted lesions completely abolished sound localization in the contralesional hemifield). Thus, there appears to be some support for the idea that different portions of auditory cortex have different functions and further investigation on additional animals appears warranted.

In cats, the significance of the tonotopic arrangement of auditory cortex for sound localization has been investigated by compromising the blood supply to restricted frequency bands in primary auditory cortex (Jenkins & Merzenich, 1984). The results indicate that such lesions impair the ability of an animal to localize pure tones that fall within an affected frequency band in the hemifield contralateral to the lesion. This is an important finding, one that deserves to be replicated. Among the questions that remain to be answered are whether the results apply only to the very short duration (40 ms) pure tones used in the study or whether the same deficit would be found with longer duration tones and with narrow-band noise.

CONCLUDING COMMENTS

Given the present state of our knowledge, there are a number of directions for further research. One would be to explore species differences in the function of auditory cortex. As has been noted, the results of auditory cortex lesions can range from little or no effect, as in the rat, to the dramatic effects found in macaques. Not only would a knowledge of species differences shed light on the evolution of auditory cortex, but it would help avoid the problems that can arise with attempts to combine the results from one species with those of another, a procedure that can result in an "auditory chimera" (H.E. Heffner & R.S. Heffner, 2003). A second line would be to determine the effect of ablating areas outside of classical auditory cortex where some neurons are known to respond to auditory stimuli, such as the prefrontal cortex of primates (e.g., Romanski & Goldman-Rakic, 2002). We expect that such lesions would have subtle effects and, as previously noted, we are doubtful that those areas would be able to compensate for the loss of auditory cortex.

A third line of research, one that will certainly give interesting results, is the use of chemicals or cooling to reversibly inactivate auditory cortex (e.g., Lomber, 1999; Talwar et al., 2001). One of the main advantages of this technique is the ability to determine the effect of different lesions in the same animal, and to repeat the lesions, thus reducing the effects of individual differences between animals due to motivation, skill-level, and other non-auditory factors. Another advantage is that it is possible to observe the immediate effects of a lesion before any compensation has occurred. For example, partial ablation lesions of an auditory area that impair an ability, but do not abolish it, may be due to compensation by the remaining cortical tissue. With ablation lesions, it is generally necessary to wait several days for the animal to recover from the effects of the surgery, especially the damage to muscle tissue overlying the skull, the after-effects of the anesthesia, and swelling of the brain, although in some cases it is possible to test an animal 24 hrs after surgery. The use of reversible lesions will also involve the use of intensive and extensive testing with control tests designed to rule out alternative explanations. Every advance in our views came about through investigations involving multiple experiments; although an individual experiment may provide new information, it must be replicated and tested in different ways to insure that it is correctly interpreted. And should the results of reversible lesions differ from those of ablation studies, it will be necessary to make a direct comparison between the two types of lesions under the same experimental conditions.

REFERENCES

Broca, P. (1861). Remarks on the seat of the faculty of articulate language, followed by an observation of aphemia (Remarques sur le siége de la facultè du langage articulé; suivies d'une observation d'aphemie; Bulletin de la société anatomique de Paris, 36th year 2ème série, tomé 6, 330–357). Trans. by G. von Bonin (1960), in Some Papers on The Cerebral Cortex (pp. 49–72). Springfield, IL: Charles C. Thomas.

Butler R.A., & Neff, W.D. (1950). Role of the auditory cortex in the discrimination of changes in frequency. American Psychologist, 5, 474.

Cranford, J.L. (1979). Detection versus discrimination of brief tones by cats with auditory cortex lesions. Journal of the Acoustical Society of America, 65, 1573–1575.

Elliott, D.N., & Trahiotis, C. (1972). Cortical lesions and auditory discrimination. Psychological Bulletin, 77, 198–222.

Estes, W.K., & Skinner, B.F. (1941). Some quantitative properties of anxiety. Journal of Experimental Psychology, 29, 390–400.

Evarts, E.V. (1952). Effect of auditory cortex ablation on frequency discrimination in monkey. Journal of Neurophysiology, 15, 443–448.

Ferrier, D. (1875). Experiments on the brain of monkeys. – No. I. Proceedings of the Royal Society of London, Series B, 23, 409–432.

Flourens, P. (1824). Investigations of the properties and the functions of the various parts which compose the cerebral mass (Recherches Expérimentales sur les Propiétiés et les Fonctions du Système Nerveux dans les Animaux Vertébrés) (Paris, Chez Chevot, 1824, pp. 85–122). Trans. by G. von Bonin (1960), in Some Papers on The Cerebral Cortex (pp. 3–21). Springfield, IL: Charles C. Thomas.

Fritsch, G., & Hitzig, E. (1870). Über die elektrische Erregbarkeit des Grosshirns. Archives für Anatomie Physiologie und Wissenshaftlicke Medicin, 37, 300–332. Trans. by G. von Bonin (1960), in Some Papers on The Cerebral Cortex (pp. 73–96). Springfield, IL: Charles C. Thomas.

Harrington, I.A. (1999). Can sensory deficits explain the aphasia-like behavioral of Japanese macaques (Macaca fuscata)? Unpublished Masters Thesis, University of Toledo.

Harrington, I.A. (2002). Effect of auditory cortex lesions on discriminations of frequency change, amplitude change and sound location by Japanese macaques (Macaca fuscata). Unpublished Doctoral Dissertation, University of Toledo.

Harrington, I.A., Heffner, R.S., & Heffner, H.E. (2001). An investigation of sensory deficits underlying the aphasia-like behavior of macaques with auditory cortex lesions. Neuroreports, 12, 1217–1221.

Heffner, H. (1978). Effect of auditory cortex ablation on localization and discrimination of brief sounds. Journal of Neurophysiology, 41, 963–976.

Heffner, H.E. (1987). Ferrier and the study of auditory cortex. Archives of Neurology, 44, 218–221.

Heffner, H.E. (1997). The role of macaque auditory cortex in sound localization. Acta Oto-Laryngologica Supplement, 532, 22–27.

Heffner, H.E., & Heffner, R.S. (1986a). Hearing loss in Japanese macaques following bilateral auditory cortex lesions. Journal of Neurophysiology, 55, 256–271.

Heffner, H.E., & Heffner, R.S. (1986b). Effect of unilateral and bilateral auditory cortex lesions on the discrimination of vocalizations by Japanese macaques. Journal of Neurophysiology, 56, 683–701.

Heffner, H.E., & Heffner, R.S. (1989). Unilateral auditory cortex ablation in macaques results in a contralateral hearing loss. Journal of Neurophysiology, 62, 789–801.

Heffner, H.E., & Heffner, R.S. (1990a). Effect of bilateral auditory cortex lesions on absolute thresholds in Japanese macaques. Journal of Neurophysiology, 64, 191–205.

Heffner, H.E., & Heffner, R.S. (1990b). Effect of bilateral auditory cortex lesions on sound localization in Japanese macaques. Journal of Neurophysiology, 64, 915–931.

Heffner, H.E., & Heffner, R.S. (1995). Conditioned avoidance. In G.M. Klump, R.J. Dooling, R.R. Fay, & W.C. Stebbins (Eds.), Methods in Comparative Psychoacoustics (pp. 73–87). Basel: Birkhäuser.

Heffner, H.E., & Heffner, R.S. (2003). Audition. In S.F. Davis (Ed.), Handbook of Research Methods in Experimental Psychology (pp. 413–440). Malden, MA: Blackwell.

Heffner, R.S., & Heffner, H.E. (1984). Hearing loss in dogs after lesions of the brachium of the inferior colliculus and medial geniculate. The Journal of Comparative Neurology, 230, 207–217.

Heffner, H., & Masterton, B. (1978). Contribution of auditory cortex to hearing in the monkey *(Macaca mulatta)*. In D.J. Chivers & J. Herbert (Eds.), Recent advances in primatology – Vol. I, Behaviour (pp. 735–754). New York: Academic Press.

James, W. (1890). The principles of psychology. New York: Henry Holt.

Jenkins, W.M., & Merzenich, M.M. (1984). Role of cat primary auditory cortex for sound-localization behavior. Journal of Neurophysiology, 52, 819–847.

Jerger, J., Weikers, N.J., Sharbrough, F.W. III, & Jerger, S. (1969). Bilateral lesions of the temporal lobe: A case study. Acta Otol-Laryngologica Supplement, 258, 1–51.

Kavanagh, G.L., & Kelly, J.B. (1986). Midline and lateral field sound localization in the albino rat *(Rattus norvegicus)*. Behavioral Neuroscience, 100, 200–205.

Kavanagh, G.L., & Kelly, J.B. (1987). Contributions of auditory cortex to sound localization by the ferret *(Mustela putorius)*. Journal of Neurophysiology, 57, 1746–1766.

Kelly, J.B. (1970). The effects of lateral lemniscal and neocortical lesions on auditory absolute thresholds and frequency difference thresholds of the rat. Unpublished Doctoral Dissertation, Vanderbilt University.

Kelly, J.B., & Whitfield, I.C. (1971). Effects of auditory cortical lesions on discriminations of rising and falling frequency-modulated tones. Journal of Neurophysiology, 34, 802–816.

Lomber, S.G. (1999). The advantages and limitations of permanent or reversible deactivation techniques in the assessment of neural function. Journal of Neuroscience Methods, 86, 109–117.

Massopust, L.C., Jr., Wolin, L.R., & Frost, V. (1970). Increases in auditory middle frequency discrimination threshold after cortical ablations. Experimental Neurology, 28, 299–305.

Masterton, R.B. (1992). Role of the central auditory system in hearing: the new direction. Trends in Neuroscience, 15, 280–285.

Masterton, R.B. (1993). Central auditory system. ORL Journal of Otorhinolaryngology and Related Specialities, 55, 159–163.

Masterton, R.B. (1997). Neurobehavioral studies of the central auditory system. Annals of Otology, Rhinology, and Laryngology, 106, 31–34.

Masterton, R.B., & Diamond, I.T. (1964). Effects of auditory cortex ablation on discrimination of small binaural time differences. Journal of Neurophysiology, 27, 15–36.

Masterton, R.B., & Diamond, I.T. (1973). Hearing: central neural mechanisms. In E.C. Carterette & M.P. Friedman (Eds.), Handbook of Perception, Vol. III, Biology of perceptual systems (pp. 408–448). New York: Academic.

Masterton, R.B., Heffner, H., & Ravizza, R. (1969). The evolution of human hearing. Journal of the Acoustical Society of America, 45, 966–985.

May, B.J., Moody, D.B., & Stebbins, W.C. (1988). The significant features of Japanese macaque coo sounds: a psychophysical study. Animal Behavior, 36, 1432–1444.

Meyer, D.R., & Woolsey, C.N. (1952). Effects of localized cortical destruction on auditory discriminative conditioning in cat. Journal of Neurophysiology, 16, 149–162.

Neff, W.D. (1960). Role of the auditory cortex in sound discrimination. In G.L. Rasmussen & W.F. Windle (Eds.), Neural mechanisms of the auditory and vestibular systems (pp. 211–216). Springfield, IL: Charles C. Thomas.

Neff, W.D., Diamond, I.T., & Casseday, J.H. (1975). Behavioral studies of auditory discrimination: central nervous system. In W.D. Keidel & W.D. Neff (Eds.), Handbook of sensory physiology. Auditory system Vol. V/2 (pp. 307–400). New York: Springer-Verlag.

Neff, W.D., Fisher, J.F., Diamond, I.T., & Yela, M. (1956). Role of auditory cortex in discrimination requiring localization of sound in space. Journal of Neurophysiology, 19, 500–512.

Ohl, F.W., Wetzel, W., Wagner, T., Rech, A., & Scheich, H. (1999). Bilateral ablation of auditory cortex in Mongolian Gerbil affects discrimination of frequency modulated but not of pure tones. Learning & Memory, 6, 347–362.

Petersen, M.R., Beecher, M.D., Zoloth, S.R., Moody, D.B., & Stebbins, W.C. (1978). Neural lateralization of species-specific vocalizations by Japanese macaques (*Macaca fuscata*). Science, 202, 324–327.

Rauschecker, J.P., & Tian, B. (2000). Mechanisms and streams for processing of "what" and "where" in auditory cortex. Proceedings of the National Academy of Sciences USA, 97, 11800–11806.

Ravizza, R.J., & Masterton, R.B. (1972). Contribution of neocortex to sound localization in the opossum (*Didelphis virginiana*). Journal of Neurophysiology, 35, 344–356.

Romanski, L.M., & Goldman-Rakic, P.S. (2002). An auditory domain in primate prefrontal cortex. Nature Neuroscience, 5, 15–16.

Sherrington, C.S. (1926). Brain. The Encyclopædia Britannica, 13th edition, pp. 391–413.

Talwar, S.K., Musial, P.G., & Gerstein, G.L. (2001). Role of mammalian auditory cortex in the perception of elementary sound properties. Journal of Neurophysiology, 85, 2350–2358.

Thompson, G.C., & Cortez, A.M. (1983). The inability of squirrel monkeys to localize sound after unilateral ablation of auditory cortex. Behavioral Brain Research, 8, 211–216.

Thompson, G., Heffner, H., & Masterton, B. (1974). An automated localization chamber. Behavior Research Methods and Instrumentation, 6, 550–552.

Thompson, R.F. (1960). Function of auditory cortex of cat in frequency discrimination. Journal of Neurophysiology, 23, 321–334.

Whitfield, I.C. (1980). Auditory cortex and the pitch of complex tones. Journal of the Acoustical Society of America, 67, 644–647.

Woolsey, C.N. (1960). Organization of cortical auditory system: A review and a synthesis. In G.L. Rasmussen & W.F. Windle (Eds.), Neural mechanisms of the auditory and vestibular systems (pp. 165–180). Springfield, IL: Charles C. Thomas.

8. NON-ACOUSTIC INFLUENCE ON NEURAL ACTIVITY IN AUDITORY CORTEX

Michael Brosch, Henning Scheich

Auditory cortex, similar to other sensory cortices, is generally considered to be unimodal, that is, to be involved in processing and representing various aspects of sound. In this article we attempt to give an overview on studies on awake animals, including humans, that challenge this view and that show that early auditory cortical areas are affected by a host of non-acoustic factors. The influence can be of sensory but non-auditory origin, can be of non-sensory origin, and can be related to movements. The functional consequences of non-acoustic influences are far from being understood. Still they clearly indicate that auditory cortex cannot be considered to be merely a sophisticated analyzer of sound that provides a reliable representation of the acoustic environment. Rather the analysis in auditory cortex also seems to involve the multimodal context of sounds, the significance of sound, and the behavioral consequences of sound.

MODULATION OF NEURONAL ACTIVITY IN AUDITORY CORTEX BY NON-ACOUSTIC FACTORS

A comparably large proportion of earlier studies on auditory cortex were conducted on awake and behaving subjects and aimed at exploring how auditory cortical activity varied with the task the animals were performing. An influence of attention was reported as early as 1959 when Hubel and colleagues (1959) observed that some neurons in the auditory cortex of cats responded to specific acoustic stimuli only when cats clearly paid attention to them. After this seminal report a number of studies more quantitatively analyzed differences in auditory responses between conditions in which animals actively listened to auditory stimuli or were passively exposed to the same stimuli. In one of their initial studies, Miller and colleagues (1972) found that auditory cortex neurons responded more strongly to acoustic stimuli when a monkey was performing an auditory detection task, compared to the responses when the monkey was passively stimulated with the same stimuli. In the task condition, monkeys had to press a telegraph key at the onset of a light stimulus for a few seconds and to release the key at onset of a simple acoustic stimulus to earn a reward. In a subsequent study this group found that, among 21 neurons recorded from primary auditory cortex (AI) and caudal and lateral belt areas, more than half exhibited increases in their responses when monkeys were switched from the non-performance to the performance condition (Ryan et al., 1984). The average response gain was ~30% in these neurons, which was often accompanied by a moderate increase of the intertrial firing and by slightly (3.4 ms) decreased response latencies.

Task-dependent changes of auditory responses were also reported by other groups. Benson and colleagues (1981) found that 22% of 122 neurons exhibited an enhanced response and 7% exhibited a suppressed response when animals had to localize or to detect a sound played at one out of five different locations. In a study performed by Gilat and Perlman (1984), two thirds out of 28 neurons in AI either exhibited an enhanced or suppressed response to simple auditory stimuli. The authors found similar characteristics in neurons recorded from the medial geniculate body. Task-dependent changes were also observed in auditory short term memory tasks (Gottlieb et al., 1989; Sakurai, 1990, 1994).

Benson and Hienz (1978) showed that task-dependent changes of auditory responses were due to attention specifically allocated to the auditory modality and not to general attention, vigilance, or arousal shifts. The investigators trained monkeys to respond to specific sounds presented either to the right or to the left speaker of a headphone, irrespective of background sounds played at the opposite side. In recordings from 77 cells in auditory core and lateral belt areas they found 14 cells whose response was on average 37% stronger when the sound was presented to the attended ear compared to the unattended ear. Changes in firing rate occurred as early as 20 ms after sound onset.

These findings were confirmed with other training paradigms. Miller and colleagues (1980) compared auditory responses in different task conditions. They presented acoustic and light stimuli simultaneously and instructed monkeys to respond to one of the stimuli only. In recordings from 25 neurons, most of which were from AI and the caudo-lateral belt, 15 neurons demonstrated stronger responses to acoustic stimuli when the monkeys were performing the auditory detection task, compared to responses seen in the visual task condition. The average response gain was ~23% and thus comparable to the responses that are found when auditory task performance was compared with the non-performance condition (Ryan et al., 1984). Furthermore, Miller et al. (1980) observed that response latencies were shorter during the auditory attention condition than during the visual attention condition.

The influence of specific auditory attention on auditory cortex was also addressed by Hocherman and colleagues (1976) who trained monkeys on a bimodal discrimination task. Animals had to discriminate either a noise burst from a pure tone of any frequency or a light on the left side from a light on the right side, and to signal their decision by pushing a lever to the left or to the right. In each trial, the stimuli from the two modalities were randomly paired such that the stimulus of the task-irrelevant and the task-relevant modality were associated with the same lever movements or that the irrelevant and relevant stimulus were associated with opposite movements. In recordings from 72 units in auditory core and caudal belt about two thirds of the neurons exhibited a task-dependence of their responses to acoustic stimuli. When stimuli from the two modalities indicated the same lever movement, neuronal responses were usually larger compared to the situation when stimuli indicated opposite movements, suggesting an interaction between the visual and auditory modality.

Groh and colleagues (Werner-Reiss et al., 2003) reported that attending to visual stimuli can alter receptive field properties of single neurons in auditory core areas. Monkeys were trained to maintain fixation on a visual stimulus at a randomly chosen location in the horizontal plane, while a noise burst was presented at one of four locations. With this paradigm, eye position was found to affect the activity of about one third of a total of 113 neurons. In one third of them the spontaneous activity changed, whereas in the remaining neurons the azimuth sensitivity changed. The degree of influence by eye position appeared to range along a continuum, and the nature of that influence was complex, but could neither be explained by a transformation of auditory space into head- or eye-centered space nor by maintenance of auditory space, irrespective of eye position. Similar results were reported by Fu and colleagues (2002). If auditory cortex is truly involved in spatial hearing and orientation, as advocated by these and other authors (Rauschecker & Tian, 2000), visual and vestibular influences are expected to play a role in auditory cortex.

Alterations of spectrotemporal receptive field properties of neurons in auditory cortex also occurs when animals are switched between auditory detection and discrimination tasks, as described in detail by Fritz et al. (2004).

Selective auditory attention was also found to be reflected in the immediate-early gene cFos, which reveals activation processes in the nuclei of neurons. Sakata and colleagues (2002) simultaneously presented acoustic and light stimuli to rats. In one training group, the animals discriminated between high and low frequency tones, irrespective of the light stimulus. The other training group discriminated between a light either on the left or on the right side, irrespective of the acoustic stimulus. After acquisition of the task rats were sacrificed and the cortex was labeled for cFos. The authors found that more cFos was expressed in AI of rats that attended to acoustic stimuli than in rats that attended to light stimuli. By contrast, rats performing the visual task expressed more cFos in primary visual cortex than rats performing the auditory task.

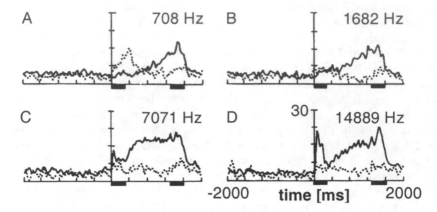

Fig. 8.1. Firing in auditory cortex related to auditory short term memory. The peristimulus time histograms represent the activity of a unit in response to two tones, while the monkey is passively exposed to the two tones (dotted line) and while a monkey performs a working memory task (solid line) in which it has to decide whether the first tone has the same or a different frequency as the second tone. The frequency of the first tone is indicated above each histogram. Occurrence of the first and the second tone is indicated by black bars. (Modified from Gottlieb et al., 1989).

MEMORY-RELATED ACTIVITY IN AUDITORY CORTEX

Although it seems to be established in textbooks that auditory cortex is part of the auditory memory system (e. g. Squire, 1987), we are aware of only a few electrophysiological studies that have found firing in auditory cortex that was related to auditory short term memory. Effects of long term memory have been reviewed by Weinberger (2004). Gottlieb et al. (1989) trained a baboon on an auditory short term memory task in which the monkey had to signal whether two subsequent tones (300 ms duration, 1 s intertone interval) were alike or had different frequencies. Among 17 neurons recorded from AI and 103 neurons recorded from posterior belt areas the investigators found that 80 neurons fired stronger and 2 weaker during the intertone interval when the animal was performing the memory task, compared to the corresponding period in which the monkey was passively exposed to the same stimuli (Fig. 8.1). Half of these neurons exhibited firing that depended on the frequency of the first tone, suggesting that their firing represented a memory trace of the frequency of the first tone which may be operational for the performance of the same/different task. The other neurons without frequency specific firing may reflect attentional shifts or expectation of the forthcoming second tone. The responses of 22% of the neurons differed between trials in which the two tones had the same frequency and trials in which they were dissimilar. No such match-dependent differences were observed in non-performance trials. As the authors did not perform additional controls they could not distinguish whether the match-dependent firing reflected information on the similarity of the tones, or whether it was related to the decision or to the preparation and execution of the motor response.

Similar results were reported by Sakurai (1994) who trained rats to perform either a working memory task or a reference memory task on a sequence of tones in which the frequency was randomly switched between 2 kHz and 10 kHz. Tone duration was 15 s, and intertone intervals were 5 s. In the working memory condition, animals were rewarded when they pressed a response panel during the initial 4 s after tone onset if this tone was different from the preceding tone. In the reference memory condition, animals were rewarded for a response to the 10-kHz tone only. Sakurai found 3 out of 54 neurons in auditory cortex that maintained elevated firing during the intertone interval when animals were engaged in the working memory task, but not when animals performed the reference memory task. The author also found match-dependent responses in 5 neurons.

Influences of short term memory on neuronal responses were also found in experiments in which acoustic stimuli were associated with light stimuli. Hocherman and colleagues (Hocherman et al., 1981; Hocherman & Yirmiya 1990) trained monkeys to discriminate between a pure tone and a noise burst by moving a lever either to the right or to the left, respectively. In each trial, the acoustic signal was preceded by a light that was briefly flashed either on the right or the left side. The light appeared in 75% of the trials at the side to which the lever movement had to be executed and in 25% of the trials it was at the opposite side. The visuo-auditory stimulus pairing affected the monkeys' task performance. The differences in performance were associated with different responses to the acoustic stimuli of neurons in AI and surrounding belt areas. About half the neurons responded differently to the acoustic stimulus when the more frequent visuo-auditory stimulus pairing was compared to the less frequent pairing. In most cases, differences were stimulus-specific, for example, they were present either only for the pure tone response or for the noise response. Merely two neurons exhibited such differences for both stimuli.

Opposite pairings, that is, presenting a light stimulus after an acoustic stimulus also seems to invoke memory-related firing in auditory cortex. Shinba and colleagues (1995) trained rats to respond to a light stimulus which was presented 1.4 s after a brief tone. In recordings from 36 cells in auditory cortex they found 9 cells that exhibited an elevated firing in the period between tone offset and the onset of the light stimulus. Unfortunately, the authors tested only three of these cells with the same stimuli outside the behavioral task and found that two of them did not exhibit such firing during the interstimulus period.

MOTOR- AND SET-RELATED FIRING IN AUDITORY CORTEX

Vaadia and colleagues (1982) found that the firing of neurons in auditory cortex could depend on the association between a sound and the behavioral response to this sound. In their study, a monkey was required to press a lever to trigger a pure tone or a noise burst, which then had to be discriminated by shifting the lever either to the right or to the left. The auditory-motor association was varied in blocks of 100–150 trials such that, in one block, a pure tone required leftward shifts and noise bursts required rightward shifts while in the subsequent block the association was reversed. Among 146 neurons the authors recorded from auditory core and lateral belt areas, 23 neurons responded differently to the auditory stimulus, depending on whether the stimulus was associated with a right or a left lever shift.

Auditory-motor associations were also reported by Durif and coworkers (2003). The investigators trained monkeys to respond to a high frequency tone with a right key press and to a low frequency tone with a left key press or vice versa, depending on which pairing was currently rewarded. After each correct key press the tone was repeated. It was found that the responses of about one third of the neurons recorded from AI and middle lateral belt depended on the behavioral consequences of the tone, i.e., they responded differently to the tone when it prompted a motor response compared to the situation in which the same stimulus was repeated after correct trials and thus did not require a motor response.

Opposite interactions, from motor actions on sound processing, have been found in several studies, in which activity in auditory cortex was recorded while subjects where speaking or vocalizing (Curio et al., 2000; Eliades & Wang, 2003; Houde et al., 2002; Müller-Preuss & Ploog, 1981). These findings are reviewed in detail by Eliades and Wang (2004).

Influences of self-produced sounds on auditory cortex activity have also been observed in musicians while playing a tune on a manipulated keyboard which did not emit any tone. Under this experimental condition, Altenmüller and coworkers (Bangert et al., 2001) found electrical DC potentials that were generated in the auditory cortex although no sound had been produced. This finding suggests that already the expectation of hearing sound or the intention to produce sound can activate auditory cortex in some conditions.

Very recently, Brosch and coworkers (Brosch et al., 2003) found that auditory cortex neurons can exhibit firing that is related to arm movements. Monkeys were trained to discriminate the direction of a pitch change in a sequence of pure tones (Brosch et al., 2004). The monkeys were cued by a light emitting diode, after which they could initiate the tone sequence by reaching a touch bar with their hand and holding it for at least 2.2 s. The first three tones in the sequence had the same frequency. These tones were followed by three tones of lower frequency, either immediately or after three to six intermittent tones of higher frequency. The monkeys were required to withdraw their hand from the touch bar not later than 1.4 s after the occurrence of the first tone of lower frequency in the sequence. Figure 8.2 shows a peri-event time histogram (PETH) of a multiunit recorded in AI. The firing of this unit was triggered on the instant of time at which the monkey made contact with the touch bar. The PETH exhibits a broad peak around the origin of the histogram, which became

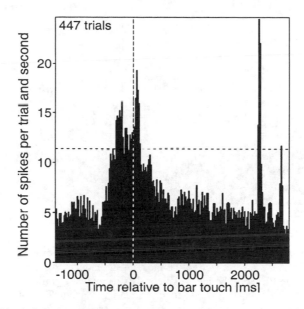

Fig. 8.2. Multiunit in primary auditory cortex whose firing was related to hand movements and tactile stimulation. The peri-event time histogram was triggered at the moment the monkey's hand contacted the touch bar. It thus shows how the neuronal firing varied with respect to this event of the behavioral procedure. Note that starting from 300 ms before bar touch, the firing was significantly increased above the intertrial firing (dashed line marks three standard deviations above this firing). Also note the additional phasic increase in firing shortly after bar touch, due to somatosensory stimulation of the hand.

significant 300 ms before bar touch and remained significant for the following 420 ms. As there was no acoustic signal before the bar touch and the multiunit firing was neither contaminated by electrical interferences nor by muscle artifacts we concluded that the firing was related to the movement of the hand towards the touch bar.

In our study, we also found motor-related firing in auditory cortex when the monkey released the touch bar. An example is given in Figure 8.3 which shows a PETH triggered on bar release. The PETH exhibits several peaks. To identify which of the peaks indicate motor-related firing, we compared trials with fast responses to the occurrence of the falling pitch direction with trials with slow responses. This was done by calculating two PETHs, one from trials in which the monkeys responded before the median reaction time, and another one from trials in which the monkeys responded after the median reaction time (Fig. 8.3). Both PETHs consist of five peaks, of which the four initial ones are shifted against each other and only the last peaks are in register. This means that the last peak is independent of reaction time and thus indicates firing time-locked to bar release. The four initial peaks in the PETH, by contrast, represent auditory responses, and are shifted due to 'incorrectly' triggering on the bar release.

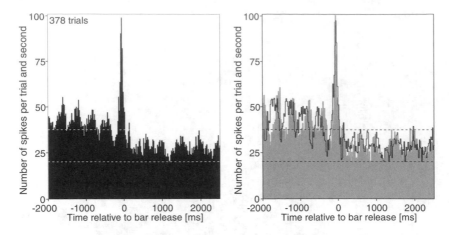

Fig. 8.3. Movement-related firing of a multiunit in auditory cortex. The peri-event time histogram (PETH) is synchronized to the moment the monkey withdraws its hand from the touch bar. The PETH in the left panel consists of several significant peaks, of which the last one indicates firing that is related to the hand movement. The four initial ones, by contrast, indicate firing evoked by the tones in the sequence. The distinction between peaks becomes obvious in the right panel in which two PETHs are shown. The gray PETH was calculated from trials in which the monkey responded early (< median reaction time) to the go-event, that is, the falling pitch direction in the tone sequence. The black curve was calculated from trials in which the monkey responded late (> median reaction time) to the go-event. Same conventions as in Figure 8.2.

In total, in 316 multiunits and 63 single units recorded from AI and posterior belt areas we observed movement-related firing in a considerable number of units. With regard to the grasping of the touch bar, 108 multiunits and 14 single units fired before the hand reached the touch bar. The number of units with movement-related firing was higher when we analyzed their firing with respect to the release of the touch bar. 184 multiunits and 25 single units fired before this event. Among the units that exhibited movement-related firing there were 8 multiunits and 2 single units that failed to respond to the tones in the sequence. The firing of these neurons rather seems to be associated with the behavioral consequences of auditory stimuli.

Evidence for neuronal firing related with bar release was also found by Yin and coworkers (2001) in the fields AI and R. The investigators trained rhesus monkeys to perform a simple auditory discrimination task, in which monkeys had to release a bar when they heard a four-note melody made up of tones below 1 kHz and hold the bar for other sounds.

Villa and associates (1999) reported that neuronal firing in auditory cortex before hearing an auditory stimulus could predict how a subject will behaviorally respond to subsequent auditory stimuli. Details of this and other experiments are reviewed by Villa (2004).

ACTIVITY IN AUDITORY CORTEX EVOKED BY VISUAL AND SOMATOSENSORY STIMULI

In our experiments we also found neuronal activity in auditory cortex that was related to visual and somatosensory stimuli. An example of a multiunit that responded to a visual stimulus is given in Figure 8.4. The PETH, which was triggered on the onset of the cue-light, exhibits a peak 60–100 ms after onset of the cue-light. Such responses to the cue-light were seen in 39 of 316 multiunits and in 1 of 63 single units. The median latency of light responses was 100 ms which corresponds well to response latencies observed in early visual cortical areas under similar conditions. In most units, responses to the cue-light were only observed when the monkeys subsequently grasped the touch bar, by which they signaled their readiness to listen to the tone sequence. Figure 8.4 gives an example of the task-dependence of light responses in auditory cortex.

The task-dependence of visual responses may explain why other studies have failed to see visual responses in auditory cortex although it was explicitly searched for them. No responses to light stimuli were found in animals performing an auditory task, in which visual stimuli were part of the behavioral procedure (Hocherman et al., 1976; Stewart & Starr, 1970; Vaadia et al., 1982). In AI of anesthetized cats, DeRibaupierre and colleagues (1973) found no indication for visual responses and Kral and colleagues (2003) reported slow modulations of neuronal firing in less than 1% of their recordings. In posterior auditory association cortex of awake monkeys, Schroeder and Foxe (2002) found that visual stimuli could evoke local field potentials and multiunit

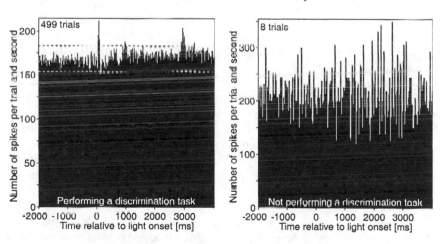

Fig. 8.4. Responses to visual stimuli in auditory cortex. Left panel shows a PETH synchronized to the onset of a cue-light, which signaled the monkey that it could initiate a tone sequence by making contact with a touch bar. Note the peak 60–100 ms after onset of the cue-light. This peak was observed in trials in which the monkey did not grasp the touch bar after the cue-light had been turned on (right panel).

responses. The finding of light responses in auditory cortex is complemented by earlier reports demonstrating acoustic responses in primary visual cortical areas 17–19 of anesthetized cats (Fishman & Michael, 1973; Morrell, 1972).

In addition to light responses, auditory cortical neurons also respond to tactile stimuli. An example of such firing is included in Figure 8.2. As described earlier this PETH shows that the units commenced firing 300 ms before bar touch which is indicative of movement-related firing. Closer inspection of the PETH reveals that a narrow peak was superimposed on the broader pedestal. This peak indicates that the unit rapidly increased its firing 20 ms after the contact with the touch bar. The following arguments indicate that this firing after the grasp is likely evoked by tactile stimulation at the moment of bar touch. There was no sound generated by the bar touch. A sudden increase of neuronal firing is not expected to occur at this time for the motor control of arm movements. The onset of this firing is similar to response latencies found in somatosensory cortex.

Somatosensory responses in auditory cortex have also been seen by Schroeder and associates. In their first study in awake but non-performing monkeys (Schroeder et al., 2001), they found that electrical stimulation of the median nerve of the contralateral hand affected the firing of neurons as well as intracortical slow wave field potentials. Such responses occurred at the same sites in caudomedial belt areas where auditory responses were seen, but not at any recording site in AI. In a subsequent study in anesthetized monkeys (Fu et al., 2003), this group could confirm that the caudomedial belt area, but not AI, responded to proper somatosensory stimuli. A single unit that responded both to auditory and tactile stimuli is given in Figure 8.5. In the caudomedial belt, 72% of the recording sites responded to some form of tactile stimulation. Somatosensory receptive fields were mostly located on the face. Thus far no clear relationship between somatosensory and auditory receptive fields could be established.

Somatosensory influences of auditory cortex activity have also been found in non-invasive imaging studies in humans. Foxe and colleagues (2000) compared event-related electrical potentials evoked by stimulation with a 1-kHz tone alone to potentials evoked by electrical stimulation of the median nerve of the hand, and to potentials evoked by combined stimulation. They found that the combined stimulation resulted in potentials, presumably generated in auditory cortex, that were larger than the sum of the potentials evoked by the two unimodal stimuli.

Selective visual activation of auditory cortex have also been found in fMRI studies with simple visual stimuli (Laurienti et al., 2002) or while subjects were watching a videotape of a face silently mouthing (Calvert et al., 1997). Although the authors claim that the activation involved Brodmann areas 41, 42, 22, and 20 further studies are needed to confirm that early auditory cortical areas are actually activated.

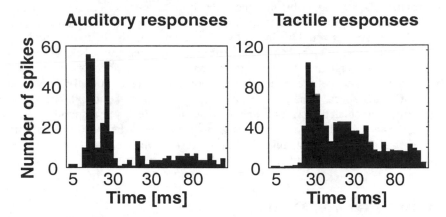

Fig. 8.5. Peristimulus time histograms for auditory (left) and somatosensory (right) responses of a neuron in the caudomedial auditory cortex. Somatosensory stimuli were air puffs delivered to the dorsal surface of the contralateral hand. Auditory stimulation was delivered through bone conduction, by tapping the exposed skull, at a rate of one per second. The tympanic membrane was completely destroyed bilaterally in this monkey to control for the possibility that the tactile response was evoked by slight noise associated with the air puff. (Modified from Fu et al., 2003)

CROSS-MODAL REPRESENTATION IN THE AUDITORY CORTEX OF DEAF SUBJECTS

There is strong experimental evidence for cross-modal processing in the auditory cortex of subjects with a long history of deafness. In humans, a magnetoencephalographic study in a congenitally deaf adult (Levänen et al., 1998) revealed that vibrotactile stimuli, applied on the palm and fingers, activated his auditory cortices bilaterally, and that the evoked magnetic fields varied with the vibration frequency. Non-invasive imaging studies have furthermore revealed that in a congenitally deaf subject the supratemporal gyri of both hemispheres are activated while the subject is watching sign language words (Nishimura et al., 1999). In profoundly deaf subjects, Finney and colleagues (2001) found that simple visual stimuli, like moving dot patterns, activated various cortical fields of the right auditory cortex, presumably involving Brodmann areas 41, 42, and 22. An electrophysiological mapping study in congenitally deaf cats, by contrast, found no evidence for cross-modal responses in AI (Kral et al., 2003), neither with visual nor with tactile stimuli.

That a cross-modal reorganization of auditory cortex can be functionally relevant has thus far only been demonstrated in animal studies, whereas such support is still limited in humans (Cohen et al., 1997). In ferrets, Sur and colleagues (Sharma et al., 2000; Sur et al., 1988; von Melchner et al., 2000) induced retinal cells to project into the medial geniculate body in newborn pups by ablating the superior colliculus and visual cortical areas 17 and 18. After this manipulation they found many cells in the auditory thalamus of adult animals, as well as in AI that could be driven by visual stimuli. Cells in rewired auditory cortex were found to be bimodal and to display visual receptive field properties like orientation and direction selectivity that are typical for normal primary visual cortex, and cells encode a two-dimensional, retinotopically organized map of visual space. When the remaining visual pathway through the visual thalamus was ablated rewired animals could still detect and respond to light stimuli. This capability, however, was grossly impaired when also the auditory cortex was ablated in these animals. Similar results were reported by Frost and associates in hamsters (Ptito et al., 2001).

SUMMARY AND CONCLUSION

This review summarizes in detail results from about fifty articles, in which a large variety of different non-acoustic influences on the neural activity in auditory cortex have been described. Although these findings do not seem to be widely acknowledged in the community of auditory cortex researchers (which may not be too surprising in the light of a total of 5000 articles or more that have been published on 'auditory cortex,' according to a Medline search) their implications for functional roles of auditory cortex may be tremendous, even if most of them may remain unclear at present. In the following we address a few implications of these findings.

Influences of non-acoustic events on auditory cortex activity seem to be quite common and strong. They have been seen in all types of neural signals, including action potentials, intracortical local field potentials, electrical and magnetic scalp recording, and imaging of glucose metabolism and cerebral blood flow. They can be found in anesthetized, awake but non-performing subjects, in subjects performing an auditory task, and in subjects with a long history of deafness. They can be induced by stimuli from other modalities, the motor realm, memory processes, selective auditory attention, and auditory learning. This suggests that auditory cortex cannot be considered to be merely a sophisticated processor for complex sound (Kaas & Hackett, 2000; Rauschecker & Tian, 2000). Rather it appears that the analysis of sound in auditory cortex is carried out in the context of stimuli of other modalities, and that the processing also involves the behavioral consequences of auditory stimuli.

Non-acoustic influences are also found at subcortical stages of the auditory system, like in the auditory thalamus (Gabriel et al., 1975; Gilat & Perlman, 1984; Hocherman & Yirmiya, 1990; Ryan et al., 1983; Sur et al., 1988) and inferior colliculus (Aitkin et al., 1981; Ryan et al., 1984). Therefore, some of the non-acoustic influences in auditory cortex will likely reflect activity of multimodal subcortical brain structures which is conveyed into auditory cortex. Some non-acoustic influence may be exerted by direct projections between different sensory cortical areas. Such connections have been demonstrated to run from auditory belt and parabelt areas and to some degree also from auditory core areas to visual cortical areas V2 and V1 (Falchier et al., 2002; Rockland & Ojima, 2003). These two studies, however, disagree whether there is also a reciprocal projection from early visual cortical areas into auditory cortex. Hackett and colleagues (2003) recently reported first data suggesting that auditory belt areas are innervated from the somatosensory area II and from polysensory nuclei of the thalamus.

Two types of non-acoustic influences may be discerned. In the first type, responses of auditory cortex neurons to auditory stimuli are modulated, resulting in an either stronger or weaker response to the same stimulus depending on the non-acoustic context, which sometimes is accompanied by alterations of receptive field properties. The modulations of auditory responses may be related to attentional effects, facilitate the processing of specific auditory stimuli, may adjust the sensitivity of neurons in auditory cortex, may contribute to the evaluation of the behavioral significance of stimuli, or may be involved in multimodal integration (Stein & Meredith, 1993).

The second type of non-acoustic influence is one in which auditory cortex is activated by non-acoustic stimuli or is active during movements, in the absence of acoustic stimuli. On the single cell level, neurons were found that responded only to acoustic stimuli, fired to acoustic stimuli and to non-acoustic stimuli or during movements, and that fired only during non-acoustic events but not to acoustic stimuli. This suggests that auditory cortex may contain purely auditory neurons, sensory but non-auditory neurons, motor-related neurons, polysensory neurons, and audio-motor neurons.

The activation related to non-acoustic events is often transient and can occur at latencies comparable to those in early visual and somatosensory cortex. Consequently when one only considers the activity of auditory cortex neurons, the activity evoked by non-acoustic events appears indistinguishable from the activity evoked by acoustic stimuli. This may have substantial consequences for the functional significance of neuronal firing in auditory cortex. Normally it is assumed that the firing of neurons in the auditory system signals the presence of an acoustic stimulus in the environment. This view is challenged by the existence of neurons in auditory cortex that are activated by non-acoustic events. Such neurons may be involved in processes other than creating a representation of the acoustic environment of an individual.

ACKNOWLEDGMENTS

We would like to express our thanks to Elena Selezneva, Elena Oshurkova, and Dr. Armenuhi Melikyan for their help during experiments, and to Dr. André Brechmann and the reviewers for their helpful suggestions on this manuscript. This research was supported by the State of Saxony-Anhalt, BMBF, and the German Research Foundation (Deutsche Forschungsgemeinschaft, DFG).

REFERENCES

Aitkin L.M., Kenyon C.E., & Philpott P. (1981). The representation of the auditory and somatosensory systems in the external nucleus of the cat inferior colliculus. The Journal of Comparative Neurology, 196, 25–40.

Bangert, M., Haeusler, U., & Altenmuller, E. (2001). On practice: how the brain connects piano keys and piano sounds. Annals of the New York Academy of Science, 930, 425–428.

Benson, D.A., & Hienz, R.D. (1978). Single-unit activity in the auditory cortex of monkeys selectively attending left vs. right ear stimuli. Brain Research, 159, 307–320.

Benson, D.A., Hienz, R.D., & Goldstein, M.H., Jr. (1981). Single-unit activity in the auditory cortex of monkeys actively localizing sound sources: Spatial tuning and behavioral dependency. Brain Research, 219, 249–267.

Brosch, M., Selezneva, E., Bucks, C., & Scheich, H. (2004). Macaque monkeys discriminate pitch relationships. Cognition, 91, 259–272.

Brosch, M., Selezneva, E., Oshurkova, E., Melikyan, A., Goldschmidt, J., & Scheich, H. (2003). Neuronal activity in monkey auditory cortex during the performance of an auditory discrimination task. Abstracts – Society for Neuroscience. Volume 33, p. 488.2.

Calvert, G.A., Bullmore, E.T., Brammer, M.J., Campbell, R., Williams, S.C., McGuire, P.K., Woodruff, P.W., Iversen, S.D., & David, A.S. (1997). Activation of auditory cortex during silent lipreading. Science, 276, 593–596.

Cohen, L.G., Celnik, P., Pascual-Leone, A., Corwell, B., Falz, L., Dambrosia, J., Honda, M., Sadato, N., Gerloff, C., Catala, M.D., & Hallett, M. (1997). Functional relevance of cross-modal plasticity in blind humans. Nature, 389, 180–183.

Curio, G., Neuloh, G., Numminen, J., Jousmaki, V., & Hari, R. (2000). Speaking modifies voice-evoked activity in the human auditory cortex. Human Brain Mapping, 9, 183–191.

DeRibaupierre, F., Goldstein, M.H., Jr., & Yenikomshian, G. (1973). Lack of response in primary auditory neurons to visual stimulation. Brain Research, 52, 370–373.

Durif, C., Jouffrais, C., & Rouiller, E.M. (2003). Single-unit responses in the auditory cortex of monkeys performing a conditional acousticomotor task. Experimental Brain Research, 153, 614–627.

Eliades, S.J., & Wang, X. (2003). Sensory-motor interaction in the primate auditory cortex during self-initiated vocalizations. Journal of Neurophysiology, 89, 2194–2207.

Eliades, S.J., & Wang, X. (2004). Dynamics of vocalization-induced sensory-motor interactions in the primate auditory cortex. In R. König, P. Heil, E. Budinger, & H. Scheich (Eds.), The Auditory Cortex – A Synthesis of Human and Animal Research. Hillsdale, NJ: Lawrence Erlbaum Associates.

Falchier, A., Clavagnier, S., Barone, P., & Kennedy, H. (2002). Anatomical evidence of multimodal integration in primate striate cortex. Journal of Neuroscience, 22, 5749–5759.

Finney, E.M., Fine, I., & Dobkins, K.R. (2001). Visual stimuli activate auditory cortex in the deaf. Nature Neuroscience, 4, 1171–1173.

Fishman, M.C., & Michael, P. (1973). Integration of auditory information in the cat's visual cortex. Vision Research, 13, 1415–1419.

Foxe, J.J., Morocz, I.A., Murray, M.M., Higgins, B.A., Javitt, D.C., & Schroeder, C.E. (2000). Multisensory auditory-somatosensory interactions in early cortical processing revealed by high-density electrical mapping. Cognitive Brain Research, 10, 77–83.

Fritz, J., Elhilai, M., & Shamma, S. (2004). Task-dependent adaptive plasticity of receptive fields in primary auditory cortex of the ferret. In R. König, P. Heil, E. Budinger, & H. Scheich (Eds.), The Auditory Cortex – A Synthesis of Human and Animal Research. Hillsdale, NJ: Lawrence Erlbaum Associates.

Fu, K.M., Johnston, T.A., Shah, A.S., Arnold, L., Smiley, J., Hackett, T.A., Garraghty, P.E., & Schroeder, C.E. (2003). Auditory cortical neurons respond to somatosensory stimulation. Journal of Neuroscience, 23, 7510–7515.

Fu, K.M., Shah, A.S., O'Connell, N.O., McGinnes, T.M., & Schroeder, C.E. (2002). Integration of auditory and eye position in auditory cortex. Abstracts – Society for Neuroscience, Volume 32, p. 220.12.

Gabriel, M., Saltwick, S.E., & Miller, J.D. (1975). Conditioning and reversal of short-latency multiple-unit responses in the rabbit medial geniculate nucleus. Science, 189, 1108–1109.

Gilat, E., & Perlman, I. (1984). Single unit activity in the auditory cortex and the medial geniculate body of the rhesus monkey: Behavioral modulation. Brain Research, 324, 323–333.

Gottlieb, Y., Vaadia, E., & Abeles, M. (1989). Single unit activity in the auditory cortex of a monkey performing a short term memory task. Experimental Brain Research, 74, 139–148.

Hackett, T., Smiley, J., & Schroeder, C. (2003). Multisensory integration in primate auditory cortex. Advances in Primate Auditory Neurophysiology, Satellite Symposium at the Society for Neuroscience Annual Meeting, p. 8.

Hocherman, S., Benson, D.A., Goldstein, M.H., Jr., Heffner, H.E., & Hienz, R.D. (1976). Evoked unit activity in auditory cortex of monkeys performing a selective attention task. Brain Research, 117, 51–68.

Hocherman, S., Itzhaki, A., & Gilat, E. (1981). The response of single units in the auditory cortex of rhesus monkeys to predicted and to unpredicted sound stimuli. Brain Research, 230, 65–86.

Hocherman, S., & Yirmiya, R. (1990). Neuronal activity in the medial geniculate nucleus and in the auditory cortex of the rhesus monkey reflects signal anticipation. Brain, 113, 1707–1720.

Houde, J.F., Nagarajan, S.S., Sekihara, K., & Merzenich, M.M. (2002). Modulation of the auditory cortex during speech: An MEG study. Journal of Cognitive Neuroscience, 14, 1125–1138.

Hubel, D.H., Henson, C.O., Rupert, A., & Galambos, R. (1959). Attention units in the auditory cortex. Science, 129, 1279–1280.

Kaas, J.H., & Hackett, T.A. (2000). Subdivisions of auditory cortex and processing streams in primates. Proceedings of the National Acadamy of Sciences USA, 97, 11793–11799.

Kral, A., Schroder, J.H., Klinke, R., & Engel, A.K. (2003). Absence of cross-modal reorganization in the primary auditory cortex of congenitally deaf cats. Experimental Brain Research, 153, 605–613.

Laurienti, P.J., Burdette, J.H., Wallace, M.T., Yen, Y.F., Field, A.S., & Stein, B.E. (2002). Deactivation of sensory-specific cortex by cross-modal stimuli. Journal of Cognitive Neuroscience, 14, 420–429.

Levänen, S., Jousmäki, V., & Hari, R. (1998). Vibration-induced auditory-cortex activation in a congenitally deaf adult. Current Biology, 8, 869–872.

Miller, J.M., Dobie, R.A., Pfingst, B.E., & Hienz, R.D. (1980). Electrophysiologic studies of the auditory cortex in the awake monkey. American Journal of Otolaryngology, 1, 119–130.

Miller, J.M., Sutton, D., Pfingst, B., Ryan, A., Beaton, R., & Gourevitch, G. (1972). Single cell activity in the auditory cortex of Rhesus monkeys: Behavioral dependency. Science, 177, 449–451.

Morrell, F. (1972). Visual system's view of acoustic space. Nature, 238, 44-46.

Müller-Preuss, P., & Ploog, D. (1981). Inhibition of auditory cortical neurons during phonation. Brain Research, 215, 61–76.

Nishimura, H., Hashikawa, K., Doi, K., Iwaki, T., Watanabe, Y., Kusuoka, H., Nishimura, T., & Kubo, T. (1999). Sign language 'heard' in the auditory cortex. Nature, 397, 116.

Ptito, M., Giguere, J.F., Boire, D., Frost, D.O., & Casanova, C. (2001). When the auditory cortex turns visual. Progress in Brain Research, 134, 447–458.

Rauschecker, J.P., & Tian B. (2000). Mechanisms and streams for processing of "what" and "where" in auditory cortex. Proceedings of the National Acadamy of Sciences USA, 97, 11800–11806.

Rockland, K.S., & Ojima, H. (2003). Multisensory convergence in calcerine visual areas in macaque monkey. International Journal of Psychophysiology, 50, 19–26.

Ryan, A.F., Miller, J.M., Pfingst, B.E., & Martin, G.K. (1984). Effects of reaction time performance on single-unit activity in the central auditory pathway of the rhesus macaque. Journal of Neuroscience, 4, 298–308.

Sakata, S., Kitsukawa, T., Kaneko, T., Yamamori, T., & Sakurai, Y. (2002). Task-dependent and cell-type-specific Fos enhancement in rat sensory cortices during audio-visual discrimination. European Journal of Neuroscience, 15, 735–743.

Sakurai, Y. (1990). Cells in the rat auditory system have sensory-delay correlates during the performance of an auditory working memory task. Behavioral Neuroscience, 104, 856–868.

Sakurai, Y. (1994). Involvement of auditory cortical and hippocampal neurons in auditory working memory and reference memory in the rat. Journal of Neuroscience, 4, 2606–2623.

Schroeder, C.E., & Foxe, J.J. (2002). The timing and laminar profile of converging inputs to multisensory areas of the macaque neocortex. Cognitive Brain Research, 14, 187–198.

Schroeder, C.E., Lindsley, R.W., Specht, C., Marcovici, A., Smiley, J.F., & Javitt, D.C. (2001). Somatosensory input to auditory association cortex in the macaque monkey. Journal of Neurophysiology, 85, 1322–1327.

Sharma, J., Angelucci, A., & Sur, M. (2000). Induction of visual orientation modules in auditory cortex. Nature, 404, 841–847.

Shinba, T., Sumi, M., Iwanami, A., Ozawa, N., & Yamamoto, K. (1995). Increased neuronal firing in the rat auditory cortex associated with preparatory set. Brain Research Bulletin, 37, 199–204.

Squire, L.R. (1987). Memory and Brain. New York: Oxford University Press.

Stein, B.E., & Meredith, M.A. (1993). The merging of the senses. Boston: MIT.

Stewart, D.L., & Starr, A. (1970). Absence of visually influenced cells in auditory cortex of normal and congenitally deaf cats. Experimental Neurology, 28, 525–528.

Vaadia, E., Gottlieb, Y., & Abeles, M. (1982). Single-unit activity related to sensorimotor association in auditory cortex of a monkey. Journal of Neurophysiology, 48, 1201–1213.

Villa, A.E.P. (2004). Spatio-temporal patterns of spike occurrences in freely-moving rats associated to perception of human vowels. In R. König, P. Heil, E. Budinger, & H. Scheich (Eds.), The Auditory Cortex – A Synthesis of Human and Animal Research. Hillsdale, NJ: Lawrence Erlbaum Associates.

Villa, A.E, Tetko, I.V., Hyland, B., & Najem, A. (1999). Spatiotemporal activity patterns of rat cortical neurons predict responses in a conditioned task. Proceedings of the National Acadamy of Sciences USA, 96, 1106–1111.

von Melchner, I., Pallas, S.L., & Sur, M. (2000). Visual behaviour mediated by retinal projections directed to the auditory pathway. Nature, 404, 871–876.

Weinberger, N.M. (2004). Specific long-term memory traces in primary auditory cortex. Nature Reviews Neuroscience, 5, 279–290.

Werner-Reiss, U., Kelly, K.A., Trause, A.S., Underhill, A.M., & Groh, J.M. (2003). Eye position affects activity in primary auditory cortex of primates. Current Biology, 13, 554–562.

Yin, P.B., Fritz, J.B., Dam, C.L., & Mishkin, M. (2001). Differential distribution of spectrotemporal response patterns in A1 and R, and presence of task-related responses, in the primary auditory cortex of the alert rhesus monkey. Abstracts – Society for Neuroscience. Volume 31.

9. THE POSTEROLATERAL SUPERIOR TEMPORAL AUDITORY FIELD IN HUMANS: FUNCTIONAL ORGANIZATION AND CONNECTIVITY

John F. Brugge, Igor O. Volkov, Richard A. Reale,
P. Charles Garell, Hiroto Kawasaki, Hiroyuki Oya, Qingyu Li,
Matthew A. Howard III

INTRODUCTION

The numbers, locations, boundaries, and connectivity of fields making up human auditory cortex are not well known. Cytoarchitectonic studies have identified a koniocortical field on the transverse gyrus (or gyri) of Heschl (hereafter referred to simply as HG) and several other fields around it (Brodmann, 1909; Galaburda & Sanides, 1980; Hackett et al., 2001; Morosan et al., 2001; Rademacher et al., 1993, 2001; von Economo & Koskinas, 1925). The koniocortical 'core' areas in humans have their counterparts in non-human primates (Hackett et al., 2001). As many as eight fields having distinct locations and histochemical characteristics, and presumably auditory in function, have been shown to occupy mainly the superior temporal plane (Chiry et al., 2003; Clarke & Rivier, 1998; Rivier & Clarke, 1997; Wallace et al., 2002). One of these fields is typically located on the mesial aspect of HG and is considered to be the location of the human primary auditory area (AI). The multiple fields comprising the 'belt' of cortex surrounding the core area are responsive to acoustic stimulation (Binder et al., 2000; Talavage et al., 2000; Wessinger et al., 2001). Although such a belt of cortex has been identified cytoarchitectonically (Hackett et al., 1998, 2001) and electrophysiologically (Rauschecker et al., 1995) in non-human primates, homologies remain highly speculative. In monkey a parabelt area lies on the lateral surface of the superior temporal gyrus

(STG) adjacent to the belt region from which it receives a cortico-cortical projection (Hackett et al., 1998). Cortex making up the lateral surface of the STG in humans is activated widely by a variety of speech and non-speech sounds (see Binder et al., 2000). This active area appears to include on its caudal aspect an auditory field we refer to as posterior lateral superior temporal field (PLST, Howard et al., 2000). Although it has been shown that PLST can be separated from presumed AI on physiological grounds, little more is known of its functional organization. Whether PLST, or any other auditory field on the lateral STG, should be considered a homologue of a monkey parabelt field is yet to be determined.

Anatomical studies in non-human primates show that auditory fields of the superior temporal gyrus are richly interconnected in what appears to be a hierarchical fashion. This arrangement could provide part of an anatomical framework for serial processing of acoustic information transmitted to cortical fields over cortico-cortical pathways operating in parallel with transmission over thalamic routes (Kaas & Hackett, 1998; Kaas et al., 1999; Rauschecker et al., 1997; Rauschecker, 1998). A hierarchical auditory processing model has also been posited for human cortex (Binder et al., 2000; Wessinger et al., 2001). Little is known, however, about the anatomical connections between human cortical auditory fields that would underlie such an organizational framework. The anatomical tract-tracing methods that have been used so effectively in mapping auditory cortical connectivity in the living monkey brain cannot be used in the human. Although limited to short distances, the use of carbocyanine dyes in postmortem human specimens has revealed both intrinsic and extrinsic cortico-cortical connections within the auditory domain of the STG (Galuske et al., 1999; Galuske et al., 2000; Tardif & Clarke, 2001). An alternative method of tracing auditory cortical pathways, used effectively in the past, involves focal electrical stimulation of one cortical site while systematically mapping the resultant evoked activity from distant sites (Bignall, 1969; Bignall & Imbert, 1969; Bremer et al., 1954; Downman et al., 1960; Howard et al., 2000; Imbert et al., 1966; Liegeois-Chauvel et al., 1991). Although this approach provides no direct information on the cellular origins, anatomical trajectories or terminal distributions of neural pathways, it does give direct information in the living brain on the functional connectivity between the site of electrical stimulation and the site(s) of recording (Brown et al., 1973; Yeomans, 1990). We have adopted this method and have used it in combination with electrophysiological recording of auditory evoked activity to study in human epilepsy-surgery patients the functional connections between physiologically identified auditory cortical fields. Here we describe results of this combined approach from an ongoing study of possible cortico-cortical processing streams between what we interpret to be primary auditory cortex and what might be considered a higher-order associational auditory field, PLST, on the posterolateral surface of the STG.

METHODS

Experiments involve direct cortical recording and electrical stimulation in patients undergoing surgical treatment for medically intractable epilepsy. Evoked potentials (EPs) are recorded from multi-contact subdural recording arrays that are chronically implanted directly on the surface of the left or right cerebral hemisphere. Surface recording grids consist typically of 64 platinum-iridium disc electrodes (contact diameter 1.5 mm) arranged in an 8 x 8 array and embedded in a silicon membrane. The center-to-center spacing of the electrodes on a grid is either 4 or 5 mm. EPs and multi-neuronal responses are also recorded from multi-contact modified depth electrodes inserted into HG (Howard et al., 1996). Depth electrodes are approximately 1.7 mm in diameter and 4.0 cm in length. Intraoperative photographs, magnetic resonance imaging (MRI) and x-ray aid electrode localization. Electrode placements are based on clinical considerations. Research protocols introduce no additional risks to the patients and have been approved by the University of Iowa Institutional Review Board.

The output from each electrode is amplified, filtered, digitized, displayed on-line, and stored for off-line analysis. Evoked potentials shown in this paper are the result of averaging 50–100 stimulus trials. Negativity is plotted upward in all figures. During recording sessions patients are awake and sitting upright in their hospital bed or resting comfortably in a chair. Acoustic stimuli consist of clicks, 300 ms tone bursts, 300 ms noise bursts and consonant vowel (CV) speech tokens presented every two seconds via inserted earphones. Stimuli are delivered to both ears at a suprathreshold level that is comfortable for each patient, which is typically 50 dB above detection threshold.

Once the location and approximate boundaries of PLST are determined using acoustic stimulation, we initiate electrical-stimulation mapping experiments. An electrical stimulus (0.2 ms charge-balanced biphasic pulse repeated every 1 or 2 s) is applied in bipolar fashion to adjacent acoustically active cortical sites while recording from distant cortical sites. Stimuli are held below after-discharge threshold, and the subjects report no resulting sensations. Additional details on methods used are found in Howard et al. (2000) and Brugge et al. (2003).

RESULTS

Area PLST is activated by a wide range of acoustic stimuli

A region of cortex on the posterior lateral aspects of the STG, referred to as PLST, is activated robustly by a wide range of acoustic stimuli, including click trains, tone bursts, noise bursts and CV sounds. Results of one experiment in which these stimuli were employed are shown in Figure 9.1. The location of the 64-channel recording grid is shown superimposed on a 3D MRI of this subject.

Below are four response maps derived from activity evoked by the four stimuli indicated on the respective map. Each response on a given map corresponds to a location on the grid. Each response waveform begins at stimulus onset and continues for 700 ms. These results are derived from a larger data set in which each of the stimulus classes was studied in a parametric fashion. The results shown are also representative of data obtained from a large number of subjects studied this way.

These maps show four response properties that characterize PLST. First, for each of the stimuli employed robust polyphasic evoked responses are recorded within a circumscribed area on the posterior lateral STG. We call such a region activated by a stimulus a 'response field.' Second, for any given effective stimulus the waveform of the polyphasic EP varies across a response field. Usually there is one recording site where the overall amplitude of the EP is greatest; amplitude then declines with distance from this site. We have seen, however, instances in which there was more than one focus of high-amplitude EPs separated by a region in which the EP was of lower amplitude (see e.g., Fig. 9.2C). These variations in waveform impart a spatio-temporal pattern of activity on a response field. Although we have always been successful in recording from a region of maximal responsiveness, we have not always been successful in determining the full extent of the response field, as it often extends beyond the edges of the recording grid. Third, at any given active recording site the shape of the waveform varies with the acoustic stimulus, as can be seen when comparing responses to the four different classes of sounds used in these experiments. Finally, the response fields derived from each of the stimulus classes are essentially coextensive on the STG. In other words, within the limits of the spatial resolution of our recording grid there is no evidence from data collected so far for spatially segregated representations of these diverse classes of stimuli. We postulate that, instead, within PLST it is the difference in sound-evoked spatio-temporal patterns that underlies such segregation.

Area PLST is activated by electrical stimulation of mesial HG

In seven subjects a depth electrode was inserted into the first transverse of Heschl's gyrus, in addition to the 64-channel grid array that was implanted over posterior STG. The depth electrode had as many as 20 high and low impedance contacts distributed along its length thereby allowing us to study acoustic response properties of auditory cortex on HG and map their mediolateral organization. In doing so we localized the primary field to the mesial aspect of HG (see Howard et al., 1996). Once the activities recorded through the depth electrode and the surface array were characterized we turned to electrical stimulation mapping of possible functional connections between HG and PLST.

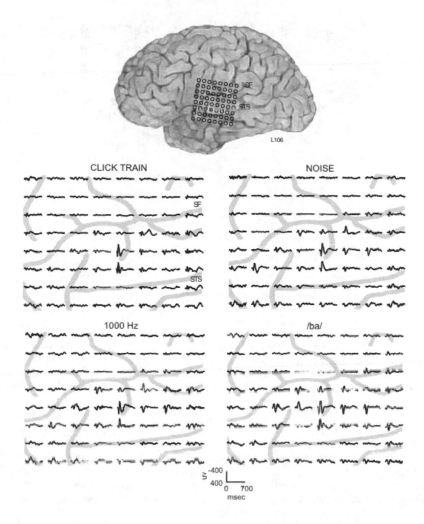

Fig. 9.1. Acoustic response maps on the posterolateral superior temporal gyrus (STG). The MRI shows the location of the recording grid on the lateral surface of the hemisphere. The grid overlaid the posterior aspect of the superior temporal gyrus. Grey lines represent the locations of major sulci including the Sylvian fissure (SF) and superior temporal sulcus (STS). Stimuli were clicks (5 clicks, 100 Hz), 1/3 octave band noise bursts with center frequency of 1000 Hz, 1000 Hz tone bursts, and CV (/ba/) tokens. Averaged evoked potentials were derived from 100 repetitions of the respective stimuli. In this and all subsequent figures negative voltage is up. Relative positions of recorded waveforms on the maps represent the relative positions of the electrodes on the recording grid. Spatial resolution was enhanced by employing a spline-Laplacian (see e.g., Nunez & Pilgreen, 1991).

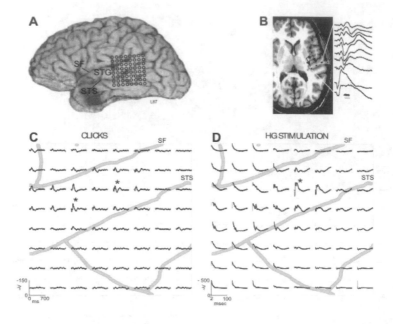

Fig. 9.2. Response fields on posterior lateral superior temporal gyrus (STG) to acoustic stimulation and to electrical stimulation of Heschl's gyrus (HG). **A**. MRI showing the location of recording grid on the lateral surface of the hemisphere. The grid overlaid the posterior aspect of the superior temporal gyrus (STG). **B**. Horizontal MRI section at the level of the HG showing the trajectory of the depth electrode, recorded EPs to click train stimulation, and the location of the bipolar stimulation sites within HG. **C, D**. Response fields on lateral STG resulting from click-train stimulation and electrical stimulation of mesial HG. Grey lines represent the locations of major sulci including the Sylvian fissure (SF) and superior temporal sulcus (STS). Averaged evoked potentials derived from 100 repetitions of the respective stimuli. Relative positions of recorded waveforms on the maps of C, D represent the relative positions of the electrodes on the recording grid shown in A. Asterisks mark the sites of maximal response within the two response fields.

Figure 9.2 illustrates our major findings with respect to electrical stimulation tract tracing for one subject. The location of the 64-channel recording grid is shown superimposed on a 3D MRI of this subject (A). To the right (B) is a horizontal MRI section showing a reconstruction of the trajectory of the depth electrode in HG, the evoked potentials obtained following click-train stimulation at each recording site and the bipolar stimulus sites (arrows). EPs exhibited maximal amplitude in the mesial 2/3 of HG, which is consistent with their location in AI. Below (C) is shown a response map of averaged EPs obtained from the surface grid by the same click-train stimulus that evoked the waveforms recorded in HG shown in B. Polyphasic evoked potentials to click stimulation were distributed over the posterior lateral aspect of the STG – area PLST – as also shown in Figure 9.1. Comparison between click maps of PLST obtained from the two subjects (Figs. 9.1 and 9.2) also illustrates differences we noted between subjects in maps derived from the use of the same acoustic stimulus.

The map shown in Figure 9.2D was obtained by applying bipolar electrical stimuli to mesial HG sites (see Fig. 9.2B). We can make three observations. First, the response field on STG obtained under these conditions overlapped considerably the one obtained with click stimulation. Second, the EP recorded at each site following HG electrical stimulation consisted of a series of positive and negative deflections occurring within about 50 ms of stimulus presentation. A stimulus artifact is clearly evident mainly on the left half of the grid, which tended to obscure possible early evoked activity at these sites. Third, like the acoustic response field, there was a cortical recording site where the EP to electrical stimulation exhibited the greatest amplitude. This is marked on the electrical response field by an asterisk. This site corresponds to one of the two sites of maximal response within the acoustic response field.

Waveforms recorded on PLST to mesial HG stimulation

In all subjects, mesial HG stimulation resulted in a polyphasic waveform that, at the PLST electrode site of maximal amplitude, was characterized by having an initial positive deflection followed by twin negative waves. Figure 9.3 illustrates two cases where the stimulus artifact was very brief, and the *onset time* of an even earlier positive deflection (arrow) was detected in addition to the positive-negative-negative deflection triad. We estimated from the waveforms in Figure 9.3A,B that the onset of this earliest positive deflection occurred at 1.7 and 2.3 ms, respectively. Because in most instances the stimulus artifact obscured this very early activity evoked by mesial HG stimulation, we were unable to map systematically the spatial distribution of this early positive wave, which we interpret to be the initial invasion of afferent input(s) to PLST activated by mesial HG stimulation. Latencies to each deflection in the wave triad are also shown. For five subjects studied this way, peak latency of the positive deflection varied from 3.2–6.0 ms, that of the first negative deflection from 8.4–13.5 ms, and that of the second negative wave from 17.9–24.8 ms. The interval between the twin negative peaks varied, on average, from 8.1 to 11.3 ms. Although waveforms having twin negative deflections tended to be most prominent at or near the site of maximal amplitude of response, systematic change in this waveform pattern could be seen across the map (see Brugge et al., 2003).

Effects of varying interstimulus interval and stimulus site

The exact mechanisms by which electrical stimulation of HG cortex activates neural pathways functionally connected to lateral STG cortex are not fully understood. It seems likely, however, that the major deflections in the electrically evoked waveforms we recorded on lateral STG represent the sequential activation of intracortical circuitry within STG or of one or more

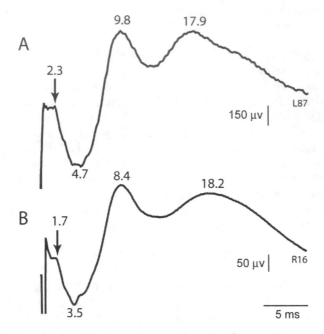

Fig. 9.3. Averaged waveforms recorded at the site of maximal amplitude of the acoustic response in the posterior lateral superior temporal auditory area (PLST) in two subjects in response to an electrical stimulus applied to mesial Heschl's gyrus (HG). In these cases the stimulus artifact did not obscure the time of onset of the early positive component (arrows). Average onset and peak latency are shown for each waveform.

afferent streams originating in mesial HG. We hypothesized that if this were the case then these deflections may exhibit different sensitivities to the rate of electrical stimulation, to the site of stimulation along HG, or to both. Results of an experiment that explored these possibilities are shown in Figure 9.4.

Figure 9.4A shows the position of the recording grid from which the response field in Figure 9.4B was derived. The bipolar stimulus configuration is shown in the schematic drawing of the superior temporal plane in Figure 9.4C. Like the results shown for another subject (see Fig. 9.2), the response field was confined to the posterior lateral STG and within the field there was a site where the polyphasic EP exhibited maximal amplitude (asterisk). Figure 9.4C illustrates the effects of shortening the interstimulus interval (ISI) on the waveform recorded from the site of maximal amplitude. At an ISI of 1000 ms, which corresponds to the 1/s-stimulus rate typically used in our mapping studies, the early onset deflection (arrow) followed by the usual triad of an early positive wave and later twin negative deflections, was evident. Reducing the ISI to 500 ms had little effect on the shape of the EP, but when the ISI was reduced to 200 ms a marked change in the waveform was observed. The early onset deflection and positive wave of the triad remained relatively unaffected, with a peak latency around 3.5 ms. However, the first of the successive negative deflections diminished in amplitude and lengthened in latency, whereas the amplitude of the second negative deflection was only marginally affected. A similar pattern was seen when the ISI was reduced even further, to 100 ms. The differential effect of changing stimulus rate on the response waveform suggests that these negative deflections arise from activation of different intracortical circuits, different afferent inputs, or some combination of the two.

The data presented so far provide evidence for a functional connection (or connections) between the putative site of AI on mesial HG and area PLST on the lateral surface of the STG. Histochemical cytoarchitectonic analyses (Chiry et al., 2003; Clarke & Rivier, 1998; Rivier & Clarke, 1997; Wallace et al., 2000) and functional imaging (Binder et al., 2000; Wessinger et al., 2001) have suggested a belt field in human that occupies a territory between the two, on the lateral aspect of HG adjacent to AI. We hypothesized that the functional connectivity between each of them and PLST would differ. We could test this hypothesis as the contacts positioned along the shaft of our depth electrode spanned the distance between mesial HG and the pial surface thereby allowing us to systematically stimulate successive sites in presumed AI and in the adjacent lateral cortex on HG while recording from the even more lateral PLST.

Data shown in Figure 9.4D were recorded from the same electrode location as the data presented in Figure 9.4C. With electrical stimulation of successively more lateral HG sites the response field on the posterior STG remained in evidence although the shape of the evoked waveform within it changed demonstrably. Stimulation of site A resulted in the familiar triad of a positive wave followed by twin negative deflections. With successive lateral shifts in stimulus location the latency of the first negative deflection shortened systematically. At this PLST recording site there was an average latency difference of 1.2 ms (from 9.4 to 8.2 ms) between the most mesial and most lateral stimulation sites. Furthermore, as the HG stimulus site was shifted successively to more lateral locations the amplitude of the second negative deflection became progressively smaller, until with the most lateral stimulation it was hardly in evidence. The rather abrupt reduction or disappearance of the second negative deflection in the waveform between stimulus sites B and C suggests that a functional boundary exists between auditory cortex on mesial HG and cortex located more laterally on HG on the supratemporal plane.

Summarizing these results, it appears that both negative deflections in the electrically evoked waveform arise from activating a cortico-cortical pathway, or pathways, originating in mesial HG. The more lateral HG cortex apparently contributes little to the second negative deflection, as this wave is essentially absent following stimulation of lateral HG sites. The first negative deflection is present regardless of the stimulus site. Its systematic decrease in latency with decreasing distance between stimulation and recording sites may suggests that we may have been stimulating axons of passage that originate in mesial HG and run within the white matter beneath the stimulating electrode. Changes shown in

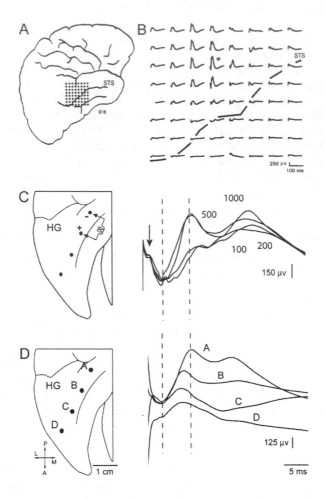

Fig. 9.4. Effects of changing electrical interstimulus interval and stimulus location on the waveform recorded at the site of maximal amplitude in the posterior lateral superior temporal auditory area (PLST). **A, B**. Grid position and response map on posterior lateral sperior temporal gyrus (STG) to mesial Heschl's gyrus (HG) stimulation at a stimulus rate of 1/s. Schematic diagrams in C and D, derived from horizontal MRI sections (see Fig. 9.1), show the sites on the surface of the superior temporal plane which when stimulated electrically resulted in the accompanying waveforms. Anterior-posterior and medial-lateral orientation are shown in D. **C**. Effect of changing interstimulus interval (ISI). Each of the four superimposed waveforms was obtained at the ISI shown on the waveform. HG stimulus location was constant at sites shown to the left. The arrow points to the onset of the evoked waveform. **D**. Effect of changing stimulus location on the evoked waveform. Each of the four superimposed waveforms was obtained by stimulating a different site along HG as indicated on the waveform. (Negative pole of the bipolar stimulus indicated on diagram of superior temporal plane.)

the evoked waveform to changes in interstimulus interval and stimulus site are robust and have been observed in several other subjects (Brugge et al., 2003).

A functional projection from PLST to HG

We also explored the possibility that PLST sends a projection to HG. This was done by stimulating electrically sites within PLST while recording the response evoked by that electrical stimulus at various sites along the depth electrode in HG. The major findings are shown for two subjects in Figure 9.5. The PLST stimulation sites illustrated in the left-hand panel were chosen to be at or near the site of maximal amplitude response to mesial HG electrical stimulation. In both subjects, the response maps to clicks (not shown) overlapped substantially the maps obtained by stimulation of mesial HG. To the right are schematic drawings of the superior temporal plane showing the recording sites within HG and the EPs recorded from each of them in response to PLST stimulation. In both subjects, PLST stimulation resulted in a polyphasic waveform having its greatest amplitude in the mesial half of HG. A major positive deflection occurred some 25–30 ms after electrical stimulation followed by a large negative wave around 60–70 ms. This positive-negative complex was in some cases preceded by a smaller negative deflection at about 12 ms. The overall amplitude of this waveform complex increased mediolaterally until a transition zone was reached within which the waveform altered its shape and diminished substantially in amplitude. An arrow marks the site of this transition. The results of these experiments indicate that area PLST projects functionally, though not uniformly, over most, if not all, of the length of HG. Furthermore, we interpret the transition in the shape of the evoked waveform that occurs along HG to mean that a functional boundary was crossed between auditory cortex on mesial HG and an auditory belt situated more laterally on HG.

DISCUSSION

PLST is organized according to spatio-temporal response fields

A circumscribed area on the posterior lateral STG (area PLST) of human is activated by a wide range of acoustic signals, including clicks, noise, tones, and CV tokens. Activity described here takes the form of an event-related slow wave potential recorded from an array of electrodes on the brain surface. It is generally accepted that a voltage waveform recorded at an electrode on the brain surface reflects the summation of potentials generated by ionic current flowing within the cortex and mainly beneath the recording electrode. These currents are created by the invasion of stimulus-evoked input arriving over one or more afferent pathways, which may in turn activate local cortical circuits. This waveform varies in magnitude and polarity over time depending on the timing, strength and location of afferent input and subsequently on the timing, strength,

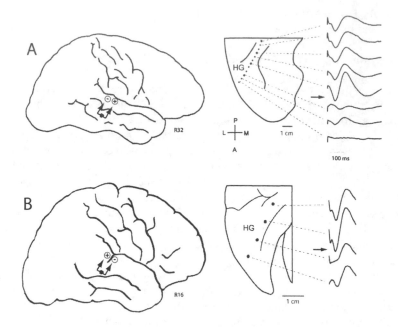

Fig. 9.5. Functional projection from the posterior lateral superior temporal auditory field (PLST) to Heschl's gyrus (HG). The figure shows waveforms evoked along HG by bipolar electrical stimulation of the most acoustically active site on PLST for two subjects (**A,B**). Location and polarity of bipolar stimulation are shown on a diagram of the lateral surface of the mapped hemisphere. Arrow points to site along HG where the evoked waveform changed abruptly. High impedance contacts are represented by small filled circles, low impedance sites by large filled circles. See legend of Figure 9.4 for explanation of diagrams of superior temporal plane.

and location of these synaptic current sinks and sources (see Arezzo et al., 1986; Mitzdorf, 1985, 1991, 1994; Mitzdorf & Singer, 1978; Vaughan & Arezzo, 1988). A spatio-temporal response field may thus be interpreted as the surface representation of underlying ionic currents distributed in both time and space.

The evoked waveform within PLST was found to be sensitive to both the nature of the acoustic signal and locus of activation within the field. At any given recording site the EP elicited by each of the four classes of acoustic stimuli used differed in its wave shape. The response fields encompassing these stimulus-dependent waveforms overlapped spatially to the extent that they could be considered essentially coextensive, at least at the moderate sound levels used. Hence, within the limits of spatial resolution of our recording grids we found no evidence for a spatial segregation within PLST of activity related to these stimulus classes. Instead we found that functional segregation in the representation of these (and other) stimuli may be achieved by expressed differences in spatially overlapping spatio-temporal patterns of presumed synaptic activity within this cortical field. The distribution of evoked activity that defines area PLST can be described in terms of space and time, and PLST can, thus, be characterized as being organized functionally as a stimulus-related 'spatio-temporal response field.' The fact that different spatio-temporal patterns are expressed over the same area of cortex when different sounds are presented also suggests that many of the same neural elements within PLST actively participate in processing wide range of acoustic stimuli, albeit in different spatio-temporal sequences.

This type of functional representation of sound requires no cortical 'place' mechanism for stimulus-related segregation. Nor does it imply a 'hierarchical' assembly of afferent inputs. Indeed, it is quite reasonable to suggest that the spatio-temporal patterns expressed within PLST are, in part, due to the spatio-temporal convergence of afferent input from different sources. One (or more) of those sources appears to be auditory cortex on HG.

HG and PLST are functionally connected

Electrical stimulation of HG results in polyphasic evoked activity on posterolateral STG, within 50 ms of stimulus onset. The electrically induced response field overlaps the acoustic response field that defines area PLST. The most robust and complex waveform results from stimulation of sites within about the mesial ½ of HG, the presumed site of AI in human. These results provide *prima facie* evidence for a functional projection from auditory cortex on HG to an associational auditory cortex, PLST, on the lateral surface of the STG in human. This finding is consistent with earlier electrophysiological results in non-human primates (Bailey et al., 1943, Bignall, 1969; Sugar et al., 1948; Ward et al., 1946). Liegeois Chauvel et al. (1991) reported that electrical stimulation of mesial HG in human evoked activity on laterally adjacent HG cortex as well as on the planum temporale. These are areas that subsequently have been identified both anatomically and functionally as part of an auditory belt (Chiry et al., 2003; Clarke & Rivier, 1998; Rivier & Clarke, 1997; Talavage et al., 2000; Wallace et al., 2002; Wessinger et al., 2001) that surrounds an auditory core.

A waveform complex composed of an initial positive deflection followed by one or more negative waves is typically recorded on the posterior lateral STG in response to electrical stimulation of presumed AI. The shape of the evoked waveform, including the magnitude, number, and latency of the deflections, depends on the recording site on STG and the rate of electrical stimulation. The earliest deflection we detected with any consistency evoked by mesial HG stimulation was a surface positive wave having an average onset latency of around 2 ms and an average peak latency ranging across subjects from about 3–6 ms. We interpret this early positive wave as representing a deep sink with a superficial source created by the first invading afferent volley evoked by mesial HG stimulation. This interpretation is consistent with what is known of auditory cortico-cortical projections to layers III and IV in owl monkey (Fitzpatrick &

Imig, 1980) and with current source density profiles of auditory cortex in rhesus monkey (Steinschneider et al., 1992). We may speculate that the later negative waves represent shallow cortical depolarizations within supragranular layers. These results would suggest that the two negative waves arise over separate circuits. If this is the case then the proposed convergent input is segregated temporally, as the differences in peak latency would imply. Whether there is spatial segregation as well is something that is yet to be determined.

From latency measurements of the major deflections in the waveform complex, from estimates of the length of axons between mesial HG and PLST, and from making certain assumptions about the caliber (Bishop & Smith, 1964; Tardif & Clarke, 2001) and conduction velocity of cortico-cortical axons (Waxman & Swadlow, 1977), we tentatively conclude that the timing of the initial positive deflection is compatible with an indirect cortico-cortical connection with a possible intervening synaptic delay in adjacent belt fields. This does not exclude the possibility that a component of this functional projection may be direct. Interpreting the sources of input that result in the later negative deflections is even less straightforward. The latency of the first of the negative wave (8.4–13.5 ms) could be accounted for by input arriving over the smallest diameter cortico-cortical axons with or without intervening synaptic delay and ending in superficial cortical layers where they would create a superficial current sink. Alternatively, both negative deflections could be accounted for by later-arriving afferent input arriving over longer interhemispheric or cortico-thalamo-cortical pathways that are likely activated by mesial HG stimulation. If in the human the HG cortex lateral to presumed AI projects preferentially to more anterior sites on STG as it does in monkey (Hackett et al., 1998) we may not have seen it as we often did not have grids in that location and even when we did we usually focused the experiments on the posterior recording sites. If this turns out to be the case, then the robust PLST response to stimulation of mesial HG may be either the result of a direct projection from AI to PLST or an indirect one with synaptic relay in a belt area that we did not stimulate. One of the posterior belt fields identified histochemically by Rivier and Clarke (1997) and Wallace et al. (2000) – perhaps their field LA on the planum temporale – would be a candidate for such an intermediate synaptic station, which is consistent with the results of Liegeois-Chauvel et al. (1991) showing that electrical stimulation of mesial HG evokes a response on the planum temporale. We might speculate further that a distinct area situated lateral to LA – referred to as area STA by Rivier and Clarke (1997) – may correspond, at least in part, to our area PLST.

We found that stimulation of sites within the response field on posterior lateral STG evoked responses all along HG. These results are in accord with the early observations of Bailey et al. (1943) in chimpanzee and Sugar et al. (1948) in rhesus monkey that strychnization of area 22 causes spikes to appear in the primary auditory cortex. In mesial HG, the waveform was characterized by an early small negativity followed by a large positive wave having a peak latency around 20–25 ms. These latencies are compatible with finding in monkey of a polysynaptic pathway from PLST to mesial HG and of a paucity of connections from the lateral association area back to the primary auditory cortex (Hackett et al., 1998a; Pandya et al., 1969). There was an abrupt change in the waveform around the middle of HG. This may have signaled the presence of a transition zone between an auditory belt and presumed AI. These results taken together suggest that the pathways making up the PLST-HG projection are fundamentally different from those that underlie the HG-PLST circuits.

Further functional studies that include more of the supratemporal plane and the lateral STG are underway to clarify where PLST is to be placed in a serial processing stream emerging from the auditory core. This new information will also be critical in determining the extent to which the anatomical framework of auditory cortical organization derived from studies in monkey can be successfully applied to the human.

ACKNOWLEDGMENTS

Supported by NIH Grants DC04290, DC00657, DC00116, HD03352 and by the Hoover Fund and Carver Trust.

REFERENCES

Arezzo, J.C., Vaughan, H.G., Jr., Kraut, M.A., Steinschneider, M., & Legatt, A.D. (1986). Intracranial generators of event related potentials in the monkey. In R.Q. Cracco & I. Bodis-Wollner (Eds.), Evoked Potential Frontiers of Clinical Neuroscience (pp. 174–189). New York: Alan R. Liss.

Bailey, P., Von Bonin, G., Carol, H.W., & McCulloch, W.S. (1943). Functional organization of temporal lobe of monkey (Maccaca Mulatta) and chimpanzee (Pan Satyrus). Journal of Neurophysiology, 6, 121–128.

Bignall, K.E. (1969). Bilateral temporofrontal projections in the squirrel monkey: origin, distribution and pathways. Brain Research, 13, 319–327.

Bignall, K.E., & Imbert, M. (1969). Polysensory and cortico-cortical projections to frontal lobe of squirrel and rhesus monkeys. Electroencephalography and Clinical Neurophysiology, 26, 206–215.

Binder, J.R., Frost, J.A., Hammeke, T.A., Bellgowan, P.S., Springer, J.A., Kaufman, J.N., & Possing, E.T. (2000). Human temporal lobe activation by speech and nonspeech sounds. Cerebral Cortex, 10, 512–528.

Bishop, G.H., & Smith, J.M. (1964). The sizes of nerve fibers supplying cerebral cortex. Experimental Neurology, 9, 481–501.

Bremer, F., Bonnet, V., & Terzuolo, C. (1954). Etude electrophysiologiaque des aires auditives corticales chez le chat. Archives Internationale Physiologie, 62, 390–428.

Brodmann, K. (1909). Vergleichende Lokalisationslehre der Großhirnrinde. Leipzig: J.A. Barth.

Brown, P.B., Smithline, L., & Halpern, B. (1973). Stimulation techniques. In P.B. Brown, B.W. Maxfield, & H. Moraff (Eds.), Electronics for Neurobiologists (pp. 300–373). Cambridge, MA: MIT Press.

Brugge, J.F., Volkov, I.O., Garell, P.C., Reale, R.A., & Howard, M.A. (2003).

Functional connections between auditory cortex on Heschl's gyrus and on the lateral superior temporal gyrus in humans. Journal of Neurophysiology, 90, 3750–3763.

Chiry, O., Tardif, E., Magistretti, P.J., & Clarke, S. (2003). Patterns of calcium-binding proteins support parallel and hierarchical organization of human auditory areas. European Journal of Neuroscience, 17, 397–410.

Clarke, S., & Rivier, F. (1998). Compartments within human primary auditory cortex: Evidence from cytochrome oxidase and acetylcholinesterase staining. European Journal of Neuroscience, 10, 741–745.

Downman, C.B., Woolsey, C.N., & Lende, R.A. (1960). Auditory areas I, II and Ep: Cochlear representation, afferent paths and interconnections. Bulletin of the Johns Hopkins Hospital, 106, 127–142.

Fitzpatrick, K.A., & Imig, T.J. (1980). Auditory cortico-cortical connections in the owl monkey. The Journal of Comparative Neurology, 192, 589–610.

Galaburda, A.M., & Sanides, F. (1980). Cytoarchitectonic organization of the human auditory cortex. The Journal of Comparative Neurology, 190, 597–610.

Galuske, R.A., Schlote, W., Bratzke, H., & Singer, W. (2000). Interhemispheric asymmetries of the modular structure in human temporal cortex. Science, 289, 1946–1949.

Galuske, R.A.W., Schuhmann, A., Schlote, W., Bratzke, H., & Singer, W. (1999). Interareal connections in the human auditory cortex. NeuroImage, 9, S994.

Hackett, T.A., Preuss, T.M., & Kaas, J.H. (2001). Architectonic identification of the core region in auditory cortex of macaques, chimpanzees, and humans. The Journal of Comparative Neurology, 441, 197–222.

Hackett, T.A., Stepniewska, I., & Kaas, J.H. (1998). Subdivisions of auditory cortex and ipsilateral cortical connections of the parabelt auditory cortex in macaque monkeys. The Journal of Comparative Neurology, 394, 475–495.

Howard, M.A., Volkov, I.O., Abbas, P.J., Damasio, H., Ollendieck, M.C., & Granner, M.A. (1996a). A chronic microelectrode investigation of the tonotopic organization of human auditory cortex. Brain Research, 724, 260–264.

Howard, M.A., Volkov, I.O., Granner, M.A., Damasio, H.M., Ollendieck, M.C., & Bakken, H.E. (1996). A hybrid clinical-research depth electrode for acute and chronic in vivo microelectrode recording of human brain neurons. Technical note. Journal of Neurosurgery, 84, 129–132.

Howard, M.A., Volkov, I.O., Mirsky, R., Garell, P.C., Noh, M.D., Granner, M., Damasio, H., Steinschneider, M., Reale, R.A., Hind, J.E., & Brugge, J.F. (2000). Auditory cortex on the posterior superior temporal gyrus of human cerebral cortex. The Journal of Comparative Neurology, 416, 76–92.

Imbert, M., Bignall, K.E., & Buser, P. (1966). Neocortical interconnections in the cat. Journal of Neurophysiology, 29, 382–395.

Kaas, J.H., & Hackett, T.A. (1998). Subdivisions of auditory cortex and levels of processing in primates. Audiology and Neurootology, 3, 73–85.

Kaas, J.H., Hackett, T.A., & Tramo, M.J. (1999). Auditory processing in primate cerebral cortex. Current Opinion in Neurobiology, 9, 164-170.

Liegeois-Chauvel, C., Musolino, A., & Chauvel, P. (1991). Localization of the primary auditory area in man. Brain, 114, 139–151.

Mitzdorf, U. (1985). Current source-density method and application in cat cerebral cortex: Investigation of evoked potential and EEG phenomena. Physiological Reviews, 65, 37–100.

Mitzdorf, U. (1991). Physiological sources of evoked potentials. Electroencephalography and Clinical Neurophysiology (Suppl.), 42, 47–57.

Mitzdorf, U. (1994). Properties of cortical generators of event-related potentials. Pharmacopsychiatry, 27, 49–51.

Mitzdorf, U., & Singer, W. (1978). Prominent excitatory pathways in the cat visual cortex (A 17 and A 18): A current source density analysis of electrically evoked potentials. Experimental Brain Research, 33, 371–394.

Morosan, P., Rademacher, J., Schleicher, A., Amunts, K., Schormann, T., & Zilles, K. (2001). Human primary auditory cortex: cytoarchitectonic subdivisions and mapping into a spatial reference system. NeuroImage, 13, 684–701.

Nunez, P. L., & Pilgreen, K. L. (1991). The spline-Laplacian in clinical neurophysiology: A method to improve EEG spatial resolution. Journal of Clinical Neurophysiology, 8, 397–413.

Rademacher, J., Caviness, V., Steinmetz, H., & Galaburda, A. (1993). Topographical variation of the human primary cortices: Implications for neuroimaging, brain mapping and neurobiology. Cerebral Cortex, 3, 313–329.

Rademacher, J., Morosan, P., Schormann, T., Schleicher, A., Werner, C., Freund, H.J., & Zilles, K. (2001). Probabilistic mapping and volume measurement of human primary auditory cortex. NeuroImage, 13, 669–683.

Rauschecker, J.P., Tian, B., & Hauser, M. (1995). Processing of complex sounds in the macaque non-primary auditory cortex. Science, 268, 111–114.

Rauschecker, J.P., Tian, B., Pons, T., & Mishkin, M. (1997). Serial and parallel processing in rhesus monkey auditory cortex. The Journal of Comparative Neurology, 382, 89–103.

Rauschecker, J.P. (1998). Parallel processing in the auditory cortex of primates. Audiology and Neurootology, 3, 86-103.

Rivier, F., & Clarke, S. (1997). Cytochrome oxidase, acetylcholinesterase, and NADPH-diaphorase staining in human supratemporal and insular cortex: Evidence for multiple auditory areas. NeuroImage, 6, 288–304.

Steinschneider, M., Tenke, C.E., Schroeder, C.E., Javitt, D.C., Simpson, G.V., Arezzo, J.C., & Vaughn, H.G. (1992). Cellular generators of the cortical auditory evoked potential initial component. Electroencephalography and Clinical Neurophysiology, 84, 196–200.

Sugar, O., French, J.D., & Chusid, J.G. (1948) Corticocortical connections of the superior surface of the temporal operculum in the monkey (Macaca mulatta). Journal of Neurophysiology, 11, 175–184.

Talavage, T.M., Ledden, P.J., Benson, R.R., Rosen, B.R., & Melcher, J.R. (2000). Frequency-dependent responses exhibited by multiple regions in human auditory cortex. Hearing Research, 150, 225–244.

Tardif, E., & Clarke, S. (2001). Intrinsic connectivity of human auditory areas: a tracing study with DiI. European Journal of Neuroscience, 13, 1045-1050.

Vaughan, H.G., Jr., & Arezzo, J.C. (1988). The neural basis of event-related potentials. In T.W. Picton (Ed.), Human Event-related Potentials (pp. 45–96). Amsterdam: Elsevier.

von Economo, C., & Koskinas, G.N. (1925). Die Cytoarchitektonik der Hirnrinde des erwachsenen Menschen. Berlin: Julius Springer.

Wallace, M.N., Johnston, P.W., & Palmer, A.R. (2002). Histochemical identification of cortical areas in the auditory region of the human brain. Experimental Brain Research, 143, 499–508.

Ward, A.A., Peden, J.K., & Sugar, O. (1946). Cortico-cortical connections in the monkey with special reference to area 6. Journal of Neurophysiology, 9, 453–462.

Waxman, S.G., & Swadlow, H.A. (1977). The conduction properties of axons in central

162 *Brugge, Volkov, Reale, Garell, Kawasaki, Oya, Li, Howard III*

white matter. Progress in Neurobiology, 8, 297–324.
Wessinger, C.M., Vanmeter, J., Tian, B., Van Lare, J., Pekar, J., & Rauschecker, J.P.
(2001). Hierarchical organization of the human auditory cortex revealed by
functional magnetic resonance imaging. Journal of Cognitive Neuroscience, 13, 1–7.
Yeomans, J.S. (1990). Principles of Brain Stimulation. Oxford: Oxford University Press.

10. VOICE PROCESSING IN HUMAN AUDITORY CORTEX

Pascal Belin, Robert J. Zatorre

The human voice is the most important sound category our auditory system has to analyze. How the wealth of information it contains – linguistic as well as paralinguistic – is processed by the auditory cortex is a complex, important, and still unresolved issue. In this chapter we review recent neuroimaging studies that suggest the involvement in voice processing of several parts of the superior temporal sulcus (STS) bilaterally. The significance of these "voice-selective" activations, as well as their possible functional roles, is discussed hereafter.

THE HUMAN VOICE: AN "AUDITORY FACE"

The voice carries speech and its infinite number of possible meanings, and this makes us a unique species. Yet, the voice is more than "simply" speech; it can also be considered as an "auditory face," also carrying a wealth of information on the identity and the affective state of the speaker: We can often easily tell the gender and approximate age of a person simply by hearing a short voice sample, as for a face briefly viewed, and interjections such as laughs or cries, although they are not speech, obviously contain rich information on a person's emotional state comparable to the facial expressions of emotion.

We are all experts at processing voice. Our auditory system enables us to perform an exquisitely fine analysis of the vocal signal, and to rapidly and effortlessly extract several types of information it carries: speech information, as well as non-speech, speaker-related information. Speech perception has been extensively studied using various techniques and methodologies, and the neuronal organization of the parallel and distributed network of cortical areas involved in speech perception is increasingly well understood (Samson et al.,

2001; Scott & Johnsrude, 2003; Zatorre & Binder, 2000). In contrast, little is known on the neuronal bases of "voice perception," that is, our ability to perceive the non-linguistic information contained in these auditory faces.

Does voice involve a specific network of cortical regions?

This question arises quite naturally given the complexity of the neuronal computations involved in voice analysis and identification, and is supported by several considerations.

First of all, some of our auditory abilities apply *only* to sounds of voice, such as telling the gender of a speaker, or his/her approximate age, for instance; sounds other than vocal sounds do not bear such information. Speaker recognition can be viewed as just a particular case of the auditory system's ability to recognize auditory objects, but it is made particularly difficult by the highly similar physical structure of vocal sounds compared to other sounds of our auditory world.

Second, the ability to extract identity- and emotion-related information from voice is present very early in life, long before the linguistic message carried by voice can be understood, perhaps even in-utero (DeCasper & Fifer, 1980; Gerhardt & Abrams, 2000).

Finally, unlike speech perception, we share voice perception abilities with other species. For example, many species of mammals are able to recognize conspecific individuals based on their vocalizations (Rendall et al., 1998), and this ability plays an important role in survival, especially for social species such as apes. Thus, it seems quite likely that our varied and highly complex voice perception abilities, deeply rooted in evolutionary history, are made possible by a specific neuronal machinery.

Voice processing and face processing

The question about voice-dedicated cortical networks appears even more pertinent if one looks at a very dynamic field in visual sciences, the research on face perception. Cellular recordings in non-human primates have shown the existence of face-selective cells along the superior temporal sulcus (STS) that respond preferentially to faces compared to other visual objects and are selective to specific viewing orientations (Perrett et al., 1992). Neuroimaging experiments in humans have yielded nicely converging results, with evidence of face-selective regions in the fusiform gyrus and posterior STS (Haxby et al., 2000; Kanwisher et al., 1999; Puce et al., 1995). According to these studies, face perception and recognition is subserved by an extensive network of cortical areas that includes regions thought to be dedicated exclusively to face processing, although this point is still a hot matter of debate (Gauthier et al., 2000).

Interestingly, the highly complex computational problems posed by voice perception are very similar in nature to those posed to the visual system by face perception – differentiation of highly similar physical structures, extraction of invariants in ever-changing stimuli – which suggests that evolution may have found a similar solution to these problems. This observation, combined to the fact that the basic principles of cortical organization (columns, topography) are similar in visual and auditory cortex (Mountcastle, 1997), again suggests that voice perception, as face perception, could be subserved by a dedicated network of cortical areas.

What is the current evidence for cortical areas specialized in voice processing?

Studies in non-human primates have shown that the auditory cortex, particularly in the left hemisphere, is necessary for discriminating conspecific vocalizations (Heffner & Heffner, 1986). Numerous electrophysiological recording studies in monkeys have evidenced responses to conspecific vocalizations in primary auditory cortex (A1; Wang et al., 1995) as well as lateral belt neurons (Tian et al., 2001). However, in most cases these responses have not been compared to those elicited by other equally-complex, non-vocal environmental sounds. Thus it is difficult to evaluate the degree of specificity of this vocalization-sensitive response.

In humans, most of the research on the neural bases of auditory cognitive abilities has focused on speech perception or on music perception, two (arguably) uniquely human abilities. Only little research has focused on the representation of non-linguistic voice perception abilities. Assal and colleagues (1976) were the first to assess the effects of brain lesions on a voice discrimination task, and their results suggested a more important role of the right hemisphere in this task (Assal et al., 1976). Van Lancker and Canter (1982) confirmed this finding by examining the recognition of famous faces and voices in brain-damaged patients: they found that impairments at both the face or voice recognition tasks were more prevalent after lesion to the right hemisphere, and introduced the term "phonagnosia" for pathological voice recognition (Van Lancker & Canter, 1982). They later found a dissociation between discrimination of unfamiliar voices and recognition of known voices, similar to the one known for faces (Van Lancker & Kreiman, 1987).

Thus, these clinical studies suggest that voice perception abilities might rely on a specific neural substrate, and emphasize the dissociation with speech perception which was essentially normal in most patients with a right hemispheric lesion. Unfortunately, these early studies did not provide much neuroanatomical detail, and interest in the neural bases of non-linguistic voice perception abilities seemed to fade, until the recent appearance of neuroimaging techniques.

CORTICAL REGIONS SENSITIVE TO VOICE?

Functional magnetic resonance imaging (fMRI) appeared only a decade ago, but soon became the reference technique in neuroimaging studies: It rapidly prevailed over positron emission tomography (PET) because of its lower cost, greater availability and better signal-to-noise ratio, allowing robust, non-invasive measure of cortical activation in single subjects in a one-hour session (Turner & Jezzard, 1994).

FMRI is based on the rapid acquisition of series of successive brain volumes measuring blood oxygenation (the blood oxygenation level-dependent signal, or "BOLD" signal), an indirect index of brain activity. An important drawback for functional studies of the auditory system, though, is the very loud (> 100 dB sound pressure level, SPL) acquisition noise of the scanner, due to mechanical constraints on rapidly-switching gradient coils for ultra-rapid image acquisition (echo-planar imaging). Researchers have devised different methods to circumvent the noise artifact. One efficient method is the "sparse sampling" method, based on a long interval between successive volume acquisitions (time of repetition TR = 10 s), that ensures low contamination of brain images by scanning noise-induced activity, and allows presentation of stimuli on a silent background (Belin et al., 1999; Hall et al., 1999). This method has been used in all experiments described hereafter, except the study on species-specificity of voice processing. In that study, an event-related design was used, involving presentation of auditory stimuli at about 5-seconds intervals, with continuous brain image acquisition implying a constant background noise.

Vocal vs. non-vocal sounds

We used fMRI to investigate the question of "voice-selective areas" in the cerebral cortex. We first asked whether cortical regions could be found in which neuronal activity is greater when processing sounds of voice than when processing other sounds. Eight normal volunteers were scanned while they listened passively to a variety of sound stimuli divided in two basic categories based on their "voiceness": *vocal* sounds vs. *non-vocal* sounds.

The vocal sounds consisted of speech sounds (words, connected speech in several languages) produced by a large variety of speakers, as well as a variety of non-speech vocal sounds such as emotional interjections (laughs, cries, screams, etc.), coughing, or sneezing sounds. We aimed to stimulate subjects with the largest possible variety of sounds that would share the single common property of being produced by a human vocal tract. We also included sounds that were unequivocally produced by a voice with vibrating vocal folds; unvoiced vocal sounds such as whispering or whistling were excluded for a more conservative comparison.

The non-vocal sounds consisted of a variety of mechanical, industrial or environmental sounds from various sources, and were matched to the vocal sounds in number of sources and overall energy (RMS). Stimuli were arranged in 20-seconds blocks each composed of 12 sounds from a same category, and presented in a pseudo-random order with a 10-seconds silent inter-block interval. There were 21 vocal blocks and 21 non-vocal blocks (252 sounds in each category). As shown in Figure 10.1a, brain images were acquired at 10-seconds intervals – synchronized with the beginning of the blocks – for a scanning time of 21 minutes (Belin et al., 2000).

The comparison of images acquired during sound stimulation to those acquired after a silent interval revealed in each subject, as expected, a large pattern of auditory activation extending anteriorly and posteriorly along the superior temporal gyrus (STG), with maximal activation located in most subjects along the posterior transverse sulcus delimitating the posterior wall of Heschl's gyrus. Of greater interest was the comparison of images acquired during stimulation with the two categories of sounds: We found in each subject focal regions in which activity was significantly greater for the vocal sounds compared to the non-vocal sounds. Importantly, no region in any subject showed greater response to the non-vocal sounds (Belin et al., 2000).

Figure 10.1b illustrates the variability in the localization of this voice-sensitive response in three subjects. In some subjects the voice-responsive areas were unilateral, for some other significant foci were present in both hemispheres. In some subjects the voice-sensitive foci were quite anterior, in some cases they were posterior to Heschl's gyrus. An important regularity emerged from this apparent variability, however: Peak responses were in most cases (7 out of 8 subjects) located along the upper bank of the superior temporal sulcus (STS). Figure 10.1c shows the group-average of the vocal > non-vocal contrast: Several voice-sensitive regions can be found in the STG, with several peaks located close the upper bank of the STS, posteriorly to Heschl's gyrus and extending up to planum temporale on the left side, as well as anteriorly towards the temporal pole. Peaks of highest significance were located in both left and right hemisphere in the anterior part of the STS (Talairach coordinates: left: x = −62, y = −14, z = 0; right: x = 63, y = −13, z = −1).

Two features of this group-average map of "voice-sensitivity" are worth noticing. First, areas of significant voice-sensitive activation were located outside Heschl's gyrus, suggesting that primary auditory cortex responded similarly on average to the two sound categories. Thus, the diversity of sounds used (each of the 252 sounds in each category came from a different speaker/source) as well as the energy normalization appeared successful in equating the two categories in low-level acoustic features, yielding comparable response at the level of primary auditory cortex. Second, the group-average activation was greater and more extensive in the right hemisphere which is somewhat counter-intuitive considering the classical left-hemisphere dominance for speech.

In sum, whereas most of auditory cortex – including A1 – responded equally to the vocal and non-vocal sounds, discrete cortical areas were found in each subject, mostly located along the STS, with stronger response to the vocal sounds.

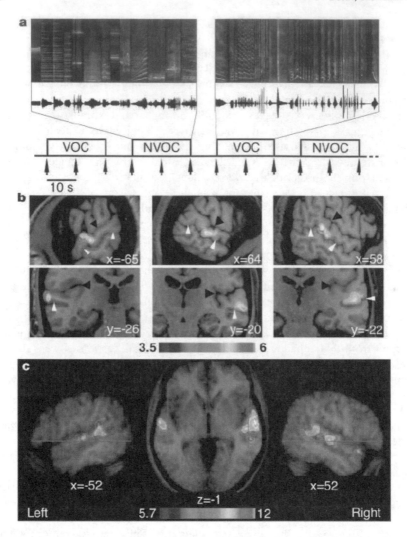

Fig. 10.1. a) Experimental paradigm. Spectrograms (0–4 kHz) and amplitude waveforms of examples of auditory stimuli. Vocal (VOC) and non-vocal (NVOC) stimuli are presented in 20-s blocks with 10-s silent inter-block intervals, while scanning (arrows) occurs at regular 10-s intervals. **b)** Individual voice-sensitive activations. Maxima of vocal and non-vocal activation maps from three subjects are indicated in grayscale (t-value) on anatomical images in sagittal (upper panel) and coronal (lower panel) orientations (x and y: Talairach coordinates). Arrows indicate relative positions of the Sylvian fissure (black arrows) and of the superior temporal sulcus (white arrows). **c)** Voice-sensitive activation in the group average. Regions with significantly ($p < 0.001$) higher response to human voices than to energy-matched non-vocal stimuli are shown in grayscale (t-value) on an axial slice of the group-average MR image (center, Talairach coordinate $z = -1$) and on sagittal slices of each hemisphere (sides, Talairach coordinates $x = -52$ and $x = 52$).

SELECTIVITY OF VOICE-SENSITIVE ACTIVATIONS

Before being able to interpret those discrete areas of voice-enhanced activation as evidence for voice-selective neuronal computations in auditory cortex, several alternative explanations need to be ruled out. The above pattern of results could reflect genuine voice-selectivity, but it could also reflect more subtle differences between the vocal and the non-vocal sounds that were used, other than "voiceness." We performed additional experiments to test the selectivity of the voice-sensitive response, in which we used several categories of control sounds.

Scrambled voices and amplitude-modulated noise

Two categories of "acoustic" control sounds were used: amplitude-modulated noise (AM-noise) and "scrambled sounds." AM-noise has shown its effectiveness as a control sound in previous neuroimaging experiments (Zatorre et al., 1994) and is obtained by modulating white noise by the amplitude envelope of the original stimulus. It results in a waveform very similar in shape to the original stimulus, but with a nearly flat spectrum (Fig. 10.2). "Scrambled sounds" have been devised for the purpose of this experiment, inspired from the "scrambled objects" or "scrambled faces" widely used as control stimuli in vision research (e.g., Puce et al., 1995). Scrambled sounds were obtained by scrambling the sound spectrogram within each temporal window (vertical band): A Fourier transform is performed and phase and amplitude components in the frequency domain are randomly intermixed in each window, and re-transformed in the time domain using an inverse Fourier transform (Belin et al., 2002). This results in a sound with same energy and envelope – provided the size of the window used in the Fourier transforms is small enough, that is, about 10–20 ms and composed of the same low level acoustic features as the original sound (Fig. 10.2), but totally unrecognizable and sounding like flowing water. These two control sound categories had relatively preserved temporal structure, but a much degraded spectral structure. They will thus allow to test whether the pattern of results of Experiment 1 can be explained mostly by the temporal structure of the vocal sounds.

Control for spectral distribution of energy was obtained by frequency filtering. Both vocal and non-vocal sound were passed through band-pass filters, one keeping only low frequencies (center frequency: 200 Hz, bandwidth: 50 Hz), and another keeping higher frequencies (center frequency: 1600 Hz, bandwidth: 200 Hz). This allowed to obtain, in each of these two cases, filtered vocal and non-vocal sounds with very similar average spectral distribution (Belin et al., 2000). Thus, any difference observed in cerebral response to the filtered vocal vs. non-vocal sounds could not be due to differences in average spectral distribution. Additionally, these filters were chosen so that they would keep frequencies principally reflecting the contribution of the source (vocal fold vibration) for low frequencies, versus the filter (supralaryngeal vocal tract) for

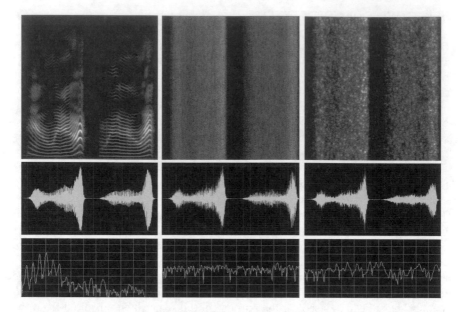

Fig. 10.2. Scrambled voices and amplitude-modulated noise. Original voice stimulus (left column), amplitude-modulated noise (middle column), and scrambled voice (right column). **Upper row:** Spectrograms (abscissa: 0–1900 ms; ordinate: 0–11025 Hz). **Middle row:** Amplitude waveform (arbitrary units). **Lower row:** Short-term Fourier transform at t = 800 ms (abscissa: 0–11025 Hz; ordinate: 0–96 dB). Note the similar amplitude waveforms of the two control sounds, but very different spectral profiles.

middle frequencies, thus allowing to evaluate the respective contribution of these two main acoustic components of vocal sounds on the cortical response.

Bells and human non-vocal sounds

More "psychological" control sound categories were also used. One category consisted of a collection of varied sounds from one homogeneous category: bell sounds. Indeed, whereas the vocal sounds used in the first experiments could all be classified within one category – sounds of human voice – it was not the case with the non-vocal sounds that were composed of sounds from several different categories: musical sounds, natural sounds, mechanical sounds, and so on. The issue of level of categorization is still a much debated one in vision research, and it has been proposed that the "face-selective" areas identified in visual cortex might in fact be involved in fine-level categorization at the subordinate level of any object category (e.g., a face among other faces, or a chair among other chairs) rather than really dedicated to face processing (Gauthier et al., 2000). Thus, it seemed important to use a sound category similar to the vocal sounds used in the first experiment, in the sense of presenting many various exemplars of a same sound category, bells or voices. Another control category consisted of human non-vocal sounds, that is, sounds that were clearly recognizable as produced by humans but not produced with the vocal tract, such as footsteps, handclapping, and so on. This sound category was included to test the hypothesis that the voice-sensitive areas observed in the first experiment might in fact be responsive to any sound of human origin, vocal or not.

These different categories of control sounds were used to probe the selectivity of the voice-sensitive activation. Again, subjects were scanned while passively listening to blocks of auditory stimuli from a single category separated by 10-s silent intervals. Comparison of BOLD signal changes induced by the different sound categories was performed at the cortical locations yielding maximal voice-sensitive activation in each hemisphere in Experiment 1.

A clear pattern emerged: in both left and right voice-sensitivity maxima, the response to vocal sounds was found to be significantly ($p < 0.001$) greater than to AM-noise, scrambled voices, bell sounds, and human non-vocal sounds. Additionally, the greater response to vocal sounds compared to non-vocal sounds was preserved even after frequency filtering preserving low or middle frequencies (Belin et al., 2000). Thus, the enhanced response to voice was maintained through comparison with a number of control non-vocal sounds.

The smaller response to each control category also allowed to rule out possible explanations for the voice-sensitive activation. The presence of specific temporal modulations in the amplitude envelope of the vocal sounds was not sufficient to induce this activity, as those were conserved in the scrambled voices and AM noise. Similarly, specific frequency components more present in vocal sounds compared to non-vocal sounds could not account for all of the enhanced response to voice since it was preserved after frequency filtering that equated vocal and non-vocal stimuli in average spectral distribution.

On a more cognitive level, the reduced response to human non-vocal sounds shows that the voice-sensitive response did not generalize to human sounds of non-vocal origin. It does probably not reflect discrimination and categorization at a subordinate level within a sound category, or comparable activation would then have been expected with another homogeneous sounds category, bells.

Thus, neuronal activity in anterior STS regions appears not only to be sensitive to sounds of voice, but also highly selective. It responded to a combination of acoustic features – temporal modulation, frequency components in the low and middle frequency range – characteristic of voice, each of which appearing to have lead to significant activation compared to silence. However, it is only when all these features were combined in a true vocal stimulus that maximal activation was observed. An interesting follow-up experiment will use vocal synthesizers to independently manipulate the most relevant acoustic features of vocal signals – frequency of phonation, formant structure, breathiness, harshness, and so on. – to evaluate their respective importance and elucidate the probably complex and non-linear interaction mechanisms that lead to the enhanced response to voices. The experiments described in the next section involve several, more natural categories of vocal sounds, from non-human vocalizations to speech.

RESPONSE OF VOICE-SENSITIVE CORTEX: FROM ANIMAL VOCALIZATIONS TO HUMAN SPEECH

The above experiments contrasted the cortical response to vocal sounds and to several categories of acoustical and psychological control sounds. They clearly showed that in each subject, discrete regions of auditory cortex, mostly located along the STS, respond maximally to sounds of voice. The next question is: How do these regions respond to stimulation with different categories of vocal sounds? Are the voice-selective areas equally activated by human speech, animal vocalizations, or human non-speech emotional vocalizations?

Speech vs. non-speech

In one experiment, subjects were scanned while listening to sounds of human voice separated in two categories: 1) *speech sounds*, consisting of isolated words and syllables or connected speech in various languages; 2) *non-speech vocal sounds*, such as humming, singing without words, emotional interjections, that is, various sounds that were clearly produced with a human vocal tract but did not carry linguistic information. The scrambled versions of these two sound categories were also played to the subjects as low-level acoustical controls with similar energy and temporal envelope as the vocal sounds, but without their typical spectral structure. Response to these sound categories were compared to one another at the voice-selective locations previously identified as well as in left and right A1.

Speech sounds were found to elicit the strongest response at all cortical locations tested. Moreover, they induced significantly greater response than their scrambled version at every location except the most posterior region of right STS. Non-speech vocal sounds, in contrast, elicited smaller cortical responses, that were not distinguishable from the response to their scrambled version in left or right A1 or anywhere in the left hemisphere. Greater response to non-speech vocal sounds than to their scrambled version was found only in right anterior STS regions (Belin et al., 2002).

The generalized stronger response to speech sounds compared to non-speech vocal sounds or scrambled voices is not really surprising given their comparatively greater acoustic complexity – with their large number of different phonemes in rapid succession – and the importance of speech in human communication. It is interesting that this greater response was observed even at the level of A1, which suggests that primary auditory cortex is sensitive not only to temporal variations in sound envelope that were similar for speech sounds and scrambled speech, but also in the spectral information that was present only in speech sounds.

Of particular interest was the response of right anterior STS regions. These regions might underlie neuronal computations that are not only dedicated to linguistic analysis of the vocal sounds, since they show voice-selective activation even when there is no linguistic information. This finding is consistent with several neuroimaging studies that explored non-linguistic voice-perception abilities. One PET-study of emotion and speaker recognition found that the anterior temporal lobes were more active bilaterally during speaker discrimination than during emotion discrimination (Imaizumi et al., 1997). The same group reported that the right anterior temporal pole was more active during discrimination of familiar voices than during control discriminations, and that activity in this region correlated with subject's identification performance (Nakamura et al., 2001). Thus, current evidence suggests that the right anterior temporal lobe could be involved in tasks requiring analysis of paralinguistic information contained in the human voice.

Animal vs. human vocalizations

Do the voice-selective areas respond to any animal vocalization, or do they respond only to sounds of human voice? To answer this question, human vocal sounds (24 speech and 24 non-speech sounds) were compared in another experiment to two categories of animal vocalizations: cat vocalizations (n = 24) and mixed vocalizations from different species (n = 24). A category of non-vocal sounds (n = 24) was used as a control condition. Subjects (n = 14) were asked to listen passively to the different sounds. Here, an event-related design was used instead of the classical block design: brain volumes were acquired continuously (TR = 2.6 s) while stimuli were presented individually in a pseudo-random order with a 5-seconds inter-onset-interval. This paradigm allowed to model the hemodynamic response to each of the 5 categories of auditory stimuli, thus providing additional temporal information. We asked whether the voice selective areas, identified by contrasting vocal to non-vocal sounds in the group of subjects, would also respond to animal vocalizations (Fecteau et al., 2003).

First, this experiment replicated the previous findings. Whereas primary auditory cortex responded similarly to the 5 sound categories, human vocal sounds induced greater cortical response than control non-vocal sounds in STS bilaterally. Thus, the enhanced response of STS to sounds of voice has now been confirmed in several groups of subjects, using different sets of stimuli and scanning paradigms. However, when animal vocalizations – cat or mixed vocalizations – were compared to the non-vocal sounds, no significant difference was observed anywhere in auditory cortex. This finding was confirmed by investigating the response of the STS voice-selective locations to the animal sound categories: Paired sample comparisons showed that the response to animal vocalizations was significantly smaller than to the vocal sounds, speech as well as non-speech.

Thus, the voice-selective areas along STS are not responsive to vocalizations in general, but are really selective to human vocalizations. This finding is very similar to results from the visual literature, that show that the face-selective areas of visual cortex respond more to human faces than to animal faces (Kanwisher et al., 1999).

FUNCTIONAL ROLE OF THE VOICE-SELECTIVE REGIONS

Overall, the above experiments provide converging evidence that there are voice-selective regions in secondary auditory cortex, that are selectively activated by sounds of human voices but not by non-vocal stimuli or vocalizations from other species. Now, what is the exact functional role of these voice-selective regions? Are the different voice-selective areas responsible for processing specific types of information from voice: speech, emotion- or identity-related information?

The next experiment looked at the neuronal representation of vocal identity. We are all able to recognize speakers from the sound of their voice, even though the acoustic signal is never the same. Speaker recognition, as a particular case of auditory object recognition, implies some kind of long-term representation of each familiar speaker's vocal characteristics. This representation of vocal identity is probably computed by extracting a combination of acoustic features that show high inter-individual, but low intra-individual variability, to be compared to incoming vocal signals. Although the format of this putative representation is still largely unknown, a recent neurocognitive model of cerebral function posted the existence of an «area specialized for identifying individual voice patterns» (Mesulam, 1998), by analogy with the «area specialized for face encoding» of visual cortex.

We asked whether we could find evidence for such neuronal representation of speaker's identity in auditory cortex. We used the recently introduced "adaptation paradigm" (Grill-Spector & Malach, 2001), that exploits the property of neuronal population to reduce their firing rate for repeated stimulation. Subjects (n = 14) were scanned while passively listening to 20-s auditory blocks composed of spoken syllables.

As shown in Figure 10.3, there were two conditions corresponding to two types of blocks: "adapt-syllable" blocks in which a same syllable was spoken by 12 different speakers, and "adapt-speaker" blocks in which 12 different syllables were spoken by a same speaker. Thus, one type of block maximized variability in speaker-related information while minimizing variability in syllabic information (adapt-syllable), while it was the reverse for the other type of block (adapt-speaker). Overall, the two conditions were very similar: The same 144 stimuli (12 syllables x 12 speakers) were presented, simply with a different order of presentation. Yet, we predicted that these two conditions would elicit significant activity differences in restricted parts of auditory cortex.

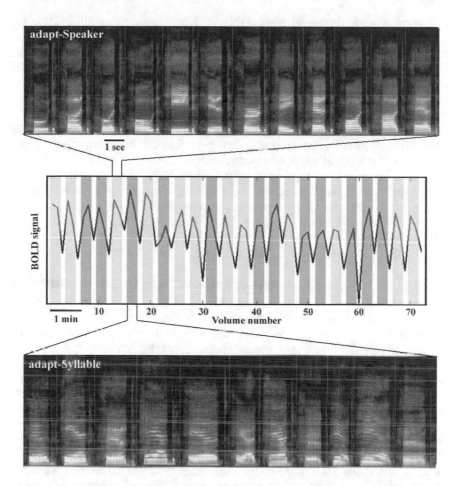

Fig. 10.3. Experimental design of the adaptation study. **Upper and lower panels:** Spectrograms (0–5 kHz, 20 s) of examples of auditory blocks for the two main adaptation conditions. *Adapt-speaker:* Same speaker says 12 different syllables. *Adapt-syllable:* Same syllable is spoken by 12 different speakers. **Middle panel:** BOLD signal time-course from one voxel in primary auditory cortex of a representative subject, across the whole scan duration (12 min). Dark and light gray vertical bars: *Adapt-speaker* and *adapt-syllable* blocks, respectively (20 s); white bars: silence (10 s). Note acoustic features that remain constant across different words for a same speaker (*adapt-speaker*), such as spacing of horizontal striations in the spectrogram, or the dark band at mid-height corresponding to a 'hole' at about 3 kHz in the spectral distribution of acoustic energy for this particular speaker.

Only one region of auditory cortex showed different activation in the two conditions. This region, falling in right anterior STS 2 mm away from one of the previously identified peaks of voice-sensitivity, showed reduced activation when all syllables were spoken by a same speaker, or, conversely, greater activation when syllables were spoken by different speakers (Belin & Zatorre, 2003). This differential activation was thought to arise from adaptation, or repetition-suppression effects related to the repetition of a same voice, and was interpreted as evidence for a representation of speaker's identity in right anterior temporal-lobe. Although this result is preliminary and clearly needs to be substantiated by additional experiments, there is converging evidence that the right anterior temporal-lobe plays an important role in the paralinguistic aspects of voice processing, such as the study by Nakamura et al. (2001) mentioned above. This finding is also in line with the particularly high response of right anterior STS regions to non-speech vocal sounds.

Thus, voice-selective regions of right anterior STS might play an important role in the representation of speaker's identity and in speaker recognition. Future research will now aim to better understand the functional role of the different voice-selective areas, and their interactions in processing speech, identity- and emotion-related information from voice.

CONCLUSION: VOCALIZATION-SELECTIVE AREAS IN NON-HUMAN PRIMATES?

Homo sapiens is not the only species in which accurate processing of conspecific vocalizations plays a critical role. If speech perception appears to be unique to humans, the ability to extract useful information from conspecific vocalizations is found in numerous other species of vertebrates such as oscines, primates, and aquatic mammals (Fitch, 2000). For example, northern fur seals have the ability to form vocal signatures that allow them to recognize their offspring or parents from their vocalizations over a 4-years period (Insley, 2000). In primates, formant frequencies in vocalizations provide useful information on the size of the caller (Fitch, 2000), and rhesus monkeys have been shown to be able to recognize individuals and kin based on their calls (Rendall et al., 1996). Thus, neuronal structures of auditory cortex dedicated to analyzing conspecific vocalizations are probably quite old phylogenetically.

These considerations lead to the following prediction (from human to non-human, which is unusual): One should be able to find "vocalization-selective" cells or areas in the auditory cortex of non-human primates. These cells are likely to be found along the STS, which is one of the phylogenetically oldest sulcal structure in the primate brain (it is found even in species where only few sulci are present) and where face-selective cells have been found in the macaque brain (Perrett et al., 1992). As noted earlier, cells responding to conspecific vocalizations are easy to find in the auditory cortex of many species. In general, conspecific vocalizations are good stimuli that evoke robust responses throughout auditory cortex (e.g., Tian et al., 2001). However, the *selectivity* of these responses has seldom been tested using non-vocal control sound categories, and it is not clear whether other sounds might drive cell activity to a comparable or even greater level of activity. Interestingly, one area of the prefrontal cortex of the macaque seems to contain cells that respond preferentially to vocalizations over other sound categories (Romanski & Goldman-Rakic, 2002), but it would be interesting to look for similar patterns of response in auditory cortex.

Finally, we would like to end on a conclusive note on the cerebral lateralization of the voice specific processes in the brain. One of the most established finding in neuropsychology is the "dominance" of the left hemisphere for language, and this has led many researchers to look for a similar pattern of lateralization in non-human primates. However, there is increasing evidence that this left-hemisphere superiority is mostly concerned with phonological and lexico-semantic processes. Other abilities, such as the perception of emotional information, or speaker recognition, seem on the contrary to rely more on right-hemisphere structures (Belin & Zatorre, 2003; Nakamura et al., 2001). As vocalization perception in non-human primates is probably much closer to our non-verbal voice perception abilities than to speech perception, one would rather expect a right-lateralized cortical network to process conspecific vocalizations in non-human primates.

ACKNOWLEDGMENTS

Research supported by the National Science and Engineering Council of Canada, the Canadian Institute of Health Research, the Canadian Foundation for Innovation and the Fonds de Recherche en Santé du Québec.

REFERENCES

Assal, G., Zander, E., Kremin, H., & Buttet, J. (1976). Discrimination des voix lors des lesions du cortex cerebral. Archives Suisses de Neurologie, Neurochirurgie et Psychiatrie, 119, 307–315.

Belin, P., & Zatorre, R.J. (2003). Adaptation to speaker's voice in right anterior temporal lobe. Neuroreport, 14, 2105-2109.

Belin, P., Zatorre, R.J., & Ahad, P. (2002). Human temporal-lobe response to vocal sounds. Cognitive Brain Research, 13, 17–26.

Belin, P., Zatorre, R.J., Hoge, R., Pike, B., & Evans, A.C. (1999). Event-related fMRI of the auditory cortex. Neuroimage, 10, 417 429.

Belin, P, Zatorre, R.J., Lafaille, P., Ahad, P., & Pike, B. (2000). Voice-selective areas in human auditory cortex. Nature, 403, 309–312.

DeCasper, A.J., & Fifer, W.P. (1980). Of human bonding: newborns prefer their mothers' voices. Science, 208, 1174–1176.

Fecteau, S., Armony, J.L., Joanette, Y., Lepore, F., & Belin, P. (2003). Is voice processing species-specific? Journal of Cognitive Neuroscience, 10, Suppl., E59.

Fitch, W.T. (2000). The evolution of speech: a comparative review. Trends in Cognitive Sciences, 4, 258–267.

Gauthier, I., Tarr, M.J., Moylan, J., Skudlarski, P., Gore, J.C., & Anderson, A.W. (2000). The fusiform "face area" is part of a network that processes faces at the individual level. Journal of Cognitive Neuroscience, 12, 495–504.

Gerhardt, K.J., & Abrams, R.M. (2000). Fetal exposures to sound and vibroacoustic stimulation. Journal of Perinatology, 20, S21–S30.

Grill-Spector, K., & Malach, R. (2001). fMR-adaptation: a tool for studying the functional properties of human cortical neurons. Acta Psychologica, 107, 293-321.

Hall, D., Haggard, M.P., Akeroyd, M.A., Palmer, A.R., Quentin Summerfield, A., Elliott, M.R., Gurney, E.M., & Bowtell, R.W. (1999). "Sparse" temporal sampling in auditory fMRI. Human Brain Mapping, 7, 213–223.

Haxby, J.V., Hoffman, E.A., & Ida Gobbini, M. (2000). The distributed human neural system for face perception. Trends in Cognitive Science, 4, 223–233.

Heffner, H.E., & Heffner, R.S. (1986). Effect of unilateral and bilateral auditory cortex lesions on the discrimination of vocalizations by japanese macaques. Journal of Neurophysiology, 56, 683–701.

Imaizumi, S., Mori, K., Kiritani, S., Kawashima, R., Sugiura, M., Fukuda, H., Itoh, K., Kato, T., Nakamura, A., Hatano, K., Kojima, S., & Nakamura, K. (1997). Vocal identification of speaker and emotion activates different brain regions. Neuroreport, 8, 2809–2812.

Insley, S.J. (2000). Long-term vocal recognition in the northern fur seal. Nature, 406, 404–405.

Kanwisher, N., Stanley, D., & Harris, A. (1999). The fusiform face area is selective for faces not animals. Neuroreport, 10, 183–187.

Mesulam, M.M. (1998). From sensation to cognition. Brain, 121, 1013–1052.

Mountcastle, V.B. (1997). The columnar organization of the neocortex. Brain, 120, 701–722.

Nakamura, K., Kawashima, R., Sugiura, M., Kato, T., Nakamura, A., Hatano, K., Nagumo, S., Kubota, K., Fukuda, H., Ito, K., & Kojima, S. (2001). Neural substrates for recognition of familiar voices: a PET study. Neuropsychologia, 39, 1047–1054.

Perrett, D.I., Hietanen, J.K., Oram, M.W., & Benson, P.J. (1992). Organization and functions of cells responsive to faces in the temporal cortex. Philosophical Transactions of the Royal Society of London, Series B. Biological Sciences, 335, 23–30.

Puce, A., Allison, T., Gore, J.C., & McCarthy, G. (1995). Face-sensitive regions in human extrastriate cortex studied by functional MRI. Journal of Neurophysiology, 74, 1192–1199.

Rendall, D., Owren, M.J., & Rodman, P.S. (1998). The role of vocal tract filtering in identity cueing in rhesus monkey (Macaca mulatta) vocalizations. Journal of the Acoustical Society of America, 103, 602–614.

Rendall, D., Rodman, P.S., & Edmond, R.E. (1996). Vocal recognition of individuals and kin in free-ranging rhesus monkeys. Animal Behaviour, 51, 1007–1015.

Romanski, L.M., & Goldman-Rakic, P.S. (2002). An auditory domain in primate prefrontal cortex. Nature Neuroscience, 5, 15–16.

Samson, Y., Belin, P., Thivard, L., Boddaert, N., Crozier, S., & Zilbovicius, M. (2001). Auditory perception and language: functional imaging of speech sensitive auditory cortex. Revue Neurologique, 157, 837–846.

Scott, S.K., & Johnsrude, I.S. (2003). The neuroanatomical and functional organization of speech perception. Trends in Neurosciences, 26, 100–107.

Tian, B., Reser, D., Durham, A., Kustov, A., & Rauschecker, J.P. (2001). Functional specialization in rhesus monkey auditory cortex. Science, 292, 290–293.

Turner, R., & Jezzard, P. (1994). Magnetic resonance studies of brain functional activation using echo-planar imaging. In R.W. Thatcher, M. Hallett, T. Zeffiro, E. R. John, & M. Huerta (Eds.), Functional Neuroimaging. Technical Foundations (pp. 69–78). San Diego, CA: Academic Press.

Van Lancker, D.R., & Canter, G.J. (1982). Impairment of voice and face recognition in patients with hemispheric damage. Brain and Cognition, 1, 185–195.

Van Lancker, D.R., & Kreiman, J. (1987). Voice discrimination and recognition are separate abilities. Neuropsychologia, 25, 829–834.

Wang, X., Merzenich, M.M., Beitel, R., & Schreiner, C.E. (1995). Representation of a species-specific vocalization in the primary auditory cortex of the common marmoset: temporal and spectral characteristics. Journal of Neurophysiology, 74, 2685–2706.

Zatorre, R.J., & Binder, J.R. (2000). Functional and Structural Imaging of the Human Auditory System. In A.W. Toga & J.C. Mazziotta (Eds.), Brain Mapping: The Systems (pp. 365–402). San Diego, CA: Academic Press.

Zatorre, R.J., Evans, A.C., & Meyer, E. (1994). Neural mechanisms underlying melodic perception and memory for pitch. The Journal of Neuroscience, 14, 1908–1919.

11. CEREBRAL ORGANIZATION OF SPEECH SOUND PERCEPTION: HEMISPHERIC LATERALIZATION EFFECTS AT THE LEVEL OF THE SUPRATEMPORAL PLANE, THE INFERIOR DORSOLATERAL FRONTAL LOBE, AND THE CEREBELLUM

Hermann Ackermann, Ingo Hertrich, Werner Lutzenberger, Klaus Mathiak

INTRODUCTION: FUNCTIONAL COMPONENTS OF SPEECH SOUND PROCESSING

Within some limits, the various classes of speech sounds (phonemes) of any human language system, that is, the respective inventory of consonants and vowels, can be characterized in terms of fairly specific features of the acoustic signal. For example, the spectrogram of isolated vowels or stationary vocalic segments shows rather distinct steady-state maxima of spectral energy distribution (formants). Initial rapid up- or down-going shifts of these formant structures extending across a few tens of milliseconds (formant transitions) cue the voiced stop in consonant-vowel (CV) concatenations such as /ba/ and /da/ (Liberman, 1996; Fig. 11.1). These CV units represent the most frequent syllables across the world's languages and are mastered first during speech development. Formant transitions have been assumed to represent the acoustic correlates of articulatory lip and tongue movements, for example, the shift from bilabial contact to the subsequent configuration of vowel /a/ during production of /ba/. Most noteworthy, the various acoustic "information-bearing elements" (Suga, 1994) of spoken utterances exhibit considerable variability: The same

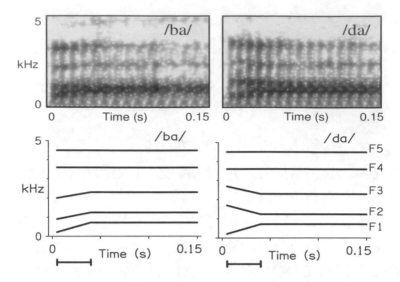

Fig. 11.1. Upper panels: Spectrogram (frequency resolution ca. 150 Hz) of spoken (natural) /ba/ and /da/ utterances (initial part of the stimuli = 150 ms). **Lower panels:** Displays of the formant structure (F1 - F5 = first to fifth formant) of the synthesized /ba/ and /da/ templates, exclusively differing in the initial shift of F1, F2, and F3 (horizontal bar = duration of formant transitions). Stationary vocalic segments, as in this case, or isolated vowels exhibit rather constant center frequencies of the formants.

phoneme may be signaled by quite different acoustic patterns depending upon preceding and succeeding sounds (coarticulation effects) or even within the same linguistic context (trading relations; for an example, see Fig. 11.2, right panel). Listeners, therefore, have to integrate multiple cues, within the time constraints of ongoing verbal communication, to extract speech sound categories from the acoustic signal.

As a response to the problem of "lacking acoustic-linguistic invariances", Liberman and colleagues (see Liberman, 1996) assumed, based on a series of psychoacoustic experiments, that perception of CV syllables depends upon a "phonetic module" mapping the acoustic speech signal onto representations of articulatory (!) gestures ("motor theory of speech perception"). Whereas this mechanism does not extend to all classes of speech sounds, sparing, for example, isolated vowels, encoding of (at least some) phonemes, nevertheless, is assumed to be mediated by the representation of articulatory (motor) routines, a process distinct from any other auditory-perceptual operation and allegedly unique to human beings ("as echolocation is to the bat or song is to the bird;" Liberman, 1996, p. 26). As an alternative, other psycholinguistic models suggest speech and non-speech complex sounds to share the same encoding mechanisms (e.g., "fuzzy logical theory of perception"; Massaro, 1998). Under these premises, acoustic-linguistic invariances are sought at a more fine-grained level of signal analysis. And allegedly speech-specific phenomena such as categorical

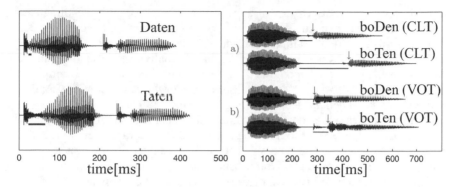

Fig. 11.2. Left panel: Speech oscillograms of the German words "Daten" and "Taten", exclusively differing in voice onset time (VOT) of the initial stop consonant (underlined). **Right panel:** Prototypical examples of two series of "Boden" / "Boten" utterances (test materials of the fMRI experiment). The first two waveforms (a) differ in closure time (CLT), that is, the (underlined) pause signaling word-medial /d/ (first waveform) or /t/ (second waveform), all the other components of the acoustic speech signal being identical (arrows = voice onset of the second syllable). The utterance with short CLT (boDen) is recognized as the German word "Boden" (English "floor"), its cognate with long CLT (boTen) as "Boten" ("messengers"). The lower two signals (b) differ only in VOT, that is, the (underlined) noise segment extending from consonant burst to the beginning of the vocalic segment (arrows = onset of the schwa vowel). Thus, the difference between two sounds, in this case /d/ and /t/, can be cued even within the same linguistic context by two different acoustic parameters (trading relations).

perception have been assumed to reflect the operation of general auditory-perceptual mechanisms. In line with this proposal, other mammals and even birds are, for example, able to discriminate speech sounds after appropriate training in a way similar to human listeners (for a review, see Kuhl, 1987).

Besides linguistic-contextual effects, verbal utterances show considerable between-talker differences at the level of the acoustic speech signal (Johnson & Mullennix, 1997). Rather than nuisance, this source of variability provides a basis for a listener to derive speaker-related, that is, indexical information (identity, age, gender). Among others, pitch represents an important indexical aspect of acoustic communication that, within some limits, constitutes an orthogonal dimension to speech sounds.

In addition to organized sequences of speech sounds (segments), verbal utterances are characterized by distinct suprasegmental features such as intonation contours or rhythmic structures. Apart from their contribution to the meaning of a sentence, for example, the differentiation of declarative and interrogative utterances, the suprasegmental dimension of speech production contributes to a speaker's emotional expression (affective prosody). For example, utterances spoken in a happy or sad tone differ, as a rule, in their extent of pitch fluctuations. The "parallel-processing hypothesis" suggests rather early separation of the encoding of linguistic and indexical aspects of the acoustic speech signal. However, a variety of more recent psycholinguistic studies were able to document distinct interferences between these two data structures such as, for example, considerable implicit memory for indexical information during verbal recognition tasks. Alternative models, for example, the "voice connotation hypothesis", assume, therefore, that the encoding of speech stimuli is bound to episodic (sensory) memory traces encompassing fine-grained perceptual details (see Johnson & Mullennix, 1997).

Taken together, the acoustic speech signal is characterized by considerable "informational richness" encompassing segmental and suprasegmental linguistic as well as indexical data structures. The present chapter focuses on temporal aspects of verbal utterances (rapid shifts of spectral energy distribution, durational parameters of the oscillogram) cueing distinct consonantal sounds.

CEREBRAL HEMISPHERIC LATERALIZATION EFFECTS OF SPEECH SOUND PROCESSING

Superior parts of the temporal lobe

In contrast to the anterior and posterior language zones of the perisylvian cortex, that is, Broca's and Wernicke's area, unilateral lesions of primary auditory cortex fail to elicit clinical deficits, at least within the context of neurological bedside evaluation. Damage to the supratemporal plane of both hemispheres and/or the respective afferent projections may give rise, however, to the syndrome of pure word deafness (Ackermann & Mathiak, 1999). This rather rare constellation is characterized by impaired auditory speech comprehension, repetition of verbal material as well as writing to dictation whereas spontaneous speech production and reading largely remain unaffected. Thus, higher-order (supramodal) aspects of speech perception must be preserved. To varying degrees, recognition of nonverbal (environmental) sounds, perception of musical tunes, temporal resolution of sequential auditory cues and/or spatial localization of acoustic events are compromised as well. Sometimes, pure word deafness is preceded by mostly transient cortical deafness, that is, complete hearing loss.

Dichotic listening (DL) tasks are considered a probe of functional hemispheric lateralization effects arising at the level of the temporal lobe (Hugdahl, 2003). CV syllables with an initial stop consistently yield a right-ear advantage indicating superior left-hemisphere processing of these items. There is, furthermore, some evidence that selective damage to the left, but not the right half of the brain compromises the discrimination of speech sounds incorporating rapidly changing spectral cues (for a review, see Tallal et al., 1993). Based on a DL experiment including systematically varied CVC syllables as test materials, Studdert-Kennedy and Shankweiler (1970) attributed the observed right-ear advantage of the initial consonant to a left-hemisphere phonetic/linguistic device rather than lateralized central-auditory mechanisms of spectral/temporal analysis. Nevertheless, a variety of psychoacoustic studies both in healthy subjects and in clinical populations indicate higher capabilities of the left hemisphere in processing dynamic acoustic cues operating across speech and non-speech domains (Fitch et al., 1997; Tallal et al., 1993). As an alternative to the concept of a phonetic module, enhanced left-hemisphere processing of CV syllables just might originate from a higher proficiency of the respective temporal lobe for the discrimination of any rapidly changing acoustic events, including, among others, formant transitions.

As a synthesis of the behavioral/psychoacoustic data referred to, Poeppel (2001) assumed that, first, both superior temporal lobes participate in speech perception, i.e., the integration of acoustic data into appropriate representations that subsequently enter the mental lexicon, but that, second, the two hemispheres exhibit lateralization effects in that the left side preferentially extracts information over time domains (25–50 ms) corresponding to the duration of formant transitions. This model of functional asymmetry within a framework of bilateral processing capabilities gains some support by animal data. In Japanese macaques left-sided ablation of superior temporal cortex gives rise to transient deficits in the discrimination of species-characteristic vocalizations whereas contralateral excision fails to elicit any disorders. By contrast, damage to both sides permanently compromises the processing of these calls (H.E. Heffner & R.S. Heffner, 1990).

So far, only few functional hemodynamic imaging studies (positron emission tomography = PET, functional magnetic resonance imaging = fMRI) implicitly or explicitly addressed the processing of the acoustic characteristics of speech sounds. PET measurements by Hughdahl and collaborators (for a review, see Hugdahl, 2003) found bilateral hemodynamic activation at the level of the superior temporal sulcus concomitant with left larger than-right responses within the planum temporale area during dichotic application of (spoken) CV syllables. A recent fMRI investigation revealed an even more pronounced multi-patched activation pattern in association with speech sound perception (Jäncke et al., 2002): CV stimuli controlled for their acoustic structure elicited, among others, both bilateral symmetric as well as left- and right-lateralized responses, in comparison to sine tones or white noise (subtraction approach), within superior parts of the temporal lobe (planum temporale and superior temporal sulcus).

Frontal cortex including Broca's area

The "motor theory" proposes that the assumed phonetic module pertains to the perisylvian "language apparatus" of the human brain (Liberman, 1996) and, thus, argues, at least implicitly and at least with respect to CV syllables, for lateralized mechanisms of speech sound perception. Motor aspects of speech production are assumed to be associated with the "anterior language zones" rostral to the central sulcus, for example, Broca's area, and/or the anterior insular cortex of the left hemisphere (Ackermann, 1999). Since the motor theory suggests that the representation of articulatory gestures mediates speech sound recognition, the assumed phonetic module should be bound to frontal and/or intrasylvian structures. In subjects undergoing brain surgery, electrical stimulation of the exposed anterior perisylvian cortex at sites giving rise to speech arrest, indeed, disrupted speech perception as well (Ojemann, 1983). Furthermore, compromised phoneme or syllable discrimination/identification have been documented in subgroups of patients with Broca's aphasia, a syndrome commonly bound to anterior perisylvian lesions (Blumstein, 1995). However, the profile of performance deficits in these subjects seems to indicate impaired "activation" of linguistic representations rather than disrupted "extraction" of the respective acoustic information-bearing elements.

Functional hemodynamic imaging studies provided further evidence for a contribution of brain areas outside the superior temporal cortex to the decoding of the sound structure of verbal utterances. Thus, a seminal PET study by Zatorre and colleagues (1992) found increased blood flow at the level of Broca's area during a phonetic discrimination task as compared to passive listening to the same items (hierarchical subtraction design). Several, but not all subsequent PET investigations addressing phonetic/phonological processing such as rhyming of letter names or detection of pre-specified phonemes found left-frontal activity during these tasks (Poeppel, 1996). Most noteworthy, there is some evidence that recruitment of left-frontal areas during speech sound encoding depends upon pre-linguistic aspects of signal analysis rather than the representation of phonological data structures: Detection of CV syllables and CVC words as well as tone triplets yielded significant left-hemispheric frontal-opercular hemodynamic responses whereas, in contrast, relatively long steady-state vowel targets (duration = 250 ms) failed to show a similar effect (Fiez et al., 1995). Both within the speech and non-speech domain, any stimulus type encompassing rapidly changing spectral cues, thus, seems to elicit enhanced neural activity within the anterior perisylvian area of the language-dominant hemisphere.

Conclusions

Behavioral data obtained in clinical populations (pure word deafness) indicate that the acoustic cortex of either side possesses the capabilities to encode linguistic and indexical aspects of the sound structure of verbal utterances. Nevertheless, at least the processing of CV syllables is characterized by distinct lateralization effects, most presumably due to a higher left-hemisphere proficiency in the encoding of formant transitions, that is, rapid shifts of spectral energy distribution. Besides lesion studies, functional imaging techniques provide a further approach to investigate brain-behavior relationships. Recent PET and fMRI studies revealed multi-faceted patterns of bilateral as well as predominantly left- and right-sided responses within the superior parts of the temporal lobe during the processing of CV items. Conceivably, these various components of hemodynamic activation represent different stages of the general-auditory and/or linguistic encoding of the sound structure of verbal utterances. Because of better temporal resolution as compared to hemodynamic functional imaging, electrophysiological techniques should provide a well-suited tool to further elucidate early aspects of speech sound encoding bound to the extraction of the respective information-bearing elements of the acoustic signal.

ENCODING OF THE ACOUSTIC SPEECH SIGNAL AT THE LEVEL OF THE SUPRATEMPORAL PLANE: WHOLE-HEAD MAGNETOENCEPHALOGRAPHY (MEG) STUDIES

Methodological background: Electrophysiological correlates of central-auditory processing

Any series of auditory events, as a rule, evokes a positive EEG deflection arising about 50 ms after stimulus onset (P50) as well as a subsequent negative one peaking at ca. 100 ms (N1) (Näätänen & Winkler, 1999). Randomly interspersed rare stimuli (deviants) within a sequence of homogeneous events (standards) elicit an additional component, the mismatch negativity (MMN), representing the difference signal between the evoked responses to standards and deviants. These brain activities can also be detected by means of MEG recordings, a more recent technology as compared to EEG (M50, M100, and mismatch field (MMF) = MEG analogues of P50, N1, and MMN; Ackermann et al., 2001; Hertrich et al., 2002; Mathiak et al., 2000). Mismatch responses even arise in the absence of attention directed toward the auditory channel and, thus, may reflect early cognitive processes in terms of pre-attentive comparison of an incoming deviant stimulus with a stored sensory memory trace of the preceding standard events. Based on a comprehensive review of the pertinent literature, Näätänen and Winkler (1999) proposed a functional interpretation of these various EEG/MEG components in terms of distinct levels of central-auditory processing: The event-related N1 response arising at the level of the supratemporal plane is assumed to reflect detection of single acoustic features such as signal periodicity whereas neural activity within the MMN/MMF domain might portray the earliest representational stage of auditory input bound to sensory memory functions. Among others, thus, mismatch activity appears to represent a correlate of "language-specific phonetic traces" stored within sensory memory buffers and serving as recognition models for speech sounds during auditory perception (Näätänen, 2001).

As compared to EEG recordings, MEG technology shows rather selective sensitivity to superficial, tangentially-oriented neural currents and, therefore, allows for a rather focused study of the activity of the supratemporal plane including acoustic projection areas (Hari & Lounasmaa, 1989). Furthermore, event-related magnetic fields in response to discrete acoustic stimuli are less distorted by the skull and the skin as compared to EEG signals. Whole-head

MEG devices allow for simultaneous recordings of evoked magnetic fields over both hemispheres and, therefore, are capable to detect rather subtle lateralization effects of cerebral functions at a high spatial and temporal resolution. As a consequence, these techniques should provide a suitable tool for a further elucidation of the time course of the processing of dynamic acoustic events (formant transitions) at the level of the supratemporal plane.

Left-hemisphere lateralization effects of formant transition encoding: Sensory memory representations

Tallal and coworkers (Fitch et al., 1997; Tallal et al., 1993) suggested the higher proficiency of the left hemisphere in processing CV syllables to reflect superior temporal resolution capabilities within the auditory domain allowing for enhanced detection of formant transitions. Thus, a general-auditory device operating across linguistic and non-linguistic domains is assumed to account for these functional asymmetry effects. Based on the observation of "generalization" phenomena across different vowel contexts, Studdert-Kennedy and Shankweiler (1970) assumed, in contrast, the right-ear advantage of stop consonant perception to occur at the level of phonetic/linguistic analysis rather than spectral/temporal processing. The extent, to which the neurobiological representation of speech depends upon complex acoustic properties, on the one hand, and linguistic content, on the other, is still a matter of ongoing debate (Fitch et al., 1997).

Event-related N1 components arising at the level of the supratemporal plane have been proposed to reflect detection of single acoustic features such as signal periodicity whereas neural activity within the MMN/MMF domain might portray the earliest representational stage of auditory input (see above). Based on these suggestions, left-hemisphere mechanisms of spectral/temporal processing must be expected to operate as early as the N1/M100 activity whereas phonetic/linguistic decoding, characterized by the integration of multiple primary acoustic cues, should be restricted to later stages such as the MMF.

Using whole-head MEG technology, Shtyrov and coworkers (2000) had found semi-synthetic CV syllables to yield left-hemisphere prominence of MMF. To further elaborate these findings, a recent MEG study of our group (Hertrich et al., 2002) recorded evoked magnetic brain fields in response to CV syllables using also a whole-head device (CTF, Vancouver, Canada; 151 sensors, sampling rate = 250 Hz, anti-aliasing filter cutoff = 80 Hz; sound-attenuated, magnetic-shielded booth; 20 right-handed subjects). Both CV syllables produced by a human speaker and exclusively synthetic items differing in strictly controlled formant transitions served as test materials (Fig. 11.1). Stimuli were applied within the framework of an oddball design, that is, a pseudo-random sequence of frequent (standards = binaural /ba/, 80% of the total of stimuli) and rare stimuli (deviants = dichotic /ba/-/da/ or /da/-/ba/, 10% each; previous studies had provided some evidence that dichotic presentation of

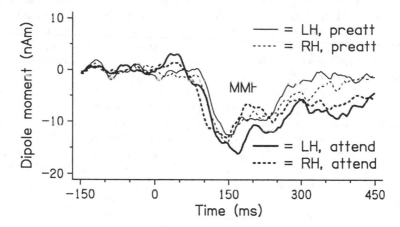

Fig. 11.3. Time course of mismatch field (MMF) strength (subspace projection onto the dipole structure derived from the difference wave between standards and deviants) averaged across all subjects: Interactions of attentional load (preatt = visual distraction, attend = stimulus detection task) and hemisphere (RH, LH = right, left hemisphere). Note that attentional demands influence (1) the timing of MMF onset at about 100 ms and (2) lateralization of the center of the mismatch reaction (150–200 ms).The time scale refers to stimulus onset (= 0 ms).

deviants might unmask functional cerebral asymmetries of speech sound processing; see Mathiak et al., 2000). First, a bilateral position-symmetric pair of dipoles was fitted to the grand average across the entire group of subjects in order to obtain a noise-insensitive estimate of the M50 sources. As a second step of analysis, the time course of dipole strength was calculated. The mismatch fields, finally, were derived by subtraction of the averaged responses to standard stimuli from the averaged signal across rare events. To explicitly assess the influence of attentional demands on evoked magnetic fields, mismatch activity was measured either during controlled visual distraction or during a task requiring overt identification of the applied auditory items.

The M100 field, a component assumed to reflect detection of single acoustic features, did not show any hemispheric side-differences in latency or amplitude. As concerns mismatch fields, synthetic items gave rise to an earlier onset of this deflection (around 100 ms) over the left hemisphere during preattentive processing, but failed to elicit any later lateralization effects. During the stimulus identification task, that is, directed attention towards the auditory channel, synthetic deviants elicited an enlarged MMF peak over the left hemisphere resembling the pre-attentive response to natural syllables (Fig. 11.3). Thus, electrophysiological correlates of lateralized CV syllable encoding, first, were restricted to MMF, that is, a representational stage of formant transient encoding which has been assigned to linguistic operations (Näätänen, 2001). Second, the development of the MMF lateralization effect across time was found to be influenced both by stimulus characteristics (spectral "richness") and attentional demands. Obviously, thus, the "depth" of signal analysis depends upon an interaction between bottom-up (stimulus-driven) and top-down (instruction-driven) processes ("audition versus cognition," see Plomp, 2002).

An early MMF component (around 100 ms), lateralized towards the right hemisphere side, emerged in response to natural syllables during pre-attentive processing and to synthetic stimuli in case of directed attention. Conceivably, these effects indicate right-hemisphere operations bound to the extraction of periodicity information and indexical data (Mathiak et al., 2002b). A subsequent study, therefore, aimed at a further clarification of lateralized pitch processing within the domain of the fundamental frequency of acoustic speech signals. Unexpectedly, it turned out that these investigations may shed further light on the processing of CV syllables.

Functional segregation of aperiodic and periodic acoustic signal components across the two hemispheres

In case of harmonic sounds such as spoken vowels or musical tones, perceived pitch, that is, a distinct aspect of auditory perception characterized by an inherent low/high dimension, corresponds to the fundamental frequency (F0) of these events, that is, the spectral distance between neighboring harmonics or the inverse of periodicity across time. DL data provided first evidence for a higher proficiency of the right hemisphere in encoding harmonic sounds (Sidtis, 1984). By contrast, pure sine waves failed to show a similar effect. Even after removal of the spectral F0 component by means of high-pass filtering, a complex tone approximately matches in pitch a sine wave of a periodicity equal to its missing fundamental. Clinical findings indicate that lesions of the right auditory cortex (Heschl's gyrus) impair discrimination of the pitch of complex tones in the absence of a spectral F0 component (missing fundamental) as well as the determination of the direction of pitch changes when subjects were asked to indicate whether the second tone of a pair was higher or lower than the first one (for a review, see Zatorre, 2003). By contrast, pitch discrimination based on tones encompassing spectral F0 seems to be preserved subsequent to damage to the auditory cortex, in case that the task considered lacks relevant working memory load. As a consequence, Zatorre (2003) assumed the right primary auditory cortex to predominantly support fine-grained representation of tonal materials or the scaling of sounds according to their pitch, respectively. At some variance with these clinical data, at least two functional imaging studies revealed, however, predominant right-hemisphere activation of Heschl's gyrus during passive listening to pure tones (Pugh et al., 1996; Tzourio et al., 1997; see Celsis et al., 1999).

Besides vocal musical performance, pitch represents an important aspect of verbal utterances, conveying both linguistic (e.g., sentence accent and mode, tone languages) and indexical information (e.g., a speaker's age and gender). The sparse clinical and functional imaging data available so far indicate higher right-hemisphere proficiency in the processing of intonational aspects of speech utterances (see Belin & Zatorre, 2004).

Two classes of pitch-extracting procedures have been proposed so far: Besides pattern-matching on tonotopic structures or spectral representations (see Pantev et al., 1996), pitch can be derived from the temporal organization of neural activity (Langner & Schreiner, 1988; Schreiner & Langner, 1988). In humans, a recent MEG study documented pitch-related phasing of the 40-Hz component of steady-state responses over the right, but not the left hemisphere (Patel & Balaban, 2001). Conceivably, thus, lateralization effects during complex pitch processing might reflect right-hemisphere representation of the periodic structure of acoustic signals. MEG steady-state responses do not provide, however, further information about the time course and the processing stage of lateralized pitch encoding. By contrast, transient evoked MEG responses allow for the investigation of cortical activity at a rather high temporal resolution.

In order to delineate the cortical processing stages of lateralized representation of periodicity pitch, a further MEG study of our group recorded evoked magnetic fields in response to rippled noise (RN) stimuli (20 subjects) using again a whole-head device (Hertrich et al., 2004). It is widely recognized that RN predominantly addresses temporal mechanisms of pitch processing. These events are generated by a delay-and-add procedure: A segment of random noise is copied, delayed and added back to the original signal two or more times. This approach imposes a partial periodic structure (temporal regularity) on the noise signal. RN events, therefore, give rise to simultaneous perception of a hiss sound, the perceptual correlate of the noise component of the signal, and a buzzy tone corresponding in pitch to the inverse of the delay interval. Most importantly, the original noise and the RN derivates exhibit a similar spectral energy distribution. Since simple tonotopic representations of pitch are largely masked under these conditions, pitch encoding must be expected primarily to depend upon time-domain mechanisms (Griffiths et al., 2001). As a consequence, the RN paradigm should represent a feasible tool for the investigation of pitch encoding within the temporal domain. Fundamental frequencies within the range of speech communication were selected for analysis (111 Hz and 133 Hz). Stimulus application again relied on a dichotic design (see Experiment 1). Since previous studies had found evoked magnetic fields to interact with attentional demands (Hertrich et al., 2002), the measurements were performed either during visual distraction or during an auditory pitch detection task. In order to separate the various effects caused by the noise and the pitch components of the RN stimuli, two control experiments recorded MEG responses to pulse trains (harmonic sounds), pulse trains mixed with noise, and "pure" noise segments.

Three novel electrophysiological effects of central-auditory processing in response to periodic and aperiodic acoustic signal components could be documented:

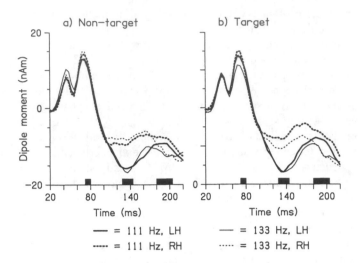

Fig. 11.4. Time course of evoked magnetic fields (subspace projection onto group dipoles, time in ms post stimulus onset): Interactions of pitch (111 Hz versus 133 Hz) with hemisphere (LH, RH = left, right hemisphere) depending on the target status of the respective stimuli.

(a) Both RN stimuli and the harmonic sounds (pulse trains) elicited stronger MEG fields in response to the higher-pitched tones (133 Hz) as compared to their lower (111 Hz) cognates ("pitch scaling"). In case of harmonic stimuli, high-pitch salience emerged over both hemispheres as early as the M100 time domain. By contrast, RN events elicited within this interval a similar effect solely at the right side depending upon subjects' attentional setting (Fig. 11.4). Neuropsychological models of the visual system propose an early cortical short-term buffer that, rather than a passive storage device, amplifies distinct features of visual objects such as edges, facilitating figure-ground segregation (e.g., Kosslyn, 1999). Similar principles may characterize sensory memory operations of the central-auditory system giving rise, among others, to an inherent scaling of auditory features such as pitch. Conceivably, this effect represents an electrophysiological correlate of the "markedness" of high-pitch stimuli as compared to their lower cognates within the linguistic context. For example, peaks of the intonation contour of verbal utterances signal, among others, word and sentence accents.

(b) In line with previous studies, harmonic stimuli (control experiment) elicited larger right- than left-hemisphere M100 fields. Unexpectedly, RN events yielded, however, significantly stronger left-sided responses peaking at a latency of 136 ms (Fig. 11.4). The control sessions, furthermore, revealed the latter lateralization effects to be bound to the noise rather than the pitch aspect of RN stimuli (predominant left-sided representation of aperiodic acoustic energy).

(c) Stimuli encompassing noise intermixed with a regular-impulse component gave rise to an interaction between aperiodic and periodic signal components within the M100 time domain: Subtle differences between succeeding noise stimuli had an effect on this component only in the presence of an additional pitch component.

Taken together, the present study provides first evidence for functional hemispheric segregation of the cortical processing of complex acoustic signals such as RN within a time domain centered around 136 ms post stimulus onset: Periodicity information seems to be bound predominantly to the right hemisphere while the left side maintains spectral templates of the applied stimuli. Functional hemispheric segregation of periodic (right hemisphere) and aperiodic signal components (left hemisphere) might allow for parallel representation of these two different (periodic versus aperiodic) data structures. For example, Suga (1988) assumed that the auditory cortex maintains the "raw data" of acoustic signals either as a backup mechanism or as a supplement to information processing in more specialized areas. Since noise stimuli elicited stronger left-hemisphere evoked magnetic fields, the respective auditory areas might subserve broadband spectral representation of the applied RN stimuli awaiting further analysis.

Besides these lateralization effects, an interaction of pitch and noise could be documented providing, conceivably, the basis for pitch-synchronous spectral signal evaluation within the left hemisphere, triggered by the right-hemisphere periodicity representation. Pitch-synchronous spectral evaluation represents a widely recognized procedure within the areas of automatic speech recognition enhancing or facilitating the extraction of formant trajectories from the acoustic signal. Thus, left-hemisphere spectral/temporal signal evaluation of the RN "raw data" might be triggered by the separately stored right-hemisphere periodicity information updating spectral representations in synchrony with a neuronal reference signal bound to pitch period markers. And, conceivably, this mechanism contributes to lateralization effects observed during speech sound recognition tasks such as predominant left-hemisphere processing of CV syllables. Since the residual noise component does not encompass, after periodicity extraction, any further information-bearing elements, the evoked activity at the cortical level can be expected to break down earlier than during the encoding of speech stimuli (see above).

Although the suggested pitch-synchronous spectral evaluation mechanism actually limits temporal resolution to the length of single pitch periods, this procedure might well serve to evaluate complex changes of the spectral envelope within the 20–40 ms domain. This assumption of left-dominant evaluation of spectral patterns is corroborated by intracranial recordings within the auditory cortex in humans (Liegeois-Chauvel et al., 2001). Whereas the earliest neural activity, arising about 50 ms after stimulus onset, showed a quite symmetric tonotopic distribution within both hemispheres, secondary representations within a time-interval of 80 ms to 100 ms exhibited considerable side-differences: The right hemisphere showed sharp tuning to single best

frequencies whereas the left hemisphere displayed bimodal or wideband
frequency response curves rather than simple tonotopy.

"HEARING BEYOND THE TEMPORAL LOBE:" THE CONTRIBUTION OF LEFT-FRONTAL AND RIGHT-CEREBELLAR STRUCTURES TO THE PROCESSING OF DURATIONAL PARAMETERS OF THE ACOUSTIC SPEECH SIGNAL

A classical tenet of clinical neurology, tracing back to the early 19th century,
proposes cerebellar lesions and diseases to compromise motor capabilities such
as the coordination of voluntary movements and the control of balance, but to
spare sensory and cognitive functions (Ackermann & Daum, 2003). Contrary to
this notion, Ivry and Keele (1989) first noted disrupted time perception in
patients with cerebellar pathology: Subjects performed worse when asked to
compare a pair of time intervals bound by two clicks each, the second item
being either shorter or longer than the first one. Subsequent studies found, in
addition, impaired representation of temporal information within the
somatosensory and visual domains. Since at least some cerebellar motor
deficits, for example, increased variability of finger tapping in response to
external stimuli, might be due to disordered central pacing mechanisms, the
"generalized timing hypothesis" (Ivry & Fiez, 2000) considers the cerebellum
an "internal clock" supporting precise temporal representation across motor and
sensory functions.

Besides transient and steady-state components of spectral energy
distribution, durational measures contribute to phoneme specification. The
generalized timing hypothesis predicts impaired processing of those features of
the acoustic speech signal. Indeed, a clinical study found cerebellar atrophy to
compromise distinct temporal aspects of speech perception. For example, the
English word "rabbit" involves a short period of silence (closure time = CLT)
signaling the intraword stop consonant /b/. Prolongation of CLT gives rise to a
phoneme-boundary effect: Stimuli with short intra-word pause (< 40 ms) are
recognized as the lexical item "rabbit" whereas closure intervals above
approximately 80 ms yield the percept "rapid" (Liberman, 1996). Using a
German analogue of the "rabbit"/"rapid" paradigm ("Boden" (floor) [bodn] =
short CLT, versus "Boten" (messengers) [botn] = long CLT; Fig. 11.2, right
panel), patients with diffuse cerebellar atrophy, indeed, failed to exhibit any
significant phoneme-boundary effect (Ackermann et al., 1997). Thus, these
subjects were unable to identify these words based on an exclusively durational
parameter. Besides CLT, voice onset time (VOT) represents a further temporal
measure contributing to the specification of speech sounds. For example, the
syllables [da] and [t^{h}a] differ in VOT of the initial stop consonant, that is, the
interval between initial burst and vowel onset (see Fig. 11.2, left panel).
English-speaking adults asked to label monosyllabic stimuli extending in VOT
from less than 10 ms (yielding the percept [da]) to 80 ms (recognized as [t^{h}a])

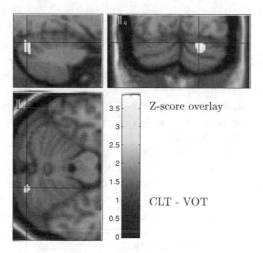

Fig. 11.5. Significant BOLD effects at the level of the cerebellum (lateral aspects of right-hemisphere Crus I) during the "Boten"/"Boden" identification task (subtraction approach: CLT minus VOT condition; Z-score overlay on normalized anatomical images, threshold at $Z > 3.1$, corresponds to $p < 0.001$, uncorrected). This cerebellar response was associated with an activation cluster adjacent to Broca's area.

show a rather abrupt shift between these two response categories at a value of about 30 ms. Similar identification curves across a continuum of verbal utterances varying in VOT of the initial stop consonant have been documented in cerebellar subjects and their controls (Ackermann et al., 1997). It is well established that listeners may utilize all available acoustic cues of the speech signal during phonological encoding. In case of VOT processing, the sound energy of the aspiration phase, that is, the loudness of this noise segment, can contribute to the perceived voicing contrast of stop consonants such as /d/ and /t/ (see Ackermann et al., 1997, for further references). Consequently, categorical VOT distinction may merely reflect intrasegmental backward masking, that is, aspiration noise must exceed a given intensity threshold in order to be detected. In contrast to CLT, categorical VOT representations, therefore, do not necessarily require explicit time measurements.

Functional magnetic resonance imaging (fMRI) enables detection and localization of cerebellar hemodynamic responses bound to specific motor or cognitive tasks. Therefore, this technique was used in order to identify the cerebellar subsystem engaged in the encoding of temporal aspects of verbal utterances (Mathiak et al., 2002a). In analogy to the clinical study on speech perception in cerebellar disorders, a series of 15 stimuli systematically varying in the durational parameter CLT was generated, extending from a prototypical item of "Boden" (CLT = 27 ms) at one extreme to "Boten" (CLT = 167 ms) at the other (see Fig. 11.2). Recognition of these items was required during the active condition. Besides CLT, the difference in sound structure between the words "Boden" and "Boten" may be signalled by the VOT of the word-medial stop consonants /d/ and /t/ ([bodən] versus [bot^{h}ən], the /t/-sound being characterized by an aspiration noise preceding the "schwa" vowel; Fig. 11.2). As a control condition, thus, a second series of verbal utterances with constant CLT but systematically varied word-medial VOT was generated. Subjects had to distinguish the lexical items "Boden" and "Boten," therefore, either by analysis of the durational parameter CLT (active condition) or by the characteristics of the noise segment VOT (reference condition). This design minimizes any interferences with other cognitive functions. Using a subtraction approach, the main contrast, that is, responses to CLT blocks minus the VOT runs, yielded a single cluster of hemodynamic activation rostral to the horizontal fissure within lateral Crus I of the right cerebellar hemisphere (Fig. 11.5). Right-hemisphere cerebellar activation was associated with left-prefrontal responses anterior and inferior to Broca's area at the level of supratentorial structures. The reversed contrast (VOT - CLT) yielded a single significant cluster within the left supratemporal plane, but failed to elicit any significant cerebellar activation spots.

CONCLUSIONS: DISTRIBUTED MECHANISMS SUBSERVE THE ENCODING OF TEMPORAL ASPECTS OF THE ACOUSTIC SPEECH SIGNAL (DYNAMIC AND DURATIONAL PARAMETERS EXTENDING ACROSS SEVERAL TENS OF MILLISECONDS)

A variety of behavioral data obtained in healthy subjects and in clinical populations indicates a higher proficiency of the left hemisphere in the encoding of CV syllables characterized by distinct formant transitions such as /ba/ and /da/. Recordings of evoked magnetic fields in response to synthetic formant structures and to RN stimuli by means of whole-head MEG indicate, tentatively, two successive mechanisms of the central-auditory system that contribute to these lateralization effects: (a) enhanced left-hemisphere detection of formant transitions by means of pitch-synchronous evaluation of spectral energy distribution and (b) predominant left-hemisphere representation of the time course of formant transitions within sensory memory.

Besides rapid shifts of spectral energy distribution, the duration of pauses, noise segments and vowels represents a further temporal information-bearing element of the acoustic speech signal. Recent clinical and functional imaging data provided first evidence that the resolution of pauses (e.g., word-medial occlusion time) and stretches of noise (e.g., VOT) depends on different encoding mechanisms. Whereas VOT processing seems to be bound to the left supratemporal plane, a right-cerebellar/left-prefrontal network was found engaged in the determination of segment lengths such as word-medial pauses. Most presumably, these cerebellar/frontal interconnections subserve generalized explicit time measurements operating across the domains of speech and non-speech auditory stimuli (Mathiak et al., 2004).

In summary, rather than an "encapsulated" phonetic module, a multitude of central-auditory mechanisms seem to mediate the encoding of the information-bearing elements of the acoustic speech signal (see Ivry & Lebby, 1998). The MEG and fMRI studies referred to indicate at least two procedures contributing to the resolution of temporal aspects, within a time domain of several tens of milliseconds, of the acoustic speech signal: left-supratemporal pitch-synchronous evaluation of spectral energy distribution, based on a functional segregation of periodic and aperiodic data structures across the two hemispheres, and explicit measurements of durational parameters subserved by a right-cerebellar/left-prefrontal generalized timing device. These findings do not imply that speech perception in any case recruits all components of this distributed network. Depending upon a listener's expectations and knowledge about the context of a conversation, the analysis of the sound structure of verbal utterances as a prerequisite to lexical access may vary in extent and depth (Plomp, 2002).

ACKNOWLEDGMENTS

This work was supported by grants of the German Research Foundation (DFG-SPP "ZIZAS," DFG-SFB 550). We thank Maike Borutta for excellent assistance.

REFERENCES

Ackermann, H. (1999). Acquired disorders of articulation: Classification and intervention. In F. Fabbro (Ed.), Concise encyclopedia of language pathology (pp. 261 268). Amsterdam: Elsevier.

Ackermann, H., & Daum, I. (2003). Neuropsychological deficits in cerebellar syndromes. In M.A. Bédard, Y. Agid, S. Chouinard, S. Fahn, A.D. Korczyn & P. Lespérance (Eds.), Mental and behavioral dysfunction in movement disorders (pp. 147–156). Totowa, NJ: Humana Press.

Ackermann, H., Gräber, S., Hertrich, I., & Daum, I. (1997). Categorical speech perception in cerebellar disorders. Brain and Language, 60, 323–332.

Ackermann, H., Hertrich, I., Mathiak, K., & Lutzenberger, W. (2001). Contralaterality of cortical auditory processing at the level of the M50/M100 complex and the mismatch field: A whole-head magnetoencephalographic study. Neuroreport, 12, 1683–1687.

Ackermann, H., & Mathiak, K. (1999). Syndromes, pathologic-anatomical basis, and pathophysiology of central hearing disorders (pure word deafness, auditive agnosia, cortical deafness). Fortschritte der Neurologie-Psychiatrie, 67, 509–523 (German).

Belin, P., & Zatorre, R.J. (2004). Voice processing in human auditory cortex. In R. König, P. Heil, E. Budinger, & H. Scheich (Eds.), The Auditory Cortex – A Synthesis of Human and Animal Research. Hillsdale, NJ: Lawrence Erlbaum Associates.

Blumstein, S.E. (1995). The neurobiology of the sound structure of language. In M.S. Gazzaniga (Ed.), The cognitive neurosciences (pp. 915–929). Cambridge, MA: MIT Press.

Celsis, P., Boulanouar, K., Doyon, B., Ranjeva, J.P., Berry, I., Nespoulous, J.L., & Chollet, F. (1999). Differential fMRI responses in the left posterior superior temporal gyrus and left supramarginal gyrus to habituation and change detection in syllables and tones. NeuroImage, 9, 135–144.

Fiez, J.A., Raichle, M.E., Miezin, F.M., Petersen, S.E., Tallal, P., & Katz, W.F. (1995). PET studies of auditory and phonological processing: Effects of stimulus characteristics and task demands. Journal of Cognitive Neuroscience, 7, 357–375.

Fitch, R.H., Miller, S., & Tallal, P. (1997). Neurobiology of speech perception. Annual Review of Neuroscience, 20, 331–353.

Griffiths, T.D., Uppenkamp, S., Johnsrude, I., Josephs, O., & Patterson, R.D. (2001). Encoding of the temporal regularity of sound in the human brainstem. Nature Neuroscience, 4, 633–637.

Griffiths, T.D., & Warren, J.D. (2002). The planum temporale as a computational hub. Trends in Neuroscience, 25, 348–353.

Hari, R., & Lounasmaa, O.V. (1989). Recording and interpretation of cerebral magnetic fields. Science, 244, 432–436.

Heffner, H.E., & Heffner, R.S. (1990). Role of primate auditory cortex in hearing. In W.C. Stebbins (Ed.), Comparative perception. Vol. II: Complex signal (pp. 279–310). New York, NY: John Wiley.

Hertrich, I., Mathiak, K., Lutzenberger, W., & Ackermann, H. (2002). Hemispheric lateralization of the processing of consonant-vowel syllables (formant transitions): Effects of stimulus characteristics and attentional demands on evoked magnetic fields. Neuropsychologia, 40, 1902–1917.

Hertrich, I., Mathiak, K., Lutzenberger, W., & Ackermann, H. (2004). Time course and hemispheric lateralization effects of complex pitch processing: Evoked magnetic fields in response to rippled noise stimuli. Neuropsychologia, 42, 1814–1826.

Hugdahl, K. (2003). Dichotic listening in the study of auditory laterality. In K. Hugdahl & R.J. Davidson (Eds.), The asymmetrical brain (pp. 441–475). Cambridge, MA: MIT Press.

Ivry, R.B., & Fiez, J.A. (2000). Cerebellar contributions to cognition and imagery. In M.S. Gazzaniga (Ed.), The new cognitive neurosciences (pp. 999–1011). Cambridge, MA: MIT Press.

Ivry, R.B., & Keele, S.W. (1989). Timing functions of the cerebellum. Journal of Cognitive Neuroscience, 1, 136–152.

Ivry, R.B., & Lebby, P.C. (1998). The neurology of consonant perception: Specialized module or distributed processors. In M. Beeman & C. Chiarello (Eds.), Right hemisphere language comprehension: Perspectives from cognitive neuroscience (pp. 3–25). Mahwah, NJ: Lawrence Erlbaum.

Jäncke, L., Wüstenberg, T., Scheich, H., & Heinze, H.-J. (2002). Phonetic perception and the temporal cortex. NeuroImage, 15, 733–746.

Johnson, K., & Mullennix, J.W. (Eds.). (1997). Talker variability in speech processing. San Diego, CA: Academic Press.

Kosslyn, S.M. (1994). Image and brain: The resolution of the imagery debate. Cambridge, MA: MIT Press.

Kuhl, P.K. (1987). The special-mechanisms debate in speech research: Categorization tests on animals and infants. In S. Harnad (Ed.), Categorical perception: The groundwork of cognition (pp. 355–386). Cambridge, UK: Cambridge University Press.

Langner, G., & Schreiner, C.E. (1988). Periodicity coding in the inferior colliculus of the cat: I. Neuronal mechanisms. Journal of Neurophysiology, 60, 1799–1822.

Liberman, A.M. (1996). Speech: A special code. Cambridge, MA: MIT Press.

Liegeois-Chauvel, C., Giraud, K., Badier, J. M., Marquis, P., & Chauvel, P. (2001). Intracerebral evoked potentials in pitch perception reveal a functional asymmetry of the human auditory cortex. Annals of the New York Academy of Sciences, 930, 117–132.

Massaro, D.W. (1998). Perceiving talking faces: From speech perception to a behavioral principle. Cambridge, MA: MIT Press.

Mathiak, K., Hertrich, I., Grodd, W., & Ackermann, H. (2002a). Cerebellum and speech perception: A functional magnetic resonance imaging study. Journal of Cognitive Neuroscience, 14, 902–912.

Mathiak, K., Hertrich, I., Grodd, W., & Ackermann, H. (2004). Discrimination of temporal information at the cerebellum: Functional magnetic resonance imaging of nonverbal auditory memory. NeuroImage, 21, 154–162.

Mathiak, K., Hertrich, I., Lutzenberger, W., & Ackermann, H. (2000). Encoding of temporal speech features (formant transients) during binaural and dichotic stimulus application: A whole-head magnetencephalography study. Brain Research. Cognitive Brain Research, 10, 125-131.

Mathiak, K., Hertrich, I., Lutzenberger, W., & Ackermann, H. (2002b). Functional cerebral asymmetries of pitch processing during dichotic stimulus application: A whole-head magnetoencephalography study. Neuropsychologia, 40, 585–593.

Näätänen, R. (2001). The perception of speech sounds by the human brain as reflected by the mismatch negativity (MMN) and its magnetic equivalent (MMNm). Psychophysiology, 38, 1–21.

Näätänen, R., & Winkler, I. (1999). The concept of auditory stimulus representation in cognitive neuroscience. Psychological Bulletin, 125, 826–859.

Ojemann, G.A. (1983). Brain organization for language from the perspective of electrical stimulation mapping. Behavioral and Brain Sciences, 6, 189–230.

Pantev, C., Elbert, T., Ross, B., Fulitz, C., & Terhardt, E. (1996). Binaural fusion and the representation of virtual pitch in the human auditory cortex. Hearing Research, 100, 164–170.

Patel, A. D., & Balaban, E. (2001). Human pitch perception is reflected in the timing of stimulus-related cortical activity. Nature Neuroscience, 4, 839–844.

Plomp, R. (2002). The intelligent ear: On the nature of sound perception. Mahwah, NJ: Lawrence Erlbaum Associates.

Poeppel, D. (1996). A critical review of PET studies of phonological processing. Brain and Language, 55, 317–351.

Poeppel, D. (2001). Pure word deafness and the bilateral processing of the speech code. Cognitive Science, 25, 679–693.

Pugh, K.R., Shaywitz, B.A., Shaywitz, S.E., Fulbright, R.K., Byrd, D., Skudlarski, P., Shankweiler, D.P., Katz, L., Constable, R.T., Fletcher, J., Lacadie, C., Marchione, K., & Gore, J.C. (1996). Auditory selective attention: An fMRI investigation. NeuroImage, 4, 159–173.

Schreiner, C.E., & Langner, G. (1988). Periodicity coding in the inferior colliculus of the cat: II. Topographical organization. Journal of Neurophysiology, 60, 1823–1840.

Shtyrov, Y., Kujala, T., Palva, S., Ilmoniemi, R.J., & Näätänen, R. (2000). Discrimination of speech and of complex nonspeech sounds of different temporal structure in the left and right cerebral hemispheres. NeuroImage, 12, 657–663.

Sidtis, J.J. (1984). Music, pitch perception, and the mechanisms of cortical hearing. In M. Gazzaniga (Ed.), Handbook of cognitive neuroscience (pp. 91–114). New York: Plenum Press.

Studdert-Kennedy, M., & Shankweiler, D. (1970). Hemispheric specialization for speech perception. Journal of the Acoustical Society of America, 48, 579–594.

Suga, N. (1988). What does single-unit analysis in the auditory cortex tell us about information processing in the auditory system? In P. Rakic & W. Singer (Eds.), Neurobiololgy of neocortex (pp. 331–349). Chichester: Wiley & Sons.

Suga, N. (1994). Multi-function theory for cortical processing of auditory information: Implications of single-unit and lesion data for future research. Journal of Comparative Physiology A, 175, 135–144.

Tallal, P., Miller, S., & Fitch, R.H. (1993). Neurobiological basis of speech: A case for the preeminence of temporal processing. Annals of the New York Academy of Sciences, 682, 27–47.

Tzourio, N., Massioui, F.E., Crivello, F., Joliot, M., Renault, B., & Mazoyer, B. (1997). Functional anatomy of human auditory attention studied with PET. NeuroImage, 5, 63–77.

Zatorre, R.J. (2003). Hemispheric asymmetries in the processing of tonal stimuli. In K. Hugdahl & R.J. Davidson (Eds.), The asymmetrical brain (pp. 411–440). Cambridge, MA: MIT Press.

Zatorre, R.J., Evans, A.C., Meyer, E., & Gjedde, A. (1992). Lateralization of phonetic and pitch processing in speech perception. Science, 256, 846–849.

PART II

CODING OF SOUNDS

12. INTRODUCTION: CODING OF SOUNDS

Michael Brosch

The contributions contained in this section are a non-exhaustive representation of the increasing breadth of research on "Coding of Sound in Auditory Cortex". They demonstrate a range in invasive and non-invasive methodologies, which include recordings of single cell discharge and intracortical electrical slow wave field potentials, and optical imaging of intrinsic signals as well as recordings of electro- and magnetoencephalographic signals and imaging hemodynamic responses. The goal of this introduction is to provide the reader with a non-technical overview of the topics, general hypotheses, and conclusions of the authors. In an effort to organize these chapters into a cohesive picture, we have distilled a few overriding issues recurring throughout the contributions and specific to this section of this book.

The chapters of this section cast some light on what leading researchers in the field consider possible functional roles of auditory cortex. While in some contributions it is, implicitly and sometimes explicitly, assumed, that auditory cortex is involved in low-level automatic processing of sound, others assume that auditory cortex differs qualitatively from earlier stations of the auditory pathway. Lower levels up to the auditory midbrain are thought to basically provide a high-fidelity representation of the acoustic structure of sound. Auditory cortex, by contrast, performs a more abstract processing on sound. This may include the segregation of the sounds simultaneously emanating from different auditory objects that superimpose at the ear or the extraction of sound invariances from the large number of different realizations of the same auditory object. These processes may facilitate the classification and recognition of sounds and may enable access to auditory memory. In addition to utilizing efficient mechanisms for sound representation, auditory cortex may also process sound under other primarily non-auditory premises, which may involve the environmental and communicative importance of sound and the control of self-produced sounds, including vocalizations and speech signals.

As much as there are different views on functional roles of auditory cortex, there is variety of approaches how coding in auditory cortex can be understood. Studies have used simple stimuli like pure tones, noise bursts, modulated sounds, and complex sound like speech, which are presented monaurally, binaurally, or dichotically at various sound pressure levels. This is done with the intention to characterize response properties of individual neurons or large groups of neurons or to obtain transfer functions which allow to predict the neural response to arbitrary acoustic signals.

Inseparable from the question which sound features are coded in auditory cortex is the question of how auditory cortex encodes and decodes information. Put in other words, this is equivalent to asking what are the appropriate parts of auditory cortex and the neural observables that are crucial for coding and what features of the neural observables provide the neuronal codes. In the following contributions, a number of observables are explored, ranging from the firing of single neurons and of ensembles of neurons to slowly varying electric and magnetic fields on a mesoscopic or macroscopic scale, to hemodynamic responses. The latter provides an indirect measure of neural activation with a relatively high spatial but poor temporal resolution. Gross electric and magnetic fields have the advantage of yielding a high temporal resolution in the millisecond range and may yield a spatial resolution of centimeters or millimeters. While these non-invasive techniques allow to observe the activity of large brain regions, the recordings of the firing of neurons provide only a very restricted picture of brain activation, limited by the number of electrodes that can be brought into the regions of interest. Nevertheless recording of action potentials offers the unique opportunity to get insights on neuronal transformations and calculations on the single cell level.

Neurons transmit information, which can be quantified using information theory once one 'knows' what 'symbol' in the neural activity codes for it. Potential coding symbols are the average firing rate, interspike intervals, precise spike times, spike bursts, synchronized spikes across neuronal populations on the level of the firing of neurons, and amplitudes, frequency content and phase relationship on the level of electric and magnetic fields. One powerful approach to examine what features of neural activity provide a code is to compare these features with perception or behavior, which has been done in normal subjects or in subjects with specific deficits. Despite the progress that has already been made in finding potential coding parameters it is still unclear who 'reads' the neuronal activity and how perception emerges from neuronal activity.

In the following chapters of this section a number of potential codes and coding mechanisms will be critically described and analyzed. Heil and Neubauer put forward arguments how the detection of simple stimuli may be based on the occurrence of the first spikes generated in the auditory nerve. Middlebrooks, Furukawa, Stecker, and Mickey review work, mostly performed on cats, suggesting that the discharge patterns of cell assemblies in auditory cortex provide the code utilized for sound localization and that caudal auditory cortex might play a more important role in spatial representation than other parts of auditory cortex. Wible, Nicol, and Kraus describe experiments that show that reading impairments in children may result from an underdeveloped hemispheric and regional specialization for the processing of simple acoustic signals and speech signals. Eggermont reviews basic features of neuronal assemblies defined by synchronously firing neurons and argues that neuronal synchrony may be of functional importance in auditory cortex, particularly for the extraction of stimulus invariances with high signal-to-noise ratios. Villa describes experiments, performed on behaving rats, designed to understand neuronal mechanisms, particularly precise spatio-temporal spike patterns, underlying speech sound perception. Ahissar and Ahissar propose a model for the decoding of the temporal envelope of speech signals that is consistent with perceptual phenomena seen in normal and reading impaired subjects: an array of intrinsic cortical oscillators set at adjustable frequencies in the range of natural frequencies of syllables sets a pace for syllabic segmentation and their spectral analysis. Taniguchi, Sugimoto, Hess, Horikawa, Hosokawa, and Scheich describe experiments they have performed with voltage-sensitive dyes and with pharmacological manipulation of synaptic transmission, which demonstrate how different synaptic transmission systems contribute to the generation of differential spatio-temporal activity patterns in response to various acoustic stimuli. Nelken, Las, Ulanovsky, and Farkas review their experimental findings and that of others in favor of their theoretical accounts that auditory cortex is involved in the processing of more abstract features of the structure of acoustic signals. Finally, Eliades and Wang exploit concepts of a more stimulus representation in auditory cortex and review findings that auditory cortex is actively involved in the control of vocalizations and speech and in the distinction between self-produced sounds and other environmental sounds. Note that some other issues of the coding of sound are covered in the chapters of other sections of this book.

13. TOWARD A UNIFYING BASIS OF AUDITORY THRESHOLDS

Peter Heil, Heinrich Neubauer

INTRODUCTION

One of the major goals of auditory neuroscience is to explain psychophysical performance in terms of neuronal processing (see Nelken et al., 2004). While this can be attempted for psychophysical tasks of various complexities and at all processing levels of the auditory system, it would seem reasonable to start with seemingly easy paradigms, for example, the detection of simple stimuli in quiet. A detailed knowledge of how the system at the perceptual level and of how individual neurons, e.g. in auditory cortex, reach threshold in response to sounds is likely to also promote a more thorough understanding of sound coding by individual neurons and populations.

Among physiologists it is common practice to specify neuronal thresholds in terms of pressure only, e.g. in dB SPL. Thresholds expressed this way for pure tones and plotted as a function of tone frequency yield the well-known frequency tuning curves found in numerous articles and textbooks on hearing. This practice implies that thresholds of auditory neurons are sufficiently characterized by that pressure and are independent of stimulus duration. However, at the perceptual level, the SPL needed to detect a stimulus decreases as stimulus duration increases in every species examined (for reviews see Fay, 1992; O'Connor et al., 1999). Such a trading relationship between a sound's amplitude and its duration is consistent with the notion that the auditory system integrates sound over time. It is frequently believed that the physical quantity of sound ultimately integrated by the system is sound intensity, $I(t)$ (e.g., Au, 1988; Brown & Maloney, 1986; Clark & Bohne, 1986; Clock Eddins et al., 1993; Clock Eddins & Peterson, 1999; Dooling, 1976; Ehret, 1976; Fay & Coombs, 1983; Garner, 1947; Gerken et al., 1990; Gollisch et al., 2002; Green, 1985;

Johnson, 1968; Klump & Maier, 1990; O'Connor et al., 1999; Plomp & Bouman, 1959; Ronacher et al., 2000; Schmidt & Thaller, 1994; Solecki & Gerken, 1990; Syrlykke et al. 1988; Tougaard, 1996; Watson & Gengel, 1969; Zwislocki, 1960). $I(t)$ is the sound power transmitted per unit area and, for pure tones, is proportional to the square of the peak pressure or the pressure envelope, $P(t)$ (Buser & Imbert, 1992). Since $I(t)$ integrated over time yields energy density, the common interpretation of the perceptual data therefore implies that the auditory system has a threshold that is best specified in terms of the sound's acoustic energy density, and not its pressure. The energy density of threshold stimuli generally increases with increasing stimulus duration, a time-dependence which has often been attributed to leaky integration of $I(t)$. This interpretation, however, encounters serious problems because of the very long time constants, up to several hundreds of milliseconds, needed to describe the increase in threshold energy with increasing duration (for summaries see Gerken et al., 1990; O'Connor et al., 1999). Such long time constants contrast with the short membrane time constants of neurons in the auditory periphery (deBoer, 1985; Clock et al., 1993; Golding et al., 1995; Green, 1985; Viemeister & Wakefield, 1991) and are also difficult to reconcile with the high temporal resolution of the auditory system. Some ideas have been proposed to resolve this "resolution-integration paradox," such as that temporal resolution is mediated by peripheral processing and temporal integration by processing high up in the central auditory system (Gerken et al., 1990; Watson & Gengel, 1969; Zwislocki, 1960), that the system only acts as if it were an integrator but instead takes "multiple looks" (Viemeister & Wakefield, 1991), or that the system performs a running cross-correlation of the activity pattern triggered by a particular threshold stimulus with a stored template of a pattern produced by some suprathreshold version of that stimulus (Dau et al., 1996a, 1996b). These central, memory-based, models are difficult to assess physiologically. And, they contrast with findings of clear parallels of the perceptual trading relationship between the SPL of a threshold stimulus and its duration in neuronal responses at very peripheral levels of the auditory system, viz. cochlear nucleus (Clock Eddins et al., 1993; Kitzes et al., 1978) and auditory nerve (Clock Eddins et al., 1998; Dunia & Narins, 1989), suggesting that integration is accomplished at, or peripheral to, the auditory nerve.

Here we take a different approach to arrive at a unifying description of auditory thresholds at the physiological and perceptual levels, but also to disclose the parameter that is really traded for stimulus duration, and to aid the identification of the processes by which thresholds are reached. Most of the findings reported here have been published elsewhere (e.g., Heil & Neubauer, 2003).

Our approach is from physiology and is based on the rationale that the first spike of an auditory neuron following the onset of a stimulus is triggered when the stimulus reaches the neuron's threshold and that it occurs with some fixed "transmission delay" thereafter (Fig. 13.1a). Thus, the stimulus-dependent timing of this first and for auditory cortical neurons often only spike (e.g., deWeese et al., 2003; Heil, 1997b; Phillips, 1988) can be exploited to derive their thresholds. We have previously used this approach to show that thresholds of primary (AI) and other auditory cortical neurons and of auditory-nerve (AN) fibers are not specified in terms of fixed pressures (Heil, 1997a; Heil & Irvine, 1996, 1998; Heil & Neubauer, 2001). In fact, the instantaneous value of $P(t)$ at which the first spike was triggered during the onset decreased as first-spike latency increased, a trading relationship consistent with temporal summation (Figs. 13.1a, 13.1b). Here we show that integration of $P(t)$ provides a better descriptor than integration of $I(t)$ for thresholds of AI neurons as well as for perceptual thresholds.

METHODS

Electrophysiology

Spikes from well-isolated single AI neurons and AN fibers were recorded in a sound-attenuating chamber from adult barbiturate-anaesthetized cats (Heil, 1997a; Heil & Irvine, 1997). AI neurons respond preferentially at sound onset (e.g., Brugge et al., 1969; deWeese et al., 2003; Heil, 1997a, 1997b; Phillips, 1988), where $I(t)$ and $P(t)$ both increase dynamically, but differently, because $I(t) \propto P^2(t)$. To exploit these differences, we stimulated each neuron with tones, at its characteristic frequency (CF), of different onset functions and systematically varied both the time to the steady-state SPL (onset time or rise time) and the SPL. Onset functions were either linear (Fig. 13.1b), i.e. $P(t)$ increased linearly with time, t, during the onset time, t_r, to the maximum, P_{max}: $P(t) = P_{max} \cdot t/t_r$, with onset times of 1, 5, 10, 50, and 100 ms; or cosine-squared (cos²) (Fig. 13.1a), that is, $P(t) = P_{max} \cdot \sin^2(\pi/2 \cdot t/t_r)$, with onset times of 1.7, 4.2, 8.5, 17, 42, 85, and 170 ms. The SPL was increased from low to high values (usually 0–90 dB SPL during steady-state) in 5- or 10-dB steps. Each stimulus was repeated 20–50 times. Tone durations were 400 ms (AI) or 200 ms (AN). Tones were presented at 1 Hz (AI) or 2 Hz (AN) through sound-delivery tubes sealed into the external meati.

Psychoacoustics

Detection thresholds (in dB SPL) for 11 human subjects (4 tested twice) and 5 cats were kindly given to us by G.M. Gerken and measured as detailed elsewhere (Gerken et al., 1990; Solecki & Gerken, 1990). Thresholds were obtained to sets of single- and multiple-burst stimuli differing in duration and envelope characteristics (Fig. 13.2a). The carrier frequency was 3.125 kHz for humans and 6.25 kHz for cats. The shortest stimulus (stimulus 1) was composed only of onset and offset portions of 4.16 ms each ($P(t)$ of cos² function). Multiple-burst stimuli were composed of stimulus 1 repeated to form stimuli

P. Heil, H. Neubauer

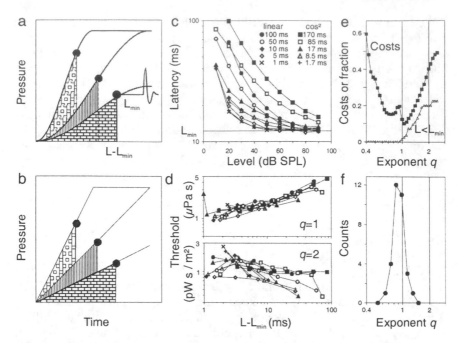

Fig. 13.1. Thresholds of AI neurons can be extracted from the stimulus-dependent timing of their responses and are better described as being reached by temporal integration of $P(t)$ than of $I(t)$. **a, b.** Onset envelopes, $P(t)$, of the tonal stimuli followed cosine-squared (a) or linear functions (b). Onset times to steady-state SPL and SPL were varied. Filled dots mark the times, $L - L_{min}$, and corresponding instantaneous amplitudes at which a hypothetical neuron´s response to these stimuli would be triggered. The spike is measured with a constant "transmission delay", L_{min}, thereafter (shown for one stimulus in a). Filled areas underneath pressure envelopes represent pressure envelope integration thresholds. **c.** Mean first spike latency, used to derive threshold, plotted against SPL for different onset times and onset functions of a single cat AI neuron tested at its CF of 22 kHz (see key). **d.** Individual thresholds (key as in c) for that AI neuron plotted against the time-to-threshold, $L - L_{min}$. The vertical scatter of individual thresholds and the systematic differences between mean thresholds obtained with different rise functions are smaller when thresholds are expressed in terms of the temporal integral of $P(t)$ ($q = 1$; top) than of $I(t)$ ($q = 2$; bottom). L_{min}, the only free parameter of the fits, was 12.21 ms for $q = 1$ and 12.57 ms for $q = 2$. **e.** Costs (filled squares) and proportion of data points for which $L_{min} < L$ (open triangles) as a function of the exponent q of $P(t)$. **f.** Distribution of the optimal q obtained from 32 neurons tested with different onset functions. The geometric mean was 0.914 with an error interval of 0.791–1.054.

that differed either in number of bursts (multiple-burst series: stimuli 1–5) or in interburst interval (interval series: stimuli 3, 21–24). A single-burst series (stimuli 6–14) was created by adding a constant amplitude plateau in the middle of the stimulus; and an onset–offset series (stimuli 1, 15–20) by varying onset and offset times.

RESULTS

AI thresholds are well described by temporal integration of $P(t)$

We first derived thresholds of AI neurons from the stimulus-dependence of their mean first-spike latency, L. Figures 13.1c-e show the data for one representative neuron. Panel c reveals that for each onset function, L decreased with increasing SPL for a given rise time and decreased with decreasing rise time for a given SPL, finally approaching a minimum, L_{min}, the neuron-specific constant transmission delay (Heil, 1997a,b; Heil & Irvine, 1996, 1997, 1998).

Based on our previous experience with AN fibers (Heil & Neubauer, 2001), whose latencies behave qualitatively similarly (Heil & Irvine, 1997), we phenomenologically modeled the data by assuming that threshold, T, is equal to the temporal integral, from stimulus onset, $t = 0$, to the trigger time of the first spike, $t = L - L_{min}$, of $P(t)$ raised to a power, q:

$$T(L - L_{min}) = \int_{0}^{L-L_{min}} P^q(t)\, dt \qquad (1)$$

with $T(L - L_{min})$, L_{min}, and q as free parameters. For $q = 1$, $T(L - L_{min})$ can be conceptualized as an area underneath the stimulus pressure envelope $P(t)$ (the differently shaded areas in Figs. 13.1a, 13.1b), and for $q = 2$, as an area underneath the intensity envelope $I(t)$, since $I(t) \propto P^2(t)$. Note that T in Equation 1 is a function of $L - L_{min}$, meaning that threshold defined this way must not necessarily be constant, but may constitute some function of the time it takes to reach T (the differently shaded areas in Figs. 13.1a, 13.1b may differ in size). We will first deal with the value of q in the right-hand term of Equation 1, i.e., with the issue of whether $P(t)$ or $I(t)$ is integrated to reach threshold, both at the AI neuronal and the perceptual level. We will then turn to the time-dependence of the thresholds defined in this way.

The optimal exponent q of $P(t)$ for a given AI neuron was obtained by minimizing a cost function which depended on q and L_{min}. The cost function was defined such that its minimum was obtained when the spread of thresholds at any given integration time, $L - L_{min}$, and systematic differences between the thresholds obtained with linear and with $\cos^2$ onset functions were minimal (explained in more detail in Heil & Neubauer, 2003). This approach only postulates that thresholds to those CF tones of different onset function, onset time, and SPL which elicit responses with identical $L - L_{min}$ should be identical (e.g., the two brick-filled areas in Figs. 13.1a, 13.1b should be identical in size, because in this schematic the two corresponding stimuli evoke responses at identical times after onset). The approach imposes no *a priori* constraints on thresholds for different values of $L - L_{min}$ (e.g., the vertically hatched and the brick-filled areas in Fig. 13.1a or in Fig. 13.1b could differ in size, because the corresponding stimuli evoke responses at different times after onset). This approach thus allows T to be constant or to form any function of $L - L_{min}$.

The cost function of the example neuron has its global minimum near $q = 1$ (Fig. 13.1e). Furthermore, with increasing q, the estimated L_{min} also increases. This results in an increase in the proportion of stimuli for which the measured latency L is shorter than L_{min} from near zero for $q \leq 1$ to ~20% for $q = 2$ (Fig. 13.1e, open triangles). Since for a good model, L_{min} should be shorter than all measured values of L, this result renders temporal integration of $I(t)$ rather implausible. Figure 13.1d shows that when the thresholds (obtained from best fits) to all tones for this neuron are plotted against $L - L_{min}$, the vertical scatter of the data points is appreciably smaller for $q = 1$ (top) than for $q = 2$ (bottom). Across our AI sample, the optimal values of the exponent q of $P(t)$ were narrowly distributed around 1, and not 2 (Fig. 13.1f). These findings demonstrate that thresholds of AI neurons, like AN fibers (Heil & Neubauer, 2001), can be well described as being reached by temporal integration of $P(t)$, and better than by temporal integration of $I(t)$. This description shall not imply that thresholds are in fact reached by an integration process in the literal or physical sense. In other words, we do not assume the existence of a response which is directly proportional to the continuously increasing integral of $P(t)$ or of $P(t)$ raised to some power and which could be measured during a given trial. We rather assume that temporal integration is a statistical summation process (see below, and Heil & Neubauer, 2003).

Perceptual thresholds are also well described by temporal integration of $P(t)$

To also distinguish between integration of $P(t)$ and of $I(t)$ at the perceptual level, we next re-analyzed perceptual thresholds for both cats and humans tested with a large set of single- and multiple-burst tones (original data from Gerken et al., 1991; Solecki & Gerken, 1990) that differed in duration and envelope characteristics (Fig. 13.2a). The results (Figs. 13.2b-f) show clearly that also at this level the integral of $P(t)$ provides a much better fit to the data than the integral of $I(t)$. We start by considering the dependence of thresholds, expressed in dB SPL (corresponding to the peak amplitude), on stimulus duration. We define stimulus duration as the total duration during which sound is present. This definition thus excludes all silent intervals and it does not weight the durations of onsets and offsets any different than the duration of a plateau. In both humans and cats, the threshold SPL decreased with increasing number of bursts (stimuli 1–5 in Fig. 13.2a; open circles), with increasing plateau duration (stimuli 1, 6–14; filled circles), and, tested in humans only, with increasing onset–offset times for a single burst without plateau (stimuli 1, 15–18; plus-signs; Fig. 13.2b). These trading relationships between threshold SPL and stimulus duration are all consistent with thresholds reached by temporal summation. Threshold SPL did not differ for time-reversed versions of stimuli with temporally asymmetric envelopes (stimuli 19–20) or for multiple-burst stimuli differing in interburst interval, from 4.16 ms to 66.56 ms (stimuli 3, 21–24; the five crosses representing the threshold SPLs for these stimuli in Figs. 13b-e essentially fall on top of one another). The latter result is inconsistent

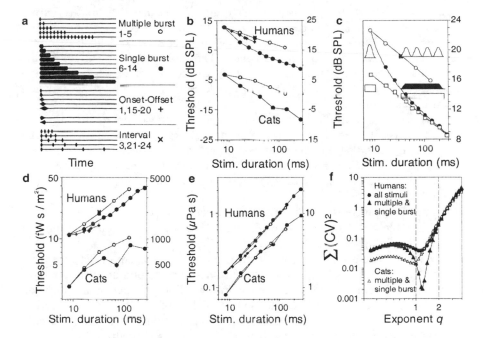

Fig. 13.2. Perceptual thresholds are also better described as being reached by temporal integration of *P(t)* than of *I(t)*. **a**. Pressure envelopes of the stimuli for which detection thresholds were obtained. Multiple-burst series (open circles): stimuli 1–5; single-burst series (filled circles): 6–14; onset–offset series (plus-signs): 1, 15–20; and interval series (crosses): 3, 21–24. The same symbols are used in b–e. Abscissa duration, 275 ms. Modified and reprinted with permission from Gerken et al., Auditory temporal integration and the power function model, Journal of the Acoustical Society of America 88(2), 767–778, 1990. Copyright 1990, Acoustical Society of America. **b**. Grand means of threshold SPL plotted against stimulus duration for human subjects (right ordinate) and cats (left ordinate). Stimulus duration excludes interburst intervals. **c**. Threshold SPL plotted against stimulus duration for theoretical rectangular stimuli (grey squares). The human data from (**b**) for single-burst stimuli, multiple-burst stimuli and interval series are replotted. Straight lines are power law fits for grey and open symbols, and curved line was calculated from the former for stimuli with cos² onset and offset times of 4.16 ms. Envelopes of multiple-burst (open), single-burst (black) and rectangular (grey) threshold stimuli with durations of 8.32 ms and 33.28 ms are depicted. **d–e**. Thresholds of humans (right ordinates) and cats (left ordinates) expressed as temporal integrals of *I(t)* (i.e. as energy densities, calculated with a specific impedance of 414 Pa·s·m⁻¹) (d) and as temporal integrals of *P(t)* (e) plotted against stimulus duration. **f**. The alignment of thresholds for stimuli from the different series is best (the measure of distance, Σ(CV)², is smallest) for values of *q* near 1, in cats (open triangles) and humans (filled symbols).

with the leaky integration hypothesis, which would predict an increase in threshold SPL with increasing interburst intervals because leakage would continue during these intervals and its net effect would increase with time

(Gerken et al., 1990). Other studies have also found that threshold SPLs are independent of the interval between two short tone bursts (Carlyon et al., 1990; Krumbholz & Wiegrebe, 1998) or clicks (Viemeister & Wakefield, 1991), once the interval exceeds a few milliseconds. Threshold SPL for stimuli in the multiple-burst, single-burst and onset–offset series diverged as duration increased (Figs. 13.2b, 13.2c). Thus, threshold SPL is not an invariant function of stimulus duration.

We next expressed the same threshold data in terms of energy density, i.e., of the temporal integral of $I(t)$ (in fW·s·m^{-2}). Energy density increased as the number of bursts, plateau duration, and stimulus onset–offset times increased. Importantly, there was a pronounced divergence of the thresholds between the series (Fig. 13.2d), so that threshold energy is also not an invariant function of stimulus duration.

In contrast, there is obviously a much closer alignment of the thresholds for stimuli in the different series when expressed in terms of the temporal integral of $P(t)$ (in μPa·s; Fig. 13.2e).

We next quantified this visual impression with a measure of distance from perfect alignment, enabling us to critically assess the optimum value of q in Equation 1. The measure was derived as follows. For a given stimulus duration and for a given q, we first calculated the coefficient of variation, CV, defined as the ratio of the square root of the mean squared deviations to the mean threshold across the series. In this way, the standard deviation is normalized by the mean threshold at every stimulus duration. CV operates on the ratio level and thus requires to take the linear values of the thresholds. CV was calculated for all durations for which thresholds from at least two series were actually available or one was available and at least one other could be obtained via linear interpolation on double-log axes. In this way, a range of durations from 11.52 to 133.12 ms could be evaluated. The coefficients were then squared and summed across all durations to yield $\Sigma(CV)^2$. Functions relating $\Sigma(CV)^2$ to the exponent q are shown in Figure 13.2f. The open triangles show the results for cats, which were tested with stimuli of the multiple- and single burst series only (Solecki & Gerken, 1990). The filled symbols show the results for humans, the filled triangles the results obtained with the single- and multiple-burst series only, and the squares with all stimuli. All three functions exhibit clear minima, that is, alignment is best at values of $q = 0.90$ (cats), $q = 1.22$ (humans, single-, and multiple-bursts), and $q = 1.15$ (humans, all stimuli), i.e., close to 1. The close alignment of thresholds for $q = 1$, as revealed by these analyses, was expected from the ~6-dB difference between threshold SPLs for single- and multiple-burst stimuli of longer durations (Figs. 13.2b, 13.2c). Hence, perceptual, like neuronal, thresholds are better defined by the temporal integral of $P(t)$ than of $I(t)$.

A close alignment of pressure envelope integration thresholds for stimuli of a given duration but of different $P(t)$ is also evident from re-analysis of data reported by Booth and Cramb (1991). These investigators obtained thresholds of human listeners to 1 kHz tones of 100 ms duration, all of which but one consisted of two segments of different amplitudes. Amplitude ratios of the bi-amplitude signals were 1, 2, 3, 5, 10 dB and the higher-amplitude segment either preceded the lower-amplitude segment or vice versa. From their data, which are expressed in dB SPL, we have calculated the thresholds in terms of the temporal integral of $P(t)$ (in μPa·s). Figure 13.3d reveals that these are essentially identical.

The time-dependence of pressure envelope integration thresholds is well described by a power law

Figure 13.2c also illustrates that perceptual thresholds expressed in terms of the temporal integral of $P(t)$ increase almost linearly with stimulus duration on double-log scales for both cats and humans. Consequently, the power law

$$T(t_s) = \int_0^{t_s} P^1(t)\, dt = k \cdot t_s^{\,m} \tag{2}$$

provides an excellent descriptor of the data. Here, t_s represents the duration of the threshold stimulus as defined above, the exponent m corresponds to the slope of the increase in $T(t_s)$ with t_s in double-log scales, and the scaling factor k defines the curve's vertical position. Equation 2 leaves only 0.84% (humans) and 1.11% (cats) of the variance unexplained, which is remarkably little, given that m and k are the only two free parameters.

We also re-analyzed available perceptual thresholds from other studies of temporal summation in various mammals, birds and fish (Brown & Maloney, 1986; Clark & Bohne, 1986; Costalupes, 1983; Dallos & Johnson, 1966; Dooling, 1976; Ehret, 1976; Fay & Coombs, 1983; Johnson, 1968; Klump & Maier, 1990) and re-plotted the data accordingly (Fig. 13.3c). It is apparent that in each species the dependence of the pressure envelope integration thresholds on stimulus duration can be well described by Equation 2. The adequacy of this power law may be obscured in the conventional plot of threshold SPL vs. log duration, particularly when only single-burst stimuli with fixed onset and offset times are used. For such stimuli, threshold SPLs increase more rapidly the shorter the stimulus duration, as illustrated with high resolution for the human data in Figure 13.2c (filled circles). This curved shape could suggest an exponential function with a long time constant, but in fact results from the increase in the proportion of onset and offset times with respect to the total duration of the tone concomitant with a decrease in plateau duration. To demonstrate this, we calculated the threshold SPLs for theoretical stimuli with rectangular $P(t)$ that had durations and temporal integrals of $P(t)$ identical to those of the single-burst threshold stimuli by dividing the temporal integral of $P(t)$ of each stimulus by its duration (grey squares in Fig. 13.2c). These values fall on a straight line (line through grey squares in Fig. 13.2c) with a slope of 20 (m-1) (here: −5.33±0.09 dB/decade of duration). Threshold SPLs measured for multiple-burst stimuli fall on a line (line through open circles and crosses in Fig. 13.2c) of similar slope (−5.64±0.10 dB/decade of duration), because the

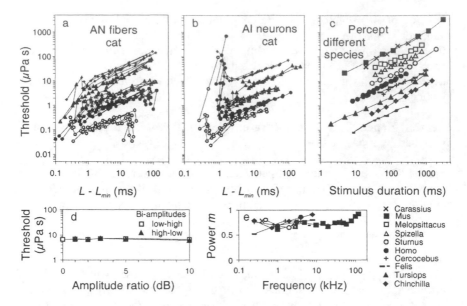

Fig. 13.3. Comparison of the pressure envelope integration thresholds for neuronal (**a-b**) and perceptual measurements (**c**). Plots of thresholds for **a.** 5 AN fibers and **b.** 5 AI neurons with different CFs (different symbols). Lines connect thresholds derived from tones of different SPLs but of the same onset function and onset time. **c.** Analogous functions for mean perceptual thresholds for a range of vertebrate species, calculated from published data (see key below panel and text for references). For the porpoise, parakeet and field sparrow, absolute thresholds could not be determined from the original articles and thus the position on the ordinate is arbitrary. **d.** For a given duration, pressure envelope integration thresholds seem rather independent of stimulus shape (here amplitude ratio of bi-amplitude signals; raw data from Booth & Cramb, 1991). **e.** The power m, obtained from perceptual measurements in different species (same key as for **c**) is largely independent of tone frequency.

proportion of onset and offset times also does not change with duration. The line is elevated by 6.15±0.22 dB, that is, a factor of ~2, relative to that for the rectangular stimuli, because the peak amplitudes of multiple-burst stimuli are twice as high as their mean amplitudes and hence as the peak amplitudes of equivalent rectangular stimuli.

The power law (Equation 2 with $L - L_{min}$ instead of t_s) can also well describe the functions relating the pressure envelope integration thresholds to time-to-threshold, i.e., to $L - L_{min}$, of cat AI neurons (Fig. 13.3b) and AN fibers (Fig. 13.3a), at least over the time range corresponding to the stimulus durations tested for perception in that species (cf. Figs. 13.3a-c). Deviations from the power law can be observed for small values of $L - L_{min}$ in some AI neurons (e.g., open and filled circles in Fig. 13.3b) and for long values in some AN fibers (e.g., open circles in Fig. 13.3a) and are readily explained as follows. In some neurons of the central auditory pathway, latency decreases with increasing

SPL for low SPLs, but for higher SPLs remains relatively constant (e.g., Covey & Casseday, 1991) or even increases with further increments in SPL (e.g., Galazuyk & Feng, 2001; Heil & Irvine, 1998; Klug et al., 2000; Phillips & Orman, 1984; Sullivan, 1982). This "paradoxical latency shift" (Sullivan, 1982) converts to the steep increase of pressure envelope integration thresholds for short integration times. The latency shift is likely mediated by fast inhibition (Galazuyk & Feng, 2001; Klug et al., 2000), a conclusion also supported by the observation that many of these AI neurons have non-monotonic spike-count versus SPL functions and respond to high-SPL short-rise time CF tones rather poorly or not at all (Heil, 1997b; Heil & Irvine, 1998; Phillips & Orman, 1984). In AN fibers, the spontaneous activity sets an upper limit to the measurable latency (Heil & Irvine, 1997; Heil & Neubauer, 2001). This upper limit, which is related to the mean interspike interval, produces roughly constant latencies to low-SPL stimuli and consequently results in a nearly vertical drop of threshold estimates for such stimuli.

The slope m of the time-dependence of pressure-envelope integration thresholds

The exponent m of Equation 2, i.e. the slope of the increase of the pressure envelope integration thresholds with stimulus duration, averaged 0.76 ± 0.09 for humans and 0.69 ± 0.06 for cats. For the other species, we obtained very similar values, ranging from 0.67 to 0.79, and, after weighting them with the number of individuals, frequencies, and stimuli tested, a mean m of 0.75. The exponent m was also largely independent of stimulus frequency, both across species and within a given species (Fig. 13.3e). Only in the mouse (raw data from Ehret, 1976) was there an increase of m with increasing frequency near the upper limit of hearing in that species (> 100 kHz; Fig. 13.3e, filled squares). A study by Florentine et al. (1988), not included in Figures 13.3e, 13.3e since we do not have the exact data, allows a similar conclusion for humans, viz. that m is largely independent of frequency (0.25–14 kHz). And, their data also allow to deduce that for 2 of the 5 subjects (DF and HF) included in the normal-hearing group, m was larger at 14 kHz than at the other frequencies and for the other subjects. Since the thresholds of DF and HF at 14 kHz were the highest in that group, and for DF actually no longer qualified as normal, the larger m may be related to presbyacusis or some other form of hearing loss (see Neubauer & Heil, 2004).

    For cat AI neurons, the values of m were more widely distributed than for perception, but for some neurons, and notably the most sensitive ones (lowest k), the values matched those for perception (not shown). The perceptual sensitivity of the cats tested by Solecki and Gerken (1990) was about 20 dB better than that of the most sensitive neurons included here and recorded by Heil and Irvine (1997), a difference likely attributable to the conditions used for neuronal recording (anesthesia; stimulation of mostly one ear only and near the tympanum, thus disenabling pinna gain). All values of m, whether from AI neurons or from perception, are < 1. This excludes a fixed pressure threshold, for which $m = 1$ and the integral $T(t_s) \sim t_s$.

DISCUSSION

Where is the integrator?

The functions relating the pressure envelope integration threshold to time-to-threshold, $L - L_{min}$, or stimulus duration for AN fibers, AI neurons and perception in the same species, viz. the cat, are very similar (cf. Figs. 13.3a-c). The similarity between AN and AI stresses the fact that cortical response properties, here the stimulus dependent response timing which is undoubtedly critical for cortical coding (Heil, 2004; see also Middlebrooks et al., 2004), can be largely inherited from the periphery. And, the most parsimonious conclusion is that the integrator is peripheral to the site of spike generation in the AN fibers. A more central origin, as proposed by others (Dau et al., 1996a, 1996b; Gerken et al., 1990; Viemeister & Wakefield, 1991; Watson & Gengel, 1969; Zwislocki, 1969), seems unnecessary to explain the data, although central processes, including attention (e.g., Dai & Wright, 1995), could modify thresholds (see comments above re differences between Figs. 13.3a and 13.3b). We can also conclude that the integrator must be central to the processes determining the inner hair cell's (IHC) membrane potential. This potential almost instantaneously follows the fine structure of the stimulus at low frequencies and the pressure envelope, $P(t)$, at higher frequencies, without any slow changes of its DC component when $P(t)$ is constant (Kros, 1996). These observations agree well with the short, ~1.4 ms (Raybold et al., 2001), IHC membrane time constants. Thus, the integration of $P(t)$ over the observed long time scales cannot have been accomplished at, or peripheral to, the level of the receptor potential. Also, the compelling evidence that each IHC is innervated by 10–30 AN fibers of different spontaneous rates and thresholds (Liberman, 1982), argues against an integrator identical for all afferent fibers of a given IHC (Heil & Neubauer, 2001). This limits the possible location of the integrator to the first synapse in the auditory pathway, between the IHC and the distal dendrite of a single AN fiber, including that distal dendrite with its additional synaptic inputs, just below the IHC, from efferent fibers of the lateral olivocochlear system (Liberman et al., 1990). This synaptic region is structurally diverse, which could readily account for the range of AN fiber sensitivities, as there are systematic relationships between morphological and physiological properties (Liberman, 1982; Liberman et al., 1990; Merchan-Perez & Liberman, 1996; Ruel et al., 2001).

How could the integrator work?

Equation 2 can be reformulated to yield the parameter, $\overline{R}$, which is actually traded for duration, i.e., that parameter which when multiplied with duration yields a constant:

$$\overline{R} \cdot t_s = const. \tag{3}$$

Here $\overline{R} = c \cdot \overline{P}^{\alpha}$, $\alpha - (1-m)^{-1}$, $c - const. \cdot (1/k)^{\alpha}$, and $\overline{P} = \left[\int_0^{t_s} P(t)\, dt\right]/t_s$, is

the mean amplitude of $P(t)$ during t_s. Because *const.* is dimensionless, $\overline{R}$ has the unit Hz. $\overline{R}$ can be interpreted as a mean rate of individual events, each of which could be very brief (point processes). Then, *const.* identifies the number of such events that need to be accumulated for threshold, and t_s the time required to accumulate that number. This view resolves the resolution–integration paradox. Because $\overline{R} \propto \overline{P}^{\alpha}$, t_s is short when $\overline{P}$ is high, indicating high temporal resolution. As $\overline{P}$ decreases, t_s increases and the temporal resolution decreases, consistent with available data (e.g., Giraudi et al., 1980). This general interpretation of this trading law does not require any assumptions about the necessary number of events nor about their distribution (homogeneous or inhomogeneous) over time. It is also important to stress that such an accumulation process of individual events is not equivalent to the temporal integration of a continuously changing quantity (e.g. of $P(t)$ or $I(t)$). Rather, on this view, the „integration" is a summation of chance events, which occur with a mean rate $\overline{R}$ or probability per unit of time $\sim P^{\alpha}$, and the "integration time" is the average waiting time required for the necessary number of such events (= *const.*) to occur. Our re-analysis of the perceptual data (Fig. 13.3c) reveals no obvious deviations from Equation 3, except maybe for a tendency of m to increase slightly at rather long durations (see data of mouse or starling in Fig. 13.3c). This increase could be accounted for by the assumption of some lower limit of the pressure which the system can detect and, in contrast to the relatively short maximum integration times (~200 ms) proposed (Green, 1985), does not require an upper limit to the "integration time". This is nicely in accord with our view of this time as a waiting time for some number of chance events to occur.

What could be the nature of these chance events? Their probability of occurrence, $\sim \overline{P}^{\alpha}$, can be viewed as a conditional probability that results from the interaction of α statistically independent sub-events, the probability of each of those occurring being proportional to $\overline{P}$. From the slopes m of the perceptual data values of α between 3 and 5 are derived. Thus, it seems meaningful to search for events, which are mediated by 3, 4 or 5 sub-events. A strong candidate for such events is exocytosis at the IHC-AN fiber synapse, which, in mouse, depends approximately on the 4th power of the intracellular Ca^{2+}-concentration, so that 4-5 Ca^{2+}-binding steps (the sub-events) are necessary (Beutner et al., 2001). The molecular steps underlying this supralinear dependence of exocytosis on the intracellular Ca^{2+}-concentration could thus constitute the basis for the phenomenon of temporal summation, which is so strikingly similar across species, from goldfish to humans (Fig. 13.3c). It is noteworthy in this context that the supralinear dependence of exocytosis on Ca^{2+} seems to be conserved in evolution, because similar exponents (between 3 and 5) have been reported, or are inferred, for the giant synapse in the squid, the bipolar neuron in the goldfish retina, the neuromuscular junction in the frog, and the calyx of Held in the rat auditory brainstem (for review see Meinrenken et al., 2003).

Does this mean that a single vesicle, or group of vesicles given the evidence for simultaneous multi-vesicular release (Fuchs et al., 2003; Glowatzki & Fuchs, 2001), which is released at a single presynaptic site of an IHC in response to a sound and which then triggers a single postsynaptic spike in the afferent AN fiber, is sufficient for perception of that sound? In the case of tactile afferents, it has been shown that a single spike in a single fiber can be perceived (Vallbo et al., 1984), but for AN fibers this is unlikely to be the case. This is so, because AN fibers are generally spontaneously active, i.e., discharge in the absence of intentional acoustic stimulation, and the most sensitive fibers have the highest spontaneous rates (which can exceed 100 spikes/s). But, if the sound triggered extra spikes at roughly the same time in a small number of AN fibers innervating the same or different IHCs, coincidence detectors at higher levels could start separating the signal from the noise. There is good evidence that such coincidence detection operates as low as the cochlear nucleus (Joris et al., 1994).

ACKNOWLEDGMENTS

We are grateful to D.R.F. Irvine in collaboration with whom the electrophysiological data were recorded, and to G.M. Gerken who generously allowed us access to his perceptual data. This study was supported by the BMBF, the state of Sachsen-Anhalt, and grants of the DFG to P.H.

REFERENCES

Au, W.W.L. (1988). Detection and recognition models of dolphin sonar systems. In P.E. Nachtigall & P.W.B. Moore (Eds.), Animal sonar: Processes and performance (pp. 753–768). New York: Plenum.

Beutner, D., Voets, T., Neher, E., & Moser, T. (2001). Calcium dependence of exocytosis and endocytosis at the cochlear inner hair cell afferent synapse. Neuron, 29, 681–690.

Booth, J.C., & Cramb, D.A. (1991). Threshold integration of bi-amplitude signals. Hearing Research, 52, 312–320.

Brown, C.H., & Maloney, C.G. (1986). Temporal integration in two species of Old World monkeys: Blue monkeys (Cercopithecus mitis) and grey-cheeked mangabeys

(*Cercocebus albigena*). Journal of the Acoustical Society of America, 79, 1058–1064.

Brugge, J.F., Dubrovsky, N.A., Aitkin, L.M., & Anderson, D.J. (1969). Sensitivity of single neurons in auditory cortex of cat to binaural tonal stimulation: Effects of varying interaural time and intensity. Journal of Neurophysiology, 32, 1005–1024.

Buser, P., & Imbert, M. (1992). Audition. Cambridge: MIT Press.

Carlyon, R.P., Buus, S., & Florentine, M. (1990). Temporal integration of trains of tone pulses by normal and cochlearly impaired listeners. Journal of the Acoustical Society of America, 87, 260–268.

Clark, W.W., & Bohne, B.A. (1986). Cochlear damage. Audiometric correlates. In: M.J. Collins, T.J. Glattke, & L.A. Harker (Eds.), Sensorineural Hearing Loss (pp. 59–82). Iowa City: University of Iowa.

Clock Eddins, A., & Peterson, J.R. (1999). Time-intensity trading in the late auditory evoked potential. Journal of Speech, Language, and Hearing Research, 42, 516–525.

Clock Eddins, A., Salvi, R.R., Saunders, S.S., & Powers, N.L. (1993). Neural correlates of temporal integration in the cochlear nucleus of the chinchilla. Hearing Research, 71, 37–50.

Clock Eddins, A., Salvi, R.R., Wang, J., & Powers, N.L. (1998). Threshold-duration functions of chinchilla auditory nerve fibers. Hearing Research, 119, 135–141.

Costalupes, J.A. (1983). Temporal integration of pure tones in the cat. Hearing Research, 9, 43–54.

Covey, E., & Casseday, J.H. (1991). The monaural nuclei of the lateral lemniscus in an echolocating bat: Parallel pathways for analyzing temporal features of sound. Journal of Neuroscience, 11, 3456–3470.

Dai, H., & Wright, B.A. (1995). Detecting signals of unexpected and uncertain durations. Journal of the Acoustical Society of America, 98, 708–896.

Dallos, P.J., & Johnson, K.R. (1966). Influence of rise-fall time upon short-tone threshold. Journal of the Acoustical Society of America, 40, 1160–1163.

Dau, T., Püschel, D., & Kohlrausch, A. (1996a). A quantitative model of the "effective" signal processing in the auditory system I. Model structure. Journal of the Acoustical Society of America, 99, 3615–3622.

Dau, T., Püschel, D., & Kohlrausch, A. (1996b). A quantitative model of the "effective" signal processing in the auditory system II. Simulations and measurements. Journal of the Acoustical Society of America, 99, 3623–3631.

deBoer, E. (1985). Auditory time constants: a paradox? In A. Michelsen (Ed.), Time Resolution in the Auditory System (pp. 141–158). Heidelberg: Springer.

deWeese, M.R., Wehr, M., & Zador, A.M. (2003). Binary spiking in auditory cortex. Journal of Neuroscience, 23, 7940–7949.

Dooling, R.J. (1976). Temporal summation of pure tones in birds. Journal of the Acoustical Society of America, 65, 1058–1060.

Dunia, R., & Narins, P.M. (1989). Temporal integration in an anuran auditory nerve. Hearing Research, 39, 287–297.

Ehret, G. (1976). Temporal auditory summation for pure tones and white noise in the house mouse (*Mus musculus*). Journal of the Acoustical Society of America, 59, 1421–1427.

Fay, R.R. (1992). Structure and function in sound discrimination among vertebrates. In D.B. Webster, R.R. Fay, & A.N. Popper (Eds.), The Evolutionary Biology of Hearing (pp. 229–263). New York: Springer.

Fay, R.R., & Coombs, S. (1983). Neural mechanisms in sound detection and temporal summation. Hearing Research, 10, 69–92.

Florentine, M., Fastl, H., & Buus, S. (1988). Temporal integration in normal hearing, cochlear impairment, and impairment simulated by masking. Journal of the Acoustical Society of America, 84, 195–203.

Fuchs, P.A., Glowatzki, E., & Moser, T. (2003). The afferent synapse of cochlear hair cells. Current Opinion in Neurobiology, 13, 452–458.

Galazyuk A.V., & Feng, A.S. (2001). Oscillation may play a role in time domain central auditory processing. Journal of Neuroscience, 21, RC147.

Garner, W.R. (1947). The effect of frequency spectrum on temporal integration of energy in the ear. Journal of the Acoustical Society of America, 19, 808–815.

Gerken, G.M., Bhat, V.K.H., & Hutchison-Clutter, M. (1990). Auditory temporal integration and the power function model. Journal of the Acoustical Society of America, 88, 767–778.

Giraudi, D., Salvi, R., Henderson, D., & Hamernik, R. (1980). Gap detection by the chinchilla. Journal of the Acoustical Society of America, 68, 802–806.

Glowatzki, E., & Fuchs, P.A. (2002). Transmitter release at the hair cell ribbon synapse. Nature Neuroscience, 5, 147–154.

Golding, N.L., Robertson, D., & Oertel, D. (1995). Recordings from slices indicate that octopus cells of the cochlear nucleus detect coincident firing of auditory nerve fibers with temporal precision. Journal of Neuroscience, 15, 3138–3153.

Gollisch, T., Schütze, H., Benda, J., & Herz, A.V.M. (2002). Energy integration describes sound-intensity coding in an insect auditory system. Journal of Neuroscience, 22, 10434–10448.

Green, D.M. (1985). Temporal factors in psychoacoustics. In Michelsen, A. (Ed.), Time Resolution in the Auditory System (pp. 122–140). Heidelberg: Springer.

Heil, P. (1997a). Auditory cortical onset responses revisited: I. First-spike timing. Journal of Neurophysiology, 77, 2616–2641.

Heil, P. (1997b). Auditory cortical onset responses revisited: II. Response strength. Journal of Neurophysiology, 77, 2642–2660.

Heil, P. (2004). First-spike latency of auditory neurons reconsidered. Current Opinion in Neurobiology, 14, 461–467.

Heil, P., & Irvine, D.R.F. (1996). On determinants of first-spike latency in auditory cortex. Neuroreport, 7, 3073–3076.

Heil, P., & Irvine, D.R.F. (1997). First-spike timing of auditory-nerve fibers and comparison with auditory cortex. Journal of Neurophysiology, 78, 2438–2454.

Heil, P., & Irvine, D.R.F. (1998). The posterior field P of cat auditory cortex: Coding of envelope transients. Cerebral Cortex, 8, 125–141.

Heil, P., & Neubauer, H. (2001). Temporal integration of sound pressure determines thresholds of auditory-nerve fibers. Journal of Neuroscience, 21, 7404–7415.

Heil, P., & Neubauer, H. (2003). A unifying basis of auditory thresholds based on temporal summation. Proceedings of the National Academy of Sciences USA, 100, 6151–6156.

Johnson, C.S. (1968). Relation between absolute threshold and duration-of-tone pulses in the bottlenosed porpoise. Journal of the Acoustical Society of America, 43, 757–763.

Joris, P.X., Smith, P.H., & Yin, T.C.T. (1994). Enhancement of neural synchronization in the anteroventral cochlear nucleus. II. Responses in the tuning curve tail. Journal of Neurophysiology, 71, 1037–1051.

Kitzes, L.M., Gibson, M.M., Rose, J.E., & Hind, J.E. (1978). Initial discharge latency and threshold considerations for some neurons in cochlear nuclear complex of the cat. Journal of Neurophysiology, 41, 1165–1182.

Klug, A., Khan, A., Burger, R.B., Bauer E.E., Hurley, L.M., Yang, L., Grothe, B., Halvorsen, M.B.. & Park, T.J. (2000). Latency as a function of intensity in auditory neurons: Influences of central processing. Hearing Research, 148, 107–123.

Klump, G.M., & Maier, E.H. (1990). Temporal summation in the European Starling (*Sturnus vulgaris*). Journal of Comparative Psychology, 104, 94–100.

Kros, C.J. (1996). Physiology of mammalian cochlear hair cells. In P. Dallos, A.N. Popper, & R.R. Fay (Eds.), The Cochlea (pp. 318–385). New York: Springer.

Krumbholz, K., & Wiegrebe, L. (1998). Detection thresholds for brief sounds - are they a measure of auditory intensity integration? Hearing Research, 124, 155–169.

Liberman, M.C. (1982). Single-neuron labeling in the cat auditory nerve. Science, 216, 1239–1241.

Liberman, M.C., Dodds, L.W., & Pierce, S. (1990). Afferent and efferent innervation of the cat cochlea: Quantitative analysis with light and electron microscopy. The Journal of Comparative Neurology, 301, 443–460.

Meinrenken, C.J., Borst, J.G.G., & Sakmann, B. (2003). The Hodgkin-Huxley-Katz Prize Lecture: Local routes revisited: The space and time dependence of the Ca2+ signal for phasic transmitter release at the rat calyx of Held. Journal of Physiology, 547, 665–689.

Merchan-Perez, A., & Liberman, M.C. (1996). Ultrastructural differences among afferent synapses on cochlear hair cells: correlations with spontaneous discharge rate. The Journal of Comparative Neurology, 371, 208–221.

Middlebrooks, J.C., Furukawa, S., Stecker, G.C., & Mickey, B.J. (2004). Distributed representation of sound-source location in the auditory cortex. In R. König, P. Heil, E. Budinger, & H. Scheich (Eds.), The Auditory Cortex – A Synthesis of Human and Animal Research. Hillsdale, NJ: Lawrence Erlbaum Associates.

Nelken, I., Las, L., Ulanovsky, N., & Farkas, D. (2004). Levels of auditory processing: The subcortical auditory system, primary auditory cortex, and the hard problems of auditory perception. In R. König, P. Heil, E. Budinger, & H. Scheich (Eds.), The Auditory Cortex – A Synthesis of Human and Animal Research. Hillsdale, NJ: Lawrence Erlbaum Associates.

Neubauer, H., & Heil, P. (2004). Towards a unifying basis of auditory thresholds: The effects of hearing loss on temporal integration reconsidered. Journal of the Association for Research in Otolaryngology, 6, I:pub ahead of print.

O'Connor, K.N., Barruel, P., Hajalilou, R., & Sutter, M.L. (1999). Auditory temporal integration in the rhesus macaque (*Macaca mulatta*). Journal of the Acoustical Society of America, 106, 954–965.

Phillips, D.P. (1988). Effect of tone-pulse rise time on rate level functions of cat auditory cortex neurons: Excitatory and inhibitory processes shaping responses to tone onset. Journal of Neurophysiology, 59, 1524–1539.

Phillips, D.P., & Orman, S.S. (1984). Responses of single neurons in posterior field of cat auditory cortex to tonal stimulation. Journal of Neurophysiology, 51, 147–163.

Plomp, R., & Bouman, M.A. (1959). Relation between hearing threshold and duration for tone pulses. Journal of the Acoustical Society of America, 31, 749–758.

Raybould, N.P., Jagger, D.J., & Housley, G.D. (2001). Positional analysis of guinea pig inner hair cell membrane conductances: implications for regulation of the membrane filter. Journal of the Association for Research in Otolaryngology, 2, 362–376.

Ronacher, B., Krahe, R., & Hennig, R.M. (2000). Effects of signal duration on the recognition of masked communication signals by the grasshopper *Chorthippus biguttulus*. Journal of Comparative Physiology A, 186, 1065–1072.

Ruel, J., Nouvian, R., Gervais d'Aldin, C., Pujol, R., Eybalin, M., & Puel, J.-L. (2001). Dopamine inhibition of auditory nerve activity in the adult mammalian cochlea European Journal of Neuroscience, 14, 977–986.

Schmidt, S., & Thaller, J. (1994). Temporal auditory summation in the echolocating bat, *Tadarida brasiliensis*. Hearing Research, 77, 125–134.

Solecki, J.M., & Gerken, G.M. (1990). Auditory temporal integration in the normal-hearing and hearing-impaired cat. Journal of the Acoustical Society of America, 88, 779–785.

Sullivan, W.E. (1982). Possible neural mechanisms of target distance coding in auditory system of the echolocating bat Myotis lucifugus. Journal of Neurophysiology, 48, 1033–1047.

Syrlykke, A., Larsen, O.N., & Michelsen, A. (1988). Temporal coding in the auditory receptor of the moth ear. Journal of Comparative Physiology A, 162, 367–374.

Tougaard, J. (1996). Energy detection and temporal integration in the noctuid A1 auditory receptor. Journal of Comparative Physiology A, 178, 669–677.

Vallbo, A.B., Olsson, K.G., Westberg, K.-G., & Clark, F.J. (1984). Microstimulation of single tactile afferents from the human hand. Brain, 107, 727–749.

Viemeister, N.F., & Wakefield, G.H. (1991). Temporal integration and multiple looks. Journal of the Acoustical Society of America, 90, 858–865.

Watson, C.S., & Gengel, R.W. (1969). Signal duration and signal frequency in relation to auditory sensitivity. Journal of the Acoustical Society of America, 46, 989–997.

Zwislocki, J.J. (1960). Theory of temporal auditory summation. Journal of the Acoustical Society of America, 32, 1046–1060.

14. DISTRIBUTED REPRESENTATION OF SOUND-SOURCE LOCATION IN THE AUDITORY CORTEX

John C. Middlebrooks, Shigeto Furukawa,
G. Christopher Stecker, Brian J. Mickey

INTRODUCTION

Normal sound localization behavior requires an intact auditory cortex. That statement is based on clinical reports of deficits following cortical lesions (Efron et al., 1983; Greene, 1929; Pinek et al., 1989; Sanchez-Longo & Forster, 1958; Zatorre & Penhune, 2001) and on results of experimental studies in animals in which the auditory cortex has been lesioned or reversibly inactivated (e.g., Heffner, H.E. & Heffner, R.S., 1990; Jenkins & Merzenich, 1994; Lomber & Malhotra, 2003). Indeed, one of the most conspicuous behavioral deficits that follows a unilateral cortical lesion in a cat or monkey is a deficit in localization of sound sources on the side opposite to the lesion. Despite the demonstrated necessary role of the auditory cortex in localization, presently little is understood of the form in which sound-source locations are represented in patterns of cortical activity, nor is there consensus on the identity of particular cortical areas that might be specialized for processing of location-related information.

One form in which sensory space can be represented in the brain is as a point-to point "topographical" map. Such maps are well known in the visual and somatosensory systems, in which locations of stimuli in visual space or on the body surface map onto locations within visual or somatosensory cortical fields. In those sensory systems, however, locations in sensory space correspond directly to locations on the respective sensory epithelia (i.e., the retina and body surface), so the cortical maps of space might simply reflect the topography of the sensory periphery. In the auditory system, the cochlear sensory epithelium maps sound frequency, not location. The peripheral representation of frequency is reflected in the presence in the auditory cortex of multiple topographic maps of sound frequency (i.e., "tonotopic" representations; e.g., Merzenich et al., 1975; Reale & Imig, 1980). Identification of sound-source location by the auditory system requires analysis and integration of multiple acoustical cues, including interaural differences in sound level and arrival time and direction-dependent spectral cues (reviewed by Middlebrooks & Green, 1991). That such an integration can be accomplished and locations coded in a topographical map is demonstrated by the presence of such a map in the superior colliculus (Middlebrooks & Knudsen, 1984; Palmer & King, 1982); the superior colliculus is a midbrain structure involved in initiation of orienting movements of the eyes and head to auditory, visual, and tactile stimuli. The topographical form of auditory space representation in the superior colliculus probably reflects constraints of other sensory and motor modalities, however, and might not be an appropriate example of basic auditory mechanisms.

Numerous studies over the past two decades have sought, either explicitly or implicitly, a topographical space map in the auditory cortex (e.g., Brugge et al., 1996; Imig et al., 1990; Middlebrooks & Pettigrew, 1981; Rajan et al., 1990). Those efforts have been uniformly unsuccessful. Several commonly observed properties of the spatial sensitivity of auditory cortical neurons conflict with the basic requirements of a point-to-point map. Most important, a point-to-point map would seem to require neurons with narrow, well defined spatial receptive fields. Contrary to that requirement, most neurons in all well studied auditory cortical areas have broad spatial receptive fields, generally extending throughout 180° to 360°. Often, narrower receptive fields can be measured at near-threshold sound levels, but the fields expand markedly at moderate sound levels at which animals and humans show accurate localization behavior. Also, a topographical map would require that the locations in space of receptive fields would shift systematically with shifts in cortical location, but no such systematic shifts have been observed.

The observed properties of auditory neurons that conflict with a topographical map can be seen to be ideal qualifications for an alternative, *distributed*, form of spatial representation. The broad spatial tuning of auditory cortical neurons raises the possibility that single neurons might vary their response patterns as a function of sound-source location within a broad receptive field, thereby transmitting information about source locations throughout as much as 360° of space. The expectation of a topographical representation is that the representation of a point in space is restricted to a limited portion of any auditory cortical field. In a putative distributed representation, in contrast, the representation of any particular sound source location would be widely distributed throughout an auditory cortical field. All the available data support this view, that sound-source locations are represented in a highly distributed manner in the auditory cortex.

In this chapter, we review our work that has characterized the distributed coding of source locations, we present results from cortical areas that appear to show some specialization for location coding, and we contrast location coding under anesthetized and awake-behaving conditions.

SPATIAL SENSITIVITY AND DISTRIBUTED CODING

Most studies of auditory spatial sensitivity in our laboratory have been conducted in cats anesthetized with α-chloralose (Middlebrooks et al., 1998). In those experiments, the cat is positioned in the center of a sound-attenuating chamber that is lined with absorbent foam to reduce sound reflections. A circular hoop, 1.2 m in radius and positioned in the horizontal plane, holds 18 loudspeakers spaced in 20° increments of azimuth. Sound stimuli are Gaussian noise bursts, 80 or 100 ms in duration. Sound levels generally vary among trials from 20 to 40 dB or more above neural thresholds. Neural responses are recorded with silicon-substrate multi-channel recording probes (Anderson et al., 1989). The probes permit simultaneous recording of spike activity from single neurons or small unresolved clusters of neurons at 16 sites positioned in a line at 100- or 150-μm intervals. The probes are inserted into the cortex, generally oriented roughly parallel to the cortical surface in the middle cortical layers.

Figure 14.1 illustrates the location of auditory cortical areas on the lateral surface of the cat's brain. Our earlier studies focused on areas A1, A2, and the anterior ectosylvian auditory area (AES) (e.g., Furukawa et al., 2000, Middlebrooks et al., 1994, 1998). Area A1 is the primary tonotopically organized field, which receives its main ascending input from the ventral

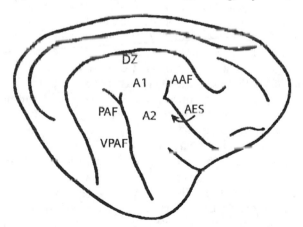

Fig. 14.1. Lateral view of the auditory areas in the cat's cerebral hemisphere. Abbreviations: A1: primary auditory cortex; A2: second auditory field; AAF: anterior auditory field; AES: anterior ectosylvian auditory area; DZ: dorsal zone of A1; PAF; posterior auditory field; VPAF: ventro-posterior auditory field.

division of the medial geniculate body. An early ablation-behavioral study indicated that area A1 might have a special role in spatial hearing (Jenkins & Merzenich, 1984), although its low-level position in cortical processing suggests that any lesion in A1 might impact function in other cortical areas. In area A2, neurons show broad frequency tuning and there is little or no tonotopic organization (Merzenich et al., 1975; Schreiner & Cynader, 1984). Psychophysical studies indicate that sounds are localized most accurately when they have broad bandwidths (Middlebrooks & Green, 1991). For that reason, it seems sensible to investigate spatial coding in an area such as A2 in which neurons appear to integrate information across broad ranges of frequency. Neurons in AES also show broad frequency tuning (Middlebrooks et al., 1998). That area is interesting for studies of auditory spatial coding because it is known to send corticofugal projections to the superior colliculus (Meredith & Clemo, 1989), which contains an auditory space map (Middlebrooks & Knudsen, 1984). Because of the differences among areas A1, A2, and AES in regard to frequency tuning and corticofugal projections, we are surprised to have found essentially no qualitative differences in the spatial sensitivity of neurons in those areas; subtle quantitative differences have been observed (Middlebrooks et al., 1998). Figure 14.2 shows examples of the spatial sensitivity of two neurons recorded from area A2. Each horizontal row of panels shows responses of one neuron, and each vertical column of panels shows responses at a particular sound level (indicated at the top of each column) relative to the neuron's threshold. The illustrated neurons are representative of the substantial majority of neurons in areas A1, A2, and AES (in the anesthetized condition) in the following respects. *First*, responses generally are restricted to a burst of spikes, ~10 to 20 ms in duration, following the onset of the noise burst. *Second*, at the lowest sound levels, neurons respond reliably to sounds located only in the frontal contralateral quadrant of azimuth. That is, there is little variation among neurons in the preferred locations of stimuli. *Third*, at more moderate sound levels, spatial receptive fields of neurons expand to encompass 360° of azimuth. Level-dependent changes in spatial sensitivity are most conspicuous at low sound levels and tend to stabilize at levels 30–40 dB above threshold. *Fourth*, response patterns of neurons vary systematically with sound-source location, particularly in the spike count, the latency to the first spike, and in some cases, in the duration of the burst of spikes. The lack of variation of preferred location and the broad spatial tuning both are inconsistent with a topographical representation. The broad spatial tuning and the location-dependent changes in spike patterns, however, both support the notion of a distributed representation.

One of the requirements of a distributed representation, as we have presented it, is that single neurons transmit stimulus-related information throughout broad ranges of sound-source location. We tested this premise by attempting to recognize, for single neurons, the spike patterns associated with particular sound-source locations and, thereby, to estimate source locations. We have employed artificial neural networks for this task; artificial neural networks can be regarded as computer-based pattern-recognition procedures. Typically, we

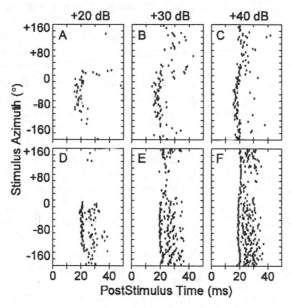

Fig. 14.2. Spatial sensitivity of two neurons recorded from area A2 (from Furukawa & Middlebrooks, 2002). Within each panel, each horizontal raster (i.e., row of dots) indicates spikes elicited by a single noise burst. The vertical position of each raster indicates the stimulus azimuth. Eight trials are represented at each azimuth. The frontal midline is plotted at 0°, and negative azimuths represent locations to the left of the midline, contralateral to the recording site. These neurons spiked only near the onset of the noise bursts; for that reason, only the first 50 ms after stimulus onset are shown.

divide a set of spike patterns into training and test sets. The training set is used to train the network, and then the trained network is used to classify the test set, resulting in estimates of the stimulus locations. Many spike patterns are classified for each stimulus location, and the distribution of estimated locations is evaluated.

Figure 14.3 shows examples of responses of neurons recorded in area A1 (top row) and shows the results of neural-network classification of spike patterns in the form of confusion matrices (bottom row). In the confusion matrices, the horizontal and vertical positions of symbols indicate, respectively, the target location and the location estimated based on the spike patterns. The area of each symbol represents the proportion of trials in which a particular location was estimated for each target location. Perfect identification of all targets would yield a line of large circles lying on the positive major diagonal. Although perfect identification never is observed, there is in many cases a strong tendency of data to clump near the diagonal. The example in Figures 14.3A and 14.3D showed quite accurate localization throughout most of the frontal hemifield (i.e., −90° to 90°), with less accuracy in the rear hemifield. The example in Figures 14.3B and 14.3E showed many responses near the positive major diagonal plus a subset of responses lining up along the negative minor diagonal from target −180°, response 0° to target 0°, response −180°. That minor diagonal corresponds to the loci of points for which front and back locations were confused. Front/back confusions are often encountered in human psychophysical studies (e.g., Makous & Middlebrooks, 1990; Wightman & Kistler, 1989). The example in Figures 14.3C and 14.3F is representative of many neurons that accurately distinguished right from left, but showed little discrimination within each half of space.

The representation of spatial coding in the form of confusion matrices, as in Figure 14.3, leads easily to the computation of transmitted information. Transmitted information, in our application, is the information about sound-source location that is transmitted by the cat's auditory pathway, resulting in cortical spike patterns that then are interpreted by our neural-network procedure (Furukawa & Middlebrooks, 2002; Stecker et al., 2003). Perfect identification of targets that were randomly distributed among 18 possible locations would transmit ~4.2 bits of information. One bit of information could indicate perfect discrimination of two locations or could indicate somewhat imperfect

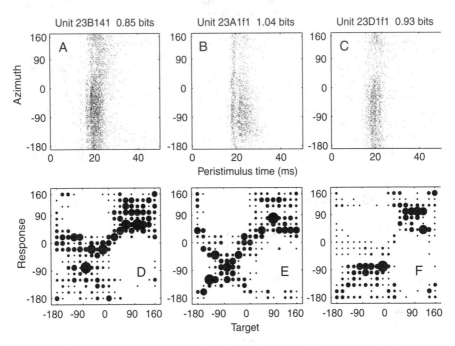

Fig. 14.3. Spatial sensitivity of 3 neurons recorded from A1. **A, B, C:** Responses of 3 units shown as raster plots. Each panel is labeled with the unit number and the amount of information (in bits) that it transmitted about sound-source location. **D, E, F:** Stimulus/ response confusion matrices show the stimulus locations estimated by automated recognition of the spike patterns shown in parts A, B, and C.

identification of a larger number of locations. In the sample of neurons in areas A1 and A2 studied in the anesthetized condition, neurons typically transmitted 0.5 to 1.2 bits of information about sound-source location. As a general rule, nearly all neurons tended to transmit stimulus-related information with varying degrees of accuracy throughout as much as 360° of azimuth. We refer to this as "panoramic" coding of azimuth by single neurons (Middlebrooks et al., 1994). The finding of panoramic neurons throughout areas A1, A2, and AES leads to the inference that information about any particular source location is widely distributed throughout those areas and probably extends beyond to areas not yet explored. The accuracy of spatial representation presumably is enhanced by the combination of information transmitted by multiple neurons. For instance, we showed that a simple pattern recognition scheme based on responses of 128 cortical neurons could transmit sound locations about as accurately as a cat could localize sounds in behavioral trials (Furukawa & Middlebrooks, 2000).

Many neurons exhibit stimulus-dependent changes in the latency from the onset of the stimulus to the first spike. We attempted to quantify the information about stimulus azimuth that is transmitted by first spike latencies by disrupting the stimulus dependence of latencies and then noting the loss in total transmitted information. We eliminated the stimulus dependence of spike timing by forming a distribution of all the recorded spike times for a particular neuron, then forming "shuffled" spike patterns in which each spike pattern was replaced by a pattern containing the original number of spikes but with times drawn randomly from the distribution of all times. This had the effect of preserving the first-order distribution of spike times and preserving any information that might be transmitted by spike counts while disrupting any relationship between specific stimulus locations and spike times. Figure 14.4 compares the information transmitted by full spike patterns (plotted in the horizontal dimension) with the information transmitted by shuffled patterns (vertical dimension); data were recorded from well isolated single units in area A2 (Furukawa & Middlebrooks, 2002). One can see that most of the points lie well below the diagonal, indicating a substantial reduction in transmitted information. On average, transmitted information was reduced by 17–53% when stimulus-related temporal information was eliminated from spike patterns.

CORTICAL SPECIALIZATION FOR SPATIAL REPRESENTATION

Studies of cortical areas A1, A2, and AES in the anesthetized condition have demonstrated spatial sensitivity that qualitatively is quite similar among areas. The observation of rather uniform spatial sensitivity among those areas has led us to speculate that auditory spatial processing is largely complete within the auditory brainstem and that the special role of the cortex in spatial processing is restricted to routing spatially coded information to cortical areas that might have more or less spatial functions (Middlebrooks et al., 2002). That speculation was founded partially on the premise that knowledge of the location of sound

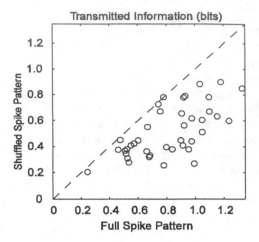

Fig. 14.4. Stimulus-related information transmitted by full spike patterns (horizontal dimension) and by spike patterns in which spike timing was degraded (from Furukawa & Middlebrooks, 2002).

sources is beneficial for many auditory tasks, including those that are explicitly spatial in nature (e.g., discrimination of source locations; orientation toward sound sources) and others that are less so (e.g., recognition of communication sounds amid spatially distinct distracters). We recently have obtained data that conflict with the notion that spatial sensitivity is uniform across all the auditory cortical areas (Stecker et al., 2003; Stecker & Middlebrooks, 2003). We find rather distinctive spatial sensitivity in the posterior auditory field (PAF) and in the dorsal zone (DZ) of area A1.

Area PAF is located posterior to the posterior ectosylvian sulcus, extending onto the bank of that sulcus (see Fig. 14.1). In previous studies in the anesthetized cat (Phillips & Orman, 1984), PAF has been shown to have a larger proportion of neurons that show non-monotonic rate-level functions. That finding is pertinent to studies of spatial representation because, at least in area A1, non-monotonic neurons tend to show the most restricted spatial tuning (Barone et al., 1996, Imig et al., 1990). Also, neurons in PAF tend to show relatively complex frequency response areas (Heil & Irvine, 1998; Loftus & Sutter, 2001). Such complexity might reflect a specialization for processing spectral cues for the vertical and front/back locations of sounds.

Neurons recorded from PAF show a greater variety of spatial tuning than that encountered in other areas studied in anesthetized conditions (Stecker et al., 2003). Figure 14.5 shows three examples. The neuron in Figure 14.5A showed two strong temporally discrete bursts of spikes (latencies ~25 and 35 ms) to sound sources restricted to a contralateral quadrant, and a later, more diffuse, burst to ipsilateral sounds. The neuron in Figure 14.5B had a spatial receptive field sharply bounded within the ipsilateral half of space. The neuron in Figure 14.5C showed spatial tuning centered about 80° contralateral to the frontal

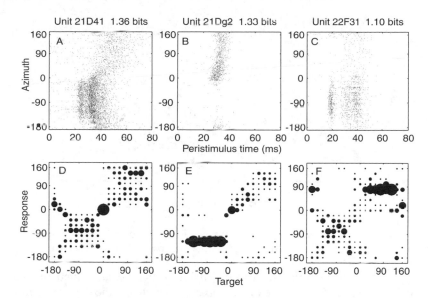

Fig. 14.5. Spatial sensitivity of 3 neurons recorded from PAF. Same format as Figure 14.3 (adapted from Stecker et al., 2003).

midline compared to neurons in areas A1, A2, and AES studied in the anesthetized condition, PAF neurons showed greater modulation of spike counts by sound-source location and showed narrower tuning width. Moreover, the distribution of spatial preferences in PAF covered space more uniformly than that measured in A1, A2, or AES.

A striking feature of responses in PAF is their long latencies and the strong modulation of first-spike latency by stimulus location. The median of first spike latencies in PAF is 29 ms, compared to 18 ms in A1. The median value of the range of first-spike latencies across all stimulus locations is 10.7 ms in PAF compared to 3.2 ms in A1. We compared areas A1 and PAF in regard to the location-related information transmitted by spike count alone or by the latency to the first spike (Stecker et al., 2003). Figure 14.6 shows that for both cortical areas, first-spike latency transmits more information than does spike count (i.e., the majority of data points lies above the diagonal). The relative importance of latency is considerably greater in PAF, however, in which the ratio of information transmitted by latency versus spike count was 1.7:1 compared to 1.3:1 in A1. The difference between A1 and PAF is most pronounced in respect to neurons that transmit the largest amount of information. In A1, many of the most informative neurons transmitted more information by spike count than by latency (i.e., many points on the right half of the left panel of Fig. 14.6 lie below the diagonal) whereas in PAF it was a general trend that first-spike latency tends to transmit more information than does spike count.

Area DZ is found at the dorsal margin of area A1, near the ventral bank of the suprasylvian sulcus. Similar to more ventral regions of A1, DZ receives a

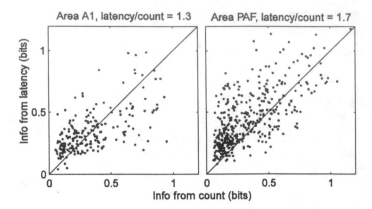

Fig. 14.6. Stimulus-related information transmitted by first-spike latency (vertical axis) or spike count (horizontal axis) computed from A1 (left panel) or PAF (right panel).

strong thalamic input from the ventral division of the medial geniculate body, but in the case of DZ the source of that input is restricted to the dorsal cap of the ventral division (Middlebrooks & Zook, 1983). Compared to more ventral regions of area A1, neurons in DZ show broad frequency tuning that is biased toward high frequencies, and many DZ neurons respond only to sounds presented simultaneously to both ears (Middlebrooks & Zook, 1983). The latter property suggests that DZ might show a preponderance of tuning for locations near the midline.

In recent studies of spatial sensitivity in DZ, we have found examples of spatial tuning that is more restricted than that usually seen elsewhere in A1 or in A2 (Stecker & Middlebrooks, 2003). A distinctive characteristic of spatial sensitivity in DZ is that nearly half of the neurons show spatial tuning centered in the ipsilateral half of space. Often, along a recording penetration in DZ, we encounter a sequence of several neurons tuned to contralateral locations, then tuning abruptly shifts to ipsilateral tuning, then back to contralateral, and so on.

Figure 14.7 shows examples of sequences of recordings in DZ. In the figure, each neuron is represented by an azimuth "centroid" which is a spike-count-weighted center of mass of a spike-count-vs-azimuth function. The spatial sensitivity seen in PAF and DZ suggests that those cortical areas might play a more important role in spatial representation than do areas A2, AES, or A1 ventral to DZ. In the case of PAF, that suggestion is supported by a recent study that demonstrated following reversible inactivation of PAF a striking deficit in sound localization performance in cats (Lomber & Malhotra, 2003). That study also showed that inactivation of the anterior auditory field (AAF) produced a deficit in a task requiring identification of a temporal pattern but produced no localization deficit. The latter result is consistent with our unpublished physiological observations that AAF seems to show no particular specialization for location coding.

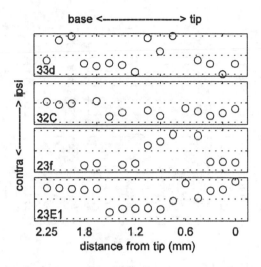

Fig. 14.7. Preferred locations as a function of recording position for 4 electrode penetrations in DZ. Each open circle shows the azimuth preference of a single neuron represented by its azimuth centroid, the spike-count-weighted center of mass of spatial tuning. Electrode penetrations were oriented from lateral to medial down the ventral bank of the suprasylvian sulcus. The vertical axis plots the location of the azimuth centroids in the contra- or ipsilateral hemifields (from Stecker & Middlebrooks, 2003).

A widely cited hypothesis (Rauschecker & Tian, 2000) asserts, by analogy with the primate visual system, that the primate auditory cortex contains two hierarchically organized auditory processing streams. One of the hypothetical pathways, the "what" stream, is said to lie anterior to the primate area A1 and to be specialized for identifying sounds. The other, "where" stream, lies posterior to A1 and is hypothesized to specialize in processing of spatial aspects of sounds. It is difficult to draw homologies between cortical areas in cats and primates. Nevertheless, because of the lateral expansion of the temporal lobe in the primate, the anterior-posterior locations of cortical areas in primates seem to be reversed relative to those in cats. That means that area PAF in the cat, which appears to show some specialization for localization, is more likely to correspond to an anterior area in the primate. Indeed, the Rauschecker group has speculated that PAF is part of a putative feline "what" pathway and AAF part of a "where" pathway (Tian & Rauschecker, 1998). Our present results in the cat, and the behavioral results from the Lomber group (Lomber & Malhotra, 2003), conflict with that assignment of PAF and AAF, respectively, to what and where streams. Because of uncertainty in cortical-field homologies in cats and primates, our present results cannot be said to refute conclusively the dual stream hypothesis as stated for the primate, but neither do our results support that hypothesis.

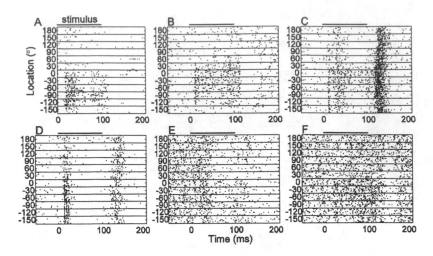

Fig. 14.8. Spatial sensitivity of 6 neurons recorded from A1 in awake cats (from Mickey & Middlebrooks, 2003).

SPATIAL REPRESENTATION IN AN AWAKE PREPARATION

With few exceptions (Ahissar et al., 1992; Benson et al., 1981; Eisenman, 1974; Recanzone et al., 2000), studies of spatial sensitivity in the auditory cortex have used anesthetized preparations. The use of anesthesia offers many advantages in experimental design, but one always must be concerned that the true nature of the cortical representation of auditory space might be masked by the presence of anesthetic agents. We recently have begun to study spatial representation in the auditory cortex of unanesthetized cats (Mickey & Middlebrooks, 2003). In our protocol, the cat is only loosely restrained. The cat's head is free to move. The cat performs a simple auditory discrimination, in which it is rewarded by discriminating a periodic 200-Hz click train from an ongoing sequence of broadband noise bursts that vary in location. The purpose of the auditory task is simply to insure that the cat is listening to sounds. There is no reward contingency related to the locations of the sounds. The cat is implanted with a 16-channel recording probe similar to that described above. During recording sessions, the cat has a tracking device attached to its head that permits measurement of the orientation of the head relative to the loudspeaker array. All stimulus locations are corrected for head orientation, yielding stimulus locations in head-centered coordinates. The cats generally maintain their pinnae in a forward position while doing the auditory task, so variation in pinna position adds only minimal uncertainty to the interpretation of results. Our present data set in the awake preparation is limited to recordings in area A1.

Figure 14.8 shows examples of responses of 6 neurons (or clusters o. neurons) in area A1 in the awake condition. In contrast with responses in the anesthetized condition which usually are restricted to a short burst of spikes near the stimulus onset, these responses show a variety of temporal patterns. The illustrated examples include responses primarily near the stimulus onset (Fig. 14.8A), responses sustained throughout the stimulus duration (Fig. 14.8B), responses that were strongest after the stimulus offset (Fig. 14.8C), and responses to both stimulus onset and offset (Fig. 14.8D). In some cases, neurons showed relatively high rates of spontaneous activity that was suppressed either by stimulus onset (Fig. 14.8E) or offset (Fig. 14.8F).

As in the anesthetized preparation, spatial receptive fields of neurons in the awake condition generally were broad, typically 150° to 180° wide in azimuth. Also like the anesthetized condition, there was no indication of spatial topography. Those two observations, while somewhat disappointing, reassured us that previous failures to demonstrate point-to-point auditory space maps in A1 were not simply a consequence of the use of anesthesia. Several other properties of spatial sensitivity in area A1 were quite different between the anesthetized and awake conditions. *First*, the modulation of spike counts by sound-source location generally was greater in the awake condition and spatial tuning was sharper, largely because of suppression of spontaneous activity at non-optimum locations. *Second*, there was a greater diversity of temporal spike patterns, as indicated above. *Third*, the awake condition showed a greater diversity of preferred stimulus locations, including spatial tuning centered throughout the contralateral hemifield, in the ipsilateral hemifield, and on the midline in the front and in the back. In A1 in the anesthetized condition, in contrast, most neurons show tuning centered in the frontal contralateral quadrant, in front of the axis of greatest sensitivity of the contralateral pinna (Middlebrooks & Pettigrew, 1981). *Finally*, spatial tuning in the awake condition was considerably less sensitive to changes in stimulus level. Across the population sampled in the awake condition, there was little or no systematic increase or decrease in spatial tuning width or in the amount of stimulus-dependent modulation of spike count. (Mickey & Middlebrooks, 2003). In contrast, neurons in A1 in the anesthetized condition consistently react to increases in stimulus level with a decrease in the modulation of spike counts by stimulus location and an increase in the breadth of spatial tuning (Stecker et al., 2003).

The present data in the awake condition were obtained while the cats were engaged in a task that demanded only minimal attention to sound. In future studies, it will be of interest to test the degree to which the demands of the behavioral task influence the cortical representation of space. For instance, might we expect the sharpness of spatial sensitivity to increase under conditions in which the animal must attend to the locations of sounds? If reward is paired with a particular sound source location, how might that affect the representation of rewarded and of unrewarded locations?

SUMMARY AND CONCLUSIONS

In all auditory cortical areas studied so far, spatial receptive fields tend to be broad, although somewhat sharper spatial tuning and narrower spatial receptive fields are seen in PAF and DZ than in ventral A1, A2, or AES. In none of these areas is there consistent evidence of point-to-point spatial topography.

Response patterns of neurons vary systematically with source location, such that neurons can be said to code space "panoramically". The accuracy of panoramic coding appears to be considerably greater in PAF and DZ than in ventral A1, A2, and AES, at least under anesthetized conditions. In PAF and DZ, panoramic location coding is particularly conspicuous in the form of modulation of spike latencies by stimulus location. By inference, the representation of any point in auditory space is distributed across widespread neural populations, within and among cortical fields. There is some indication of specialization for spatial processing in PAF and, perhaps, in DZ, but any of the cortical areas studied so far display considerable capacity for spatial representation.

In the awake condition, neurons in A1 show sharper spatial tuning and greater diversity of temporal spike patterns than in the anesthetized condition. Even so, spatial receptive fields in the awake condition often occupy nearly 180° of azimuth, and there is no indication of point-to-point spatial topography. The model of distributed coding developed in the anesthetized preparation appears to apply equally to the awake condition.

The greater diversity of spatial tuning observed in PAF (in the anesthetized condition) and in A1 in the awake condition indicates that coordinated activity of even small numbers of neurons in those areas potentially could signal sound-source location with accuracy comparable to reported behavioral performance. In ongoing studies, we are eager to evaluate spatial sensitivity in area PAF to test the hypothesis that it is particularly adapted for distributed representation of sound-source location.

REFERENCES

Ahissar, M., Ahissar, E., Bergman, H., & Vaadia, E. (1992). Encoding of sound-source location and movement - activity of single neurons and interactions between adjacent neurons in the monkey auditory cortex. Journal of Neurophysiology, 67, 203–215.

Anderson, D.J., Najafi, K., Tanghe, S.J., Evans, D.A., Levy, K.L., Hetke, J.F., Xue, X., Zappia, J.J., & Wise, K.D. (1989). Batch-fabricated thin-film electrodes for stimulation of the central auditory system. IEEE Transactions of Biomedical Engineering, 36, 693–704.

Barone, P., Clarey, J.C., Irons, W.A., & Imig, T.J. (1996). Cortical synthesis of azimuth-sensitive single-unit responses with nonmonotonic level tuning: A thalamocortical comparison in the cat. Journal of Neurophysiology, 75, 1206–1220.

Benson, D.A., Hienz, R.D., & Goldstein, Jr. M.H. (1981). Single-unit activity in the auditory cortex of monkeys actively localizing sound sources: Spatial tuning and behavioral dependency. Brain Research, 219, 249–267.

Brugge, J.F., Reale, R.A., & Hind, J.E. (1996). The structure of spatial receptive fields of neurons in primary auditory cortex of the cat. Journal of Neuroscience, 16, 4420–4437.

Efron, R., & Crandall, P.H. (1983). Central auditory processing II. Effects of anterior temporal lobectomy. Brain and language, 19, 237–253.

Eisenman, L.M. (1974). Neural encoding of sound location: An electrophysiological study in auditory cortex (AI) of the cat using free field stimuli. Brain Research, 75, 203–214.

Furukawa, S., & Middlebrooks, J.C. (2002). Cortical representation of auditory space: Information-bearing features of spike patterns. Journal of Neurophysiology, 87, 1749–1762.

Furukawa, S., Xu, L., & Middlebrooks, J.C. (2000). Coding of sound-source location by ensembles of cortical neurons. Journal of Neuroscience, 20, 1216–1228.

Greene, T.C. (1929). The ability to localize sound: A study of binaural hearing in patients with tumor of the brain. Archives of Surgery, 18, 1825–1841.

Heffner, H.E., & Heffner, R.S. (1990). Effect of bilateral auditory cortex lesions on sound localization in Japanese macaques. Journal of Neurophysiology, 64, 915–931.

Heil, P., & Irvine, D.R.F. (1998). The posterior field P of cat auditory cortex: Coding of envelope transients. Cerebral Cortex, 8, 125–141.

Imig, T.J., Irons, W.A., & Samson, F.R. (1990). Single-unit selectivity to azimuthal direction and sound pressure level of noise bursts in cat high-frequency primary auditory cortex. Journal of Neurophysiology, 63, 1448–1466.

Jenkins, W. M., & Merzenich, M.M. (1984). Role of cat primary auditory cortex for sound-localization behavior. Journal of Neurophysiology, 52, 819–847.

Loftus, W., & Sutter, M. (2001). Spectrotemporal organization of excitatory and inhibitory receptive fields of cat posterior auditory field neurons. Journal of Neurophysiology, 86, 475–491.

Lomber, S., & Malhotra, S. (2003). Double dissociation of "what" and "where" processing in auditory cortex. In E. Budinger & B. Gaschler-Markefski (Eds.), Proceedings of the International Conference on Auditory Cortex – Towards a Synthesis of Human and Animal Research (p. 33). Aachen: Shaker-Verlag.

Makous, J.C., & Middlebrooks, J.C. (1990). Two-dimensional sound localization by human listeners. Journal of the Acoustical Society of America, 87, 2188–2200.

Meredith, M.A., & Clemo, H.R. (1989). Auditory cortical projection from the anterior ectosylvian sulcus (field AES) to the superior colliculus in the cat: An anatomical and electrophysiological study. The Journal of Comparative Neurology, 289, 687–707.

Merzenich, M.M., Knight, P.L., & Roth, G.L. (1975). Representation of cochlea within primary auditory cortex in the cat. Journal of Neurophysiology, 38, 231–249.

Mickey, B. J., & Middlebrooks, J. C. (2003). Representation of auditory space by cortical neurons in awake cats. Journal of Neuroscience, 23, 8649–8663.

Middlebrooks, J.C., Clock, A.E., Xu, L., & Green, D.M. (1994). A panoramic code for sound location by cortical neurons. Science, 264, 842–844.

Middlebrooks, J.C., & Green, D.M. (1991). Sound localization by human listeners. Annual Review of Psychology, 42, 135–159.

Middlebrooks, J.C., & Knudsen, E.I. (1984). A neural code for auditory space in the cat's superior colliculus. Journal of Neuroscience, 4, 2621–2634.

Middlebrooks, J.C., & Pettigrew, J.D. (1981). Functional classes of neurons in primary auditory cortex of the cat distinguished by sensitivity to sound location. Journal of

Neuroscience, 1, 107–120.

Middlebrooks, J.C., Xu, L., Eddins, A.C., & Green, D.M. (1998). Codes for sound-source location in nontonotopic auditory cortex. Journal of Neurophysiology, 80, 863–881.

Middlebrooks, J.C., Xu, L., Furukawa, S., & Mickey, B.J. (2002). Location signaling by cortical neurons. In D. Oertel, A. Popper, & R.R. Fay (Eds.), Integrative Functions in the Mammalian Auditory Pathway (pp. 319–357). New York: Springer-Verlag.

Middlebrooks, J.C., & Zook, J.M. (1983). Intrinsic organization of the cat's medial geniculate body identified by projections to binaural response-specific bands in the primary auditory cortex. Journal of Neuroscience, 3, 203–224.

Palmer, A.R., & King, A.J. (1982). The representation of auditory space in the mammalian superior colliculus. Nature, 299, 248–249.

Phillips, D.P., & Orman, S.S. (1984). Responses of single neurons in posterior field of cat auditory cortex to tonal stimulation. Journal of Neurophysiology, 51, 147–163.

Pinek, B., Duhamel, J.R., Cave, C., & Brouchon, M. (1989). Audio-spatial deficits in humans: Differential effects associated with left versus right hemisphere parietal damage. Cortex, 25, 175–186.

Rajan, R., Aitkin, L.M., & Irvine, D.R.F. (1990). Azimuthal sensitivity of neurons in primary auditory cortex of cats. II. Organization along frequency-band strips. Journal of Neurophysiology, 64, 888–902.

Rauschecker, J.P., & Tian, B. (2000). Mechanisms and streams for processing of "what' and "where" in auditory cortex. Proceedings of the National Academy of Sciences USA, 97, 11800–11806.

Reale, R.A., & Imig, T.J. (1980). Tonotopic organization in auditory cortex of the cat. The Journal of Comparative Neurology, 192, 265–291.

Recanzone, G.H., Guard D.C., Phan, M.L., & Su, T.K. (2000). Correlation between the activity of single auditory cortical neuroms and sound-localization behaviour in the macaque monkey. Journal of Neurophysiology, 83, 2723–2739.

Sanchez-Longo, L.P., & Forster, F.M. (1958). Clinical significance of impairment of sound localization. Neurology, 8, 119–125.

Schreiner, C.E., & Cynader, M.S. (1984). Basic functional organization of second auditory cortical field (AII) of the cat. Journal of Neurophysiology, 51, 1284–1304.

Stecker, G.C., Mickey, B.J., Macpherson, E.A., & Middlebrooks, J.C. (2003). Spatial sensitivity in field PAF of cat auditory cortex. Journal of Neurophysiology, 89, 2889–2903.

Stecker, G.C., & Middlebrooks, J.C. (2003). Distributed coding of sound location in the auditory cortex. Biological Cybernetics, 89, 341–349.

Tian, B., & Rauschecker, J.P. (1998). Processing of frequency-modulated sounds in cat's posterior auditory field. Journal of Neurophysiology, 79, 2629–2642.

Wightman, F.L., & Kistler, D.J. (1989). Headphone simulation of free-field listening. II: Psychophysical validation. Journal of the Acoustical Society of America, 85, 868–878.

Zattore, R.J., & Penhune, V.B. (2001). Spatial localization after excision of human auditory cortex. Journal of Neuroscience, 21, 6321–6328.

15. ENCODING OF COMPLEX SOUNDS IN AN ANIMAL MODEL: IMPLICATIONS FOR UNDERSTANDING SPEECH PERCEPTION IN HUMANS

Brad Wible, Trent Nicol, Nina Kraus

INTRODUCTION

An understanding of the biological foundations of speech perception demands a corresponding appreciation of the neural encoding of complex sounds. Our interests span a range of topics in these interrelated fields of auditory perception and neurophysiology. Among them are the encoding of complex sounds in auditory midbrain, thalamus, and cortex. The evoked response approach permits measurement, with precise timing, of phasic and tonic aspects of the encoding of such sounds. Of particular interest is the aggregate neural response to speech. Many of these responses include both transient and sustained components, much like a speech signal itself. Inasmuch as it may be an oversimplification to equate features of speech, such as consonants and vowels, with transient and sustained evoked responses, there are certain parallels. Just as perception of consonant sounds is much more vulnerable to disruption with background noise, the analogous neural transient response is degraded by noise. Likewise, phase-locked responses are hallmarks of subcortical auditory pathways and may be measured in scalp recordings from humans and direct intracranial recordings in an animal model. Temporal and spectral analyses of these responses have been shown to directly reflect some of the analogous characteristics of the corresponding stimuli, for example the fundamental frequency and some harmonic structures of a vowel.

In one particular population – learning-disabled children – abnormally poor perception of auditory signals has been demonstrated, with respect to normal-learning peers, and these perceptual deficits have been linked to accompanying abnormalities in the encoding of sounds by both transient and sustained components of auditory evoked responses (Cunningham et al., 2001; Hayes et al., 2003; King et al., 2001; Kraus et al., 1996; Wible et al., 2002). Based on such findings, it has been proposed that, among such subsets of learning-disabled children, poor sensory encoding of the subtle acoustic distinctions that distinguish speech signals results in pronounced ambiguity and uncertainty associated with the internal representations of utterances, which ultimately impairs the fidelity with which such representations of the phonemes, thus syllables and thus words, can be meaningfully related to linguistic, orthographic, conceptual and expressive processes.

The guinea pig model is useful for a number of reasons. Recording of evoked responses from electrodes placed within guinea pig auditory pathway allows observation of highly-localized patterns of activation within anatomical structures that are thought to be analogous to those contributing to the scalp recorded responses we measure in children. For example, the inferior colliculus is thought to be a major contributor to scalp recordings of transient and phasic brainstem activity (Jacobson, 1985). Across the frequency regions spanned by the stimuli in which we are interested, guinea pig hearing thresholds are comparable to those demonstrated by human listeners. Guinea pig communication calls contain acoustic structures analogous to those observed in human speech, such that the guinea pig auditory system can be assumed to incorporate mechanisms optimized for processing of such signals. We are specifically interested in low-level "automatic" coding of the acoustic structure of the signal (i.e., *not* interested in effects of "higher" processes such as those subserving attentional, linguistic, or other cognitive functions). In seeking to isolate mechanisms of basic auditory encoding, it can be safely assumed that human speech does not activate any processes in the guinea pig that are dedicated to representing the linguistic content of the signal. Likewise, it can be safely assumed that the use of anesthesia eliminates any remote potential for the guinea pig to "understand" or attend to the signals. In addition to understanding normal processing, the guinea pig model has been useful in providing insight into the sources of abnormal processing such as that observed in learning-impaired children. Based on our own observations of human evoked responses and on further descriptions in the literature stimulus parameters are manipulated to emulate conditions under which auditory processing by the learning-impaired children might be thought to suffer.

Here we consider two lines of investigation. First, we describe how encoding of speech sounds is disrupted by background noise and by rapid stimulation. Second, we discuss how encoding and perception can be improved by incorporation of acoustically-enhanced speech cues. In parallel designs, we have been studying these issues in both animals and school-age children.

REPETITION RATE AND BACKGROUND NOISE

Increased talker rate and background noise are two conditions known to adversely affect accurate perception and recognition of speech. These detrimental effects have been shown to be especially pronounced in learning-impaired subjects. Wible and colleagues investigated cortical (Wible et al., 2002) and subcortical (Wible et al., 2004) responses to rapidly repeated speech sounds, both in quiet and noisy backgrounds in children with learning problems (LP) and normal controls (NL). Ongoing studies are investigating these phenomena in guinea pig models of the normal mammalian auditory pathway. These studies are summarized herein.

Methods, Human

LP children (cortical experiment: n = 13, subcortical experiment: n = 11) performed poorer than NL children (n = 12, 9) on a measure of single word reading and spelling (Wilkinson, 1993), and on a test of discrimination of speech sounds (/da/-/ga/; Carrell et al., 1999). Four-token stimulus trains were presented monaurally to the right ear by earphone. The 40 ms synthesized syllable /da/ was presented at 80 dB, separated within the trains by an interstimulus interval (ISI: time from offset of stimulus to onset of subsequent stimulus) of 360 ms (cortical experiment) or 12 ms (subcortical). Intertrain intervals (ITI: time separating the offset and onset of subsequent trains) of 1060 ms and 30 ms were used during cortical and subcortical experiments, respectively. A continuous white noise masker (115 dB signal-to-noise ratio (SNR)) was added to half of the trials. Evoked potentials in response to the first and fourth stimuli in a train were compared. Recordings of cortical activity were from an electrode placed over left temporal lobe (TL: midway between T4 and T6), used the nose as reference, had gain of 5000, and were band pass filtered from 0.05 to 50 Hz. Recordings of subcortical activity were from an electrode placed at the vertex (Cz), used right mastoid as reference, had gain of 5000, and were bandpass filtered from 100 to 2000 Hz. Forehead served as ground. Impedances were less than 5 kOhm. Correlation between initial and repeated cortical responses (over the range spanning 10–60 ms post-stimulus-onset) reflected relative change in timing of responses. The subcortically generated frequency-following response (FFR), measured from 11.4 to 46.4 ms post-stimulus-onset, was investigated by Fourier analysis. The FFR reflects the periodic structure of the stimulus (Sohmer et al., 1977), in this case the transition from the onset of the consonant to the vowel. This response was isolated by frequency into components corresponding to the stimulus' fundamental frequency (F_0, 125 Hz) and first formant (F_1, 220–720 Hz).

Methods, Animal

Evoked potentials were recorded from left primary auditory cortex (A1; 10 kOhm silver ball electrode) and central nucleus of the inferior colliculus (IC; stereotaxically positioned 1 MOhm tungsten needle), in 11 adult (~350 g), albino, ketamine/xyaline anesthetized guinea pigs. Responses were amplified 5000 times, and band pass filtered from 5 to 3000 Hz. Stimulation was according to paradigms described above, with ISIs of 350, 50, 24, and 12 ms, and ITI of 600 ms. Correlations between A1 responses to the first and fourth stimuli in a train were measured over the 10–50 ms latency range. FFRs from IC were measured from 17.20–42.75 ms, and analyzed according to frequency components described above.

Cortical Responses, Human

Similar to previous findings (Wible et al., 2002) describing long-latency responses recorded from the vertex (Cz), these earlier responses from TL, reflecting initial activation of auditory cortex, demonstrated differences between NL and LP children. LP children demonstrated lower correlations between the initial and repeated responses in noise than in quiet (Fig. 15.1, Right). NL children demonstrated no differences between quiet and noise. Relatively high inter-response correlations were maintained by LP children in quiet, similar to NL children in both quiet and in noise, suggesting that the timing of response generators was maintained, and demonstrating that effects of repetition alone did not segregate LP from NL children. The marked decrease in correlations, likely reflecting diminished synchronization of response generators, was particular to the representation of repeated stimuli in noise in LP children.

Cortical Responses, Animal Model

Patterns of correlation of guinea pig responses recorded at 350 ms ISI provided a model for the responses demonstrated by NL children. Given the established literature reporting abnormal temporal processing as a basis for learning problems, increasing the temporal demands upon the normal system was thought to be a reasonable approach to model processing in the abnormal, LP-like system. In other words, we speculated that rather than representing entirely novel aspects of processing, perhaps the LP system represents a poor-performing tail of the distribution of normal processing, such that a "normal" system could be made to demonstrate "LP-like" characteristics by forcing it to process under conditions falling toward a tail of the distribution of normal performance. Responses recorded at a decreased ISI of 50 ms were used to model the LP system. Overall magnitudes of inter-response correlations were larger in the animals than in humans, due to differences in recording techniques

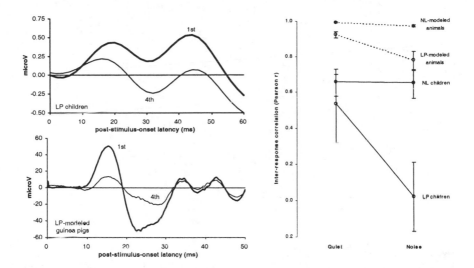

Fig. 15.1. Top left: Average responses to first and fourth stimuli in train, in quiet, recorded over temporal lobe in LP children. **Bottom left:** Average responses to first and fourth stimuli in train, in noise, recorded over guinea pig primary auditory cortex, with LP-modeled 50 ms ISI. **Right:** Correlations between cortical responses to first and fourth stimuli, presented in quiet and noise, in NL and LP children, and in NL- and LP-modeled guinea pigs. Error bars reflect standard errors of the means.

that provided larger response amplitudes with respect to background noise. Under ISI and SNR conditions similar to the human study, the guinea pig A1 responses maintained similar inter-response correlations in noise with respect to quiet, much like the NL controls (Fig. 15.1, Right). At the shorter, LP modeled ISI, inter-response correlations in noise were lower than in quiet, similar to the pattern observed in LP children. As also demonstrated by the human data, stimulus repetition alone, in quiet, did not dramatically degrade processing at the LP-modeled faster rate; correlations at the LP-modeled rate were relatively high in quiet, and were not profoundly dissimilar from the correlations at the NL-modeled rate in both quiet and noise. It was rapid repetition in combination with background noise that resulted in greatly diminished inter-response correlations at the faster LP-modeled rate. The processing of a faster rate by the normal system appears to have been a reasonable choice to model abnormal processing of a slower rate by the LP system.

Subcortical Responses, Human

The primary component of the /da/-evoked FFR corresponds in frequency to the stimulus' F_0. No differences in the magnitude of the F_0 component of the FFR were observed between LP and NL children. However, at higher frequencies

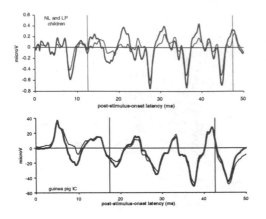
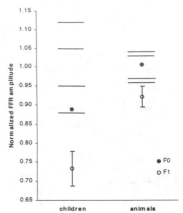

Fig. 15.2. Top left: Averaged brainstem responses to the first stimulus in the train, in NL (thick line) and LP (thin) children. The FFR was measured over the range indicated between the dashed lines. **Bottom left:** Averaged IC responses to the first (thick line) and second (thin) stimuli in the train, at ISI 24 ms, in guinea pig. The FFR was measured over the range indicated between the dashed lines. **Right (children):** Mean FFR amplitudes for LP children, shown as percentage of NL response amplitude, over frequency ranges corresponding to /da/ stimulus F_0 (solid circle) and F_1 (open circle). LP error bars reflect standard error of the mean. Normal ranges (+/− standard error of NL) are shown for F_0 (solid line) and F_1 (dashed line). **Right (animals):** Mean FFR amplitudes in response to second stimulus in train, at 24 ms ISI, shown as percentage of response to first stimulus, over frequency ranges corresponding to /da/ stimulus F_0 (solid circle) and F_1 (open circle). F_1 error bars reflect standard error of the mean. Normal ranges (+/− standard error of first response) are shown for F_0 (solid line) and F_1 (dashed line).

corresponding to F_1, LP children demonstrated diminished FFR activity (Fig. 15.2, Right: normalized to NL responses, LP responses are below the normal range for F_1, within the normal range for F_0). Responses in noise were not analyzed, due to excessive degradation of responses. These group differences were observed in response to the fourth stimulus, but also in response to the first stimulus in the train, prior to the within-train stress of repetition.

Subcortical Responses, Animal Model

Given the established literature implicating sensitivity to rapid stimulation as a basis for auditory processing deficits in LP children, we speculated that the response component that was shown to be abnormally represented in the LP response to the first stimulus in the train (F_1) would be likely to demonstrate noticeable effects of rapid stimulation in an animal model, while the F_0

component, which was not degraded in the LP response, would be similarly unaffected in animals.

In guinea pig IC, thought to be a generator of the human scalp-recorded FFR (Sohmer et al., 1977), comparison of the first two responses in a train, separated by 24 ms, provided a model of the normal effects of a similar interval, 30 ms, which was used to separate the final and initial stimuli in subsequent trains in the human study. As described for the guinea pig models of the human cortical response, a decreased ISI (in this case, 12 ms) was used to attempt to model the particular response patterns demonstrated by LP children. The F_0 component of the guinea pig IC FFR was largely unchanged by rapid repetition of the stimulus at both 24 and 12 ms ISI. In contrast, the frequencies corresponding to F_1 were diminished by repetition at both rates (Fig. 15.2, Right: normalized to first responses, the responses to repeated stimuli appear below the normal range for F_1, within the normal range for F_0). The different ISIs (12, 24 ms) did not provide a differentiation between responses akin to the observed NL/LP differences. Still, it is informative and interesting that differences in processing between NL and LP children were observed on the component that demonstrated sensitivity to rapid stimulation (F_1), while similar processing among NL and LP groups was demonstrated on the component that did not reflect effects of rapid stimulation (F_0). In other words, were one to predict differences in processing between NL and LP children, based on the established temporal-deficit literature and on the present guinea pig data, the temporally-sensitive F_1 component of the FFR would present a more likely candidate than the F_0 component, which is precisely the pattern that was observed in human data.

In combination, the human and guinea pig results suggest that the impairments seen in LP children may be due to an inability of their auditory systems to precisely respond under conditions of rapid stimulation that are relatively unchallenging to the NL children. This deficit was simulated in the guinea pig model by using exaggerated repetition rates and by investigating temporal sensitivity of different spectral components of the response. Both human and animal studies implicated degraded processing at subcortical as well as cortical levels as contributing to the auditory perceptual difficulties, and subsequent higher-level language problems, experienced by the LP children.

CUE-ENHANCEMENT

In adverse listening conditions such as noisy environments, as well as when addressing non-native or hearing-impaired listeners, talkers naturally alter their speech in order to make it clearer. Two cue enhancements involving stop consonants are increased stop-gap duration and increased amplitude of plosive consonants (Picheny et al., 1986). Cunningham and colleagues (Cunningham et al., 2001) measured syllable discrimination abilities in school-age children, using two synthesized continua containing conversational and cue-enhanced (clear) variants of a speech sound, presented in quiet and in background noise. Both cortical and subcortical speech-evoked responses were recorded and comparisons were made between normal controls and LP children who performed poorly on the discrimination task (Figure 15.3, Left). A guinea pig physiology model was employed to help elucidate the underlying human cue-enhancement results (Cunningham et al., 2002).

Methods, Human

Behavioral just-noticeable-differences were assessed with four /ada/-to-/aga/ continua. A 'conversational' continuum had a stop-gap duration of 50 ms and a consonant-vowel (CV) intensity ratio of −18 dB. In a 'clear' continuum, the stop-gap and CV ratio were increased to 230 ms and −8 dB, respectively. Two more continua employed each of those cue enhancements separately. All continua were presented at 65 dB SPL binaurally under headphones (Sennheiser HD-540) in quiet and with a white noise masker presented at a signal-to-noise ratio of +5 dB. It was found that for these subject groups and stimuli, the increased CV intensity ratio was much more effective than the increased stop-gap duration. Therefore, the initial vowel /a/ was removed and 40-ms duration conversational and clear /da/ syllables, differing only in CV intensity ratio, were used for human evoked response recording

Cortical and subcortical auditory evoked responses were differentially amplified and recorded from Cz, referenced to nose and earlobe, respectively. Stimuli were delivered monaurally to the right ear at 80 dB SPL both with and without a white noise background masker presented at a +5 dB signal-to-noise ratio. For subcortical responses, stimuli were delivered with a repetition rate of 11/s and responses were recorded for 60 ms post-stimulus. Responses were digitized at 20 kHz and online bandpass filtered from 0.1 to 2 kHz. Latency of the onset response was measured, and the sustained response was evaluated by Fourier analysis and stimulus-to-response correlation. Cortical responses were recorded separately using a repetition rate of 1.7/s, a response window of 500 ms post-stimulus, and bandpass filters of 0.1 to 100 Hz. Latencies and amplitudes of the major cortical responses in the 50–250 ms latency range, in particular P2 and N2, were measured.

Methods, Animal

In guinea pigs, far-field auditory evoked responses were recorded from left primary auditory cortex, and near-field evoked responses were recorded from primary subdivisions of left medial geniculate nucleus and inferior colliculus. The conversational and clear /ada/ stimuli were delivered to the right ear at 85 dB SPL with and without a white-noise masker at a signal-to-noise ratio of +5 dB. Repetition rate was 1/s and the response window was 500 ms post-stimulus. Responses were online bandpass filtered from 0.05 to 1000 Hz. Amplitudes of the onset responses were measured at the three recording sites. Subcortical sustained responses also were compared between stimulus conditions and among the anatomical levels by means of RMS amplitude, Fourier analysis and stimulus-to-response correlation.

Syllable Perception, Human

NL and LP children were similar in their abilities to discriminate conversational /ada/-/aga/ syllables when presented in quiet. The addition of background noise markedly degraded performance of LP children with respect to NL children. The inclusion of clear-speech cue enhancements in these syllables presented in background noise improved LP performance, which returned to levels demonstrated by NL children (Fig. 15.3, Left).

Cortical Response, Human

Cortical P2-to-N2 amplitudes for the two subject groups were equivalent in response to the conversational /da/ in quiet. The addition of background noise, however, led to a much more severe response degradation in the LP group. Maintaining the background noise, the cue-enhanced /da/ stimulus restored the response amplitude in LPs to the same level as that of the NL controls (Fig. 15.3, Right).

Subcortical Response, Human

Latencies of the onset response, occurring at about 8 ms post-stimulus-onset, demonstrated a pattern similar to that of the cortical response. That is, in response to the conversational /da/ presented in quiet, onset latencies were equivalent between subject groups, and the addition of background noise delayed the onset response in LPs relative to the normal controls. Onset latencies between the two groups again became equivalent in response to the clear /da/ in noise.

The frequency-following response, however, demonstrated a different pattern from that of the cortical and subcortical onset responses. The frequency composition of the sustained response was equivalent between the two groups to conversational /da/ in quiet. With background noise, the higher-frequency components (450–750 Hz) were diminished in the LP group, relative to the NL controls but this deficit was not restored by the clear /da/. A similar pattern was seen using a stimulus-to-response correlation technique. This technique revealed a deficit in the LP group frequency following response observed in noise, but this deficit was not restored by cue enhancement.

Animal Model

In the guinea pig, because the full /ada/ stimulus was used there were two discrete onset/sustained responses. The initial /a/ portion of the stimulus was

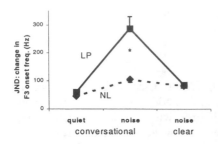 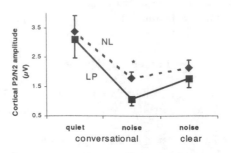

Fig. 15.3. Physiological and behavioral outcomes of noise and cue enhancement. **Left:** Syllable Discrimination: LP subjects discriminate as well as NL controls on a conversational /ada/ to /aga/ continuum when stimuli are presented in quiet. With the addition of background noise, LPs perform significantly worse. When cue-enhancement strategies are added to the stimuli, LP performance in the same background noise improved to match that of the NL controls. **Right:** The same pattern of results is demonstrated with cortical response amplitude. The LPs differ from the NL controls only in the conversational stimulus in noise condition. (Figures modified from Cunningham et al., 2001.)

unaltered between the conversational and clear stimuli, thus analyses were confined to the response evoked by the /da/. The response to the conversational /da/ in quiet was considered the basis for comparison of the responses to the conversational and clear stimuli in noise.

Onset responses, Animal

When noise was added to the conversational stimulus, the onset responses were dramatically reduced at all three recording sites. However, there was a definite hierarchy of diminution among the levels. The inferior colliculus response amplitude was least affected and the cortex amplitude was most affected. Moreover, the cortical response amplitude benefited most from the clear stimulus manipulation (Fig. 15.4).

Sustained responses, Animal

The frequency-following response to the voiced portion of the /da/ stimulus was present only at the two subcortical recording sites. In general, RMS amplitude of the steady-state portion of the response was unaffected by the noise masker at both sites. More specifically, however, Fourier analysis of the inferior colliculus response revealed that while the lower-frequency components of the response were diminished by the noise masker, the higher-frequency components, corresponding to F_1 in the vowel, were stable. Though representation of lower-frequency components was diminished in amplitude by the addition of noise, the temporal precision of these components was preserved to a degree sufficient to

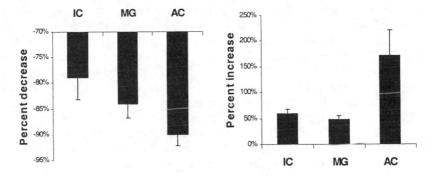

Fig. 15.4. Onset response amplitudes recorded from three levels along the auditory pathway (IC = inferior colliculus; MG = medial geniculate nucleus; AC = auditory cortex). **Left:** Effect of Noise: Background noise most affected the amplitude of the onset response at auditory cortex. **Right:** Effect of Cue Enhancement: The clear stimulus had the most impact at auditory cortex. (Figures modified from Cunningham et al., 2002.)

maintain similar levels of stimulus-to-response correlation across noise conditions. As observed in the children, the clear /da/ stimulus resulted in no improvements in the steady-state response at either recording location on any measure.

Both manipulations – the addition of background noise and the subsequent cue-enhancement of the speech token – impacted the cortical response most, in both children and in the guinea pig model. The subcortical response seen in human subjects, inferred by the scalp-recorded frequency-following response, was consistent with the subcortical responses recorded intracranially in the animal model: both were much less affected by noise when compared to cortex. Results in both subject groups provide evidence for the independence of the underlying neural processes that manifest themselves as transient onset and sustained frequency-following responses. Furthermore, the resilience of the subcortical sustained response in the LP group in adverse listening conditions, in contrast to the dramatic disruption of the cortical evoked responses, furnishes evidence that auditory-based learning problems in this group likely have an origin in the cortical encoding of acoustic transients in speech. Though not as pronounced as the effects in cortical encoding of acoustic transients, subcortical representation of the periodicity of the vowel component also indicated modest deficits in the LP children. Finally, the use of stimulus manipulation to promote restoration of normal-like responses, both behaviorally and physiologically, may help to inform effective remediation strategies.

DIFFERENTIATION OF PROCESSING, PATHWAYS, FUNCTION

Presentation of single, discrete stimuli has been observed to elicit multiple, independent patterns of neural activation, corresponding to different stimulus features. An example of this phenomenon comes from the literature examining anatomical and functional differences in the neural processing of the identification and location of a stimulus, or distinguishing "what" from "where." While much of this research has been performed in the visual system (Ungerleider & Mishkin, 1982), anatomically distinct pathways have recently been shown to contribute to the differentiation of analogous features of auditory stimuli (Clarke et al., 2002; Rauschecker & Tian, 2000; Zatorre et al., 2002). Differentiation of processing has also been demonstrated with respect to the acoustic structure of the stimulus, for example selective activation in response to simple tones versus complex vocalizations, and phasic versus tonic encoding of stimulus structure (for review, see Popper & Fay, 1992). In all of these cases, functional organization is evident, hallmarked by the efficient distribution of processes among multiple centers and circuits, each optimized for a particular function, contributing to integration into a perceptual whole.

Independence of patterns seen in the onset and sustained responses has been a repeated finding in the research conducted in this lab, some examples of which have been detailed here. Certain stimulus manipulations, such as repetition, masking noise and cue enhancement, differentially affect the transient and periodic response elements. Given the above-described literature addressing differentiation of pathways, function and corresponding perceptual ramifications, perhaps the differences between transient and periodic encoding presented here can be understood to reflect similarly organized assemblies of pathways and functions, evolved to extract and process information dependent upon its acoustic structure and/or environmental and communicative importance. For example, much information about the identity, intent and emotional condition of the speaker is contained in the fundamental frequency and harmonic structure of the utterance, which would be robustly represented by the periodic encoding at subcortical levels. Vast amounts of information about the phonetic content of the utterance, for example representation of fricatives and stops, are included in the transient portions of the response, reflected with remarkable precision in aggregate subcortical neural activity, and for which encoding in auditory cortex has been demonstrated to be ideally suited. While our hypotheses, and subsequent experimental designs, are not intended to specifically address such issues of differentiation, consideration of our findings within such a framework could prove insightful.

CONCLUSIONS

In the designs presented here, the human subject groups contained children with clinically diagnosed language-based learning problems. Several instances of abnormal processing of sounds have been described as likely contributing to the learning problems experienced by these children. These deficits were observed at multiple levels of the auditory pathway and affected different portions of the encoded signal. For example, the auditory encoding deficits seen in this group are very apparent in the presence of substantial levels of masking noise. Not coincidentally, it is in such listening conditions, for example in noisy classrooms, where many such children experience the most perceptual difficulty.

As a model of the human auditory system, the guinea pig has proven to be a useful tool. Localized recording from discrete subcortical nuclei permits confirmation of inferences resulting from scalp recordings in humans. This model permits an approximation of the "normal" system. Given reasonable assumptions about the nature of the "impaired" system, stimulus manipulations and investigations of particular sensitivities of response components can also model, to a degree, mechanisms that may contribute to abnormal cortical and subcortical processing in humans.

An interesting finding from the study of effects of stimulus repetition and noise on cortical processing in NL and LP children, and supported by guinea pig models of normal and impaired processing, is that perhaps abnormal encoding of auditory stimuli does not reflect an altogether novel, degraded process, and thus entirely different underlying mechanisms, but that it instead reflects a tail end of exceedingly poor processing along the distribution of normal performance. Such a perspective has appeared elsewhere in the literature concerning learning problems. Rather than representing a distinctly "impaired" mode from a bimodal distribution of reading ability, dyslexia can be described as reflecting a poor-performing tail of unimodal normal distribution of reading ability (Shaywitz et al., 1992). Likewise, our data could support such a notion, that the "abnormal" encoding demonstrated by LP children is in fact similar to "normal" encoding that would be demonstrated by NL children under exaggerated conditions, when normal processing was stressed over a more extreme range of performance.

Also of particular interest are our multiple descriptions of deficits in subcortical processing that were observed in the LP children. While not entirely unheard of previously, the literature describing brainstem processing in relation to learning disabilities pales in comparison to studies of cortical phenomena. That differences are observed at such an early, primary level of encoding is vastly interesting. In many respects, such investigations may have been overlooked, as low-level encoding has long been described as so relatively robust that it may not have been considered as fraught with potential abnormalities as more sensitive, complex processing in cortex. Disruptions in such low levels of encoding speak to the distinctly auditory-perceptual nature of these problems, as opposed to effects observed in cortical auditory responses, that are often confounded by longer-latency, simultaneously-evolving attentional, linguistic, and cognitive responses.

ACKNOWLEDGMENTS

Supported by NIH–NIDCD R01 DC01510-09, T32 DC00015-17, and F31 DC04546-01.

REFERENCES

Carrell, T.D., Bradlow, A.R., Nicol, T.G., Koch, D.B., & Kraus, N. (1999). Interactive software for evaluating auditory discrimination. Ear & Hearing, 20, 175–176.

Clarke, S., Bellman Thiran, A., Maeder, P., Adriani, M., Vernet, O., Regli, L., Cuisenaire, O., & Thiran, J.P. (2002). What and where in human audition: Selective deficits following focal hemispheric lesions. Experimental Brain Research, 147, 8–15.

Cunningham, J., Nicol, T., King, C.D., Zecker, S.G., & Kraus, N. (2002). Effects of noise and cue enhancement on neural responses to speech in the auditory midbrain, thalamus and cortex. Hearing Research, 169, 97–111.

Cunningham, J., Nicol, T., Zecker, S.G., Bradlow, A., & Kraus, N. (2001). Neurobiologic responses to speech in noise in children with learning problems: deficits and strategies for improvement. Clinical Neurophysiology, 112, 758–767.

Hayes, E., Warrier, C.M., Nicol, T., Zecker, S.G., & Kraus, N. (2003). Neural plasticity following auditory training in children with learning problems. Clinical Neurophysiology, 114, 673–684.

Jacobson, J.T. (1985). The Auditory Brainstem Response. San Diego, CA: College Hill.

King, C., Warrier, C.M., Hayes, E., & Kraus, N. (2001). Deficits in auditory brainstem encoding of speech sounds in children with learning problems. Neuroscience Letters, 319, 111–115.

Kraus, N., McGee, T.J., Carrell, T.D., Zecker, S.G., Nicol, T.G., & Koch, D.B. (1996). Auditory neurophysiologic responses and discrimination deficits in children with learning problems. Science, 273, 971–973.

Picheny, M.A., Durlach, N.I., & Braida, L.D. (1986). Speaking clearly for the hard of hearing. II: Acoustic characteristics of clear and conversational speech. Journal of Speech & Hearing Research, 29, 434–446.

Popper, A., & Fay, R. (1992). The Mammalian Auditory System, Vol. II. New York: Springer-Verlag.

Rauschecker, J.P., & Tian, B. (2000). Mechanisms and streams for processing of "what" and "where" in auditory cortex. Proceedings of the National Academy of Sciences USA, 97, 11800–11806.

Shaywitz, S.E., Escobar, M.D., Shaywitz, B.A., Fletcher, J.M., & Makuch, R. (1992). Evidence that dyslexia may represent the lower tail of a normal distribution of reading ability. New England Journal of Medicine, 326, 145–150.

Sohmer, H., Pratt, H., & Kinarti, R. (1977). Sources of frequency following responses (FFR) in man. Electroencephalography and Clinical Neurophysiology, 42, 656–664.

Ungerleider, L., & Mishkin, M. (1982). Two cortical visual systems. In D.Ingle, M. Goodale, & Mansfield R. (Eds.), Analysis of visual behavior (pp. 549–586). Cambridge, MA: MIT Press.

Wible, B., Nicol, T.G., & Kraus, N. (2002). Abnormal neural encoding of repeated speech stimuli in noise in children with learning problems. Clinical Neurophysiology, 113, 485–494.

Wible, B., Nicol, T., & Kraus, N. (2004). Atypical brainstem representation of onset and formant structure of speech sounds in children with language-based learning problems. Biological Psychology, 67, 299–317.

Wilkinson, G. (1993). Wide range achievement test-3. Wilmington, DE: Jastak.

Zatorre, R. J., Bouffard, M., Ahad, P., & Belin, P. (2002). Where is 'where' in the human auditory cortex? Nature Neuroscience, 5, 905–909.

16. CORRELATED NEURAL ACTIVITY: EPIPHENOMENON OR PART OF THE NEURAL CODE?

Jos J. Eggermont

INTRODUCTION

Cortical neurons receive their inputs only for a small fraction from specific thalamic afferents and for a much larger fraction from other cortical neurons. The same could be said for the sensory thalamus, where the majority of inputs is not from collicular afferents but from centrifugal cortical neurons. Yet, by analyzing single-unit stimulus-response functions, such as the frequency-tuning curve (FTC) or the spectro-temporal receptive field (STRF), one regards the sensory system as a simple single-input-single output system. One reason that this works fairly well is because the specific thalamic afferents to cortical neurons are synchronized by the stimulus, whereas the majority of other neural inputs arrive asynchronously. Abeles (1991) was one of the first to draw attention to the power of synchronously arriving inputs in activating cortical neurons. In simplified terms, the amplitude of the post-synaptic potentials (PSP) resulting from synchronized inputs is proportional to the number of inputs, whereas the PSP amplitude from asynchronously arriving inputs is only proportional to the square root of their number. Assume that the synaptic connection strengths and firing rates for thalamic cells combined are a factor 3–4 higher than those of cortico-cortical cells, which is not an unreasonable assumption (Gil et al., 1999). Then, even only 30 synchronously firing specific afferents (the putative number converging on a cortical cell, Miller et al., 2001), which produce compound PSPs that are 3–4 times larger than for cortico-cortical cells and effectively produce 90–120 amplitude units of PSP, would still be as effective as 9000 asynchronously firing non-specific cortico-cortical inputs that produce $\sqrt{9000} \cong 95$ amplitude units of PSP.

What can one infer about the cortical network when only extracellular recordings of spike trains are made and when only a very partial sampling of the number of contributing neurons to the firings of the target neuron is available? In other words, how can one interpret pair correlation functions, and how does the neural connectivity matrix enter into the neural code, the putative representation of invariant stimulus features in cortex? Neural synchrony also plays an important role in the generation of scalp-recorded evoked electric potentials or magnetic fields. For instance, the amplitude of these signals is proportional to the number of activated pyramidal cells and the degree of synchrony in their excitatory post-synaptic potentials (EPSPs) and excitatory post-synaptic currents (EPSCs).

In the following sections I will systematically evaluate what, generally pairwise, neural correlations have elucidated about the thalamo-cortical information transfer, about stimulus dependence of neural synchrony, and about the role of correlated neural activity in neural coding.

SYNCHRONOUS FIRING OF NEURONS

Correlated neural activity results from above chance level synchronous firings of single units. Figure 16.1 shows, in the left part, a 10-second section of spontaneous firings of four simultaneously recorded neurons, three of which fire rather frequently, and the fourth rather sparsely.

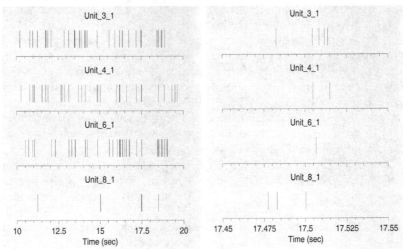

Fig. 16.1. A 10-second section of spontaneous activity for four simultaneously recorded neurons from cat primary auditory cortex (left). On the right a 100-ms part around the time mark of 17.5 s shows synchronous firing within 5–10 ms.

The right part of Figure 16.1 shows a stretch of 100 ms long taken from the left part around the time mark of 17.5 s that illustrates that several pair combinations of neurons show near coincident firing, that is, within 5–10 ms. It is those firings that constitute the correlated neural activity that we will discuss. A cross-correlogram (as shown in Fig. 16.2) is a histogram that shows the firings of one neuron relative to the firings of another neuron (the trigger neuron). The time base has a bin size that is as large as possible but small enough that it is unlikely that more than one spike would fall in that bin for a given trigger neuron spike. Typically, a bin size of 1 or 2 ms is used (upper part of the sections in Fig. 16.2). However, to get an impression of secondary effects such as oscillatory phenomena often bin sizes of 10 ms or larger are used (lower part of the sections in Fig. 16.2). The large bin sizes violate the Poisson assumption (low probability of bin filling) that is used in the calculation of the peak cross-correlation coefficient, R, of the correlogram. The calculation of R is typically the same as for the Pearson correlation coefficient familiar from statistics. The difference here is that R is a function of the lead and lag time (τ). The R values are calculated from the peak number of coincidences, $R_{AB}(\tau)$, by first subtracting the expected value under the assumption of independent firings of neurons 1 and 2, and then dividing by the product of the number of spikes in both spike trains (Eggermont, 1992a). In formula, the cross-correlation function between units A and B is, if firing rates are below 20 spikes/s, to a very good approximation equal to:

$$R(\tau) = [(R_{AB}(\tau) - E] / [N_A N_B]^{0.5} \tag{1}$$

Here $E - N_A N_B / N_{bin}$ is the estimated number of spikes in a bin under the assumption that the firings of neurons A and B are independent. The Poisson assumption enters when we calculate the standard deviation (SD) of the bin filling process. For a Poisson process, the SD equals the square root of the mean value, which in this case is $[N_A N_B / N_{bin}]^{0.5}$. If we would enter the SD in the numerator, we would get a z-score. The cross-correlation coefficient is related to the z-score (Eggermont, 1992a) by:

$$R(\tau) = Z_{AB}(\tau) / [N_{bin}]^{0.5} \tag{2}$$

The standard deviation for $R(\tau)$ is given by : $SD(R) = [(1 - E/N_{bin}) / N_{bin}]^{0.5}$.

For large number of bins, that means for long recording times, which in our case is typically 15 minutes, i.e., 450,000 or 900,000 bins, this reduces to

$$SD(R) = [1 / N_{bin}]^{0.5}. \tag{3}$$

For a 2 ms-bin correlogram, the SD is 0.0015. We typically take 4 SD as the boundary for significance (indicated in Fig. 16.2 by dashed lines), which results in R values that have to exceed 0.006 to be significantly different from zero.

The peak of the cross-correlograms obtained in auditory cortex is typically around zero-lag time. This is usually taken as an indication of shared input by the two neurons involved. If the peak is displaced from the zero time point by one synaptic delay and is asymmetric, that is, shaped as the time-derivative of the EPSP, then the correlogram can be interpreted as due to monosynaptic excitation. This is very rarely observed for extracellular recordings in cortex, especially if they are done with separate electrodes.

MEASURING NEURAL CORRELATION FOR THE PURPOSE SKETCHED ABOVE REQUIRES MULTI-ELECTRODE RECORDINGS

Correlated neural activity can be calculated for neurons recorded on single electrodes, but problems arise because of overlap of waveforms and of the dead time of the sorting, that is, when one waveform is assigned to a particular class, the next item has to come one "waveform duration" later. This results in a dead time, of the order of 1 ms, in the cross correlogram. Recording population neural activity requires the use of microelectrode arrays, either with independently movable electrodes or consisting of electrodes with fixed distances. Spike sorting was reviewed recently (Lewicki, 1998), as was the potential of multi-electrode recordings (Devilbiss & Waterhouse, 2002) and problems therewith (Zhu et al., 2002).

ASSESSMENT OF MONOSYNAPTIC NEURAL CONNECTIVITY

Because of the divergence of thalamic cell outputs, and consequently the convergence of inputs from more than one thalamic cell upon a cortical target neuron in deep layer III or layer IV, simultaneous recordings of thalamic projection neurons and auditory cortical neurons have been of interest for a long time (Creutzfeldt et al., 1980). Several studies have addressed the number of thalamic cells that contribute to the firing of cortical target cells. This number has been established to about 30 in both visual and auditory systems (Abeles, 1991; Miller et al., 2001). Most cross-correlation studies in sensory cortex based on extra-cellular recordings register only the effects of common excitatory input. A common excitatory input reflects the number of inputs (synapses) from the thalamo-cortical or cortico-cortical cell axons that are shared between the two neurons. This is dependent on the degree of branching of these axons and weighted by the firing rates of the neurons and the strengths of the synapses. It is rare to observe excitatory or inhibitory monosynaptic connection using cross-correlation studies based on extracellular recordings. One reason for this could be that the effects of excitatory connections may be drowned under the larger common input from asynchronously firing cortical neurons. One expects the excitatory synaptic effects to become stronger with increased stimulus level and should thus be clearer to observe. The difficulty is then that these strong stimulus-locked spikes are subsequently removed by correction procedures such as the shift predictor or the joint peri-stimulus time histogram (JPSTH) predictor (Eggermont, 1994) that aim at purifying the correlogram from stimulus-locked events. Only the "uninteresting" asynchronous inputs that are poorly locked to the stimulus may survive and show up in the corrected correlogram.

THE ROLE OF CORRELATED NEURAL ACTIVITY IN THE TRANSMISSION OF INFORMATION

Correlated neural activity in sensory and motor cortex in vast majority is the result of common input either from divergent connections of thalamic cells, or from cortical interconnectivity. As a result, network properties such as oscillations synchronized over large (alpha rhythms) or more restricted (beta and gamma rhythms) cortical areas will affect the preferred timing of synchronous spiking and thus could be precursors for precise synchrony. Gamma-band oscillations in auditory cortex have been shown for unit recordings (Brosch et al., 2002) and for local field potentials (LFPs) (MacDonald & Barth, 1995). However, the only dominant oscillations in the auditory system are the alpha-spindles that may limit temporal coding (Eggermont, 1992b; Horikawa et al., 1994; Kenmochi & Eggermont, 1997) and appear to be largely a slow wave sleep (SWS) or anesthesia phenomenon (Cotillon-Williams & Edeline, 2003).

Neurons transmit information, and this information can be quantified using information theory once one does know what "symbol" in neural spike trains codes for it. This is the problem of neural coding (Dayan & Abbott, 2001), and potential coding symbols are average firing rate, interspike intervals, precisely timed spike latencies, spike bursts, synchronized spikes across a neural population, and so on. One could compute what symbol is most efficient, and assuming that nature prefers efficiency this would suggest the neural code. It is also understandable that independence of symbols is better to transmit information since more symbols are available. Independently firing neurons would then also be able to transmit more information than spike trains with serial correlation between the intervals. However, as reviewed below, correlated neural activity is not always bad for information transfer.

Calculations of information transmission based on neural synchrony become rapidly unwieldy if the number of neurons involved in the ensemble increases. Rolls et al. (2003) described a way to reduce this dimensionality problem. They expanded the information transmitted in time interval t, $I(t)$, in powers of t (up to second order) by using a Taylor expansion that effectively equates transmission of information with the sum of the rate and acceleration of information transmission.

The rate of information transmission appears to be independent of neural interaction and is only dependent on average firing rates for each stimulus. The correlation terms appear in the acceleration of information transmission. Two different correlation terms are distinguished: *noise* correlation, based on fluctuations around the mean for a given stimulus, or for silence, and *signal* correlation, based on the mean response of neurons calculated over the entire set of stimuli, i.e., based on tuning curve overlap of the individual neurons. Signal and noise correlations can potentially annihilate each other.

CORRELATED NEURAL ACTIVITY EXTRACTS STIMULUS INVARIANTS

Information transfer is an important requisite of a sensory system, however, stimulus recognition and assigning meaning to a stimulus may be even more important. It is likely that stimuli are stored in memory in an incomplete way: Only invariants in the neural representation of a stimulus are stored. The remainder is filled in during recall or recognition and depends on context. So, incomplete information about the stimulus may still result in recognition. Assigning symbols that provide maximum information transfer to the most likely code to be used by the sensory system may therefore be wrong, transferring the information that leads to reliable recognition or classification is all that is needed. Classification is based on stimulus invariants, i.e., most likely the stimulus contours as these play an important role in stimulus recognition. Thus, access to stimulus memory may be based on information about the contours and on correlated neural activity, either between simultaneously activated sensory neurons or between sensory neurons and memory neurons. This may also form the basis for extracting invariants and reconstructing the stimulus (Eggermont, 1990). In this way the correlation between neural activity representing stored stimulus invariants and neural activity evoked by the current stimulus may act as the code to reconstruct the stimulus, i.e., recognize it or categorize it. Consequently, any mechanism that extracts stimulus invariants may provide a neural code that allows this recognition. The correlated neural activity across a neural population may do precisely that, regardless whether it is not optimal in transmitting information.

CORRELATED NEURAL ACTIVITY IN AUDITORY CORTEX

The pioneering studies in auditory cortex by Dickson and Gerstein (1974) followed a decade later by Frostig et al. (1983) indicated only a minority of cases with evidence for stimulus-dependent correlograms, i.e., where the shape of the correlogram changed. Later, Espinoza and Gerstein (1988), Ahissar et al. (1992), and Eggermont (1994) showed stimulus dependent changes in the cross-correlation coefficient (R). Subsequently, deCharms and Merzenich (1996) showed that neural correlation is enhanced, without a change in shape, during continuous tones whereas firing rates were not above the spontaneous level, and Brosch and Schreiner (1999) demonstrated that correlation strength was strongly associated with similarities in binaural and temporal response properties

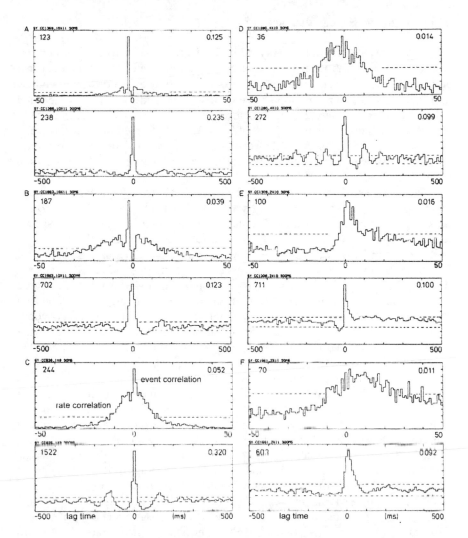

Fig. 16.2. Examples of cross-correlograms for units recorded on the same electrode (**A, B**) and on separate electrodes (**C-F**). The upper part of each block shows results on a time scale of −50 to 50 ms (1 ms bins) and the lower part shows a time scale of −500 to 500 ms using 10-ms bins. The dashed lines indicate ±4 SD from the expected value under independence. Reproduced from Eggermont (1992a) with permission from the publisher.

between the neurons. In the following, I will review our work on cross-correlation studies in cat auditory cortex over the past decade and present some recent results as well.

Effect of inter-electrode distance

Electrode distance can functionally be divided into three ranges. 1) Unit pairs recorded on one electrode comprise distances between neurons within a cortical column (< 100 µm distance), 2) unit pairs recorded at electrodes separated by more than 200 µm but within the same cortical area, and 3) unit pairs recorded from electrodes in different cortical fields. Distance can also be expressed in CF difference or amount of receptive field overlap. Units recorded on the same electrode and isolated using spike-sorting techniques show on average higher correlation strength than units with the same CF but recorded on separate electrodes (Eggermont, 1992a).

Figures 16.2A, B show two single-electrode pair correlograms for recordings under spontaneous conditions, both on a 50-ms (1-ms bins) and 500-ms (10-ms bins) lag/lead time and 101 bins. The number of coincidences in a bin is shown in the left hand corner and the peak cross-correlation coefficients (R) are shown in the top right corner of each panel. By comparing the upper and lower part of Figure 16.2A one observes that the number of coincidences and the R-values are dependent on the bin size. Because for 10-ms bins (the lower parts of the Figure sections) more than one spike can occur in the same bin these large-bin correlograms should only be used qualitatively, that is, to show secondary aspects such as the oscillations shown in the lower part of Figure 16.2D of the spiking activity of the two neurons. The dashed lines indicate the expected value ±4 SD of the correlation under the assumption of independent Poisson processes. The example in part A shows a single 1-ms wide peak at –2 ms from zero lag time. This likely represents different arrival times of the common input to both cells as a result of different conduction velocities or different axonal branch lengths. Previously (Eggermont, 1992a) I interpreted this as a sign of monosynaptic excitation between the two units, however, in that case the shape of the peak should reflect the time derivative of the EPSP and thus be asymmetric. The R-value of 0.125 indicates that on average 12.5% of the spikes result from this common input. The example in part B shows a broad pedestal with a superimposed narrow peak (R = 0.039), suggesting again some small difference in spike arrival times from one driver unit combined with activity from asynchronous arriving spikes likely from other cortical units. As we will see later, the pedestal can be considered as arising from the covariation in firing rate of the two neurons, whereas the sharp peak indicates event correlations contributed to a few strongly synchronized driver neurons. Figures 16.2C-F illustrate pair correlograms from neurons recorded on separate electrodes. Here the peak of the correlogram is much broader than for single electrode pairs and the peak correlation coefficients are smaller. The example shown in part C, which shows a symmetric correlogram, again can be interpreted as due to rate covariance and event correlation. The long-range correlogram shows oscillatory features, which are likely due to 8-Hz spindling in the EEG as the period between the primary and secondary peaks is about 125 ms. This is also obvious in part D, albeit that the oscillation period here is about 100 ms. The example shown in parts E and F show asymmetric correlograms likely due to prolonged bursting of the second neuron. Here only rate covariance remains and there is very little if any event correlation. Removal of the effects of bursting and secondary aspects typically results in symmetric and fairly narrow correlograms (Eggermont & Smith, 1996).

When comparing the common input type correlations for single vs. dual electrode recordings, the average correlation strength, R, for 1 ms bins was 0.021 for single electrode pairs, which is twice as large as for dual electrode pairs with the same CF (R = 0.010). For dual-electrode pairs there was no further dependence on CF difference up to 1.75 octaves (Eggermont, 1992a) which roughly corresponds to a distance of about 2 mm in the direction of the tonotopic gradient. The drop in R-value in the first 200 μm (change from single-electrode to dual electrode pairs) may largely be due to a sharp reduction in the number of event correlations due to branching axonal inputs. All what is left in most dual electrode pairs could be some form of rate covariance resulting from common input of many asynchronously firing cortical neurons. In a later study (Eggermont, 1994), also using 1-ms bins, slightly higher values for spontaneous correlation strengths were found: 0.059 for single electrode pairs and 0.014 for dual electrode pairs (independent of CF differences up to 3 octaves). Correlation strengths were significantly smaller for units recorded with electrodes in different cortical areas, but were still of the order of 0.01 (Eggermont, 2000). In our studies, single electrode correlations rarely exceeded 0.3 and in the vast majority were below 0.1 whereas dual electrode correlations rarely exceeded 0.03 (Eggermont, 1992a, 1994, 2000). One could thus say that within a cortical column neurons fire synchronously with on average about 6% of their spikes in perfect coincidence (the peak correlation strength in a 1-ms bin) and occasionally showing 30% or more of the spikes coincident. For electrode separations exceeding 200 μm the average peak correlation strength is on average 0.014 and only occasionally reaches 0.03 (3% of spikes in perfect coincidence). These are very small numbers, however, the widths of the correlogram peaks for dual-electrode pairs are much larger than those for same-electrode pairs, as Figure 16.2 illustrates. When all the "coincidences" in the central peak are added up, there is no longer a difference between the percentage of correlated events for units within a cortical column or units far apart (Eggermont, 1992a). This suggests that the smaller peak values found for dual electrode pairs are likely the result of less synchronous arrivals of the common inputs. As long as the "coincidences" are within the temporal integration window of the receiving neurons, that is, within 15–30 ms, the degree of synchrony likely does not matter that much.

Stimulus effects and correction methods

In order to appreciate the effects that stimulation has on cross-correlograms it is appropriate to distinguish between neural synchrony and neural correlation. *Neural synchrony* is equated here with the cross-correlation under stimulus conditions, that is, the number of coincidences is converted into a cross-corrrelation coefficient in the same way as for spontaneous activity. *Neural correlation* is the correlation under spontaneous conditions or after correction for stimulus related correlations on the basis of a shift predictor. It is important to realize that neural synchrony is the measure that matters for efficiently transmitting neuron-invariant information or for grouping neurons into assemblies. Corrections for stimulus-locked correlations were inspired by the idea that stimulus induced spikes and spontaneous spikes were generated independently, and by the belief that the estimate of the neural correlation under various stimulus conditions could demonstrate stimulus-dependent neural connection strengths. Only under some assumptions about the integration of neural input by a neuron and about the shape of the neuron's response curve can one estimate the synaptic strength. Furthermore, the estimate of the synaptic strength is very sensitive to the shape and working point of the neuron's response curve (Melssen & Epping, 1987). Therefore it is generally pointless to equate the strength of the neural correlation with the synaptic strength. Changes in neural correlation strength without changes in the shape of the correlogram corrected for stimulus-locked contributions are generally the result of a change in the working point on the neuronal response curve. In that case one expects that larger R-values are correlated with larger firing rates. As shown in Eggermont (1994), the additivity assumption for stimulus-induced and connectivity effects to neural synchrony may well be the weakest link in the reasoning that leads to the interpretation of stimulus-dependent neural correlation.

The interpretation of neural synchrony strength is more straightforward and informative (Eggermont, 1994) as the following example shows. For three different amplitude-modulated stimuli, namely periodic click trains, sinusoidally-amplitude-modulated noise bursts and sinusoidally-amplitude-modulated tone bursts the average R values for 52 single-electrode pairs were respectively 0.14, 0.14, and 0.08 compared to 0.06 for spontaneous activity. Obviously, the spectrally broadband stimuli increased the correlation much more than the amplitude modulated tones.

For 57 dual-electrode pairs the differences were also about 3 fold and for the same sequence of stimuli were respectively 0.045, 0.037, and 0.039 compared to 0.014 for spontaneous conditions. It is interesting that the difference between broadband and narrow-band stimuli disappears here. The differences in peak correlation strength, before and after stimulus correction, were generally accompanied by changes in the shape of the correlograms (Fig. 16.3). In this Figure, for pairs recorded on the same electrode, the left hand column of each section reflects neural synchrony (during stimulation), the right hand column neural correlation (during post-stimulus silence). Each section consists of two parts; the bottom graph shows the raw correlogram and the shift predictor (black), the top graph shows the difference histogram (raw correlogram minus the shift predictor) and a line corresponding to 4 SD of the shift predictor. In the right hand corner the values of R are indicated. One notices that the correlation

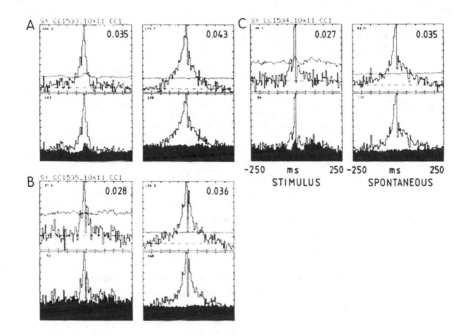

Fig. 16.3. Examples of cross-correlograms for unit pairs recorded on the same electrode under different stimulus conditions (left-hand column of each part) and post-stimulus spontaneous activity (right-hand column of each part). The bottom part of each section shows neural raw correlation and shift predictor (black), the top part the difference and the 4 SD function of the shift predictor. The stimuli were periodic click trains (**A**), amplitude-modulated noise (**B**) and amplitude modulated tones (**C**). Adapted from Eggermont (1994) with permission.

under stimulus conditions is generally smaller than the corresponding neural correlation during silence. The changing shape of the difference histogram under stimulus conditions is strongly indicative of stimulus-dependent neural correlation and suggestive of a role of correlated neural activity in the transmission of information.

For electrode pairs in different cortical areas (AI, AAF, or AII), the neural synchrony was typically a factor 3–4 higher than the correlation during spontaneous activity. The neural correlation between cortical areas was significantly lower than found for within area dual-electrode pairs and not dependent on the distance (Eggermont, 2000).

The effects of intrinsic neural response properties and thalamo-cortical network properties

Correlated neural activity is the result of connectivity between neurons and is determined by intra-cortical and thalamo-cortical network properties, that is, the

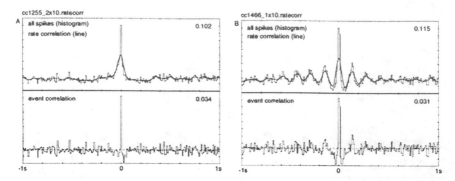

Fig. 16.4. Examples of cross-correlograms of unit pairs recorded on separate electrodes with separation of the contributions from rate covariance (drawn line in upper sections) and event correlation (bottom sections). The numbers in the upper right of each box are the peak cross-correlation coefficients. Adapted from Eggermont and Smith (1995).

shape of the cross-correlogram is affected by the auto-correlation structure of the spike trains, that is, periodicities in the firing of the individual neurons will be reflected in the cross-correlogram as secondary features. Burst firing of neurons (reflecting cortical ripples) will generally affect the central peak in the cross-correlogram. In addition, as we have seen in Figure 16.2, the cross-correlogram reflects the sum of rate covariance between the two neurons (broad peaks or pedestals) and event-correlation (coincident firing). We found that both under spontaneous and stimulus conditions, secondary effects from burst firing, global synchrony related to LFPs and stimulus-related effects largely obscure any underlying correlation produced by event correlation, that is, reflecting direct connectivity (Eggermont & Smith, 1996).

One could assume that the LFP-mediated firings produce slow changes in the covariance of the firing rates of the two neurons. A simple way to take care of this is to low-pass filter the spike trains, e.g., use a sliding 50 ms window advancing in 5 ms steps (the bin width of the cross-correlogram) and cross-correlate the resulting spike number sequences (Eggermont & Smith, 1995). This results in a predictor of the effect of rate covariance on the correlogram (Fig. 16.4). In part A, the rate covariance produces the smooth correlogram and subtracting that from the overall correlogram reveals the event correlation for this dual electrode pair. In part B, the LFP-spindles produce a periodic correlogram, the rate predictor explains all of this and the subtraction shows the event related part of the correlogram. Rate-covariance comprised about 73% of the peak correlation for single-electrode pairs and 67% for dual-electrode pairs, whereas secondary effects were generally accounted for completely (Eggermont & Smith, 1995). Secondary effects, such as those resulting from LFP spindles, can be effectively removed by deconvolving the cross-correlogram with the autocorrelogram of the trigger unit (Eggermont & Smith, 1996). The effect of burst firing could be estimated by comparing cross-correlograms obtained for

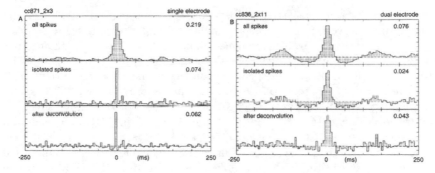

Fig. 16.5. Example of correcting cross-correlograms for burst-firing and periodicities resulting from network properties. The top part represents a single-electrode pair, the bottom part is for a dual-electrode pair. The numbers in the upper right of each box are the peak cross-correlation coefficients. Adapted from Eggermont and Smith (1996) with permission.

"isolated" spikes (no spike preceding or following within 30 ms) with those for all spikes. Alternatively, one could only use the first spike of bursts together with isolated spikes.

Figure 16.5 illustrates the combined burst removal and deconvolution procedure. Part A illustrates that asymmetric correlograms often become symmetric after removal of burst spikes and deconvolution. In part B, the effect of burst firing is small, whereas the periodicities can be removed by deconvolution. The combined deconvolution and burst correction procedure resulted in very little effect on spontaneous firing correlograms. However, for stimulus conditions, there was a factor 4 reduction in the strength of the neural synchrony for single electrode pairs and a factor 6 for dual electrode pairs (Eggermont & Smith, 1996) suggesting that especially for dual electrode pairs secondary effects dominate the neural synchrony. Correcting for these effects becomes important when investigating the role of neural synchrony in neural coding. A sleeping brain typically shows higher neural correlations that extend over larger distances than an awake brain or a brain that is processing information (evidence reviewed in Eggermont, 1990).

One could say that the neurons in a sleeping brain are part of one large assembly. In contrast one may assume that in an information processing brain, regardless whether it is under light anesthesia or not, neurons with different response properties will be very unlikely doing the same thing at the same time and thus will show less synchronized firings.

NEURAL SYNCHRONY AND JOINT RECEPTIVE FIELD PROPERTIES

One can split the spikes recorded during stimulation into those that contribute to the receptive field and those that do not. For spikes contributing to the receptive field the peak correlation strength between two neurons will likely depend strongly on the overlap of the receptive fields of these neurons, whereas spikes firing "spontaneously" would not. This might explain why for spontaneously firing neurons the dependence on CF-distance was small and even under stimulus conditions no strong dependence on CF distance was noted (Brosch & Schreiner, 1999; Eggermont, 1994). The procedure for selecting spikes contributing to the STRF (in-RF spikes) and those that do not (out-RF spikes) is illustrated in Figure 16.6. Each of the 4 panels shows an STRF obtained with 15-minute multi-frequency stimulation (Blake & Merzenich, 2002) in the cat posterior auditory field. The region of interest of the excitatory RFs is indicated (ellipses) and spike firings that exceed the mean value of the STRF (here shown as the frequency-dependent PSTH) are selected. Cross-correlograms were then calculated (Table 16.1) between all six pairs of in-RF spikes of the 4 recordings represented here, and also between the six pairs of out-RF spikes. One observes that the synchrony between electrodes 1, 2, and 3 is relatively strong (R values from 0.024–0.043), but that those pairs involving electrode 4 are lower (0.005−0.019). Only part of this is due to RF overlap.

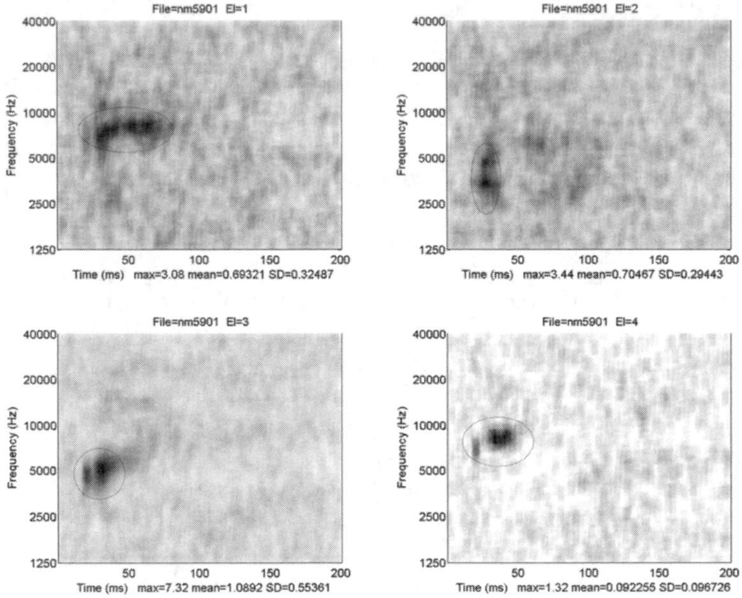

Fig. 16.6. Spectro-temporal receptive fields for 4 simultaneously recorded units. The horizontal axis represents time, the vertical axis frequency (log scale) between 1250 Hz and 40 kHz. Darker areas represent stronger responses. The spikes contributing to regions within the ellipses (in-RF spikes) are separated from those outside the STRF (out-RF spikes). The cross correlation coefficients are shown in Table 16.1.

Table 16.1: Cross-correlation coefficients for spikes from within the STRF and those for spikes from outside the STRF.

Unit pair	In-RF	Out-RF
1 x 2	0.024	0.039
1 x 3	0.037	0.032
1 x 4	0.019	0.010
2 x 3	0.043	0.028
2 x 4	0.005	0.008
3 x 4	0.006	0.011

The cross correlation between pairs of out-RF spikes, likewise is also strong between electrodes 1, 2, and 3 and low between pairs involving electrode 4. STRF overlap was measured by taking the contour line representing 30% of the difference between the maximum response and the mean value of the STRF for each of the neurons, calculating the number of pixels within that contour line for each neuron's STRF as well as the number of overlapping pixels.

The weighted excitatory STRF overlap was defined as (overlap/geometric mean of the number of pixels for the two units) and scaled between 0 (no overlap) and 1 (complete overlap). Figure 16.7 shows results obtained for a particular set of recordings using two 8-micro-electrode arrays, from one of which the previous example was taken. The left panel shows the scattergram between R and the weighted overlap for in-RF and out-RF spikes for all pairs from the 15 responsive electrodes in the two electrode arrays and for 15-minute steady-state multi-frequency stimulation. The right panel shows results for a 15 minute silence condition for the same electrodes and location. One observes that the correlation is strongest for the in-RF spikes ($r^2 = 0.4$) and weakest for the spontaneous spike pairs ($r^2 = 0.06$) although the dependence was still significant ($p < 0.05$). Although the in-RF spike pairs showed a stronger dependence on RF overlap this was by no means the only aspect determining the correlation. For instance in the overlap range from 0.3–0.4, the R-values obtained during stimulation ranged from 0.005 to 0.45, that is, about 10 fold. Note that R-values under spontaneous conditions could be higher than under stimulus conditions. On average the R-values were 0.016 (silence), 0.017 (in-RF) and 0.010 (out-RF), and only the difference with the out-RF value was significant ($p < 0.0001$). Stimulation may thus disrupt the correlation observed under spontaneous firing conditions. This could potentially be the result of abolishing the spindles in this slow-wave-sleep state, that is, by "arousing" the cat and thereby breaking up the large-assembly state into a large number of smaller, mutually independent, assemblies that represent a dynamic state resembling that observed in an alert animal (Miller & Schreiner, 2000). The shape of the correlograms was different for in-RF and out-RF pairs, mostly resulting in larger width at half-peak amplitude for out-RF pairs, suggesting that stimulation synchronizes spikes within a smaller temporal range. These results, albeit for one recording, are typical for our findings in auditory cortex.

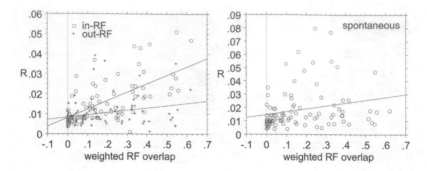

Fig. 16.7. Dependence of the peak cross-correlation coefficient (R) on receptive field (RF) overlap for in-RF spikes and out-RF spikes (left) and spikes recorded under spontaneous conditions (right).

ARE COINCIDENT FIRINGS SPECIAL?

Where do coincident firings occur in the STRFs? From the cross-correlograms we selected spikes that occurred within 5 ms of each other on any pair of electrodes (i.e., within ±5 ms from zero lag time; termed coincident spikes), which across the 4 recordings shown in Figure 16.6 represented 50.4% of the spikes. We reconstructed the STRFs for coincident spikes and compared them to the STRFs for spike firings that were not within ±5 ms (termed non-coincident spikes), and because of nearly equal number of spikes for the two conditions the resulting STRFs had similar background noise levels. The results are shown in Figure 16.8, where the 50% contour lines of the excitatory parts of the STRFs are shown (compare with Fig. 16.6). The solid lines are for coincident spikes and the dotted ones for non-coincident spikes. Note the differing time and frequency axes because the STRFs were zoomed in here to center and enlarge their receptive fields. Note also that the minimum latencies of the coincident-spike STRFs are within 5 ms from 30 ms, but that in the upper left example coincident spikes also appear in the 55–70 ms range. These spikes could potentially be strongly correlated with the short latency spikes in the same STRF, but the correlograms did not show secondary peaks in the 25–40 ms range.

The non-coincident spike STRFs showed in two cases latencies around 20 ms and formed a subsection of the overall STRF. Coincident spikes appeared responsible for those parts of the STRF with the highest firing rates. As shown in Figure 16.8, the parts of the STRF that result from well synchronized spikes can have the same frequency range as those that result from less synchronized spikes. Thus, a coincident assembly of neurons would be able to focus on the RF centers.

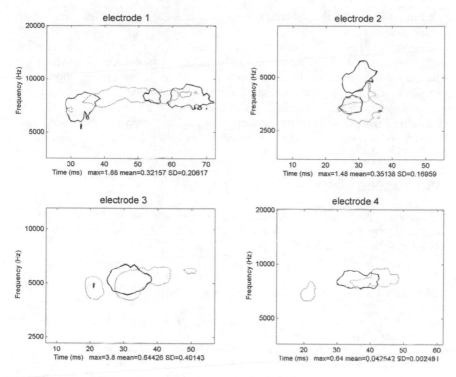

Fig. 16.8. Coincident spikes (±5 ms) contribute differently to the STRFs (solid contour lines) then do less coincident spikes (> 5 ms, dotted contour lines). Compare with the full STRFs shown in Figure 16.6 and note the differences in the time axes. For details see text.

CONCLUSIONS

Correlated neural activity is in a sense an epiphenomenon of the large interconnectivity of cortical neurons; however, it is the functional changes in this network as reflected in changes in neural synchrony and caused by state changes in the brain and by stimulation that may become part of the neural code. The main question then is: Are correlated neural events a part of the neural code or do they extract information about stimuli that becomes part of the neural code? From the modest stimulus dependence of the shape of the correlograms one expects only minor contributions to the amount of transmitted information above that provided by firing rates. However, the ability of selecting specific parts of the STRFs on the basis of the window of coincident firing suggests that neural synchrony is important to extract stimulus invariants with high signal-to-noise ratios. These invariants form the basis of stimulus recognition and classification. The firing rates associated with those parts of the stimulus ensemble selected by the synchrony condition are transmitting the information contained therein.

Synchrony in cortex under silence mainly reflects the ongoing network oscillations; stimulation disrupts this and results in often decreased synchrony reflecting the reduced neural assemblies in a stimulus-processing brain. This once more illustrates that stimulation does not add spikes to a spontaneous background but actively redistributes the timing of the spontaneous activity. This refutes the use of stimulus correction procedures based on the assumption of additivity of spontaneous activity and stimulus-evoked spikes.

ACKNOWLEDGMENTS

This work was supported by the Alberta Heritage Foundation for Medical Research, the National Sciences and Engineering Research Council of Canada, and the Campbell McLaurin Chair for Hearing Deficiencies.

REFERENCES

Abeles, M. (1991). Corticonics: Neural circuits of the cerebral cortex. London: University Press.

Ahissar, M., Ahissar, E., Bergman, H., & Vaadia, E. (1992). Encoding of sound-source location and movement: Activity of single neurons and interactions between adjacent neurons in the monkey auditory cortex. Journal of Neurophysiology, 67, 203–215.

Blake, D.T., & Merzenich, M.M. (2002). Changes in AI receptive fields with sound density. Journal of Neurophysiology, 88, 3409–3420.

Brosch, M., Budinger, E., & Scheich, H. (2002). Stimulus-related gamma oscillations in primate auditory cortex. Journal of Neurophysiology, 87, 2715–2725.

Brosch, M., & Schreiner, C.E. (1999). Correlations between neural discharges are related to receptive field properties in cat primary auditory cortex. European Journal of Neuroscience, 11, 3517–3530.

Cotillon-Williams, N., & Edeline, J.-M. (2003). Evoked oscillations in the thalamo-cortical auditory system are present in anesthetized but not in unanesthetized rats. Journal of Neurophysiology, 89, 1968–1984.

Creutzfeldt, O.D., Hellweg, F.-C., & Schreiner, C.E. (1980). Thalamocortical trans-formation of responses to complex auditory stimuli. Experimental Brain Research, 39, 87–104.

Dayan, P., & Abbott, L.F. (2001). Theoretical neuroscience. Cambridge, MA: The MIT Press.

deCharms, R.C., & Merzenich, M.M. (1996). Primary cortical representation of sound by coordination of action-potential timing. Nature, 381, 610–613.

Devilbiss, D.M., & Waterhouse, B.D. (2002). Determination and quantification of pharmaceutical, physiological, or behavioral manipulations on ensembles of simultaneously recorded neurons in functionally related neural circuits. Journal of Neuroscience Methods, 121, 181–198.

Dickson, J.W., & Gerstein, G.L. (1974). Interaction between neurons in auditory cortex of the cat. Journal of Neurophysiology, 37, 1239–1261.

Eggermont, J.J. (1990). The Correlative Brain. Berlin: Springer-Verlag.

Eggermont, J.J. (1992a). Neural interaction in cat primary auditory cortex. Dependence on recording depth, electrode separation and age. Journal of Neurophysiology, 68, 1216–1228.

Eggermont, J.J. (1992b). Stimulus induced and spontaneous rhythmic firing of single units in cat primary auditory cortex. Hearing Research, 61, 1–11.

Eggermont, J.J. (1994). Neural interaction in cat primary auditory cortex II. Effects of sound stimulation. Journal of Neurophysiology, 71, 246–270.

Eggermont, J.J. (2000). Sound induced correlation of neural activity between and within three auditory cortical areas. Journal of Neurophysiology, 83, 2708–2722.

Eggermont, J.J., & Smith, G.M. (1995). Rate covariance dominates spontaneous cortical unit-pair correlograms. Neuroreport, 6, 2125–2128.

Eggermont, J.J., & Smith, G.M. (1996). Neural connectivity only accounts for a small part of neural correlation in auditory cortex. Experimental Brain Research, 110, 379–392.

Espinoza, I.E., & Gerstein, G.L. (1988). Cortical auditory neuron interactions during presentation of 3-tone sequences: effective connectivity. Brain Research, 450, 39–50.

Frostig, R.D., Gottlieb, Y., Vaadia, E., & Abeles, M. (1983). The effects of stimuli on the activity and functional connectivity of local neuronal groups in the cat auditory cortex. Brain Research, 272, 211–221.

Gil, Z., Connors, B.W., & Amitai, Y. (1999). Efficacy of thalamocortical and intracortical synaptic connections: Quanta, innervation and reliability. Neuron, 23, 385–397.

Horikawa, J., Tanahashi, A., & Suga, N. (1994). After-discharges in the auditory cortex of the mustached bat; no oscillatory discharges for binding auditory information. Hearing Research, 76, 45–52.

Kenmochi, M., & Eggermont, J.J. (1997). Autonomous cortical rhythms affect temporal modulation transfer functions Neuroreport, 8, 1589–1593.

Lewicki, M.S. (1998). A review of methods for spike sorting: The detection and classification of neural potentials. Network, 9, R53–R78.

MacDonald, K.D., & Barth, D.S. (1995). High frequency (gamma-band) oscillating potentials in rat somatosensory and auditory cortex. Brain Research, 694, 1–12.

Melssen, W.J., & Epping, W.J.M. (1987). Detection and estimation of neural connectivity based on crosscorrelation analysis. Biological Cybernetics, 57, 403–414.

Miller, L.M., Escabi, M.A., Read, H.L., & Schreiner, C.E. (2001). Functional convergence of response properties in the auditory thalamocortical system. Neuron, 32, 151–160.

Miller, L.M., & Schreiner, C.E. (2000). Stimulus-based state control in the thalamo-cortical system. Journal of Neuroscience, 20, 7011–7016.

Rolls, E.T., Franco, L., Aggelopoulos, N.C., & Reece, S. (2003). An information theoretic approach to the contributions of the firing rates and the correlations between the firing of neurons. Journal of Neurophysiology, 89, 2810–2822.

Zhu, Z., Lin, K., & Kasamatsu, T. (2002). Artifactual synchrony via capacitance coupling in multi-electrode recording from cat striate cortex. Journal of Neuroscience Methods, 115, 45–53.

17. SPATIO-TEMPORAL PATTERNS OF SPIKE OCCURRENCES IN FREELY-MOVING RATS ASSOCIATED TO PERCEPTION OF HUMAN VOWELS

Alessandro E. P. Villa

INTRODUCTION

The cerebral cortex is a highly interconnected network of neurons in which the activity of each cell is necessarily related to the combined activity in the neurons that are afferent to it. Due to the presence of reciprocal connections between cortical areas and between the cortex and the thalamus, re-entrant activity through chains of neurons is likely to occur. Certain pathways through the network may be favored by preferred synaptic interactions between the neural elements as a consequence of developmental and/or learning processes. In cell assemblies interconnected in this way, some ordered, and precise (in the order of few ms) interspike interval relationships referred to as 'spatio-temporal firing patterns', may recur within spike trains of individual neurons, and across spike trains recorded from different neurons. If functional correlates of spatio-temporal neural coding exist, one would expect that whenever the same information is presented, the same temporal pattern of firing would be observed. Electrical stimulation with complex stimuli that include amplitude and frequency modulation revealed remarkable invariance in the firing times of the tested neurons *in vitro* and indicated a high degree of reliability of their response (Bryant & Segundo, 1976; Mainen & Sejnowski, 1995). Experimental evidence exists that correlated firing between single neurons recorded simultaneously in the primate frontal cortex may evolve within tens of milliseconds in systematic relation to behavioral events without modulation of the firing rates (Vaadia et al., 1995). Precise firing sequences have been described in relation to particular temporal relationships to stimuli (Villa & Abeles, 1990), or movement (Abeles et al., 1993), or differentially during the delay period of a delayed response task (Prut et al., 1998; Villa & Fuster, 1992; Villa et al., 1999b).

Acoustical information is carried by very precise temporal features, such that complex sounds, and speech sounds in particular, provide good candidates for a set of stimuli aimed to investigate the rationale of a precise temporal coding in the auditory cortex. The limited temporal and spatial resolution of most brain imaging techniques available to date makes it difficult to perform such investigation in human subjects. Conversely, recordings performed by means of microelectrodes provide the requested technical resolution but are much too invasive to be applied in human subjects. Then, the study of speech sound perception by non-human species appears necessary for at least two reasons. Firstly, this study investigates the neural coding of complex stimuli in the auditory system in a general way. Secondly, this study allows to determine whether the sensory processing of speech sounds rests upon general properties of the auditory system or on unique human capabilities.

Studies on animal responses to speech sounds have been carried out in cats (Dewson, 1964), chinchillas (Burdick & Miller, 1975), monkeys (Kuhl, 1991), budgerigars (Dooling & Brown, 1990), blackbirds and pigeons (Hienz et al., 1981), quails (Kluender et al., 1987), and starlings (Kluender et al., 1998). Although there is interest in the rat's auditory capabilities (Syka et al., 1996; Talwar & Gerstein, 1999) its ability to discriminate complex sounds has not yet been fully investigated. Psychophysical tests of synthetic vowel formant frequencies discrimination by non-human species indicate that animal performances are only slightly below that of humans (Hienz et al., 1996; Sinnot & Kreiter, 1991; Sommers et al., 1992). These studies provide a behavioral counterpart to electrophysiological studies aimed at determining how complex sounds (Nelken et al., 1999; Villa et al., 1999b) and vowels (Blackburn & Sachs, 1990; Delgutte & Kiang, 1984; Sachs & Young, 1979) are encoded in the auditory system. A current hypothesis (Conley & Keilson, 1995; May et al., 1996) is that humans as well as non-human species discriminate vowel formant changes using a profile analysis based on the mean discharge rate of auditory nerve fibers (Green, 1988).

Natural sounds are not invariant, however, and the recognition and categorization of meaningful sounds has an important survival value for many species. Hence, in addition to being able to make fine discriminations, animals, including humans, must be able to determine which cues carry information and which are irrelevant. There is no one-to-one correspondence between a given physical acoustic pattern and a corresponding speech sound. Thus, listeners need to assign a phonemic label to an acoustic pattern based on known categories of speech signals, referred to as equivalence classes. A fundamental issue in research on speech perception is to determine to which extent *equivalence classes* are innate and species-specific or associated with an experience-driven process.

The present study aims to investigate whether discrimination of vowel categories could be learned by rats and whether spatio-temporal firing patterns associated with speech sounds could be observed in the auditory cortex. We tested two vowel categories: /ɛ/, as in "head", and /ɔ/, as in "hawed". The testing procedure involved a Go/NoGo behavioral paradigm and the stimuli were all synthetic vowels whose fundamental and formant frequencies were varied in a systematic way (with formants and fundamental frequency shifted in the same direction) to cover the range of variation recorded in human speech. After initial training with a small set of exemplars from each vowel category, we tested the ability of the rats to generalize to a larger set. After reaching a steady-state performance the subjects were chronically implanted in the auditory cortex and multiple spike trains were recorded during various phases of the behavioral task (Eriksson et al., 1999; Villa et al., 2001).

MATERIALS AND METHODS

Subjects

The subjects were six Long-Evans male rats *Rattus norvegicus*, aged 6–8 months at the beginning of the experiment. The rats were housed individually with free access to water and restricted food supply. The rats were rewarded by sunflower seeds during the experimental sessions and were given supplemental pellets at the end of each session so to maintain their body weight at least at 90% of the *ad libitum* weight. All experimental procedures were carried out in accordance with the international guidelines for the care and use of laboratory animals and with governmental veterinary authorization.

Apparatus

The subjects were trained in a black box (750 mm wide, 800 mm long, 400 mm high) inside a sound-proof room (Fig. 17.1). The box was open at the top and had two principal areas: (i) the stimulus delivery area, and (ii) the feeder area. The stimulus delivery area was fitted with two loudspeakers (20 Watts, impedance 4–8 Ohms, Poly Planar Inc., Warmingto, PA, USA) mounted on either side. At one extremity the box had a narrow section (80 mm). A dispenser of sunflower seeds was mounted above the box at this extremity. A plastic tube connected to the dispenser was mounted in order to deliver a seed close to the extremity wall of the box. At this extremity, a transparent window (80 mm width, 60 mm height), at 10 mm from ground level, was fitted in the box wall. A stroboscope flash was placed outside the box, in front of the window.

The box had movable parts and could be configured in order to define either a short (Fig. 17.1a) or a long path (Fig. 17.1b) between the stimulus delivery area and the feeder area. Three infrared beams (IRB1-IRB3) were used to monitor the subject's position. IRB1 and IRB3 signal the presence of the subject in the stimulus delivery and feeder areas, respectively. IRB2 was used in the

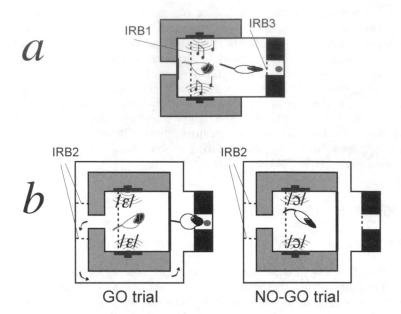

Fig. 17.1. Schematic diagram of the top view of the behavioral apparatus. (a) Short-path setup. (b) Long-path setup. The infra-red beams are labeled IRB1, IRB2, and IRB3. The small arrows indicate movement from the stimulus delivery area.

long path configuration, and signals the exit from the stimulus delivery area. The reaction time (RT) corresponded to the interval between the onset of sound delivery and IRB2 crossing. A video camera on the ceiling was used to observe the rat's behavior from the outside of the sound-proof room. Digital pulses were generated when the IRBs were interrupted and the time stamp of these occurrences was recorded by a Macintosh (Apple Computers, Cupertino, CA) personal computer equipped with digital acquisition boards (National Instruments, Austin, TX). Control and recording of occurrences of the acoustical stimulation onset, activation of the stroboscopic flash and of the food dispenser were also performed by the same microcomputer running in house programs developed using LabView software (National Instruments, Austin, TX). All events were recorded at a time resolution of 1 ms and stored digitally for off-line analysis.

Acoustic stimuli

The stimuli consisted of eighteen synthetic vowels /ɛ/, as in "head", and /ɔ/, as in "hawed" whose fundamental frequencies ($f0$s) and formant frequencies were manipulated. The stimuli, labeled ε_i and $ɔ_i$ (i = 1..9), were characterized by $f0$s ranging from 125 to 325 Hz in steps of 25 Hz. The first three formants were taken from Peterson and Barney (1952) estimated at a reference fundamental frequency ($f0_{ref}$) of 200 Hz. The formant peaks were shifted by 1/3 of the $f0$ in log units (Miller, 1989), e.g. $F1_i = F1_{ref,o} (f0_i / f0_{ref})^{1/3}$. Figure 17.2 shows the power spectra of ten vowels used. Neither the formant bandwidths nor the amplitudes were modified or adjusted as $f0$ was shifted. It is important to notice that for these stimuli, an increase in the fundamental frequency $f0$ does not correspond to an increase in the ratios *F1/F2* and *F1/F3*.

The stimuli were digitally generated with a Klatt (1980) synthesizer with a 45 kHz sampling frequency. Each stimulus was 400 ms in duration and had an amplitude rise-fall time of 30 ms. The formant frequencies were fixed during the stimulus (Table 17.1) but the fundamental frequency was frequency modulated following a sinusoidal contour starting with $f0$ at 0 ms, with a maximum of $1.04 \times f0$ at 133 ms and a minimum of $0.96 \times f0$ at 400 ms, for naturalness. The digitized stimuli were normalized such that their root-mean-square values of sound pressure levels were equal. A custom-built sound generator (Federal Institute of Technology, Lausanne, Switzerland) was used to deliver the stimuli. The sound generator was calibrated using pure tone stimuli (range 100–8000 Hz) and measuring the output of the speakers in the box.

The intensity response varied with the location of measurement but was adjusted to produce a response that was relatively flat (±4 dB) where the animals positioned themselves to wait for the stimulus. The sequence of the stimuli was randomized, as was the stimulus intensity (65±3 dB SPL).

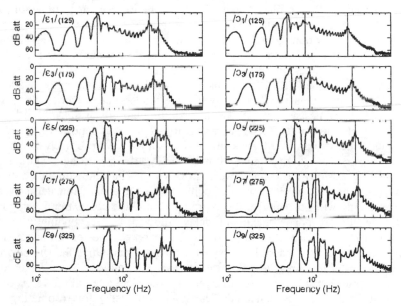

Fig. 17.2. Power spectra of ten of the vowels used in the experiment. /ε/ are displayed on the left column and /ɔ/ are displayed on the right column. The fundamental frequency $f0$ is indicated in parentheses. The vertical lines indicate the formant frequencies *F1*, *F2*, and *F3*.

Table 17.1. Characteristic frequencies for the two sets of stimuli.

Vowel	$f0$ (Hz)	$F1$ (Hz)	$F2$ (Hz)	$F3$ (Hz)
$\mathfrak{I}_1$	125	513	838	2565
$\mathfrak{I}_2$	150	545	890	2726
$\mathfrak{I}_3$	175	574	937	2869
$\mathfrak{I}_4$	200	600	980	3000
$\mathfrak{I}_5$	225	624	1019	3120
$\mathfrak{I}_6$	250	646	1056	3223
$\mathfrak{I}_7$	275	667	1090	3336
$\mathfrak{I}_8$	300	687	1122	3434
$\mathfrak{I}_9$	325	705	1152	3527
ε_1	125	513	1966	2565
ε_2	150	545	2090	2726
ε_3	175	574	2200	2869
ε_4	200	600	2300	3000
ε_5	225	624	2392	3120
ε_6	250	646	2478	3223
ε_7	275	667	2558	3336
ε_8	300	687	2633	3434
ε_9	325	705	2704	3527

Sound-reward association

Two habituation sessions of 15–30 minutes were conducted prior to training, in which the animals were placed individually in the experimental apparatus and allowed to move unhindered. The first step of training was aimed at conditioning the subjects to stay quietly in the stimulus delivery area and wait for an auditory stimulus before entering the feeder area and retrieve a sunflower seed. This training was conducted with the box initially set up in the short path configuration (Fig. 17.1a). During this phase a white noise stimulus of 200 ms duration was delivered simultaneously to both loudspeakers. During the first 2 sessions (20 minutes/session), the acoustical stimulation was self-paced by the subject upon entering the feeder area and the sound was repeated in order to strengthen the sound-reward association. The subjects were trained to exit the feeder area before a maximum allowed delay of 15 seconds. During the following 2 sessions the animals were trained to go into the stimulus delivery area. The stimulus presentation was controlled by the experimenter and was delivered only when the subject was roaming around the box extremity opposite to the feeder area. The maximum delay allowed for responding after the acoustical stimulation was initially set to 15 seconds. The remaining sessions were computer-controlled and self-paced by the subject. Once the subjects had retreated to the rest area, a timer was started. The subjects were required to remain within this area for a variable randomized time interval (6–15 seconds) before the stimulus was delivered. The maximum delay for responding was decreased from 15 to 5 seconds in 4 sessions. Steady-state performance was determined by 3 successive sessions with performances over 90%. Overall, 7–10 sessions (at a rate of 2 sessions/day at 4 hours interval) were necessary to complete this phase. Before discrimination training began the configuration of the box was changed such that the animals had to move along the longer path (Fig. 17.1b). Seven sessions using the white noise stimulus were given before proceeding to the discrimination phase. All subjects got used to the new configuration in 1–2 sessions.

Discrimination training

The discrimination training consisted of the association of a set of stimuli to the Go response (positive stimuli, giving access to the reward) and of the other set of stimuli to the NoGo response (negative stimuli). In this phase the stimuli were two sets of vowels with $f0$ of 175 and 275 Hz, i.e., ε_3, ε_7, $\jmath_3$ and $\jmath_7$ (Table 17.1). To ensure that the subjects did not use intensity cues to learn the discrimination, the range of presentation levels was extended in the training phase (7 levels, i.e., 65±6 dB, by steps of 3 dB). In each trial a variable (6–15 s) waiting period preceded an auditory stimulus, and the maximally allowed response time was set to 9 s. If the animal moved away from the stimulus delivery area during the waiting period, the trial was aborted. Three subjects were assigned set ε as the positive (rewarded) stimulus set (ε^+) and $\jmath$ as negative set (ε^-), while for the other three the assignments were $\jmath^+$ and ε. The sequence of stimulus delivery was randomized using a stimulus selection algorithm that has been described elsewhere (Villa et al., 1999a). A session lasted until the animal had made 27 correct responses to the positive stimuli. Overall, 26 sessions (at a rate of 1 session/day) were necessary to complete this phase with performances steadily > 80%.

Generalization testing

The ability of the subjects to generalize the categorization was tested by using the full set of stimuli, nine from each vowel category, that is, ε_i ($i = 1..9$) and $\jmath_i$ ($i = 1..9$). Each stimulus was presented three times per session. A session began with 12 practice runs involving the initial four stimuli. A typical session lasted for about 30 to 40 minutes. This test was conducted over 9 sessions, for a total of 27 trials per stimulus. After this period of time the subjects were surgically operated for the implantation of the microelectrodes.

Chronic Implantation of recording electrodes

The subjects (weighing 280–330 g) were anesthetized with a mixture of ketamine (57 mg/kg) and xylazine hydrochloride (8 mg/kg) and mounted in a stereotaxic frame without ear-bars. Holes were drilled in the skull over the temporal cortex of both hemispheres. We preferentially aimed at areas Te1 on one hemisphere and Te2, Te3 on the other hemisphere, but the localization was assessed only after histological analysis of the site of electrolytic lesions performed before the sacrifice of the subjects. An epidural earth contact (flattened silver-wire) was introduced through a separate hole in the frontal bone. Bundles of four Teflon-insulated tungsten microwire electrodes were lowered into the cortex under electrophysiological recording-control at an angle of approximately 30 degrees from vertical (approaching normal to the cortical surface), to a depth where spike discharges of greatest signal-to-noise ratio were detected (usually around 700–1200 µm from the surface). Units were tested for responses to simple tone stimuli delivered from microphones (Bruel & Kjaer 4134) in the auditory canals. Electrodes were fixed in place with non-irritating carboxylate cement, and the contact sockets for electrodes and earth lead stabilized with acrylic cement.

Single unit recordings

A headstage containing unity-gain preamplifiers was plugged in prior to each session. Signals from all electrodes were led via an ultra-flexible cable and multichannel swivel unit to the recording apparatus, where they were amplified (×50k) and filtered (0.7–10 kHz bandwidth). The actual weight of the headstage was 5 g, but the cable was counterbalanced by using pulleys and weights such that the effective weight of the cable and headstage together was 0 g. After being band-passed filtered the analog electrophysiological signals were fed into commercially available spike sorting devices (MultiSpike Detector, Alpha Omega Engineering, Nazareth, Israel), which use digital signal processing units and an on-line template matching algorithm to detect and sort spike waveforms. Digital pulses were generated whenever a waveform corresponding to one of the selected templates was recognized, and the time stamp of these occurrences was recorded by a Macintosh computer at a time resolution of 1 ms and stored digitally for off-line analysis together with the behavioral events. Up to three different extracellular waveforms (corresponding to discharges of three cells) could be discriminated on each of the wires, with a maximum number of 15 spike trains being recorded per session. All subjects could perform the task at preoperative levels of performance after one week post-operative time.

Spatio-temporal pattern analysis

Firing sequences were detected by applying the Pattern Grouping Algorithm (PGA), designed to identify and evaluate the statistical significance of temporal patterns of spikes formed by three or more different events with slight differences in spike timing (Tetko & Villa, 2001a, 2001b).

The PGA algorithm can search and cluster individual patterns which differ from each other by a small jitter in spike timing of the order of few ms. The estimation of significance of the detected patterns is done according to three different tests. The first test is an extension of the Pattern Detection Algorithm, PDA (Abeles & Gerstein, 1988), which does not rest on the assumption that the spike trains behave like Poisson processes, but just on the assumption that at any time instance t the probability of getting one pre-specified pattern is very low. However, such assumption is not valid for spikes occurring in a burst that can be modeled by non-stationary Poisson processes with high firing rate fluctuation.

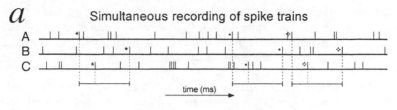

a   Simultaneous recording of spike trains

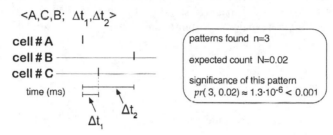

b   Detection of statistically significant spatiotemporal firing patterns

<A,C,B; $\Delta t_1, \Delta t_2$>

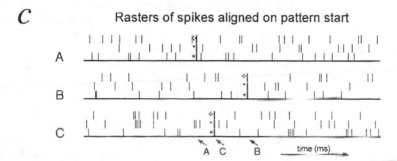

c   Rasters of spikes aligned on pattern start

Fig. 17.3. Outline of the general procedure followed by pattern detection algorithms. (**a**) Analysis of a set of simultaneously recorded spike trains. Three cells, labeled A, B, and C, participate in a patterned activity. In this example three occurrences of a precise pattern are detected. Each occurrence of the pattern has been labeled by a specific marker in order to help the reader to identify the corresponding spikes. (**b**) Estimation of the statistical significance of the detected pattern. (**c**) Display of pattern occurrences as a raster plot aligned on the pattern start.

Two additional tests of significance, FPD, a modified version of Favored Pattern Detection (Dayhoff & Gerstein, 1983), and JTH, Joint Triplet Histogram (Prut et al., 1998) were applied and only those patterns that passed the three tests were kept for further analysis.

The three adjustable parameters in PGA include the maximal duration of the pattern measured as a delay between the first and the last spike in the sequence of spikes (i.e., the window duration, *w*), the level of significance to be used for detection of significant groups and the upper bound of allowed jitter applied to all the groups, designated as *J*. The criteria for identifying potential patterns were that they included at least 3 spikes (triplets), either within the spike train of a single cell or across spike trains from different cells, repeated at least 7 times over the data sample, lasted less than 1000 ms (*window* duration), and repeated with an accuracy of ±3 ms. Figure 17.3 illustrates the application of PGA to a case study.

The Fano Factor was also calculated for all data sets. It may be used to characterize the variability of the spike train and it is equal to 1 for time series following a Poisson distribution (Softy & Koch, 1993). A de-convolution procedure (Tetko & Villa, 2001a) is applied to the spike trains in order to avoid any overestimation of pattern significance due to deviations from Poisson processes, often revealed by significant peaks in auto- and cross-correlation histograms.

RESULTS

Synthetic vowels discrimination

The initial set of stimuli contained two exemplars of the vowels (*f0* of 175 and 275 Hz). The performances were very similar across subjects irrespective of the vowel associated to the reward and all subjects could successfully discriminate between positive and negative stimuli following the training procedure described above. The *reaction times* were comprised between 400 and 6000 ms. Because of the excellent performance to the task, most motor responses towards the feeder were correct responses that followed a Go stimulus. In much fewer cases the subjects responded incorrectly and went into the feeder area after a NoGo stimulus. Irrespective of the vowel associated with the reward and irrespective of the fundamental frequency *f0*, we observed that normalized reaction times in the incorrect trials were significantly slower than those in the correct trials (Mann-Whitney, $p < 0.01$ and $p < 0.05$ for the low and high *f0*, respectively).

In the second phase of training the subjects had to generalize the response from the initial set and had to discriminate 18 stimuli, 9 of which were associated with the reward after the Go response. The ability of the subjects to generalize the discrimination is shown by a similar performance to the four stimuli used during the first phase and to the novel fourteen test stimuli (Fig. 17.4). It is worth mentioning that performance to both sets of stimuli slightly increased along this phase, but not in a significant way. The number of false alarm responses was insufficient to compare reaction times between correct and incorrect Go responses for each *f0*.

The reaction time data were grouped into three samples corresponding to low (*f0* equal to 125, 150, and 175 Hz), medium (*f0* equal to 200, 225, and 250 Hz), and high (*f0* equal to 275, 300, and 325 Hz) formants. The reaction times were significantly faster during correct Go trials of medium and high formant vowels (Mann-Whitney, $p < 0.01$) but not for low formant trials.

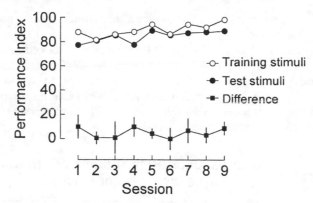

Fig. 17.4. Session-by-session cumulative performance of all rats during the generalization test. Performance indexes are shown separately for the four stimuli used in the previous training phase and for the fourteen novel test stimuli. The bottom trace shows the mean (±SD) of the difference between performances to training and novel stimuli.

Spatio-temporal patterns

A total of 1190 single units were recorded during 81 sessions from the cortical auditory areas of both hemispheres of six rats. The recording for each new session is automatically referred to as "new units". Most spike trains included at least 10000 events. The total recording time was approximately 2 hours per session and we recorded over 8 billion spikes. The firing rate of the single units ranged between 0.08 and 11.23 spikes/s. The results here focus on the spatio-temporal firing patterns that were found in the interval that followed the stimulus onset. We found 78 patterns of discharges that corresponded to significant sequences of two intervals, i.e. triplets. No patterns of complexity larger than 3 were detected using the settings of PGA indicated here. A total of 180 single units were recorded along 14 sessions lasting 2 hours each in two control rats, naive with respect to the vowel stimuli and that were not trained to the behavioral task. In these control sessions the 18 vowels were presented in a random order. We found 7 patterns overall in the control sessions and none related to a recognizable class of stimuli.

About half of the patterns that we found could neither be related to a stimulus feature nor to a motor behavior. Twenty-seven patterns were related to the behavioral response, that is, associated to a Go or to a NoGo response irrespective of its correctness. The most striking result with respect to the goal of this study was the finding of 16 (20%) significant patterns associated to some class of stimuli. Figure 17.5a shows an example of a pattern of 3 spikes repeating 9 times during the session, and starting with a spike of cell A, then after 190 ms a spike of cell 1 with a jitter ±3 ms and then after 218±3 ms a spike of cell 6. Figure 17.5b illustrates that this pattern occurred exclusively after an ε vowel which corresponded to the reinforced stimulus for this subject. Notice that the pattern was observed twice after ε_1, twice after ε_3, once after ε_4, once after ε_7, once after ε_8, and twice after ε_9.

The firing pattern displayed in Figure 17.5 is not time-locked to the stimulus onset as it occurs with variable delays ranging between 800 ms and more than 10 seconds. Notice that only one pattern was associated to an incorrect Go response, that is, an ε stimulus followed by a NoGo behavior. Overall 137 ε-stimuli (Go) were presented during this session, with an error rate of 21%, and 122 ɔ-stimuli (NoGo) with an error rate of 11%.

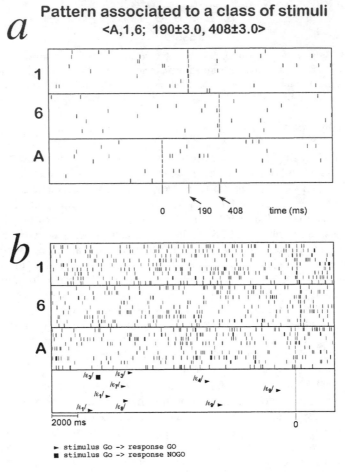

Fig. 17.5. (a) Raster display of the activities of three cortical neurons: Cells 1 and 6 were recorded in Te1 from the left hemisphere from different electrodes, and cell A in Te3 from the right hemisphere. The rasters are aligned by displaying the first spike in the pattern <A,1,6; 190±3, 408±3> at time 0. The pattern is repeated 9 times with a jitter of ±3 ms. **(b)** The same triplet is plotted in a different time scale such to show the corresponding stimuli onset. Notice that the pattern always follows stimuli of type /ε/.

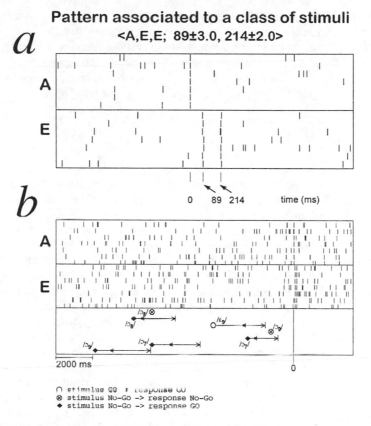

Pattern associated to a class of stimuli
<A,E,E; 89±3.0, 214±2.0>

Fig. 17.6. (a) Raster display of the activities of two cortical neurons: cells A and E were recorded in Te3 from the right hemisphere from different electrodes. The rasters are aligned by displaying the first spike in the pattern <A,E,E; 89±3, 214±2> at time 0. The pattern is repeated 7 times. (b) The same triplet is plotted in a different time scale such to show the corresponding stimuli onsets. Notice that the pattern follows stimuli of type /ɔ/, but one, with f0 higher than or equal to 275 Hz.

Based on these numbers we should expect to observe at least 1 pattern following an incorrect NoGo stimulus, and no patterns following an incorrect Go stimulus if the pattern were purely 'motor' related. In addition, the latencies of the pattern to the stimulus onset is significantly different from a random latency occurring in the 0–10 seconds post-stimulus interval (*t*-test, $p < 0.05$).

We found spatio-temporal patterns of spikes that were associated to a restricted class of stimuli, represented not only by a vowel equivalence class but also to specific sets of pitches. Such an example is illustrated in Figure 17.6. The firing pattern is formed by a sequence of two intervals repeating 7 times. A spike of cell A occurred at first (*t* = 0), followed by a spike of cell E 89±3 ms later, then by another spike of cell E 303±2 ms from the pattern onset (Fig. 17.6a). In this example the firing pattern was associated to ɔ stimuli with *f0* higher than

250 Hz (see Fig. 17.6b). However 5 out of 7 occurrences were associated to puzzling responses, four of which were Go responses that followed an ɔ stimulus (that was normally triggering a NoGo response) and one occurrence of the pattern followed a ε₉ stimulus and a Go response. The example of Figure 17.6 is also an illustration of the difficulty to attribute firing patterns to easily definable sets of stimuli or to sets of behavioral responses.

DISCUSSION

The present study reports experimental observations that demonstrate the ability of rats to discriminate between human categories of speech signals, referred to as equivalence classes, and the existence of electrophysiological correlates of these classes recorded in the auditory cortex. The rat is a common experimental subject but virtually no attempts have been made to test this animal in behavioral tasks involving other than simple auditory stimuli. A possible explanation for this choice may be that the audiogram of *Rattus norvegicus* (Fay, 1988; Heffner et al., 1994) is significantly different from that of humans and of other species used in auditory research such as monkey, cat, guinea pig, or birds. Many rat vocalizations are in a range of frequencies well above that of sound stimuli of interest in human speech research, and thus the rat auditory system is likely to be optimized for those calls.

Discrimination experiments involving several animal species indicate that difference thresholds for vowel formant changes are similar or better cue than difference thresholds for pure tones (Hienz et al., 1996; Sinnot & Kreiter, 1991; Sommers et al., 1992). Discrimination of vowels differing mainly in *F1* frequencies, usually below 1 kHz, represents a difficult task for rats. Rats should be capable of discriminating formant changes of 70 Hz at 1 kHz, 80 Hz at 2 kHz, and near 200 Hz at 3 kHz (Syka et al., 1996). Hirahara and Kato (1992) showed that changes in *f0* and formant frequencies produced different effects in perception of synthetic vowels according to the *F1/F2* ratio. In the results reported here we observed a similar performance to both sets of vowels, irrespective of the fact that they were associated to a Go or a NoGo behavioral response. All three formants (*F1, F2, F3*) were changed in the same direction, thus increasing further the likelihood that the individual stimuli could be discriminated.

In an initial phase, the subjects had to learn a discrimination using two exemplars from each vowel category, /ε/ and /ɔ/. In the next phase the rats could generalize to a larger set of exemplars from the same vowel sets from the start of the experimental session (Fig. 17.4). No difference in performance to the novel stimuli relative to the training stimuli was observed over successive sessions. Which were the actual cues used by rats to achieve such a behavior? One hypothesis might be that the discrimination to novel stimuli occurred during the first session of the generalization test. The learning of the training stimuli required several days and only four exemplars were used. It is unlikely that all novel stimuli (fourteen new exemplars) may be learned in just one session. An alternative hypothesis is that the observed results reflect the ability of the subjects to generalize following the previous training. Open-ended categorization (Herrnstein, 1990), as opposed to simple discrimination, implies that stimuli which can be discriminated are treated equivalently. This is the basic principle of equivalent class perception. Hence, the question is raised whether the subjects generalized to novel stimuli because they attended to the right stimulus properties or whether they did so because they could not distinguish between various exemplars within each category. Moreover, the small sample of subjects and stimuli does not allow to hypothesize that the same cues are used by all subjects. New experimental paradigms based on manipulations of formant ratios in opposite directions to $f0$ are needed to determine which the actual relevant cues are. However, it appears that speech related issues involving learning, representations ("prototypes"), categorization, and possibly pitch perception, may be investigated in experiments with rats and their corresponding electrophysiological correlates may shed new light on the higher levels of stimulus processing.

The presence of certain spatially and temporally organized sequences of intervals between spikes defines a precise spatio-temporal firing pattern. Spatio-temporal patterns do in fact occur by chance, spontaneously, but occur recurrently and in a more stable way, in particular association with stimuli, movement or cognitive tasks (Tetko & Villa, 2001c; Villa & Abeles, 1990; Villa & Fuster, 1992; Villa et al., 1999a; Villa, 2000). The results reported in this study represent a demonstration that spatio-temporal firing patterns occur reliably with relation to equivalence classes under particular behavioral conditions. These patterns are extremely rare to detect with current techniques because the evaluation of significance of each single pattern is carefully done with the goal to avoid including spurious patterns in the analysis. Then, a legitimate question could be to consider what is the level of significance of finding a certain class of patterns over the total sample, for example, 27 'motor' patterns (i.e., related to the Go or NoGo response irrespective of its correctness) over a sample of 78 spatio-temporal patterns identified in this study. The answer to such a question is not trivial because the question itself is ill-posed.

The detection of patterns is not simply a count of events. The spatio-temporal firing patterns are "rare" events and the matter of the level of significance is crucial at the time to decide whether a specific firing sequence is occurring by chance or not (Tetko & Villa, 2001a, 2001b). During a session we observe thousands of repeating sequences of spike intervals, but almost all of them are discarded by the statistical estimation of significance. This procedure is carried out in such a way to increase the risk of rejecting valid events (say, discard 95% of really valid firing patterns), and to decrease the risk of including false events (say, accept 5% of spurious patterns occurring by chance). Then, all patterns detected by PGA must be considered like valid patterns and the ratio becomes meaningless. All 78 patterns are significant and the question becomes how to classify a pattern into a certain 'type', like a 'motor' pattern, instead of a 'stimulus-triggered' or 'behavior-predicting' pattern. Such classification is indeed difficult and certainly represents the active debate around the significance of the spatio-temporal patterns.

It has been proposed (Ferster & Spruston, 1995) that clear proofs for a temporal code would require that distinct stimuli could reliably produce different temporal spike patterns. This restrictive view consists to assimilate the temporal code to a kind of "Morse alphabet" and it cannot account for the complex dynamics existing in the brain. In our view, it is not envisaged that the specific intervals that we find could in themselves be "read out" as bearing any particular information. They are instead seen as signposts towards a much larger integrated dynamic occurring in the cortex. Because of the complexity of this dynamics, patterns are not equal and may be associated to very different brain processes. In some cases patterns may be considered as parts of "templates" generated by processes activated in order to extract the useful information from the sensory cues (auditory "objects" in cognitive contexts requiring difficult discriminations). We do not know which equivalence classes exist in the brain of the subjects, but according to our findings we may suggest that open-ended categorization is a mental task that can be achieved by the rats (Fig. 17.5).

The relevance of pitch in the detection process is not discarded by the above statement, as several dimensions of the stimuli certainly contribute to the representation of the auditory percept. Spatio-temporal firing patterns related to certain pitches, irrespective of the motor responses and correctness of the task related decision-making are in favor of the latter hypothesis (Fig. 17.6). The sample of firing patterns that was detected so far is still too small to raise questions about the respective roles of core and belt auditory cortical areas. This is also true for further speculations about the size of the re-entrant loops that are likely to sustain the activity of cell assemblies such to keep precisely ordered sequences of discharges and the exact meaning of the intervals (Hahnloser et al., 2002).

In conclusion, with respect to the issue in determining to which extent equivalence classes are either innate and species-specific or associated with an experience-driven process, the present study supports the experience-driven process hypothesis and suggests that the mechanisms for human voice perception may rely on general properties of auditory coding mixed with learning mechanisms in the higher centers of the nervous system. The finding of timed electrophysiological activity in the auditory cortex related to equivalence classes demonstrates that the auditory percept is represented, at least partly, by an extremely precise temporal pattern of discharges. This result is not contradictory with response profiles based on neural coding characterized by frequency of discharges instead of timing of discharges. Rather, it shows that the representation of complex percepts is likely to require coding properties necessary for fine sensorimotor associations that population coding based only on firing rates are not able to account for.

ACKNOWLEDGMENTS

The author is particularly indebted to Dr. Jan L. Eriksson for his contribution to vowel generation, behavioral analysis, and his participation to the electrophysiological recordings. Parts of these data were collected for his PhD Dissertation. Dr. Igor V. Tetko, Abdellatif Najem, Javier Iglesias, and Tania Rinaldi are acknowledged for their contributions to the experimental sessions and data analysis.

REFERENCES

Abeles, M., Bergman, H., Margalit, E., & Vaadia, E. (1993). Spatiotemporal firing patterns in the frontal cortex of behaving monkeys. Journal of Neurophysiology, 70, 1629–1638.

Abeles, M., & Gerstein, G. (1988). Detecting spatiotemporal firing patterns among simultaneously recorded single neurons. Journal of Neurophysiology, 60, 909–924.

Blackburn, C.C., & Sachs, M. B. (1990). The representation of the steady-state vowel /e/ in the discharge patterns of cat anteroventral cochlear nucleus neurons. Journal of Neurophysiology, 63, 1191–1212.

Bryant, H.L., & Segundo, J.P. (1976). Spike initiation by transmembrane current: a white noise analysis. Journal of Physiology (London), 260, 279–314.

Burdick, C.K., & Miller, J.D. (1975). Speech perception by the chinchilla: Discrimination of sustained /a/ and /i/. Journal of the Acoustical Society of America, 58, 415–427.

Conley, R.A., & Keilson, S.E. (1995). Rate representation and discriminability of second formant frequencies for /ɛ/-like steady-state vowels in cat auditory nerve. Journal of the Acoustical Society of America, 98, 3223–3234.

Dayhoff, J.E., & Gerstein, G.L. (1983). Favored patterns in spike trains. I. Detection. Journal of Neurophysiology, 49, 1334–1348.

Delgutte, B., & Kiang, N.Y.S. (1984). Speech coding in the auditory nerve. I. Vowel-like sounds. Journal of the Acoustical Society of America, 75, 866–878.

Dewson, J.H. (1964). Speech sound discrimination by cats. Science, 144, 555–556.

Dooling, R.J., & Brown, S.D. (1990). Speech perception by budgerigars (Melopsittacus undulatus): Spoken vowels. Perception and Psychophysics, 47, 568–574.

Eriksson, J.L., Villa, A., & Najem, A. (1999). Discrimination by rats of variable instances of vowels. Abstracts of the 22nd Midwinter Research Meeting of the Association for Reseach in Otolaryngology, p. 74.

Fay, R.R. (1988). Hearing in vertebrates: A psychophysics databook. Winnetka, IL: Hill-Fay.

Ferster, D., & Spruston, N. (1995). Cracking the neural code. Science, 270, 756–757.

Green, D.M. (1988). Profile analysis. Oxford, UK: Oxford University Press.

Hahnloser, R.H., Kozhevnikov, A.A., & Fee, M.S. (2002). An ultra-sparse code underlies the generation of neural sequences in a songbird. Nature, 419, 65–70.

Heffner, H.E., Heffner, R.S., Contos, C., & Ott, T. (1994). Audiogram of the hooded norway rat. Hearing Research, 73, 244–247.

Herrnstein, R.J. (1990). Levels of stimulus control: A functional approach. Cognition, 37, 133–166.

Hienz, R.D., Aleszczyk, C.M., & May, B.J. (1996). Vowel discrimination in cats: Threshold for the detection of second formant changes in the vowel /ɛ/. Journal of the Acoustical Society of America, 99, 3656–3668.

Hienz, R.D., Sachs, M.B., & Sinnot, J.M. (1981). Discrimination of steady-state vowels by blackbirds and pigeons. Journal of the Acoustical Society of America, 70, 699–706.

Hirahara, T., & H. Kato (1992). The effect of F0 on vowel identification. In Y. Tohkura, E. Vatikiotis-Bateson, & Y. Sakisaka (Eds.), Speech Perception, Production and Linguistic Structure. Tokyo: Ohmusha Ltd.

Klatt, D.H. (1980). Software for a cascade/parallel formant synthesizer. Journal of the Acoustical Society of America, 67, 971–995.

Kluender, K.R., Diehl, R.L., & Killeen, P.R. (1987). Japanese quail can learn phonetic categories. Science, 237, 1195–1197.

Kluender, K.R., Lotto, A.J., Hold, L.L., & Bloedel, S.L. (1998). Role of experience for language-specific functional mappings of vowel sounds. Journal of the Acoustical Society of America, 104, 3568–3582.

Kuhl, P.K. (1991). Human adults and human infants show a 'perceptual magnet effect' for the prototypes of speech categories, monkeys do not. Perception and Psychophysics, 50, 93–107.

Mainen, Z.F., & Sejnowski, T.J. (1995). Reliability of spike timig in neocortical neurons. Science, 268, 1503–1506.

May, B.J., Huang, A., Prell, G.L., & Hienz, R.D. (1996). Vowel formant frequency discrimination in cats: Comparison of auditory nerve representations and psychophysical thresholds. Auditory Neuroscience, 3, 135–162.

Miller, J.D. (1989). Auditory-perceptual interpretation of the vowel. Journal of the Acoustical Society of America, 85, 2114–2134.

Nelken, I., Rotman, Y., & Yosef, O.B. (1999). Responses of auditory-cortex neurons to structural features of sounds. Nature, 397, 154–157.

Peterson, G.E., & Barney, H.L. (1952). Control methods used in a study of vowels. Journal of the Acoustical Society of America, 24, 175–184.

Prut, Y., Vaadia, E., Bergman, H., Haalman, I., Slovin, H., & Abeles, M. (1998). Spatiotemporal structure of cortical activity - Properties and behavioral relevance. Journal of Neurophysiology, 79, 2857–2874.

Sachs, M.B., & Young, E.D. (1979). Encoding of steady-state vowels in the auditory nerve: Representation in terms of discharge rate. Journal of the Acoustical Society of America, 66, 471–479.

Sinnot, J.M., & Kreiter, N.A. (1991). Differential sensitivity to vowel continua in old world monkeys (Macaca) and humans. Journal of the Acoustical Society of America, 89, 2421–2429.

Softky, W.R., & Koch, C. (1993). The highly irregular firing of cortical cells is inconsistent with temporal integration of random EPSPs. Journal of Neuroscience, 13, 334–350.

Sommers, M.S., Moody, D.B., Prosen, C.A., & Stebbins, W.C. (1992). Formant frequency discrimination by japanese macaques (Macaca fuscata). Journal of the Acoustical Society of America, 91, 3499–3510.

Syka, J., Rybalko, N., Brozek, G., & Jilek, M. (1996). Auditory frequency and intensity discrimination in pigmented rats. Hearing Research, 100, 107–113.

Talwar, S.K., & Gerstein, G.L. (1999). Auditory frequency discrimination in the rat. Hearing Research, 126, 135–150.

Tetko, I.V., & Villa, A.E.P. (2001a). Pattern grouping algorithm and de-convolution filtering of non-stationary correlated Poisson processes. Neurocomputing, 38–40, 1709–1714.

Tetko, I.V., & Villa, A.E.P. (2001b). A pattern grouping algorithm for analysis of spatiotemporal patterns in neuronal spike trains. 1. Detection of repeated patterns.

Journal of Neuroscience Methodes, 105, 1–14.

Tetko, I.V., & Villa, A.E.P. (2001c). A pattern grouping algorithm for analysis of spatiotemporal patterns in neuronal spike trains. 2. Application to Simultaneous Single Unit Recordings. Journal of Neuroscience Methods, 105, 15–24.

Vaadia, E., Haalman, I., Abeles, M., Bergman, H., Prut, Y., Slovin, H., & Aertsen, A. (1995). Dynamics of neuronal interactions in monkey cortex in relation to behavioural events. Nature, 373, 515–518.

Villa, A.E.P. (2000). Empirical evidence about temporal structure in multi-unit recordings. In R. Miller (Ed.), Time and the Brain (pp. 1–51). Chur, CH: Harwood Academic Publishers.

Villa, A.E.P., & Abeles, M. (1990). Evidence for spatiotemporal firing patterns within the auditory thalamus of the cat. Brain Research, 509, 325–327.

Villa, A. E. P., Eriksson, J., Eriksson, C., Haeberli, C., Hyland, B., & Najem, A. (1999a). A novel go/nogo conflict paradigm in rats suggests an interaction between stimulus evaluation and response systems. Behavioral Processes, 48, 69–88.

Villa, A.E.P., & Fuster, J.M. (1992). Temporal correlates of information processing during visual short-term memory. Neuroreport, 3, 113–116.

Villa, A.E.P., Najem, A., Iglesias, J., Tetko, I.V., & Eriksson, J.L. (2001). Spatiotemporal patterns of spike occurrences in freely-moving rats associated to perception of human vowels. Abstracts – Society for Neuroscience, 27, 166.18.

Villa, A.F.P., Tetko, I.V., Hyland, B., & Najem, A. (1999b). Spatiotemporal activity patterns of rat cortical neurons predict responses in a conditioned task. Proceedings of the National Academy of Sciences USA, 96, 1006–1011.

18. PROCESSING OF THE TEMPORAL ENVELOPE OF SPEECH

Ehud Ahissar, Merav Ahissar

INTRODUCTION

The temporal envelope of speech contains low-frequency information, which is crucial for speech comprehension. This information is essential for identification of phonemes, syllables, words, and sentences (Rosen, 1992). The temporal envelope of speech defines slow variations of the spectral energy of a spoken sentence, variations that are usually below 8 Hz (Houtgast & Steeneken, 1985). Comprehension of speech depends on the integrity of its temporal envelope between 4 and 16 Hz (Drullman et al., 1994; van der Horst et al., 1999). The mechanisms by which this information is extracted and processed are not yet known.

Speech comprehension does not depend on the exact frequency of the temporal envelope. In fact, the temporal envelope of normal speech can be compressed to 0.5 of its original duration before comprehension is significantly affected (Foulke & Sticht, 1969; Beasley et al., 1980). Thus, brain mechanisms normally responsible for speech perception can adapt to different input rates within a certain range (see Dupoux & Green, 1997; Miller et al., 1984; Newman & Sawusch, 1996). This on-line adaptation is crucial for speech perception, since speech rates vary between different speakers, and change according to the emotional state of the speaker.

The ability of listeners to follow fast speech rates varies significantly. In particular, reading disabled subjects (RDs) are usually more vulnerable to the time compression of sentences than good readers (Freeman & Beasley, 1978; Riensche & Clauser, 1982; Watson et al., 1990), although not always (McAnally et al., 1997). Deficiency of RDs in perceiving time-compressed speech might be related to their impaired processing of successive auditory signals (Ahissar et al., 2000b; Amitay et al., 2002a; Aram et al., 1984; Banai & Ahissar, 2004; Bishop, 1992; Farmer & Klein, 1995; Hari et al., 1999b; Helenius et al., 1999; Shapiro et al., 1990; Tallal et al., 1993; Tallal & Piercy, 1973). Inadequacies of RDs in comprehending time-compressed speech appear to emerge at the cortical level (Welsh et al., 1982). One sign of such impaired processing is probably reduced cortical reactivity to speech signals (Renvall & Hari, 2002).

Here we review and interpret our previously reported data that demonstrates that auditory cortical activity in humans follows the temporal envelope of speech, and that stimulus-response temporal locking correlates with speech comprehension. We will consider two components of temporal locking: frequency matching and phase-locking. Our data is consistent with comprehension of short sentences depending primarily on a-priori matching between the sentence envelope and an intrinsic frequency, and secondarily on on-line phase-locking. Further analysis of our data demonstrates that the ability to comprehend short sentences depends on the existence of a cortical frequency mode that is equal to, or higher than, the highest frequency mode of the envelope. Moreover, accuracy of reading non-words also correlated with the maximal cortical frequency mode. The novel psychophysical data presented here demonstrate that RDs are less tolerant than good readers to accelerated speech.

Based on our data and those of others, we hypothesize that the brain sets time intervals for analysis of individual speech components by intrinsic oscillations that are pre-tuned to an expected speech rate, and re-tuned during continuous speech processing by locking to the temporal envelope. By analogy with the somatosensory system, we suggest that such temporal locking is achieved by thalamocortical phase-locked loops, which may involve the non-lemniscal thalamic pathway. Such loops also extract temporal information contained in the envelope signal and recode it by rate. Such rate-coded signals could be used for further, temporally-loose processing, and for closing the sensory-motor loop. Here we present, schematically, the primary function of this hypothetical algorithm, which is to time syllable processing.

COMPREHENSION OF TIME-COMPRESSED SPEECH BY READING-DISABLED SUBJECTS AND GOOD READERS

So far, deficiencies of RDs in comprehending time-compressed speech were demonstrated for time compressions of 0.5 or 0.6 of normal rate. At these compressions, speech comprehension is still above chance level, and, as a result, a complete psychometric curve could not be constructed. Thus shifts in psychometric curves of time-compressed speech between RDs and good readers could not be estimated. To obtain complete psychometric curves, we applied a novel time-scale compression algorithm that kept the spectral and pitch content intact across compression ratios down to 0.1 of the original rate (Ahissar et al., 2001).

Table 18.1. Sentences for psychophysics experiment (1: true; −1: false).

1.	Six is greater than three	1
2.	Three is greater than six	−1
3.	Two plus three is five	1
4.	Two plus six is nine	−1
5.	Three plus six is nine	1
6.	Three plus three is three	−1
7.	Six is smaller than three	−1
8.	Three is smaller than six	1
9.	Five and five are ten	1
10.	Five and nine are ten	−1

We tested 6 RDs (native English speakers, ages 20–45, with documented history of reading disability), and 7 good readers (5 post-doctorate fellows and students, and 2 staff members of the Keck Center at UCSF; 5 were native English speakers, and English was the second language of the other 2; ages 29–45) for comprehension of time-compressed speech. Ten sentences (Table 18.1) were compressed to 6 different rates (0.1, 0.2, 0.3, 0.4, 0.5, and 1 of their original duration). The compression rate of 1 (i.e., no compression) was presented to all RDs, and to 3 of the 7 good readers. Each compression was presented 20 times. Thus, subjects were given either 100 trials (compressions 0.1, 0.2, 0.3, 0.4, and 0.5) or 120 trials (compressions 0.1, 0.2, 0.3, 0.4, 0.5, and 1). Comprehension was quantified using a Comprehension Index (CI) = [($N_{correct}$ − $N_{incorrect}$) / N_{total}], where N equals the number of trials. CI could have values between −1 (all incorrect) and 1 (all correct), where 0 was the chance level.

Compared to good readers, RDs showed poorer comprehension at all speech rates, except for 0.1 at which both groups were at chance level, and 1 at which both groups showed similar performance (Fig. 18.1A). RDs were still at chance level at a compression of 0.2, whereas good readers started to show some comprehension, and RDs exhibited marginal comprehension at 0.3, whereas good readers already comprehended about 75% of the sentences (CI = 0.5). In general, between compression levels of 0.1 and 0.5, the comprehension curve of RDs was shifted by 0.1 towards weaker compressions.

The impaired comprehension of the RDs appeared to be specific to three of the ten sentences used (sentences 2, 6, and 7) across most comprehension levels. CI averaged across all compression levels is depicted in Figure 18.1B.

Within-session improvement occurred in both the RD and good reader groups (Fig. 18.1C). Since compression levels, which determine task difficulty, were randomized for each subject, these levels distributed differently along the session for different subjects. Thus, comprehension normalized with regard to the average compression level presented to each subject is a better representation of within-session improvement (Fig. 18.1D). Examination of the two within-session comprehension plots suggests that the comprehension of RDs improves significantly during sessions, starting at chance level and approaching the performance of good readers in the second half of the session.

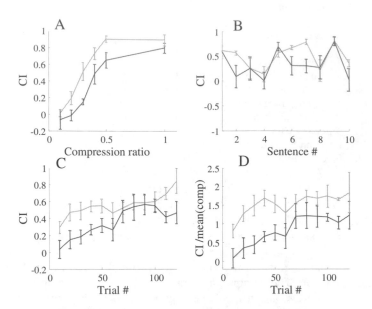

Fig. 18.1. Psychophysical evaluation of comprehension of time-compressed speech sentences by RDs (n = 6, black) and good readers (n = 7, gray). **A.** Mean comprehension as a function of compression level. **B.** Mean comprehension as a function of sentence number (Table 18.1). **C.** Within session improvement; mean comprehension as a function of trial number. Data were smoothed by a moving average window of 20 trials, shifted in steps of 10 trials. **D.** Within session improvement, normalized comprehension; Mean(comprehension)/mean(compression) was computed for each 20-trials window for each subject before averaging. Same smoothing as in C.

MAGNETOENCEPHALOGRAM (MEG) RECORDINGS

Thirteen subjects (4 good readers and 9 RDs, 7 males and 6 females, 11 native English speakers and English was the second language of the other 2, ages 25–45; one of the RDs also participated in the psychophysical experiment described above) volunteered to participate in this MEG experiment. Reading abilities were again heterogeneous, ranging from 81 to 122 in a word-reading test, and 78 to 117 in a non-word reading test, with 100 being the population average (Woodcock, 1987).

Three balanced sets of sentences were used (Table 18.2). Subjects were exposed to the sentences before the experiment, and the mapping between each sentence and its associated correct response (true or false) was clarified to them. During the experiment, the sentences were played at compressions of 0.2, 0.35, 0.5, and 0.75 (in some cases, compression of 1.0 instead of 0.75 was presented). Average sentence duration at compression 1.0 (i.e., without compression) was about 1 s. For each sentence, subjects responded by pressing one of three buttons corresponding to true, false, or don't know, using their left hand.

Table 18.2. Sentences for MEG experiment (1: true; –1: false).

Set 1

1.	Two plus six equals nine	–1
2.	Two plus three equals five	1
3.	Three plus six equals nine	1
4.	Three plus three equals five	–1

Set 2

1.	Two minus two equals none	1
2.	Two minus one equals one	1
3.	Two minus two equals one	–1
4.	Two minus one equals none	–1

Set 3

1.	Black cars can all park	1
2.	Black cars can not park	–1
3.	Black dogs can all bark	1
4.	Black dogs can not bark	–1
5.	Black cars can all bark	–1
6.	Black cars can not bark	1
7.	Black dogs can all park	–1
8.	Black dogs can not park	1
9.	Playing cards can all park	–1
10.	Playing cards can not park	1

Magnetic fields were recorded from the left hemisphere in a magnetically-shielded room, using a 37-channel biomagnetometer array with SQUID-based first-order gradiometer sensors (Magnes II; Biomagnetic Technologies, Inc.). Data acquisition epochs were 3000 ms in total duration with a 1000 ms pre-stimulus period. Data were acquired at a sampling rate of 297.6 Hz. For each subject, data were first averaged across all artifact-free trials. After which, a singular value decomposition was performed on the averaged time-domain data for the channels in the sensor array, and the first three principal components (PCs) calculated. These three PCs, which typically accounted for more than 90% of the variance within the sensor array, were used for all computations related to that subject. The basic phenomena described here could usually be observed in a single PC, usually PC1. Thus, for clarity, all examples presented here include only one PC.

In each set of sentences, envelopes of the sentences were selected such that they had similar temporal patterns (Ahissar et al., 2001). Thus, responses to different sentences could be averaged. The data presented here were obtained by averaging trials of all sentences for each compression level.

For each subject, there were 371–800 trials, resulting in, on the average, 93–200 trials per compression level. Sentences were composed in English and

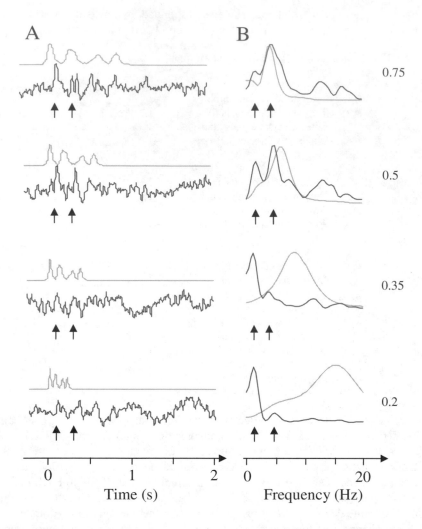

Fig. 18.2. Constancy of cortical frequencies. Data of PC1 of an RD subject, MS. **A.** PC1 (black) and stimulus envelope (gray) as a function of time from sentence onset for all 4 compressions. For each compression, data for all sentences were averaged. Arrows indicate the onsets of the first two response peaks. **B.** Power spectra of PC1 and envelope. Arrows indicate the first two frequency modes of the response. Fast Fourier Transforms (FFTs) were computed using windows of 1 s and overlaps of 0.5 s. Power scale is 0 to maximum power. Compression levels indicated on the right.

tested on English speakers. Since typical speech rates are similar across languages, we expect that our results regarding the processing of the temporal envelope of speech can be generalized to other languages.

Relationship between auditory cortical activity and the temporal envelope

When responses of different trials with the same compression level were averaged, they often showed clear fluctuations between 4 to 10 Hz, with the latency of the first response peak being close to 100 ms (Fig. 18.2A, an RD subject). These fluctuations added up across trials, which indicates that they are time-locked to the stimulus: either each of these fluctuations is driven by a stimulus syllable, or a burst of intrinsic oscillations is triggered (or reset) by the sentence onset. To differentiate between these two possibilities, we compared the frequencies of the stimulus envelope and cortical responses over different compression levels; if driven by the stimulus, cortical responses to syllables should follow the syllabic frequency. But this is not the case; in this subject cortical activity exhibited two major frequency modes, one below 2 Hz and one around 5 Hz. These modes do not follow the stimulus frequency; they are stationary, albeit their relative amplitudes vary. This can also be seen in the time domain (Fig. 18.2A); the inter-peak intervals remained more-or-less constant (arrows) despite more than 3-fold compression of the stimulus envelope.

Frequency matching between the auditory cortex and temporal envelope

Constant-frequency behavior was observed in almost all thirteen subjects for all 3 PCs. To demonstrate this phenomenon, we present the data of all the subjects that participated in this experiment. We divide the subjects into 3 groups according to the PC that exhibited the largest frequency mode for each subject. Data from the eight subjects in which PC1 exhibited the largest frequency mode are depicted in Figure 18.3. For each subject, the power spectra of the stimulus envelope and PC1 of the cortical response are plotted for each compression level (4 top rows), and her/his CI is plotted as a function of compression (lowest row). In all eight subjects, the PC1 spectra contain several modes between 0 and ~10 Hz. The main difference between responses to various speech rates was not in the location, i.e., frequency, of the modes, but rather in their relative amplitudes. In only one case (subject KR, compression 0.5), a slight shift of the ~5-Hz mode towards the peak of the envelope can be observed.

Thus, the oscillatory cortical activity does not appear to be directly driven by the syllables of the sentence. Rather, the stimulus appears to hit upon an existing set of intrinsic oscillations. In which case, what might constrain a subject's comprehension? Previously, we showed that the difference between the frequencies of the envelope and cortical mode constrains the comprehension of a subject (Ahissar et al., 2001). Examination of the relationships between these two variables (Fig. 18.3) shows that comprehension is good when cortical frequencies are the same as, or higher than, the envelope frequencies, and becomes poorer as this relationship reverses. For example, subject RB loses comprehension already at compression of 0.5, when his cortical power drops to very low frequencies; subjects MS, KR, and KB lose comprehension at

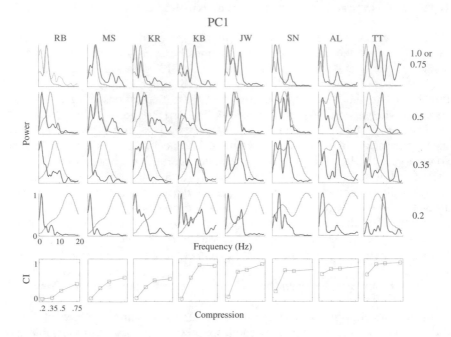

Fig. 18.3. Power spectra and comprehension index (CI) of 8 subjects whose highest frequency mode was expressed by PC1. SN and AL were tested with compression of 1 instead of 0.75. Five subjects (left five) were tested with sentences of set 3; SN and AL with set 2, and TT with set 1. Compression levels indicated on the right.

compression of 0.35, when their cortical power is mainly contained in frequencies that are lower than those of the envelope; and JW and SN lose comprehension only at compression of 0.2, when their cortical frequency becomes too low for the syllabic frequency.

These data also demonstrate that, within this range (~4–10 Hz), the higher the maximal intrinsic frequency generated by a cortex, the better the comprehension of the subject. This was true not only with regard to accelerated speech, but also for comprehension at normal speech rates (compressions of 0.75 or 1). In Figure 18.3, subjects were arranged (from left to right) according to increased comprehension (comprehension at 0.35 was arbitrarily chosen for ranking). In accordance with this gradient of comprehension, the maximal frequency generated by the left auditory cortex of these subjects, across all compression levels, also increased from left to right; from ~5 Hz with RB to ~10 Hz with the three subjects on the right. In other words, comprehension correlated with the maximal frequency that the left auditory cortex of a given subject generated when challenged with accelerated speech in our task. This arrangement revealed another signature of poor speech perceivers (in this case RB, MS, and KR), they lack the ~10-Hz mode. The impairment of these three

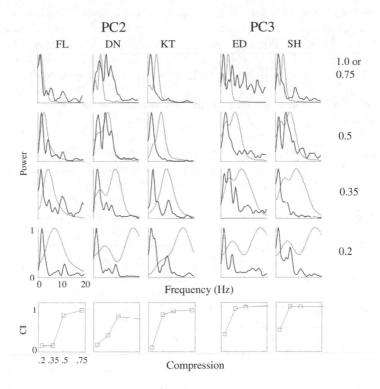

Fig. 18.4. Power spectra and comprehension index (CI) of subjects whose highest frequency modes were expressed by PC2 (3 subjects) and PC3 (2 subjects). DN, SH and ED were tested with compression of 1 instead of 0.75. KT was tested with sentences of set 3; DN, SH and ED with set 2; and FL with set 1. Compression levels indicated on the right.

poor speech perceivers was not limited to accelerated speech, their comprehension of normal speech rates was also significantly impaired.

Data on the other five subjects, in which the maximal recorded frequencies were exhibited by their PC2 or PC3, are depicted in Figure 18.4. Although some correlation between maximal cortical frequency and comprehension was seen in these groups, it was less pronounced than that exhibited by the PC1 group (Fig. 18.3). For example, two subjects (KT and SH) exhibited excellent comprehension without a significant match between the frequencies of the stimulus envelope and the recorded cortical responses. Subject AL also exhibited good comprehension at compression of 0.2 without such a match (Fig. 18.3). Perhaps these three subjects use other mechanisms or, alternatively, similar frequency-matching dependent mechanisms, but in other cortical areas, for example, the right auditory cortex.

Interestingly, the stimulus set that had a bimodal power distribution, also often induced bimodal power distributions in cortical activity (set 2; subjects SN, AL, DN, SH, and ED). In subject ED, frequency matching with the lower mode correlated with comprehension (Fig. 18.4); in this subject, cortical frequency clearly tracked changes in that frequency mode as speech accelerated.

Correlation of maximal cortical frequency mode with speech comprehension and reading

Previously, we examined the correlation between comprehension of accelerated speech and stimulus-cortex frequency matching using two quantitative measures for frequency matching: (i) Fdiff (frequency difference = modal frequency of the evoked cortical signal minus the modal frequency of the stimulus envelope), and (ii) Fcc (frequency correlation coefficient = the correlation coefficient between the power spectra of the stimulus envelope and the cortical signal in the range of 0–20 Hz). Both these measures of frequency matching correlate highly with comprehension: Fcc, $r = 0.87 \pm 0.12$, $p < 0.0001$; Fdiff, $r = 0.94 \pm 0.07$, $p < 0.0001$ (Ahissar et al., 2001).

We now examined the correlation between comprehension of accelerated speech and maximal frequency mode (maxFmode) in the cortical response. MaxFmode in the cortical response of a subject was defined as the highest frequency mode observed (by visual inspection of the power spectra) while a subject listened to the sentences at any of the compression levels in any of the 3 PCs. Comprehension of accelerated speech was represented as the compression "threshold" level at which comprehension was at 50% of its span (CL@50%, i.e., CL for CI = min(CI)+0.5[max(CI)-min(CI)]). The correlation between maxFmode and CI@50% (Fig. 18.5A) was apparent, but on the threshold of being statistically significant ($R2 = 0.28$, $p = 0.063$). As the threshold level

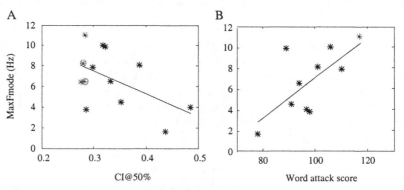

Fig. 18.5. Correlation between the frequency of the highest mode (maxFmode) recorded from a subject and his/her comprehension threshold (CL@50%) of time-compressed speech (Panel A; $R^2 = 0.28$, $p = 0.06$, $n = 13$) and accuracy of reading non-words (word attack score; Panel B; $R^2 = 0.47$, $p = 0.027$, $n = 10$). RDs represented by black and good readers by gray asterisks. Data from the two non-native English speakers are circled.

increased, correlation with maxFmode decreased (CL@25%, R2 = 0.35, p = 0.034; CL@50%, R2 = 0.28, p = 0.063; CL@75%, R2 = 0.06, p = 0.4). The correlation of maxFmode with accuracy of reading non-words ("word attack") was strong: R2 = 0.47, p = 0.027 (Fig. 18.5B).

The higher correlation of maxFmode with reading, than with comprehension of accelerated speech, might suggest that reading impairment and cortical rhythms do not necessarily link via mechanisms of speech perception. It is possible that both reading and speech perception depend on cognitive mechanisms related to the cortical alpha rhythm. Indeed, RDs exhibit deficiencies in perceiving successive stimuli, not only for auditory, but also for visual sequences (Amitay et al., 2002b; Ben-Yehudah et al., 2001; Hari et al., 1999a).

Phase locking and speech comprehension

The relevance of phase locking to speech comprehension was examined by determining the cross-correlation between the two time domain signals: the temporal envelopes of the speech input and of the recorded cortical response. The strength of phase locking was quantified as the peak-to-peak amplitude of the cross-correlation function, filtered at ±1 octave around the stimulus modal frequency at 0 to 0.5 s. This measure, which represents stimulus-response phase locking at the stimulus frequency band, correlated highly with comprehension (Ahissar et al., 2001).

The low signal-to-noise ratio of MEG signals prevented a trial-by-trial analysis. Despite this constraint, some trial specific information was obtained by comparing "correct" trials to "incorrect" and "don't know" trials. This comparison revealed that stimulus-response phase locking was significantly higher during "correct" than during "incorrect" trials or "don't know" trials, whereas frequency matching was not (Ahissar et al., 2001). This finding can be explained as follows. With short sentences, such as those presented here, presumably there is not sufficient time for the brain to change its response frequency and fully track the stimulus frequency, therefore it was crucial that the input frequency would fall within the operational range of *a priori* tuned cortical oscillating frequencies. However, the temporal patterns of the envelopes were not regular, even though they exhibited clear frequency modes. The phase-locking data indicate that comprehension was better when cortical fluctuations correlated with the pattern of the temporal envelope, not only with its average frequency. Such temporal locking could occur by chance, or due to some limited active tracking, which might still occur during these short sentences. Whatever the reason, in trials where the temporal patterns of the speech input and recorded cortical response matched, comprehension was better.

Thus, speech comprehension in these experiments appeared to depend on pre-tuned cortical oscillations whose mean frequencies were equal to or higher than the envelope frequencies, and was facilitated by accurate temporal matching. The ability of auditory cortical neurons to follow modulations at the frequency-range of speech envelopes was demonstrated in many studies (e.g., Eggermont, 1998; Schreiner & Urbas, 1988). Moreover, neurons of the primary auditory cortex of monkeys phase lock to the envelope of a portion of a species-specific vocalization, which is centered around their characteristic frequencies (Wang et al., 1995). Interestingly, the results of these studies indicate that the strongest response locking of cortical neurons to a periodic input is usually achieved for stimulus rates (envelope frequencies) that are within the dominant range of spontaneous and evoked cortical oscillations, i.e., for frequencies below 16 Hz (Ahissar & Vaadia, 1990; Cotillon et al., 2000). This is also the frequency range in which AM modulations evoke the strongest fMRI responses in the human auditory cortex (Giraud et al., 2000). Our results suggest that cortical response locking to the temporal structure of the speech envelope is a prerequisite for speech comprehension. This stimulus-response phase correspondence may enable internal segmentation of sentence components, mainly syllables.

DECODING OF THE TEMPORAL ENVELOPE: A HYPOTHESIS

Since cortical frequencies did not simply follow the input frequencies, we assume that they are generated by intrinsic mechanisms. Evidence for such intrinsic cortical mechanisms, which are capable of generating alpha range oscillations, is sound (e.g., Ahissar et al., 1997; Ahissar & Vaadia, 1990; Gray & McCormick, 1996; Llinas et al., 1991; Silva et al., 1991). The observed locking of post-stimulus cortical oscillations to speech onset (and hence not being averaged out across trials), indicates that intrinsic oscillatory sources must be triggered, or reset, by speech onset. Our results indicate that comprehension of short sentences depends on the relationship between the frequencies of these intrinsic oscillations and those of the sentence envelope: For good comprehension, cortical frequency has to be equal to or higher than the input frequency. Furthermore, our results indicate that comprehension improves when phase-locking between the sentence envelope and cortical oscillations increases.

Here, we present a hypothesis that can account for the perception of short sentences, and also continuous speech in general. Based on existing neurophysiological data and our findings, we hypothesize that arrays of intrinsic cortical oscillators, which possess frequencies in the range of plausible syllabic rates (~4 to ~16 Hz), are involved in speech perception. We speculate that the role of these arrays of cortical oscillators is to set the clock for spectral syllable processing (Fig. 18.6). Clearly, processing of the spectral content of a syllable must be done at the time in which this information is valid. Thus, the brain might extract this time from a feedforward derivative processing of syllable onset (Fishbach et al., 2001), in which case some information carried by, or close in time to, syllable onset might be lost. Alternatively, the brain could initiate syllabic processing based on an internal prediction of the time of

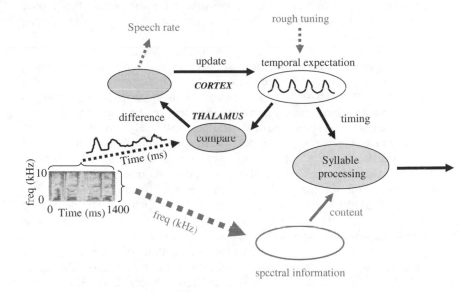

Fig. 18.6. Hypothesized scheme for processing of the temporal envelope of speech and its function in syllable processing. We postulate that the temporal envelope of the speech signal is processed in parallel to pre-processing of its spectral content, possibly by the non-lemniscal and lemniscal systems, respectively. In this scheme, the temporal envelope is compared against a cortical reference (temporal expectation) implemented by neuronal oscillations. The comparison occurs in the (non-lemniscal) thalamus, and its output (which is proportional to the temporal difference between the two signals) is fed back to the cortex, where it eventually updates the reference signal. The entire thalamocortical loop is a negative feedback loop that functions as a neuronal phase-locked loop (Ahissar, 1998). The signal that represents the temporal difference, which contains information about input speech rate, might be further processed (dashed arrow, top left). Cortical oscillations, which express an expectation for timing of the next syllable, send this timing information to a postulated "syllable processor", which processes dynamic spectral information contained in a syllable. The cortical oscillations can be pre-tuned by expectations of speech rate ("rough tuning").

arrival of the next syllable, in which case typically no information would be lost, and which we propose here.

We suggest that a postulated "syllabic processor" receives its timing from a cortical "temporal predictor," which is basically a bank of oscillators. These oscillators have some intrinsic frequencies that are adjustable: They can be increased by excitation and decreased by inhibition (Ahissar, 1998). Before speech is received, these oscillators can be tuned by internal processes to be in the expected (or slightly higher) rate of speech. If tuned appropriately, the syllabic processor will be able to process the incoming syllable(s). Moreover, our data suggest that an *a priori* rough tuning, even if slightly different from the frequency of the envelopes, is sufficient for reasonable comprehension of short sentences (see Fig. 18.3). However, a consistent frequency difference over longer sentences should eventually impair comprehension, as cortical timing will lose input timing.

Thus, a mechanism that will force such intrinsic oscillators to lock to the actual syllabic rate is required. We propose that such a function is implemented by a mechanism similar to the phase-locked loop (PLL; Ahissar, 1998). The algorithm of the PLL is based on comparison and update (Fig. 18.6). Timing of the actual input envelope is compared with the predicted one, and the temporal difference is encoded by some neuronal variable, most-likely spike-count, which is used to update the period of the next oscillatory cycle. Such a mechanism times the syllabic processor before the next syllable arrives, thus allowing efficient processing of the entire syllable, including its information-rich onset segment. Prediction of timing cannot be achieved with open-loop mechanisms, such as a bank of band-pass filters. However, a PLL, which is itself an adaptive band-pass filter, provides both efficient filtering of the actual envelope and an updated prediction about the timing of the next syllable.

The algorithm and possible neuronal implementations of such a loop were previously discussed in detail (Ahissar, 1998; Ahissar & Arieli, 2001; Ahissar et al., 1997; Ahissar & Vaadia, 1990; Ahissar & Zacksenhouse, 2001; Kleinfeld et al., 1999; Kleinfeld et al., 2002), and thus, are not described here. Since auditory implementations of the PLL algorithm have not been proposed before, we will suggest auditory sites that appear plausible for such implementation. Our suggestions are based on known auditory anatomy and physiology, and on an analogy with the tactile system of the rat, in which some predictions of the PLL algorithm were recently tested and confirmed (Ahissar & Arieli, 2001; Ahissar et al., 1997; Ahissar et al., 2000a; Kleinfeld et al., 1999; Sosnik et al., 2001).

In principle, PLLs might be implemented by many neuronal circuits, including sub-cortical and cortico-cortical loops. We hypothesize that envelope-related PLLs, like those in the tactile system, are implemented by thalamocortical loops, and that a temporal comparison takes place in the thalamus, most likely the non-lemniscal nuclei. As in the vibrissal tactile system, the auditory non-lemniscal thalamus exhibits larger temporal dispersion (He & Hu, 2002; Hu, 2003) and spatial (spectral) integration (Hu, 2003; Malmierca et al., 2002; Steriade et al., 1997) than the lemniscal thalamus. Both these features, together with typical thalamic gating mechanisms (McCormick & von Krosigk, 1992; Sherman & Guillery, 1996) and strong corticothalamic feedback (Ojima, 1994), make the non-lemniscal thalamus optimal for temporal comparison functions (Ahissar, 1998; Ahissar & Arieli, 2001). According to this hypothesis, the signal indicating timing differences, produced by the non-lemniscal thalamus, is fed back to the cortex where it is used to update the frequency of the intrinsic oscillators. The entire loop should be connected as a negative feedback loop, via thalamic (Yu et al., 2004) or cortical inhibition. Such a negative feedback loop would force the cortical oscillations to phase-lock to the envelope of the speech signal. Thus, with longer spoken sentences we predict that cortical oscillations will not stick to their original frequencies, but will adapt to the actual envelope frequencies.

Spectral analysis of syllables must be coordinated with syllable timing. In fact, Giraud et al. (2000) suggested that "Slow oscillations (2–10 Hz) could signal the temporal limits of syllables." Our hypothesis, which is fully consistent with this, goes further by suggesting that these slow oscillations are intrinsic, and actually serve as temporal expectations. It is the intrinsic "clock" that sets the pace for segmentation, and not the incoming signal. The rate of the incoming signal only updates the intrinsic clock, and makes it a better predictor of the following input rate. The existence of such an intrinsic clock is consistent with another phenomenon often related to speech perception, that of perceptual center (P-center; Goswami et al., 2002; Morton et al., 1976). The P-center of a signal, such as a syllable, "corresponds to its psychological moment of occurrence" (Morton et al., 1976). The experimental definition of a P-center of a speech signal depends on a comparison, by a listener, between such psychological moments of occurrence and an internal "temporal ruler," or pacemaker (Morton et al., 1976; Scott, 1993). Our model describes such a process: the rate of an input stream of syllables is compared against an internal temporal ruler, which takes the form of intrinsic oscillations.

SUMMARY AND CONCLUSIONS

We have extended our previous report on processing of the temporal envelope of speech by demonstrating the difference between poor and good readers in comprehending accelerated speech, and demonstrating the correlation of the maxFmode recorded from the auditory cortex with reading and with comprehension thresholds for accelerated speech. Our hypothesis about the processing of speech rate, and its possible role in speech comprehension, is described in detail. Based on our hypothesis, we suggest that the ability of listeners to adapt to varying speech rates depends on the dynamic range of their cortical oscillations. Further experimental testing will determine whether these dynamic ranges can be increased by training, and whether such increases will facilitate comprehension of varying-rate speech.

ACKNOWLEDGMENTS

Sentences were time-compressed by Athanassios Protopapas; MEG experiments were conducted together with Srikantan Nagarajan, Henry Mahncke, and Michael M. Merzenich. Manuscript was reviewed by Barbara Schick. Supported by the US-Israel Binational Science Foundation, Edith Blum Foundation, Esther Smidof Foundation, and Volkswagen Foundation. E.A. is the incumbent of the Helen and Sanford Diller Family Professorial Chair of Neurobiology.

REFERENCES

Ahissar, E. (1998). Temporal-code to rate-code conversion by neuronal phase-locked loops. Neural Computation, 10, 597–650.

Ahissar, E., & Arieli, A. (2001). Figuring space by time. Neuron, 32, 185–201.

Ahissar, E., Haidarliu, S., & Zacksenhouse, M. (1997). Decoding temporally encoded sensory input by cortical oscillations and thalamic phase comparators. Proceedings of the National Academy of Sciences USA, 94, 11633–11638.

Ahissar, E., Nagarajan, S., Ahissar, M., Protopapas, A., Mahncke, H., & Merzenich, M. (2001). Speech comprehension is correlated with temporal response patterns recorded from auditory cortex. Proceedings of the National Academy of Sciences USA, 98, 13367–13372.

Ahissar, M., Protopapas, A., Reid, M., & Merzenich, M.M. (2000b). Auditory processing parallels reading abilities in adults. Proceedings of the National Academy of Sciences USA, 97, 6832–6837.

Ahissar, E., Sosnik, R., & Haidarliu, S. (2000a). Transformation from temporal to rate coding in a somatosensory thalamocortical pathway. Nature, 406, 302–306.

Ahissar, E., & Vaadia, E. (1990). Oscillatory activity of single units in a somatosensory cortex of an awake monkey and their possible role in texture analysis. Proceedings of the National Academy of Sciences USA, 87, 8935–8939.

Ahissar, E., & Zacksenhouse, M. (2001). Temporal and spatial coding in the rat vibrissal system. Progress in Brain Research, 130, 75–88.

Amitay, S., Ahissar, M., & Nelken, I. (2002a). Auditory processing deficits in reading disabled adults. Journal of the Association for Research in Otolaryngology, 3, 302–320.

Amitay, S., Ben-Yehudah, G., Banai, K., & Ahissar, M. (2002b). Disabled readers suffer from visual and auditory impairments but not from a specific magnocellular deficit. Brain, 125, 2272–2285.

Aram, D.M., Ekelman, B.L., & Nation, J.E. (1984). Preschoolers with language disorders: 10 years later. Journal of Speech & Hearing Research, 27, 232–244.

Banai, K., & Ahissar, M. (2004). Poor frequency discrimination probes dyslexics with particularly impaired working memory. Audiology & Neuro-otology, 9, 328–340.

Beasley, D.S., Bratt, G.W., & Rintelmann, W.F. (1980). Intelligibility of time-compressed sentential stimuli. Journal of Speech & Hearing Research, 23, 722–731.

Ben-Yehudah, G., Sackett, E., Malchi-Ginzberg, L., & Ahissar, M. (2001). Impaired temporal contrast sensitivity in dyslexics is specific to retain-and-compare paradigms. Brain, 124, 1381–1395.

Bishop, D.V.M. (1992). The underlying nature of specific language impairment. Journal of Child Psychology & Psychiatry & Allied Disciplines, 33, 2–66.

Cotillon, N., Nafati, M., & Edeline, J.M. (2000). Characteristics of reliable tone-evoked oscillations in the rat thalamo- cortical auditory system. Hearing Research, 142, 113–130.

Drullman, R., Festen, J.M., & Plomp, R. (1994). Effect of temporal envelope smearing on speech reception. Journal of the Acoustical Society of America, 95, 1053–1064.

Dupoux, E., & Green, K. (1997). Perceptual adjustment to highly compressed speech: effects of talker and rate changes. Journal of Experimental Psychology – Human Perception and Performance, 23, 914–927.

Eggermont, J.J. (1998). Representation of spectral and temporal sound features in three cortical fields of the cat. Similarities outweigh differences. Journal of Neurophysiology, 80, 2743–2764.

Farmer, M.E., & Klein, R.M. (1995). The evidence for a temporal processing deficit linked to dyslexia: A review. Psychonomics Bulletin & Review, 2, 460–493.

Fishbach, A., Nelken, I., & Yeshurun, Y. (2001). Auditory edge detection: A neural model for physiological and psychoacoustical responses to amplitude transients. Journal of Neurophysiology, 85, 2303–2323.

Foulke, E., & Sticht, T.G. (1969). Review of research on the intelligibility and comprehension of accelerated speech. Psychological Bulletin, 72, 50–62.

Freeman, B.A., & Beasley, D.S. (1978). Discrimination of time-altered sentential approximations and monosyllables by children with reading problems. Journal of Speech & Hearing Research, 21, 497–506.

Giraud, A.L., Lorenzi, C., Ashburner, J., Wable, J., Johnsrude, I., Frackowiak, R., & Kleinschmidt, A. (2000). Representation of the temporal envelope of sounds in the human brain. Journal of Neurophysiology, 84, 1588–1598.

Goswami, U., Thomson, J., Richardson, U., Stainthorp, R., Hughes, D., Rosen, S., & Scott, S.K. (2002). Amplitude envelope onsets and developmental dyslexia: A new hypothesis. Proceedings of the National Academy of Sciences USA, 99, 10911–10916.

Gray, C.M., & McCormick, D.A. (1996). Chattering cells: superficial pyramidal neurons contributing to the generation of synchronous oscillations in the visual cortex. Science, 274, 109–113.

Hari, R., Saaskilahti, A., Helenius, P., & Uutela, K. (1999b). Non-impaired auditory phase locking in dyslexic adults. Neuroreport, 10, 2347–2348.

Hari, R., Valta, M., & Uutela, K. (1999a). Prolonged attentional dwell time in dyslexic adults. Neuroscience Letters, 271, 202–204.

He, J., & Hu, B. (2002). Differential distribution of burst and single-spike responses in auditory thalamus. Journal of Neurophysiology, 88, 2152–2156.

Helenius, P., Uutela, K., & Hari, R. (1999). Auditory stream segregation in dyslexic adults. Brain, 122, 907–913.

Houtgast, T., & Steeneken, H.J.M. (1985). A review of the MFT concept in room acoustics and its use for estimating speech intelligibility in auditoria. Journal of the Acoustical Society of America, 77, 1069–1077.

Hu, B. (2003). Functional organization of lemniscal and nonlemniscal auditory thalamus. Experimental Brain Research, 153, 543–549.

Kleinfeld, D., Berg, R.W., & O'Connor, S.M. (1999). Anatomical loops and their electrical dynamics in relation to whisking by rat. Somatosensory & Motor Research, 16, 69–88.

Kleinfeld, D., Sachdev, R.N., Merchant, L.M., Jarvis, M.R., & Ebner, F.F. (2002). Adaptive filtering of vibrissa input in motor cortex of rat. Neuron, 34, 1021–1034.

Llinas, R.R., Grace, A.A., & Yarom, Y. (1991). In vitro neurons in mammalian cortical layer 4 exhibit intrinsic oscillatory activity in the 10- to 50-Hz frequency range. Proceedings of the National Academy of Sciences USA, 88, 897–901.

Malmierca, M.S., Merchan, M.A., Henkel, C.K., & Oliver, D.L. (2002). Direct projections from cochlear nuclear complex to auditory thalamus in the rat. Journal of Neuroscience, 22, 10891–10897.

McAnally, K.I., Hansen, P.C., Cornelissen, P.L., & Stein, J.F. (1997). Effect of time and frequency manipulation on syllable perception in developmental dyslexics. Journal of Speech Language & Hearing Research, 40, 912–924.

McCormick, D.A., & von Krosigk, M. (1992). Corticothalamic activation modulates thalamic firing through glutamate "metabotropic" receptors. Proceedings of the National Academy of Sciences USA, 89, 2774–2778.

Miller, J.L., Grosjean, F., & Lomanto, C. (1984). Articulation rate and its variability in spontaneous speech: a reanalysis and some implications. Phonetica, 41, 215–225.

Morton, J., Marcus, S., & Framkish, C. (1976). Perceptual centers (P-centers). Psychological Review, 83, 405–408.

Newman, R.S., & Sawusch, J.R. (1996). Perceptual normalization for speaking rate: effects of temporal distance. Perception & Psychophysics, 58, 540–560.

Ojima, H. (1994). Terminal morphology and distribution of corticothalamic fibers originating from layers 5 and 6 of cat primary auditory cortex. Cerebral Cortex, 4, 646–663.

Renvall, H., & Hari, R. (2002). Auditory cortical responses to speech-like stimuli in dyslexic adults. Journal of Cognitive Neuroscience, 14, 757–768.

Riensche, L.L., & Clauser, P.S. (1982). Auditory perceptual abilities of formerly misarticulating children. Journal of Auditory Research, 22, 240–248.

Rosen, S. (1992). Temporal information in speech: acoustic, auditory and linguistic aspects. Philosophical Transactions of the Royal Society of London. Series B – Biological Science, 336, 367–373.

Schreiner, C.E., & Urbas, J.V. (1988). Representation of amplitude modulation in the auditory cortex of the cat. II. Comparison between cortical fields. Hearing Research, 32, 49–63.

Scott, S.K. (1993). P-centers – an acoustic analysis. PhD thesis, University College London.

Shapiro, K.L., Ogden, N., & Lind-Blad, F. (1990). Temporal processing in dyslexia. Journal of Learning Disabilities, 23, 99–107.

Sherman, S.M., & Guillery, R.W. (1996). Functional organization of thalamocortical relays. Journal of Neurophysiology, 76, 1367–1395.

Silva, L.R., Amitai, Y., & Connors, B.W. (1991). Intrinsic oscillations of neocortex generated by layer 5 pyramidal neurons. Science, 251, 432–435.

Sosnik, R., Haidarliu, S., & Ahissar, E. (2001). Temporal frequency of whisker movement. I. Representations in brain stem and thalamus. Journal of Neurophysiology, 86, 339–353.

Steriade, M., Jones, E.G., & McCormick, D.A. (1997). Thalamus. Vol. I: Organisation and function. Amsterdam: Elsevier.

Tallal, P., Miller, S., & Fitch, R.H. (1993). Neurobiological basis of speech: A case for the preeminence of temporal processing. Annals of the New York Academy of Science, 682, 27–47.

Tallal, P., & Piercy, M. (1973). Defects of non-verbal auditory perception in children with developmental aphasia. Nature, 241, 468–469.

van der Horst, R., Leeuw, A.R., & Dreschler, W.A. (1999). Importance of temporal-envelope cues in consonant recognition. Journal of the Acoustical Society of America, 105, 1801–1809.

Wang, X., Merzenich, M.M., Beitel, R., & Schreiner, C.E. (1995). Representation of a species-specific vocalization in the primary auditory cortex of the common marmoset: Temporal and spatial characteristics. Journal of Neurophysiology, 74, 2685–2706.

Watson, M., Stewart, M., Krause, K., & Rastatter, M. (1990). Identification of time-compressed sentential stimuli by good vs poor readers. Perceptual Motor Skills, 71, 107–114.

Welsh, L.W., Welsh, J.J., Healy, M., & Cooper, B. (1982). Cortical, subcortical, and brainstem dysfunction: A correlation in dyslexic children. Annals of Otology Rhinology & Laryngology, 91, 310–315.

Woodcock, R. (1987). Woodcock Reading Mastery Tests – Revised. Circle Pines, MN: American Guidance Service.

Yu, Y., Xiong, Y., Chan, Y., & He, J. (2004). Corticofugal gating of auditory information in the thalamus: An in vivo intracellular recording study. Journal of Neuroscience, 24, 3060–3069.

19. SPATIO-TEMPORAL PATTERNS OF RESPONSES TO PURE TONES AND FREQUENCY-MODULATED SOUNDS IN THE GUINEA PIG AUDITORY CORTEX

Ikuo Taniguchi, Shunji Sugimoto, Andreas Hess,
Junsei Horikawa, Yutaka Hosokawa, Henning Scheich

INTRODUCTION

A major role of tonotopic organization in primary auditory cortex (AI) is to analyze sound frequency. To date, we have a good understanding of the responses to pure tones (PT) in the auditory cortex. Electrophysiological studies have revealed a tonotopic organization and isofrequency contours in AI, and variations of neuronal properties like frequency tuning, rate-intensity functions to PT, binaural and azimuthal tuning, and distribution of these neurons along and across the isofrequency contours. We also start to have an insight into how AI represents frequency modulated sounds (FM). However, we have not yet understood the dynamic properties of the responses of neuron populations of AI to PTs and FMs, that is, spatial and temporal developments of the responses within the tonotopic organization. Therefore, we studied in AI of guinea pigs the relationship between PT and FM responses, both obtained by an optical recording technique using a voltage sensitive dye. This article describes the similarity and difference of the spatiotemporal patterns of responses to PTs and FMs and possible synaptic mechanisms producing such spatiotemporal patterns in AI.

MATERIALS AND METHODS

We used optical recording by a voltage-sensitive dye because this technique has advantages over other methods in that spatiotemporal activity and dynamic properties of neural circuitry in the auditory cortex can be monitored with submillisecond time resolution (Horikawa et al., 1996; Taniguchi et al., 1992).

Guinea pigs were anesthetized with Nembutal (30 mg/kg initial and 10 mg/kg/h supplementary) combined with neuroleptanalgesic drugs (pentazocine 1 mg/kg/h and droperidol 0.3 mg/kg/h). Next, the auditory cortex was exposed and stained with a voltage-sensitive dye RH795 (0.2 mg/ml saline). The auditory cortex was epi-illuminated by a light (480–580 nm) and fluorescent signals (> 620 nm) from the cortex were detected by 144-channel square (Hamamatsu Photonics) or 464-channel hexagonal (Neuroplex, Red Shirt Imaging Inc.) photodiode arrays at a rate of 0.5 ms/frame (Hamamatsu) or 0.58 ms/frame (Neuroplex) and a 16-bit resolution of A/D converters. Each photodiode channel recorded signals from a 250-μm (Hamamatsu) and 188-μm (Neuroplex) cortical square, respectively. The measuring microscope was focused at a depth of 0.2 mm from the surface in order to dominantly measure the signals from the layers II and III. The recorded signals were intensity-coded and superimposed on a vascular reference picture of the cortical surface.

The stimuli used were pure tones (PT: 1, 2, 4, 8, 12, and 16 kHz; 50 and 100-ms durations; 10-ms rise-fall times) and frequency modulated tones (upward FM: swept from 4 to 16 kHz, downward FM: swept from 16 to 4 kHz; 100-ms duration; 10-ms rise-fall times). All sounds were presented to the ear contralateral to the recording side at 70–75 dB SPL every 2 s by a loudspeaker. Typically, responses to 5 stimulus presentations were averaged.

In order to study the synaptic mechanisms of the responses, excitatory- and inhibitory-receptor blockers were applied to the bath over the auditory cortex. Bicuculline methiodide (BMI, 4 μM), 2-amino-5-phosphonovalerate (APV, 100 μM) and 6-cyano-7-nitroquinoxaline-2,3-dione (CNQX, 5 μM) were dissolved in the voltage-sensitive dye solution. They were applied to the cortex for 10 min and then washed out. From former studies it is known that the drugs act directly and therefore recordings started immediately and lasted for 10 min. After that the drug was washed out and the reversibility of the drug effects was controlled, but the data are not shown here for all cases.

MULTIPLE AUDITORY FIELDS OF THE GUINEA PIG AUDITORY CORTEX

The guinea pig auditory cortex consists of two core fields and several belt fields surrounding them (Fig. 19.1A). The fields were previously identified by the response characteristics to PT such as tonotopic organization, response latency and duration obtained by electrical (Hellweg et al., 1977; Redies et al., 1989; Wallace et al., 1999, 2000) and optical (Horikawa et al. 2001; Taniguchi et al.,

1992) recordings. The core fields consist of the primary auditory field (AI) located rostrally with the shortest response latency among the fields (Fig. 19.1B), and the dorso-caudal field (DC: by Redies et al. 1989; or called the area II by Hellweg et al. 1977; the area II does not correspond to the AII of cats) showing the second shortest latency. These two fields share a common high frequency border. The belt fields consist of the dorso-caudal (DCB), ventro-caudal (VCB), dorso-rostral (DRB) and ventro-rostral (VRB) belt fields (Redies et al., 1989; Wallace et al., 1999, 2000). Using optical recordings these belt

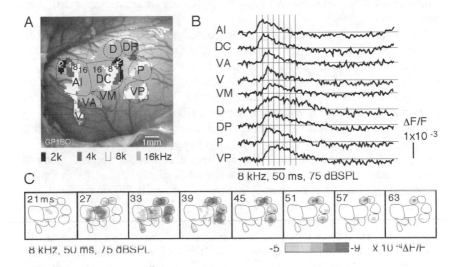

Fig. 19.1.A. Tonotopic organization as shown by superimposing the areas responding to 2, 4, 8, and 16 kHz (50-ms duration, 10-ms rise-fall time, 75 dB SPL) 35 ms after the onset of the stimulus. The responding areas over 60% of the maximum response to each frequency were superimposed. The overlapped areas in the superimposition are not shown. Multiple auditory fields identified by the tonotopic organization, latency and duration are outlined. AI: primary auditory field, DC: dorso-caudal field, D: dorsal field, DP: dorso-posterior field, P: posterior field, VP: ventro-posterior field, VM: ventro-medial field, and VA: ventro-anterior field. Scale bar = 1 mm. (Adapted from Fig. 2 of Horikawa et al., 2001). The dorso-anterior field (DA) was not observed in this animal. **B.** Traces of the optical response in each field to an 8-kHz tone burst (50-ms duration, 10-ms rise-fall time, 75 dB SPL). The response signal was inverted because the optical intensity decreased with a depolarizing potential. The horizontal lines indicate the level at rest and the vertical thin lines indicate certain times shown in C. The horizontal bar at the bottom indicates the tone burst stimulation. The magnitude of the response is represented as $\Delta F/F$ where ΔF is the change in optical intensity and F is the background optical intensity. **C.** Spatiotemporal responses to an 8-kHz tone burst in multiple auditory fields. Borders of the multiple auditory fields are superimposed on the responses. Numbers in the panels indicate time after the onset of the stimulus. The response from 60% ($-5 \cdot 10^{-4}$) to 100% ($-9 \cdot 10^{-4}$) of the maximum response was intensity-coded. In B and C it can be seen, that the response appears first in the core fields (AI and DC) and then systematically in the belt fields (see text).

fields could be further divided into the dorso-posterior (DP) and posterior (P) fields, ventro-posterior (VP) and ventro-medial (VM) fields, dorsal (D) and dorso-anterior (DA) fields, and ventro-anterior (VA) and ventral (V) fields, respectively (cf. Figs. 1 and 2 in Horikawa et al., 2001). The shapes and sizes, and even the existence of these fields differed among individuals; the core fields AI and DC and the belt fields D, DP, P, VA, and VP were observed in all animals studied (n = 11), but VM and V in 75% and DA in just 35% of them (Horikawa et al., 2001). Field S was not observed in optical recording, because it is located inside the pseudosylvian sulcus below large vessels which makes it difficult to obtain optical signals.

The relative location of the AI of the guinea pig is opposite to that of other rodents such as rats (Sally & Kelly, 1988) and gerbils (Thomas et al., 1993), and macaque monkeys, in which the AI is located caudal to the other core fields. The tonotopic gradient of the guinea pig AI is also opposite to that of other rodents, but resembles that of monkeys in which the low to high frequencies are represented in the rostral-to-caudal direction (Kaas & Hackett, 2000). AI and DC have pronounced tonotopic organization of optical responses, although the response bands at near frequencies are overlapping to different extents. The overlap was measured by the ratio of the width of the overlap along the tonotopic axis between the response bands (clipped at 60% of the maximum response) to 2 and 4, 4 and 8, and 8 and 16 kHz at 70 dB SPL to the total width of 4-16 kHz response bands. It was larger in DC (the ratio: 0.67) than in AI (0.44). The belt areas have a larger overlap of response bands to pure tones (> 0.7). The gradual shift of the center of gravity of the response areas as a function of shifting the stimulation frequency also indicates tonotopic organization in VA, P and VP. Such shifts were not clearly observed in the other belt fields. Concentric overlap observed in D and DP may indicate a concentric tonotopic organization (Horikawa et al., 2001), as seen in the gerbil auditory cortex (Thomas et al., 1993). But this will need more investigations.

The latency and the duration of responses vary among those multiple areas. This is demonstrated for the response to an 8-kHz PT based on continuous time profiles of optical responses for the different fields (Fig. 19.1B) and snapshots of the spatial activation pattern at certain times (Fig. 19.1C). These times are given by the lines in Figure 19.1B and are numbered in ms in Figure 19.1C. The response appeared first in the core fields (AI and DC, 18–20 ms) and then with a 6–13 ms longer latency in the belt fields. Within the belt fields, the response appeared first in D and VM (26 ms) and in VA (27 ms), then in DP and P (29 ms), and last in VP and V (32 ms). Those differences in latency might be consistent with different pathways of spreading the activity into the belt fields. Specific functions for different belt areas might be indicated by the different response durations. Generally, the activity duration was longer for the belt areas than for the core fields. The response was maintained longer especially in D, DP, and VP (more than 63 ms), compared to AI and DC (less than 57 ms).

There is some electrophysiological evidence of functional differences among the core and belt fields. Within the core fields, basic response characteristics are

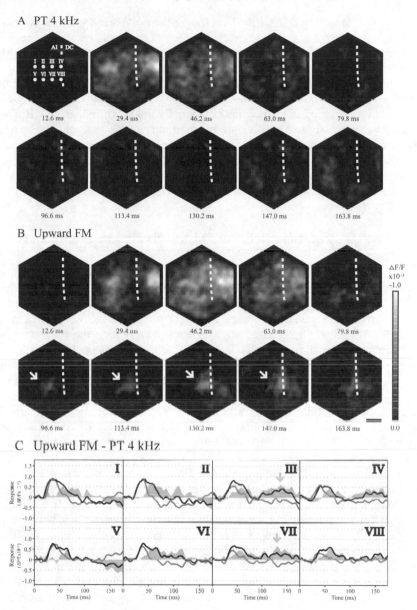

Fig. 19.2. Spatiotemporal response patterns for a 100-ms 4-kHz PT (**A**) and a 100-ms 4–16-kHz upward FM (**B**) obtained in the same animal. Arrows in B indicate spatially-focused activities moving along the tonotopic axis. Dashed lines: border between AI (left) and DC (right). Scale bar: 1 mm. (**C**) A comparison of signal traces for PT (gray lines) and FM (black lines). Time-histograms show differences between PT and FM signals. The signals were obtained at 8 pixel positions (I-VIII in A). Further descriptions in text.

similar: The latency in DC is only 1 ms longer than in AI, and the time course of the responses, frequency tuning and distribution of thresholds is similar between the fields (Redies et al., 1989; Tanaka et al., 1994; Wallace et al., 1999, 2000). Weaker tonotopic organization, larger overlaps of response bands and better responses to noise (Wallace et al., 1999) in the belt fields suggest that the belt fields process integrated frequency information, although the kind of frequency integration performed in the belt fields is largely unknown. For the VCB it was found, that it is more sensitive to binaural difference than the core fields (Hosokawa et al., 2004). This suggests that the VCB performs sound location analysis. These results obtained in guinea pigs are comparable to those obtained in monkeys showing that the caudal belt is more sharply tuned to sound locations (Rauschecker, 2002; Rauschecker & Tian, 2002; Tian et al., 2001).

SPATIOTEMPORAL PATTERNS OF FM RESPONSES IN COMPARISON TO PT RESPONSES

Figure 19.2 shows a comparison between responses to a 4-kHz PT (Fig. 19.2A) and a 4–16-kHz upward FM (Fig. 19.2B). For the PT, the response spread widely around the area of frequency of 4 kHz in AI and DC (29.4–46.2 ms in Fig. 19.2A) and was suppressed after 63.0 ms even though the PT stimulation still continued (duration: 100 ms). Only in 25% of all cases for PT (4, 8, and 16 kHz) some responses remained in the area corresponding to that of stimulus frequency. This is different from optical recording of intrinsic signals in which the PT responses spread upon the tonotopic gradients over much longer periods (Hess & Scheich, 1996). In contrast to PT, the FM response always consisted of an onset excitatory spread and a late activation (Fig. 19.2B). The onset excitation for FM was stronger and longer-lasting than that for PT (29.4–63.0 ms in Fig. 19.2B, compared to Fig. 19.2A), while they are very similar in spatial configuration. The late activation for FM consisted of spatially focused responses moving along the tonotopic axis in AI and DC presumably reflecting the instantaneous frequency of FM (white arrows at 96.6–147.0 ms in Fig. 19.2B). They appeared as several excitatory patches, maximally 0.3–1.0 mm in diameter. Figure 19.2C shows signal traces for PT (gray lines) and FM (black lines) obtained from 8 pixel positions denoted in Figure 19.2A. The differences between the two traces (histograms in Fig. 19.2C) confirm that in general the response to FM is stronger compared to PT (compare also Figs. 19.2A, 19.2B). Moreover they show that the late activation for FM appears broadly distributed over AI, especially around the ending frequency of FM (arrows in III and VII in Fig. 19.2C).

Similar differences were also found comparing the response pattern for a 16 kHz PT with that for a 16–4-kHz downward FM (Fig. 19.3). Again, suppressive effects were observed after the onset response to the 16-kHz PT (after 63.0 ms). This suppression was generally stronger for the higher stimulus frequencies (gray lines in Fig. 19.3C) than for the lower stimulus frequencies (gray lines in

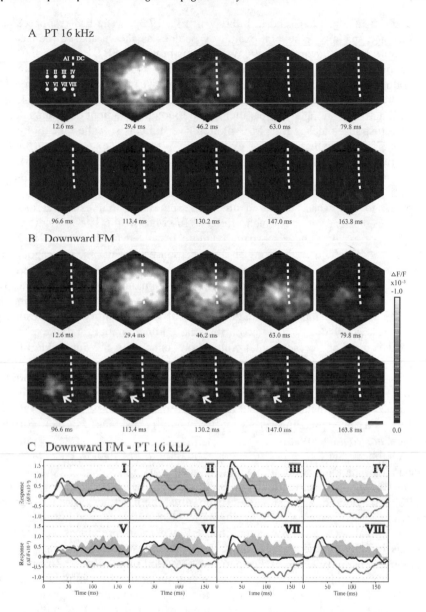

Fig. 19.3. Spatiotemporal response patterns for the 16-kHz PT (**A**) and the 16–4-kHz downward FM (**B**) obtained in the same animal as in Figure 19.2. The other parameters are the same as those of Figure 19.2.

Fig. 19.2C). Conversely, the onset and late responses to downward FM are merged in the time course of them, while those to upward FM were separated especially around the area of its ending frequency (compare, e.g., histograms in

III and VII in Fig. 19.2C and in I and V in Fig. 19.3C). The FM responses are represented spatially in several excitatory patches as shown also in the case of downward FM (white arrows at 96.6–147.0 ms in Fig. 19.3B).

In order to disentangle thalamo-cortical from intrinsic cortical excitatory components of the activation for PT and FM we applied an N-methyl-D-aspartate (NMDA) receptor blocker (APV) to the cortex. In Figure 19.4, the cortical activities along a line parallel to the tonotopic gradient cutting spatially the late response patches for FM is plotted over time as so called location-time images. They show that while PT evoked only a spread of excitation during the onset response (Fig. 19.4A: up to 55 ms and Fig. 19.4D: up to 85 ms) FM evoked further patchy activations after this onset response (Fig. 19.4B: up to 125 ms and Fig. 19.4E: up to 150 ms). After the application of APV, the onset response to FM was reduced in amplitude but its spatial extent across the tonotopic gradient was not much affected. In contrast, the late activations for FM became weaker and also spatially more restricted (white arrows in Figs. 19.4C, 19.4F). This reduction of late responses seems to correspond to inhibition of cortico-cortically propagated activities normally mediated by NMDA receptors. After APV application the remaining activities could be mainly due to non-NMDA receptor-mediated activities induced by direct inputs from auditory thalamus. The spatial extent of the excitatory onset response might be largely due to the direct thalamo-cortical inputs, and the cortico-cortical vertical and/or horizontal connections enhancing the amplitude of this response. In contrast, the late activations seem to be induced by three components: (1) remaining activities caused by the onset excitation (cortico-cortical vertical and/or horizontal activation), (2) activities by the instantaneous frequency of FM (thalamo-cortical but also cortico-cortical *vertical* activation), and (3) activities spreading across the frequency bands caused by (2) (cortico-cortical *horizontal* activation).

A stronger and longer-lasting onset activation to FM than to PT is probably due to the spatiotemporal summation of excitatory postsynaptic potentials of successive inputs by FM stimulation because the $GABA_A$ mediated inhibition is not effective before approximately 10 ms after the excitatory onset of the PT response (Horikawa et al., 1996; Sugimoto et al., 2002). In addition, electro-physiological studies have shown that PT presentation induces suppressive effects broadly around the area of spike generation thereby creating stronger response sensitivity to the earlier parts of FM (Heil et al., 1992a; Zhang et al., 2003). This is quite comparable to the present result in which inhibitory effects were observed in large areas slightly after the onset excitation spread for PT (Figs. 19.2, 19.3). Indeed, considering the broad onset spread of subthreshold depolari-zation, we can assume that inhibitory effects appear in each area proportionally to the strength of onset excitation, rather than as flanking inhibitory sidebands outside the excitatory frequency area (cf. Wehr & Zador, 2003).

However, if inhibitory effects induced by the onset excitation for FM were as strong as those observed during PT presentation, few neurons might show

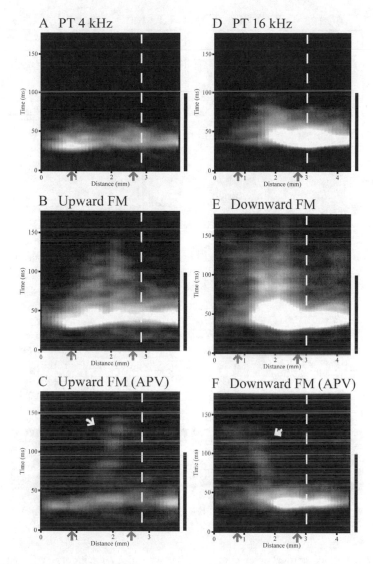

Fig. 19.4. Effects of an NMDA antagonist (APV) on upward and downward FM responses shown in 2 animals. The location-time images per animal (one column) have been obtained along the same line parallel to the tonotopic axis for all conditions. Scaling is the same as that in Figure 19.2. Dashed lines indicate the border between AI and DC. Vertical bars indicate the position of sound stimuli. Gray arrows at X-axis indicate the position of the maximal response to 4 and 16-kHz PTs, respectively. White arrows indicate FM responses restricted spatially and appearing as more distinct patches after the application of APV. It can be also seen that the amplitude of the onset response of FM was reduced but its spatial extent across the tonotopic gradients was not much affected by APV.

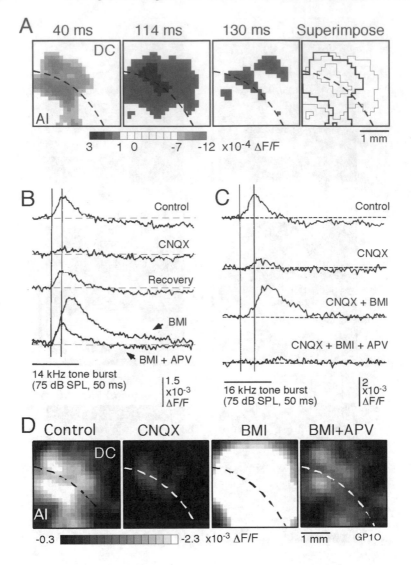

Fig. 19.5. Cortico-cortical interactions of PT revealed by excitatory- and inhibitory-receptor blockers. **(A)** Excitatory (40 ms) and inhibitory areas (114 and 130 ms) in AI and DC to a 14-kHz tone burst (50-ms duration, 75 dB SPL) are shown after the onset of the stimulus. The area over 60% maximum and under 60% minimum was picked up. Superimpose: The contours of excitatory response at 40 ms (thick lines) and the inhibitory response at 114 ms (thin lines) were superimposed. **(B)** The effect of application of CNQX, BMI and APV to the auditory cortex on the response to a 14-kHz PT. CNQX suppressed the early excitatory response (B: CNQX). The response recovered 1 h after washing out CNQX (B: Recovery). BMI enhanced the late response (B: BMI) and concomitant application of BMI and APV suppressed this enhanced response but not the early response (B: BMI+APV). **(C)** A different order of antagonist application.

CNQX suppressed the early response (C: CNQX). Concomitant application of CNQX and BMI enhanced the late response (C: CNQX+BMI) and further application of APV suppressed this response (C: CNQX+BMI+APV). Vertical lines indicate the onset and peak of the control response. **(D)** Response maps to a 14-kHz PT are shown after application of CNQX, BMI and BMI+APV to the auditory cortex. The responses 40 ms after the onset of the stimulus are shown. The data are the same as those shown in B. CNQX suppressed the response (D: CNQX). BMI enhance the responses in the wide areas of AI and DC (D: BMI). Concomitant application of BMI and APV suppressed this enhanced response (D: BMI+APV).

spike generation within their frequency response areas. In fact, this is not the case in electrophysiological studies where spikes were generated when (sometimes as soon as) the effective frequency of FM was within the excitatory frequency area of a given neuron (Heil et al., 1992b; Schulze et al., 1997). Moreover, the present study showed that inhibitory effects were reduced and cortico-cortical horizontal (and/or vertical) activation was induced in large areas during FM presentation (Figs. 19.4B, 19.4E, compare to Figs. 19.4C, 19.4F). This indicates that depolarization by cortico-cortical horizontal (and/or vertical) activation for FM may contribute to an increase in sensitivity to the successive inputs by the instantaneous frequency of FM.

The patchy excitation in FM responses shown in this study probably reflects the columnar structure in the auditory cortex shown in previous morphological studies (Ojima et al., 1991; Wallace et al., 1991). Such patchy excitation has also been observed in response to the second tone of asynchronous two-tone stimuli with the onset delay of 15–20 ms (Sugimoto et al., 2002) and is therefore thought to be a common feature in response to sequential cortical inputs.

CORTICO-CORTICAL INTERACTIONS OF PURE TONES REVEALED BY EXCITATORY- AND INHIBITORY-RECEPTOR BLOCKERS

The spatiotemporal pattern of the response to FM in AI appears to be different from that to PT as described above. However, they can be explained by the same synaptic mechanisms of the neural circuitry in AI, which were revealed by the studies on the effects of excitatory- and inhibitory-receptor blockers on the response to PT (Horikawa et al., 1996).

In response to PT, the onset excitation appeared in a band-like structure in AI and DC (40 ms in Fig. 19.5A), followed by inhibition appearing over the excitatory band (114 ms and superimpose in Fig. 19.5A). In some cases inhibitory effects appeared also in a band-like structure (130 ms in Fig. 19.5A). The onset excitation is proven to be mediated mostly by thalamo-cortical inputs via non-NMDA receptors as shown by nearly complete loss of activity after the application of CNQX, a non-NMDA receptor blocker onto the cortex (CNQX in Figs. 19.5B, 19.5C, and 19.5D). The inhibition following the onset excitation is mediated by $GABA_A$ receptors, as demonstrated by the application of BMI, a

GABA$_A$ receptor blocker onto the cortex (BMI in Figs. 19.5B, 19.5D). The enhancement of the excitation by BMI occurred widely in AI and DC (BMI in Fig. 19.5D). This enhanced excitation is mediated by cortico-cortical inputs via NMDA-receptors, because the application of BMI concomitant with APV onto the cortex suppressed this enhanced response (BMI+APV in Figs. 19.5B, 19.5D) while concomitant application of CNQX and BMI did not suppress the late response (CNQX+BMI in Fig. 19.5C). Moreover, additional application of APV diminished almost all excitation (CNQX+BMI+APV in Fig. 19.5C).

Thus, cortico-cortical horizontal connections across the frequency bands in layers II-III of the core fields are mostly mediated by NMDA receptors and suppressed by GABA$_A$ receptors under normal conditions. This GABA$_A$ inhibition prevents horizontal spread of the excitation beyond stimulus frequency band and is called "horizontal inhibition." Without GABA$_A$ inhibition a local excitation in AI spreads throughout the field and even across the whole auditory cortex as shown by 2-deoxyglucose labeling (Richter et al., 1999).

A MODEL OF THE LAYER II-III NEURAL CIRCUITRY IN AI AND A POSSIBLE EXPLANATION OF THE PT AND THE FM RESPONSES

A simplified scheme of the layer II-III neural circuitry of the auditory cortex, based on our results (present study and Horikawa et al., 1996) and on previous physiological and anatomical data (Huntley et al., 1994; Mitani et al., 1985; Ojima et al., 1991; Prieto et al., 1994a, 1994b; Richter et al., 1999), is shown in Figure 19.6. In this scheme, the isofrequency bands are considered to consist of numbers of columns. The previous physiological and anatomical data showed that pyramidal neurons (open triangles) in layer II/III receive excitatory inputs from layer IV and/or the MGB and inhibitory inputs from surrounding interneurons (filled circles) in the layer. Our optical recording results suggest that these pyramidal neurons receive both non-NMDA and NMDA receptor-mediated excitatory inputs from layer IV and/or the MGB. The NMDA receptor-mediated excitation is functionally counteracted by GABA-ergic inhibition from surrounding interneurons. Our results also showed that the layer II/III pyramidal neurons receive GABAergic inhibition and NMDA receptor-mediated excitation from areas wider than an isofrequency column.

This circuitry is based on the results of PT but it also explains the results of FM. The onset excitation to FM spreading widely over the cortex is mediated by non-NMDA receptors and initiates inhibition. Inhibitory effects lead to a spatial focusing of the responses to the instantaneous frequency of FM. The APV application narrows the spatial extent of the late activation for FM. This is explained by the suppression of NMDA receptor-mediated cortico-cortical activation within the layers. This activation is thought to increase excitatory FM responses across the frequency bands, competing with inhibitory effects.

However, the above explanations may lead to an over-simplification of the nature of spatiotemporal patterns of PT and FM responses in the AI. The neural

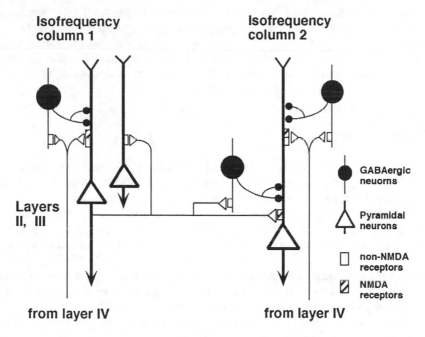

Fig. 19.6. Neural circuitry, based on our results and those of previous physiological and anatomical data. Pyramidal neurons (unfilled triangles) in layer III receive non-NMDA and NMDA receptor-mediated excitatory inputs from layer IV and/or the MGB and those in layer II receive inputs from layer III. The pyramidal neurons in layers II-III receive NMDA-receptor-mediated intracortical connections across the isofrequency columns, which are functionally quiescent as a result of GABAergic inhibition by surrounding interneurons (filled circles). When GABAergic inhibition is removed, the excitation spreads beyond the isofrequency columns. (From Fig. 7 of Horikawa et al., 1996.)

circuitry in the layers II-III is more complicated than that explained above. Along the tonotopic axis, neurons tuned to different characteristic frequencies are arranged systematically. These neurons have a soma of 20–30 μm diameter and 300–500 μm wide dendritic arborizations, and thus the dendritic arborizations of each neurons along the tonotopic axis are largely overlapping. Therefore, the wide activity to PT observed by optical recording is certainly not only due to the horizontal cortico-cortical connections but also to the dendritic arborization of each neuron and consequently to the activity of neurons with deviating characteristic frequencies (CFs) responding to the supra-threshold stimuli (20–30 dB above the threshold). For supra-threshold FM stimuli, a neuron with a given CF will respond not only when the instantaneous frequency of the FM reaches to the CF but also before and after reaching to the CF. Therefore, the optically determined response to FM should be considered as the temporally and spatially integrated sliding response of a neuron population activated by the vertical inputs (from thalamo-cortical projections and cortico-cortical connections from the layer IV to the layers II-III) of previous, instantaneous and subsequent FM frequencies and by horizontal inputs (by cortico-cortical connections within the layers) from the adjacent frequency bands activated previously and subsequently. The horizontal inhibition prevents the horizontal spread of activity after the onset response and spatially focuses the active area of the late response in the AI.

CONCLUSIONS

Our optical recording studies using excitatory and inhibitory receptor blockers have shown that the response patterns to PT and FM observed in the layers II-III of the core fields can be explained by the same neural mechanisms.

The onset response to PT is induced by non-NMDA-receptor mediated (thalamo-cortical) inputs and the following inhibition is mediated by $GABA_A$-receptors which also suppresses horizontal spread of NMDA-receptor-mediated (cortico-cortical) excitatory responses. The onset response to FM is induced also by non-NMDA-receptor-mediated (thalamo-cortical) inputs. The late activation for FM is induced by both non-NMDA-receptor-mediated thalamo-cortical and NMDA-receptor-mediated cortico-cortical inputs. This study implied that the late activation was reduced by GABAergic inhibition and thus formed spatially-focused responses (Horikawa et al., 1998).

The non-NMDA-receptor mediated onset process may play a role to detect initiation of sounds and to induce inhibition in wide areas of AI in order to spatially focus later activations. The non-NMDA receptor-mediated secondary process may play a role for processing the instantaneous frequency of FM and the NMDA receptor-mediated (cortico-cortical) secondary process would play a role to send information to other frequency columns and to integrate frequency information across the isofrequency bands. Thus, it is speculated that the non-NMDA receptor-mediated within-frequency and the NMDA receptor-mediated across-frequency processes in the core fields work together to produce specific spatio-temporal response patterns to be sent to the belt areas, which might be specialized for more complex auditory information.

ACKNOWLEDGMENTS

The work was supported by Grants-in-Aids for Scientific Research (13035019, 13480096, and 15300057) and the 21st Century COE Program "Intelligent Human Sensing" from the Ministry of Education, Science, Sports and Culture, Japan.

REFERENCES

Heil, P., Langner, G., & Scheich, H. (1992a). Processing of frequency-modulated stimuli in the chick auditory cortex analogue: evidence for topographic representations and possible mechanisms of rate and directional sensitivity. The Journal of Comparative Physiology A, 171, 583–600.

Heil, P., Rajan, R., & Irvine, D.R.F. (1992b). Sensitivity of neurons in cat primary auditory cortex to tones and frequency modulated stimuli. I. Effects of variation of stimulus parameters. Hearing Research, 63, 108–134.

Hellweg, F.C., Koch, R., & Vollrath, M. (1977). Representation of the cochlea in the neocortex of guinea pigs. Experimental Brain Reasearch, 29, 467–474.

Hess, A., & Scheich, H. (1996). Optical and FDG mapping of frequency-specific activity in auditory cortex. Neuroreport, 7, 2643–2647.

Horikawa, J., Hess, A., Nasu, M., Hosokawa, Y., Scheich, H., & Taniguchi, I. (2001). Optical imaging of neural activity in multiple auditory cortical fields of guinea pigs. Neuroreport 12, 3335–3339.

Horikawa, J., Hosokawa, Y., Kubota, M., Nasu, M., & Taniguchi, I. (1996). Optical imaging of spatiotemporal patterns of glutamatergic excitation and GABAergic inhibition in the guinea-pig auditory cortex in vivo. Journal of Physiology (London), 497, 629–638.

Horikawa, J., Nasu, M., & Taniguchi, I. (1998). Optical recording of responses to frequency-modulated sounds in the auditory cortex. Neuroreport, 9, 799–802.

Hosokawa, Y., Sugimoto, S., Kubota, M., Taniguchi, I., & Horikawa, J. (2004). Optical imaging of binaural interaction in multiple fields of the guinea pig auditory cortex. Neuroreport 15 (in press).

Huntley, G.W., Vickers, J.C., & Morrison, J.H. (1994). Cellular and synaptic localization of NMDA and non-NMDA receptor subunits in neocortex: organizational features related to cortical circuitry, function and disease. Trends in Neuroscience, 17, 536–543.

Kaas, J.H., & Hackett, T.A. (2000). Subdivisions of auditory cortex and processing streams in primates. Proceedings of the National Academy of Sciences USA, 97, 11793–11799.

Mitani, A., Shimokouchi, M., Itoh, K., Nomura, S., Kudo, M., & Mizuno, N. (1985). Morphology and laminar organization of electrophysiologically identified neurons in the primary auditory cortex in the cat. The Journal of Comparative Neurology, 235, 430–447.

Ojima, H., Honda, C.N., & Jones, E.G. (1991). Patterns of axon collateralization of identified supragranular pyramidal neurons in the cat auditory cortex. Cerebral Cortex, 1, 80–94.

Prieto, J.J., Peterson, B.A., & Winer, J.A. (1994a). Morphology and spatial distribution of GABAergic neurons in cat primary auditory cortex (AI). The Journal of Comparative Neurology, 344, 349–382.

Prieto, J.J., Peterson, B.A., & Winer, J.A. (1994b). Laminar distribution and neuronal targets of GABAergic axon terminals in cat primary auditory cortex (AI). The Journal of Comparative Neurology, 344, 383–402.

Rauschecker, J.P. (2002). Cortical processing of complex sounds. Currrent Opinon in Neurobiology, 8, 516–521.

Rauschecker, J.P., & Tian, B. (2000). Mechanisms and streams for processing of "what" and "where" in auditory cortex, Proceeding of the National Academy of Sciences USA, 97, 11800–11806.

Redies, H., Sieben, U., & Creutzfeldt, O.D. (1989). Functional subdivisions in the auditory cortex of the guinea pig. The Journal of Comparative Neurology, 282, 473–488.

Richter, K., Hess, A., & Scheich, H. (1999). Functional mapping of transsynaptic effects of local manipulation of inhibition in gerbil auditory cortex. Brain Research, 831, 184–199.

Sally, S.L., & Kelly, J.B. (1988). Organization of auditory cortex in the albino rat: sound frequency. Journal of Neurophysiology, 59, 1627–1638.

Schulze, H, Ohl, F.W., Heil, P., & Scheich, H. (1997). Field-specific responses in the auditory cortex of the unanaesthetized Mongolian gerbil to tones and slow frequency modulations. Journal of Comparative Physiology A, 181, 573–589.

Sugimoto, S., Hosokawa, Y., Horikawa, J., Nasu, M., & Taniguchi, I. (2002). Spatial focusing of neuronal responses induced by asynchronous two-tone stimuli in the guinea pig auditory cortex. Cerebral Cortex, 12, 506–514.

Tanaka, H., Komatsuzaki, A., & Taniguchi, I. (1994). Spatial distribution of response latency in the anterior field of the auditory cortex of the guinea pig (in Japanese). Audiology Japan, 37, 222–228.

Taniguchi, I., Horikawa, J., Moriyama, T., & Nasu, M. (1992). Spatio-temporal pattern of frequency representation in the auditory cortex of guinea pigs. Neuroscience Letters, 146, 37–40.

Thomas, H., Tillein, J., Heil, P., & Scheich, H. (1993). Functional organization of auditory cortex in the Mongolian gerbil (Meriones unguiculatus). I. Electrophysiological mapping of frequency representation and distinction of fields. European Journal of Neurosciene, 5, 992–897.

Tian, B., Reser, D., Durham, A., Kustov, A., & Rauschecker, J.P. (2001). Functional specialization in rhesus monkey auditory cortex. Science, 292, 290–293.

Wallace, M.N., Kitzes, L.M., & Jones, E.G. (1991). Intrinsic inter- and intralaminar connections and their relationship to the tonotopic map in cat primary auditory cortex. Experimental Brain Research, 86, 527–544.

Wallace, M.N., Rutkowski, R.G., & Palmer, A.R. (1999). A ventrorostral belt is adjacent to the guinea pig primary auditory cortex. Neuroreport, 10, 2095–2099.

Wallace, M.N., Rutkowski, R.G., & Palmer, A.R. (2000). Identification and localization of auditory areas in guinea pig cortex. Experimental Brain Research, 132, 445–456.

Wehr, M., & Zador, A.M. (2003). Balanced inhibition underlies tuning and sharpens spike timing in auditory cortex. Nature, 426, 442–446.

Zhang, L.I., Tan, A.Y., Schreiner, C.E., & Merzenich, M. M. (2003). Topography and synaptic shaping of direction selectivity in primary auditory cortex. Nature, 424, 201–205.

20. LEVELS OF AUDITORY PROCESSING: THE SUBCORTICAL AUDITORY SYSTEM, PRIMARY AUDITORY CORTEX, AND THE HARD PROBLEMS OF AUDITORY PERCEPTION

Israel Nelken, Liora Las, Nachum Ulanovsky, Dina Farkas

INTRODUCTION

One of the major research programs in auditory neuroscience is the attempt to explain psychophysical performance in terms of neuronal processing (see review in Delgutte, 1996). Some of the basic phenomena in hearing can be roughly explained using the known anatomy and physiology of the auditory periphery and early central stations. For instance, the critical bands of psychoacoustics are related to the narrow tuning of auditory nerve fibers (Pickles, 1975) or of neurons in the inferior colliculus (Ehret & Merzenich, 1988). Similarly, the representation of interaural time differences (ITD) and binaural unmasking phenomena may be related to the calculation of cross-correlation between the peripheral representations of sounds in the two ears (Colburn, 1996), neurally implemented in the superior olive (Brand et al., 2002; Grothe, 2003; Yin & Chan, 1990) and clearly present at the level of the inferior colliculus (IC; Fitzpatrick et al., 2002; Shackleton et al., 2003).

However, some of the most important auditory phenomena are still resistant to this program. For example, we do not have a good auditory theory for the perception of speech sounds, although the representation of vowels and consonants in the auditory nerve and the cochlear nucleus has been extensively studied (Delgutte, 1996; Eggermont, 2001). Similarly, regularities in the inter-spike intervals of auditory nerve fibers probably underlie pitch perception

(Cariani & Delgutte, 1996a, 1996b), and there is strong evidence for the cortical representation of such regularity in humans (Gutschalk et al., 2002; Krumbholz et al., 2003; Langner et al., 1997). Nevertheless, correlates of pitch have not been convincingly described at the single neuron level in higher auditory stations. Even spatial perception, which is based on binaural cues that are known to be extracted early in the central auditory system (Colburn, 1996), has still a large number of mysteries, such as the representation of multiple concurrent sound sources.

In this chapter, some of the features of these 'hard questions' of auditory perception will be reviewed. We will argue that speech perception, pitch perception and space perception share a number of properties that suggest a late, presumably cortical, involvement. Finally, the possible role of primary auditory cortex in these processing tasks will be evaluated and a model for hierarchical processing in the auditory system will be proposed.

SOME HARD PROBLEMS OF AUDITORY PERCEPTION: SPEECH, PITCH, AND SPACE

Studies of the neural coding of speech signals have a long and distinguished past (Eggermont, 2001). However, these studies did not give rise to an even approximately complete model for the representation of speech in the auditory system. For example, except for a single case (the voice onset time, Eggermont, 1995; Eggermont & Ponton, 2002; Steinschneider et al., 1994, 1999, 2003), the categorical perception of speech sounds does not have neural correlates, perhaps due to the fact that most neuronal response properties vary continuously with changes of physical parameters.

In some respects, an account for the representation of speech sounds in neural activity should have been easy. Consider an experimental setting in which the speech signal is the only relevant sensory input. In order to avoid the influence of semantic context, the chosen speech sound is a simple consonant-vowel-consonant (CVC) non-sense syllable. Finally, assume that in order to correctly identify the CVC syllable, it is necessary to correctly identify each of the three component phonemes (Allen, 1996). We are therefore looking for a brain signal that will be unambiguously related to each of the phonemes. There is a finite number of vowels and consonants in each language (30–200; Moore, 2003), and these phonemes differ from each other on a large number of features that have clear acoustic correlates. Thus, a small set of neurons, sensitive to the acoustic correlates of phonemes, should be able to perform the task.

This is, of course, a naïve view of speech perception given the complexity in the structure of real speech sounds. Nevertheless, most electrophysiological studies of speech coding are performed under even more relaxed assumptions. Such studies identified features that could be used by a (admittedly, half mythical) 'next layer' that should be activated according to the phonemic identity of the speech sounds (Chi et al., 1999; Ru et al., 2003; Versnel &

Shamma, 1998). However, a brain signal that actually finishes the job, by representing in an invariant way a single phoneme, has not been described.

Similar problems are associated with pitch perception. As a basic task, we can consider the identical pitch values that are perceived when listening to a 200 Hz pure sine wave, and to iterated ripple noise (IRN) generated with a delay of 5 ms and high-pass filtered at 1000 Hz. The two stimuli are very different. The sine wave is perfectly periodic and is narrowband (and if low in amplitude presumably excites only a restricted set of auditory nerve fibers around its frequency). On the other hand, the IRN stimulus is aperiodic and wideband, presumably exciting at least all auditory nerve fibers with best frequencies of 1000 Hz and above. Nevertheless, the two stimuli generate an excess of interspike intervals of 5 ms in auditory nerve fibers (Cariani & Delgutte, 1996a) and in some neurons of the cochlear nucleus (Winter et al., 2001), thus presumably signaling the same pitch. However, this excess of interspike intervals occurs, for each sound, in different neuronal populations. Therefore, it has to be decoded by another (again, half mythical) 'next layer'. Beyond the auditory nerve and the cochlear nucleus, there are few suggestions for neural correlates of pitch, and none of them is as yet fully convincing (but see Fishman et al., 2000; Schulze & Langner, 1997; Schulze et al., 2002). One of the most important problems in finding the putative pitch detectors is the fact that they should be wideband. They should generalize the temporal regularity associated with pitch stimuli across frequency, or look for a specific spectral template across frequency, but in either case they need to process information across multiple peripheral channels (Moore, 2003, p. 231).

The perception of space also shares some of these difficulties. As the basic task, consider the lateralization of a 100-Hz tone presented with an interaural time difference of 0.5 ms, left ear leading, and a sinusoidally amplitude modulated 4-kHz tone, modulated at 100 Hz, with envelope interaural difference of 0.5 ms, left ear leading. The two sounds evoke activity in very different peripheral channels, but are nevertheless lateralized to the same side. As in the case of pitch, different neuronal populations code for these sounds in the early auditory system. Thus, the crucial cue (in this case, ITD) that is extracted and represented in the activity of narrowband neurons (Brand et al., 2002; Yin et al., 1990) must be abstracted across frequency. Whereas within-channel extraction of binaural disparities is reasonably well understood both psychoacoustically and electrophysiologically, the integration of these measurements across frequency is not yet convincingly understood in mammals (although wideband integration of ITD cues has been explicitly demonstrated in avians, as shown in the barn owl by Wagner et al., 1987).

What are the features that make it so hard to provide a neurobiological explanation for our abilities to perform these three tasks? We would like to suggest three reasons here: (1) the wideband character of speech, pitch and space perception; (2) the generalizing nature of the resulting percepts; and (2) the effects of temporal context.

(1) A basic difficulty in accounting for speech perception from the point of view of an auditory physiologist is the fact that the identity of even a simple steady-state vowel sound depends on information in a wide frequency band, consisting of many octaves. For example, telephone lines transmit sound energy between about 500 Hz and 4000 Hz – a 3-octave band. In contrast, the basic auditory perceptual channel, the critical band, has a width of about 1/6 octave in humans. Critical bands are often considered to be related to the bandwidth of auditory neurons in the auditory nerve (Pickles, 1975) or in the inferior colliculus (Ehret & Merzenich, 1988). If speech is processed through the same channels, the output of a single neuron in the core, mostly narrowband pathway of the auditory system cannot be used for speech perception on its own. The perceptual correlate of this statement is the fact that decomposing a speech sound into its critical band components results in many signals, none of which alone can be robustly understood as speech. Thus, in some sense, speech is a non-linear construct of multiple non-speech components.

Pitch and space are wideband in the same sense. For example, the pitch of a sound composed of the sum of multiple resolved harmonics cannot be extracted, in principle, from the activity in any single auditory channel, at least if the sound is not too loud. Similarly, lateralization depends on integration across frequency. For example, a sound presented with an interaural time delay is usually lateralized to the side of the leading ear. However, the lateralized position of a narrow noise band centered at 500 Hz, with the left ear leading by 1.5 ms, is to the right and not to the left. Increasing the bandwidth of such noise results in the lateralized position of the image moving to the left (Trahiotis & Stern, 1989).

(2) Another obvious problem in accounting for speech, pitch and space perception is the fact that sounds with very different physical structures can give rise to the same percept. In the context of speech, the phoneme detectors must generalize across many physical realizations of the same speech sound. For example, a given vowel can be produced by an adult or a child, by an adult male or female, voiced or whispered, or it can be synthesized by low-quality speech synthesis software. These realizations of the same phoneme 'sound' different – we are certainly able to tell them apart, but they share the same phonemic label. Neurons in the auditory system are certainly sensitive to these variable, 'nuisance' parameters, and in the early auditory stations the representation of the variable parameters may be stronger than that of the phonemic label. Thus, we have in fact a pretty good description of why different realizations of the same phoneme sound different but only rough ideas about the neural correlates of the invariant features of the same sounds.

Precisely the same problems are readily apparent in the study of pitch and space coding in the auditory system. The differences between responses evoked in the auditory nerve by a 200-Hz pure tone and by the high-pass IRN with 5-ms delay are probably much larger than the similarities. Similarly, the 100-Hz tone and the 4-kHz sinusoidally amplitude-modulated tone discussed above are both lateralized to the same side, but are represented in the early auditory system very differently. This example may be somewhat trivial, in that we know that both will excite presumably the 0.5 ms, left-leading coding neurons in their respective frequency band, and it is only necessary to add up all of these neurons in order to generate a lateralization neuron (as presumably done in the barn owl, Wagner et al., 1987). However, there are additional examples in which the physical invariance is much less trivial. For example, some wideband dichotic sounds may be lateralized to the middle of the head (e.g., clicks with opposing ITD and ILD cues, Moore, 2003, p. 245). There are probable differences in the representation of diotic clicks and such compensated dichotic clicks in the early binaural processing stations, which may underlie the ability of listeners to discriminate between them. However, eventually these sounds are perceived at the same location, requiring a non-trivial generalization.

(3) However, the most cited reason for the hard nature of speech perception is co-articulation (Holt & Kluender, 2000). Speech sounds belonging to the same phonemic category may differ because of their temporal context. Inversely, the same physical sound can receive two different phonemic labels, according to the context in which it is presented. Thus, the phonemic identity of a sound depends on a temporal context that may last as long as a few hundreds of milliseconds. For the electrophysiologist, this means that the mythical phoneme detectors must be influenced not only by the current sound input, but also by past, and possibly also future, context.

Pitch perception is also context-dependent. This can be seen, for example, from the possibility of changing the pitch of a harmonic complex with one mistuned partial by capturing the mistuned partial into a different auditory stream (Ciocca & Darwin, 1993; Darwin et al., 1995).

Finally, spatial perception also shows contextual effects. For example, when presenting two pairs of clicks with a very short time interval between them, each pair with a different interaural time difference, the perception of the second one is suppressed (the precedence effect, Litovsky et al., 1999). When the second burst is loud enough, it is nevertheless heard, and the minimal level above which the second click is perceived is called the echo threshold. This threshold is not fixed, and can be manipulated: a long series of click pairs, in which the lagging pair would come from the left, would increase the echo threshold, whereas if the position of the lagging click pair is suddenly shifted, it will be perceived at lower levels (Freyman et al., 1991).

ARE SPEECH, PITCH, AND SPACE EARLY OR LATE IN THE AUDITORY SYSTEM?

The three properties described above that are common to speech, pitch, and space perception have analogs in other senses. In vision, face recognition shares many of the properties of speech recognition: It is based on information possibly scattered over large parts of the visual field, it is highly robust to variable 'nuisance parameters' such as illumination level and direction or angle of rotation, and it shows context sensitivity: stimuli that are not perceived as faces under some conditions, can be perceived as faces if appropriately primed (Bentin & Golland, 2002; Sagiv & Bentin, 2001). These properties caused vision researchers to assume that face perception occurs in higher visual areas, beyond primary visual cortex. In fact, face sensitive neurons have been described in the anterior infero-temporal cortex (Desimone et al., 1984; Rolls, 1992), relatively high in the visual processing hierarchy. Moreover, evoked potential components related to face recognition have been described at a latency of about 170 ms, more than 100 ms after the first arrival of the visual information to the visual cortex.

In contrast, when discussing the auditory system there is a tendency to assign the extraction of phonemic identity, pitch and spatial location to early processing stages. For example, most studies of speech and pitch processing have been performed in the auditory nerve, with a small number in the cochlear nucleus (Cariani & Delgutte, 1996a, 1996b; Sachs et al., 1988; Wang & Sachs, 1993; Winter & Palmer, 1990; Winter et al., 2001), see Eggermont (2001) for review. Similarly, it is often stated explicitly or implicitly that the extraction of space is done in the superior olive, where binaural disparities are processed within narrow frequency channels. As discussed above, such a statement downplays the more difficult issues of spatial perception.

Part of this difference in emphasis seems to be related to the difference between correlates of perceptual phenomena on the one hand, and the resulting percepts on the other hand. Thus, pitch is related to periodicity, and periodicity is relatively strongly represented in the auditory nerve and the cochlear nucleus (Cariani & Delgutte, 1996a; Winter et al., 2001). However, pitch is much more than periodicity: binaural pitch does not require periodicity in any peripheral channel (Culling et al., 1998) and pitch is influenced by temporal context (Ciocca & Darwin, 1993; Darwin et al., 1995). In fact, information that is not present in the activity of auditory nerve fibers cannot be created de novo in higher auditory centers, and therefore it is expected that correlates of all perceptual phenomena should be present already in the auditory nerve (bilaterally, if binaural phenomena are to be accounted for). However, these acoustic cues, as represented in the early auditory system, are only partially correlated with the resulting percepts.

This discrepancy between low-level correlates and high-level percepts is emphasized when sounds come in mixtures. Double-vowel recognition studies, for example, suggest that common ITD is only a weak cue for grouping formants (Akeroyd & Summerfield, 2000; Culling & Summerfield, 1995). These studies can be interpreted as indicating that grouping based on other cues is performed first, and only then the lateralization is assigned to the combined object. For example, the cues that are used for grouping in double-vowel experiments certainly include harmonic relationships between partials (de Cheveigne et al., 1995; Summerfield & Assmann, 1991), suggesting that these are used before the spatial cues are integrated. Studies of simultaneous segregation and grouping are rare in the literature, but these are precisely the kind of studies that can constrain the order and levels at which the various parameters are processed.

Physiologically, the properties of most neurons below the level of the IC are mostly inconsistent with the requirements of wideband processing, generalization capabilities and long (more than about 100 ms) context dependence. These neurons are mostly narrowband, they are extremely sensitive to the precise physical structure of the sounds, and they don't show contextual effects on time scales that are longer than a few tens of ms (e.g., Spitzer & Semple, 1998). This statement, like any other general statement about the physiology of the auditory system, needs to be qualified. Even at the level of the cochlear nucleus, relatively wideband integration is performed (Jiang et al., 1996; Winter & Palmer, 1995). In fact, possible correlates of pitch have been described in some subclasses of neurons of the cochlear nucleus (Winter et al., 2001). However, these neurons do not explicitly code pitch – they form a middle layer, in which the pitch correlate (in this case, an excess of interspike intervals of the appropriate value) is enhanced and becomes more independent of variations in the physical structure of the sound. Other neurons have to read these interspike intervals and extract pitch.

In the IC, the situation starts to change. Context dependence first appears (Spitzer & Semple, 1993), but the neurons are still highly sensitive to the physical structure of sounds, although possibly in more complex ways than in the periphery. For example, in the IC, a small class of neurons is highly selective to rare patterns in random sets of sounds used to compute spectro-temporal receptive fields (Escabi & Schreiner, 2002). Similarly, duration sensitivity is arguably first expressed in its full form above the brainstem, and may depend on processing mechanisms in the nuclei of the lateral lemniscus and in the IC (Casseday & Covey, 1996; Covey & Casseday, 1999; Faure et al., 2003). Spatially organized sensitivity to modulation rate also appears in the IC (Schreiner & Langner, 1997). These 'feature detectors' may be to some extent segregated to different parts of the IC, as has been shown for modulation rate and for other features (Ehret et al., 2003). Binaural sensitivity is also widely found in the IC, and neuronal best ITD just-noticeable differences in the IC, extracted by ideal observer analysis, are comparable to behavioral performance (Shackleton et al., 2003). Thus, in parallel to its anatomical location as an obligatory station of the auditory pathway, it seems that the IC also represents all of the features extracted in the brainstem and possibly additional features extracted from sounds in the lateral lemniscus and arguably in the IC itself.

Thus, up to the level of the IC, speech, pitch and space cannot be fully 'solved', although the low-level correlates of these percepts are extracted and enhanced. We hypothesize that the same is true in the IC itself. In fact, phonemic encoding has never been attributed to the IC. Similarly, true sensitivity to space in mammals is thought to be first synthesized in the projection from the IC to the deep layers of the superior colliculus (as shown by King et al., 1998, in the ferret). The situation for pitch is more complicated – there are some good reasons to believe that at least some of the generalization inherent in the perception of pitch is already performed at the level of the IC (Griffiths et al., 2001). However, in the central nucleus of the IC, processing is still overwhelmingly narrowband (Casseday et al., 2002), and at the single neuron level there are no good candidates for 'pitch detectors'.

The answer to the question at the beginning of this section therefore seems to be that speech, pitch and space are both early and late – early in the sense that relevant low-level features are extracted in the brainstem and midbrain, but late in the sense that no auditory station, up to and presumably including the IC, has the right properties for fully representing any of these percepts.

AUDITORY PROCESSING ABOVE THE IC

The situation in medial geniculate body (MGB), the thalamic station of the auditory pathway, and in primary auditory cortex (A1), is in many respects very different. Neurons in MGB and A1 have a number of features that differentiate them from neurons in auditory stations up to and including the IC. Most standard characterizations of auditory neurons show degradation when going from IC to A1. Tuning curves tend to be wider, temporal response properties become more sluggish, and responses are much more labile (Malone et al., 2002; Miller et al., 2002; Ulanovsky et al., 2003). Thus, to paraphrase Douglas Adams (Adams, 2002), in terms of standard auditory characterizations, auditory cortex is almost, but not quite, as interesting as the auditory nerve.

Auditory cortex has however a number of redeeming features that makes it a natural place for dealing with more abstract problems in auditory processing. Neurons in A1 have an exquisite sensitivity to small changes in their auditory input. For example, adding a low-level tone to strong slowly fluctuating noise strongly suppresses envelope locking to the noise, even at extreme signal-to-noise ratios. Although weak effects are seen in the IC at similar signal-to-noise ratios, they are highly amplified at the level of MGB and A1 (Nelken et al., 2003). Conversely, low levels of background noise may dramatically modify the responses of A1 neurons to bird calls consisting of a single, main tonal component (Bar-Yosef et al., 2002). These effects, which are highly idiosyncratic even across neurons with the same best frequency, strongly reduce the informational redundancy between neurons in MGB and A1 relative to the IC (Nelken et al., 2003).

Both the effect of a weak tone on the responses to strong fluctuating noise, and the effects of low-level noise on dominant tonal vocalizations, requires across-frequency integration. They are therefore a prima facie indication of wideband integration. This integration has, however, a peculiar property – it is highly sensitive to weak acoustic components. We hypothesize that these effects are due to a transformation in the representation of sounds: while in the IC sounds are presumably represented by a combination of acoustic features, in MGB and A1 sounds at least start to be represented in terms of auditory objects or of auditory sources (Nelken et al., 2003).

In addition to these effects of simultaneous spectro-temporal interactions, that are present both in MGB and in A1, neurons in A1 show temporal context sensitivity that goes beyond anything described below A1, both in terms of the time scales involved and in terms of the parameter sensitivity. Thus, in blocks consisting of tones of two frequencies that are only 10% apart, a majority of A1 neurons show differentially higher adaptation to the frequency that appears more commonly (Ulanovsky et al., 2003). This effect still persists in some A1 neurons even for tones that are 4% apart, and disappears only when the interstimulus interval is longer than 2 seconds. This hyperacuity of A1 neurons, measured by the differential adaptation profiles, is not present in the MGB at the same parameter ranges (Ulanovsky et al., 2003).

Thus, in contrast to IC, where processing is mostly narrowband, neurons in MGB and A1 show strong across-frequency effects, even when they are narrowband as judged by tonal responses (Bar-Yosef et al., 2002). Furthermore, they show strong context sensitivity under circumstances where such context sensitivity is not found in IC or MGB. As discussed above, these are two of the properties required for solving the hard problems of auditory perception.

One property that A1 neurons seem to lack, at least in the contexts in which we tested them, is invariance to acoustic features. In fact, in our hands, the reverse seems to occur: some small perturbations of sounds, as described above, have inordinately large effects on the responses of MGB and A1 neurons. However, this hypersensitivity is apparent when mixing two signals. Under these circumstances, object-sensitive neurons are in fact expected to show some sort of hypersensitivity, since small changes in the sound can change its perceived source composition.

IMPLICATIONS: THE ROLE OF PRIMARY AUDITORY CORTEX IN AUDITORY PERCEPTION

Neurons that code for speech, pitch, or space should have properties that mirror the properties of the resulting percepts. The activity of such neurons should be affected by sound energy in a sufficiently wide frequency band; these neurons should be sensitive to context; and they should be insensitive to some, possibly large, changes in the physical structure of sounds, while being extremely sensitive to other, possibly small, changes, provided that these changes have to do with the global aspects of sound encoded by these neurons.

Our results suggest therefore that speech, pitch, and space are not encoded as such in the activity of neurons in primary auditory cortex. Rather, primary auditory cortex builds auditory objects, to which later processing can assign pitch, spatial location, or phonemic identity. Primary auditory cortex is therefore at an intermediate stage in the processing hierarchy – whereas it is already sensitive to spectro-temporal context, this sensitivity is related to the representation of auditory objects rather than to the computation of their properties.

The role of primary auditory cortex is therefore pivotal in the auditory system. Whereas lower processing stages (at least up to the IC) seem to encode with high fidelity the physical properties of sounds, activity in primary auditory cortex seems to be related already to the interpretation of the physical structure of sounds, rather than to the physical structure itself. We hypothesize therefore that primary auditory cortex supplies the object representation on which all further auditory processing operates. The extensive anatomical projections from primary auditory cortex to lower processing stations, such as the auditory thalamus and the IC, as well as to higher auditory areas, seem to support its central position both within the bottom-up processing hierarchy, and within a reverse, top-down interpretation hierarchy.

How should we expect speech, pitch, and space to be encoded in A1? We hypothesize that properties related to these percepts will be encoded in a double scheme. On the one hand, rough sensitivity to the appropriate features does exist, as shown in a large number of studies. However, none of these studies used sound mixtures, and studying neuronal responses to mixtures are the crucial experiments for our hypothesis. We therefore hypothesize that low-level correlates of pitch, space, and phonemic identity may strongly influence A1 activity when they can be used for auditory segregation and grouping.

For example, since periodicity, probably the most important low-level correlate of pitch, is a strong grouping cue, it is conceivable that periodicity would affect neuronal responses when it is important for auditory object formation, in spite of the fact that pitch in all its generality and invariance would not be explicitly represented in A1. Similarly, wideband spectro-temporal patterns that are related to phonemic identity, such as formants, formant transitions, and transients related to plosives, may affect the coding of sound components within the frequency response area of a cortical neuron in essential ways. Finally, it is conceivable again that the importance of cortical responses for the coding of auditory space resides not in the coding of space itself, which is usually considered as represented in the superior colliculus (SC), but rather by the relation to auditory objects, to which spatial position can be assigned. Thus, we predict that cortical modulation of SC activity would be maximal when testing responses to sound mixtures.

What happens to the auditory information beyond A1? Given the current information about two streams of anatomical connections starting in the core auditory cortex areas of primates and projecting to the temporal lobe and to the parietal lobe respectively, it has been hypothesized that these two streams represent 'where' and 'what' pathways of the auditory system (Rauschecker & Tian, 2000; Romanski et al., 1999). Some supporting electrophysiological evidence has been accumulated (Tian et al., 2001), although the case is far from closed. If these two processing streams indeed exist, it is appealing to hypothesize that the posterior stream assigns spatial location to the auditory objects generated in A1, while the anterior stream assigns properties such as pitch or phonemic category.

SUMMARY

The model presented here for the auditory system consists of three parts. Low-level acoustic features related to important percepts are extracted early, and are hypothesized to be fully represented at the level of the IC. MGB and A1 deal with the creation of auditory objects, using across-frequency integration and contextual information at multiple time scales (Nelken et al., 2003), at least up to 1–2 seconds. Finally, later processes assign perceptual qualities to these objects, and create the physical invariance that is one of the hallmarks of the hard problems of auditory perception. Many details of this model are unverified, and investigations and discussions related to the interrelationships between A1, the subcortical auditory system, and higher cortical areas will continue for a long time. We believe that explicitly presenting a conceptual model of this kind is useful since it can guide experiments as well as motivate collaborations between psychophysicists, cognitive psychologists and electrophysiologists.

ACKNOWLEDGMENTS

Supported by grants from the Israeli Science Foundation (ISF) and by the Volkswagen-Stiftung.

REFERENCES

Adams, D. (2002). The ultimate hitchhiker's guide to the galaxy. New York: Del Rey.

Akeroyd, M.A., & Summerfield, A.Q. (2000). Integration of monaural and binaural evidence of vowel formants. Journal of the Acoustical Society of America, 107, 3394–3406.

Allen, J.B. (1996). Harvey Fletcher's role in the creation of communication acoustics. Journal of the Acoustical Society of America, 99, 1825–1839.

Bar-Yosef, O., Rotman, Y., & Nelken, I. (2002). Responses of neurons in cat primary auditory cortex to bird chirps: Effects of temporal and spectral context. Journal of Neuroscience, 22, 8619–8632.

Bentin, S., & Golland, Y. (2002). Meaningful processing of meaningless stimuli: the influence of perceptual experience on early visual processing of faces. Cognition, 86, B1–14.

Brand, A., Behrend, O., Marquardt, T., McAlpine, D., & Grothe, B. (2002). Precise inhibition is essential for microsecond interaural time difference coding. Nature, 417, 543–547.

Cariani, P.A., & Delgutte, B. (1996a). Neural correlates of the pitch of complex tones. I. Pitch and pitch salience. Journal of Neurophysiology, 76, 1698–1716.

Cariani, P.A., & Delgutte, B. (1996b). Neural correlates of the pitch of complex tones. II. Pitch shift, pitch ambiguity, phase invariance, pitch circularity, rate pitch, and the dominance region for pitch. Journal of Neurophysiology, 76, 1717–1734.

Casseday, J.H., & Covey, E. (1996). A neuroethological theory of the operation of the inferior colliculus. Brain, Behavior & Evolution, 47, 311–336.

Casseday, J.H., Fremouw, T., & Covey, E. (2002). The Inferior Colliculus: A Hub for the Central Auditory System. In D. Oertel, R.R. Fay & A.N. Popper (Eds.), Integrative functions in the mamalian auditory pathway (pp. 238–318). New York: Springer.

Chi, T., Gao, Y., Guyton, M.C., Ru, P., & Shamma, S. (1999). Spectro-temporal modulation transfer functions and speech intelligibility. Journal of the Acoustical Society of America, 106, 2719–2732.

Ciocca, V., & Darwin, C.J. (1993). Effects of onset asynchrony on pitch perception: adaptation or grouping? Journal of the Acoustical Society of America, 93, 2870–2878.

Colburn, H.S. (1996). Computational Models of Binaural Processing. In H.L. Hawkins, T.A. McMullen, A.N. Popper & R.R. Fay (Eds.), Auditory Computation (pp. 332–400). New York: Springer.

Covey, E., & Casseday, J.H. (1999). Timing in the auditory system of the bat. Annual Reviews of Physiology, 61, 457–476.

Culling, J.F., & Summerfield, A.Q. (1995). Perceptual separation of concurrent speech sounds: Absence of across-frequency grouping by common interaural delay. Journal of the Acoustical Society of America, 98, 785–797.

Culling, J.F., Summerfield, A.Q., & Marshall, D.H. (1998). Dichotic pitches as illusions of binaural unmasking. I. Huggins' pitch and the "binaural edge pitch". Journal of the Acoustical Society of America, 103, 3509–3526.

Darwin, C.J., Hukin, R.W., & al-Khatib, B.Y. (1995). Grouping in pitch perception: evidence for sequential constraints. Journal of the Acoustical Society of America, 98, 880–885.

de Cheveigne, A., McAdams, S., Laroche, J., & Rosenberg, M. (1995). Identification of concurrent harmonic and inharmonic vowels: A test of the theory of harmonic cancellation and enhancement. Journal of the Acoustical Society of America, 97, 3736–3748.

Delgutte, B. (1996). Physiological Models for Basic Auditory Percepts. In H.L. Hawkins, T.A. McMullen, A.N. Popper & R.R. Fay (Eds.), Auditory Computation (pp. 157–220). New York: Springer.

Desimone, R., Albright, T.D., Gross, C.G., & Bruce, C. (1984). Stimulus-selective properties of inferior temporal neurons in the macaque. Journal of Neuroscience, 4, 2051–2062.

Eggermont, J.J. (1995). Representation of a voice onset time continuum in primary auditory cortex of the cat. Journal of the Acoustical Society of America, 98, 911-920.

Eggermont, J.J. (2001). Between sound and perception: reviewing the search for a neural code. Hearing Research, 157, 1–42.

Eggermont, J.J., & Ponton, C.W. (2002). The neurophysiology of auditory perception: from single units to evoked potentials. Audiology & Neuro-Otology, 7, 71–99.

Ehret, G., Egorova, M., Hage, S.R., & Muller, B.A. (2003). Spatial map of frequency tuning-curve shapes in the mouse inferior colliculus. Neuroreport, 14, 1365–1369.

Ehret, G., & Merzenich, M.M. (1988). Complex sound analysis (frequency resolution, filtering and spectral integration) by single units of the inferior colliculus of the cat. Brain Research, 472, 139–163.

Escabi, M.A., & Schreiner, C.E. (2002). Nonlinear spectrotemporal sound analysis by neurons in the auditory midbrain. Journal of Neuroscience, 22, 4114–4131.

Faure, P.A., Fremouw, T., Casseday, J.H., & Covey, E. (2003). Temporal masking reveals properties of sound-evoked inhibition in duration-tuned neurons of the inferior colliculus. Journal of Neuroscience, 23, 3052–3065.

Fishman, Y.I., Reser, D.H., Arezzo, J.C., & Steinschneider, M. (2000). Complex tone processing in primary auditory cortex of the awake monkey. II. Pitch versus critical band representation. Journal of the Acoustical Society of America, 108, 247–262.

Fitzpatrick, D.C., Kuwada, S., & Batra, R. (2002). Transformations in processing interaural time differences between the superior olivary complex and inferior colliculus: beyond the Jeffress model. Hearing Research, 168, 79–89.

Freyman, R.L., Clifton, R.K., & Litovsky, R.Y. (1991). Dynamic processes in the precedence effect. Journal of the Acoustical Society of America, 90, 874–884.

Griffiths, T.D., Uppenkamp, S., Johnsrude, I., Josephs, O., & Patterson, R.D. (2001). Encoding of the temporal regularity of sound in the human brainstem. Nature Neuroscience, 4, 633–637.

Grothe, B. (2003). New roles for synaptic inhibition in sound localization. Nature Review Neuroscience, 4, 540–550.

Gutschalk, A., Patterson, R.D., Rupp, A., Uppenkamp, S., & Scherg, M. (2002). Sustained magnetic fields reveal separate sites for sound level and temporal regularity in human auditory cortex. NeuroImage, 15, 207–216.

Holt, L.L., & Kluender, K.R. (2000). General auditory processes contribute to perceptual accommodation of coarticulation. Phonetica, 57, 170–180.

Jiang, D., Palmer, A.R., & Winter, I.M. (1996). Frequency extent of two-tone facilitation in onset units in the ventral cochlear nucleus. Journal of Neurophysiology, 75, 380–395.

King, A.J., Jiang, Z.D., & Moore, D.R. (1998). Auditory brainstem projections to the ferret superior colliculus: anatomical contribution to the neural coding of sound azimuth. The Journal of Comparative Neurology, 390, 342–365.

Krumbholz, K., Patterson, R.D., Seither-Preisler, A., Lammertmann, C., & Lütkenhöner, B. (2003). Neuromagnetic evidence for a pitch processing center in Heschl's gyrus. Cerebral Cortex, 13, 765–772.

Langner, G., Sams, M., Heil, P., & Schulze, H. (1997). Frequency and periodicity are represented in orthogonal maps in the human auditory cortex: Evidence from magnetoencephalography Journal of Comparative Physiology A, 181, 665–676.

Litovsky, R.Y., Colburn, H.S., Yost, W.A., & Guzman, S.J. (1999). The precedence effect Journal of the Acoustical Society of America, 106, 1633–1654.

Malone, B.J., Scott, B.H., & Semple, M.N. (2002). Context-dependent adaptive coding of interaural phase disparity in the auditory cortex of awake macaques. Journal of Neuroscience, 22, 4625–4638.

Miller, L.M., Escabi, M.A., Read, H.L., & Schreiner, C.E. (2002). Spectrotemporal receptive fields in the lemniscal auditory thalamus and cortex. Journal of Neurophysiology, 87, 516–527.

Moore, B.C. (2003). An introduction to the psychology of hearing, 5th edition. London: Academic Press.

Nelken, I., Ulanovsky, N., Las, L., Bar-Yosef, O., Anderson, M., Chechik, G., Tishby, N., & Young, E.D. (2003). Transformation of stimulus representation in the ascending auditory system. In D. Pressnitzer, A. de Cheveigne, S. McAdams, & L. Collet (Eds.), Auditory signal processing: Physiology, psychoacoustics and models (pp. 358–416). New York: Springer Verlag.

Pickles, J.O. (1975). Normal critical bands in the cat. Acta Otolaryngologica, 80, 245–254.

Rauschecker, J.P., & Tian, B. (2000). Mechanisms and streams for processing of "what" and "where" in auditory cortex. Proceedings of the National Academy of Sciences USA, 97, 11800–11806.

Rolls, E.T. (1992). Neurophysiological mechanisms underlying face processing within and beyond the temporal cortical visual areas. Philosophical Transactions of the Royal Society of London. Series B. Biological Sciences, 335, 11–20.

Romanski, L.M., Tian, B., Fritz, J., Mishkin, M., Goldman-Rakic, P.S., & Rauschecker, J.P. (1999). Dual streams of auditory afferents target multiple domains in the primate prefrontal cortex. Nature Neuroscience, 2, 1131–1136.

Ru, P., Chi, T., & Shamma, S. (2003). The synergy between speech production and perception. Journal of the Acoustical Society of America, 113, 498–515.

Sachs, M.B., Winslow, R.L., & Blackburn, C.C. (1988). Representation of speech in the auditory periphery. In G.M. Edelman, W.E. Gall & W.M. Cowan (Eds.), Auditory Function: Neurobiological Bases of Hearing (pp. 747–774). New York: John Wiley & Sons.

Sagiv, N., & Bentin, S. (2001). Structural encoding of human and schematic faces: Holistic and part-based processes. Journal of Cognitive Neuroscience, 13, 937–951.

Schreiner, C.E., & Langner, G. (1997). Laminar fine structure of frequency organization in auditory midbrain. Nature, 388, 383–386.

Schulze, H., Hess, A., Ohl, F.W., & Scheich, H. (2002). Superposition of horseshoe-like periodicity and linear tonotopic maps in auditory cortex of the Mongolian gerbil. European Journal of Neuroscience, 15, 1077–1084.

Schulze, H., & Langner, G. (1997). Periodicity coding in the primary auditory cortex of the Mongolian gerbil *(Meriones unguiculatus)*: Two different coding strategies for pitch and rhythm? Journal of Comparative Physiology A, 181, 651–663.

Shackleton, T.M., Skottun, B.C., Arnott, R.H., & Palmer, A.R. (2003). Interaural time difference discrimination thresholds for single neurons in the inferior colliculus of Guinea pigs. Journal of Neuroscience, 23, 716–724.

Spitzer, M.W., & Semple, M.N. (1993). Responses of inferior colliculus neurons to time-varying interaural phase disparity: Effects of shifting the locus of virtual motion. Journal of Neurophysiology, 69, 1245–1263.

Spitzer, M.W., & Semple, M.N. (1998). Transformation of binaural response properties in the ascending auditory pathway: Influence of time-varying interaural phase disparity. Journal of Neurophysiology, 80, 3062–3076.

Steinschneider, M., Fishman, Y.I., & Arezzo, J.C. (2003). Representation of the voice onset time (VOT) speech parameter in population responses within primary auditory cortex of the awake monkey. Journal of the Acoustical Society of America, 114, 307–321.

Steinschneider, M., Schroeder, C.E., Arezzo, J.C., & Vaughan, H.G., Jr. (1994). Speech-evoked activity in primary auditory cortex: Effects of voice onset time. Electroencephalography and Clinical Neurophysiology, 92, 30–43.

Steinschneider, M., Volkov, I.O., Noh, M.D., Garell, P.C., & Howard, M.A., 3rd (1999). Temporal encoding of the voice onset time phonetic parameter by field potentials recorded directly from human auditory cortex. Journal of Neurophysiology, 82, 2346–2357.

Summerfield, Q., & Assmann, P.F. (1991). Perception of concurrent vowels: Effects of harmonic misalignment and pitch-period asynchrony. Journal of the Acoustical Society of America, 89, 1364–1377.

Tian, B., Reser, D., Durham, A., Kustov, A., & Rauschecker, J.P. (2001). Functional specialization in rhesus monkey auditory cortex. Science, 292, 290–293.

Trahiotis, C., & Stern, R.M. (1989). Lateralization of bands of noise: Effects of bandwidth and differences of interaural time and phase. Journal of the Acoustical Society of America, 86, 1285–1293.

Ulanovsky, N., Las, L., & Nelken, I. (2003). Processing of low-probability sounds by cortical neurons. Nature Neuroscience, 6, 391–398.

Versnel, H., & Shamma, S.A. (1998). Spectral-ripple representation of steady-state vowels in primary auditory cortex. Journal of the Acoustical Society of America, 103, 2502–2514.

Wagner, H., Takahashi, T., & Konishi, M. (1987). Representation of interaural time difference in the central nucleus of the barn owl's inferior colliculus. Journal of Neuroscience, 7, 3105–3116.

Wang, X., & Sachs, M.B. (1993). Neural encoding of single-formant stimuli in the cat. I. Responses of auditory nerve fibers. Journal of Neurophysiology, 70, 1054–1075.

Winter, I.M., & Palmer, A.R. (1990). Temporal responses of primarylike anteroventral cochlear nucleus units to the steady-state vowel /i/. Journal of the Acoustical Society of America, 88, 1437–1441.

Winter, I.M., & Palmer, A.R. (1995). Level dependence of cochlear nucleus onset unit responses and facilitation by second tones or broadband noise. Journal of Neurophysiology, 73, 141–159.

Winter, I.M., Wiegrebe, L., & Patterson, R.D. (2001). The temporal representation of the delay of iterated rippled noise in the ventral cochlear nucleus of the guinea-pig. Journal of Physiology, 537, 553–566.

Yin, T.C., Carney, L.H., & Joris, P.X. (1990). Interaural time sensitivity in the inferior colliculus of the albino cat. The Journal of Comparative Neurology, 295, 438–448.

Yin, T.C., & Chan, J.C. (1990). Interaural time sensitivity in medial superior olive of cat. Journal of Neurophysiology, 64, 465–488.

21. DYNAMICS OF VOCALIZATION-INDUCED SENSORY-MOTOR INTERACTIONS IN THE PRIMATE AUDITORY CORTEX

Steven J. Eliades, Xiaoqin Wang

INTRODUCTION

Studies of perception and stimulus encoding have yielded a great deal of information about the functions of the auditory system. However, our knowledge of auditory functions related to self-generated sounds, including both human speech and primate vocalization, is limited. Such sensory inputs often have important behavioral effects. Humans continuously, and unconsciously, monitor their speech in order to compensate for any perturbations in acoustic structure. Shifts in the spectral profile of speech feedback, for example, result in compensatory changes in both the produced fundamental and formant frequencies (Burnett et al., 1998; Houde & Jordan 1998). Animals show similar feedback-dependant vocal control behavior, including temporal patterning in birdsong (Leonardo & Konishi, 1999), frequency in bat echolocation sounds (Smotherman et al., 2003) and amplitude in primate vocalizations (Sinnott et al., 1975). The neural mechanisms underlying this type of sensory-motor control and the function of the auditory system during vocal production remain largely unknown.

In the bat, echolocation-related activity has been largely studied in the brainstem, particularly the lateral leminiscal and nearby nuclei (Smotherman et al., 2003; Suga & Shimozawa, 1974). In humans and non-human primates, studies of auditory-vocal interactions have been primarily focused on the auditory cortex. Magnetoencephalogram studies in humans have shown a reduction in auditory cortical signal during speech production, compared to passive listening, that is largely absent from auditory-brainstem recordings

(Houde et al., 2002). PET imaging studies have also shown reduced cortical activation during speech (Paus et al., 1996). Physiologic evidence for reduced auditory cortex activation has been previously recorded in primates electrically-stimulated to vocalize (Müller-Preuss & Ploog, 1981). We have investigated the role of sensory-motor interaction in the auditory cortex of a vocal primate, the common marmoset (*Callithrix jacchus*), using single-unit recordings during spontaneous, self-initiated, vocalizations. This article summarizes and extends our previous findings on this subject (Eliades & Wang, 2003).

We recorded from two animals in an awake, non-sedated condition. Recordings were performed in a sound attenuated chamber with the animals' heads restrained. Because of the sparse occurrence of vocalization under these conditions, other physiological experiments were performed concurrently with this study, characterizing auditory response properties of the sampled units. This resulted in overlap between vocalization and auditory stimulation, in some cases, however the vocalization-induced modulation affected both spontaneous and stimulus-driven activities similarly. A detailed explanation of recording conditions can be found in our original paper (Eliades & Wang, 2003).

VOCALIZATION-INDUCED MODULATIONS OF THE AUDITORY CORTEX

The activities of auditory cortical neurons, including both spontaneous and stimulus-driven discharges, are modulated during voluntarily produced vocalizations. The most prevalent response observed was a suppression of cortical neurons (Fig. 21.1A). Vocalization-induced suppression began several hundred milliseconds *prior to* the onset of vocal production (median 220 ms) and continued for the duration thereof (Fig. 21.1B). The median reduction in firing rate by this suppression was 71%. The onset of suppression before vocalization suggests a neurally-mediated inhibition caused by signals from vocal control centers. The absence of auditory feedback before vocal onset rules out an explanation by sound-induced inhibition, though it may contribute to further modulation once vocalization has begun. A second, smaller, group of neurons displayed excitation during vocalization (Fig. 21.1C). Unlike suppression, this excitation did not begin until after the start of vocal production and is likely an auditory response to feedback of the produced sound (Fig. 21.1D).

MODULATIONS DURING STRINGS OF VOCALIZATION

While the majority of vocalizations recorded during this study consisted of a single phrase (Figs. 21.1A, 21.1C), one quarter of vocalizations contained multiple phrases. These multi-phrase marmoset vocalizations showed the same types of vocalization induced modulations (suppression + excitation) as single-phrase ones (Figs. 21.2A, 21.2B). The degree of suppression or excitation was

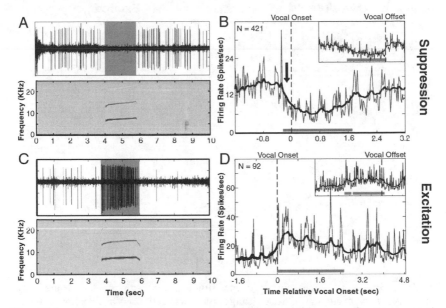

Fig. 21.1. Vocalization-induced suppression and excitation. **A, C:** Representative examples of both response types are shown. **B, D:** Population average response histograms, constructed from vocal onset aligned spike-times, demonstrate the magnitude and timing of modulations. The insets show response histograms aligned by vocal offset. Thick bars along the horizontal axis indicate duration of statistically significant (p < 0.01) rate changes. Adapted from Eliades and Wang (2003).

generally consistent between both of the phrases (Fig. 21.2C). During the interval between phrases, however, a burst of spikes was commonly seen, particularly when the vocalization was suppressive (Fig. 21.2A). This activity may indicate a brief return to baseline neural firing between phrases, consistent with the rapid offset seen during single-phrase vocalizations (Fig. 21.1B). It may also represent a rebound release from inhibition.

MODULATIONS OF NEURAL ACTIVITY VARY WITH THE ACOUSTIC CHARACTERISTICS OF VOCALIZATION

In addition to being either single or multi-phrased, vocalizations also varied in both amplitude and frequency, both within and between phrase categories (Fig. 21.3A). Multi-phrase vocalizations were, in general, of both higher average energy and mean frequency than single phrase ones, though a small overlap was observed, particularly for frequency. The average energy and mean frequency of a vocalization were highly correlated, with vocalizations of higher frequency containing more energy (r = 0.91, Fig. 21.3B). We examined the dependence of

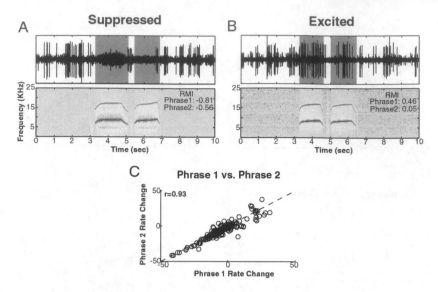

Fig. 21.2. Strings of vocalizations induce similar responses. **A, B:** Examples of suppression and excitation during strings of vocalization. Vocalization response modulations were quantified by RMI = $(R_{voc} - R_{pre\text{-}voc}) / (R_{voc} + R_{pre\text{-}voc})$, where $R_{pre\text{-}voc}$ and R_{voc} are the firing rates before and during vocalization (suppression: RMI < 0, excitation: RMI > 0), and are indicated for each phrase on the plots. **C:** Response modulations, measure by changes in firing rate, were highly consistent between the two phrases of these vocalizations.

vocalization-induced neural modulations upon these two acoustic parameters. Although there were variations from unit to unit, many individual neurons showed strong correlation between response modulation index and vocalization energy or frequency (Fig. 21.3C). Most units, particularly those that were suppressed, had an inverse relationship to vocal energy or frequency (Fig. 21.3C, left), and were more suppressed by louder than softer vocalizations. Units with positive correlation, including those that were either bimodal or purely excited or suppressed, were also seen (Fig. 21.3C, middle and right). These units showed greater excitation (or less suppression) at higher energies and mean frequencies. A linear correlation coefficient was calculated for each unit to quantify the relationship between modulation index and vocalization energy/frequency. Negative correlations were observed to be more prevalent in the sampled units (Fig. 21.3D).

It is unclear how these vocalization-dependant modulations relate to tone-derived receptive field properties of these units. It might be expected, for example, to find positive correlation between modulation index and energy in units with monotonic rate-level functions. However this was not always the case, as several monotonic units were found to have negative correlations. Additionally, many units were found to be excited by vocalizations whose acoustic energy was far outside their tonal receptive fields.

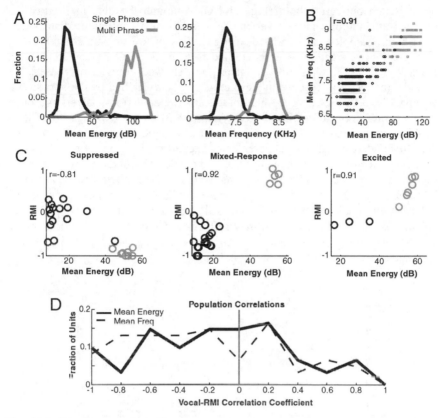

Fig. 21.3. Distribution of vocalization acoustic parameters and their relationship with response modulation. **A:** The distributions of average energy (left) and mean frequency (right) of vocalizations are shown for both single and multi-phrase vocalizations. Grey symbols or lines correspond to multi-phrase vocalizations, while black represents single phrase ones. These two parameters were highly correlated in the recorded vocalization samples **(B)**. **C:** Examples of three representative single-units in which response modulation index (RMI) was dependent upon vocal acoustics. These units exhibited dominantly suppressed (left), excited (right), or bimodal (middle) response modulation characteristics. **D:** In untis sampled with > 3 vocalizations the correlation coefficient between frequency or energy and RMI was calculated. Population histograms for these single-unit coefficients show a bias toward negative correlation.

DISTRIBUTION OF POPULATION MODULATIONS IN THE AUDITORY CORTEX

In the majority of the 79 single-units studied, more than one vocalization was captured. Most of these units with multiple vocalization samples showed a general consistency in their vocalization-induced modulation, either suppression or excitation but rarely both (Fig. 21.4A). Although the data in Figure 21.4 (median modulation index) gives the impression of a continuous distribution, most highly sampled units showed strong tendencies towards either suppression or excitation. A fraction of units studied had small median vocal modulation indexes, and large modulation variances, and showed bimodal responses. The bimodal modulation response in these units can be explained by the variation in vocalization acoustics (Fig. 21.3C, middle). The population analysis presented in our earlier publication (Eliades & Wang, 2003), and shown again in Figure 21.4A, did not take into account acoustic variations of vocalization, and therefore underestimates the suppressed or excited modulations of many units.

Anatomically, units with suppressed and excited modulations were observed in part of the primary auditory cortex as well as in lateral belt areas. There was, however, a greater proportion of suppressed units in the upper cortical layers, but roughly equal numbers of suppressed and excited units in deeper layers (Eliades & Wang, 2004), which may reflect cortico-cortical projections as the source of suppressive signals. There was no correlation between unit spontaneous rate and suppression/excitation.

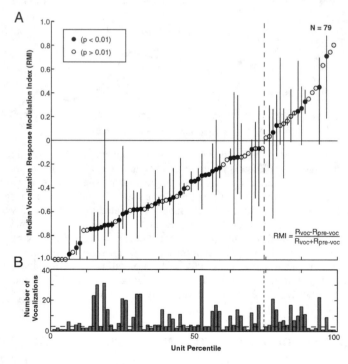

Fig. 21.4. Distribution of response modulations for auditory cortical units. **A:** The distribution of the median response modulation (RMI) for each unit. Error bars represent the inter-quartile range; filled circles are those units that had statistically significant modulations (p < 0.01). **B:** The number of vocalization samples recorded for each unit plotted in A is shown. Dashed line is n = 3. Adapted from Eliades and Wang (2003).

COMPARISON OF SINGLE NEURON RESPONSES AND GLOBAL CORTICAL ACTIVITY

Although the single-unit responses we have recorded in the non-human primate auditory cortex have revealed the existence of two types of vocalization-induced cortical responses, suppressed and excited, most human studies have thus far reported only dampened activation (MEG: Houde et al., 2000; PET: Paus et al., 1996; intra-operative electrocorticography: Crone et al., 2001). These measurements show that there is increased activity in auditory areas during speaking, but that the level of activity is smaller than that observed when the same speech sound is played back to the listener passively. Given the nature of the methods used to record from the human brain, the observations in these studies may reflect globally summed neural activities. In our previous publication (Eliades & Wang, 2003) only well-isolated single units were included in the analysis. In order to reconcile our neurophysiological studies with those in humans we have further analyzed the population properties of both single units and simultaneously recorded multi-unit clusters (Fig. 21.5). Well-isolated single-unit recordings, based on large-size action potentials, showed strongly suppressed responses in 75% of units (Fig. 21.5A). Previously unanalyzed units of smaller action potential size, likely more distant from the recording electrode, exhibited a similar ratio of suppressed and excited units, but with a smaller magnitude of inhibition (compare solid and dashed lines in Fig. 21.5A). Poorly isolated multi-units, however, showed a further reduction in suppression and an increased proportion and magnitude of excitation. These findings suggest that inhibitory modulation due to self-produced vocalization can be masked if a broader range of neural activities is included in the measurement.

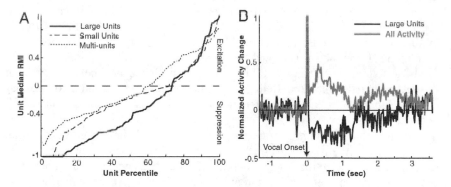

Fig. 21.5.A: The distribution of median RMI for units of different isolation qualities. "Large units": well-isolated single-units with large action potential size (signal-to-noise ratio > 10 dB). "Small units": sorted single-units with smaller action potential size. "Multi-units": multi-unit clusters. **B:** The summed activity of all large units showing onset activity followed by sustained inhibition. Summed activity from units of all three categories shows an overall excitation.

During speech, measures of human auditory cortex activity show weak activation, activation that is dampened, however, compared to the activity in response to playback of recorded speech sounds. Similarly, our broadest measure of cortical activity, the sum of responses from both single and multi-unit categories, reveals an overall weakly excitatory pattern (Fig. 21.5B). In contrast, the sum of responses from only well-isolated single-units was suppressed during vocalization. This suggests that the dampened excitation reported in humans likely represents the weakly excitatory aggregate activity of populations of both suppressed and excitatory neurons, while the reduced strength of the net activation in humans may be attributable to the presence of a large population of suppressed neurons. The reason we see an overall excitation pattern despite a large proportion of suppressed neurons is the asymmetry of neural excitation and inhibition, especially for the low spontaneous discharge rates of most auditory cortical neurons. The maximum amount of discharge rate reduction observable by extracellular recordings is bounded by zero (no firing), while sound driven rates can be many times higher than spontaneous. This asymmetry allows a much smaller number of excitatory neurons to mask the larger number of inhibited ones when sampled as a group.

FUNCTIONAL MODELS FOR SENSORY-MOTOR INTERACTION DURING VOCALIZATION

Sensory-motor interaction has been described in a number of sensory systems. In each, a neural signal, termed an efference copy or corollary discharge, relays information from motor control areas to influence activities of sensory neurons. The precise form of this signal is unclear, though it has been suggested to contain a representation of the expected sensory product of a motor action (Bell, 1989; Poulet & Hedwig, 2003). These discharges act, almost universally, to inhibit sensory neurons. In the weakly electric fish, perhaps the most well characterized model of neuronal sensory-motor interactions, electric organ discharges have been shown to influence central sensory neurons through GABA-mediated inhibition (Bell, 1989). Such findings are similar to auditory cortical suppression, and suggest parallel mechanisms for modulation during vocalization.

The possible functions of efference copy mediated inhibition are twofold. First, it may play a role in distinguishing self-generated from external sensory stimuli. Central electrosensory neurons in the fish perform a subtractive comparison of efferent and afferent signals, the output of which reflects environmental stimuli, but not the fish's own electric discharges (Bell, 1989). The cricket cercal system is suppressed during stridulation (rubbing of the wings to generate sound) in order to prevent saturation of auditory neurons by self-generated sounds and the resulting loss of acoustic sensitivity (Poulet & Hedwig, 2003). Efferent signal mediated inhibition is also seen in mammalian somatosensory and visual cortices and has been implicated in the processing of sensory information (Blakemore et al., 1998; Judge et al., 1980). The auditory cortex is likely suppressed by a similar efferent mechanism, however the processing of external auditory stimuli during vocalization may not be related to such suppression. Limited evidence suggests that suppressed auditory neurons respond poorly to external sounds during vocalization, while excited neurons, that may not receive as strong an inhibitory signal, respond to acoustic stimuli similarly during vocalization and quiet (Eliades & Wang, 2003).

The second possible function of efferent-mediated sensory-motor interaction is self-monitoring for the control of motor behavior, the auditory equivalent of which is the monitoring of vocal/speech feedback to maintain desired production characteristics (frequency, amplitude, etc.). For example, brainstem neurons in nuclei surrounding the bat lateral lemniscus are suppressed during the production of bat echolocation sounds (Metzner, 1993), similar to what we have observed in primate cortex. These nuclei, which may represent a specialized adaptation for echolocation, are involved in the control of echolocation frequency production when presented with frequency-shifted feedback, a phenomenon known as Doppler-shift compensation (Smotherman et al., 2003). Sensory input also plays a role in controlling many other motor phenomena, including occulomotor control (Sperry, 1950). While sensory feedback has an important function in regulating human and primate vocalization, the involvement of efferent signals is unclear. Subtraction of an expected sensory consequence of vocalization could result in a signal representing deviations in production or feedback, an error signal that could then be used to regulate future vocal production. Whether the suppression observed in the auditory cortex serves such a function remains to be seen.

The observed correlation of vocalization-induced modulations with acoustic parameters of vocalization is interesting given the role of auditory feedback in controlling vocal production. While such correlation is not the evidence that auditory cortical neurons are actively participating in self-monitoring of feedback, it demonstrates that they are at least capable of encoding variations in vocalization production, despite being suppressed. It is unclear whether this correlation observed in auditory cortex results from feedback or from neural signals containing parameters for vocal production (i.e., the corollary discharge). The latter would be consistent with an efferent-afferent comparison being performed within the auditory cortex. The former, on the other hand, would suggest that the comparison takes place elsewhere, perhaps directly in vocal control centers where behavioral access would be the most direct, since it would likely arise from a general suppression lacking specific efferent information. If this were the case, the suppression in the auditory cortex might reflect an alteration in auditory receptive fields to maximize the ability of neurons to encode incoming feedback for later comparison. Such alterations in receptive fields have been observed perisaccadically in parietal visual areas (Kusunoki & Goldberg, 2003).

SUMMARY

We have observed sensory-motor interaction at the level of single neurons in the auditory cortex of primates during self-initiated vocalizations. The predominant response was vocalization-induced suppression beginning prior to the onset of vocal production. A smaller fraction of neurons exhibited excitation during vocalization, likely the result of sensory feedback. Responses during strings of vocalization show that suppression is temporally synchronized to each phrase of vocal production. The suppression and excitation of many neurons was correlated with the acoustic structure of self-produced sounds, which may reflect feedback sensitivity. These two neural populations, suppressed and excited, may play different functional roles in two important tasks during vocalization or speaking (if they also exist in human auditory cortex), self-monitoring for vocal production and environmental monitoring to maintain hearing sensitivity, respectively. Finally, by summing together the cortical activities of both single and multi-units, we can relate the vocalization-induced suppression observed in electrophysiological experiments in non-human primates to the dampened excitation observed by gross measurements during human speech production.

REFERENCES

Bell, C.C. (1989). Sensory coding and corollary discharge effects in mormyrid electric fish. Journal of Experimental Biology, 146, 229–253.

Blakemore, S.J., Wolpert, D.M., & Frith, C.D. (1998). Central cancellation of self-produced tickle sensation. Nature Neuroscience, 1, 635–640.

Burnett, T.A., Freedland, M.B., Larson, C.R., & Hain, T.C. (1998). Voice F0 responses to manipulations in pitch feedback. Journal of the Acoustical Society of America, 103, 3153–3161.

Crone, N.E., Hao, L., Hart, J., Boatman, D., Lesser, R.P., Irizarry, R., & Gordon, B. (2001). Electrocorticographic gamma activity during word production in spoken and sign language. Neurology, 57, 2045–2053.

Eliades, S.J., & Wang, X. (2003). Sensory-motor interaction in the primate auditory cortex during self-initiated vocalizations. Journal of Neurophysiology, 83, 2194–2207.

Eliades, S.J., & Wang, X. (2004). The role of auditory-vocal interaction in hearing. In D. Pressnitzer, A. de Cheveigne, S. McAdams, & L. Collet (Eds.), Auditory signal processing: Physiology, psychoacoustics, and models (pp. 244–250). New York: Springer Verlag.

Houde, J.F., & Jordan, M.I. (1998). Sensorimotor adaptation in speech production. Science, 279, 1213–1216.

Houde, J.F., Nagarajan, S.S., Sekihara, K., & Merzenich, M.M. (2002). Modulation of the auditory cortex during speech: An MEG study. Journal of Cognitive Neuroscience, 14, 1125–1138.

Judge, S.J., Wurtz, R.H., & Richmond, B.J. (1980). Vision during saccadic eye movements. I. Visual interactions in striate cortex. Journal of Neurophysiology, 43, 1133–1155.

Kusunoki, M., & Goldberg, M.E. (2003). The time course of perisaccadic receptive field shifts in the lateral intraparietal area of the monkey. Journal of Neurophysiology, 89, 1519–1527.

Leonardo, A., & Konishi, M. (1999). Decrystallization of adult birdsong by perturbation of auditory feedback. Nature, 399, 466–470.

Metzner, W. (1993). An audio-vocal interface in echolocating horseshoe bats. Journal of Neuroscience, 13, 1899–1915.

Müller-Preuss, P., & Ploog, D. (1981). Inhibition of auditory cortical neurons during phonation. Brain Research, 215, 61–76.

Paus, T., Perry, D.W., Zatorre, R.J., Worsley, K.J., & Evans, A.C. (1996). Modulation of cerebral blood flow in the human auditory cortex during speech: role of motor-to-sensory discharges. European Journal of Neuroscience, 8, 2236–2246.

Poulet, J.F., & Hedwig, B. (2003). A corollary discharge mechanism modulates central auditory processing in singing crickets. Journal of Neurophysiology, 89, 1528–1540.

Sinnott, J.M., Stebbins, W.C., & Moody, D.B. (1975). Regulation of voice amplitude by the monkey. Journal of the Acoustical Society of America, 58, 412–414.

Smotherman, M., Zhang, S., & Metzner, W. (2003). A neural basis for auditory feedback control of vocal pitch. Journal of Neuroscience, 23, 1464–1477.

Sperry, R.W. (1950). Neural basis of the spontaneous optokinetic responses produced by visual inversion. Journal of Comparative Physiology and Psychology, 43, 482–489.

Suga, N., & Shimozawa, T. (1974). Site of neural attenuation of responses to self-vocalized sounds in echolocating bats. Science, 183, 1211–1213.

PART III

PLASTICITY, LEARNING, AND COGNITION

22. INTRODUCTION: PLASTICITY, LEARNING, AND COGNITION

Reinhard König

During the last two decades or so, the once strongly held point of view that enduring changes in cortical properties are only possible in the *developing* brain has made room for the now widely accepted concept that this holds for the *adult* brain as well. The capacity for plasticity or functional re-organization in adult brains has now been documented for different sensory modalities (visual, auditory, and somatosensory), from cortex to sub thalamic levels. Plasticity in the adult brain has been most frequently studied in primary sensory and motor areas which therefore serve as model systems for cortical plasticity (Calford, 2002).

The term plasticity refers to changes of neuronal properties occurring under various circumstances and on different levels of complexity. Altered neuronal properties are sometimes manifested as a re-organization of sensory or motor representations. Additional attributes identify the assumed origin or cause of the changes, like injury-induced or use-dependent plasticity, or plasticity associated with experience, learning, and memory. Possible circumstances that may cause these different types of plasticity span from, for example, peripheral lesions and sensory injuries to behavioral training and learning.

Cortical plasticity denotes both structural and functional changes. It includes alterations of cortical properties that occur on different temporal and spatial scales. The time scales on which plasticity can occur extend over several orders of magnitude, basically from seconds to a whole life time. The spatial extent of plasticity may range from a molecular or sub-cellular level (changes in synaptic transmission) to the modification of connections in a neural network or changes of topographic maps.

Plasticity, however, is not the sole phenomenon which – on the basis of emerging experimental evidence – has influenced a re-thinking of the role and importance of sensory cortices. Also, cognitive functions traditionally attributed to higher cortical regions are at least to a certain extent assigned to sensory cortices, and of particular interest here, to the auditory cortex. There is, for example, strong evidence that the potential of the auditory cortex clearly reaches beyond the mere analysis of acoustic stimuli. This quality, in turn, may distinguish the auditory cortex from sub-cortical stations of the auditory pathway. Learning-induced plasticity in the auditory cortex is one prominent example of this superior capacity of the auditory cortex. Other cognitive functions associated with the auditory cortex, include, for example, the learning of a demanding task or the formation of (acoustic) categories (see, e.g., Edeline, 1999; Weinberger, 2004, and references therein).

Thus, one key problem to be tackled by future research is to establish the connection of cognitive functions or psychological concepts like learning with a physiological concept like plasticity. The challenge of such studies is to set up a relationship between findings made with different methodological approaches (accentuating either behavioral or cognitive aspects) and constraint by different boundary conditions (invasiveness of experimental techniques). In this context, a synthesis of human and animal research might be a particularly worthwhile exercise because it could achieve a more detailed picture and an improved understanding of the functioning of the auditory cortex.

The following chapters contribute to various types or aspects of plasticity, learning, and cognitive processing. They also reveal their interconnections. Edeline discusses possible underlying mechanisms of experience-dependent plasticity in the auditory system. The core issue of this contribution deals with different coding strategies of fundamental sound properties and their relevance for the description of sensory plasticity. The comparison of a rate code (firing rate) with temporal codes (temporal organization of neuronal discharges) and their possible mutual influence also provides a strong link to the chapters in the preceding section on "Coding of sounds". Irvine, Brown, Martin, and Park review their studies on humans and animals and critically reflect on aspects of perceptual learning as a result of training on an auditory discrimination task. Furthermore, they compare their findings to possible changes of neural correlates of perceptual learning with the results obtained from different species.

The primary objective of the chapter by Fritz, Elhilai, and Shamma is to establish a relationship between behavioral performance and auditory cortical plasticity. Findings of behavioral studies on tone detection and tone discrimination tasks, along with observed patterns of changes of spectro-temporal receptive fields are interpreted in terms of a task-dependent adaptive plasticity. Rüsseler, Nager, Möbes, and Münte contribute to the discussion on temporal aspects of plasticity, that is, of the relevant time scales for the observation of plasticity. They study event-related potentials and magnetic fields as indices for neuroplasticity and discuss to which extent their findings of auditory processing in professional musicians can be interpreted in terms of plasticity.

The concepts of categorization and generalization, and the relationship between category learning and neuronal plasticity form key topics of the chapter by Ohl, Scheich, and Freeman. The authors introduce an animal model of category learning and discuss parallels among their psychological (behavioral) and physiological findings. Aspects of stimulus-response associations play a crucial role in the analysis and interpretation of category learning experiments, and are further elaborated in the chapter by Scheich, Ohl, Schulze, Hess, and Brechmann. Here, the authors emphasize that the spatiotemporal patterns of neuronal processing in auditory cortex are not solely the result of "bottom-up" processing within the ascending auditory system. Rather, cognitive demands, such as selective attention, object formation, categorization, and concept formation strongly influence the auditory cortex in a "top-down" manner. They suggest possibilities how the problems associated with this duality of processing might be solved in auditory cortex.

REFERENCES

Calford, M.B. (2002). Dynamic representational plasticity in sensory cortex. Neuroscience, 111, 709–738.

Edeline, J.-M. (1999). Learning-induced physiological plasticity in the thalamo-cortical sensory systems: A critical evaluation of receptive field plasticity, map changes and their potential mechanisms. Progress in Neurobiology, 57, 165–224.

Weinberger, N.M. (2004). Specific long-term memory traces in primary auditory cortex. Nature Reviews Neuroscience, 5, 279–290.

23. LEARNING-INDUCED PLASTICITY IN THE THALAMO-CORTICAL AUDITORY SYSTEM: SHOULD WE MOVE FROM RATE CODE TO TEMPORAL CODE DESCRIPTIONS?

Jean-Marc Edeline

INTRODUCTION AND AIMS

At the beginning of the 60s', the pioneering studies by Wiesel and Hubel (1963) opened large avenues of researches aimed at understanding the mechanisms underlying functional reorganizations in sensory systems. However, these outstanding studies also had a drastic impact on the conception of sensory cortex: for more than two decades the general view, both in the field of sensory physiology and in the field of learning, was that sensory representations could be subjected to experience-dependent plasticity only during development, not in adulthood. This dogma was progressively reconsidered in the middle of the 80s' when some studies pointed out that reorganizations can take place in the adult sensory cortex after deafferentations (e.g., Merzenich et al., 1983; for review see Weinberger, 1995). In the auditory system, the first demonstration of such reorganizations came from the work by Robertson and Irvine (1989). One month after localized damages of the cochlea, leading to important increase in threshold for a particular frequency range, cortical territories normally allocated to the deafferented frequency range were responding to adjacent frequencies. Similar reorganizations were recently described at the thalamic level (Kamke et al., 2003) and patchy reorganizations were also reported at the level of the inferior colliculus (Irvine & Rajan, 1994). Thus, it seems that, from the cortex to subthalamic stations, sensory systems remain capable to display functional reorganizations in adult brains. This view now prevails in any sensory modality. This is not a surprise for investigators who for decades have described the impact of learning on auditory evoked responses (see for review, Weinberger and Diamond, 1987). However, as explained below, most, if not all, of the studies describing experience-dependent plasticity in sensory systems based their findings on the firing rate collected during a time window related to stimulus presentation. This contrasts with a long tradition in auditory physiology which emphasizes the fact that temporal organizations of neuronal discharges code for basic properties of a sound (frequency, intensity) more efficiently than rate coding does (Hind et al., 1963). As I shall defend in the last section, describing results exclusively in terms of firing rate, or exclusively in terms of temporal coding, probably contributes to keep separated lines of research which should rather cooperate to reach a major goal: unravelling the neural code and its plasticity.

LEARNING-INDUCED PLASTICITY IN THE AUDITORY SYSTEM

Starting from the seventies, numerous studies have described changes in evoked responses in the thalamo-cortical auditory system of awake animals engaged in various learning tasks. Such effects were reported using evoked potentials, multi-unit or single units recordings during both aversive and appetitive tasks (see for review Edeline, 1999; Weinberger & Diamond, 1987). However, these initial studies did not attack the fundamental question of whether these modifications reflect changes in neuronal excitability or changes in information processing. At the end of the eighties, a set of decisive experiments provided an answer to this question. By discovering that, after a brief training session during which a particular frequency predicted the occurrence of an aversive event, the frequency receptive field (RF) of auditory cortex neurons could be re-tuned to the significant frequency, Weinberger and colleagues provided the first evidence that sensory coding can be modified by learning (Diamond & Weinberger, 1986, 1989). Initial findings came from the secondary auditory areas (AII and VE in cat), but several subsequent studies have confirmed and extended these effects to primary auditory cortex. In the guinea-pig primary auditory cortex, an important percentage of neurons exhibited increased evoked response for the conditioned stimulus (CS) and decreased responses for the initial cell's best frequency (BF), which led to re-tune the neuron to the CS frequency (Bakin & Weinberger, 1990; Edeline et al., 1993). Selective re-tuning was also observed after instrumental training (Bakin et al., 1996), and after a 2-tone discrimination protocol (Edeline & Weinberger, 1993)[1]. Two points are important to be kept in mind. First, these RF modifications emerge rapidly: They can be detected after 5–15 training trials (Edeline et al., 1993). Second, they are not transient: They were systematically detected one hour after training (Edeline & Weinberger, 1993), 24 hours after training in some experiments (Bakin & Weinberger, 1990)

[1]Using a particular experimental protocol, other types of selective effects were described in primary auditory cortex (Ohl & Scheich, 1996).

and even reported for periods up to two months (Weinberger et al., 1993). These RF reorganizations were also described at subcortical levels. Immediately post-training, they were expressed, with the same selectivity, in the three main divisions of the auditory thalamus (ventral, dorsal and medial). However, they were not long-lasting in the ventral, tonotopic division, whereas they were long-lasting in the dorsal and medial, non-tonotopic, divisions (Edeline & Weinberger, 1991a, 1991b, 1992). Selective RF modifications were also detected in the bat inferior colliculus (IC) after tone-shock pairing (Gao & Suga, 1998, 2000). On the basis of results obtained during cortical inactivation, these authors proposed that the collicular plasticity is partly mediated by the corticofugal system, and they envisioned a complex timing of sequential events to explain the occurrence and duration of experience-induced RF modifications in the IC (see for review Suga et al., 2002). Lastly, it is crucial to mention that sensory plasticity does not require the use of aversive unconditioned stimulus (US): it was obtained during appetitive conditioning (Birt et al., 1979; Birt & Olds, 1981; Maho & Hennevin, 2002) and selective RF modifications were also reported after pairing protocols involving as US a stimulation of the medial forebrain bundle (Kisley & Gerstein, 2001), an area known to induce self-stimulation.

Because in each of the aforementioned experiments, neuronal re-tuning was obtained for non-negligible proportions (35–70%) of recorded cells, these effects should have considerable impact on the cortical map organization: if neurons which have initially their BF close to the CS frequency shift their BF to the CS frequency, the consequence should be an expansion of the tonotopic map in favor of the CS frequency. This prediction was verified. After 2–3 months of training in a perceptive discrimination task, an enlargement of the tonotopic map was observed in favor of the trained frequency (Recanzone et al., 1993). More recently, another study demonstrated the relationship between stimulus importance and the amount of cortical tissue allocated to a particular frequency band. By manipulating the motivational level of thirsty rats to bar press for water at presentation of a 6-kHz tone, it was found that the percentage of auditory cortex tuned to this frequency was directely related with the animals' behavioral performance (Rutkowski et al., 2002).

It is tempting to propose a simple, coherent, synthesis of these results based on a strict "rate code" point of view. After a brief training experiment (a few tens of trials), only a fraction of the neurons within a given structure are re-tuned to the frequency of the behaviorally significant stimulus, but the daily accumulation of these neuronal re-tuning is responsible for the massive reorganizations observed after months of training when tonotopic maps are evaluated under general anesthesia. However, as already discussed (Edeline, 2003) direct links between RF plasticity and map reorganizations should not be oversimplified, for the following reasons. First, selective RF re-tuning was usually reported at suprathreshold intensities whereas map reorganizations were assessed at threshold, which is a problem because, in auditory cortex, the cortical area responsive to a suprathreshold stimulus cannot be predicted from the threshold map (Phillips et al., 1994, discussed in Calford, 2002). However, in some experiments, cases of RF modifications were detected at, or around threshold, suggesting potential map reorganizations after a brief training experiment (Edeline et al., 1993; Galvan & Weinberger, 2002).

Second, as extensively discussed by Weinberger (in press), perceptual learning (leading to map reorganizations) and rapid associative learning (leading to RF modifications) should be distinguished, even if they both trigger plasticity in sensory cortex. A brief associative learning can trigger RF plasticity and nothing further would develop, i.e., there would be no perceptual learning unless the subject were challenged to make finer and finer discrimination. Selective RF plasticity triggered by associative learning might subserve rapid associative memory, whereas map reorganization triggered by perceptual learning might only help analyzing the same stimulus with a finer grain (Weinberger, in press). Lastly, a brief learning experience and perceptual learning might engage the constitutive elements of cortical maps (cell assemblies and/or cortical columns) in very different operations: Adapting to the CS predictive value in the first case, tracking small differences in activation of cells population in the second case.

As discussed below, the "rate code view" in the field of learning-induced sensory plasticity is complemented by two sets of data: (i) those coming from the plasticity induced by the neuromodulatory systems and (ii) those coming from the trauma-induced reorganizations.

PLASTICITY INDUCED BY NEUROMODULATORY SYSTEMS

An impressive amount of studies has described the effects produced by pairing protocols between a sensory stimulus and a neuromodulatory system; only a few key findings of this vast literature will be mentioned here. The rationale of this line of research is clear: since the historical implication of the noradrenergic and cholinergic system in the visual cortex developmental plasticity, neuromodulators are viewed as permissive factors controlling the emergence of sensory plasticity. More specifically, in the auditory system, a conceptual model has been formulated (Weinberger et al., 1990) proposing testable hypotheses about the role of the cholinergic system in learning-induced cortical plasticity.

Using iontophoretic applications of acetylcholine (ACh), or stimulations of the nucleus basalis (NB) initial studies have demonstrated the potency of ACh in promoting long-lasting facilitations of evoked responses (Metherate et al., 1988; Tremblay et al., 1990). Subsequent studies demonstrated that this plasticity can be selective for the stimulus associated with the presence of neuromodulators. Studies performed in auditory cortex have shown that pairing either ACh application or NB stimulation with a particular frequency can induce very specific alterations in the neurons RFs. When ACh application was used, both selective increases and decreases were observed at the paired frequency (Metherate & Weinberger, 1989, 1990), whereas only selective increases were obtained after NB stimulations (Bakin & Weinberger, 1996; Bjordahl et al., 1998; Dimyan & Weinberger, 1999). Looking at map reorganizations provided complementary evidences to the results obtained with RF analysis. After 3–4 weeks of repetitive pairing (300–500 trials per day) between a tone frequency and NB stimulation, massive reorganizations of the primary auditory cortex (AI) were reported (Kilgard & Merzenich, 1998a). The isofrequency band of the paired stimulus increased from about 250 μm in naive animals up to 1 mm in the experimental ones (over 85% of AI responded to the paired frequency at 50 dB). As pointed by the authors, the map reorganizations generated by NB activation are far more extensive than those typically observed after several months of behavioral training (Recanzone et al., 1993). Subsequent studies demonstrated that the "repetition rate transfer function" of AI neurons can also be modified by repeated NB stimulations: The initial low-pass characteristics of AI neurons can be either extended toward higher frequencies (15 Hz) or restricted to the low frequency range (5 Hz) depending on the repetition rate associated with NB stimulation (Kilgard & Merzenich, 1998b).

Thus, neuromodulators seem capable to trigger RF plasticity and map reorganizations that are as selective and as extensive as those obtained after behavioral training. The responses to both spectral and temporal parameters of acoustic stimuli can be affected by neuromodulators. Although most of these studies involved the cholinergic system, extensive map reorganizations were also obtained after repetitive activation of dopaminergic neurons of the ventral tegmental area (Bao et al., 2001).

LIMITATIONS OF FIRING RATE AND TOPOGRAPHIC MAPS

In all the literature reviewed above, the firing rate was the unique code considered for the transmission of information within the central nervous system, probably because it is the easiest to measure and to think about. According to the rate code description, the more a neuron is firing action potentials at presentation of a given stimulus, the more efficiently it is suspected to process the information concerning this stimulus. In a similar vein, it is also assumed that the larger is the number of neurons responding to a stimulus in a given brain region, the more efficient is the processing of that stimulus over the whole region. Therefore, extensions of topographic map were always considered as benefit for processing a particular stimulus. In a way, this view is justified when looking at evolution. When a species makes extensive use of a particular region of the sensory epithelium for its daily behavior, the amount of cortical tissue responding to this peripheral region is dramatically expanded. Rodents make extensive use of their vibrissea in their daily behavior and the rodent barrel cortex extents on large territories whose counterpart is the hand representation in primates. In the auditory system, the cortical area responding to the bat vocalization frequency occupies 50% of its primary auditory cortex, whereas the human auditory cortex contains large territories responding to

500–2000 Hz, the frequency range the most represented in speech. However, considering that experience-induced plasticity replicates, on a short-time scale, the adaptive selection operating through evolution, might turn to be too simplistic.

As mentioned in the introduction, in the auditory system, several studies have demonstrated map reorganizations after peripheral lesions in adult animals (see for review Irvine et al., 2000). However, the relationships between peripheral loss, cortical reorganizations and perceptual consequences of these reorganisations are still unclear. First, some idiopathic hearing losses do not result in plastic changes in tonotopic organization (Rajan, 1998; discussed in Irvine et al., 2000). Second, in human subjects, the consequences of potential reorganizations seem to have little effects on the subject's perceptual abilities. The psychophysic performance of human subjects exhibiting hearing loss similar to those inducing massive cortical reorganizations in animals was tested in three experiments. In two of them (McDermott et al., 1998; Thai-Van et al., 2002), the smallest discriminable differences in frequency showed a local minimum in the region of the cut-off frequency: This modest effect was significant, but was not present in all subjects. In a third experiment (Buss et al., 1998), the performance of hearing-impaired subjects was studied in a range of tasks (frequency sweep detection, intensity discrimination, gap detection and discrimination). In none of these tasks there was compelling evidence that hearing-impaired subjects had better performance than normal subjects. Thus, it seems that in the auditory system, there is still little evidence for correlation between perceptual phenomena and the occurrence of map reorganization. Without denying the importance of cortical maps in sensory processing (Kaas, 1997), these results may indicate that factors, other than the firing rate and the extent of cortical areas, underly the neural code and behavioral performance.

THE MULTIPLE FACETS OF THE NEURAL CODE: TEMPORAL ASPECTS OF NEURONAL DISCHARGES

No doubt that, today, most of the neuroscientists will accept the idea that firing rate is only one of the actors allowing information to be encoded in the central nervous system. It is not possible to develop here the various facets by which neurons might code information (see for reviews Eggermont, 1998, 2001), but a few examples taken from the auditory system will illustrate that important aspects of sensory coding might be missed by focusing exclusively our attention on firing rate.

It is first necessary to point out that within the central auditory system the temporal code probably fundamentally differs from the one which operates at the level of the eight nerve: At this level the temporal occurrence of action potentials directly reflects the sound frequency (for stimuli with fundamental frequency less than about 4 kHz). In contrast, we should also consider that, in the central auditory system, several non-exclusive levels of temporal organization can be envisioned behind the words "temporal coding". These different levels correspond to "who" is considered as sender and receiver of information: a single neuron, a small group of neurons, or a large population of cells.

At the single cell level, temporal coding can mean that the exact time of occurrence of the action potentials, and/or the succession of the interspike intervals, give an accurate representation of a stimulus. Actually, that temporal aspects of neuronal responses code for parameters of auditory stimuli has been proposed since the 1960s. Based on unit recordings from the inferior colliculus it was shown that latency and latency variability are more reliable to code a given sound frequency than the neurons firing rate (Hind et al., 1963). In auditory cortex, the critical parameter for the first-spike latency seems to be the acceleration of peak pressure at tone onset rather than the rise-time or the sound pressure level per se (Heil & Irvine, 1996; Heil, 1997). Over a neuronal population, this property could be used to track instantaneous properties of transients, and thus might contribute to the instantaneous coding of transients thought to underlie the categorical perception of speech and some non-linguistic sounds (see discussion in Heil, 1997). In addition, several studies provided evidence that auditory cortex neurons code stimulus location using more the temporal structure of spike trains than the rate of discharge of individual neurons (Middlebrooks et al., 1994, 1998). When an artificial neural network is trained to recognize a stimulus location among 18 possible sources using as inputs the neuron spike trains, it appeared that, for most of the cells, azimuth coding by complete spike pattern is more accurate than by spike count, probably because of additional stimulus-related information contained in the timing of spikes.

At the level of small cell assemblies, temporal coding can be expressed by the short-time scale coordinations of neuronal discharges as assessed by cross-correlograms. Auditory cortex neurons can exhibit precise neuronal coordinations that are selective for a stimulus location or a stimulus movement (Ahissar et al., 1992). Furthermore, short time-scale interactions between neuronal discharges were found to be related with sound frequency independently of the firing rate: neurons can synchronize their firing rate without firing more action potentials (deCharms & Merzenich, 1996).

At the level of large populations of cells, the spatio-temporal patterns of fast oscillations triggered by acoustic stimuli might also be part of the neural code (Sukov & Barth, 1998, 2001): By synchronizing neuronal populations that respond to different parameters of a given stimulus (the carrier frequency, the frequency modulation, the first- and second-order amplitude modulation), these fast oscillations might solve the "binding" problem, that is, the integration of different sensations in a single percept.

Thus, at several levels of integration, temporal aspects of neuronal discharges participate to the neural code. However, before taking into account these data in the field of sensory plasticity, some considerations deserve attention. Most of our knowledge concerning the temporal coding comes from

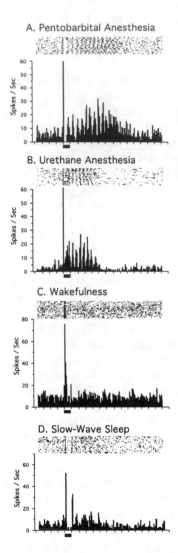

Fig. 23.1: Presence of tone-evoked oscillations in anesthetized states, but not in non-anesthetized states. The peri-stimulus time histograms (PSTHs, 10-ms bin size) display tone-evoked responses at a recording site in auditory cortex under Pentobarbital and Urethane anesthesia (**A** and **B**), and in undrugged conditions, during Wakefulness and slow-wave sleep (**C** and **D**). The PSTHs and rasters are based on 55 tone presentations (ITI: 2.5 s). The horizontal bar under the histograms indicates the tone period (100 ms, 9 kHz, 80 dB). Note that during anesthesia, the "on" phasic response was followed by regularly spaced discharges observed both on rasters and PSTHs. The oscillation frequency was 12 Hz under Pentobarbital and 15 Hz under Urethane. There was no tendency for such oscillations in waking and slow-wave sleep.

anesthetized preparations, and there is evidence that the temporal aspects of neuronal discharges notably differ between awake and anesthetized animals. This is the case for the large scales temporal synchonizations between cells. Although many studies have described evoked oscillations in auditory cortex of anesthetized animals (e.g., Brosch et al., 2002; Sukov & Barth, 1998, 2001), such oscillations were not detected in unanesthetized animals (Fig. 23.1; Cotillon-Williams & Edeline, 2003).

This is also the case for the fine grain structure of spike trains which are composed of both single action potentials (AP) and bursts, i.e., groups of AP emitted at high frequency (200–400 Hz). An increasing literature considers that high-frequency bursts are a way to (i) increase the reliability of synaptic transmission, (ii) sharpen neuronal selectivity, and (iii) induce "natural" synaptic plasticity (Lisman, 1997; Sherman, 2001; Swadlow & Gusev, 2001; Steriade & Timofeev, 2003). Although bursts were recently found in waking animals, their proportion is much lower than in anesthetized states (less than 5% in waking vs. more than 16% under anesthesia; Massaux & Edeline, 2003, Massaux et al., 2004). But, even if bursts sparingly occur during waking, their occurrence can have drastic impact on the timing of evoked responses: Both latency and latency variability are decreased when a cell responds by a burst compared with responses composed of isolated spikes (Fig. 23.2). Surprisingly, this effect is not observed under various anesthetics (Pentobarbital, Urethane, Ketamine). Altogether, these data indicate that cautions have to be exerted before considering that the temporal aspects of neuronal discharges can be transferred from anesthetized animals to unanesthetized ones.

GOING BEYOND RATE CODE DESCRIPTION OF SENSORY PLASTICITY

Examination of some of the data published in the field of learning-induced plasticity revealed that temporal aspects of neuronal discharges can exhibit plasticity. For example, studies describing increased auditory evoked responses during behavioral training have reported decreases in response latencies (McEchron et al., 1996; Quirk et al., 1995, 1997). Also, examining the time course of firing probability in the gerbil auditory cortex clearly revealed differences between reinforced and non-reinforced tones (Ohl & Scheich, 1997). Lastly, the short- and long-time scale synchronizations between neuronal discharges can be modified by learning (Quirk et al., 1995). But here too, the temporal dynamic should not be lost. Functional coupling can evolve very quickly over time, and therefore, they should not be taken as indicators of static, permanent, changes in synaptic efficacy. In the cortex of monkeys performing a Go/(No-Go) task, functional coupling between neurons evolved in tens of milliseconds with totally different patterns during the Go and the No-Go trial (Vaadia et al., 1995). These effects occurred without changes in firing rate and without changes in the functional coupling when quantified over several

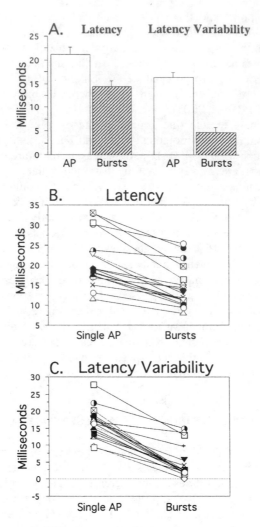

Fig. 23.2: Bursts occurrence changes the latency and latency variability of auditory thalamus cells during waking. **A.** Group data for the 18/100 cells recorded in the auditory thalamus which exhibited a burst percentage above 20% during evoked activity. For these cells, the frequency tuning was tested at 70–80 dB and the bursts were automatically detected based on the presence of an interspike interval ≤ 5 ms preceeded by a period of silence of at least 100 ms. The initial spike train was separated in a "single action potential" spike train and a "burst" spike train, and the latency and latency variability were calculated from these two spike trains. The latency and latency variability were significantly reduced when cells were in burst mode compared with single AP mode. **B** and **C.** Individual data for these 18 cells, showing that each individual cell exhibited decreased latency and decreased latency variability when emitting evoked bursts.

seconds. Thus, descriptions focusing only on firing rate probably miss important reorganizations emerging from the temporal structure of neuronal discharges.

That learning-induced plasticity impacts either the rate or the temporal aspects of sensory processing can present several advantages. In brain areas where the exact timing of action potentials is essential for a particular function, modulation of rate coding is a way to preserve essential information while signaling the relevance of a stimulus. For example, in the first levels of the auditory system where timing of the first spikes is crucial for sound localization, adding more spikes to evoked discharges can signal which sound localization is significant. Also, changing the rate coding representation of sound frequency in the auditory cortex is a way to specify the importance of a frequency whose representation can be read in the first auditory relays. Lastly, an advantage of affecting the temporal code is that it should not require an averaging as the rate code: A single presentation might allow to distinguish between two stimuli which trigger the same number of spikes.

Last but not least, considering exclusively the neurons' firing rate to describe sensory plasticity can lead to paradoxical results as illustrated in Figure 23.3. After 30 trials of tone alone presentations, this auditory cortex neuron was submitted to a pairing protocol where each tone was presented during a brief (1 second) ejection of noradrenaline (NA) at the immediate vicinity of the cell. Based on firing rate, we should consider that this pairing protocol resulted in a large attenuation of the responses during the last two blocks of pairing trials: The responses decreased from 25 spikes to 12 and 14 spikes. But by looking at the temporal aspects of the responses one can clearly see that the response is concentrated in time in such a way that its latency and latency variability are much lower. In fact, this response is made of high-frequency bursts of action potentials which are known to be much more efficient to discharge post-synaptic cells, and thus facilitate stimulus detection. This dilemma means that a response made of fewer spikes grouped in high-frequency bursts is more efficient than a response made of more spikes with longer interspike-intervals. A rate code description of this experiment will consider that NA produces a decrease in evoked response, which in this particular case lasted for about 10 minutes and was specific of the paired frequency (Manunta & Edeline, 2004). In contrast, a temporal code description of this experiment will consider that NA promotes high frequency inputs to the target cells, which can potentially induce a facilitated synaptic transmission. The effect described here at the single cell level can also be detected at the level of a small assembly of cells. Current source-density analyses performed in the somatosensory cortex during locus coeruleus activation revealed that noradrenergic activation concentrates in time the current sink in supragranular layers and reduces multiunit and single unit response latency (Lecas, 2001).

To summarize, it seems unwise to claim that neural code is based only on the rate or only on the temporal aspects of neuronal discharges. Important efforts are required to integrate rate and temporal aspects of the neuronal discharges in a single unified neural code.

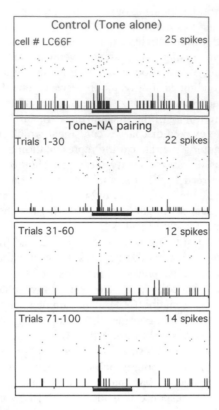

Fig. 23.3: Modification of rate code and temporal code during iontophoretic application of NA. For this cell (LC66f) recorded in auditory cortex, each histogram (2 ms bin size) and rasters represent the evoked responses during 30 repetitions of a contralateral tone (100 ms in duration, 10 kHz, 70 dB). **A.** In control conditions, the response exhibits a large latency variability leading to a response that is spread over the first 50 ms of the tone. **B.** During pairing, a brief (1 s) pulse of noradrenaline (NA, 40 nA) was iontophoretically applied at the vicinity of the cell before each tone presentation. As soon as the first block of pairing, the response latency was less variable and all the spikes were concentrated in a temporal window of 10–15 ms. **C** and **D.** Similar effects were observed even when the response of the cell was largely reduced.

CONCLUSION

Over the last 15 years, an important concept has been validated by many laboratories: Adult sensory systems can exhibit plastic changes under various circumstances ranging from peripheral lesions to behavioral training. In three recent review articles, the relationships between sensory code and memory code were extensively discussed (Weinberger, 2001a, 2001b, 2003). Memory code was described as a particular input-output function which transforms a set of sensory input patterns into a memorized percept. The strength and richness of this hypothesis is to explicitly state that when a neural code is modified by a learning experience, it becomes part of a memory code, thus reinforcing the inseparability between sensory plasticity and memory. As recently recognized, in addition to rate memory code, there are probably many other types whose nature might encompass any neurobiological process involved in the storage of experience (Weinberger, 2003). Thus, explaining and clarifying the intrinsic relationships between sensory code and memory code using rate code descriptions is, at first, the most rational starting point from which we can progress toward any other aspects of the neural code. Changes in latency, changes in the internal structure of the bursts, changes in synchronization between cortical columns or between large thalamo-cortical populations should also be considered as part of the memory code because they can have dramatic impacts on long-lasting cell properties and therefore on the neuronal substrat of memorized information.

Obviously, the use of complex artificial stimuli such as the "dynamic ripples" is a powerful way to assess functional properties of auditory neurons (Fritz et al., 2003). However, because the "neural code" probably evolved over evolution to allow precise and reliable processing of sounds that are of survival value, a straightforward approach to understand it would be to use natural stimuli such as vocalizations. Dissecting the neural code used by awake animals to extract information from natural stimuli and understanding how this code is changed by experience is a colossal challenge, but it is a task we should be pride to participate in.

ACKNOWLEDGMENTS

I am pleased to thank Norman Weinberger and Elizabeth Hennevin for detailed and helpful comments on an earlier version of this paper. I am also grateful to Yves Manunta, Nathalie Cotillon and Aurélie Massaux for participation to some of the experiments reported in this chapter.

REFERENCES

Ahissar, M., Ahissar, E., Bergman, H., & Vaadia E. (1992). Encoding of sound-source location and movement: activity of single neurons and interactions between adjacent neurons in the monkey auditory cortex. Journal of Neurophysiology, 67, 203–215.

Bakin, J.S., South, D.A., & Weinberger N.M. (1996). Induction of receptive field plasticity in the auditory cortex of the guinea pig during instrumental avoidance conditioning. Behavioral Neuroscience, 110, 905–913.

Bakin, J.S., & Weinberger, N.M. (1990). Classical conditioning induces CS-specific receptive field plasticity in the auditory cortex of the guinea pig. Brain Research, 536, 271–286.

Bakin, J.S., & Weinberger, N.M. (1996). Induction of a physiological memory in the cerebral cortex by stimulation of the nucleus basalis. Proceedings of the National Academy of Sciences USA, 93, 11219–11224.

Bao, S., Chan V.T., & Merzenich, M.M. (2001). Cortical remodelling induced by activity of ventral tegmental dopamine neurons. Nature, 412, 79–83.

Birt, D., Nienhuis, R., & Olds, M. (1979). Seperation of associative from non-associative short-latency changes in medial geniculate and inferior colliculus during differential conditioning and reversal in rats. Brain Research, 167, 129–138.

Birt, D., & Olds, M. (1981). Associative response changes in the lateral midbrain tegmentum and medial geniculate during differential appetitive conditioning. Journal of Neurophysiology, 46, 1039–1055.

Bjordahl, T.S., Dimyan, M.A., & Weinberger, N.M. (1998). Induction of long-term receptive field plasticity in the auditory cortex of the waking guinea pig by stimulation of the nucleus basalis. Behavioral Neuroscience, 112, 467–479.

Brosch, M., Budinger, E., & Scheich, H. (2002). Stimulus-related gamma oscillations in primate auditory cortex. Journal of Neurophysiology, 87, 2715–2725.

Buss, E., Hall III, J.W., Grose, J.H., & Hatch, D.R. (1998). Perceptual consequences of peripheral hearing loss: do edge effects exist for abrupt cochlear lesions? Hearing Research, 125, 98–108.

Calford, M.B. (2002). Dynamic representational plasticity in sensory cortex. Neuroscience, 111, 709–738.

Cotillon-Williams, N., & Edeline, J.-M. (2003). Evoked oscillations in the thalamo-cortical auditory system are present in anesthetized but not in unanesthetized rats. Journal of Neurophysiology, 89, 1968–1984.

deCharms, R.C., & Merzenich, M.M. (1996). Primary cortical representation of sounds by the coordination of action-potential timing. Nature, 381, 610–613.

Diamond, D.M., & Weinberger, N.M. (1986). Classical conditioning rapidly induces specific changes in frequency receptive fields of single neurons in secondary and ventral ectosylvian auditory cortical fields. Brain Research, 372, 357–360.

Diamond, D.M., & Weinberger, N.M. (1989). Role of context in the expression of learning-induced plasticity of single neurons in auditory cortex. Behavioral Neuroscience, 103, 471–494.

Dimyan, M.A., & Weinberger, N.M. (1999). Basal forebrain stimulation induces discriminative receptive field plasticity in the auditory cortex. Behavioral Neuroscience, 113, 691–702.

Edeline, J.-M. (1999). Learning-induced physiological plasticity in the thalamo-cortical sensory system: A critical evalutation of receptive field plasticity and maps changes and their potential mechanisms. Progress in Neurobiology, 57, 165–224.

Edeline, J.-M. (2003). The thalamo-cortical auditory receptive fields: Regulation by the states of vigilance, learning and the neuromodulatory systems. Experimental Brain Research, 153, 554–572.

Edeline, J.-M., Pham, P., & Weinberger, N.M. (1993). Rapid development of learning-induced receptive field plasticity in the auditory cortex. Behavioral Neuroscience, 107, 539–551.

Edeline, J.-M., & Weinberger, N.M. (1991a). Subcortical adaptive filtering in the auditory system: Associative receptive field plasticity in the dorsal medial geniculate body. Behavioral Neuroscience, 105, 154–175.

Edeline, J.-M., & Weinberger, N.M. (1991b). Thalamic short-term plasticity in the auditory system: Associative retuning of receptive fields in the ventral medial geniculate body. Behavioral Neuroscience, 105, 618–639.

Edeline, J.-M., & Weinberger, N.M. (1992). Associative retuning in the thalamic source of input to the amygdala and auditory cortex: Receptive field plasticity in the medial division of the medial geniculate body. Behavioral Neuroscience, 106, 81–105.

Edeline, J.-M., & Weinberger, N.M. (1993). Receptive field plasticity in the auditory cortex during frequency discrimination training: Selective retuning independent of task difficulty. Behavioral Neuroscience, 107, 82–103.

Eggermont, J.J. (1998). Is there a neural code? Neuroscience and Biobehavioral Reviews, 22, 355–370.

Eggermont, J.J. (2001). Between sound and perception: reviewing the search for a neural code. Hearing Research, 157, 1–42.

Fritz, J., Shamma, S., Elhilali, M., & Klein, D. (2003). Rapid task-related plasticity of spectrotemporal receptive fields in primary auditory cortex. Nature Neuroscience, 11, 1216–1223.

Galvan V.V., & Weinberger, N.M. (2002). Long-term consolidation and retention of learning-induced tuning plasticity in the auditory cortex of the guinea pig. Neurobiology of Learning and Memory, 77, 78–108.

Gao, E., & Suga, N. (1998). Experience-dependent corticofugal adjustment of midbrain frequency map in bat auditory system. Proceedings of the National Academy of Sciences USA, 95, 12663–12670.

Gao, E., & Suga N. (2000). Experience-dependent plasticity in the auditory cortex and the inferior colliculus of bats: role of the corticofugal system. Proceedings of the National Academy of Sciences USA, 97, 8081-8086.

Heil, P. (1997). Auditory cortical onset responses revisited. I. First-spike timing. Journal of Neurophysiology, 77, 2616–2641.

Heil, P., & Irvine, D.R. (1996). On determinants of first-spike latency in auditory cortex. Neuroreport, 7, 3073–3076.

Hind, J.E., Goldberg, J.M., Greenwood, D.D., & Rose, J.E. (1963). Some discharge characteristics of single neurons in the inferior colliculus of the cat. II. Timing of discharges and observations on binaural stimulation. Journal of Neurophysiology, 26, 321–341.

Irvine, D.R., & Rajan, R. (1994). Plasticity in the mature auditory system. In G.A. Manley, G.M. Klump, C. Köppl, H. Fastl, & H. Oeckinghaus (Eds.), Advances in Hearing Research (pp. 3–23). Singapore: World Scientific Publishing.

Irvine, D.R., Rajan, R., & McDermott, H.J. (2000). Injury-induced reorganization in adult auditory cortex and its perceptual consequences. Hearing Research, 147, 188–199.

Kaas, J.H. (1997). Topographic maps are fundamental to sensory processing. Brain Research Bulletin, 44, 107–112.

Kamke, M.R., Brown, M., & Irvine, D.R. (2003). Plasticity in the tonotopic organization of the medial geniculate body in adult cats following restricted unilateral cochlear lesions. The Journal of Comparative Neurology, 459, 355–367.

Kilgard, M.P., & Merzenich, M.M. (1998a). Cortical map reorganization enabled by nucleus basalis activity. Science, 279, 1714–1718.

Kilgard, M.P., & Merzenich, M.M. (1998b). Plasticity of temporal information processing in the primary auditory cortex. Nature Neuroscience, 1, 727–731.

Kisley, M.A., & Gerstein, G.L. (2001). Daily variation and appetitive conditioning-induced plasticity of auditory cortex receptive fields. European Journal of Neuroscience, 13, 1993–2003.

Lecas, J.C. (2001). Noradrenergic modulation of tactile responses in rat cortex. Current source-density and unit analyses. Comptes Rendus de l'Academie des Sciences. Serie III. Sciences de la Vie, 324, 33–44.

Lisman, J.E. (1997). Bursts as a unit of neural information: Making unreliable synapses reliable. Trends in Neuroscience, 20, 38–43.

Maho, C., & Hennevin, E. (2002). Appetitive conditioning-induced plasticity is expressed during paradoxical sleep in the medial geniculate, but not in the lateral amygdala. Behavioral Neuroscience, 116, 807–823.

Manunta, Y., & Edeline, J.-M. (2004). Noradrenergic induction of selective plasticity in the frequency tuning of auditory cortex neurons. Journal of Neurophysiology, 92, 1445–1463.

Massaux A., Dutrieux G., Cotillon-Williams, N., Manunta, Y., & Edeline, J.-M. (2004). Auditory thalamus bursts in anesthetized and non-anesthetized states: Contribution to functional properties. Journal of Neurophysiology, 91, 2117–2134.

Massaux, A.E., & Edeline, J.-M. (2003). Bursts in the Medial Geniculate Body: A comparison between anesthetized and unanesthetized states in guinea pig. Experimental Brain Research, 153, 573–578.

McDermott, H.J., Lech, M., Kornblum, M.S., & Irvine, D.R. (1998). Loudness perception and frequency discrimination in subjects with steeply sloping hearing loss: Possible correlates of neural plasticity. Journal of the Acoustical Society of America, 104, 2314–2325.

McEchron, M.D., Green, E.J., Winters, R.W., Nolen, T.G., Schneiderman, N., & McCabe, P.M. (1996). Changes of synaptic efficacy in the medial geniculate nucleus as a result of auditory classical conditioning. Journal of Neuroscience, 16, 1273–1283.

Merzenich, M.M., Kaas, J.H., Wall, J., Nelson, R.J., Sur, M., & Felleman, D. (1983). Topographic reorganization of somatosensory cortical areas 3b and 1 in adult monkey following restricted deafferentation. Neuroscience, 8, 33–55.

Metherate, R., Tremblay, N., & Dykes, R.W. (1988). Transient and prolonged effects of acetylcholine on responsiveness of cat somatosensory cortical neurons. Journal of Neurophysiology, 59, 1253–1275.

Metherate, R., & Weinberger, N.M. (1989). Acetylcholine produces stimulus-specific receptive field alterations in cat auditory cortex. Brain Research, 480, 372–377.

Metherate, R., & Weinberger, N.M. (1990). Cholinergic modulation of responses to single tones produces tone-specific receptive field alterations in cat auditory cortex. Synapse, 6, 133–145.

Middlebrooks, J.C., Clock, A.E., Xu, L., & Green, D.M. (1994). A panoramic code for sound localisation by cortical neurons. Science, 264, 842–844.

Middlebrooks, J.C., Xu, L., Clock, A.E., & Green, D.M. (1998). Codes for sound-source location in nontonotopic auditory cortex. Journal of Neurophysiology, 80, 863–868.

Ohl, F., & Scheich, H. (1996). Differential frequency conditioning enhances spectral contrast sensitivity of units in the auditory cortex (field AI) of the alert mongolian gerbil. European Journal of Neuroscience, 8, 1001–1017.

Ohl, F., & Scheich, H. (1997). Learning-induced dynamic receptive field changes in primary auditory cortex (AI) of the unanaesthetized mongolian gerbil. Journal of Comparative Physiology A, 181, 685–696.

Phillips, D.P, Semple, M.N., Calford, M.B., & Kitzes, L.M. (1994). Level-dependent representation of stimulus frequency in cat primary auditory cortex. Experimental Brain Research, 102, 210–226.

Quirk, G.J., Armony, J.L., & LeDoux, J.E. (1997). Fear conditioning enhances different temporal components of tone-evoked spike trains in auditory cortex and lateral amygdala. Neuron, 19, 613–624.

Quirk, G.J., Repa, C., & LeDoux, J.E. (1995). Fear conditioning enhances short-latency auditory responses of lateral amygdala neurons: Parallel recordings in the freely behaving rat. Neuron, 15, 1029–1039.

Rajan, R. (1998). Receptor organ damage causes loss of cortical surround inhibition without topographic map plasticity. Nature Neuroscience, 1, 138–143.

Recanzone, G.H., Schreiner, C.E., & Merzenich, M.M. (1993). Plasticity in the frequency representation of primary auditory cortex following discrimination training in adult owl monkeys. Journal of Neuroscience, 13, 87–103.

Robertson, D., & Irvine, D.R. (1989). Plasticity of frequency organization in auditory cortex of guinea pigs with partial unilateral deafness. The Journal of Comparative Neurology, 282, 456–471.

Rutkowski, R., Than, K., & Weinberger, N.M. (2002). Evidence for area of frequency representation encoding acquired stimulus importance in rat primary auditory cortex. Abstracts – Society for Neuroscience, 24, 80.3.

Sherman, S.M. (2001). Tonic and burst firing: dual modes of thalamocortical relay. Trends in Neuroscience, 24, 122–126.

Steriade, M., & Timofeev, I. (2003). Neuronal plasticity in thalamocortical networks during sleep and waking oscillations. Neuron, 37, 563–576.

Suga, N., Xiao, Z., Ma, X., & Ji, W. (2002). Plasticity and corticofugal modulation for hearing in adult animals. Neuron, 36, 9–18.

Sukov, W., & Barth, D.S. (1998). Three-dimensional analysis of spontaneous and thalamically evoked gamma oscillations in auditory cortex. Journal of Neurophysiology, 79, 2875–2884.

Sukov, W., & Barth, D.S. (2001). Cellular mechanisms of thalamically evoked gamma oscillations in auditory cortex. Journal of Neurophysiology, 85, 1235–1245.

Swadlow, H.A., & Gusev, A.G. (2001). The impact of 'bursting' thalamic impulses at neocortical synapse. Nature Neuroscience, 4, 402–408.

Thai-Van, H., Micheyl, C., Norena, A., & Collet, L. (2002). Local improvement in auditory frequency discrimination is associated with hearing-loss slope in subjects with cochlear damage. Brain, 125, 524–537.

Tremblay, N., Warren, R.A., & Dykes, R.W. (1990). Electrophysiological studies of acetylcholine and the role of the basal forebrain in the somatosensory cortex of the cat. II. Cortical neurons excited by somatic stimuli. Journal of Neurophysiology, 64, 1212–1222.

Vaadia, E., Haalman, I., Abeles, M., Bergmen, H., Prut, Y., Slovin, H., & Aertsen, A. (1995). Dynamics of neuronal interactions in monkey cortex in relation to behavioural events. Nature, 373, 515–518.

Weinberger, N.M. (1995). Dynamic regulation of receptive fields and maps in the adult sensory cortex. Annual Review of Neuroscience, 18, 129–158.

Weinberger, N.M. (2001a). Receptive field plasticity and memory in the auditory cortex: Coding the learned importance of events. In J.E Steinmetz, M.A. Gluck, & P.R. Solomon (Eds.), Models systems and the neurobiology of associative learning: A festschrift in honor of Richard F. Thompson (pp. 187–216). London: Lawrence Erlbaum Associates.

Weinberger, N.M. (2001b). Memory code: A new concept for an old problem. In P.E. Gold & W. Greenough (Eds.), Memory consolidation: Essays in honor of James L. McGaugh (pp. 321–342). Washington DC: American Psychological Association.

Weinberger, N.M. (2003). The nucleus basalis and memory codes: Auditory cortical plasticity and the induction of specific associative behavioral memory. Neurobiology of Learning and Memory, 80, 268–284.

Weinberger, N.M. (in press). Experience-dependent response plasticity in the auditory cortex: Issues, characteristics, mechanisms and functions. In T. Parks, E. Rubel, A. Popper, & R. Fay (Eds.), Springer handbook of Auditory Research. New York: Springer-Verlag.

Weinberger, N.M., Ashe, J.H., Metherate, R., McKenna, T.M., Diamond, D.M., & Bakin, J. (1990). Retuning auditory cortex by learning: A preliminary model of receptive field plasticity. Concepts in Neurosciences, 1, 91–132.

Weinberger, N.M., & Diamond, D.M. (1987). Physiological plasticity in auditory cortex: Rapid induction by learning. Progress in Neurobiology, 29, 1–55.

Weinberger, N.M., Javid, R., & Lepan, B. (1993). Long-term retention of learning-induced receptive-field plasticity in the auditory cortex. Proceedings of the National Academy of Sciences USA, 90, 2394–2398.

Wiesel, T.N., & Hubel, D.H. (1963). Single-cell responses in striate cortex of kittens deprived of vision in one eye. Journal of Neurophysiology, 26, 1003–1017.

24. WHAT IS REFLECTED IN AUDITORY CORTEX ACTIVITY: PROPERTIES OF SOUND STIMULI OR WHAT THE BRAIN DOES WITH THEM?

Henning Scheich, Frank W. Ohl, Holger Schulze,
Andreas Hess, André Brechmann

Sensory cortical activity is manifest in spatio-temporal patterns. These patterns are usually conceived as representations of stimuli in maps. Various lines of evidence suggest, however, that these map-based patterns also depend on the specific cognitive or behavioral purpose served by the cortical processing. Therefore, a broader concept of the function of sensory neocortex seems to be required. Several principles are illustrated, how bottom-up and top-down processing of stimuli convey in auditory cortex maps. Top-down functions, so far, have been addressed in terms of prefrontal, parietal and cingulate cortical areas which obviously control these functions. With respect to selective auditory percepts and perceptual comparisons, which are the objects of cognitive top-down processing, the executive influences from these areas seem to use special organizations of maps and to modify auditory cortical representations of stimuli in these maps.

INTRODUCTION: THE DUALITY PROBLEM

Sensory cortex maps can be conceived to interface two complementary functions, bottom-up and top-down controlled processing of sensory information. This duality is not new and both aspects, more or less separately, have been subject of investigation since decades. But relatively little attention has been paid to the fact that the interfacing itself is not clear and demands a new look on the concept of sensory maps. On the one hand cortex maps serve the specification of sensory input information (stimulus attributes or features) by individual neuronal and network mechanisms. This can be considered as the implicit aspect of pattern recognition (*bottom-up principle*). Maps of this type are the way in which sensory cortex copes with separable features of the stimulus world and their variability generating orderly spatial representations of what is similar and dissimilar. On the other hand mechanisms and organization of sensory maps may also serve cognitive functions to make sensory information explicit and available in different contexts, namely by selective attention and discrimination, object constitution, categorization, and concept formation, as well as by selective long-term storage, recollection of information of interest and mental imagery (*top-down principle*). The bottom-up process is the result of polysynaptic sequential and parallel processing along the modality-specific sensory pathway with certain hierarchically concluding steps specific to cortex. The substrate for top-down control is much less clear but may occur by known feed-back interactions of sensory cortex fields in a given modality chiefly with other forebrain sources which have been implied in cognitive and motivational control and storage of information.

An exemplary substrate for the top-down control of sensory cortex may be structures and pathways which have been identified to serve in working memory (WM), because this function is thought "to provide an interface between perception, long-term memory and action" (Baddeley, 2003, for review). Key structures, which have been shown to be involved in working memory in monkeys and humans, comprise dorsolateral and middle prefrontal areas, dorsal parietal areas and anterior cingulate cortex. Dorsolateral prefrontal cortex is thought to be related to sequential comparisons and to the delay aspect of sequential information thus to the load of temporary memory in WM, anterior cingulate cortex more to the difficulty of decision making in the task, and parietal cortex to the storage and rehearsal aspects of the task (Baddeley, 2003; Barch et al., 1997; Cabeza & Nyberg, 2000; Knight et al., 1989; Olesen et al., 2004; Pessoa et al., 2002; Smith et al., 1998).

Within a modality-specific sensory cortex, which is usually parcellated into primary-like and multiple higher order fields, reciprocal feedback systems seem to be typical. Across this hierarchy feedback allowing top-down influences may reach all the way down to the primary fields and beyond. For instance in auditory cortex a system with core fields, belt and parabelt fields has been described with such interconnectivities. In this system especially the higher order (parabelt) areas also maintain connectivities with the aforementioned prefrontal, parietal and cingulate areas (Budinger et al., 2000; Kaas & Hackett, 2000; Romanski et al., 1999). Thus, for the functions of WM a neural interfacing substrate is available which could, in principle, be used to compare specific attributes of actual percepts with foregoing percepts of sounds.

There is a prevailing conceptual tendency in the literature to keep bottom-up processing in sensory cortex maps "clean" of cognitive processing, i.e. to allocate relevant mechanisms at least in higher order "association areas". This is particularly obvious for primary visual, auditory, and somatosensory cortex. But no principle reason would exclude the existence of duality even in primary sensory areas except that it has proven extremely demanding to experimentally disentangle the interfacing of such processes in sensory cortex maps. Thereby it is only part of the problem that most studies of sensory cortex have been carried out in anesthetized animals, thus revealing only the strongest bottom-up inputs. Even in an awake brain of a behaving subject any analysis of this sort has a unidirectional bias: One cannot exclude or abolish the bottom-up processing to determine the top-down contribution because basic feature analysis will be impaired. It is only possible to minimize or to largely vary the top-down demands to have an estimate of the bottom-up prerequisite. Consequently, lesions encroaching on fields with early sensory processing will abolish bottom-up mechanisms unless functions can be fulfilled by subcortical centers (cf. discussion in Ohl et al., 1999).

Nevertheless, a concept of duality in sensory cortex has previously been put forward with respect to memory, to selective attention, and to mental imagery. The study of organization of various types of memory has generated the view that a number of systems, especially limbic structures and prefrontal and parietal cortex, are essential for selection and intermediate retention of to be stored information. But it has long been recognized that "memory is stored in the same neuronal systems that ordinarily participate in perception, analysis and processing" of this information, thus in sensory cortex (Squire et al., 1990, p. 15).

Similar conclusions are drawn for attention (Posner 1997, p. 617): "When attention operates during task performance, it will operate at the site where the computation involved in the task is usually performed. Thus, when subjects attend to color, form, or motion of a visual object they amplify blood flow in various extrastriate areas (Corbetta et al., 1991)". Thus, in contrast to the above mentioned problem in lesion and functional imaging research there are results from brain imaging studies supporting duality in sensory cortex. Results of this type are also available in the case of mental imagery (Farah, 1997; Wheeler et al., 2000).

In spite of these convictions how parallel bottom-up and top-down functions are enabled in sensory cortex has not been well conceptualized. In a certain sense the brain itself may have a problem of distinguishing the results of bottom-up and top-down processing in the same structure. If the two are intermingled in the same neurons, stimulus identity may not be secured across stimulus representations, the flow of fresh information may be interrupted by top-down processing and the distinction of what is real and what is imagination may be jeopardized, to name only a few problems.

We propose here a concept for auditory cortex illustrated by several examples by which the duality problem might be solved by sensory cortex. Solutions may be:

A) Representation of different stimulus features in separate maps if top-down cognitive demands or behavioral consequences are different for the recognition of these features. Conversely, representation of different stimulus features in the same map if usual top-down demands are the same.

B) Orderly spatial organization of neuronal ensembles devoted to different top-down recognition needs in the form of superimposed maps in the same space.

C) Sequential order of representations of bottom-up and top-down information by different activity states in the same maps.

It should be clear that the issue of these components reflects working hypotheses rather than firm propositions. Furthermore, some of the arguments in the following may not yet be experimentally testable but are rather based on comparative evidence in animal and human cortex, that is, on evolutionary arguments.

MAPS AND STATES

At this point it seems important to make the crucial distinction of how a cortex map is usually constructed experimentally from stimulus response data of individual neurons and what this view subsequently predicts about the total representation of a single stimulus in the map as a basis of identification: In a given location a neuron is tested with an array of stimuli providing the response profile (or receptive field) of that neuron. Variations in a certain stimulus class are made along its different feature dimensions separately (like pure tone frequency, amplitude modulation frequency, fundamental frequency bandwidth etc., or color, shape, orientation, etc.) to explore the tuning to variants of a given feature and the selectivity for different features. The procedure is repeated with multiple locations in a raster across the presumed map. In this way multiple response profiles are obtained from which a response space could be constructed over the raster with the dimensionality of the number of feature dimensions. In practice this is rarely done but instead singularities of response profiles, like maximum excitation or inhibition, are selectively used to connect locations with comparable response properties in the map (iso-stimulus contours). Thereby, within a map the information about the global distribution of a response to any given stimulus is usually lost.

This selection of the seemingly most important response aspects entails only *local views of the response distribution in the map*. It is important to point out that this type of map characterization is useful to estimate where in the map maximal contrasts between feature variants can be expected as long as it is not implied that local views constitute stimulus "finger prints". Since these local views are, in essence, arbitrary classification procedures, it becomes impossible to determine from them the complete representation of a given stimulus by neurons in a map, which neurons are involved and whether the stimulus has a unique representation in the map (global view). This shortcoming is particularly obvious in optical recording and human brain imaging techniques in which "direct contrast" of activations by two stimuli is commonly derived by subtraction methods. Local views of the map similar to units of receptive field properties are selective bottom-up aspects of stimulus processing (Lee et al., 2004; Phillips & Singer, 1997). They do not allow by themselves to address a stimulus or one of its features as an entity, i.e. to make it explicit.

From a local view, "artificial" problems may arise which are less salient in a global view of the map's activation pattern, namely whether flexible ensembles of feature-selective neurons have to be generated to recognize stimuli (Hardcastle, 1994) or whether recognition relies on "expert neurons" (Sigala & Logothetis, 2002; Hasegawa & Miyashita, 2002). Advantages of the alternative *global view* of maps (unique stimulus representation by global activation patterns) have long been recognized (for review, Freeman, 2000). It has also been recognized by electrophysiological techniques and by optical imaging that local response features in maps show spatial shifts during the time course of the response to any given stimulus (Arieli et al., 1996; DeMott, 1970; Hess & Scheich, 1996; Horikawa et al., 1996, 1998; Hosokawa et al., 1999; Lilly, 1954; Taniguchi & Nasu, 1993; Uno et al., 1993). This strongly argues for the relevance of a global view of maps because stimulus representational aspects of neuronal responses are non-stationary. The global spatiotemporal activation pattern of a complete map is called here a state of the map.

GLOBAL VIEWS, MAP SUPERPOSITION, AND TOP-DOWN DEMANDS

A global view of a given map would produce a unique representation of any stimulus if a sufficient diversity of unit response properties (receptive fields) is provided in the map. When behavioral or cognitive demands require to single out (make explicit) a particular stimulus feature and its relevant variation (e.g. of color, tone frequency, sound periodicity), a separate map in the cortex would be one strategy to provide a global view of this feature (Kaas, 1982, 1993). Alternatively, a global view may still be provided if another, correspondingly specialized, map is superimposed on a given map (superposition maps) (e.g. Cohen & Knudsen, 1999; Schreiner, 1995, 1998). It should be pointed out that the process of making a particular feature explicit by the top-down demand may imply putting the recruited global activity state (actual state) into relation to the other non-recruited activity states (potential states) represented in the superposition maps. Thus, a map, in the global view of a top-down perspective, may be the specific geometric or topological frame for the cognitive construction of an explicit feature. It should also be noted that a global view of the activity distributions within the frame of a map offers relatively simple ways to "read out" information about stimuli.

THE AUDITORY CORTEX: A TEST GROUND FOR VIEWS ON CORTICAL MAPS

Before embarking on these topics a few principles of auditory cortex organization and open questions related to this organization are described which become relevant during the course of this article. One of the most conservative organizational principles in the auditory pathway of mammals are tonotopic maps which reflect the place code for frequency channel analysis in the cochlea up to cortex (Merzenich & Brugge, 1973; Merzenich et al., 1975; Scheich, 1991; Scheich et al., 1993; Thomas et al., 1993). The geometry of these bottom-up tonotopic maps basically consists of a tonotopic gradient along which neurons show an orderly change of highest sensitivity (characteristic frequency CF) and of highest discharge rate (best frequency BF) in response to systematically varied pure tone frequencies. Orthogonal to this tonotopic gradient neurons have roughly the same CF or BF. This isofrequency dimension of the maps obtained with pure tones does not reflect the analytical potential of neurons but rather a common dominant subcortical input from the tonotopic frequency channel. Neurons along an isofrequency dimension have highly varied sensitivities for additional single or complex acoustic parameters (Bonham et al., 2004; Heil et al., 1992, 1994; Ohl & Scheich, 1997b; Read et al., 2002; Schreiner, 1995, 1998; Schreiner et al., 2000).

A characteristic property of auditory cortex in all mammalian species is the multiplicity of maps distinguished with tone stimuli. Usually several of these maps are tonotopically organized. (The failure to show this so far in some species is presumably due to insufficient mapping.) Size and geometries of these tonotopic maps (spatial relationship between tonotopic and isofrequency dimension) and spatial characteristics of non-tonotopic maps which still show tone responsiveness of most neurons are species-specific. Geometries are also characteristically different among the multiple maps of a species.

The reasons for multiple representations of cochlear place information have been sought in the separate brain analysis of various complex acoustic parameter spaces (stimulus features like amplitude modulations (AM), frequency modulations (FM), noise bandwidths, segmentations, harmonic structures, spectral envelopes). But in the best studied cases with this bottom-up concept, cat, monkey and gerbil auditory cortex, mapping experiments have shown that representation of any feature is not exclusive to any particular map (Eggermont, 1998; Rauschecker et al., 1995; Schreiner & Urbas, 1988; Schulze et al., 1997). Thus, these differences between maps may only be gradual.

On the other hand there is a detailed analysis of the highly specialized maps in auditory cortex of the mustache bat which suggests indeed the principle of parametric representation of different features of echo sounds in separate maps (for review, see Suga, 1994). Interestingly, this apparent counterexample to cat, monkey and gerbil may prove the case for a subtle yet important distinction of what multiple maps in auditory cortex represent. Variations of echo features from the bat's own voice reflected from obstacles and prey are not simply stimulus features serving pattern recognition. They manifest at the same time detailed behavioral meaning for the hunter. Namely, information about size, surface structure, relative speed and direction of objects which is derived from such features subsequently entails adequate specific behavioral acts. Consequently, in the mustache bat stimulus features represent qualities equivalent to behavioral categories. While for the special case of the bat a cognitive generalization for a particular behavior can be made from one or very few stimulus features, for less specialized and more opportunistic animals this cognitive generalization can only be made from heterogeneous auditory objects with numerous stimulus features which may vary dependent on the environment. This may be the reason why their different maps appear to be much less feature-specific.

In summary, the specialized case of the bat auditory cortex which presumably evolved on the basis of self-generated "predictable" sound patterns (in contrast to individually unpredictable acoustic environments of most other animals) may still imply a common principle with multiple maps in auditory cortex of other animals: Their significance may chiefly lie in cognitive demands of different behavioral tasks. The consequences of this distinction will become clear by examples in the following from Mongolian gerbil and human auditory cortex. There it will be shown (1) that neurons organized in a given map may derive information of comparable behavioral relevance from different stimulus features and (2) conversely, that different tasks executed on the same stimulus material lead to activation of different maps or to different states of a map. Such functional aspects of maps are not easily reconciled with a strict bottom-up concept of stimulus specification but rather point to a decisive influence of top-down processing in constitution and use of such maps.

EXAMPLES OF SUPERIMPOSED MAPS IN AUDITORY CORTEX

Evidence for map superposition in auditory cortex

The primary auditory cortex (AI) map because of its rigid tonotopic input organization is a suitable example to demonstrate the principle of top-down influences on this framework. One aspect is its parcellation into multiple ensembles of task-dedicated neurons or submaps. An early example described in cat are ensembles of neuron types related to binaural processing (EE, EI) originally thought to form multiple stripes orthogonal to tonotopic organization (Middlebrooks et al., 1980; Schreiner, 1991) but in essence may be irregular patches of similar neuron types (Phillips & Irvine, 1983; for review, Clarey et al., 1991). Furthermore, in cat multiple representations of complex features related to frequency tuning overlaying the best frequency (BF) organization was described (Schreiner & Sutter, 1992). Also this organization related to specification of stimulus feature may consist of patches with different spatial order in individual animals (Heil et al., 1992). These organizational principles already suggest a tendency in AI to map and thereby separate the results of multiple filter properties of neurons which are generated stepwise along the auditory pathway. For instance space maps of auditory sources are found in inferior and superior colliculi (Knudsen et al., 1987), but spectral aspects of the localized sounds do not seem to be distinguished in detail. Similarly, periodicity of sounds is mapped in inferior colliculus presumably serving complex pitch discrimination (Langner, 1992), but this processing step is not yet sufficient for the use of periodicities for object constitution or foreground-background discrimination.

Therefore, it is of considerable interest that map principles are found in AI which can be considered as strategies to orderly disentangle separable stimulus features, i.e. to make them more explicit. This is the case in the following examples in which a superimposed map is either independent of the tonotopic organization or exists in a specific relation to the tonotopic gradient.

Superimposed tonotopic and periodicity maps

Using optical imaging of intrinsic signals as well as electrophysiological mapping of the primary auditory cortex (AI) of the gerbil we recently described a representation of sound periodicity with a continuous, almost cyclic functional gradient superimposed on the tonotopic organization (Fig. 24.1 right panel; Schulze et al., 2000). This is particularly interesting because periodicity is a non-cyclic parameter. As previously pointed out (Nelson & Bower, 1990; Scheich, 1991), the geometry of a topographic stimulus representation has implications for the neuronal computations that can be carried out within a map, in other words, different types of computations require different map constructs. According to Nelson & Bower (1990) continuous maps are those in which the computationally relevant parameter is represented along a simple functional gradient. Computations carried out in such maps are characterized by predominantly local interactions in the problem space, for example, lateral inhibition.

With reference to these postulates we suppose that the cyclic geometry of the functional gradient in this map is the result of computational requirements beyond simple local interactions: The cyclic arrangement of stimulus representations, such as periodicities, allows for equivalent interconnection across the center of the map between neurons which represent a certain value of a stimulus parameter with the remaining neurons representing all other values of that parameter. Such a pattern of interconnections facilitates computational algorithms for which global synchronous interactions between arbitrary distances in the parameter space are critical. Thus, a cyclic map could provide a pattern of interconnections that facilitates the extraction of a particular value of the represented parameter from a mixture of other values by a neuronal implementation of a "winner-take-all" algorithm (Haken, 1991; Schmutz & Banzhaf, 1992; Waugh & Westervelt, 1993) in addition to the local lateral interaction mechanism thought to operate in linear topographic maps. In such linear maps, for example, tonotopic maps, only the contrast between neighboring neurons (and stimulus representations) is enhanced. There are also other examples of cyclic maps: The map of stimulus amplitudes composed of two facing half-cycles of amplitude representation in the auditory cortex of the mustached bat (Suga, 1977) and the pinwheel-like arrangement of the iso-orientation domains in the visual cortex (Bonhoeffer & Grinvald, 1991) may also provide a substrate for a winner-takes-all computation.

The identification of individual signals from a mixture is a common task for the auditory systems of all vocalizing species (Bodnar & Bass, 1999). Gerbils are social animals living as family groups in elaborate burrows, with many such groups in close vicinity in a given area (Ågren et al., 1989; Thiessen & Yahr, 1977). They have a rich repertoire of vocalizations, of which a particular group of alarm calls (Yapa, 1994) is characterized by harmonic spectra with periodicities in the range represented in the cortex map reported here. Gerbils

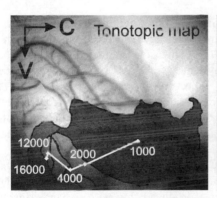 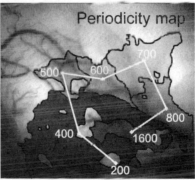

Fig. 24.1. Topography of tonotopic and periodicity map in gerbil AI. Best-stimulus representations from one animal from optical recording of intrinsic signals are shown using pure tones or amplitude modulated stimuli with different periodicities. Areas of strongest tone frequency responses or modulation frequency responses are given in different shades of gray and centers of gravity with numbers in Hz are connected by white lines to show the gradients increasing BF or periodicity, respectively. The maps are superimposed on an image of the cortical surface. v = ventral, c = caudal. Scale bar, 0.5 mm. (Modified after Schulze et al., 2000.)

may therefore use a winner-takes-all algorithm in their periodicity map for selecting the vocalizations of individuals within a group. It remains to be seen whether an area in rostral human auditory cortex activated by foreground-background decomposition tasks (Scheich et al., 1998) contains a map for extracting the periodicity (fundamental) of a specific speaker's voice in noisy situations such as cocktail parties (von der Malsburg & Schneider, 1986).

Interestingly, sound periodicities in the range below about 100 Hz, which are perceptually different form sounds with high periodicities (see below), are not represented within the described cyclic map but are represented via a temporal code (phase-locking) in AI. Neurons that code for sound periodicity via this temporal code, are not continuously distributed across AI but form a scattered, non-topographic map instead (Schulze & Langner, 1997). Obviously, there are two different maps for one sound parameter (periodicity) in the auditory cortex, one which is continuous and represents high periodicities that elicit the percept of certain pitches and one which is scattered and represents low periodicities which are perceived as rhythm or roughness (cf. Schulze & Langner, 1997). While from the point of view of the continuous parameter space of periodicities (bottom-up view) there would be no need to generate separate representations, this parcellation becomes understandable from a top-down point of view, since the two submaps represent stimuli from different perceptual categories and therefore may serve different purposes.

Superimposed tonotopic and vowel maps

A further example of superposition of maps shedding light on the issue of local vs. global views of maps is given by the case of vowel representation in the auditory cortex (Ohl & Scheich, 1997b). This study aimed at solving the problem that on the one hand psychophysical experiments have shown that the discrimination of human vowels chiefly relies on the frequency relationship of the first two peaks of a vowel's spectral envelope, the so-called formants F1 and F2 (Peterson & Barney, 1952), but that on the other hand all previous attempts to relate this 2-dimensional (F1, F2)-relationship to the known one-dimensional topography of cortical tonotopic maps had failed.

A first linear hypothesis would have predicted that in a tonotopic map the activation pattern evoked by a 2-formant vowel would resemble the superposition of the activation patterns produced by narrow-band signals centered around the frequencies F1 and F2, respectively. This view was plausible because single units' activities in the peripheral auditory system (as measured by rate or synchrony codes (Young & Sachs, 1979)) when plotted over their characteristic frequency give indeed a profile similar to the power spectrum of a vowel. Instead, we found a different unique activation pattern that held no obvious relationship to patterns produced by single formants. We first showed that in a part of gerbil primary auditory cortex field AI single units showed nonlinear spectral interaction mechanisms as a function of varied F2-F1 spectral distance. Second, these response properties formed a new map, superposed on the tonotopic map, in which a nonlinear transformation of the psychophysically determined (F1, F2)-relationship was represented as a spatial gradient. The transformed relationship was isomorphic to the original (F1, F2)-relationship with respect to identification and classification of vowels (Ohl & Scheich, 1997b).

This finding helped to identify an interpretational bias inherent in earlier attempts, namely the a-priori assumption, that single units in a map contribute to the coding predominately of those parts of the vowel spectrum that corresponded to their characteristic frequencies (*"feature extraction"*). Consequently, this view entails the problem that those individually coded features subsequently have to be put into relation to each other again (*"feature binding"*) by yet unknown mechanisms. Alternatively, it has been argued (Ohl & Scheich, 1998) that the availability of a global activity pattern in the above described transformed map eliminates the need for feature extraction and rebinding processes during vowel recognition and classification. By emphasizing the relevance of the activity state over the map geometry even the requirement for isomorphism between activity patterns and perception has been disputed (Pouget & Sejnowski, 1994; Freeman, 2000).

TOP-DOWN PROCESSING

Same stimuli, different tasks

It was recently shown in the Mongolian gerbil that right (but not left) auditory cortex is essential for the distinction of rising versus falling direction of frequency modulated tones (FM). Gerbils trained in a shuttle box to well discriminate directionally mirror imaged frequency sweeps lose the capability after lesion of right but not of left auditory cortex and are no longer able to acquire this discrimination (Wetzel et al., 1998a). Gerbils are capable, however, of learning pure tone discriminations after auditory cortex lesions (Ohl et al., 1999).

These results gave rise to the question whether human auditory cortex might be specialized in a similar way. Right human auditory cortex specializations for certain aspects of FM discrimination might be suspected because there are numerous reports on deficits of right brain lesioned patients with respect to the distinction of prosodic information in speech (e.g., Ackermann et al., 1993; Joanette et al., 1990). Prosody is the dimension of speech which chiefly conveys information about emotions, intentions, personal attitudes of the speaker towards the content of his speech and towards the communication partners and various other social and biological attributes of individual speakers independent of the linguistic content of speech. Thereby, modulation of voice fundamental frequency within words and across sentences (speech contour) as well as some variations of spectral motion of vowel formants seem to play an important role.

The question of FM directional discrimination was addressed in human auditory cortex by low noise fMRI using the same type of FM stimuli as in the gerbil experiments (Brechmann & Scheich, 2004). The first task (control task) was to listen to a collection of FM sweeps randomly varying in frequency range and direction and to determine any commonality among the stimuli. Subjects easily identified the concept of the stimuli describing them as tones with changing pitch. Responses in auditory cortex were measured in a so-called block design integrating activation across the whole period of presentation of the stimulus set. This experiment depending on the individual generated either balanced activation in right and left auditory cortex or a left dominance of activation (Fig. 24.2, left panel).

Subsequently, the same stimulus selection was presented again, but subjects were informed that they had to identify the rising FM samples (respectively the falling FM samples) by key pressing. This task amounts to a categorization because direction had to be determined independent of frequency range. The result was different from the previous experiment in spite of hearing the same stimuli. Activation of right auditory cortex was stronger than in the listening control (Fig. 24.2, right panel). The redistribution of activity towards right auditory cortex was specific to secondary fields which shall not be described here. The shift of activation upon categorization of FM direction was specific to this task as demonstrated with another stimulus set in which long and short as well as rising and falling FM sweeps were present. Categorization of the stimulus duration aspect generated stronger left auditory cortex, activation compared to categorization of direction while categorization of direction caused stronger right auditory cortex activation compared to categorization of duration.

In the light of the gerbil experiment showing that the rodent right auditory cortex is indispensable for the discrimination of FM direction the fMRI results suggest at least a special role of right human auditory cortex in this respect in humans. The most important point to make here is that mechanisms related to FM directional processing are only engaged when this stimulus feature is to be explicitly distinguished not simply upon stimulus presentation. This demonstrates that top-down influences can dominate the activation in auditory cortex to the extent that even a change of hemispheric lateralization will result.

Different cues, same task

Foreground-background decomposition. Periodicity analysis provides one possible cue by which certain classes of auditory objects which coincide in time may be distinguished. Above a superposition map was described in gerbil AI which not only allows the systematic mapping of periodicity but may also select among coinciding objects with different periodicities. While these mechanisms presumably allow to discriminate certain classes of competing auditory objects, the fundamental concept of object constitution in a mixture of sounds is more general and more demanding. In its best known form this capability has been addressed as the "cocktail party effect" (Cherry, 1953; von der Malsburg & Schneider, 1986). While Cherry (1953) who coined the name, was under the assumption that the effect is a sound localization problem, it is clear now that the problem of foreground-background decomposition can also be solved monaurally (Yost & Sheft, 1993). But it requires selective attention to the features of an individual voice in a mixture of concurrent voices and is a good example of top-down influence. An important cue for the distinction are periodicities in the attended voice represented by vowel fundamental frequencies together with all harmonics. Several other mechanisms of spectral and temporal discrimination beside periodicity analysis may be used, presumably in an opportunistic fashion, a matter of ongoing research in this and other laboratories.

Some lines of experiments with low noise (48 dB SPL) fMRI in human auditory cortex have led to the concept that a rostral area on the dorsal surface of the temporal lobe, anterior to Heschl's gyrus, may be an area of central importance in foreground-background decomposition. Several mechanisms relevant in this context may converge in this area named territory TA (T1a).

One of our experiments addressed the question how in a series of complex tones (notes of different musical instruments) matching pairs (instrument and note identical) are identified in the presence of a continuous background. This background consisted of a saw tooth frequency modulation of a tone which strongly masked fundamental and lower harmonic frequencies of the instrument notes (Scheich et al., 1998). This constellation is a simplified version of the task of a conductor when monitoring different instruments in an orchestra piece.

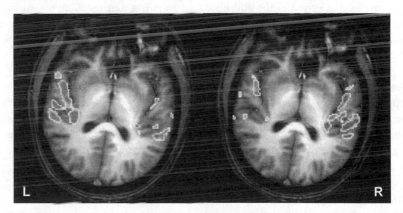

Fig. 24.2. Task-dependent fMRI activation in a subject during listening to the same series of linearly frequency modulated tones varied in frequency range and direction of sweep. Left panel, left-lateralized activation: by uninformed attentive listening to the series of stimuli. Right panel, right-lateralized activation: Identification of the sweeps with downward direction. (Modified after Brechmann & Scheich, 2004.)

In the first experiment the total effect of instrument notes, background and discrimination task was determined in auditory cortex as referred to interval periods without any stimulation. This revealed strong bilateral activation in all previously known primary and non-primary subdivisions of auditory cortex.

The second experiment served to isolate the effect of the foreground-dependent task. The described situation was the same but the background alone continued though the reference periods. Thereby the FM background had been calibrated in such a way that it maximally activated primary-like areas in auditory cortex. Consequently, by referring foreground plus background to the background alone it was expected that much of the primary-like activation in auditory cortex would cancel out. This was indeed the case. Of the original activation determined in the first experiment merely the activity in the rostral area TA was maintained in the second experiment. That activity in TA was not significantly different in the two experiments. This suggests that in contrast to the other areas the background alone had very little direct influence on TA and did not appreciably influence the effect of the foreground task in this area.

The properties of TA do not depend on particular stimuli. This became apparent in a study on level-dependent activation of human auditory cortex with a large set of different rising and falling FM sweeps (Brechmann et al., 2002). TA in contrast to other auditory cortex areas showed little activation and no level dependent change of activation for intermediate and high levels of stimuli. Only when the FM level (36 dB SPL) fell below the level of the background noise of the MR scanner (48 dB SPL) was TA activation strongly increased. Thus, activation of this area increased when the targets had to be retrieved from a louder yet distinguishable scanner noise. This is a result similar to the previous experiments and provides the additional information that mechanisms in TA are challenged especially if the background strongly interferes with the foreground targets.

A motion-selective map in auditory cortex. If principles of a map organization strongly relate to the constitution of behavioral meaning of stimuli (top-down demands) in addition to the analysis of a particular stimulus feature one should expect that neurons in this map derive information of comparable behavioral relevance from different stimulus features. This seems to be the case in a motion-selective area on the lateral planum temporale of human auditory cortex (Baumgart et al., 1999). This area, sometimes dominantly activated on the right side, was identified with fMRI using motion percepts generated by time-variant interaural cues through headphones and later confirmed by head-related transfer functions (Warren et al., 2002). One motion cue is a changing interaural level relationship of stimuli (interaural intensity difference, IID). In this case a slow amplitude modulation of a carrier sound was generated which in the motion case had a slowly varying phase angle and in the case of the control stimulus had the same phase of the modulation cycle at the two ears. The sound of the control stimulus was not perceived as having any specific location in space. Conversely, if amplitude-phase cycles of the identical stimuli were slowly shifted interaurally the percept was that of a sound source slowly moving back and forth in azimuth in front of the listener.

With fMRI these two stimuli generated very strong and spatially similar activations in primary and non-primary areas of auditory cortex. The subtraction of the two activation patterns, however, yielded a reliable signal intensity increase by the motion stimulus laterally on the right planum temporale (Fig. 24.3, left panel). Interestingly, a very similar activation increase was obtained with a different interaural cue and a different type of carrier stimulus (Fig. 24.3, right panel). These were short tone bursts of constant frequency presented with simultaneous onset at the two ears (control) or with successively changing onset between the two ears (motion). The latter contains interaural time differences (ITD) as a motion cue. While the control condition did not generate any location percept of the sound source the ITD cue led to the percept of small azimuthal jumps of source location.

The similarity of the spatial location of signal increase for IID and ITD cues in the right planum temporale is relevant for assumed hemispheric specializations for extracorporal space analysis by the right hemisphere. Obviously, not only visual space cue analysis and multimodal space cue processing is lateralized to the right hemisphere (Bisiach & Berti, 1997; Bisiach & Vallar, 1988) but also auditory space cue analysis (Griffith et al, 1998). Whether this relates in any way to a proposed "dorsal stream" of auditory space analysis in auditory cortex (Romanski et al., 1999) remains to be determined.

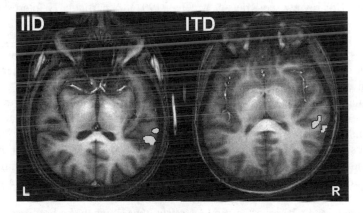

Fig. 24.3. Parameter-independence of movement-selective fMRI activation in human auditory cortex. The activations in the white areas on the right planum temporale in two subjects were obtained during perceived motion of an auditory object generated by interaural phase shifts of envelops of an amplitude-modulated sound (interaural intensity difference, IID, left), or by changing interaural onset delays of a pure tone (interaural time difference, ITD, right), respectively. (Modified after Baumgart et al., 1999.)

The immediate relevance to the present subject is that the motion-selective area in right auditory cortex is neither stimulus specific nor motion-cue specific, thus does not fulfill the criterion of an area specialized for specific acoustic features in a bottom-up concept. Rather the generation of explicit motion percepts seems to be the common denominator. This is further underlined by fMRI experiments using a third motion cue, namely head-related transfer functions using a moving sound source, which generates a vivid space percept of a movement all around the head.

Categorization

The concept of multiple overlaying maps in the same neuronal substrate raises the question in which ways activity states coexisting in this substrate can be organized (a) to avoid confusion by interference effects and (b) to allow the relation of a given activity state to any particular map. We propose that the *sequential temporal order of recruitment* of neural activity states is one mechanism for the disentanglement of maps. While the types of overlaying maps discussed in section 5 are typically obtained in a particular and widely used experimental approach to uncover regularities in map organization ("mapping experiment") we will argue in this section that in more natural circumstances activity states emerge to serve particular needs of the behaving organism or subject.

Since decades electrophysiological studies in human auditory cortex have described the succession of events related to different aspects of stimulus analysis (for review see Kraus & McGee, 1991). A particularly interesting field concerned with the temporal interplay of bottom-up and top-down aspects of information processing is the analysis of *selective attention*. Here, a subject focuses attention on a selected subset of the environmental (or proprioceptive) inputs at the expense of less relevant inputs (for review, see Posner, 1997). Clearly, the attribution of relevance during selection and maintenance of a focus constitutes a top-down modulation of bottom-up information processing. There has been some debate about whether this modulation occurs only at "late" stages (several 100 ms) of information processing or already affects "early" stimulus processing. Advances in neuroimaging studies have revealed that selective attention can affect both early and late components of information processing (Hillyard et al., 1995). While there is multiple evidence that selective attention involves cortical (rather than more peripheral) mechanisms, attention becomes effective already 20 ms after stimulus onset, that is, when the bottom-up-evoked neural activity arrives in the cortex. Although this demonstrates that top-down modulations can occur at the earliest possible time of cortical stimulus processing, it should not be overlooked that in an experimental setting with stimulus repetition they are the result of initial experiences which lead to focusing of attention and expectancy.

A clear example of temporal separation between bottom-up and top-down aspects of neuronal representation is given by recent findings on the neuronal correlates of auditory categorization learning (Ohl et al., 2001, 2003a, 2003b). In single-trial analyses of high-resolution electrocorticograms, "early" (20-50 ms) neural activity states representing stimulus-related, mainly bottom-up-relayed, information could be discerned from "late" (several 100 ms to few seconds) states representing category-related information. In this experiment, Mongolian gerbils, a rodent species especially well suited for complex learning tasks (Ohl & Scheich, 1996, 1997a; Schulze & Scheich, 1999) were trained to sort novel, previously unknown, frequency-modulated (FM) sounds into the categories "rising" or "falling", respectively, depending on the direction of the frequency modulation (low pitch to high pitch or vice versa) of the sound (Wetzel et al., 1998b). Discrimination of modulation direction has been demonstrated to be cortex-dependent (Ohl et al., 1999).

First, in behavioral analyses (Wetzel et al., 1998b) it was shown that gerbils can learn this categorization upon training a sequence of pairwise discriminations with a number of sound prototypes (rising vs. falling). In each training block of the sequence, the discrimination of a particular pair of a rising and a falling FM tone is trained until criterion. This is followed by a subsequent training block with another stimulus pair. During this so-called *discrimination phase* animals will show (a) a gradual increase in discrimination performance for each new prototype pair of FM tones and (b) a gradually declining generalization gradient for gradually varying FM tones taken from the stimulus continuum between the learned prototypes. After training continued for a few blocks, a sudden transition in behavior occurs after which novel stimuli are immediately identified as belonging to either the rising or falling category. This so-called *categorization phase* is characterized by (a) immediate stimulus identification and (b) categorical perception (sigmoid psychometric functions) instead. The transition from the discrimination phase to the categorization phase occurs abruptly at a point in time during the training history that is specific to the individual animal (Fig. 24.4).

This behavioral state transition is paralleled by a transition in the organization of a particular type of transient spatio-temporal activity pattern in AI that we called "*marked states*". These states were identified by tracking over time a measure of dissimilarity between the spatial activity pattern in a given trial to be analyzed and the mean pattern obtained by averaging over all trials involving stimuli of the respective other category (Figs. 24.4A, 24.4B). This measure peaks after stimulus arrival in the cortex independent of the training state (i.e., in both naive and trained animals) reflecting the perturbation of ongoing activity by the incoming stimulus (Freeman, 1994; Arieli et al., 1996). Specifically, the spatial activity pattern found in the early marked states reflects the physical stimulus characteristics represented in the tonotopically organized map of primary auditory cortex (Ohl et al., 2000a, 2000b). With training additional peaks emerged from the ongoing activity tagging additional marked

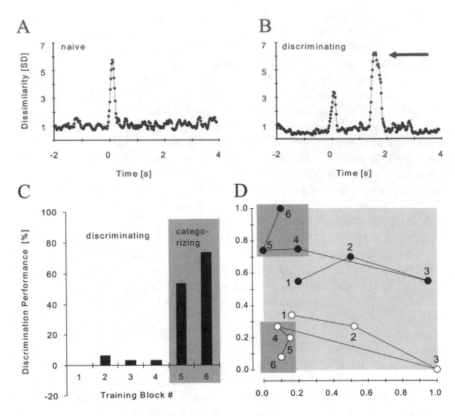

Fig. 24.4. Cortical dynamics during categorization learning of upward and downward frequency modulations (FM). (**A, B**) Dissimilarity functions in a typical trial of a naive and a discriminating animal, respectively. "Marked states" of auditory cortex are distinguished by transient maxima in these functions. (**C**) Discrimination performance in one animal obtained in the first training sessions of six consecutive training blocks with different FM pairs. In the first sessions of each training block the FM pair to be discriminated were novel to the animal. Note, in training blocks 1-4 discrimination performance was negligible in the first session (and built up gradually in later sessions, not shown) (*discrimination phase*), whereas in blocks 5 and 6, performance was already high in the first sessions (*categorization phase*). (**D**) Similarity relations between spatial activity patterns associated with marked states in the same animal. For each training block (numbers) the pattern for the category "upward" (filled circles) and the pattern for the category "downward" (open circles) is depicted. The diagram is so arranged that distances between points are proportional to the dissimilarity of the corresponding activity patterns. Note that when categorization begins between training blocks 4 and 5 (cf. C) activity patterns during marked states start to remain similar to the patterns found during the previous training block leading to a clustering in the diagram (darker rectangles). Before the clustering, interpoint distances within and between categories were of similar magnitude. (Modified after Ohl et al., 2001.)

states occurring at variable later latencies up to 4 s after stimulus presentation (Fig. 24.4B). The spatial activity patterns associated with these later peaks showed an interesting change at the transition from discrimination learning to categorization: With categorization, the patterns reflected the belongingness to the formed category rather than the physical characteristics of the stimuli. The similarity relations between spatial activity patterns during the marked states can be visualized in 2-dimensional plots, in which the dissimilarity between two patterns is proportional to the distance between the corresponding points (Fig. 24.4D). During discrimination learning (training blocks 1-4, cf. Fig. 24.4C) dissimilarities within and between categories were similar in magnitude. In contrast, the dissimilarities after the transition to categorization (blocks 4-6, cf. Fig. 24.4D) were much smaller within a category than between categories.

It is presently unknown how the later activity states forming the superimposed map of category-belongingness might form. It is currently investigated whether they dynamically spread with approximately circular isophase contours over cortical areas starting from point-like centers of nucleation which would be indicative of a self-organized process in cortex (Freeman & Barrie, 2000).

CONCLUSIONS

This chapter summarizes experimental evidence from animal and human auditory cortex in favor of the hypothesis that sensory cortex is not simply the head stage of "passive" stimulus analysis, but also the locus of "active" processes which make stimulus features cognitively explicit and available for tasks of variable demand. Cognitive functions so far have been addressed in terms of prefrontal, parietal and cingulate cortical areas which obviously control the process. With respect to percepts which are objects of cognition these executive influences seem to impinge on particular organizational feature of maps and to modify the cortical representations of stimuli in maps. Several map-inherent principles seem to be used in this context. In this feedback view prefrontal, parietal and limbic structures receive information from sensory areas for their executive function, but sensory cortex remains still the site of execution. Several organizational principles are held responsible for this bottom-up - top-down interfacing within sensory cortex. For instance, there is evidence from this and numerous other studies that cognitive processing of incoming stimuli in cortex follows the initial descriptive processing in maps and, as judgded from analysis of "cognitive potentials" in EEG and MEG, proceeds in steps.

The new hypothesis suggested here is that top-down cognitive processes create new states within maps which can still be described as spatiotemporal activation patterns but may use coordinates of cognitive similarity rather than similarity at the initial stimulus-descriptive level. Furthermore, the organizational principles of multiple separate maps in auditory cortex and of superposition maps for several stimulus features within the same area are considered in the light of this state-dependent bottom-up – top-down interfacing. Both types of maps may be regarded not simply as a way to orderly analyze distinguishable stimulus features in parallel but as principles to independently address and make explicit such features for various cognitive demands.

Local views of activity states in maps provide not more than peak activities of local neural ensembles for respective features (traditional feature analysis). It is proposed instead that global views of maps in terms of activation patterns more fully represent a given stimulus, i.e. a neuronal space with both active and non-active subregions within the frame of a map may be relevant to characterize a stimulus. Similarly, more complex activation patterns generated by map superposition may be resolved better in a global view than in local views. Consequently, it is proposed that later cognitive states of given maps also provide such global views of maps yet with a cognitive frame of reference.

REFERENCES

Ackermann, H., Hertich, I., & Ziegler, W. (1993). Prosodische Störungen bei neurologischen Erkrankungen – eine Literaturübersicht. Fortschritte der Neurologie und Psychiatrie, 61, 241–253.

Ågren, G., Zhou, Q., & Zhong, W. (1989). Ecology and social behaviour of Mongolian gerbils, Meriones unguiculatus, at Xilinhot, Inner Mongolia, China. Animal Behavior, 37, 11–27.

Arieli, A., Sterkin, A., Grinvald, A., & Aertsen, A. (1996). Dynamics of ongoing activity: Explanation of the large variability in evoked cortical responses. Science, 273, 1868–1871.

Baddeley, A. (2003). Working memory: Looking back and looking forward. Nature Reviews Neuroscience, 4, 829–839.

Barch, D.A., Braver, T.S., Nystrom, L.E., Forman, S.D., Noll, D.C., & Cohen, J.D. (1997). Dissociating working memory from task difficulty in human prefrontal cortex. Neuropsychologia, 35, 1373–1380.

Baumgart, F., Gaschler-Markefski, B., Woldorff, M.G., Heinze, H.J., & Scheich, H. (1999). A movement-sensitive area in auditory cortex. Nature, 400, 724–726.

Bisiach, E., & Berti, A. (1997). Consciousness and dyschiria. In M.S. Gazzaniga (Ed.), The cognitive neurosciences (pp. 1331–1340). Cambridge: MIT Press.

Bisiach, E., & Vallar, G. (1988). Hemineglect in humans. In F. Boller & J. Grafman (Eds.), Handbook of Neurophysiology, Vol. 1. (pp. 195–222). Amsterdam: Elesevier.

Bodnar, D.A., & Bass, A.H. (1999). Midbrain combinatorial code for temporal and spectral information in concurrent acoustic signals. Journal of Neurophysiology, 81, 552–563.

Bonham, B.H., Cheung, S.W., Godey, B., & Schreiner, C.E. (2004). Spatial organization of frequency response areas and rate/level functions in the developing AI. Journal of Neurophysiology, 91, 841–854.

Bonhoeffer, T., & Grinvald, A. (1991). Iso-orientation domains in cat visual cortex are arranged in pinwheel-like patterns. Nature, 353, 429–431.

Brechmann, A., Baumgart, F., & Scheich, H. (2002). Sound-level dependent representation of frequency modulation in human auditory cortex: A low-noise fMRI study. Journal of Neurophysiology, 87, 423–433.

Brechmann, A., & Scheich, H. (2004). Hemispheric shifts of sound representation in auditory cortex with conceptual listening. Cerebral Cortex (in press).

Budinger, E., Heil, P., & Scheich, H. (2000). Functional organization of auditory cortex in the Mongolian gerbil (Meriones unguiculatus). III. Anatomical subdivisions and corticocortical connections. European Journal of Neuroscience, 12, 2425–2451.

Cabeza, R., & Nyberg, L. (2000). Imaging Cognition II: An Empirical Review of 275 PET and fMRI studies. Journal of Cognitive Neuroscience, 12, 1–47.

Cherry, E.C. (1953). Some experiments on the recognition of speech, with one and with two ears. Journal of the Acoustic Society of America, 25, 975–979.

Clarey, J.C., Barone, P., & Imig, T.J. (1991). Physiology of thalamus and cortex. In A.N. Popper & R.R. Fay (Eds.), The Mammalian Auditory Pathway: Neurophysiology. (pp. 232–334). New York: Springer.

Cohen, Y.E., & Knudsen, E.I. (1999). Maps versus clusters: Different representations of auditory space in the midbrain and forebrain. Trends in the Neurosciences, 22, 128–135.

Corbetta, M., Miezin, F.M., Dobmeyer, S., Shulman, G.L., & Petersen, S.E. (1991). Selective and divided attention during visual discriminations of shape, color, and speed: Functional anatomy by positron emission tomography. Journal of Neuroscience, 11, 2383–2402.

DeMott, D.W. (1970). Toposcopic studies of learning. Thomas Books, Springfield.

Eggermont, J.J. (1998). Representation of spectral and temporal sound features in three cortical fields of the cat. Similarities outweigh differences. Journal of Neurophysiology, 80, 2743–2764.

Farah, M.J. (1997). The neural basis of mental imagery. In M.S. Gazzaniga (Ed.), The cognitive neurosciences (pp. 963–975). Cambridge: MIT Press.

Freeman, W.J. (1994). Neural mechanisms underlying destabilization of cortex by sensory input. Physica D, 75, 151–164.

Freeman, W.J. (2000). Neurodynamics: An exploration of mesoscopic brain dynamics. London: Springer.

Freeman, W.J., & Barrie, J.M. (2000). Analysis of spatial patterns of phase in neocortical gamma EEGs in rabbit. Journal of Neurophysiology, 84, 1266–1278.

Griffiths, T.D. Ress, G., Rees, A., Green, G.G.R., Witton, C., Rowe, D., Büchel, C., Turner, R., & Frackowiak, R.S.J. (1998). Right parietal cortex is involved in the perception of sound movement in humans. Nature Neuroscience, 1, 74–79.

Haken, H. (1991). Synergetic Computers and Cognition. Springer, Berlin.

Hardcastle, V.G. (1994). Psychology's binding problem and possible neurobiological solutions. Journal of Consciousness Studies, 1, 66–90.

Hasegawa, I., & Miyashita, Y. (2002). Categorizing the world: Expert neurons look into key features. Nature Neuroscience, 5, 90–91.

Heil, P., Rajan, R., & Irvine, D.R.F. (1992). Sensitivity of neurons in cat primary auditory cortex to tones and frequency-modulated stimuli. II: Organization of response properties along the 'isofrequency' dimension. Hearing Research, 63, 135–156.

Heil, P., Rajan, R., & Irvine, D.R.F. (1994). Topographic representation of tone intensity along the isofrequency axis of cat primary auditory cortex. Hearing Research, 76, 188–202.

Hess, A., & Scheich, H. (1996). Optical and FDG-mapping of frequency-specific activity in auditory cortex. Neuroreport, 7, 2643–2647.

Hillyard, S.A., Mangun, G.R., Woldorff, M.G., & Luck, S.J. (1995). Neural systems mediating selective attention. In M.S. Gazzaniga (Ed.), The cognitive neurosciences (pp. 665–681). Cambridge: MIT Press.

Horikawa, J., Hoskowa, Y., Kubota, M., Nasu, M., & Taniguchi, I. (1996). Optical imaging of spatiotemporal patterns of glutamatergic exictation and GABAergic inhibition in the guinea-pig auditory cortex in vivo. Journal of Physiology, 497, 620–638.

Horikawa, J., Nasu, M., & Taniguchi, I. (1998). Optical recording of responses to frequency-modulated sounds in the auditory cortex. Neuroreport, 9, 799–802.

Hosokawa, Y., Horikawa, J., Nasu, M., & Taniguchi, I. (1999). Spatiotemporal representation of binaural difference in time and intensity of sound in the guinea pig auditory cortex. Hearing Research, 134, 123–132.

Joanette, Y., Goulet, P., & Hannequin, D. (1990). In Y. Joanette, P. Gouldet, & D. Hannequin (Eds.), Right Hemisphere and Verbal Communication (pp. 132–159). New York: Springer.

Kaas, J.H. (1982). A segregation of function in the nervous system: Why do sensory systems have so many subdivisions? In W.P. Neff (Ed.), Contributions to sensory physiology (pp. 201–240). New York: Academic Press.

Kaas, J.H. (1993). Evolution of multiple areas and modules within neocortex. Perspectives in Developmental Neurobiology, 1, 101–107.

Kaas, J.H., & Hackett, T.A. (2000). Subdivisions of auditory cortex and processing streams in primates. Proceedings of the National Academy of Sciences USA, 97, 11793–11799.

Knight, R.T., Scabini, D., & Woods, D.L. (1989). Prefrontal cortex gating of auditory transmission in humans. Brain Research, 504, 338–342.

Knudsen, E.I., du Lac, S., & Esterly, S.D. (1987). Computational maps in the brain. Annual Reviews in Neuroscience, 10, 41–65.

Kraus, N., & McGee, T. (1991). Electrophysiology of the human auditory system. In A.N. Popper & R.R. Fay (Eds.), The Mammalian Auditory Pathway: Neurophysiology (pp. 335-404). New York: Springer.

Langner, G. (1992). Periodicity coding in the auditory system. Hearing Research, 60, 115–142.

Lee, C.C., Imaizumi, K., Schreiner, C.E., & Winer, J.A. (2004). Concurrent tonotopic processing streams in auditory cortex. Cerebral Cortex, 14, 441–451.

Lilly, J.C. (1954). Instanaeous relations between the activities of closely spaced zones on the cerebral cortex - electrical figures during responses and spontaneous activity. American Journal of Physiology, 176, 493–504.

Merzenich, M.M., & Brugge, J.F. (1973). Representation of the cochlear partition on the superior temporal plane of the Macaque monkey. Brain Research, 50, 275–296.

Merzenich, M.M., Knight, P.L., & Roth, G.L. (1975). Representation of the cochlea within primary auditory cortex in the cat. Journal of Neurophysiology, 38, 231–249.

Middlebrooks, J.C., Dykes, R.W., & Merzenich, M.M. (1980). Binaural response-specific bands in primary auditory cortex (AI) of the cat: Topographical organization orthogonal to isofrequency contours. Brain Research, 181, 31–48.

Nelson, M.E., & Bower, J.M. (1990). Brain maps and parallel computers. Trends in Neuroscience, 13, 403–408.

Ohl, F.W., Deliano, M., Scheich, H., & Freeman, W.J. (2003a). Analysis of evoked and emergent patterns of stimulus-related auditory cortical activity. Reviews in the Neurosciences, 14, 35–42.

Ohl, F.W., Deliano, M., Scheich, H., & Freeman, W.J. (2003b). Early and late patterns of stimulus-related activity in auditory cortex of trained animals. Biological Cybernetics, 88, 374–379.

Ohl, F.W., & Scheich, H. (1996). Differential frequency conditioning enhances spectral contrast sensitivity of units in auditory cortex (field AI) of the alert Mongolian gerbil. European Journal of Neuroscience, 8, 1001–1017.

Ohl, F.W., & Scheich, H. (1997a). Learning-induced dynamic receptive field changes in primary auditory cortex of the unanaesthetized Mongolian gerbil. Journal of Comparative Physiology A, 181, 685–696.

Ohl, F.W., & Scheich, H. (1997b). Orderly cortical representation of vowels based on formant interaction. Proceedings of the National Academy of Sciences USA, 94, 9440–9444.

Ohl, F.W., & Scheich, H. (1998). Feature extraction and feature interaction. Behavioral and Brain Sciences, 21, 278.

Ohl, F.W., Scheich, H., & Freeman, W.J. (2000a). Topographic analysis of epidural pure-tone-evoked potentials in geril auditory cortex. Journal of Neurophysiology, 83, 3123–3132.

Ohl, F.W., Scheich, H., & Freeman, W.J. (2001). Change in pattern of ongoing cortical activity with auditory category learning. Nature, 412, 733–736

Ohl, F.W., Schulze, H., Scheich, H., & Freeman, W.J. (2000b). Spatial representation of frequency-modulated tones in gerbil auditory cortex revealed by epidural electrocorticography. Journal of Physiology (Paris), 94, 549–554.

Ohl, F.W, Wetzel, W., Wagner, T., Rech, A., & Scheich, H. (1999). Bilateral ablation of auditory cortex in Mongolian gerbil affects discrimination of frequency modulated tones but not of pure tones. Learning & Memory, 6, 347–362.

Olesen, P.J., Westerberg, H., & Klingberg, T. (2004). Increased prefrontal and parietal activity after training of working memory. Nature Neuroscience, 7, 75–79.

Pessoa, L., Gutierrez, E., Bandettini, P.A, & Ungerleider, L.G. (2002). Neural correlates of Visual Working Memory: fMRI amplitude predicts task performance. Neuron, 35, 975–987.

Peterson, G.E., & Barney, H.L. (1952). Control methods used in a study of the vowels. Journal of the Acoustic Society of America, 24, 175–184.

Phillips, D.P., & Irvine, D.R. (1983). Some features of binaural input to single neurons in physiologically defined area AI of cat cerebral cortex. Journal of Neurophysiology, 49, 383–395.

Phillips, W.A., & Singer, W. (1997). In search of common foundations for cortical computation. Behavioral and Brain Sciences, 20, 657–722.

Posner, M.I. (1997). Attention in cognitive neuroscience: An overview. In M.S. Gazzaniga (Ed.), The cognitive neurosciences (pp. 615–624). Cambridge: MIT Press.

Pouget, A., & Sejnowski, T.J. (1994). Is perception isomorphic with neural activity? Behavioral and Brain Sciences, 17, 274.

Rauschecker, J.P., Tian, B., & Hauser, M. (1995). Processing of complex sounds in the Macaque nonprimary auditory cortex. Science, 268, 111–114.

Read, H.L., Winer, J.A., & Schreiner, C.E. (2002). Functional architecture of auditory cortex. Current Opinion in Neurobiology, 12, 433–440.

Romanski, L.M., Tian, B., Fritz, J., Mishkin, M., Goldman-Rakic, P.S., & Rauschecker, J.P. (1999). Dual streams of auditory afferents target multiple domains in the primate prefrontal cortex. Nature Neuroscience, 2, 1131–1136.

Scheich, H. (1991). Auditory cortex: Comparative aspects of maps and plasticity. Current Opinion in Neurobiology, 1, 236–247.

Scheich, H., Baumgart, F., Gaschler-Markefski, B., Tegeler, C., Tempelmann, C., Heinze, H.J., Schindler, F., & Stiller, D. (1998). Functional magnetic resonance imaging of a human auditory cortex area involved in foreground-background decomposition. European Journal of Neuroscience, 10, 803–809.

Scheich, H., Heil, P., & Langner, G. (1993). Functional organization of auditory cortex in the Monglian gerbil (Meriones unguiculatus): II. Tonotopic 2-deoxyglucose. European Journal of Neuroscience, 5, 898–914.

Schmutz, M., & Banzhaf, W. (1992). Rubust competitive networks. Physical Reviews A, 45, 4132–4145.

Schreiner, C.E. (1991). Functional topographies in the primary auditory cortex of the cat. Acta Otolaryngology Supplement, 491, 7–15.

Schreiner, C.E. (1995). Order and disorder in auditory cortical maps. Current Opinion in Neurobiology, 5, 489–496.

Schreiner, C.E. (1998). Spatial distribution of responses to simple and complex sounds in the primary auditory cortex. Audiology & Neuro-Otology, 3, 104–122.

Schreiner, C.E., Read, H.L., & Sutter, M.L. (2000). Modular organization of frequency integration in primary auditory cortex. Annual Review of Neuroscience, 23, 501–529.

Schreiner, C.E., & Sutter, M.L. (1992). Topography of excitatory bandwidth in cat primary auditory cortex: Single-neuron versus multiple-neuron recordings. Journal of Neurophysiology, 68, 1487–1502.

Schreiner, C.E., & Urbas, J.V. (1988). Representation of amplitude modulation in the auditory cortex of the cat. II. Comparison between cortical fields. Hearing Research, 32, 49–64.

Schulze, H., Hess, A., Ohl, F.W., & Scheich, H. (2000). Optical imaging reveals cyclic periodotopic map in gerbil auditory cortex. ARO-Abstracts, 23rd Midwinter Research Meeting, 16.

Schulze, H., & Langner, G. (1997). Periodicity coding in the primary auditory cortex of the Mongolian gerbil (Meriones unguiculatus): Two different coding strategies for pitch and rhythm? Journal Comparative Physiology A, 181, 651–663.

Schulze, H., Ohl, F.W., Heil, P., & Scheich, H. (1997). Field-specific responses in the auditory cortex of the unanaesthetized Mongolian gerbil to tones and slow frequency modulations. Journal of Comparative Physiology A, 181, 573–589.

Schulze, H., & Scheich, H. (1999). Discrimination learning of amplitude modulated tones in Mongolian gerbils. Neuroscience Letters, 261, 13–16.

Sigala, N., & Logothetis, N.K. (2002). Visual categorization shapes feature selectivity in the primate temporal cortex. Nature, 415, 318–320.

Smith, E.E., Jonides, J., Marshuetz, C., & Koeppe, R.A. (1998). Components of verbal working memory: Evidence from neuroimaging. Proceedings of the National Academy of Sciences USA, 95, 876–882.

Squire, L.R., Mishkin, M., & Shimamura, A. (Eds.). (1990). Learning and Memory. Discussions in Neuroscience. Geneva, Switzerland: Elsevier Science Publishers B.V.

Suga, N. (1977). Amplitude spectrum representation in the Doppler-shifted-CF processing area of the auditory cortex of the mustached bat. Science, 196, 64–67.

Suga, N. (1994). Multi-function theory for cortical processing of auditory information: implications of single-unit and lesion data for future research. Journal of Comparative Physiology A, 175, 135–144.

Taniguchi, I., & Nasu, M. (1993). Spatio-temporal representation of sound intensity in the guinea pig auditory cortex observed by optical recording. Neuroscience Letters, 151, 178–181.

Thiessen, D., & Yahr, P. (1977). The gerbil in behavioral investigations; Mechanisms of territoriality and olfactory communication. Austin/London: University of Texas Press.

Thomas, H., Tillein, J., Heil, P., & Scheich, H. (1993). Functional organization of auditory cortex in the Mongolian gerbil (Meriones unguiculatus): I. Electrophysiological mapping of frequency representation and distinction of fields. European Journal of Neuroscience, 5, 822–897.

Uno, H., Murai, N., & Fukunishi, K. (1993). The tonotopic representation in the auditory cortex of the guinea pig with optical recording. Neuroscience Letters, 150, 179–182.

von der Malsburg, C., & Schneider, W. (1986). A neural cocktail-party processor. Biological Cybernetics, 54, 29–40.

Warren, D.W., Zielinski, B.A., Green, G.G.R., Rauschecker, J.P., & Griffiths, T.D. (2002). Perception of sound-source motion by the human brain. Neuron, 34, 139–148.

Waugh, F.R., & Westervelt, R.M. (1993). Analog neural networks with local competition. I. Dynamics and stability. Physical Reviews E, 47, 4524–4536.

Weinberg, R.J. (1997). Are topographic maps fundamental to sensory processing? Brain Research Bulletin, 44, 113–116.

Wetzel, W., Ohl, F.W., Wagner, T., & Scheich, H. (1998a). Right auditory cortex lesion in Mongolian gerbils impairs discrimination of rising and falling frequency-modulated tones. Neuroscience Letters, 252, 115–118.

Wetzel, W., Wagner, T., Ohl, F.W., & Scheich, H. (1998b). Categorical discrimination of direction in frequency-modulated tones by Mongolian gerbils. Behavioral Brain Research, 91, 29–39.

Wheeler, M.E., Petersen, S.E., & Buckner, R.L. (2000). Memory's echo: Vivid remembering reactivates sensory-specific cortex. Proceedings of the National Academy of Sciences USA, 97, 11125–11129.

Yapa, W.B. (1994). Social behaviour of the Mongolian gerbil Meriones unguiculatus, with special reference to acoustic communication. Dissertation, University of Munich.

Yost, W.A. & Sheft, S. (1993). Auditory perception. In W.A. Yost, A.N. Popper, & R.R. Fay (Eds.), Human Psychophysics (pp. 193–236). New York: Springer.

Young, E.D., & Sachs, M.B. (1979). Representation of steady-state vowels in the temporal aspects of the discharge patterns of populations of auditory-nerve fibers. Journal of the Acoustic Society of America, 66, 1381–1403.

25. AUDITORY PERCEPTUAL LEARNING AND CORTICAL PLASTICITY

Dexter Irvine, Mel Brown, Russell Martin, Valerie Park

INTRODUCTION: PERCEPTUAL AND PROCEDURAL LEARNING

Improvement in perceptual discriminative ability with practice (perceptual learning) is a ubiquitous feature both of everyday experience and of experimental psychophysics, in which it has been well known for over a century (see Gibson, 1953; and Goldstone, 1998; for reviews). In the last 15 years, there has been increasing evidence that some forms of perceptual learning might reflect plasticity at early stages of cortical sensory processing. This proposal has commonly been based on indirect evidence, notably the specificity of improvements on some discrimination tasks to a particular parameter of the training stimulus or to the region of the receptor surface to which the training stimuli are presented. Thus, improvements in Vernier acuity and texture discrimination have been reported to be highly specific for such features as locus of retinal stimulation, stimulus orientation and size, and (in some cases) the trained eye (e.g., Ahissar & Hochstein, 1996; Fiorentini & Berardi, 1980; Gilbert, 1994; Karni & Sagi, 1991; Ramachandran & Braddick, 1973; Schoups et al., 1995). To consider a specific example, Karni and Sagi (1991) found that learning of a texture discrimination task was specific to retinal locus, the trained eye, and the orientation of the background elements, and therefore argued that the learning reflected plasticity in primary visual cortex (V1). The extensive evidence that has accumulated over the last 20 years for injury- and use-related plasticity in primary sensory cortex in adult animals (see Buonomano & Merzenich, 1998; Gilbert, 1998; Irvine & Rajan, 1996; Weinberger, 1995; for reviews) establishes that these cortical areas have the capacity to change response characteristics and organization in this fashion.

Although the specificity of some forms of perceptual learning makes an explanation in terms of primary sensory cortical plasticity attractive, it should be emphasized that such specificity does not logically entail plasticity at this level. An alternative possibility is that the observer learns which subset of central channels is most useful for making the discrimination and what weights should be attached to the outputs of the channels in the decision making process (Dosher & Lu, 1999; Mollon & Danilova, 1996). Learning of this sort would have to be repeated for each change in the stimulus or the region of the receptor to which it is applied, but would not involve any change in the properties of the channels themselves.

Any psychophysical experiment requires that the human or animal subject perform some task on which perceptual discriminative capacity is manifested. One component of improved performance on the task is therefore the subject's learning the response demands of the task itself – what has been called "procedural" learning (Robinson & Summerfield, 1996). The time course of procedural learning would be expected to vary with the complexity of the task, and improvement of this sort would be expected to transfer to any other discrimination involving the same response requirements. In addition to this procedural learning, there might or might not be an improvement in discriminative capacity itself as a consequence of training. The term perceptual learning will be used here to refer to such improvements in discriminative capacity. Whether or not perceptual learning so defined generalizes to stimuli other than those used in training is an empirical issue. Perceptual learning is normally thought to depend on extensive training, and it is therefore common to consider the early fast phase of improvement on a psychophysical discrimination task as reflecting procedural learning, and the slower later phase as reflecting perceptual learning. In fact the two forms of learning presumably occur in parallel, but on most tasks the procedural learning is likely to be rapid, and thus the major contributor to the early fast phase of learning.

This distinction between procedural and perceptual learning relates to the way in which partial generalization to stimuli other than those used in training is interpreted. Three different patterns of generalization after a change in the stimulus or in the position on the receptor surface at which it is presented are illustrated schematically in Figure 25.1. The upper panel shows a complete lack of generalization. Since procedural learning would be expected to generalize, this pattern implies that there was very little procedural learning involved, which might be the case if the task were extremely simple, as in a "pop-out" identification task such as that used by Karni and Sagi (1991), or that procedural learning was completed prior to the first training phase. In either case, this pattern indicates that the perceptual learning was totally specific to the training stimulus/position. In contrast, the interpretation of partial and complete generalization, which is shown in the lower panels, is more ambiguous. Total generalization could indicate either that there was no perceptual learning on the task, or that both procedural and perceptual learning have generalized completely, and thus that the perceptual learning was not at all specific. In the

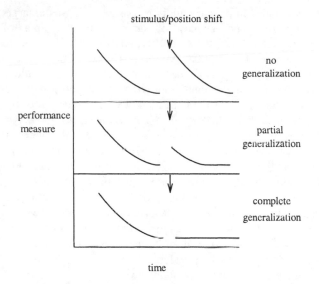

stimulus/position shift

no
generalization

performance
measure

partial
generalization

complete
generalization

time

Fig. 25.1. Schematic illustration of different patterns of generalization in perceptual learning experiments when the stimulus or the region of the receptor surface to which it is applied is changed. See discussion in text. Modified from figure in Dill (2002).

case of partial generalization, procedural learning alone could have generalized (i.e., the perceptual learning is totally specific) or some combination of procedural and perceptual learning could have generalized (i.e., the perceptual learning is partly specific). The interpretation of partial generalization can be made unambiguous only if extensive practice on the task is given prior to the first training phase, so that both it and the post-shift training phase can be assumed to be free of procedural learning. Under those conditions, partial generalization unequivocally indicates partial specificity of the perceptual learning. Neither total nor partial generalization of perceptual learning would seem to carry any implications with respect to the locus or the nature of the changes underlying perceptual learning. Either could reflect changes in a sensory processing area (not necessarily primary sensory cortex) that were not specific to the neural circuitry processing the training stimuli, but could also reflect changes of some other sort.

NEURAL CORRELATES OF PERCEPTUAL LEARNING

There is only a limited body of evidence from combined behavioral-neurophysiological studies that bears directly on the extent to which perceptual learning is associated with changes in primary sensory cortex. In a study that is described in more detail below, Recanzone et al. (1993) reported that in owl monkeys trained on a frequency discrimination task the area of representation of the training frequencies in primary auditory cortex (AI) was enlarged, and that the frequency tuning and latency of neurons in the area of enlarged representation differed from those in normal animals. Similar results were reported by Recanzone et al. (1992a, 1992b) in somatosensory cortex of monkeys trained on a frequency discrimination task using sinusoidal tactile stimuli applied to a restricted region of a single digit. Improvements in performance on this task generalized partially to the adjacent digit but not to the homologous (control) digit on the other (untrained) hand. In cortical area 3b of the trained monkeys, the area of representation of the skin region to which the stimuli were applied was significantly increased (by a factor of ~2 to ~16 relative to the homologous region on control digits and by a factor of 1.4 to 3.2 relative to that on the adjacent digit). The receptive fields (RFs) of multi-neuron clusters in the area representing the trained skin were significantly larger than those in areas representing control digits. The latter result is contrary to the usual inverse relationship between magnification factor and RF size. In two other studies involving tactile training of monkeys (but not perceptual learning), increases in area of representation were reported to be associated with decreases in RF size (Jenkins et al., 1990; Xerri et al., 1999), in accordance with the normal inverse relationship.

In contrast to these results, a number of recent studies of visual perceptual learning in monkeys have found no changes in cortical topography, and either subtle or no changes in neuronal response characteristics, in primary visual cortex (V1). Schoups et al. (2001) found that perceptual learning of an orientation discrimination task was specific to both the position and orientation of the training stimuli. In V1 of the trained monkeys, there was no change in the proportion of neurons tuned to the training orientation, and neurons tuned to that orientation exhibited lower discharge rates than neurons tuned to other orientations. The only change that appeared to provide a substrate for the improved discrimination performance was a significant change in the slope of the orientation tuning curves *at the training orientation* of neurons with preferred orientations between 12° and 20° from the training orientation. Ghose et al. (2002) also trained monkeys on an orientation discrimination task, but in contrast to Schoups et al. (2001) found that although improvements were specific to the orientation used in training they were not specific to the retinotopic position of the training stimuli. Ghose et al. (2002) observed no change in the retinotopic organization of V1 or of secondary visual cortex (V2) in trained monkeys, and no effect of training on the RF properties of neurons in either V1 or V2. The only significant effect of training was a small but statistically significant decrease in the population response in V1 to the trained orientation at the trained location, which reflected a slight decrease in the number of neurons responding best to the trained orientation. In agreement with the finding in these two studies of a decrease in the response of neurons in monkey V1 and V2 to the trained orientation, Schiltz et al. (1999) reported that in a positron emission topography study in humans, perceptual learning on an orientation discrimination task was associated with reduced activation in striate and extrastriate cortex.

In a third study, Crist et al. (2001) trained monkeys on a three-line bisection task. They did not present evidence on the specificity of perceptual learning to the training stimuli, but like Ghose et al. (2002) found no change in the retinotopic organization of V1 or in the RF and orientation tuning properties of neurons in the region of V1 activated by the training stimuli. The only effect of training was a significant change in the extent to which the responses of neurons in this region to stimuli in their RF were modified by contextual stimuli. This effect was observed only for contextual stimuli that were present in the training task, and only when monkeys were performing the bisection task.

Whether the different patterns of results across these visual system experiments, and the even greater differences between the visual system results and those in the auditory and somatosensory systems, reflect differences in the tasks employed, the particular sensory discriminations investigated, and/or differences between cortical areas, remains unclear (see Ghose et al. (2002) for a detailed and insightful discussion). This uncertainty about the neural correlates of perceptual learning, and their relationship to the specificity of the learning, has prompted us to further examine auditory perceptual learning and its neural correlates. In the following sections, evidence on the specificity of auditory perceptual learning, particularly on frequency discrimination tasks by humans and animals and on the cortical changes associated with improvements in frequency discrimination in animals, is reviewed.

AUDITORY PERCEPTUAL LEARNING

Over a number of years, there has been interest in human auditory perceptual learning with respect to the discrimination of speech sounds by normal listeners (e.g., Pisoni et al., 1982) and the progressive improvements in performance by hearing impaired people in the period following the provision of a prosthetic device (e.g., Robinson & Summerfield, 1996, Watson 1980, 1991). In almost none of these studies, however, was there a focus on the specificity of the learning to the training stimulus or on the implications of such specificity with respect to the nature of the underlying processes. In one early study, however, Zwislocki et al. (1958) reported that improvements in absolute thresholds at 1000 Hz as a consequence of training did not generalize to thresholds at 100 Hz. More recently, evidence for both specificity and generalizability of different aspects of auditory perceptual learning has been found. Tremblay et al. (1997) reported that improvements in discrimination of an unfamiliar voice onset time contrast improved as a result of training, and that this improvement generalized from one place of articulation to another (i.e., was not specific to the place of articulation of the training stimuli). In a study of temporal interval discrimination in which the intervals were bounded by brief tones, Wright et al. (1997) reported that learning-induced improvements in discrimination did not generalize to untrained intervals bounded by the same frequency, but did generalize to the trained interval bounded by a different frequency. More recently, Wright and Fitzgerald (2001) studied perceptual learning in the discrimination of interaural time and level difference (ITD and ILD, respectively) cues to auditory azimuthal position, and found different patterns of learning and generalization for the two cues. Rapid initial learning on both cues generalized widely and was attributed to procedural learning. A later slow stage of improvement was seen only with ILD training and generalized to a different ILD at the same frequency but not to the same ILD at different frequencies.

These studies have reported different patterns of generalization to untrained frequencies for discriminations on different stimulus parameters. Specificity of visual perceptual learning on a number of tasks with respect to the retinal location at which the stimuli are presented suggests that there might be an analogous specificity of auditory perceptual learning with respect to cochlear locus of activation, that is, with respect to frequency. In the following section, evidence on the specificity of perceptual learning on frequency discrimination tasks *per se* is reviewed.

PERCEPTUAL LEARNING AND AUDITORY FREQUENCY DISCRIMI-NATION

Improvements in human frequency discrimination with practice had been reported by a number of authors (e.g., Campbell & Small, 1963; Moore 1973, 1976), but Demany (1985) was the first to investigate the specificity of this learning. He trained four different groups of subjects on a frequency discrimination task at 0.2, 0.36, 2.5, and 6 kHz, and determined the effect of this training on frequency difference limens (DLFs) at 0.2 kHz. His results indicated that training at the first three frequencies resulted in similar (statistically indistinguishable) improvement in discrimination at the test frequency (0.2 kHz), whereas training at 6 kHz resulted in less improvement. He suggested that this difference might be attributable to the fact that the three lower frequencies were in the frequency range likely to be coded peripherally by temporal mechanisms, whereas the highest frequency (6 kHz) was in the place-coding range. This study involved relatively short periods of training, however, suggesting that the generalization might have largely reflected procedural rather than perceptual learning, although the fact that only partial generalization was found from 6 kHz argues against this. In contrast to Demany's (1985) report of complete or partial generalization, a brief report by Wright (1998) indicated a complete lack of generalization of learning after (longer) frequency discrimination training.

In view of these apparently discrepant results, we have conducted two studies to determine whether perceptual learning on frequency discrimination tasks using frequencies in the range coded peripherally by place rather than temporal mechanisms is specific to the training frequency. In the first experiment (D.R.F. Irvine, R. Martin, & R. Smith; unpublished), we used a reverse-training paradigm of the type commonly used in visual perceptual

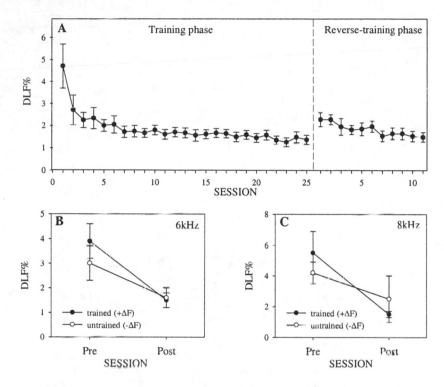

Fig. 25.2. Data from unpublished experiment by D.R.F. Irvine, R. Martin, & R. Smith showing improvement in human frequency discrimination with training. A. Changes in mean (±1 standard error of the mean (SEM)) DLF% during training and reverse training phases. Means are for 10 subjects (5 trained at 8 kHz and reverse-trained at 6 kHz and 5 trained at 6 kHz and reverse trained at 8 kHz). B and C. Pre- and post-training DLF% values for + and −ΔF discriminations at 6 kHz (B) and 8 kHz (C) for subjects trained on +ΔF discrimination.

learning experiments. In each phase of the experiment, an adaptive 3-interval, 3-alternative forced choice (3AFC) task was used to estimate DLFs. The general procedure was that subjects (N = 5 in each group) were given extensive training (25 sessions over 6–7 days, comprising 3500–4000 trials) at either 6 or 8 kHz (training phase), followed by further training (11 sessions over 3 days, and 1500–2000 trials) at the other frequency (reverse-training phase). In both phases, the subject's task was to detect the interval in which the frequency was higher (+ΔF). Figure 25.2A shows the change in the DLF (expressed as a percentage of base frequency; DLF%) averaged across both groups in the two phases. The improvement in DLF% in the training phase has a fast early component and a slower component. The frequency shift was made during the latter stage, when procedural learning was presumably complete. If this were the case, both the partial generalization and the further improvement in the reverse-

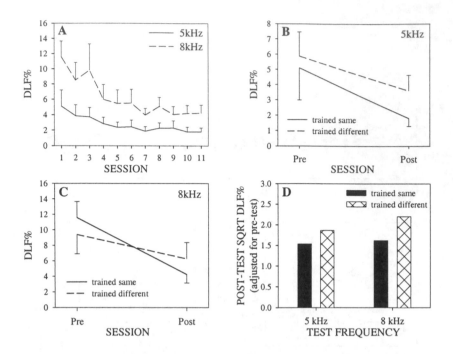

Fig. 25.3. Data from Irvine et al's. (2000) study of human perceptual learning on a frequency discrimination task. **A.** Mean functions (±1 SEM) showing learning curves for the two groups at their training frequencies. Analysis of variance yielded a significant main effect of session , but no difference between the groups. **B** and **C**. Mean (±1 SEM) pre- and post-test DLF% values at 5 and 8 kHz (**A** and **B**, respectively) for subjects trained at that frequency ("trained same") and subjects trained at the other frequency ("trained different"). Note different ordinate scales. **D.** Mean post-test square root DLF% values, adjusted for differences in pre-test values, at 5 and 8 kHz for subjects trained at the same and at the other frequency. Analysis of covariance indicated a significant difference between the trained same and trained different means, but no significant effect of training frequency. Reproduced from Irvine et al. (2000) by permission of the American Institute of Physics.

training phase shown in Figure 25.2A suggest that some component of the perceptual learning in the training phase was specific to the training frequency.

In a second experiment, Irvine et al. (2000) used the same psychophysical procedures to determine DLFs at 5 and 8 kHz, for two groups of 8 subjects before and after extensive training (6–7 hours and 4000–5000 trials over the course of a week) at one or the other frequency. In this experiment a preliminary task-practice phase during which DLFs were determined at 1 kHz was used in order to minimize the contribution of procedural learning to any improvement seen in the training phase. Figure 25.3A shows the change in DLF% during training. The improvement was more gradual than that in Figure 25.2A, presumably because all or most of the procedural learning took place during the task-practice phase and the improvement during training reflects perceptual learning. Asymptotic or near-asymptotic group performance was achieved over the last 5 sessions at each frequency. Mean pre- and post-training DLF% values at 5 and 8 kHz are shown in Figures 25.3B and 25.3C, respectively, for subjects trained at that frequency ("trained same") and at the other frequency ("trained different"). The "trained-same" lines show the substantial improvement already illustrated in Figure 25.3A. At each of the test frequencies, there is also improvement in DLF for the subjects trained at the other frequency (broken lines), indicating generalization of perceptual learning across frequencies. However, the slope of the "trained-same" line is steeper than that of the "trained-different" line in each case, indicating a greater degree of improvement at the trained frequency, and suggesting that some proportion of the improvement with practice was specific to the training frequency. This difference in slope is confounded with differences in the pre-test DLFs, so its interpretation is unclear. In order to control for the effects of pre-test scores, the data were analyzed by analysis of covariance, using pre-test scores as a covariate. In Figure 25.3D, the mean post-test square-root DLF% values, adjusted for the correlation with the pre-test covariate, are shown. For each of the test frequencies the adjusted post-test DLF% was significantly smaller for subjects trained at the same frequency. Thus, this second experiment supports the conclusion from the first experiment that although the perceptual learning component of improvements in frequency discrimination generalizes partially to an untrained frequency, a statistically significant component of the learning is specific to the training frequency. As noted above, partial generalization of this sort does not carry strong implications as to the locus of the neural changes associated with perceptual learning.

Recently, Demany and Semal (2002) tested generalization to 1.2 kHz and 6.5 kHz after training at 3 kHz, using a much larger number of training trials than in Demany's (1985) study. They reported that improvements in discrimination over the first 10 (hourly) sessions generalized totally to the untrained frequencies, but that the data obtained over sessions 11–16 showed partial generalization and indicated a degree of specificity in the improvement at the trained frequency. This result is in broad agreement with our conclusion of a degree of specificity in perceptual learning on frequency discrimination tasks.

In our two experiments, training involved large numbers of trials using $+\Delta F$. As a further test of generalization in the first experiment, the extent to which training with $+\Delta F$ generalized to discrimination with $-\Delta F$ was examined by determining thresholds with $-\Delta F$ at the frequency used in the initial phase of training before and after that phase. In Figures 25.2B and 25.2C, the changes in $-\Delta F$ thresholds are compared with those in the $+\Delta F$ thresholds. It is apparent that at each frequency there was improvement in the (untrained) $-\Delta F$ discrimination but that this improvement was less than in the (trained) $+\Delta F$ discrimination. Again, these results suggest partial but not complete generalization of learning. Because these subjects had limited experience with the task prior to the pre-test, this generalization almost certainly has a substantial procedural learning component.

Observations on the specificity of perceptual learning on frequency discrimination tasks have also been made in animal studies. Recanzone et al. (1993) reported that improvements in frequency discrimination (at 2.5, 3.0, 5.0, and 8.0 kHz) by owl monkeys were characterized by an early fast phase in which large improvements in performance were seen, and a later, slower phase in which smaller improvements occurred. Improvements in the fast phase generalized to frequencies other than that at which the monkeys were trained, and were attributed to "conceptual" learning of the task (i.e. to procedural learning). Improvements in the second, slower phase did not generalize to other frequencies, and in some cases were described as resulting in decrements in performance at other frequencies. In the owl monkey (OM2) in which specificity was studied most extensively, by interrupting training during the slow phase of learning at 2.5 kHz with an extended period of training at 8 kHz, the 2.5-kHz DLF *increased* almost threefold during the 8-kHz-training period, while that at 8 kHz decreased by approximately 70%. In another monkey (OM4) in which $-\Delta F$ trials were interpolated into $+\Delta F$ discrimination training at 5 kHz, improved performance with $+\Delta F$ was associated with decreased performance with $-\Delta F$. Thus, Recanzone et al.'s (1993) results suggest that perceptual learning not only failed to generalize to other frequencies but actually occurred at the expense of discrimination at other frequencies.

We have studied frequency discrimination in cats (Brown et al., 2004), using a Go/(No-Go) procedure based on that developed by May and his colleagues (1995). Six cats were given extensive training (12000–30000 trials over 12 months) at 8 kHz using $+\Delta F$. Three of the cats were first given an extended period of training (5000–6000 trials) at 3 kHz, in order to ensure that procedural learning was complete before the start of training at 8 kHz, while the other three were given more limited preliminary training at other frequencies. For five of the six cats frequency discrimination performance at 8 kHz improved with practice, and achieved asymptotic levels that were in accord with those reported by other investigators using similar training procedures (Hienz et al., 1993). The mean normalized learning curve for all 6 animals is shown in Figure 25.4A, and the data for two individual animals in Figures 25.4B and 25.4C.

In the cats given extensive training at 3 kHz, near-asymptotic performance was achieved at this frequency (e.g., Fig. 25.4B), and it seems reasonable to assume that procedural learning was complete well before the end of the training period. The fact that two of these three animals showed improvements at 8 kHz after the shift in frequency (e.g., Fig. 25.4B) indicates a degree of specificity in perceptual learning. However, considerable generalization of the effects of training on the 8-kHz $+\Delta F$ task was demonstrated when blocks of test trials on a $+\Delta F$ 3.0-kHz and/or a $-\Delta F$ 8-kHz discrimination task were interpolated in the 8-kHz training period. As illustrated by the data in Figure 25.4C, performance on the $-\Delta F$ discrimination improved in the course of training on the $+\Delta F$ 8-kHz task, and thresholds late in training were comparable

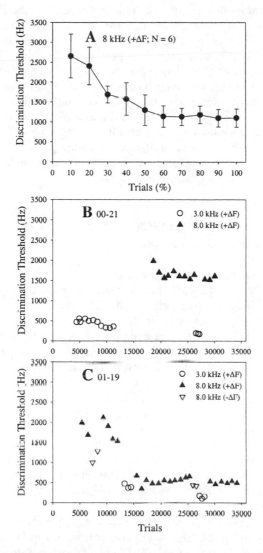

Fig. 25.4.A. Normalized mean curve (±1 SEM) showing mean change in discrimination threshold at 8 kHz (+ΔF) as a function of training in six cats. The total number of trials for each cat was normalized to 100%, and discrimination thresholds were obtained at each 10th percentile by interpolation. **B** and **C.** Change in discrimination threshold at 8 kHz as a function of training for two cats: 01–21 (**B**), which received extensive training at 3 kHz (+ΔF) prior to training at 8 kHz (+ΔF), and 01–19 (**C**), which received limited training at other frequencies prior to training at 8 kHz (+ΔF). Thresholds determined on interpolated trials testing 8 kHz (−ΔF) and 3 kHz (+ΔF) discriminations are also shown. Panels B and C reproduced from Brown et al. (2004) by permission of Oxford University Press.

to (even lower than) those on the $+\Delta F$ task. This was true of all three cats tested with interpolated $-\Delta F$ 8-kHz trials. Although the overall improvement at $-\Delta F$ includes generalization of procedural learning, the low final $-\Delta F$ values indicate that there has also been generalization of perceptual learning. This result contrasts with Recanzone et al.'s (1993) report that performance on the $-\Delta F$ discrimination became worse with improvement at $+\Delta F$. Similarly, all five of the cats tested with interpolated 3-kHz trials, showed improved discrimination in the course of training at 8 kHz (e.g., Figs. 25.5B and 25.5C), again indicating generalization of both procedural and perceptual learning. Our animal data are therefore in agreement with our human data in indicating partial generalization to other frequencies, and a degree of specificity to the training frequency, of perceptual learning on frequency discrimination tasks.

NEURAL CORRELATES OF PERCEPTUAL LEARNING ON AUDITORY FREQUENCY DISCRIMINATION TASKS

As noted above, Recanzone et al. (1993) reported that the area of representation of the training frequencies in AI of their trained owl monkeys, measured in terms of the area in which multi-unit clusters had characteristic frequency (CF; frequency at which threshold is lowest) in that frequency range, was massively enlarged (by a factor of ~7 to ~9, depending on frequency) relative to that in untrained (control) monkeys. Within the group of trained animals, larger areas of representation were associated with superior discrimination performance. The frequency tuning of multi-neuron clusters in these enlarged areas of representation was sharper, and response latency was longer, relative to that in the areas in which the same frequency ranges were represented in control animals. The expansion of the representation of training frequencies must presumably have occurred at the expense of the representation of adjacent frequencies. In accordance with these expectations, and with the reported decrease in $-\Delta F$ performance in monkey OM4 (see previous section), Recanzone et al. (1993) reported that in this animal there were no locations in AI at which the CF fell in the range used in determining the $-\Delta F$ stimuli threshold.

We (Brown et al., 2004) have also examined the frequency organization of AI in our trained cats, using conventional microelectrode mapping techniques to map in detail the entire extent of AI over which responses to the training frequency of 8 kHz could be recorded. Detailed mapping data were obtained for five of the six trained animals. At each recording site, a quantitative response area was obtained (see Brown et al. (2004) for detailed account of methods) which allowed the CF, the best frequency (BF; frequency eliciting maximum response), and other parametric features of responses and frequency tuning to be derived. The frequency map obtained for an untrained control animal is shown in Figure 25.5A; the iso-frequency contours were fitted to the CF map using an inverse distance method with contour intervals set at 0.5 kHz. The area within each 0.5-kHz band is shown in Figure 25.5B, and reveals considerable variation between these areas. Similar, but idiosyncratic, variation was seen in all untrained animals.

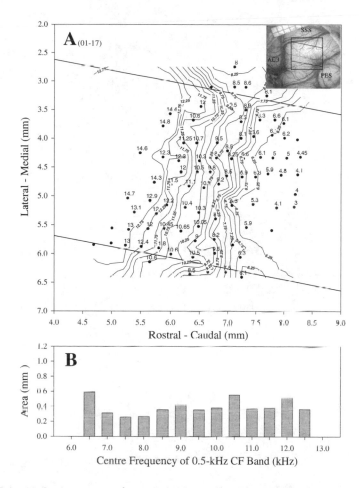

Fig. 25.5.A. AI frequency map for untrained cat (01–17). Filled circles represent the position of each electrode penetration in AI, and the number associated with each circle shows the CF determined for that penetration. Fine solid lines with small italic text show the iso-frequency contours and values fitted to the CF representation. Iso-frequency contours are set at intervals of 0.5 kHz from 6.25 to 12.75 kHz. The solid heavy parallel lines extending diagonally across the plot with a 3 mm separation show the limits of the analysis area. The insert in the top right corner of the plot shows a digital photograph of the cortical surface with the position of the plot axes and limits superimposed. The positions of the anterior ectosylvian sulcus (AES), posterior ectosylvian sulcus (PES) and the suprasylvian sulcus (SSS) are indicated on this photograph. **B.** Histogram of the area within 0.5-kHz CF iso-frequency bands within the analysis area. Bars in the histogram are centred on a frequency midway between the iso-frequency contours defining the band. Reproduced from Brown et al. (2004) by permission of Oxford University Press.

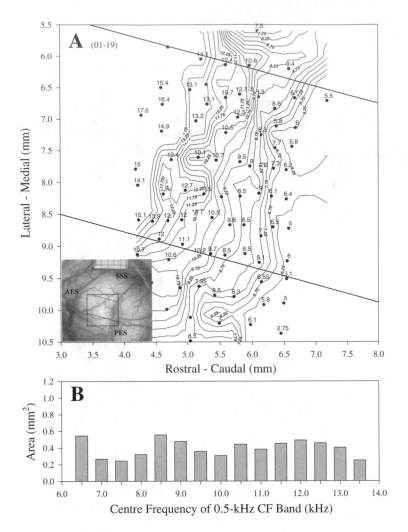

Fig. 25.6. Topographic representation of characteristic frequency (CF) in primary auditory cortex of trained cat 01–19 (**A**) and the area of 0.5-kHz iso-frequency bands within this frequency representation (**B**). Conventions as in Figure 25.5. Reproduced from Brown et al. (2004) by permission of Oxford University Press.

The CF map for trained cat 01–19, for which behavioural data are shown in Figure 25.4, is shown in Figure 25.6A, and the areas of the 0.5-kHz bands are shown in Figure 25.6B. The map is very similar to that for the untrained animal in Figure 25.5. Figure 25.6B shows a similar variation in iso-frequency-band area, with no suggestion of any increase in the area of the 8-kHz band or in the area devoted to the range of frequencies used in training on the 8-kHz discrimination. This was a consistent finding across the trained cats that showed

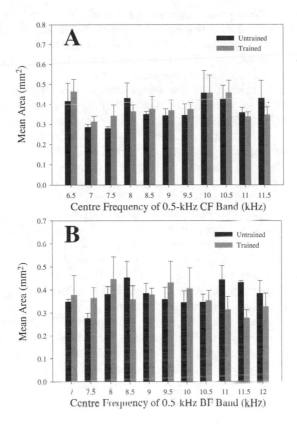

Fig. 25.7. Histograms showing the mean area of 0.5-kHz characteristic frequency (**A**) and best frequency (**B**) iso-frequency bands for four untrained cats and for the four trained cats that showed perceptual learning. Best frequency was defined as that eliciting maximum response at an intensity within the range used in generating the response area (typically 0 to 70 or 80 dB SPL). Histogram bars are centered on a frequency midway between the iso-frequency contours between which the areas are measured. Error bars show standard error of the mean. Reproduced from Brown et al. (2004) by permission of Oxford University Press.

perceptual learning at 8 kHz and for which detailed maps were obtained (N = 4), as can be seen by comparison of the mean areas for the iso-frequency bands for these and the untrained cats (N = 4) in Figure 25.7A. Although there is variation in the size of the bands at different frequencies, there is no suggestion of any systematic difference between the untrained and trained groups. This was confirmed by statistical analysis, which showed no significant difference between groups over either the 7.75 to 11.75-kHz frequency range used in training on the $+\Delta F$ task or the 6.25 to 7.75-kHz range used in testing $-\Delta F$ discrimination.

Although these results indicate that there was no change in the frequency organization of AI as reflected in CF-based maps, the fact that the cats were trained at a sound pressure level (SPL) well above threshold (viz., 60 dB SPL) suggests the possibility that there might have been changes in the area of representation of the training frequencies at this or other suprathreshold levels. To examine this possibility, the areas derived from BF maps (Fig. 25.7B) were also compared, as were the areas activated by an 8-kHz stimulus at different SPLs from 20 to 80 dB SPL. In no case was there any significant difference between the areas of representation in trained and untrained animals.

To investigate the possibility of more subtle differences in neural response properties between trained and untrained animals, the breadth of tuning of multi-neuron clusters in 1-kHz frequency bands was compared using measures of Q_{20} (CF/bandwidth at 20 dB above CF threshold) derived from the response areas. This analysis revealed no significant differences in Q_{20} values, although the means in the frequency bands centered on 9 and 10 kHz were lower in the trained than in the untrained animals and the differences approached significance (p values of 0.06 and 0.08, respectively). Our results, therefore, differ substantially from those reported by Recanzone et al. (1993), in that we found no evidence for changes in the topographic organization of AI in animals showing perceptual learning on a frequency discrimination task, and a tendency toward increased breadth of tuning in neurons with CFs higher than the training frequency, in contrast to the decrease in breadth of tuning in neurons tuned to the training frequency that they reported. Possible reasons for these different patterns of results are considered in the following section in the context of information from other sensory systems on the neural correlates of perceptual learning.

DISCUSSION AND CONCLUSIONS

There are substantial difficulties in distinguishing between procedural and perceptual learning as a consequence of training on perceptual tasks, and hence of determining the specificity of perceptual learning in cases of partial generalization to other stimuli of the effects of training with a particular stimulus. Despite these difficulties, the evidence from both the human and animal studies reviewed here supports the conclusions that perceptual learning occurs as a result of training on an auditory frequency discrimination task at a given frequency, and that while this perceptual learning generalizes partially to other frequencies, a component of it is specific to the training frequency. As argued above, partial generalization has no direct implications for either the locus or the nature of the neural changes underlying the perceptual learning.

The differences between Recanzone et al.'s (1993) and our results with respect to the occurrence of changes in AI might be a consequence of the use of different species and/or of different stimulus configurations and training paradigms. The possible effects of stimulus factors is suggested by Kilgard et al.'s (2001) report that the form of plasticity in AI neural response properties produced by pairing of stimuli with basal forebrain stimulation is differentially dependent on stimulus parameters. One notable difference in the psychophysical results of our and Recanzone et al.'s (1993) studies is that their monkeys achieved substantially lower ΔF values (120–328 Hz at 8 kHz) than did our cats (510–1850 Hz). However, while Recanzone et al.'s results are in accord with those of other studies of frequency discrimination in non-human primates (e.g., Prosen et al., 1990), ours are in accord with the only other study of cat frequency discrimination using very similar appetitive training methods (Hienz et al., 1993). The critical fact is that the cats in our study exhibited perceptual learning, and achieved asymptotic performance levels, without any change in auditory cortical topography, regardless of whether area of representation was defined in terms of CF, BF, or the area over which neurons were responsive to 8 kHz at the SPL used in training.

Our findings are in agreement with those of the recent studies of visual perceptual learning summarised in an earlier section (Crist et al., 2001; Ghose et al., 2002; Schoups et al., 2001) in indicating that perceptual learning can be associated with no or small changes in the response properties of neurons in primary sensory cortex and with no change in cortical topography. One difference between these visual system studies and those in the somatosensory and auditory systems (Recanzone et al., 1992b, 1993) that has been proposed as a possible explanation of the differences in results (e.g., Ghose et al., 2002) is that the latter experiments involved parameters that are topographically mapped throughout the sensory pathway. Our failure to find changes in cortical topography associated with perceptual learning on a frequency discrimination task indicates that this cannot be the critical difference. As Ghose et al. (2002) argue, it seems likely that details of the design and characteristics of training are likely to be important determinants of the type of cortical change associated with perceptual learning.

ACKNOWLEDGMENTS

The research presented in this chapter was supported by grants from the Australian Research Council and the National Health and Medical Research Council of Australia (Project Grant 980847).

REFERENCES

Ahissar, M., & Hochstein, S. (1996). Learning pop-out detection: Specificities to stimulus characteristics. Vision Research, 36, 3487–3500.

Brown, M., Park, V.N., & Irvine, D.R.F. (2004). Perceptual learning on an auditory frequency discrimination task by cats: Association with changes in primary auditory cortex. Cerebral Cortex, 14, 952–965.

Buonomano, D.V., & Merzenich, M.M. (1998). Cortical plasticity: From synapses to maps. Annual Review of Neuroscience, 21, 149–186.

Campbell, R.A., & Small, A.M. (1963). Effect of practice and feedback on frequency discrimination. Journal of the Acoustical Society of America, 35, 1511–1514.

Crist, R.E., Li, W., & Gilbert, C.D. (2001). Learning to see: experience and attention in primary visual cortex. Nature Neuroscience, 4, 519–525.

Demany, L. (1985). Perceptual learning in frequency discrimination. Journal of the Acoustical Society of America, 78, 1118–1120.

Demany, L., & Semal, C. (2002). Learning to perceive pitch differences. Journal of the Acoustical Society of America, 111, 1377–1388.

Dill, M. (2002). Specificity versus invariance of perceptual learning: the example of position. In M. Fahle & T. Poggio (Eds.), Perceptual Learning (pp. 219–231). Cambridge: MIT Press.

Dosher, B.A., & Lu, Z.-L. (1999). Mechanisms of perceptual learning. Vision Research, 39, 3197–3221.

Fiorentini, A., & Berardi, N. (1980). Perceptual learning specific for orientation and spatial frequency. Nature, 287, 43–44.

Ghose, G.M., Yang, T., & Maunsell, J.H.R. (2002). Physiological correlates of perceptual learning in monkey V1 and V2. Journal of Physiology, 87, 1867–1888.

Gibson, E.J. (1953). Improvement in perceptual judgments as a function of controlled practice or training. Psychological Bulletin, 50, 401–431.

Gilbert, C.D. (1994). Early perceptual learning. Proceedings of the National Academy of Sciences USA, 91, 1195–1197.

Gilbert, C.D. (1998). Adult cortical dynamics. Physiological Reviews, 78, 467–485.

Goldstone, R.L. (1998). Perceptual learning. Annual Review of Psychology, 49, 585–612.

Hienz, R.D., Sachs, M.B., & Aleszczyk, C.M. (1993). Frequency discrimination in noise: Comparison of cat performances with auditory-nerve models. Journal of the Acoustical Society of America, 93, 462–469.

Irvine, D.R.F., Martin, R.L., Klimkeit, E., & Smith, R. (2000). Specificity of perceptual learning in a frequency discrimination task. Journal of the Acoustical Society of America, 108, 2964–2968.

Irvine, D.R.F., & Rajan, R. (1996). Injury- and use-related plasticity in the primary sensory cortex of adult mammals: Possible relationship to perceptual learning. Clinical and Experimental Pharmacology and Physiology, 23, 939–947.

Jenkins, W.M., Merzenich, M.M., Ochs, M.T., Allard, T., & Guíc-Robles, E. (1990). Functional reorganization of primary somatosensory cortex in adult owl monkeys after behaviorally controlled tactile stimulation. Journal of Neurophysiology, 63, 82–104.

Karni, A., & Sagi, D. (1991). Where practice makes perfect in texture discrimination: Evidence for primary visual cortex plasticity. Proceedings of the National Academy of Sciences USA, 88, 4966–4970.

Kilgard, M.P., Pandya, P.K., Vazquez, J., Gehi, A., Schreiner, C.E., & Merzenich, M.M. (2001). Sensory input directs spatial and temporal plasticity in primary auditory cortex. Journal of Neurophysiology, 86, 326–338.

May, B.J., Huang, A.Y., Aleszczyk, C.M., & Hienz, R.D. (1995). Design and conduct of sensory experiments for domestic cats. In R. Dooling & R. Fay (Eds.), Methods of Comparative Acoustics (pp. 95–108). Basel, Switzerland: Birkhauser.

Mollon, J.D., & Danilova, M.V. (1996). Three remarks on perceptual learning. Spatial Vision, 10, 51–58.

Moore, B.C.J. (1973). Frequency difference limens for short-duration tones. Journal of the Acoustical Society of America, 54, 610–619.

Moore, B.C.J. (1976). Comparison of frequency DL's for pulsed tones and modulated tones. British Journal of Audiology, 10, 17–20.

Pisoni, D.B., Aslin, R.N., Perey, A.J., & Hennessy, B.L. (1982). Some effects of laboratory training on identification and discrimination of voicing contrasts in stop consonants. Journal of Experimental Psychology, 8, 297–314.

Prosen, C.A., Moody, D.B., Sommers, M.S., & Stebbins, W.C. (1990). Frequency discrimination in the monkey. Journal of the Acoustical Society of America, 88, 2152–2158.

Ramachandran, V.S., & Braddick, O. (1973). Orientation-specific learning in stereopsis. Perception, 2, 371–376.

Recanzone, G.H., Jenkins, W.M., Hradek, G.T., & Merzenich, M.M. (1992a). Progressive improvement in discriminative abilities in adult owl monkeys performing a tactile frequency discrimination task. Journal of Neurophysiology, 67, 1015–1030.

Recanzone, G.H., Merzenich, M.M., Jenkins, W.M., Grajski, K.A., & Dinse, H.R. (1992b). Topographic reorganization of the hand representation in cortical area 3b of owl monkeys trained in a frequency-discrimination task. Journal of Neurophysiology, 67, 1031–1056.

Recanzone, G.H., Schreiner, C.E., & Merzenich, M.M. (1993). Plasticity in the frequency representation of primary auditory cortex following discrimination training in adult owl monkeys. Journal of Neuroscience, 13, 87–103.

Robinson, K., & Summerfield, A.Q. (1996). Adult auditory learning and training. Ear and Hearing, 17, 51–65.

Schiltz, C., Bodart, J.M., Dubois, S., Dejardin, S., Michel, C., & Roucoux, A. (1999). Neuronal mechanisms of perceptual learning: changes in human brain activity with training in orientation discrimination. NeuroImage, 9, 46–62.

Schoups, A.A., Vogels, R., & Orban, G.A. (1995). Human perceptual learning in identifying the oblique orientation: Retinotopy, orientation specificity, and monocularity. Journal of Physiology, 483, 797–810.

Schoups, A., Vogels, R., Qian, N., & Orban, G. (2001). Practising orientation identification improves orientation coding in V1 neurons. Nature, 412, 549–553.

Tremblay, K., Kraus, N., Carrell, T.D., & McGee, T. (1997). Central auditory system plasticity. Generalization to novel stimuli following listening training. Journal of the Acoustical Society of America, 102, 3762–3773.

Watson, C.S. (1980). Time course of auditory perceptual learning. Annals of Otology, Rhinology and Laryngology, Supplement, 74, 96–102.

Watson, C.S. (1991). Auditory perceptual learning and the cochlear implant. American Journal of Otology, Supplement, 12, 73–79.

Weinberger, N.M. (1995). Dynamic regulation of receptive fields and maps in the adult sensory cortex. Annual Review of Neuroscience, 18, 129–158.

Wright, B.A. (1998). Generalization of auditory-discrimination learning. Association for Research in Otolaryngolgy Abstracts, Abstract 413.

Wright, B.A., Buonomano, D.V., Mahncke, H.W., & Merzenich, M.M. (1997). Learning and generalization of auditory temporal-interval discrimination in humans. Journal of Neuroscience, 17, 3956–3963.

Wright, B.A., & Fitzgerald, M.B. (2001). Different patterns of human discrimination learning for two interaural cues to sound-source location. Proceedings of the National Academy of Sciences USA, 98, 12307–12312.

Xerri, C., Merzenich, M.M., Jenkins, W., & Santucci, S. (1999). Representational plasticity in cortical area 3b paralleling tactual-motor skill acquisition in adult monkeys. Cerebral Cortex, 9, 264–276.

Zwislocki, J., Maire, F., Feldman, A.S., & Rubin, H. (1958). On the effect of practice and motivation on the threshold of audibility. Journal of the Acoustical Society of America, 30, 254–262.

26. NEURODYNAMICS IN AUDITORY CORTEX DURING CATEGORY LEARNING

Frank W. Ohl, Henning Scheich, Walter J. Freeman

INTRODUCTION

Research on learning has for historical reasons been divided mainly into behaviorally oriented studies performed on animals and more cognitively oriented studies in humans (Anderson, 2000). Accordingly, studies aimed at the presumed neurophysiological basis of learning have either exploited the full range of cognitive-phenomenological approaches in humans while being methodologically confined mainly to non-invasive imaging techniques, or alternatively, have made use of the better accessibility of the animal nervous system physiology while being restricted in the definition and analysis of the cognitive aspects involved. Consequently, our physiological understanding of learning processes is best for simple behaviors that can be studied in suited animal models (e.g., Kandel, 2001) but declines for cognitively more demanding aspects of learning.

In the present chapter we present an animal model, amenable to detailed physiological analysis, of a cognitively demanding learning task, namely the formation of categories (concept formation) and the sorting of novel stimuli into these categories. Both of these aspects are encapsulated in the term 'category learning'. We will first argue that learning phenomena having aspects beyond mere stimulus-response associations, like category learning does, are of high relevance for studying the neuronal basis of learning in general, in that they preclude explanation of learning phenomena by a broad class of simple neurophysiological models which are otherwise discussed as elemental for physiological theories of learning. Second, we introduce a new animal model for studying category learning and describe an electrophysiological correlate of category-specific processing of stimuli. Third, we argue that the physiological results derived from the category learning paradigm contribute to solving an important problem reported in the literature since the 1950s. This is the problem that in trained animals activity patterns in sensory cortices, though often stable and identifiable with high significance, do not seem to be invariant with stimuli or even with a particular training context, as required for a 'representation of a stimulus' by classic sensory physiology (Freeman, 2000, and references therein).

WHAT IS CATEGORY LEARNING ?

We define category learning as the process by which categorization of stimuli, or, more generally, of situations experienced by a subject is acquired. The term categorization describes the phenomenon that under suited conditions a (human or non-human) subject might behaviorally respond to a multitude of stimuli or situations with a considerably smaller number of response types although the stimuli itself could in principle be discriminated by the subject. (For a recent discussion of the relationship between category learning and category use, see Ashby & Ell, 2001; Markman & Ross, 2003). The nature of categorization has been subject to intellectual debates at least since Aristotle. A brief review of some of the more traditional problems which have repeatedly emerged in the context of characterizing the nature of categorization will be used to motivate the viewpoint that has been taken in planning the experiments focused on in the present chapter.

Traditional accounts of categorization

The Aristotelian view (often referred to as the 'Classical Theory') considers having or establishing a set of necessary and/or sufficient criteria to be met by stimuli or situations as being the essence of determining their membership to a category. This view, enriched by an appropriate formal framework, is also maintained by some 'artificially intelligent' approaches to the categorization problem. A main objection that was brought up against this view is that for many 'natural' categories such sets cannot in fact be found (e.g., Rosch, 1973): Neither seems category membership always be defined by features which can unequivocally be attributed to all members, nor can features always be evaluated to indicate membership or no membership to a category. Rather, varying degrees of 'typicality' of features and/or category members seem to be the rule. Consequently, a number of accounts have been proposed which can be summarized under the heading of 'prototype theories' (e.g., Posner & Keele, 1968). Prototype theories hold that some form of idealized representation of category members exists and actual membership of a given stimulus is determined by some scaling of 'similarity' of this member to the prototype. Prototype theories in some instances have faced the problem of providing a convincing framework for establishing the required similarity relations (for a discussion, see Ashby & Perrin, 1988) or could not account for the phenomenon of non-prototype members having more pronounced effects on categorization performance than the prototype itself (e.g., Brooks, 1978; Medin & Schaffer, 1978). Studies on human (Rosch, 1975) and animal categorization (Lea & Ryan, 1990) have argued that some of these problems can be mitigated by lifting the requirement for local comparisons with a singular prototype and instead requiring global comparisons with multiple (in the extreme form with all) category members (Estes, 1986; Hintzman, 1986; Nosofsky, 1986) for which reason such theories are summarized under the heading 'exemplar theories'. While historically these (and other) approaches have been initiated and put forward by their authors with very different rationales in mind they can be more objectively compared to each other using a suitably formalized reformulation (Ashby & Maddox, 1993), which can be derived from general recognition theory (Ashby & Townsend, 1986). It is particularly disturbing that many experimentally achievable observations can be accounted for by more or all of the theoretical viewpoints provided, at least if appropriate modifications to the extreme positions of such theories are allowed (Pearce, 1994).

Categorization in non-human species

While in human studies the above sketched (and other) viewpoints are maintained without questioning the existence of concepts, as mental constructs, as a possible basis for categorization, this option is not so clear for non-human species, simply because they cannot report on having a concept that might guide their categorization behavior. Research on categorization in animals has therefore to rely on operational criteria. It has been argued that defining a concept would require reference to language so that non-human species could not have concepts at all (Chater & Heyes, 1994). A less extreme viewpoint suggests that some instances of animal categorization might reflect mere discriminations albeit with very complex stimuli (Wasserman & Astley, 1994). It has been elaborated that the demonstration of concepts in non human species might be possible by suitably designed transfer experiments with appropriately constructed control stimulus sets (Lea, 1984). In designing category learning experiments for non-human species care must be taken because natural and even artificial stimuli could already have ecological relevance for the species given causing a bias in its learning behavior (Nelson & Marler, 1990). In any case, the transfer of learned behaviors to novel stimuli is a relevant criterion because it demonstrates that during an instantiation of category learning more has happened than mere associations of responses to trained particular stimuli (Lea & Ryan, 1990).

Categorization and generalization

It is appropriate to consider the terms 'categorization' and 'generalization' at this point in more detail as they are inconsistently used in the literature and have a bearing on the experiments to be described in this chapter.

When a (human or non-human) subject is trained to discriminate a stimulus
A from a stimulus B, the discrimination performance typically develops
gradually over some time as is manifest in the various forms of functions
usually referred to as 'learning curves'. A typical form is schematized in
Figure 26.1A which displays the temporal evolution of the hit rate and false
alarm rate in a Go/(No-Go) discrimination experiment. Other depictions of the
discrimination learning behavior are possible depending on the kind of
experiment performed (be these symmetric choice experiments, signal detection
approaches, etc.) and the choice of behavioral observables (e.g., the various
transformations of hit rate and false alarm rates which are suitable under given
conditions). Generally, however, the changing conditional rate of occurrence of
some behavior must be assessed at some point in the analysis. The typically
asymptotic response rate depends on various parameters (vigilance, internal
response biases, strength of the learned association, etc.) but also shows some
degree of stimulus specificity. This can be demonstrated by measuring what is
called generalization gradients: In a Go/(No-Go) experiment in which a subject
is trained to show the Go reaction in response to stimulus A and the No-Go
reaction in response to stimulus B, for example, a generalization gradient can be
assessed by measuring the conditioned response (typically quantified by its
frequency of occurrence across trials or by the strength of its expression) as a
function of a physical distance between parameters characterizing stimuli A and
B. The latter defines a path through the parameter space connecting stimuli A
and B. When physical stimulus parameters are varied along this path a more or
less gradual fall-off in the A-specific response amplitude is typically observed
and referred to as a generalization gradient (Fig. 26.1B).

Conversely, when a subject has formed categories it can recognize even
novel stimuli as representants of the learned categories. A depiction of
behavioral variables analogous to a learning curve would therefore indicate a
high discrimination performance even in the first training session (Fig. 26.1C).
The experimental demonstration of this behavior is critical for assessing
category learning and is sometimes referred to as the criterion of the 'transfer of
learned behaviors to novel stimuli' (see subsection on behavioral results in the
next section). Therefore, category learning is distinguished from simple or
discriminative conditioning also by the psychometric functions it produces.
Instead of gradual generalization gradients we find sigmoid psychometric
functions with a more or less sharp boundary at some location in the stimulus
parameter space, called the categorization boundary (cf. Ehret, 1987;
Fig. 26.1D). Learned categories develop as cognitive constructs; they epitomize
subjective 'hypotheses' that are expressible as parcellations of the set of actually
perceived or imaginable stimuli, conditions or actions, into equivalence classes
of meaning in particular contexts. Transfer of learned behaviors to novel stimuli
therefore follows the subjective laws of this parcellation, rather than being
guided by (physical) similarity relations between stimuli or stimulus features.
These are important criteria for cognitive structures that have to be accounted
for by physiological models of learning.

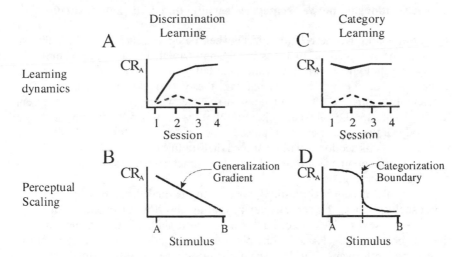

Fig. 26.1. Suitable observables differentiating discrimination learning and category learning. Learning curves (**A, C**) and psychometric functions (**B, D**) after discrimination learning (A, B) and after category learning (C, D) are shown. The A-specific conditioned response rate CR_A is typically a measure of the rate of occurrence or of the strength of the response that has been trained to be elicited by stimulus A. Solid and dashed curves in (A) and (C) depict the hit rate and false alarm rate, respectively. See subsection on categorization and generalization for details.

    In this context it could be noted that in some artificial systems (like artificial neural networks) generalization gradients emerge as a result of the used training and learning paradigm. Already in simple one-layer perceptrons generalization gradients can mimic categorization behavior when threshold operations are applied to suited state variables of the network. Typically, however, apart from the thresholding operations such systems undergo only smooth transformations under the learning paradigm unlike what has been described for category learning and we prefer to call this behavior classification. This does not imply however that artificial systems cannot in principle show category learning. It is conceivable that artificial systems can be equipped with the requisite process capacities so that their emergent behavior could in all fairness be called category learning (Kozma & Freeman, 2003; Nakamura et al., 1993).

    In a nutshell, generalization is a general feature of learned stimulus-cued behaviors reflecting the converse of stimulus specificity, while categorization is a cognitive process based on the parcellation of the represented world into equivalence classes of meaning, valid for an individual in a particular context and in a particular time.

On the relationship between category learning and neuronal plasticity

The exact nature of the relationship between category learning, or learning in general, and neuronal plasticity is highly non-trivial, because the former is a purely psychological concept while the latter is a physiological concept. Conceptual difficulties in inter-relating these two domains are therefore predictably similar to other situations in science where conceptually different levels have to be linked, like in the case of relationship between thermodynamics and statistical physics, or in the case of the 'mind-body problem'. In this section it will be argued that traditional physiological accounts for learning phenomena are insufficient to characterize the physiological basis of category learning.

If the role of neuronal plasticity for learning is considered by physiologists, it is usually seen in the capacity for re-routing the flow of excitation through neuronal networks. The case of Pavlovian conditioning, a learning phenomenon that has been intensively studied by physiologists, lends itself to this concept in a very straightforward way: Pavlovian conditioning can be described, and – in fact – has traditionally been defined, as a process by which an initially behaviorally neutral stimulus can later elicit a particular behavior, when it has previously been paired with a stimulus (US) that unconditionally triggers this behavior (Fig. 26.2A). It has proved successful to formulate models of the role of neuronal plasticity for learning which basically consist in a one-to-one translation of this idea into a neuronal substrate (Fig. 26.2B). In the case of the conditioned gill withdrawal reflex in *Aplysia*, for example, this concept is manifest in the feedforward convergence of – in the simplest case – two sensory neurons on a shared interneuron which in turn projects on a motor neuron. The concept is so straightforward, that its appraisal as a generic element of physiological models of learning has been put forward, as, for example, expressed by the metaphor of a 'cellular alphabet' (Hawkins & Kandel, 1984) or the metaphor of a 'molecular alphabet' (Kandel et al., 1995).

The claim of the elemental nature of the above sketched neuronal model for learning has been challenged by cognitive science (e.g., Schouten & De Long, 1999) where learning is viewed as a process by which an animal gains information about conditions in its environment that help it to behave in meaningful ways. It should be noted that this perspective includes, among other things, the possibility of meaningful behaviors to novel stimuli. Novel stimuli, however, have not been encountered before, specifically, they have not been associated with unconditional triggers (Fig. 26.2C). Therefore, a simple feedforward convergence scheme as in Figure 26.2A cannot be used as an explanation for such aspects of learning, that is, aspects that go beyond mere stimulus-response associations.

The current chapter focuses on an example of category learning because category learning particularly emphasizes this aspect of learning, that is, the meaningful behavior in response to novel and unfamiliar stimuli, and therefore precludes explanation by a broad class of reductionist schemes. In this sense, the

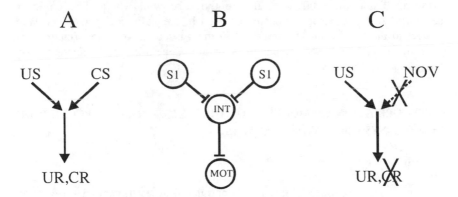

Fig. 26.2. **(A)** General scheme of flow of information before and after Pavlovian conditioning. Before conditioning, an unconditioned stimulus (US) will elicit a particular behavior, then referred to as unconditioned response (UR). After conditioning, a previously behaviorally neutral stimulus can elicit this behavior as a conditioned response (CR) and is then referred to as the conditioned stimulus (CS). **(B)** A straightforward translation of the flow of information during Pavlovian conditioning into a flow of neuronal excitation within a neuronal substrate. **(C)** The architecture in B cannot explain responses to novel stimuli (NOV), because novel stimuli have not been associated with unconditional triggers and, consequently, cannot be conditioned.

study of category learning is of general relevance to the physiological understanding of learning phenomena in general.

Moreover, the formation of categories is fundamental to cognition (Estes, 1994). Category learning transcends simple stimulus-response associations, typically studied in systems neurophysiology, in that it involves abstraction from learned particular stimulus features. Category learning leads beyond the information given (Kommatsu, 1992).

A new animal model of category learning

In this chapter the Mongolian gerbil (*Meriones unguiculatus*) is introduced as a new model of category learning (Ohl et al., 2001; Wetzel et al., 1998). The following two sections will discuss its behavioral analysis and present the physiological data obtained during the category learning behavior, respectively. As motivated in the previous subsections, the experiment is designed to shed light on the processes that give rise to the transfer of learned behaviors to novel stimuli which are located outside the generalization gradient in the perceptual space. The occurrence of the transfer of the learned behaviors to novel stimuli will be used as a marker event for the study of the physiological correlates of category learning. With respect to the issues addressed in the subsection on categorization in non-human species a stimulus set was used which is demonstratively behaviorally neutral to the naïve gerbil. Moreover, stimuli were so selected that they did not differ in the ease with which they could be associated with the particular behaviors used in the training experiments. With respect to the background summarized in the subsection on categorization and generalization, care was taken to separate generalization behavior from categorization behavior.

CATEGORIZATION OF MODULATION DIRECTION IN FREQUENCY MODULATED TONES – BEHAVIORAL ANALYSIS

Stimuli

As stimuli we used linearly frequency-modulated tones traversing a frequency range of 1 octave in 250 ms in rising or falling fashion, played at an intensity of 70 dB SPL as measured at a distance of 10 cm in front of the speaker. Due to reflections of the sound wave in the shuttle box and various possible head positions of the animal during the experiment a considerable variance of effective stimulus intensity across trials is predictable. In frequency modulated tones a number of parameters can be (co-)varied, like their duration, their intensity, the frequency ranges covered, and the modulation rate, that is, the rate of change of the tones' instantaneous frequency. By construction, most of those stimuli (all, except for those with zero modulation rate, i.e., pure tones) can be categorized as either 'rising' or 'falling frequency modulated tones', depending on whether the instantaneous frequency changes from low to high or from high to low, respectively.

For the experiment stimuli were so designed that they fell outside the generalization gradients established by training naïve animals to the two neighboring (in the parameter space) stimuli. This ensures that observed learning curves would resemble the schemes in Figures 26.1A and 26.1C thus indicating that the subject has not or has categorized the stimuli, respectively.

Apparatus and training paradigm

Training consisted of a Go/(No-Go) avoidance paradigm carried out in a 2-compartment shuttle box, with the two compartments separated by a little hurdle, ensuring a low rate of spontaneous hurdle crossings. Animals were trained to cross the hurdle in response to a rising frequency modulated tone and to stay in the current compartment in response to a falling frequency modulated tone. Training was organized in so-called 'training blocks' during which the discrimination of one particular rising frequency modulated tone from a tone traversing the identical frequency range in falling direction was trained. A training block consisted of a number of training sessions, with one session trained per day and was continued until no further changes in conditioned response rates were achieved in three consecutive sessions. Then another training block was initiated in which the discrimination of another pair of a rising and falling frequency modulated tone was trained. A training session encompassed the randomized presentation of 30 rising and 30 falling frequency modulated tones with the animals' false responses (misses and false alarms) being negatively reinforced by a mild electrodermal stimulation through a metal grid forming the cage floor. Control groups were run with the opposite contingencies to test for potential biases in this behavior which have been reported for the dog (McConnell, 1990). We showed that for the stimulus parameters tested no such biases existed for the gerbil.

Behavioral results

Animals trained on one or more training blocks never generalized to pure tones of any frequency (e.g., start or stop frequencies of the modulated tone, or frequencies traversed by the modulation or extrapolated from the modulation). This could be demonstrated by direct transfer experiments (Ohl et al., 2001, supplementary material) or by measuring generalization gradients for modulation rate which never encompassed zero modulation rates (Ohl et al., 2001).

Categorization was demonstrated by the transfer of the conditioned response behavior (changing compartment in response to tones of one category and remaining in the current compartment in response to tones of the other) to novel stimuli as measured by the response rates in the first session of a new training block. This sequential design allowed the experimenter to determine the moment in which an individual would change its response behavior from a 'discrimination phase' (Figs. 26.1A, 26.1C) to a 'categorization phase' (Figs. 26.1B, 26.1D). All animals tested were able to categorize novel frequency modulated tones but, most notably, different individuals showed the transition from the discrimination phase to the categorization phase at different points in time in their training histories, although all had been trained with the same sequence of training blocks (Ohl et al., 2001). Also, the transition from the discrimination phase to the categorization phase occurred abruptly rather than gradually, i.e., in the first session of a training block either no discrimination performance was observed (discrimination phase) or the full performance was observed (categorization phase). A third property of the transition was that after its occurrence the discrimination performance remained stable for the rest of the training blocks. These three properties of the transition, individuality of the time point of occurrence, abruptness of occurrence and behavioral stability after its occurrence, make it resemble a state transition in dynamic systems. We used this transition as a marker in the individual learning history of a subject to guide our search for physiological correlates of this behavioral state transition.

PHYSIOLOGICAL CORRELATES OF CATEGORY LEARNING

Neuronal representation of utilized stimuli

A suitable level for studying electrophysiological correlates of perceptual organization is the mesoscopic level of neurodyamics (Freeman, 2000), which defines the spatial scale of phenomena observed (Barrie et al., 1996) and provides focus on electrical phenomena emergent from the mass action of ensembles of some 10^4 to 10^5 neurons. Since it was demonstrated for the gerbil that the discrimination of the direction of frequency modulated tones requires a functional auditory cortex (Kraus et al., 2002; Ohl et al., 1999) the training procedures were combined with the parallel measurement of the neurodynamics in auditory cortex. For cortical structures, this level of description is accessible by measurement of the electrocorticogram. We have therefore combined the described category learning paradigm with the measurement of the electrocorticogram using arrays (3×6) of microelectrodes chronically implanted on the dura over the primary auditory cortex. The spatial configuration and interelectrode distance (600 μm) of the recording array were so designed to cover the tonotopic representation of the frequency modulated stimuli used and avoid spatial aliasing of electrocorticogram activity (Ohl et al., 2000a).

The spatial organization of the thalamic input into the auditory cortex can be studied by averaging electrocorticograms across multiple presentations of the same stimulus, yielding the well-known auditory evoked potential (Barth & Di, 1990, 1991). Our studies of pure-tone-induced (Ohl et al., 2000a) and frequency-modulated-tone-induced (Ohl et al., 2000b) auditory evoked potentials in primary auditory cortex, field AI, revealed that their early components (P1 and N1) are topographically organized, that is, are localized at positions within the tonotopic gradient of the field that correspond to the frequency interval traversed by the frequency modulation, while their late components (P2 and N2) are not. On a finer spatial scale, the localization of the early components of rising and falling frequency modulated tones was found to be shifted towards tonotopic representations of the respective end frequencies of the modulations, that is, toward higher frequencies for rising modulations and towards lower frequencies for falling modulations. These 'tonotopic shifts' (Ohl et al., 2000b) could be explained by the finding that single neurons are usually activated more strongly when the frequency modulation is towards the neuron's best frequency than when it is away from it (Phillips et al., 1985). In the former case, the activation of frequency channels in the neighborhood of the best frequency of a single neuron are recruited more synchronously than in the latter case, due to the increasing response latency with increasing spectral distance from the neuron's best frequency. If this asymmetry is transferred onto a tonotopically organized array of neurons a tonotopic shift as described will result. Tonotopic shifts have previously been reported in the cortex analogue of the chick (Heil et al., 1992).

Single trial analysis of electrocorticograms

Since physiological correlates of category learning could not be expected to occur time-locked to stimulus presentation, we analyzed electrocorticograms recorded during the training with a single trial type of analysis. Instantaneous spatial patterns in the ongoing cortical activity were described by state vectors (Barrie et al., 1996; Ohl et al., 2001). State vectors were formed from estimates of signal power in 120 ms time windows obtained for each channel. As the spatial pattern of signal power evolved over time, the state vector moved through the state space along a corresponding trajectory. For each trial, the Euclidean distance (parameterized by time) to a reference trajectory was calculated and termed 'dissimilarity function'. In each case the reference trajectory was the centroid over trajectories associated with trials associated with stimuli from the respective other category measured in the same training session, that is, each trajectory associated with a rising frequency modulated tone was compared to the centroid over all trajectories associated falling frequency modulated tones in the same session, and vice versa. Comparison of single trajectories with centroids of trajectories, rather than other single trajectories, ensured that, on a statistical basis, transient increases in the pattern dissimilarity (peaks in the dissimilarity function) were due to pattern changes in the observed trajectory rather than in the centroid. In naïve animals, dissimilarity functions showed a 'baseline behavior' with a sharp peak (2–7 standard deviations of baseline amplitude) after stimulus onset This peak occurred predictably because of the topographically dissimilar patterns (tonotopic shifts) of early evoked responses that rising and falling frequency modulated tones produce (Ohl et al. 2000b). With learning, additional peaks emerged from the ongoing activity, thus labeling spatial activity patterns in single trials with transiently increased dissimilarity to the reference trajectory indicating a potential relevance for representing category-specific information processing. These patterns were therefore termed 'marked states'.

To test whether marked states do in fact represent processing of category-specific information we analyzed the similarity and dissimilarity relations among them in the entire course of the training. While animals were in their discrimination phases (prior to the formation of categories), we observed that dissimilarities between marked states within categories were of the same order of magnitude than between categories. After an individual animal had entered its categorization phase, dissimilarities within a category were significantly smaller than between categories (Ohl et al., 2001). This indicated the existence of a metric which reflected the parcellation of stimuli into equivalence classes of meaning. This type of metric is therefore different from the known tonotopic, which reflects similarity relations of physical stimulus parameters, namely spectral composition, in that it reflects subjective aspects of stimulus meaning, namely its belongingness to categories formed by previous experience.

The spatial organization of the emerging marked states was analyzed in more detail and compared to that of the early evoked activity (also yielding peaks in the dissimilarity function) by a multivariate discriminant analysis, identifying the regions in the recording area which maximally contributed to the dissimilarity between the observed pattern and the reference pattern (Ohl et al., 2003b), or identifiying the regions which contribute most information about the pattern (Ohl et al., 2003a).

CONCLUSIONS

It was possible to develop an animal model of auditory category learning which demonstrated the formation of categories as a process with three main characteristics in the behavioral data: First, categorization developed abruptly rather than gradually. Second, it developed at a point in time that was specific for each individual subject in its learning history. Third, when categorization had occurred in a subject it remained stable for the rest of the subject's training experiences (unless a change in the reinforcement schedule forces a change in the meaning attributed to stimuli). A process which conforms to these characteristics is sometimes termed 'Aha'-event to indicate a change in the cognitive state of a subject.

The neurophysiological analysis revealed that the process of associating meaning to acoustic stimuli as indicated by an increasing discrimination performance in the behavioral data was paralleled by the emergence of transient activity states in the ongoing cortical activity, that could be identified on the basis of their dissimilarity to patterns found in trials associated with stimuli not belonging to the category. These activity states are the first demonstration of a 'constructive aspect' of neural activity during a categorization event.

It is noteworthy, that spatial patterns of electrocortical activity in single trials were already observed by Lilly in his toposcopic studies (Lilly & Cherry, 1954). To him it was already apparent that the long lasting dynamics was not just random 'noise', but was better described by 'figures' moving in time and space across the cortical surface. At that time the majority of research programs had already turned to the analysis of averaged data in which such spatiotemporal structures are no longer detectable. The few research programs pursuing analysis of activity patterns in single trials (e.g., DeMott, 1970; Livanov, 1977) had faced a major problem for the interpretation of such patterns: the lack of invariance with the applied stimuli. A large body of data accumulated over the last decades (summarized in Freeman, 2000) showed that such patterns might remain stable when repetitively evoked by sensory stimulation for a certain period in time, but might typically vary with behavioral context, particularly in learning situations when stimuli were associated with particular meanings. This lack of invariance of these patterns with the mere physical parameters of stimuli challenged their interpretation as 'sensory representations'. The observed metastability of the patterns was hypothesized to reflect context aspects of the stimulation as well as the perceptual history of the individual, and it was inferred that such patterns reflect subjectively relevant cognitive structures (for a summary, see Freeman, 2000, and references therein). The results described here critically confirm this interpretation: The category learning paradigm, first, allows determination of the point in time when a particular cognitive structure (the formation of the categories 'rising' and 'falling') emerges, and second, predicts that the main source of variance in the stimuli (the spectral interval traversed by the frequency modulation) is no longer a relevant feature after a subject's transition to categorization. Consequently, it was found that the dissimilarity between marked states associated with stimuli belonging to the same category was significantly reduced after the transition to categorization, although the physical dissimilarity of the corresponding stimuli was still high, as also reflected in the topographic organization of the stimulus locked peaks in the dissimilarity function and the fact the dissimilarities remained high in individuals that had not yet formed categories.

In this sense, the utilized paradigm and analysis strategy provided an objective (for the experimenter) window of a subjective cognitive structure (that of the animal).

ACKNOWLEDGMENTS

This work was supported by the BioFuture grant of the BMBF to F.W.O., and by grants from the Land Sachsen-Anhalt. We thank Brian Burke and Daniela Labra Cardero (Berkeley), as well as Kathrin Ohl and Thomas Wagner (Magdeburg) for technical assistance.

REFERENCES

Anderson, J.R. (2000). Learning and memory: An integrated approach. New York: John Wiley & Sons.

Ashby, F.G., & Ell, S.W. (2001). The neurobiology of human category learning. Trends in Cognitive Sciences, 5, 204–210.

Ashby, F.G., & Maddox, W.T. (1993). Relations between prototype, exemplar, and decision bound models of categorization. Journal of Mathematical Psychology, 7, 372–400.

Ashby, F.G., & Perrin, N.A. (1988). Toward a unified theory of similarity and recognition. Psychological Reviews, 95, 124–150.

Ashby, F.G., & Townsend, J.T. (1986). Varieties of perceptual independence. Psychological Reviews, 93, 154–179.

Barrie, J.H., Freeman, W.J., & Lenhart, M. (1996). Modulation by discriminative training of spatial patterns of gamma EEG amplitude and phase in neocortex of rabbits. Journal of Neurophysiology, 76, 520–539.

Barth, D.S., & Di, S. (1990). Three-dimensional analysis of auditory-evoked potentials in rat neocortex. Journal of Neurophysiology, 64, 1527–1636.

Barth, D.S., & Di, S. (1991). The functional anatomy of middle latency auditory evoked potentials. Brain Research, 565, 109–115.

Brooks, L. (1978). Nonanalytic concept formation and memory for instances. In E. Rosch & B.B. Lloyd (Eds.), Cognition and categorization (pp. 169–211). Hillsdale, NJ: Lawrence Erlbaum Associates.

Chater, N., & Heyes, C. (1994). Animal concepts: Content and discontent. Mind and Language, 9, 209–247.

DeMott, D.W. (1970). Toposcopic studies of learning. Springfield, IL: Thomas Books.

Ehret, G. (1987). Categorical perception of sound signals: facts and hypotheses from animal studies. In S. Harnad (Ed.), Categorical perception (pp. 301–331). Cambridge, England: Cambridge University Press.

Estes, W.K. (1986). Array models for category learning. Cognitive Psychology, 18, 500–549.

Estes, W.K. (1994). Classification and Cognition. New York: Oxford University Press.

Freeman, W.J. (2000). Neurodynamics: An exploration in mesoscopic brain dynamics. London: Springer-Verlag.

Hawkins, R.D., & Kandel, E.R. (1984). Is there a cell-biological alphabet for simple forms of learning? Psychological Reviews, 91, 375–391.

Heil, P., Langner, G., & Scheich, H. (1992). Processing of frequency-modulated stimuli in the chick auditory cortex analogue: Evidence for topographic representations and possible mechanisms of rate and directional sensitivity. Journal of Comparative Physiology A, 171, 583–600.

Hintzman, D.L. (1986). "Schema abstraction" in a multiple trace memory model. Psychological Reviews, 93, 411–428.

Kandel, E.R. (2001). The molecular biology of memory storage: A dialogue between genes and synapses. Science, 294, 1030–1038.

Kandel, E.R., Schwartz, J.H., & Jessell, T.M. (1995). Essentials of neural science and behavior. Norwalk, CT: Appleton & Lange.

Kommatsu, L.K. (1992). Recent views of conceptual structure. Psychological Bulletin, 112, 500–526.

Kozma, R., & Freeman, W.J. (2003). Basic principles of the KIV model and its application to the navigation problem. Journal of Integrative Neuroscience, 2, 125–145.

Kraus, M., Schicknick, H., Wetzel, W., Ohl, F., Staak, S., & Tischmeyer, W. (2002). Memory consolidation for the discrimination of frequency-modulated tones in Mongolian gerbils is sensitive to protein-synthesis inhibitors applied to auditory cortex. Learning & Memory, 9, 293–303.

Lea, S.E.G. (1984). In what sense do pigeons learn concepts. In H.S. Terrace, T.G. Bever, & H.L. Roitblat (Eds.), Animal cognition (pp. 263–276), Hillsdale, NJ: Lawrence Erlbaum Associates.

Lea, S.E.G. & Ryan, C.M.E. (1990). Unnatural concepts and the theory of concept discrimination in birds. In M.L. Common, R.J. Herrnstein, S.M. Kosslyn, & D.B. Mumford (Eds.), Quantitative analyses of behavior, Vol. VIII, Behavioral approaches to pattern recognition and concept formation (pp. 165–185), Hillsdale, NJ: Lawrence Erlbaum.

Lilly, J.C., & Cherry, R.B. (1954). Surface movements of click responses from acoustic cerebral cortex of cat: Leading and trailing edges of a response figure. Journal of Neurophysiology, 17, 531–537.

Livanov, M.N. (1977). Spatial organization of cerebral processes. New York: Wiley.

Markman, A.B., & Ross, B.H. (2003). Category use and category learning. Psychological Bulletin, 129, 592–613.

McConnell, P.B. (1990). Acoustic structure and receiver response in domestic dogs, Canis familiaris. Animal Behavior, 39, 897–904.

Medin, D.L., & Schaffer, M.M. (1978). Context theory of classification learning. Psychological Reviews, 85, 207–238.

Nakamura, G.V., Taraban, R., & Medin, D.L. (1993). Categorization by humans and machines: The Psychology of Learning and Motivation, Vol. 29. San Diego: Academic Press.

Nelson, D.A., & Marler, P. (1990). The perception of birdsong and an ecological concept of signal space. In W.C. Stebbins & M.A. Berkeley (Eds.), Comparative perception: Complex signals, Vol. 2 (pp. 443–477). New York: John Wiley & Sons.

Nosofsky, R.M. (1986). Attention and learning processes in the identification and categorization of integral stimuli. Journal of Experimental Psychology: Learning, Memory and Cognition, 13, 87–108.

Ohl, F.W., Deliano, M., Scheich, H., & Freeman, W.J. (2003a). Early and late patterns of stimulus-related activity in auditory cortex of trained animals. Biological Cybernetics, 88, 374–379.

Ohl, F.W., Deliano, M., Scheich, H., & Freeman, W.J. (2003b). Analysis of evoked and emergent patterns of stimulus-related auditory cortical activity. Reviews in the Neurosciences, 14, 35–42.

Ohl, F.W., Scheich, H., & Freeman, W.J. (2000a). Topographic analysis of epidural pure-tone-evoked potentials in gerbil auditory cortex. Journal of Neurophysiology, 83, 3123–3132.

Ohl, F.W., Scheich, H., & Freeman, W.J. (2000b). Spatial representation of frequency-modulated tones in gerbil auditory cortex revealed by epidural electrocorticography. Journal of Physiology (Paris), 94, 549–554.

Ohl, F.W., Scheich, H., & Freeman, W.J. (2001). Change in pattern of ongoing cortical activity with auditory category learning. Nature, 412, 733–736.

Ohl, F.W., Wetzel, W., Wagner, T., Rech, A., & Scheich, H. (1999). Bilateral ablation of auditory cortex in Mongolian gerbil affects discrimination of frequency modulated tones but not of pure tones. Learning & Memory, 6, 347–362.

Pearce, J.M. (1994). Discrimination and categorization. In N.J. Mackintosh (Ed.), Animal learning and cognition (pp. 109–134). San Diego: Academic Press.

Phillips, D.P., Mendelson, J.R., Cynader, M.S., & Douglas, R.M. (1985). Response of single neurons in the cat auditory cortex to time-varying stimuli: Frequency-modulated tones of narrow excursion. Experimental Brain Research, 58, 443–454.

Posner, M.I., & Keele, S.W. (1968). On the genesis of abstract ideas. Journal of Experimental Psychology, 77, 353–363.

Rosch, E. (1973). Natural categories. Cognitive Psychology, 4, 328–350.

Rosch, E. (1975). Cognitive reference points. Cognitive Psychology, 7, 192–238.

Schouten, M.K.D., & De Long, L. (1999). Reduction, elimination, and levels: The case of the LTP-learning link. Philosophical Psychology, 12, 237–262.

Wasserman, E.A., & Astley, S.L. (1994). A behavioral analysis of concepts: Its application to pigeons and children. Psychology of Learning and Motivation, 31, 73–132.

Wetzel, W., Wagner, T., Ohl, F.W., & Scheich, H. (1998). Categorical discrimination of direction in frequency-modulated tones by Mongolian gerbils. Behavioral Brain Research, 91, 29–39.

27. TASK-DEPENDENT ADAPTIVE PLASTICITY OF RECEPTIVE FIELDS IN PRIMARY AUDITORY CORTEX OF THE FERRET

Jonathan Fritz, Mounya Elhilali, Shihab Shamma

"Listening is not the same as hearing ... listening is an active process in which our experience, goals, and expectations constrain and control our percepts in complex ways. The transparency of the perceptual world hides the ubiquity of these representations." (Handel, 1989)

INTRODUCTION

Auditory experience leads to myriad changes in auditory processing from the periphery to the auditory cortex. Many different forms of plasticity have been described (at least nine varieties are defined by Calford, 2002). Over the past 30 years, studies of plasticity in the primary auditory cortex (A1) have revealed profound effects on the global level, notably by the reshaping of cortical maps, and on the local level, by the transformation of neuronal receptive field properties (Edeline, 1999, 2003; Suga et al., 2002; Suga & Ma, 2003; Weinberger, 2001, 2003a, 2003b, 2004). The form of cortical plasticity appears to be determined by (a) the behavioral salience or task-relevance of the spectral and temporal characteristics of the acoustic stimuli, and (b) the time course of training in perceptual learning (Recanzone et al., 1993, but see Irvine, 2004). In a non-behavioral model of salience-shaped plasticity, the form of plasticity is determined by the specific pairing of acoustic stimuli and stimulated reward pathways in cellular associative learning (Bakin & Weinberger, 1996; Kilgard et al., 2001a, 2001b, 2002; Kilgard & Merzenich, 2002). In this chapter, we focus on a particular form of plasticity, which we have called task-related plasticity (Fritz et al., 2003a, 2004), arising from behaviorally-driven rapid modulation of neuronal receptive fields in A1.

Rapid task-related plasticity

Our approach was to record from single neurons in A1 while the animal performed under different auditory task conditions, with the goal of quantitatively analyzing the nature and time-course of state-dependent adaptive plasticity in the auditory cortex on a cellular level. Once we obtained a stable recording of an isolated A1 neuron in the awake ferret, the design of our experiments was simple: (1) rapidly and comprehensively characterize the cortical spectrotemporal receptive field (STRF) in the "pre-behavioral" condition, (2) characterize the behavioral STRF while the animal was actively engaged in one type of auditory task and compare this "behavioral-STRF-1" to the initial "pre-behavioral" and subsequent "post-behavioral" quiescent STRFs, (3) if possible, characterize and compare STRF plasticity in the *same* cell while the animal performed a *different* auditory task (leading to "behavioral-STRF-2").

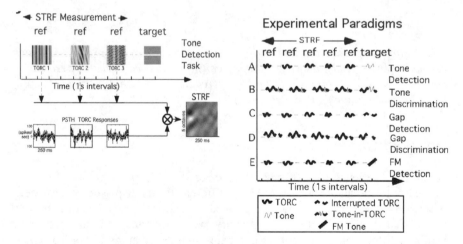

Fig. 27.1. Design of experimental stimulus presentations in conditioned avoidance tasks. **Left:** On a given trial during a behavioral session, a random number of TORCS (1–6 reference signals) is followed by a target tone. The panels illustrate spectrograms of three such TORCs and of the following target. Responses to each TORC are collected in PST histograms that are cross-correlated with the TORC spectrograms to estimate the STRF. Although the animal behaves in anticipation of the target, all spike measurements to derive the STRF are made during the presentation of the reference TORCs. **Right:** Schematic of various possible experimental paradigms. All follow the same basic design. The reference signals include TORCs used to measure the STRF. The target varies from one experiment to another. In actual experiments, the number of reference stimuli is random.

All experiments followed the same basic behavioral paradigm of conditioned avoidance (Heffner, H.E., & Heffner, R.S., 1995), which we have slightly modified in our experiments so that the animal was trained to continuously lick water from a spout during a series of similar *reference* sounds, and to *stop* licking after it heard a distinctive warning *target* in order to avoid mild shock. In all experiments, reference sounds were drawn from a class of ripple stimuli called TORCs (temporally orthogonal ripple combinations) which are temporally and spectrally rich, broadband stimuli that also serve during physiological experiments to characterize the STRF of the cell under study. By contrast, the target sound varied from one experiment to another with distinctive cues that had salient spectral or temporal, or combined spectro-temporal features. We grouped the tasks by the type of target that the animal must attend (tones, silent gaps, frequency-modulated (FM) sweeps, etc.). The major goal of the research we will describe in this chapter was to investigate auditory cortical plasticity induced by tonal targets, and to contrast their effects in two distinct behavioral contexts: tone *detection* and *discrimination*.

METHODS

Basic paradigm and training procedure

The basic behavioral paradigm is illustrated in Figure 27.1. Ferrets were trained to lick water from a spout during the presentation of a variable number of reference sounds (1–7) and learned by aversive conditioning to refrain from licking following the presentation of single target sounds, which came at the end of a sequence of reference sounds. As mentioned above, during their training, the ferrets learned a general or "cognitive" version of the detection and discrimination tasks, and reached a stable behavioral performance level in which they could perform equally well on *any* target frequencies chosen during the experiment (target frequencies were randomly chosen from a range of 125–8000 Hz). Ferrets were trained twice a day (50–100 trials/session), five days/week. Initial training on the tone detection task took 2–3 weeks for the ferrets to reach criterion (discrimination ratio > 0.65). Subsequent task variations took additional 1–2 weeks for the ferrets to learn. Some additional training was required to train the animals to switch easily between tasks. Thus, initial training to criterion in the spectral tone detection and discrimination task took about 6 weeks for each ferret. After initial training, the animal received a surgical headpost implant that allowed the head to be stably positioned. After recovery from surgery, the ferrets were retrained on the task while restrained in a cylindrical, horizontal holder, with the head fixed in place.

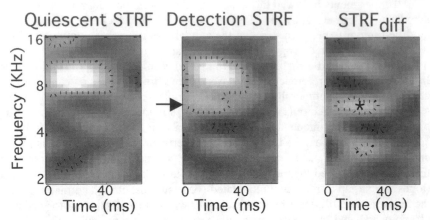

Fig. 27.2. Comparison of a pre-behavior, quiescent STRF (**left panel**) and a behavioral STRF (**middle panel**). Each panel depicts an STRF with a gray scale, representing increased-(white)-to-suppressed (black) firing about the (gray) mean. The STRF in each panel is normalized. The dashed contours depict the regions with statistically significant fluctuations (level = 3σ) from the mean. All excitatory (white) and inhibitory (black) features of the STRF discussed in subsequent figures are statistically significant by this measure. The black arrow indicates the frequency of the target tone during the detection task. The difference between the normalized quiescent and detection STRF is shown in the right panel (STRF$_{diff}$). The asterisk marks the location of maximal change: $\Delta A_{local} = 45\%$.

Stimuli and STRF measurements

In all tasks, reference stimuli were chosen from a set of 30 different TORCs (for a detailed discussion of TORCs, and the use of TORC responses to characterize neuronal STRFs using reverse correlation techniques see Depireux et al., 2001; Klein et al., 2000; Miller et al., 2002). For behavioral and control studies, stimuli were 1.25 seconds in duration, 75 dB SPL and consisted of TORCs or TORC-tone combinations. All passive STRF measurements used TORC stimuli which were 3 seconds in duration, 75 dB SPL. The STRF of an isolated unit was first measured while the animal was in a pre-behavioral, quiescent state, in which there was *no* water flow through the waterspout and *no* target was presented. This was followed by an STRF measurement made while the animal performed the detection task, ending with an STRF measurement in a post-behavioral quiescent state.

An illustration of the changes between quiescent and active STRFs of a single unit is given in Figure 27.2, which also indicates how they were quantified (since these changes are more clearly visible in color scale, rather than in the black-and-white format in this chapter, it may be useful for the interested reader to consult the color figures in Fritz et al., 2003a). In this unit, when the tonal target was placed near an excitatory region of the STRF (marked by the arrow in the middle panel) it created a new excitatory extension of the original region. To quantify this change, we computed the difference between the normalized behavioral and quiescent STRFs (STRF$_{diff}$ in Fig. 27.2). We then extracted two measures from the STRF$_{diff}$: a *local* maximum difference within ±0.25 octaves around the frequency of the target (ΔA_{local}, denoted by a black asterisk), and a *global* maximum difference (ΔA_{global}). The values of these measures are indicated in the legend of Figure 27.2. In subsequent figures, the STRF$_{diff}$ panels will be replaced by a quiescent post-behavior STRF.

Physiological Recording

Experiments were conducted in a double-walled sound attenuation chamber. Small, sterile craniotomies (< 1 mm in diameter) were made over primary auditory cortex prior to recording sessions, each of which lasted 6–8 h. Responses were recorded with tungsten microelectrodes (3–8 MΩ) and then stored, filtered and spike-sorted off-line using custom software. A typical recording site yielded 1–4 simultaneously active single units. Physiological verification of recording sites in A1 was based on the presence of distinctive A1 physiological characteristics (e.g., latency, tuning) and on the position of the neural recording relative to the cortical tonotopic map in A1 and to surface landmarks. During physiological recording, computer-generated stimuli were delivered through inserted earphones that were calibrated *in situ* at the beginning of each experiment.

STRF stability in naïve and non-behaving animals

In order to assess the stability of our STRFs in the absence of any behavioral tasks, we measured STRF pairs in a completely naïve animal that was untrained except for an initial habituation to the head-restraint holder. For the control "behavior" STRF, the animal was simply exposed to the regular TORC references and target tone, but without the presence of training, water reward or the aversive shock. This control "behavior" STRF from the naïve animal was then compared to the pre-control quiescent STRF measured earlier from the same neuron. The distribution of the STRF changes (ΔA_{local}) for 34 cells is shown in Figure 27.3 (left), where 54% of cells remained unchanged. The distribution is approximately symmetrical, with the "random" scatter off-the-midline presumably reflecting STRF changes due to uncontrolled sources of error arising from animal movement or other task-independent state changes between the two tests. A similar symmetrical distribution of ΔA_{local} was also found in data pooled from the two trained animals (12 units) when they were tested with the paradigm as in Figure 27.1, but were simply quietly listening to the sounds without performing one of the trained behavioral tasks (Fig. 27.3, right panel). These negative results in the naïve and the non-behaving trained animals, argue against the possibility that STRF changes in the detection task are the result of an auditory "oddball effect" (Ulanovsky et al., 2003), where the

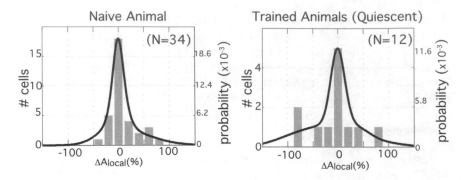

Fig. 27.3. Histogram and distributions from STRF measurements in a naïve animal (**left panel**), and from trained but non-behaving animals (**right panel**). The smoothed distributions of the population ΔA_{local} changes were computed directly from the response variability, and were derived from the corresponding histograms by (1) assuming that for each cell, the resulting ΔA_{local} was Gaussian distributed with a mean and variance computed using the bootstrap method, (2) by calculating the probability that the ΔA_{local} fell within a bin of 1% around any specific ΔA_{local} by summing over contributions from all STRFs and calculating the mean of the probability of ΔA_{local} having any particular range of values.

tone plays the role of low probability narrowband "oddball" (~25% likelihood in our procedure) in relation to the broadband background of TORCs and hence emphasize the importance of behavior in mediating these effects. However, these results also indicate that there is a subpopulation of A1 neurons which appears to show intrinsic STRF response variability and spontaneous changes in STRF shape which cannot be simply explained as behavioral in origin. The key point made in Figure 27.3 is that such intrinsic STRF population variability is symmetrical in its ΔA distribution, whereas in contrast, the ΔA distribution is clearly asymmetrical for the behavioral conditions. Although there have been few precise studies of receptive field stability in the awake animal, studies to explore receptive field lability have recently been conducted during conditions of sleep (Edeline et al., 2001) and anesthesia (Kisley & Gerstein, 2001), which suggest significant receptive field variability in the passive condition.

STRF changes in tone detection task

Data reported here were collected from two trained animals over the course of over 40 recording sessions in which we recorded 141 units. Of these, 54 units were sufficiently tested to determine their initial quiescent and behavior STRFs. In 39 cells, one or more additional post-behavior STRFs were obtained. Examples of the measured STRF changes are illustrated and quantified in Figure 27.4.

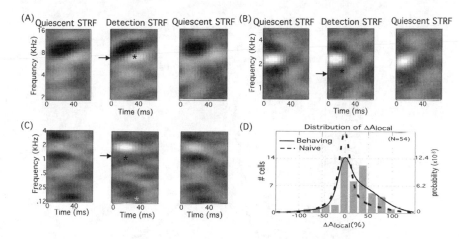

Fig. 27.4. Facilitative STRF plasticity in AI. STRFs from three single-units in A1 illustrate typical changes observed during performance of the detection task. **A.** Localized enhancement of an excitatory region in the STRF during behavior (left and middle panels). The post-behavior quiescent STRF (right panel) reverted immediately to its original shape. ΔA_{local} = 37%, ΔA_{global} = 42%. The two maxima were nearly coincident at the target frequency. **B.** Local decrease or elimination of inhibitory sidebands in the detection STRF. The inhibition recovered quickly afterwards, but the overall STRF shape was different. ΔA_{local} = 40%, ΔA_{global} = 40% (coincident maxima at target frequency). **C.** A global weakening of inhibitory fields during behavior Immediately following behavior, the STRF recovered its pre-behavior shape. ΔA_{local} = 64%, ΔA_{global} = 86%. In this example, the local maximum difference occurred at the target tone frequency, while the global maximum was located over a low frequency inhibitory field (which was also knocked out during behavior). **D.** Overall summary histogram and smoothed distribution of local STRF changes (ΔA_{local}) from all STRFs collected in preliminary experiments so far. The histogram (left ordinate) and distribution (right ordinate) are significantly skewed towards positive changes (overall mean = +20.2%).

The most common change in an STRF observed during this task was "facilitation" at the target frequency as a result of either an enhancement of its excitatory field, or a weakening of the inhibitory sidebands. Figure 27.4 illustrates examples of these kinds of changes in three single-units. Placing the target at the excitatory region of an STRF resulted in its enhancement (Fig. 27.4A). The opposite usually occurred when the target frequency coincided with STRF inhibitory sidebands, that is, it caused a reduction of the strength of the inhibition as illustrated in Figures 27.4B, 27.4C. In about half of all cases, STRF changes were local, restricted to the region of the target frequency as evidenced by the coincidence of the two asterisks in Figure 27.2 and Figures 27.4A, 27.4B. By contrast, the change depicted in Figure 27.4C was global in that all inhibitory regions of the broad STRF were significantly reduced during the task,

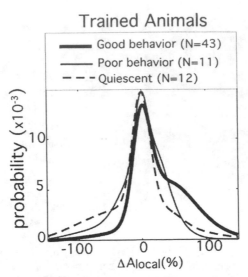

Fig. 27.5. Distribution of STRF changes in the two trained animals under three behavioral conditions: (1) No trained behavior (quiescent listening); (2) Poor behavioral performance; (3) Good behavioral performance. The commencement and improvement of behavior correlates with progressive increase in distribution asymmetry toward facilitative changes.

and the maximum change occurred away from the target tone frequency. Nevertheless, global STRF change was usually also accompanied by a local facilitation. In all units illustrated in Figure 27.4, post-behavioral quiescent STRFs were also measured, and they all tended to revert rapidly to their original pre-behavioral shape (Figs. 27.4A, 27.4C), or at least partially recover (Fig. 27.4B).

The distribution of ΔA_{local} in Figure 27.4D summarizes the STRF changes observed in 54 single-units in the two trained animals from which reliable quiescent and detection STRFs were estimated. About 72% (39/54) showed a significant STRF change throughout the tests. In these cells, in 80% (31/39) a *facilitative* or positive STRF change occurred, i.e., an enhancement of the excitatory fields or a reduction of the inhibitory sidebands during tone detection task, averaging about +46% (median = +45%) of the maximum amplitude in the STRF. Furthermore, in about half of these units (16/31), the maximum change in the STRF occurred near the frequency of the target (i.e., locations where ΔA_{local} and ΔA_{global} coincided). Finally, comparing directly the ΔA_{local} distributions in the behaving animals (Fig. 27.4D, solid line) against the "naïve" baseline (Fig. 27.4D, dashed line) reveals a clear difference showing the effect of behavior at a neuronal population level. Namely, engagement in a detection task reduced the relative number of "neutral" STRFs and increased facilitated STRFs.

Correlating Behavior with STRF changes

A primary objective of this work was to correlate plasticity and behavior. To do so, we examined the relationship between behavioral performance and the pattern of STRF changes by comparing the distribution of ΔA_{local} derived from three distinct groups of cells, which were recorded during three different behavioral conditions in the two trained animals. The first group of cells was recorded while the animals quiescently listened to the stimuli (same 12 units as in Fig. 27.4, right panel). The set of 54 units depicted earlier in Figure 27.4D were divided into a second group (11 units) recorded in sessions with poor performance (discrimination rate < 0.3 and hit rate < 80%) and a third group (43 units) recorded in sessions with better performance (hit rate > 80%). The superimposed ΔA_{local} distributions of the three groups (Fig. 27.5) show that they became progressively more asymmetric (i.e., more facilitatory) as behavior commenced or improved, consistent with the idea that there was a causal relationship between the attentive behavior (as measured by performance) of the animal and the magnitude of facilitative changes of the STRF.

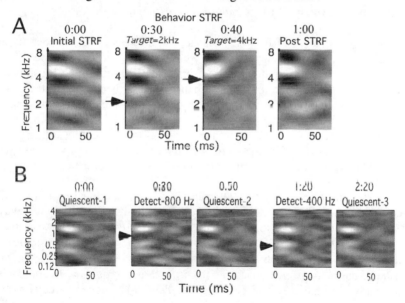

Fig. 27.6. STRF changes in a succession of tasks. **A.** The target tone was changed in the middle of the behavioral recording session from 2 kHz to 4 kHz, and an online measurement of the STRFs reflected the change. **B.** Three quiescent STRFs interleaved with two detection tasks. The target at 800 Hz reduced all four inhibitory sidebands of this STRF at a global level, as well as locally reducing inhibition at the target frequency (second panel, ΔA_{global} = 67%). The target at 400 Hz enhanced an adjacent excitatory field (fourth panel, ΔA_{global} = 36%). The STRF rapidly reverted to its original pre-behavior quiescent shape (first panel) in the post-behavior quiescent states (third and fifth panels).

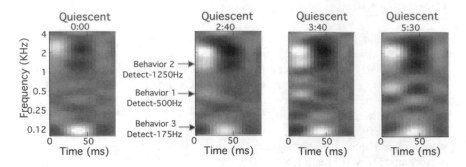

Fig. 27.7. Quiescent pre-behavioral STRF measured before (left panel), and post-behavioral STRFs (remaining panels) derived after a series of three detection tasks with different targets as indicated by the gray arrows. The STRF changes induced by the behavioral tasks persisted, to varying extents, for several hours afterwards (elapsed post-behavior time indicated above the STRF panels).

STRF plasticity for multiple, sequential targets

In some experiments, STRFs were measured in a series of tone-detection tasks with different target frequencies, which were chosen in order to probe different excitatory and inhibitory regions of the same STRF. Figure 27.6 illustrates for two units the rapid onset of STRF change during behavior, and the swift recovery afterwards. In the first unit (Fig. 27.6A), the target was changed midway through the task from 2 kHz to 4 kHz and the STRFs were constructed from three repetitions of the reference stimuli for each choice of target. As predicted, the first (2 kHz) target stretched the excitatory receptive field toward it (second panel), creating within 10 minutes a new excitatory area at the edge of the first quiescent STRF.

The second (4 kHz) target equally rapidly reduced the local inhibition (third panel). Finally, the STRF quickly returned to its initial shape following behavior (last panel). The same kind of STRF changes and recovery are demonstrated for another unit in Figure 27.6B. Note that in both behavior STRFs measured in this unit, the maximum facilitative changes observed were global, that is, occurred outside of the range of ±0.25 octaves from the target frequency. In some cases, as shown in Figure 27.6A, we speculate that the non-local change may be due to an "edge" effect, when the position of the target probe lay just "outside" the receptive field of the unit, leading to enhancement at the corresponding edge of the STRF.

Persistence of STRF changes

Once the behavioral task ceases, persistence of the receptive field changes represents a form of sensory memory (Fuster, 1995). Different forms of persistent neuronal activity following rapid plasticity have been demonstrated before in the primary motor cortex (Li et al., 2001), in the context of motor adaptation and also may be present in the somatosensory cortex (Harris et al., 2003; Romo & Salinas, 2003). About half of all cells encountered in our experiments exhibited a change that persisted after one or more tasks. Figure 27.7 illustrates a remarkable example of a recording series, in which there was a build-up of sensory memory following several behavioral tasks (detection tasks with different targets) many hours earlier.

STRF changes with spectral discrimination tasks

When an animal is *discriminating* between the frequencies of two tones (as opposed to simply detecting the presence of one tone as above), we conjecture that the STRFs could change adaptively so as to improve performance by enhancing "foreground" over "background" by facilitating the STRF at the target (foreground) frequency while suppressing it at the reference (background) frequency (Fritz et al., 2004). This hypothesis is consistent with earlier results obtained by Edeline and Weinberger (1993). In theory, another equally viable strategy to achieve discrimination might be to enhance "background" while suppressing "foreground" stimuli, since the key point for the nervous system is to enhance the contrast between the stimuli. In order to investigate this question, ferrets were trained on a tone discrimination task, which was a modified version of the earlier detection task except that now, each reference TORC was immediately followed by a *reference tone* (distinct from the target tone; Fig. 27.1). The animal learned to attend to the reference tone frequency and respond only when the frequency changed, which occurred when the target tone was presented. Figure 27.8 illustrates the changes observed in one case. The cell was

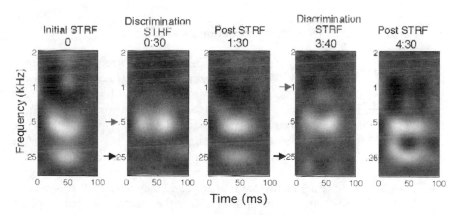

Fig. 27.8. Three quiescent STRFs interleaved with two discrimination tasks. The times at which STRFs were measured relative to the beginning of recording are shown on top of each panel. The arrows mark the reference (black) and target (gray) frequencies used. Note the disappearance of the excitatory area near 250 Hz in the STRFs measured during the discrimination tasks.

tuned to 250 Hz and 500 Hz. When the reference and target tones were placed at these two frequencies, respectively, the reference tone suppressed the excitatory field at 250 Hz, leaving 500 Hz as the only excitatory frequency. The cell recovered somewhat after the behavioral test, but the same suppression of the 250 Hz excitatory field occurred when the test was repeated with a 1000 Hz target. Subsequent, preliminary studies in 32 neurons have shown that this pattern of specific suppression of STRFs at the reference frequency was prevalent during discrimination (Fritz et al., 2003b, 2004).

Interestingly, in overall amplitude and in spectral selectivity, the average STRF change (at the reference frequency) during discrimination appeared to be exactly the opposite of the average STRF change (at the target frequency) during detection and may be operating by a common mechanism (with a sign reversal). At the population level, we have also observed an overall enhancement of the STRF at the target frequency in the discrimination task. These results from the discrimination task are consistent with receptive field changes which would be predicted as a result of an auditory "oddball effect" (Ulanovsky et al., 2003), where the reference tone plays the role of high probability standard and the target tone plays the role of low probability "oddball" (~25% likelihood in our procedure). Hence we performed a set of control studies in a naïve, untrained ferret, in which we compared an initial "quiescent" STRF, computed from neural responses to TORCs, to a subsequent "discrimination control" STRF, computed from responses in the same neuron to our "discrimination-task" (TORC-tone) stimuli (also in a non-behavioral, quiescent condition). The results from these control experiments indicate that the STRF plasticity observed in the behavioral condition in the discrimination task cannot be explained by a purely stimulus driven "oddball effect" (Fritz et al., 2004).

STRF temporal changes with gap detection tasks

We have only begun to study the STRF changes which may result from training the ferret on a temporal task. We conjectured that a gap detection task should yield faster STRF dynamics, as evidenced, for example, by shortening latencies or by a concomitant sharpening of the outlines of its excitatory and inhibitory fields along the temporal axis. The measured STRF changes in 2 units are illustrated in Figure 27.9. Figure 27.9A illustrates the changes in the sharpness of the STRF fields that imply faster temporal transitions and hence faster dynamics. Another example of the same kind of change is shown in Figure 27.9B. Although these are highly preliminary data, they suggest that it may be possible to influence both the temporal, as well as the spectral dimensions of the STRF. We are currently engaged in further research to explore this question.

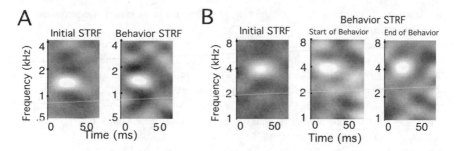

Fig. 27.9. Examples of STRF changes during a temporal gap detection task. STRFs from two units are illustrated. In each case, the initial STRF is shown, followed by the STRF during the behavior. **A.** Example of increasing contrast in STRF during behavior. **B.** Example of STRF changes during the gap detection task. Progression of the behavior induced STRF changes throughout the task. Each STRF was computed from 5 repetitions of all TORC presentations. The STRF excitatory portion became progressively sharper during the behavior.

DISCUSSION

The experiments described here suggest that *rapid auditory task-related plasticity* is an ongoing process that occurs as the animal switches between different tasks and dynamically adapts auditory cortical STRFs in response to changing acoustic demands. Rapid plasticity modifies STRF shapes in a manner consistent with enhancing the behavioral performance of the animal, monitored through externally supplied feedback signals. The specific form of the STRF change is dictated by the salient acoustic cues of the signals in the behavioral task, and is modulated by general influences reflecting the animal's state of arousal, attention, motor preparation and reward expectation. Recent studies have demonstrated the presence of neuronal responses in A1 which encode not only the acoustic features of the stimulus, but also may reflect the behavioral state of the animal in relation to the dimensions of expectation, attention, relevant non-auditory sensory cues, motor response and reward (Brosch & Scheich, 2004; Durif et al., 2003; Fu et al., 2003; Yin et al., 2001, 2004).

Our results are consistent with previous studies of A1 cortical receptive field plasticity that have shown similar rapidity of onset – we highlight three specific results from earlier experiments in this field: (1) Cortical receptive field plasticity can be induced very rapidly, within as little as 2 minutes, i.e. often within a few trials (Edeline et al., 1993; Weinberger & Diamond, 1987). (2) Such plasticity has a short-term component which is dependent for expression on the behavioral context (Edeline, 1999). (3) Receptive field plasticity can persist for 3 hours or more (following electrical stimulation in A1 or somato-sensory cortex; Ma & Suga, 2003). Since changes to organisms occur continuously in a dynamic environment, it would obviously be useful adaptively, if animals continuously modulated their nervous systems on-line (Mountcastle, 1995).

Our findings of rapid and short-lived plasticity at the onset of behavioral paradigms that usually induce long-term changes, suggest that plasticity may take place over multiple time-scales. A conceptual view that harmoniously relates these fast and slow time-scales of plasticity is that of an ongoing series of *rapid*-onset adaptive processes (seconds to a few minutes), with persistent but relatively short-lived changes that closely reflect new, changing behavioral contexts. However, if reinforced by repeated or consistent stimulation (e.g., exposure to the same target over a period of days and months) these rapid changes may accumulate and become more permanent, giving rise eventually to the widely observed long-term plastic effects. In this view, rapid-onset plasticity is the precursor process to all long-term changes. An alternate hypothesis is that these two types of plasticity may reflect different processes (Weinberger, 2003a).

However, it is still important to emphasize that many of the cortical changes we observed have short life-times, and that STRFs often returned to their original shapes soon after the behavior was over. Since most cortical sensory neurons participate in multiple behavioral contexts, it is likely that their receptive field properties are continuously being modified, against the basic scaffolding of the synaptic inputs, as the animal enters new acoustic environments and initiates new tasks. In a sense, the STRF gives "linear" snapshots of a non-linear set of adaptive transformations of the receptive field. We suggest that plasticity is part of an ongoing process that is constantly adapting and re-organizing cortical receptive fields to meet the challenges of an ever-changing environment and new behavioral demands (Edeline, 2003).

In light of previous studies, and the results of our current research, we propose three linked hypotheses that place rapid task-related plasticity in the interplay of the sensory and motor systems in behavior. The first hypothesis is strongly supported by our data:

I. Some A1 cortical cells undergo rapid, short-term, context-dependent, adaptive changes of their receptive field properties, when an animal performs an auditory task that has specific behavioral demands and stimulus feature salience (Diamond & Weinberger, 1989; Fritz et al., 2003a, 2004). Not all cortical neurons display plasticity, which may represent a cortical compromise in the trade-off between stability and adaptability of sensory information processing.

In this chapter, we have presented research designed to test the first hypothesis (our current experiments do not address the other hypotheses, which are offered as a guide to future studies). Questions arising from the following two hypotheses are the topic of ongoing research in our laboratory:

II. Such rapid task-related plasticity is adaptive and is a part of an ongoing, dynamic process that underlies normal, active listening.

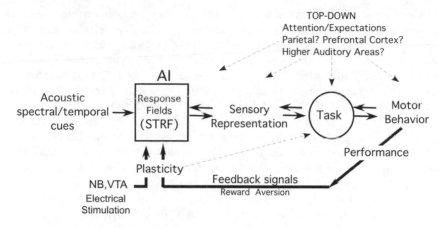

Fig. 27.10. Schematic diagram of context for rapid STRF plasticity in AI.

In this view, plasticity plays a functional role by causing a selective re-setting of the cortical circuitry. This tweaking of synaptic input strengths leads to changes in the receptive field properties of cortical neurons, which may enable the animal to achieve enhanced performance of the auditory task. The spectrotemporal receptive field (or STRF) in A1 sits at the focal juncture of this process, depicted by the highly schematic diagram in Figure 27.10. In a trained and well-behaving animal which engages in a previously-learned task, the STRF swiftly adapts so as to enhance behavioral performance, monitored through externally supplied (reward or aversive) feedback signals.

III. Rapid task-related plasticity operates on the framework of a pre-existing bi-directional sensory-to-motor map.

In our behavioral paradigm, the STRF receives *target/reference* input cues, and generates corresponding *sensory representations* that are ultimately associated with, or mapped to motor behavior. This mapping, which defines a specific learnt task or behavioral context, connects a set of stimuli and their associated sensory representations with a set of motor acts that enhance the future probability of reward or decrease the likelihood of punishment (Blake et al., 2002; Romo & Salinas, 2001). Such a learned sensori-motor mapping can be a highly specific (1-to-1), or in the case of the tasks we have used in our studies, can be a many-to-1 mapping, in which any member of a broad class of stimuli can elicit the same motor response. These tasks are "cognitive" in the sense that the animal is trained on the task with a broad range of different stimulus values, generalizes, and eventually learns the "rule" or the basic structure of the same-different task, independent of stimulus value. Although the ferret can respond appropriately to all stimuli, the specific form of task related plasticity depends upon the currently relevant stimuli or salient features as well as the structure of the learnt task.

On a highly speculative note, we conjecture that a top-down link between motor and sensory systems may constitute a very special type of behavior – a form of "invisible", or perhaps more correctly, of "internal" behavior, in which the motor system does *not* direct motor output resulting in an externally visible act, but rather influences a change in "perceptual filters", thus selectively modulating or tagging the most salient incoming sensory information for future action (Leopold & Logothetis, 1999; Maravita & Iriki, 2004).

In the case of the tone detection task, ferrets were trained to detect the presence of *any* pure tone in the context of broadband noise, and hence learned a general sensori-motor schema or mapping (which could be summarized as a rule: If you hear *any* pure tone, stop licking the waterspout for two seconds). In a particular behavioral session, where only one tonal frequency was used, the ferret performed the task and focused its attention on the salient frequency, leading to a reshaping of A1 receptive fields to enhance response at this frequency. It is important to emphasize that as many as 2/3 of cortical neurons in A1 showed such frequency-selective enhancement during tone detection task performance (Fritz et al., 2003a).

The provocative idea has been advanced that perceptual decisions arise from a subtraction between the activities of neurons with opposite sensory preferences (Lafuente & Romo, 2003). This model of decision by neuronal democracy offers a perspective on the ferret's decision to respond at the detection target frequency. Since most neurons in A1 show an enhanced response and/or suppressed inhibition at this frequency, the target frequency may "win" the popular vote in A1. Of course, A1 is not likely to be the only place where such a behavioral decision is made, but the observed STRF changes may play an important role in the evaluation of incoming sensory information and assist in behavioral performance.

Other forms of adaptive cortical plasticity

Intriguing results from motor and other sensory systems indicate that rapid adaptive task-related plasticity is a general principle of neural processing throughout the brain. The STRF plasticity found in our experiments is remarkably similar to the neuronal plasticity resulting from use-related experience observed in saccade-related neurons in the monkey superior colliculus (Dorris et al., 2000), to task-related responses in the primary visual cortex (Crist et al., 2001) and in V4 (Mazer & Gallant, 2003) and to the dynamic motor adaptation to an external force field recently described in the monkey primary motor cortex (Gandolfo et al., 2000; Li et al., 2001; for further discussion, see Fritz et al., 2003a). Another intriguing comparison is with the adaptive rapid plasticity of body schema observed in higher order parietal cortex in monkeys which had been trained to use a tool (a rake, Fig. 27.11) to retrieve distant objects (Iriki et al., 1996; Iwamura et al., 2000; Maravita & Iriki, 2004).

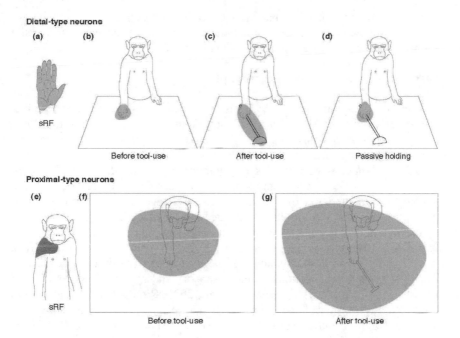

Fig. 27.11. Changes in bi-modal receptive field properties following tool use. The somatosensory receptive fields (sRF) were identified by light touch, passive joint manipulation or active hand use. The visual RF (vRF) was defined as the area in which cellular responses were evoked by visual probes moving towards the sRF. **Top panel:** (a) sRF (palmar hand surface) of the distal type bi-modal neurons shown on the left, and vRF shown (b) before tool use, (c) immediately after tool use, (d) when passively holding the rake. **Bottom panel:** (e) sRF (shoulder) of proximal-type bi-modal neurons and their vRF (f) before and (g) immediately after tool use. Adapted from Maravita & Iriki (2004) and used with permission.

In recordings from bimodal (visual and somatosensory) neurons in the IPS (intraparietal sulcus) of the monkey parietal association cortex, they demonstrated that the visual receptive fields, which were usually closely linked to their associated somatosensory receptive fields, and normally extended as far as the normal reach of the monkey's hand in space, quickly changed in size when the monkey was given a rake to use to gather food. After a few minutes of tool use, the visual receptive fields of neurons in this area extended further to include the entire reach of the rake, and expanded to cover the new accessible space. Thus the tool rapidly became an extension of the hand in both a physical and a perceptual sense. After the monkey retrieved food *without* using the rake for about three minutes, the expanded visual receptive field shrank back to its original size, even if the monkey kept grasping the tool. In short, these bimodal cells rapidly shifted the spatial boundaries of their receptive fields in accord with the new spatial range of interest to the animals during ongoing behavior.

We propose that the changing map of visual salience described in parietal cortex in these monkey experiments, is comparable to the dynamic map of acoustic salience which we have described in our experiments in ferret A1.

Search for the mechanisms of cortical plasticity

What are the candidate neural mechanisms that might underlie such selective, rapid-onset plasticity? Such dynamic changes may be mediated by top-down and/or bottom-up control (Suga & Ma, 2003) over local cortical circuitry, operating by mechanisms such as LTP or LTD to rapidly modulate synaptic efficacy or dynamics (Cruikshank & Weinberger, 1996; Dinse et al., 2003; Finnerty et al., 1999), or to unmask silent synapses (Ahissar, 1998), by rapid synaptogenesis, alteration of neuronal gain or change in the overall level of excitability (Butefisch et al., 2000; Xiao & Suga, 2002). Neuromodulators such as acetylcholine, dopamine, noradrenaline and serotonin are all influential in mediating plasticity (Gu, 2002; Manunta & Edeline, 2004). An important arena for such rapid synaptic modulation may be the set of widespread subthreshold horizontal synaptic connections found in sensory and motor neocortex (Das & Gilbert, 1995; Huntley, 1997; Laubach et al., 2000; Rioult-Pedotti et al., 1998) which exhibit plasticity and whose synaptic efficacy has been shown to strengthen in procedural motor learning (Rioult-Pedotti et al., 2000). Once temporarily formed, these rapid changes can be stabilized by slower concurrent mechanisms of long-term synaptic plasticity such as the formation of new functional connections through axonal sprouting, dendritic remodeling, or by long-term induction of changes in transmitter or receptor levels and distribution, that take place over longer periods of time (hours and days). Additional studies will be needed to clarify the cellular mechanisms of rapid-onset cortical plasticity, and its role in mediating adaptive changes in brain and behavior.

ACKNOWLEDGMENTS

We would like to thank David Klein for computational analysis, Shantanu Ray for assistance with task development and software programming, Henry Heffner for advice and guidance on behavioral training, and Tamar Vardi for help with ferret care and training. We are also grateful for the grant support of NIDCD, NIH.

REFERENCES

Ahissar, E., Abeles, M., Ahissar, M., Haidarliu, S., & Vaadia, E. (1998). Hebbian-like functional plasticity in the auditory cortex of the behaving monkey. Neuropharmacology, 37, 633–655.

Bakin, J.S., & Weinberger, N.M. (1996). Induction of a physiological memory in the cerebral cortex by stimulation of the nucleus basalis. Proceedings of the National Academy of Sciences USA, 93, 11219–11224.

Blake, D.T., Strata, F., Churchland, A.K., & Merzenich, M.M. (2002). Neural correlates of instrumental learning in primary auditory cortex. Proceedings of the National Academy of Sciences USA, 99, 10114–10119.

Brosch, M., & Scheich, H. (2004). Non-acoustic influence on neural activity in auditory cortex. In R. König, P. Heil, E. Budinger & H. Scheich (Eds.), The Auditory Cortex – A Synthesis of Human and Animal Research. Hillsdale, NJ: Lawrence Erlbaum Associates.

Butefisch, C., Davis, B.C., Wise, S.P., Sawaki, L., Kopylev, L., Classen, J., & Cohen, L.G. (2000). Mechanisms of use-dependent plasticity in the human motor cortex. Proceedings of the National Academy of Sciences USA, 97, 3661–3665.

Calford, M.B. (2002). Dynamic representational plasticity in sensory cortex. Neuroscience, 111, 709–738.

Crist, R.E., Li, W., & Gilbert, C.D. (2001). Learning to see: Experience and attention in primary visual cortex. Nature Neuroscience, 4, 519–525.

Cruikshank, S.J., & Weinberger, N.M. (1996). Evidence for the Hebbian hypothesis in experience dependent physiological plasticity of neo-cortex. A critical review. Brain Research Reviews, 22, 191–228.

Das, A., & Gilbert, C. (1995). Long-range horizontal connections and their role in cortical reorganization revealed by optical recording of cat primary visual cortex. Nature, 375, 780–784.

Depireux, D.A., Simon, J.Z., Klein, D.J., & Shamma, S.A. (2001). Spectro-temporal response field characterization with dynamic ripples in ferret primary auditory cortex. Journal of Neurophysiology, 85, 1220–1334.

Diamond, D., & Weinberger, N.M. (1989). Role of context in the expression of learning-induced plasticity of single-neurons in auditory cortex. Behavioral Neuroscience, 103, 471 494.

Dinse, H.R., Ragert, P., Pleger, B., Schwenkreis, P., & Tegenthoff, M. (2003). Pharamacological modulation of perceptual learning and associated cortical reorganization. Science, 301, 91–94.

Dorris, M.G., Parc, M., & Munoz, D.P. (2000). Immediate neural plasticity shapes motor performance. Journal of Neuroscience, 20, 1–5.

Durif, C., Jouffrais, C., & Rouiller, E.M. (2003). Single unit responses in the auditory cortex of monkeys performing a conditional acousticomotor task. Experimental Brain Research, 153, 614–627.

Edeline, J.M. (1999). Learning-induced physiological plasticity in thalamo-cortical sensory systems: A critical evaluation of receptive field plasticity, map changes and their potential mechanisms. Progress in Neurobiology, 57, 165–224.

Edeline, J.M. (2003). Thalamo-cortical auditory receptive fields: Regulation by the states of vigilance, learning and the neuromodulatory systems. Experimental Brain Research, 153, 554–572.

Edeline, J.M., Dutrieux, G., Manunta, Y., & Hennevin, E. (2001). Diversity of receptive field changes in the auditory cortex during natural sleep. European Journal of Neuroscience, 14, 1865–1880.

Edeline, J.M., Pham, P., & Weinberger, N.M. (1993). Rapid development of learning induced receptive field plasticity in the auditory cortex. Behavioral Neuroscience, 107, 539–551.

Edeline, J.M., & Weinberger, N.M. (1993). Receptive field plasticity in the auditory cortex during frequency discrimination training: Selective retuning independent of task difficulty. Behavioral Neuroscience, 107, 82–103.

Finnerty, G.T., Roberts, L.S.E., & Connors, B.W. (1999). Sensory experience modifies the short-term dynamics of neocortical synapses. Nature, 400, 367–371.

Fritz, J.B., Elhilali, M., Klein, D.J., & Shamma, S.A. (2003b). Dynamic adaptive plasticity of spectro-temporal receptive fields in the primary auditory cortex of the behaving ferret. Abstract – Society for Neuroscience.

Fritz, J.B., Elhilali, M., & Shamma, S.A. (2004). Adaptive, task-related plasticity in the active listening – differential receptive field changes in primary auditory cortex during tone detection and tone discrimination. (Submitted).

Fritz, J.B., Shamma, S.A., Elhilali, M., & Klein, D.J. (2003a). Rapid task-related plasticity of spectrotemporal receptive fields in primary auditory cortex. Nature Neuroscience, 6, 1216–1223.

Fu K.M., Johnston, T.A., Shah, A.S., Arnold, L., Smiley, J., Hackett, T.A., Garraghty, P.E., & Schroeder, C.E. (2003). Auditory cortical neurons respond to somatosensory stimulation. Journal of Neuroscience, 23, 7510–7515.

Fuster, J. (1995). Memory in the cerebral cortex: An empirical approach to neural networks in human and nonhuman primates. Cambridge, MA: MIT Press.

Gandolfo, F., Li, C., Benda, B.J., Padoa-Schioppa, C.P., & Bizzi, E. (2000). Cortical correlates of learning in monkeys adapting to a new dynamical environment. Proceedings of the National Academy of Sciences USA, 97, 2259–2263.

Gu, Q. (2002). Neuromodulatory transmitter systems in the cortex and their role in cortical plasticity. Neuroscience, 111, 815–835.

Handel, S. (1989). Listening: An introduction to the perception of auditory events. Cambridge, MA: MIT Press.

Harris, J.A., Miniussi, C., Harris, I.M., & Diamond, M.E. (2002). Transient storage of a tactile memory trace in primary somatosensory cortex. Journal of Neuroscience, 22, 8720–8725.

Heffner, H.E., & Heffner, R.S. (1995). Conditioned avoidance. In G. Klump, R. Dooling, R.R. Fay, & W.C. Stebbins (Eds.), Methods in Comparative Psychoacoustics (pp. 79–94). Basel: Birkhauser Verlag.

Huntley, G.W. (1997). Correlation between patterns of horizontal connectivity and the extent of short-term representational plasticity in the rat motor cortex. Cerebral Cortex, 7, 143–156.

Iriki, A., Tanaka, M., & Iwamura, Y. (1996). Coding of modified body schema during tool use by macaque postcentral neurons. Neuroreport, 7, 2325–2330.

Irvine, D., Brown, M., Martin, R., & Park, V. (2004). Auditory perceptual learning and cortical plasticity. In R. König, P. Heil, E. Budinger, & H. Scheich (Eds.), The Auditory Cortex – A Synthesis of Human and Animal Research. Hillsdale, NJ: Lawrence Erlbaum Associates.

Iwamura, Y., Iriki, A., Tanaka, M., Taoka, M., & Toda, T. (2000). Processing of higher order somatosensory and visual information in the intraparietal region of the postcentral gyrus. In M.J. Rowe & Y. Iwamura (Eds.), Somatosensory processing: from single neuron to brain imaging (pp. 101–112). London: Taylor and Francis Press.

Kilgard, M., & Merzenich, M.M. (2002). Order-sensitive plasticity in adult primary auditory cortex. Proceedings of the National Academy of Sciences USA, 19, 2309–2314.

Kilgard, M., Pandya P., Engineer, N.D., & Moucha, R. (2002). Cortical network reorganization guided by sensory input features. Biological Cybernetics, 87, 333–343.

Kilgard, M., Pandya, P., Vazquez, J., Gehi, A., Schreiner, C., & Merzenich, M.M. (2001a). Sensory input directs spatial and temporal plasticity in primary auditory cortex. Journal of Neuroscience, 86, 326–337.

Kilgard, M., Pandya, P., Vazquez, J., Rathbun, D.L., Engineer, N.D., & Moucha, R. (2001b). Spectral features control temporal plasticity in auditory cortex. Audiology and Neurootology, 6, 196–202.

Kisley, M.A., & Gerstein, G.L. (2001). Daily variation and appetitive conditioning-induced plasticity of auditory cortex receptive fields. European Journal of Neuroscience, 13, 1993–2003.

Klein, D.J., Depireux, D.A., Simon, J.Z., & Shamma, S.A. (2000). Robust spectrotemporal reverse correlation for the auditory system: optimizing stimulus design. Journal of Computational Neuroscience, 9, 85–111.

Lafuente, V., & Romo, R. (2003). Decisions arising from opposing views. Nature Neuroscience, 6, 792–793.

Laubach, M., Wessberg, J., & Nikolelis, M.A. (2000). Cortical ensemble activity increasingly predicts behaviour outcomes during learning of a motor task. Nature, 40, 567–571.

Leopold, D.A., & Logothetis, N.K. (1999). Multistable phenomena: changing views in perception. Trends in Cognitive Science, 3, 254–264.

Li, C.-S., Padoa-Schioppa C., & Bizzi E. (2001). Neuronal correlates of motor performance and motor learning in the primary motor cortex of monkeys adapting to an external force field. Neuron, 30, 593–607.

Ma, X., & Suga, N. (2003). Augmentation of plasticity of the central auditory system by the basal forebrain and/or somatosensory cortex. Journal of Neurophysiology, 89, 90–103.

Manunta, Y., & Edeline, J.M. (2004). Noradrenergic induction of selective plasticity in the frequency-tuning of auditory cortex neurons. Journal of Neurophysiology, 92, 1445–1463.

Maravita, A., & Iriki, A. (2004). Tools for the body (schema). Trends in Cognitive Sciences, 8, 79–86.

Mazer, J.A., & Gallant, J. (2003). Goal related activity in V4 during free viewing. Search evidence for a ventral stream visual salience map. Neuron, 40, 1241–1250.

Miller, L.M., Escabi, M.A., Read, H.L., & Schreiner, C.E. (2002). Spectrotemporal receptive fields in the lemniscal auditory thalamus and cortex. Journal of Neurophysiology, 87, 516–527.

Mountcastle, V.B. (1995). The parietal system and some higher brain functions. Cerebral Cortex, 5, 377–390.

Ohl, F.W., Scheich, H., & Freeman, W.J. (2001). Change in patterns of ongoing cortical activity with auditory category learning. Nature, 412, 733–736.

Recanzone, G., Schreiner, C., & Merzenich, M.M. (1993). Plasticity in the frequency representation of primary auditory cortex, following discrimination training in adult owl monkeys. Journal of Neuroscience, 13, 87–103.

Rioult-Pedotti, M.S., Friedman, D., & Donoghue, J.P. (2000). Learning-induced LTP in the neocortex. Science, 290, 533–536.

Rioult-Pedotti, M.S., Friedman, D., Hess, G., & Donoghue, J.P. (1998). Strengthening of horizontal cortical connections following skill learning. Nature Neuroscience, 3, 230–234.

Romo, R., & Salinas, E. (2001). Touch and go: Decision-making mechanisms in somato-sensation. Annual Review of Neuroscience, 24, 107–137.

Romo, R., & Salinas, E. (2003). Flutter discrimination: neural codes, perception, memory and decision making. Nature Reviews Neuroscience, 4, 203–218.

Suga, N., & Ma, X. (2003). Multiparametric corticofugal modulation and plasticity in the auditory system. Nature Reviews Neuroscience, 4, 783–794.

Suga, N., Xiao, Z., Ma, X., & Ji, W. (2002). Plasticity and corticofugal modulation for hearing in adult animals. Neuron, 36, 9–18.

Ulanovsky, N., Las, L., & Nelken, I. (2003). Processing of low-probability sounds by cortical neurons. Nature Neuroscience, 6, 391–398.

Weinberger, N.M. (2001). Receptive field plasticity and memory in the auditory cortex: coding the learned importance of events. In J. Steinmetz, M. Gluck, & P. Solomon (Eds.), Model systems and the neurobiology of associative learning (pp. 187–216). Hillsdale, NJ: Lawrence Erlbaum Associates.

Weinberger, N.M. (2003a). Experience dependent response plasticity in the auditory cortex: issues, characteristics, mechanisms and functions. In T. Parks, E. Rubel, A. Popper, & R. Fay (Eds.), Springer Handbook of Auditory Research. New York: Springer-Verlag.

Weinberger, N.M. (2003b). Nucleus basalis and the memory code: Auditory cortex plasticity and the induction of specific, associative, behavioural memory. Neurobiology, Learning and Memory, 80, 268–284.

Weinberger, N.M. (2004). Specific long-term memory traces in primary auditory cortex. Nature Reviews Neuroscience, 5, 279–290.

Weinberger, N.M., & Diamond, D. (1987). Physiological plasticity in auditory cortex: Rapid induction by learning. Progress in Neurobiology, 29, 1–55.

Xiao, Z., & Suga, N. (2002). Reorganization of the cochleotopic map in the bat's auditory system by inhibition. Proceedings of the National Academy of Sciences USA, 99, 15743–15748.

Yin, P.B., Fritz, J.B., Dam, C.L., & Mishkin, M. (2001). (1) Differential distribution of spectro-temporal response patterns in AI and R, and (2) Presence of task-related responses in the primary auditory cortex of the alert rhesus monkey. Abstract – Society for Neuroscience.

Yin, P.B., Fritz, J.B., & Mishkin, M. (2004). Context-related responses in the primary auditory cortex of the rhesus monkey. (Submitted).

28. COGNITIVE ADAPTATIONS AND NEUROPLASTICITY: LESSONS FROM EVENT-RELATED BRAIN POTENTIALS

Jascha Rüsseler, Wido Nager, Janine Möbes, Thomas F. Münte

INTRODUCTION

In processing stimuli from the outside world, humans are faced with several tasks: (1) They have to select those aspects of the environment that contain important information, while discarding other, less interesting aspects, (2) they have to be able to monitor the entire environment for potentially meaningful stimuli, and (3) they have to do this within milliseconds. The filter process implied in the first task is usually captured by the term selective attention, while the global surveillance required by the second task is believed to occur without selective attention, that is, preattentively. Because of the enormous temporal constraints for these selection and detection processes, methods with high temporal resolution are required. Such resolution is provided by the event-related brain potential (ERP) technique. ERP's are small voltage fluctuations that occur in response to stimuli or other events and can be extracted from the ongoing EEG by a simple averaging procedure. Importantly, it has been demonstrated that portions of the ERP vary systematically as a function of perceptual and cognitive processes (Münte et al., 2000a). They show exquisite sensitivity towards task manipulations. In this chapter we will provide a brief review of the basic ERP indexes of attentive and preattentive auditory selection. We will also discuss some studies related to auditory processing in professional musicians.

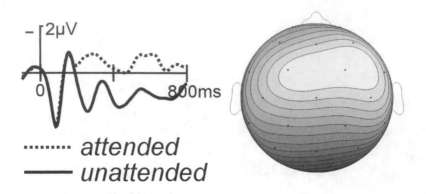

Fig. 28.1. Typical auditory attention effect. In this case, auditory channels were defined by pitch differences (1000 Hz vs. 1500 Hz) with the subject's task being to attend to one of the channels and to press a button for occasional slightly higher pitched targets within this channel. Depicted are the grand average ERPs to the standard stimuli. On the right: spline interpolated isovoltage maps of the attention effect (attended minus unattended difference wave; after data from Münte et al., 2000b).

SELECTIVE AUDITORY ATTENTION

In a typical auditory selective attention task, stimuli are represented rapidly in at least two "channels" defined by, for example, their spatial location or pitch, in order to detect rare target stimuli in the attended channel. In such a scenario, which is similar to the dichotic listening task that has been extensively used in cognitive psychology, the ERPs to attended stimuli are associated with a more negative waveform starting approximately 100 ms after the onset of the stimulus (Hansen & Hillyard, 1980). This processing negativity often extends for several hundred milliseconds and can be subdivided into subcomponents (Fig. 28.1).

While spatial location has a special status in the visual modality, this is not the case in the auditory modality, as the processing negativity is very similar for the selection according to different auditory features (e.g., pitch, timbre, loudness, duration). It has been used to investigate the processing of multidimensional auditory stimuli, that is, situations in which stimulus channels are characterized by the factorial combination of different stimulus attributes (e.g., location and pitch, Hansen & Hillyard, 1983).

PREATTENTIVE AUDITORY PROCESSING

Two different modes of preattentive auditory processing have been described. In the first situation, novel (and therefore potentially meaningful) stimuli are presented within a series of standard stimuli. An example for such an experiment would be a series of 1000 Hz tones interrupted infrequently by very different environmental sounds (honking of a car, dog's bark, etc.), i.e., each of the novel stimuli in such an experiment is different. Novel stimuli have been found to give rise to a P3a component, a positivity that occurs with a latency of about 250 to 350 ms over the frontocentral scalp (Courchesne et al., 1975). The P3a has been associated with the orienting response and the involuntary switching of auditory attention (Schröger, 1997).

Another type of preattentive auditory processing is seen in situations, in which series of unattended similar auditory stimuli are interrupted by rare deviant stimuli, with the deviant stimuli all being of a certain type (e.g., an occasional 1500 Hz tone in a series of 1000 Hz tones). Deviants are associated with a negative deflection. The mismatch negativity (MMN) is thus thought to reflect the automatic registration of the deviant feature of the incoming sound by comparing it to a sensory memory trace derived from the standard (Näätänen et al., 1980; Näätänen, 1995; Picton et al., 2000). In addition to simple physical deviants, more complex deviant events, such as the violation of a regular sequence of different sounds, have been shown to elicit an MMN (Picton et al., 2000). The preattentively registered features of sounds may serve as the basis for their further attention-mediated selection according to the goal of the listener.

While ERPs afford exquisite time-resolution on the order of 1 ms, a major drawback has been the lack of knowledge regarding the anatomical generators responsible for the different effects. With the advent of multichannel recordings, the topographical definition of ERP effects has been greatly improved. Nevertheless, it has been known since von Helmholtz (1853) that the problem of recovering the current sources from superficial electromagnetic measurements is intrinsically ill-posed. It is impossible to uniquely determine the spatial configuration of neural activity based on EEG recordings alone (Nunez, 1981). This is also known as the inverse problem.

Nevertheless, significant progress has been made in source localization by making certain a priori assumptions about the solution. A common approach is to assume that an ERP is generated by a small number of focal sources, which can be modelled by equivalent current point dipoles (ECD) (e.g., Aine et al., 2000; Miltner et al., 1994; Mosher et al., 1992; Scherg & Ebersole, 1994; Scherg et al., 1999). The location, orientation, and activity over time of each ECD are iteratively determined by minimizing the difference between the predicted and the actual ERP. Other approaches based on distributed source models are discussed in several recent publications (Phillips et al., 2002; Uutela et al., 1999). Using the estimation of equivalent current dipoles the mismatch negativity has been shown to emanate from secondary auditory cortex (Giard et al., 1990; Rinne et al., 2000). This has been corroborated by combined fMRI/ERP recordings (Opitz et al., 2002).

GENERAL METHODS

With regard to our own research presented in this chapter the following general methodological steps have been followed: For all studies, homogenous groups of normal, healthy subjects were investigated after written informed consent had been obtained. EEG was recorded with tin electrodes with a 32 channel system from the intact scalp of the subjects with electrodes placed according to the international 10/20 system. The reference electrode was placed either at the nose-tip for mismatch negativity studies or at the mastoid processes (algebraic mean of the activity at the left and right mastoid) for studies investigating attention effects. The ERPs were quantified by mean amplitude measures in time-windows defined by pilot-experiments with the mean amplitude in the 100-ms pre-stimulus baseline period serving as a reference. The mean amplitude measures were taken at electrode sites known to exhibit the maximum amplitude for a given component. These values were entered into standard analysis of variance statistics.

SELECTION AT THE COCKTAIL PARTY

For about 50 years dichotic listening has been one of the major paradigms in experimental psychology. When listening to two simultaneous speech messages played to the left and the right ear, only one of these messages can be processed for meaning. This experimental paradigm can be thus viewed as a laboratory version of the so-called "cocktail-party phenomenon". The physiological basis of this phenomenon is not fully understood but implies the enhanced processing of attended signals and the suppression of unattended parts of the signal (Bronkhorst, 2000; Woods, 1990). As has been discussed above, ERPs show robust effects of attentional selection in the auditory modality when simple auditory features (such as spatial location or pitch) defined an informational channel. Teder et al. (1993) used a more natural situation: Two simultaneous speech messages by two different human speakers were presented from two different location in a free-field situation. ERPs were triggered to the initial "k" phonemes of Finnish words of the attended and unattended speech messages and a typical attention effect was obtained. An earlier study had used task-irrelevant probe stimuli occurring at the same location as attended and unattended speech messages. Again, a typical ERP attention effect was obtained in this situation for the probe stimuli coming from the attended location (Woods et al., 1984). In a recent pilot study, we refined the probe technique: Speech messages were recorded by microphones located in the earcanals of an artificial head. Such recordings when listened to over headphones afford a very precise localization in the horizontal plane. Superimposed on these speech messages were probe stimuli that mostly came from the same location as the speech stimuli (standard probes), but sometimes were slightly displaced (deviant probes).

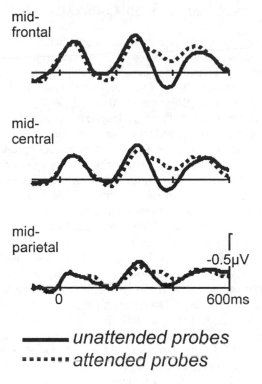

mid-
frontal

mid-
central

mid-
parietal

-0.5μV

0   600ms

———— *unattended probes*
••••••• *attended probes*

Fig. 28.2. Grand average potentials for probe stimuli in a selective listening task. The probes coinciding with the attended speaker show a typical ERP attention effect (unpublished data)

The probe stimuli comprised the syllable /da/ derived from the voices of the speakers. The ERPs were recorded using multi-channel recordings time-locked to the onset of these probe-stimuli and compared for probes coming from the attended and unattended locations. Probe stimuli occurred in a rapid sequence with about 3 probe stimuli per second. In a first pilot experiment in a group of 12 young, healthy subjects we required the subjects to attend to one of the speech messages per experimental block in order to answer questions related to this message afterwards. As is illustrated in Figure 28.2, an attentional modulation of the ERPs to the probe stimuli is present that has the typical distribution of a processing negativity. After this successful demonstration, the probe technique can now be used to investigate the factors that allow the listener to home in on one of several simultaneously active sound sources.

PREATTENTIVE PROCESSING AT THE COCKTAIL-PARTY

In everyday situations we receive acoustic input that originates from several simultaneous sound sources. The recognition of auditory events depends upon proper assignment of information to separate sound sources based on locational cues and spectral characteristics over time, a mechanism that has been termed auditory stream segregation (Bregman, 1990).

Similar to the situation in the visual system, behavioral data point to a superior role of spatial cues in auditory scene analysis (Näätänen et al., 1980). Whereas in the visual system space is represented in a retinotopic fashion all the way up to secondary visual areas, however, the auditory system has to compute spatial coordinates from interaural time and level differences (Macpherson & Middlebrooks, 2002) and by using information derived from head-related transfer functions (Langendijk & Bronkhorst, 2002).

In a recent study (Nager et al., 2003a), we asked the question to what extent the monitoring of different sound sources, a core requirement for auditory scene analysis, can take place preattentively. To this end the mismatch negativity was recorded in a situation in which sounds were played from one "standard location" and from four different "deviant" locations defined by interaural time differences. Sounds were brief band-pass filtered white noise bursts (60-ms duration, 44.1-kHz digitization rate, 250- and 750-Hz cutoff-frequencies) that were randomly presented to five spatial locations (left, mid-left, middle, mid-right, and right) defined by interaural time differences. Thus, the stimuli delivered to the two ears were physically identical except for the timing difference. Auditory input to the contralateral ear was delayed by 900 μs for the "far"-lateralized sounds and by 300 μs for the "near"-lateralized sounds. Lateral deviant sounds were heard at about 80 and 30 degrees lateral to the midline stimulus, while the frequent standard sounds (p = 0.7) occurred at the midline position (no interaural time difference). The inter-stimulus interval (ISI) varied randomly between 200 and 300 ms (rectangular distribution). Subjects took part in three runs of 1000 stimuli resulting in 225 deviants for each spatial position in the averaging procedure.

Under these conditions, location deviants, regardless of their position evoked a typical MMN peaking at about 165 ms (Fig. 28.3). This MMN was shown to be smaller for the "near" location deviants. These data indicate an automatic detection of azimuthal stimulus change, thus providing a preattentive basis for stream segregation in auditory scene analysis on the basis of location cues. This study therefore extends previous findings by Teder-Sälejärvi et al. (1999) using 7 spatial locations in a free-field setting, in which multiple cues (e.g., differential attenuation of sounds from different locations by the outer ear structures, c.f. head-related transfer functions) can be used for localization, and indicate that the human auditory system is capable to track multiple adjacent locations by interaural time differences.

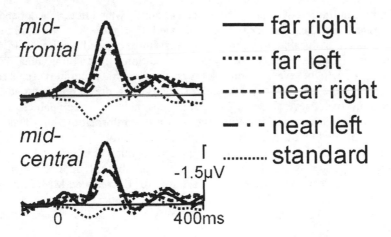

Fig. 28.3. Grand average ERPs for standard and deviant stimuli obtained in a passive listening task. Deviants were created by introducing slight interaural timing differences. Those stimuli that were localized to the far left or far right from the standard location generated a larger MMN than stimuli located nearer to the standard. (After data from Nager et al., 2003a.)

In a further experiment we asked a different question, namely whether or not the auditory system is capable of monitoring several distinct auditory streams characterized by various combinations of pitch and spatial location (Nager et al., 2003b). Three speakers were positioned in front of the subject's head at the eye-level. Left, middle and right speaker were located at −20°, 0°, and 20° according to the subjects' midsagittal plane at a distance of 90 cm. Random sequences of pure sine wave tones (60-ms duration, 5-ms rise/fall time) were presented to either one, two or three of these locations (1-, 2-, and 3-speaker condition, respectively). Tones at each location differed in pitch (800 Hz, 1000 Hz, 1400 Hz), thus forming up to three auditory streams. Deviant tones of shorter duration (36 ms) and slightly increased pitch randomly occurred on 10% of the trials (832 Hz vs. 800 Hz, 1040 Hz vs. 1000 Hz, 1456 Hz vs. 1400 Hz). The mean inter-stimulus interval (ISI) at a designated location was 167 ms in the 1-speaker condition, 333 ms in the 2-speaker condition and 500 ms in the 3-speaker condition, resulting in an overall stimulus load of 6/s for each experimental condition. The subjects were told to read a book during the recording.

The ERPs (Fig. 28.4) showed a typical MMN for each experimental condition. When stimuli were presented within a single auditory stream, a further late negativity elicited by deviant stimuli was observed from 300 ms until the end of the epoch. This late negativity is smaller when stimuli are presented in two or three auditory streams, which was confirmed by statistical analysis. The fact that an MMN was obtained for deviants in each channel indicates successful stream segregation, because the detection of a deviant requires the definition of a standard for each channel, which in turn is dependent on segregation. Thus, the experiment showed that the short term auditory sensory store is capable to monitor at least three spatial auditory streams simultaneously under free field listening conditions, resembling real world situations in which several sound sources have to be accurately separated. Furthermore, the present data strongly suggest that the spread of auditory information over several separate spatial channels is accompanied by a significant impairment in encoding the incoming information into neuronal traces as indicated by the amplitude changes of the MMN.

Due to the constant stimulus load applied in our paradigm, the ISI at a designated speaker position decreased as the number of auditory channels increased. This decrease in ISI does not account for the reduced MMN that was observed with rising number of spatial auditory channels, because no such decrement was seen when stimulus load was varied in the single speaker situation.

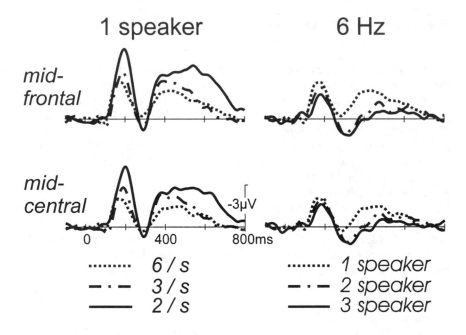

Fig. 28.4. Grand average difference waves (deviant minus standard) in a passive listening experiment. **Left side:** Effects of pitch deviants in a single speaker situation and three different presentation rates. The MMN is followed by a later long-stretched negativity. **Right side:** Effects of pitch deviants presented in the presence of no, one and two additional auditory streams. (After data from Nager et al., 2003b.)

NEUROFUNCTIONAL PLASTICITY IN PROFESSIONAL MUSICIANS

The question arises whether the electrophysiological indices of attentive and preattentive auditory processing might be used to demonstrate functional changes of auditory processing, as they may be suspected in professional musicians with longstanding training of the auditory system. Previous neurophysiological studies in trained musicians have shown that event-related potentials or event-related magnetic fields might be useful to assess training induced changes. For example, in the motor domain it has been shown that increased use of hands in string players leads to an enlargement of the cortical representation of the fingers (Elbert et al., 1995). Several studies have demonstrated a superior preattentive evaluation of sounds: Only musicians showed an MMN to impure deviant chords in a series of pure standard chords (Koelsch et al., 1999). They were also shown to have a longer temporal window of sound integration (Rüsseler et al., 2001) and appear to be able to use musical context to speed up preattentive detection of pitch anomalies (Brattico et al., 2002).

In a series of studies, we therefore asked the question, to what extent prolonged specific professional experience as a conductor or as a drummer alters the processing of auditory stimuli. With the aim to distinguish changes in ERPs specific to the specific experience from general changes related to prolonged professional musicianship we included a group of pianists as controls for the conductors and a group of woodwind players as controls for the drummers in addition to non-musicians.

In our first study we addressed the gradient of spatial auditory attention in conductors, because one of the tasks a conductor faces is to selectively attend to a sound source (a musician) at a certain location within the orchestra. To capture these requirements in an experimental task we used an array of six speakers, three located in front of the subjects and three located to the right from which rapid sequences of standard and deviant sounds were presented. Only the centermost or the most peripheral speaker were to be attended in a given run with all other speakers being irrelevant. Previous studies using similar set-ups in normal listeners (Teder-Salejärvi & Hillyard, 1998) and congenitally blind subjects (Röder et al., 1999) had demonstrated that the ability to focus on a specific location is much reduced for normal listeners in peripheral compared to central auditory space reflected by a greatly increased false alarm rate to deviant sounds from irrelevant, neighboring locations. Congenitally blind subjects on the other hand had shown an improved auditory localization in peripheral space compared to seeing control subjects. This was reflected by modulations of the ERP attention effect.

As conductors and congenitally blind subjects have in common the need to localize sound sources, we hypothesized that changes in spatial attention mechanisms should be present in conductors. In particular we predicted that they should be better in focusing stimuli and therefore should display a steeper attentional gradient, especially for peripheral auditory space both behaviorally

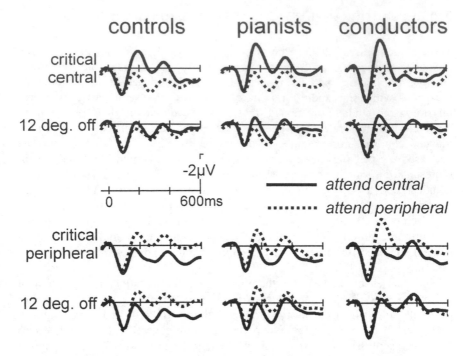

Fig. 28.5. Grand average potentials (Fz-site) for the different subject groups. Shown are ERPs to standard tones for the attended central and peripheral speakers as well as to those emanating from the second neighboring speaker (12° distance). The intermediate speakers are left out for space reasons. Clearly, all three subject groups show a gradual decline of the attention effect for the three central speakers. By contrast, in the periphery only the conductors show an attentional gradient (After data from Münte et al., 2001.)

and electrophysiologically.

This was in fact the case. When subjects were required to attend to the centermost speaker of the array, all three groups showed a similar and rather precise behavioral selectivity, indicated by the relatively low false alarm rates for the neighboring speakers. The ERPs to the standard stimuli showed a typical attention effect, that is, sounds from the attended centermost speaker were associated with an enhanced negativity when they were attended to, compared to when attention was directed to the peripheral speaker (Fig. 28.5). There was a sharp decline in the amplitude of this attention effect, i.e. the difference between ERPs from the attention central and attention peripheral condition, for neighboring speakers in the central auditory field, indicating that the spatial selectivity probably acts at the stage of perceptual selection. The effects for the central speakers are very similar to previous studies using normal (Teder-Sälejärvi & Hillyard, 1998) and congenitally blind subjects (Röder et al., 1999). By contrast, the spatial selectivity in peripheral space was much reduced both in terms of behavioral and electrophysiological effects in professional pianists and non-musicians. The conductors, however, still showed a rather good behavioral and electrophysiological selectivity for sounds in peripheral space. Their findings are thus reminiscent to previous findings obtained in a similar experiment with blind subjects (Röder et al., 1999). However, in this earlier study the distribution of the attention effect was found to be different in blind subjects and sighted controls suggesting that the electrophysiological attention effect in these two subject groups is due to the activity of at least partially different neuronal populations. This further implied functional/anatomical reorganization in the brain of blind subjects. Analysis of the scalp topography suggested that the distribution of the attention effect was indistinguishable for the three subject groups. Thus, while conductors appear to use spatial attention much more effectively than pianists or non-musicians, they apparently use the same cortical brain mechanisms to achieve the superior behavioral results.

In the current paradigm, many of the sounds occurred outside the (wider) attentional focus of the subjects. We were therefore also interested to what extent the three subject groups would show electrophysiological signs of change detection, i.e. the mismatch negativity, for stimuli coming from the unattended direction. While non-musician controls showed at best a very rudimentary MMN response, which was statistically not reliable, suggesting that they only had a very limited pre-attentive registration of deviant sounds coming from the unattended direction, both musician groups showed reliable mismatch effects (Fig. 28.6). The largest MMNs for deviants from the unattended part of the auditory scene were found in professional pianists. In conductors, a typical MMN was found albeit of smaller amplitude than in the pianists. This MMN was followed by a positivity, which showed a frontocentral distribution in the conductors. Only a rudimentary MMN was seen in the non-musician control subjects, suggesting that in this group preattentive detection of deviant stimuli was not very pronounced. Schröger (1997) has proposed a model that assigns specific processes to the MMN and P3a components during preattentive listening: According to this model the features of an incoming stimulus are initially compared with the established representation of the standard stimulus. The feature-specific mismatch signals are then integrated, giving rise to the MMN. If the integrated mismatch signal exceeds a (variable) threshold, conscious detection of the deviant takes place and initiates an involuntary attention shift, indexed by the P3a, which ultimately leads to the identification of the stimulus. This line of reasoning thus suggests that the threshold for conscious detection of the mismatch signal is exceeded only in conductors. Dipole modeling for the deviant minus standard difference waves suggested that the MMN is mainly produced by sources in the auditory cortex, while the P3a in the conductors can be attributed to an additional frontal source.

While it seems reasonable that longstanding experience as a conductor will lead to superior spatial attention abilities, percussionists and drummers, especially from the Jazz and Rock traditions, are especially taxed with regard to musical timing. In a study using evenly spaced sine tones as standard stimuli with occasional anticipations as deviant stimuli, we have been able to show that

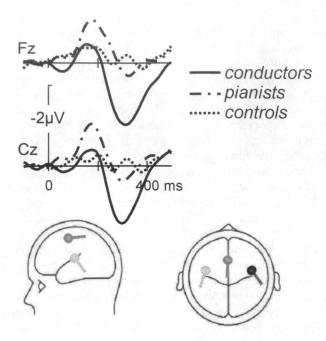

Fig. 28.6. Deviant minus standard difference waves for the peripheral stimuli (when the centermost-speaker was attended). A very different morphology of the difference waves is found for the three subject groups. The stylized heads show the location of the three dipole solutions for the mismatch potentials. While conductors and pianists showed comparable source strength for the two temporal sources, only the conductors showed activity for the medial frontal source.

professional musicians are more precise in the preattentive detection of such temporal irregularities (Rüsseler et al., 2001). Stimuli that were anticipated by 20 ms elicited a reliable mismatch negativity in musicians in a passive listening experiment, while non-musicians did not show an MMN. Stimuli that were anticipated by 50 ms led to an MMN in both groups but musicians showed a larger amplitude. In a second experiment, occasionally omitted "sounds" in an otherwise regular tone series evoked a reliable MMN at inter-stimulus intervals (ISIs) of 100, 120, 180, and 220 ms in musicians. In non-musicians, the MMN was smaller/absent in the 180- and 220-ms ISIs, respectively (Rüsseler et al., 2001).

To test the hypothesis that drummers might be even more precise in the detection of anticipations, we followed up these studies by testing 10 drummers, 10 woodwind-players, and 10 non-musician controls in a more natural task. This involved the presentation of a real drum sequence taken from a drum school. This sequence was presented as a continuous loop with no breaks. Occasionally, a beat was anticipated by 30 ms or 80 ms. The resulting sequence was presented in the format of a passive listening experiment with the attention of the subjects

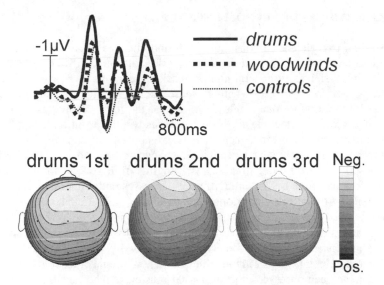

Fig. 28.7. Deviant minus standard difference waves (Cz-electrode). Anticipated drum beats give rise to a mismatch response in all three subject groups, that is bigger in the professional drummers. Moreover, for the subsequent beats additional mismatch responses are observed, which have a more frontal scalp distribution and therefore must entail the activity of at least partially different neural generators (unpublished data).

captured by a visual attention task. ERPs to standard (unaltered) parts of the sequence were subtracted from ERPs to deviant (anticipated) parts of the drum sequence. No mismatch response was found in any of the groups for the 30-ms anticipations, which can be attributed to the fact that a beat-to-beat jitter of 15 to 20 ms was present in this natural sequence. For the 80 ms anticipations, however, distinct differences were present: A typical frontocentral, slightly right preponderant MMN was seen for all groups, which was most pronounced in the drummers (see Fig. 28.7). Importantly, the subsequent beats of the sequence gave rise to additional mismatch responses, manifesting themselves as further negative peaks. These were more prominent in the drummers and had a different, more frontal distribution of the second and third peak. This pattern of results suggests that drummers' preattentive processing of temporally organized sound sequences is more profoundly disturbed. While the amplitude of the mismatch response is considerably smaller for the second and third anticipated beats in the woodwind-players and controls, this is not the case in the drummers. We therefore suggest drummers to have a more complex representation of the musical time structure than non-musicians and woodwind-players.

ERPs AS INDICES OF NEUROPLASTICITY

The present experiment demonstrates profound changes of the brain responses related to attentive and pre-attentive processing of sounds differing in spatial location in musicians in general and professional conductors in particular. The question therefore arises, whether these changes signal neuroplasticity. Obviously, there is not one single definition of the term. Neuroplasticity in its broadest sense would include all those processes which permit the adaptation of the brain to environmental factors that cannot be anticipated by genetic programming. The neural and behavioral changes attributed to plasticity have been observed on different time scales, ranging from several minutes to the whole life-time of the individual. Different processes underlie plastic changes at the extremes of this time-line. Long-term plasticity can be explained by the de novo growth of new dendrites, synapses, and neurons (e.g., Polat & Sagi, 1994), while changes on a shorter time-scale rely on the disinhibition or inhibition of preexisting lateral connections between neurons by sensory input as first suggested by Hebb (Jacobs & Donoghue, 1991). While macroscopic anatomical changes have been observed in professional musicians who began their training early in life (Münte et al., 2002; Schlaug et al., 1995a, 1995b), our own studies in musicians rather show functional adaptations and allow no direct inference about anatomical adaptations. Previously, increased amplitudes (or dipole moments) of event-related potentials/fields in musicians have been interpreted as a sign of functional anatomical reorganization of the cortex of musicians indicating the recruitment of more neurons (Pantev et al., 1998). The strength of equivalent current dipoles has even been used to estimate the number of neurons involved in a certain neurophysiological response (Elbert et al., 1995). It appears difficult, however, to draw firm conclusions as to the process underlying an increased dipole moment in evoked electromagnetic activity: Besides a de novo growth of synapses, an expansion of the receptive field by unmasking preexisting connections and a better synchronization of the activity of neural ensembles might be considered. Therefore, we would like to interpret our own findings with caution: For example, with regard to the ERP attention effect in the conductor study, no difference in the absolute, maximal amplitude was observed between the three subject groups. More importantly and unlike a similar study in blind subjects (Röder et al., 1999), no differences in the topography were observed. This implies that the same brain areas were active in supporting attentional selection in the three subject groups. How the more precise spatial tuning in the conductor group is achieved is therefore unclear. One possibility is that these reflect experience related changes at an earlier (subcortical) stage of the auditory processing cascade. The present data do not allow such a conclusion, however.

A pronounced qualitative difference between the three subject groups was seen with regard to the pre-attentive detection of deviants in the conductor study. In fact, the presence of a P3a component in the conductors only suggests that these are more tuned towards the detection of mismatching sounds than other musicians. We view this as a sign of strategic adaptation and in fact see the strength of the ERP technique in the detection of changes in cognitive processing strategies, such as differential attentional allocation.

LIMITATIONS AND FUTURE DEVELOPMENTS OF THE ERP METHOD

While the present set of data underscore the utility of the ERP method for the description of neurocognitive adaptations of the sound processing system with millisecond precision, they also point to certain limitations of this method. Its non-invasiveness limits any inferences about how the changes of neural processes at the ensemble level are related to changes at a microscopic level. Clearly, animal studies are needed to fill this gap. Also, in spite of progress in the source localization of ERP components, spatial precision of this method is limited. In other domains, we have therefore begun to combine ERP and fMRI techniques in order to describe both, the temporal and spatial characteristics of processing differences between conditions or subject groups (Rodriguez-Fornells et al., 2002). With regard to the processing of auditory stimuli, similar approaches have been proposed (Opitz et al., 2002). Thus, combined spatio-temporal imaging studies of experience-related plasticity in the auditory system are likely to appear within the next few years.

ACKNOWLEDGMENTS

We like to acknowledge the following individuals who have collaborated in these studies: Eckart Altenmüller, Oliver Rosenthal, Antoni Rodriguez-Fornells, and Ina Bohrer. Supported by grants from the DFG to TFM.

REFERENCES

Aine, C., Huang, M., Stephen, J., & Christner, R. (2000). Multistart algorithms for MEG empirical data analysis reliably characterize locations and time courses of multiple sources. NeuroImage, 12, 159–172.

Brattico, E., Winkler, I., Näätänen, R., Paavilainen, P., & Tervaniemi, M. (2002). Simultaneous storage of two complex temporal sound patterns in auditory sensory memory. Neuroreport, 13, 1747–1751.

Bregman, A.S. (1990) Auditory scene analysis: The perceptual organization of sound. Cambridge, MA: MIT Press.

Bronkhorst, A.W. (2000). The cocktail party phenomenon: A review of research on speech intelligibility in multi-talker conditions. Acoustica, 86, 117–128.

Courchesne, E., Hillyard, S.A., & Galambos, R. (1975). Stimulus novelty, task relevance, and the visual evoked potential in man. Electroencephalography and Clinical Neurophysiology, 39, 131–143.

Elbert, T., Pantev, C., Wienbruch, C., Rockstroh, B., & Taub, E. (1995). Increased cortical representation of the fingers of the left hand in string players. Science, 270, 305–307.

Giard, M.H., Perrin, F., Pernier, J., & Bouchet, P. (1990). Brain generators implicated in the processing of auditory stimulus deviance: A topographic event-related potential study. Psychophysiology, 27, 627–640.

Hansen, J.C., & Hillyard, S.A. (1980). Endogenous brain potentials associated with selective auditory attention. Electroencephalography and Clinical Neurophysiology, 49, 277–290.

Hansen, J.C., & Hillyard, S.A. (1983). Selective attention to multidimensional auditory stimuli. Journal of Experimental Psychology. Human Perception and Performance, 9, 1–19.

Jacobs, K.M., & Donoghue, J.P. (1991). Reshaping the cortical motor map by unmasking latent intracortical connections. Science, 251, 944–947.

Koelsch, S., Schröger, E., & Tervaniemi, M. (1999). Superior pre-attentive auditory processing in musicians. Neuroreport, 10, 1309–1313.

Langendijk, E.H., & Bronkhorst, A.W. (2002). Contribution of spectral cues to human sound localization, Journal of the Acoustical Society of America, 112, 1583–1596.

Macpherson, E.A., & Middlebrooks, J.C. (2002). Listener weighting of cues for lateral angle: the duplex theory of sound localization revisited. Journal of the Acoustical Society of America, 111, 2219–2236.

Miltner, W., Braun, C., Johnson, R., Simpson, G.V., & Ruchkin, D.S. (1994). A test of brain electrical source analysis (BESA): A simulation study. Electroencephalography and Clinical Neurophysiology, 91, 295–310.

Mosher, J.C., Lewis, P.S., & Leahy, R.M. (1992). Multiple dipole modeling and localization from spatio-temporal MEG data. IEEE Transactions of Biomedical Engineering, 39, 541–557.

Münte, T.F., Altenmüller, E., & Jäncke, L. (2002). The musician's brain as a model of neuroplasticity. Nature Review Neuroscience, 3, 473–478.

Münte, T.F., Kohlmetz, C., Nager, W., & Altenmüller, E. (2001). Neuroperception. Superior auditory spatial tuning in conductors. Nature, 409, 580.

Münte, T.F., Nager, W., Rosenthal, O., Johannes, S., & Altenmüller, E. (2000b). Attention to pitch in musicians and non-musicians: an event-related brain potential study. In T. Nakada (Ed.), Integrated human brain science (pp. 389–398). Amsterdam: Elsevier.

Münte, T.F., Urbach, T.P., Düzel, E., & Kutas, M. (2000a). Event-related brain potentials in the study of human cognition and neuropsychology. In F. Boller, J. Grafman, & G. Rizzolatti (Eds.), Handbook of Neuropsychology, Vol. 1 (pp. 139–235). Amsterdam: Elsevier.

Näätänen, R. (1995). The mismatch negativity – A powerful tool for cognitive neuroscience. Ear and Hearing, 16, 6–18.

Näätänen, R., Porkka, R., Merisalo, A., & Ahtola, S. (1980). Location vs. frequency of pure tones as a basis of fast discrimination. Acta Psychologica, 44, 31–40.

Nager, W., Kohlmetz, C., Joppich, G., Möbes, J., & Münte, T.F. (2003a). Tracking of multiple sound sources defined by interaural timing differences: Brain potential evidence in humans. Neuroscience Letters, 344, 181–184.

Nager, W., Teder-Sälejärvi, W.A., Kunze, S., & Münte, T.F. (2003b). Preattentive evaluation of multiple perceptual streams in human audition. Neuroreport, 14, 871–874.

Nunez, P.L. (1981). Electric fields of the brain: The neurophysics of EEG. New York: Oxford University Press.

Opitz, B., Rinne, T., Mecklinger, A., von Cramon, D.Y., & Schröger, E. (2002). Differential contribution of frontal and temporal cortices to auditory change detection: fMRI and ERP results. NeuroImage, 15, 167–174.

Pantev, C., Oostenveld, R., Engelien, A., Ross, B., Roberts, L.E., & Hoke, M. (1998). Increased auditory cortical representation in musicians. Nature, 392, 811–814.

Phillips, C., Rugg, M.D., & Friston, K. (2002). Anatomically informed basis functions for EEG source localization: Combining functional and fnatomical constraints. NeuroImage, 16, 678–695.

Picton, T.W., Alain, C., Otten, L., Ritter, W., & Achim, A. (2000). Mismatch negativity: different water in the same river. Audiology & Neuro-Otology, 5, 111–139.

Polat, U., & Sagi, D. (1994). Spatial interactions in human vision: from near to far via experience-dependent cascades of connections. Proceedings of the National Academy of Sciences USA, 91, 1206–1209.

Rinne, T., Alho, K., Ilmoniemi, R. J., Virtanen, J., & Näätänen, R. (2000). Separate time behaviors of the temporal and frontal mismatch negativity sources. NeuroImage, 12, 14–19.

Röder, B., Teder-Sälejärvi, W., Sterr, A., Rösler, F., Hillyard, S.A., & Neville, H.J. (1999). Improved auditory spatial tuning in blind humans. Nature, 400, 162–166.

Rodriguez-Fornells, A., Rotte, M., Heinze, H.J., Noesselt, T., & Münte, T.F. (2002). Brain potential and functional MRI evidence for how to handle two languages with one brain. Nature, 415, 1026–1029.

Rüsseler, J., Altenmüller, E., Nager, W., Kohlmetz, C., & Münte, T.F. (2001). Event-related brain potentials to sound omissions differ in musicians and non-musicians. Neuroscience Letters, 308, 33–36.

Scherg, M., Bast, T., & Berg, P. (1999) Multiple source analysis of interictal spikes: Goals, requirements, and clinical value. Journal of Clinical Neurophysiology, 16, 214–224.

Scherg, M., & Ebersole, J.S. (1994). Brain source imaging of focal and multifocal epileptiform EEG activity. Clinical Neurophysiology, 24, 51–60.

Schlaug, G., Jäncke, L., Huang, Y., Staiger, J. F., & Steinmetz, H. (1995a). Increased corpus callosum size in musicians. Neuropsychologia, 33, 1047–1055.

Schlaug, G., Jäncke, L., Huang, Y., & Steinmetz, H. (1995b). In vivo evidence of structural brain asymmetry in musicians. Science, 267, 699–701.

Schröger, E. (1997). On the detection of auditory deviations: A pre-attentive activation model. Psychophysiology, 34, 245–257.

Teder, W., Kujala, T., & Näätänen, R. (1993). Selection of speech messages in free-field listening. Neuroreport, 5, 307–309.

Teder-Sälejärvi, W.A., & Hillyard, S.A. (1998). The gradient of spatial auditory attention in free field: An event- related potential study. Perception & Psychophysics, 60, 1228–1242.

Teder-Sälejärvi, W.A., Hillyard, S.A., Röder, B., & Neville, H.J. (1999). Spatial attention to central and peripheral auditory stimuli as indexed by event-related potentials. Cognitive Brain Research, 8, 213–227.

Uutela, K., Hämäläinen, M.S., & Somersalo, E. (1999). Visualization of magnetoence-phalographic data using minimum current estimates. NeuroImage, 10, 173–180.

von Helmholtz, H.L.F. (1853). Ueber einige Gesetze der Vertheilung elektrischer Ströme in körperlichen Leitern mit Anwendung auf die thierisch-elektrischen Versuche. Annalen der Physik und Chemie, 89, 211–233.

Woods, D.L. (1990). Selective Attention. In J.W. Rohrbaugh, R. Parasuraman, & R. Johnson (Eds.), Event Related Brain Potentials: Basic Issues and Applications (pp. 178–209). New York: Oxford University Press.

Woods, D.L., Hillyard, S.A., & Hansen, J.C. (1984). Event-related brain potentials reveal similar attentional mechanisms during selective listening and shadowing. Journal of Experimental Psychology. Human Perception and Performance, 10, 761–777.

SUBJECT INDEX

A

AI (A1, primary auditory field) · 3–4,
9–20, 27–28, 39, 41, 46, 52, 57–60,
62–65, 68, 71, 78–85, 89, 95–105,
122, 128–138, 145–146, 150–159,
165, 167, 172–173, 184, 190, 209–
218, 227–238, 244–245, 248, 256,
265, 306, 313–328, 332, 338–341,
352, 366, 369, 389–394, 399, 412,
420–425, 438, 445–451, 457–462
AAF (anterior auditory field) · 95–105,
227, 234–235, 265
ablation · 111–123, 185, 228
accelerated speech · 296, 302–305, 309
acetylcholine · 368, 462
acetylcholinesterase (AchE) · 38,
78–79, 80, 83, 89
action potential (AP) · 138, 204, 353,
369–371, 373–375
α_1-receptor · 40, 42
α_2-receptor · 40, 42
alpha rhythm · 305
alternative forced choice (AFC) · 415
AMPA receptor · 40
amplitude modulation (AM) · 4, 371,
386, 396
animal model · 241, 246, 251, 363,
429, 435, 440
anterior auditory area (AA) · 54, 79–80
anterior auditory field *see AAF*

anterior ectosylvian sulcus (AES) · 96–
97, 227–228, 231–234, 238, 421
anterior insular auditory area (AIA) ·
79, 89
anterolateral auditory area (ALA) · 54,
59, 63–68, 79, 82
anti-localization · 112
appetitive conditioning · 367
appetitive training · 425
area LA (lateral auditory area) · 37,
54–55, 59 60, 63–64, 79–80, 82,
89, 158
area MA (medial auditory area) · 54–
55, 79–80, 82
area PA (posterior auditory area) · 55,
79–80, 82
area PAF (posterior auditory field) ·
227, 232–235, 238
area PIA (posterior insular auditory
area) · 79
area PLST (posterior lateral superior
temporal auditory area) · 146–159
area, rostral (R) · 9, 11, 78, 395–396
area, rostrotemporal (RT) · 9–11, 89
area STA (supratemporal auditory area)
· 38, 54–55, 59, 63–64, 79–80, 82,
84, 158
area Te1 · 30–46, 68, 281, 286
Te1.0 · 30, 35, 37–40
Te1.1 · 30, 37–40
Te1.2 · 38–40, 68
Te1.3 · 31, 35, 37, 40
Te2 · 30–44, 281
Te2.1 · 35, 37

N

O

P

T